DEPRESSION & MANIA

MODERN LITHIUM THERAPY

DEPRESSION
&
MANIA
MODERN LITHIUM THERAPY

Edited by
F.Neil Johnson

IRL PRESS
OXFORD · WASHINGTON DC

IRL Press
Eynsham
Oxford
England

First published 1987
Reprinted 1988

British Library Cataloguing in Publication Data

Depression and mania : modern lithium therapy
1. Lithium—Therapeutic use
I. Johnson, F. Neil
616.89'18 RC483.5.L5

ISBN 1 85221 039 7 (hardbound)
ISBN 1 85221 174 1 (softbound)

Typeset by Infotype and printed by Information Printing Ltd, Oxford, England.

CONTENTS

Pour mon ami et collègue

HENRI LÔO

En sincère hommage à ses beaux travaux, et en appréciation de son hospitalité et sa gentillesse, cette étude d'un médicament dont il est un des vrais pionniers

PREFACE

Depression and Mania: Modern Lithium Therapy is the latest in a line of books about lithium with which I have been associated — as editor or as author — over the past decade and a half. It represents a natural step in the publishing sequence, being aimed at the psychiatrist whose interests lie primarily in the practicalities of treatment rather than in research, and at the intelligent patient who wants to know something about the technicalities of his or her treatment without being burdened with excessive or esoteric detail. My earlier books tended to be addressed to the experimentalist or the research-oriented psychiatrist, and, given the many unanswered questions which existed (and still exist) about the therapeutic actions of lithium, that was perfectly proper; but even if those questions were never to be answered, the usefulness of lithium in clinical practice would be relatively unaffected. It therefore seemed to me that there was a need for a book which would focus upon contemporary usage of lithium in psychiatry and which, in doing so, would cover a number of issues of great concern to the doctor and the patient but which figure hardly at all in the research literature.

This book represents the combined efforts of 97 different authors whose brief was to try to show lithium therapy, in its many facets, as it is now.

I have organized the subject matter into nine different parts; within each part there are various sections — some quite long and others very short. To my mind, this arrangement offered greater flexibility to the text as a whole than was possible with the traditional structure of separate chapters of more or less equal weight.

The introductory part of the book gives the background to the need for lithium, by first of all discussing the kinds of conditions for which it is used, and then saying something about what kind of substance it is. The historical origins and development of lithium therapy are also outlined.

Next there is a review of the range of medical applications which lithium finds, both in psychiatry and in non-psychiatric fields, and it is only proper to look at alternative therapies to lithium.

The following five parts deal with different aspects of clinical practice — the decision processes leading up to the initiation of therapy, the technical issues governing its efficient conduct, the way in which treatment progresses and the factors which determine what problems may occur, and combinations of lithium with other treatment modalities.

Lithium, like all medications, has effects on the body over and above those which are necessary for its therapeutic action and these are reviewed in the eighth part of the book.

Finally, lithium is set into modern context, with an examination of its cost-effectiveness and its current and future status.

The style of writing differs from that usually found in books on topics such as this, and I know that many of the authors, being accustomed to the discipline of writing for learned journals, found it difficult at first to make the adjustment to a freer and less formal style. In particular, one becomes very used to supporting practically every statement with a reference to an appropriate publication in the scientific literature and this was something which was ruled out in the present text. I asked the authors to concentrate on making statements which they were prepared to regard as so well established as not to need the support of specific references, and to be very clear when statements were being made with lesser degrees of certainty. I wanted to know what could be said and what could not be said about lithium therapy as it is used *now*. The result is, I hope, a readable and honest appraisal of this treatment.

I have been very fortunate in securing the help of so many research workers and clinicians in assembling this book. My choice of contributors was by no means random. I tried first of all to choose authors who had published on a topic within the past one or two years, so as to ensure that the account they would produce would be as up-to-date as possible. Where no choice could be made on this criterion — often because nothing had, in fact, been previously published on the topic — I approached colleagues whose views I have come to value and respect and whose experience gives weight and substance to what they have to say, even on topics about which they may not previously have written.

Readers who already have some acquaintance with the literature on lithium therapy will meet some well-known names again in this book (Mogens Schou,

Amdi Amdisen, Ronald Fieve, to name just three); for the most part, however, the names will be rather less familiar because I have been more concerned to seek for fresh views and approaches than to present established dogma and doctrine for its own sake.

I hope that this book will serve several functions. Primarily it is meant to inform and guide, but I hope that it will go further than that and that it will help in some degree to shape the future of lithium therapy by making it more acceptable to patients and therapists alike. More than virtually any other psychiatric medication lithium has met with suspicion and uninformed condemnation for reasons which have more to do with history than with logic, and this (though it is less marked now than it was only five or so years ago) has led to effective treatment being denied to many who could have benefitted from it. If this book helps to break down what is left of that barrier I shall be well pleased.

Beyond that, I also aim to raise in this book a number of issues which may have far-reaching consequences, not only for the way in which treatment is carried out, but for its conceptualization: issues such as the possible superiority of a once-a-day dosage regime over a more frequent administration, and the possibilities of combining lithium with other medications to produce more effective therapies.

The successful production of a book such as this is dependent on a large number of people and it is my pleasure to make specific acknowledgement to Sylvia Sumner and Sheila Whalley who typed and retyped the various drafts, and particularly to my Editorial Assistant, Julie West. Julie has tirelessly maintained my collection of lithium literature for the past twelve years or so and has had a hand in every book I have so far produced on lithium therapy; I have come to rely heavily upon her great familiarity with the subject, the speed with which she prepares bibliographies, and the efficiency with which she organizes the complex back-up procedures which are so essential to the smooth-running of an editorial endeavour.

I am fortunate in receiving funding for my editorial assistance from Delandale Laboratories Ltd., of Canterbury, Kent. Delandale are the producers of Priadel®, a controlled-release lithium preparation, and they have always taken very seriously their responsibilities in disseminating information about lithium therapy and in encouraging the critical examination of claims made for the effectiveness of this form of treatment. John Luetchford, Keith Fanthorpe and David Trigger, in particular, have extended me every assistance and courtesy without seeking to influence my views or editorial freedom.

I must also express my gratitude to Mrs Margaret Payne, a spirited lady from Willenhall in the West Midlands of the UK, who, after learning of my work in lithium research and in the synthesis of knowledge about lithium by way of authored and edited texts, made a generous donation to my research funds which enabled me to defray the cost of postage, telephones and those many other items which so quickly drain the reserves when one engages in a publishing venture of this size.

Finally, I once again thank my long-suffering family who are, I know, heartily sick of the whole business of my editing activities, but who manage (most of the time) to hide the fact. Sorry folks — maybe this one really *is* the last.

F.Neil Johnson

LIST OF CONTRIBUTORS

M.T.Abou-Saleh, PhD, MRC Psych.
The University Department of Psychiatry,
Royal Liverpool Hospital,
PO Box 147,
Liverpool L69 3BX,
UK

Bruce Alexander, PharmD
College of Pharmacy,
University of Iowa,
Iowa City,
IA 52242,
USA

Amdi Amdisen, MD,
Psychopharmacology Research Unit,
Aarhus University Institute of Psychiatry,
Psychiatric Hospital,
Skovagervej 2,
DK-8240 Risskov,
Denmark

Raymond F.Anton, MD,
Psychiatry Service,
Veterans Administration Medical Center,
109 Bee Street,
Charleston,
SC 29403,
USA
and
Department of Psychiatry and Behavioural Sciences,
Medical University of South Carolina
SC,
USA

Hannah Ben Aryeh, PhD,
Laboratory of Oral Biology,
Department of Oral and Maxillofacial Surgery,
Rambam Medical Center,
Haifa 35254,
Israel

Ulrik Baandrup, MD, PhD,
Aarhus University Institute of Pathology,
Kommunehospitalet,
8000 Aarhus C,
Denmark

Jens Peder Bagger, MD,
Department of Cardiology,
Kommunehospitalet,
8000 Aarhus C,
Denmark

Margaret G.Baudhuin, MLS,
Lithium Information Center,
Department of Psychiatry,
University of Wisconsin Center for Health Sciences,
600 Highland Avenue,
Madison,
WI 53792,
USA

Nicholas J.Birch, PhD,
Biomedical Research Laboratory,
Wolverhampton Polytechnic,
Wolverhampton WV1 1LY,
UK

Sergio Luis Blay, MD,
Department of Psychiatry,
Escola Paulista de Medicina R.Botucatu,
740. CEP 04023 Sao Paulo,
Sao Paulo,
Brazil

B.Calon, MD,
Service de Reanimation Chirurgicale,
Hôpital de Hautepierre,
67098 Strasbourg,
France

Judith A.Carrol, MSSW,
Lithium Information Center,
Department of Psychiatry,
University of Wisconsin Center for Health Sciences,
600 Highland Avenue,
Madison,
WI 53792,
USA

M.Catalano, MD, PhD,
Institute of Clinical Psychiatry,
St Paul Hospital,
Via A.Di Rudini 8,
20142 Milan,
Italy

Steen Christensen, MD,
Copenhagen University Institute of Pharmacology,
Juliane Maries Vej,
2100 Kobenhavn 0,
Denmark

Gary D.Christian, PhD,
Department of Chemistry,
University of Washington,
Seattle,
WA 98195,
USA

C.Edward Coffey, MD,
Departments of Psychiatry and Medicine (Neurology),
Duke University Medical Center,
Durham,
NC 27710,
USA

Neil Coxhead, MB, BS, MRC Psych,
Academic Unit of Human Psychopharmacology,
Medical College of St Bartholomew's Hospital,
London EC1A 7BE,
UK

M.E.J.Curzon, PhD,
Department of Child Dental Health,
University of Leeds,
Clarendon Way,
Leeds LS2 9LU,
UK

S.Dalax, MD,
Service de Dermatologie,
Centre Hospitalier Universitaire-Bocage,
2 Boulevard Marechal de Lattre de Tassigny,
BP 1542,
21034 Dijon Cedex,
France

Lesley R.Dickson, MD,
Department of Psychiatry,
University of Kentucky College of Medicine,
820 South Limestone, Annex 2,
Lexington,
KY 40536,
USA

Ronald R.Fieve, MD,
New York State Psychiatric Institute,
Box 77,
722 West 168th Street,
New York,
NY 10032,
USA

D.Foggia, MD,
Centro Lucio Bini,
Via Crescenzio 4,
00193 Rome,
Italy

Teresita C.Frianeza-Kullberg, PhD,
Technology Department,
Lithium Corporation of America,
795 Highway 161,
Bessemer City,
NC 28016,
USA

Malcolm M.Furnell, BPharm, MRPharmS,
Pharmacy Department,
Royal Sussex County Hospital,
Eastern Road,
Brighton,
Sussex BN2 5BE,
UK

A.Galinowsky, MD,
Centre Hospitalier Sainte-Anne,
1 rue Cabanis,
75674 Paris Cedex,
France

David L.Garver, MD,
UC College of Medicine,
Department of Psychiatry,
Division of Psychobiology,
231 Bethesda Avenue,
Cincinnati,
OH 45267-0559,
USA

M.Gasperini, MD, PhD,
Institute of Clinical Psychiatry,
St Paul Hospital,
Via A. Di Rudini 8,
29142 Milan,
Italy

C.Gay, MD,
Centre Hospitalier Sainte-Anne,
1 rue Cabanis,
75674 Paris Cedex,
France

Irving H.Gomolin, MDCM, FRCPC,
Hebrew Home and Hospital,
615 Tower Avenue,
Hartford,
CT 06112-1288,
USA

Paul J.Goodnick, MD,
Department of Psychiatry,
University of Miami,
Fair Oaks Hospital at Boca/Delray,
5440 Linton Boulevard,
Delray Beach,
FL 33484,
USA

Enric Grau, MD,
Servei de Medicina Interna,
Hospital de la Santa Creu i Sant Pau,
Avinguda Sant Antoni Ma. Claret 167,
08025 Barcelona,
Spain

Waldemar Greil, MD,
University Psychiatric Hospital,
Nussbaumstrasse 7,
D-8000 Munich 2,
FRG

John H.Greist, MD,
Lithium Information Center,
Department of Psychiatry,
University of Wisconsin Center for Health Sciences,
600 Highland Avenue,
Madison,
WI 53792,
USA

Bette L.Hartley, MLS,
Lithium Information Center,
Department of Psychiatry,
University of Wisconsin Center for Health Sciences,
600 Highland Avenue,
Madison,
WI 53792,
USA

M.K.Hasan, MD, FRCP, MRP Psych,
Department of Psychiatry,
West Virginia University,
Morgantown,
WV,
USA
and
Raleigh Psychiatric Services,
PO Box 1025,
24 Mallard Court,
Beckley,
WV 25892–1025,
USA

Jonathan M.Himmelhoch, MD,
University of Pittsburgh School of Medicine,
Western Psychiatric Institute and Clinic,
3811 O'Hara Street,
Pittsburgh,
PA 15213,
USA

Freddie Ann Hoffman, MD,
Biologic Resources Branch,
Biological Response Modifiers Program,
Division of Cancer Treatment,
National Cancer Institute,
Frederick, MD 21701,
USA

Roy Hullin, PhD,
Regional Metabolic Research Unit,
Leeds Western Health Authority,
High Royds Hospital,
Menston,
Ilkley,
West Yorkshire LS29 6AQ,
UK

Kay Redfield Jamison, PhD,
Department of Psychiatry,
University of California Los Angeles School of Medicine,
Los Angeles,
CA 90024,
USA
and
1565 33rd Street N.W.,
Washington,
DC 20007,
USA

V.Chowdary Jampala, MB, BS,
Department of Psychiatry and Behavioral Sciences,
University of Health Sciences,
The Chicago Medical School,
3333 Green Bay Road,
North Chicago,
IL 60064,
USA

James W.Jefferson, MD,
Lithium Information Center,
Department of Psychiatry,
University of Wisconsin Center for Health Sciences,
600 Highland Avenue,
Madison,
WI 53792,
USA

F.Neil Johnson, PhD,
Department of Psychology,
University of Lancaster,
Fylde College,
Bailrigg,
Lancaster LA1 4YF,
UK

Peter R.Joyce, MSc, MB, ChB, MRANZCP,
Department of Psychological Medicine,
Christchurch School of Medicine,
Christchurch,
New Zealand

L.Kersten, PhD,
Institute of Pharmacology and Toxicology,
Friedrich Schiller University,
Löbderstrasse 1,
6900 Jena,
GDR

Priscilla Kincaid-Smith, MD,
Department of Medicine,
University of Melbourne,
Parkville 3052,
Victoria,
Australia

Hans Kröger, PhD, MD,
Department of Biochemistry,
Robert Koch Institute,
Nordufer 20,
D-1000 Berlin 65,
FRG

A.Kukopulos, MD,
Centro Lucio Bini,
Via Crescenzio 4,
00193 Rome,
Italy

Ihor A.Kumasz, PhD,
Foote Mineral Company,
Route 100,
Exton,
PA 19341,
USA

Chien-Suu Kuo MD,
Division of Cardiology, Room MN 670,
University of Kentucky Medical Center,
800 Rose Street,
Lexington,
KY 40536,
USA

D.Lambert, MD,
Service de Dermatologie,
Centre Hospitalier Universitaire-Bocage,
2 Boulevard Marechal de Lattre de Tassigny,
BP 1542,
21034 Dijon Cedex,
France

Jean-Michel Lemoine,
Service Hospitalo-Universitaire,
Centre Hospitalier Specialise du Rouvray,
76301 Sotteville-les-Rouen Cedex,
France

M.Lichnewsky, MD,
Service de Reanimation Chirurgicale,
Hôpital de Hautepierre,
67098 Strasbourg Cedex,
France

H.Lôo, MD,
Centre Hospitalier Sainte-Anne,
1 rue Cabanis,
75674 Paris Cedex,
France

A.Lucca, MD,
Institute of Clinical Psychiatry,
St Paul Hospital,
Via A. Di Rudini 8,
20142 Milan,
Italy

B.Ludes, MD,
Service de Reanimation Chirurgicale,
Hôpital de Hautepierre,
67098 Strasbourg Cedex,
France

Michael J.Lyons, PhD,
Department of Psychology,
Boston University,
64 Cummington Street,
Boston,
MA 02215,
USA

Alan G.Mallinger, MD,
University of Pittsburgh School of Medicine,
Western Psychiatric Institute and Clinic,
3811 O'Hara Street,
Pittsburgh,
PA 15213,
USA

Catherine A.Martin, MD,
Department of Psychiatry,
University of Kentucky Medical Center,
820 South Limestone, Annex 2,
Lexington,
KY 40536,
USA

Robin G.McCreadie, MD, FRC Psych,
Department of Clinical Research,
Crichton Royal Hospital,
Dumfries DG1 4TG,
UK

P.J.McKenna, MRC Psych,
Department of Psychiatry,
The University of Leeds,
15 Hyde Terrace,
Leeds LS2 9LT,
UK

R.H.S.Mindham, MD, FRC Psych,
Department of Psychiatry,
University of Leeds,
15 Hyde Terrace,
Leeds LS2 9LT,
UK

G.Minnai, MD,
Ospedale San Martino,
09170 Oristano,
Italy

B.Müller-Oerlinghausen, MD,
Department of Psychiatry,
Free University of Berlin,
Eischenallee 3,
D-1000 Berlin 19 (West),
FRG

D.H.Myers, FRCP(Ed), MRCP Psych,
Royal Shrewsbury Hospital,
Shelton,
Shrewsbury,
Shropshire SY3 8DN,
UK

A.G.Oswald, MB, MRC Psych,
Kingseat Hospital,
Newminster,
Aberdeen AB5 0NH,
UK

Stephen Partridge, PhD,
Biomedical Research Laboratory,
Wolverhampton Polytechnic,
Wolverhampton WV1 1LY,
UK

Paul J.Perry, PhD,
College of Pharmacy,
University of Iowa,
Iowa City,
IA 52242,
USA

Eric D.Peselow, MD,
New York University School of Medicine,
550 First Avenue,
New York,
NY 10010,
USA

Philip A.Pizzo, MD,
National Cancer Institute,
Department of Health and Human Services,
National Institute of Health,
Bethesda,
MD 20892,
USA

Robert M.Post, MD,
Biological Psychiatry Branch,
National Institute of Mental Health,
Building 10, Room 3N 212,
9000 Rockville Pike,
Bethesda,
MD 20205,
USA

T.Pottecher, MD,
Service de Reanimation Chirurgicale,
Hôpital de Hautepierre,
67098 Strasbourg Cedex,
France

Rolland I.Poust, PhD,
Burroughs Wellcome Company,
PO Box 1887,
Greenville,
NC 27835,
USA

Rudra Prakash, MD,
Department of Psychiatry,
Vanderbilt University School of Medicine,
Nashville,
TN 37232,
USA

Lawrence H.Price, MD,
Clinical Neuroscience Research Unit,
Rubicoff Research Facilities,
Connecticut Mental Health Center,
Yale University School of Medicine,
34 Park Street,
New Haven,
CT 06508,
USA

D.Reginaldi, MD,
Centro Lucio Bini,
Via Crescenzio 4,
00193 Rome,
Italy

J.A.J.Rook, NDA, MBIM,
Birdbrook Hall,
Birdbrook,
Halstead,
Essex CO9 4BJ,
UK

Donald R.Ross, MD,
The Sheppard and Enoch Pratt Hospital,
6501 North Charles Street,
Baltimore,
MD 21204,
USA

Ronald B.Salem, Pharm D,*
Department of Pharmacy Services,
University Hospital of Jacksonville,
655 W. 8th Street,
Jacksonville,
FL 32209,
USA

M.Elena Sansone, MD,
Department of Neurology,
The University of Kansas Medical Center,
39th and Rainbow Boulevard,
Kansas City,
KS 66103,
USA

Frederic J.Sautter, PhD,
UC College of Medicine,
Department of Psychiatry,
Division of Psychobiology,
231 Bethesda Avenue,
Cincinnati,
OH 45267–0559,
USA

Stephan Schmidt, MD,
University Psychiatric Hospital,
Nussbaumstrasse 7,
D-8000 Munich 2,
FRG

**Present address*
Director of Pharmacy,
Consolidated Health Care Services, Inc.,
2651 Park Street,
Jacksonville,
FL 32204,
USA

Mogens Schou,
Psychopharmacology Research Unit,
Aarhus University Institute of Psychiatry,
Psychiatric Hospital,
Skovagervej 2,
DK-8249 Risskov,
Denmark

Roderick Shelley, MRC Psych,
Department of Psychiatry,
St Brigid's Hospital,
Ardee,
Co. Louth,
Eire

Trevor Silverstone, DM, FRCP, FRC Psych,
Academic Unit of Human Psychopharmacology,
Medical College of St Bartholomew's Hospital,
London EC1,
UK

E.Smeraldi, MD, PhD,
Institute of Clinical Psychiatry,
St Paul Hospital,
Via A.Di Rudini 8,
20142 Milan,
Italy

G.A.Smythe, PhD,
Garvan Institute of Medical Research,
St. Vincent's Hospital,
Darlinghurst,
NSW 2010,
Australia

L.H.Storlien, PhD,
Garvan Institute of Medical Research,
St Vincent's Hospital,
Darlinghurst,
NSW 2010,
Australia

Klaus Thomsen, PhD, dr.med.,
Psychopharmacology Research Unit,
Aarhus University Institute of Psychiatry,
Psychiatric Hospital,
Skovagervej 2,
DK-8240 Risskov,
Denmark

L.Toro, MD,
Centro Lucio Bini,
Via Crescenzio 4,
00193 Rome,
Italy

Ming T.Tsuang, MD, PhD, DSc,
Psychiatry Service,
Brockton-West Roxbury Veterans Administration Medical Center,
940 Belmont Street,
Brockton,
MA 02401,
USA

A.Tundo, MD,
Centro Lucio Bini,
Via Crescenzio 4,
00193 Rome,
Italy

Rowan G.Walker, MD,
Department of Nephrology,
Royal Melbourne Hospital,
Parkville 3050,
Victoria,
Austalia

T.E.T.West, MD, FRCP,
Royal Shrewsbury Hospital,
Shrewsbury,
Shropshire SY3 8XF,
UK

F.Joseph Whelan, MD,
Department of Behavioural Sciences and Psychiatry,
Beckley Appalachian Regional Hospital,
306 Stanaford Road,
Beckley,
WV,
USA
and
Raleigh Psychiatric Services,
PO Box 1025,
24 Mallard Court,
Beckley,
WV 25802-1025,
USA

Ernest P.Worrall, MB, ChB, MRC Psych,
Department of Psychiatry,
Southern General Hospital,
1345 Govan Road,
Glasgow G51 4TF,
UK

Robert Y.Xie, PhD,
Department of Chemistry,
BG10,
University of Washington,
Seattle,
WA 98195,
USA

Dewey K.Ziegler, MD,
Department of Neurology,
The University of Kansas Medical Center,
39th and Rainbow Boulevard,
Kansas City,
KS 66103,
USA

Part I

INTRODUCTION

1. Mania

V.Chowdary Jampala

.... If mania is associated with joy, the patient may laugh, play, dance night and day, and go to the market crowned as if victor in some contest of skill. If it is associated with anger, the patient might tear his clothes, kill his keepers, and lay violent hands upon himself. The ideas the patients may have are infinite. Some, if intelligent and educated, believe they are experts in astronomy, philosophy or poetry ...

Aretaeus (first century AD)

Mania and melancholia were among the first psychiatric illnesses ever described, and both are referred to in the *Corpus Hippocraticum*. In what is believed to be the first treatise on psychiatric nosology, Aretaeus, a Cappadocian physician living around first century AD, described both conditions in detail.

Mania and melancholia share other things besides their history. Both are predominantly disorders of mood, perhaps representing two extremes of a continuum, and can occur at different times in the same individual or in the family of an individual suffering from one of the two. In 1854 two French psychiatrists, Jean Pierre Falret and Jules Baillarger, both from the Salpêtrière, Paris, separately described a form of 'circular' insanity in which patients suffered alternately from episodes of mania and depression, with intervening normal periods. Professor Emil Kraepelin of Munich expanded on this concept and described a group of patients with what he called manic depressive illness. By studying their clinical course, he concluded that mania and depression were part of the same illness, differing from dementia praecox by virtue of their episodic nature and preservation of intellectual function despite chronicity. Current psychiatric nosology continues to follow this classification. Mania and depression are now classified together as affective (mood) disorders, and individuals suffering from both these conditions at different times are diagnosed as having a bipolar affective disorder; when either mania or depression occur alone, the condition may be referred to as a unipolar affective disorder, though most American psychiatrists—in contrast to their European counterparts—do not see unipolar mania as a separate entity, and describe it as part of the bipolar disorder.

Although regional differences continue to exist in the diagnosis of mania, the syndrome has been noted in all cultures and races. The prevalence of mania is estimated to range between 0.1 and 0.8 per 1000 of the population. Like other affective disorders, mania is more likely to occur in women than in men, with a male to female ratio ranging from 1:1.3 to 1:2. Although the first episode of mania can occur at any age, 15–60 years is generally considered the risk period. In most cases, the first episode occurs in the second or third decade of life. Some investigators report that manics with a later age at onset are more likely to experience only manic episodes during subsequent attacks. Mania may be slighty more prevalent in higher social classes than in lower ones; the incidence of mania appears to be equal in both rural and urban areas.

In most cases of mania there are no discernible causes. Research into the occurrence of major stressful life events preceding the appearance of a manic syn-

Table 1.1 *Causes of secondary mania*

Cause	Examples
Infections	Influenza Herpes simplex encephalitis Neurosyphilis Post-St. Louis type A encephalitis Q fever
Metabolic disturbances	Postoperative states Haemodialysis Vitamin B-12 deficiency Hyperthyroidism
Structural lesions	Multiple sclerosis Parasagittal meningiomas Diencephalic gliomas Supracellar diencephalic tumour Benign spheno-occipital tumour Right intraventricular meningioma Metastases Cerebellar lesions Cortical and subcortical strokes
Medications and drugs	Bromides Calcium supplements Bronchodilators Decongestants Isoniazid Corticosteroids Procarbazine Procyclidine Phencyclidine Metoclopramide Cimetidine Levodopa

drome uncovered such events only in a small percentage of cases. There are, however, several reports of mania occurring secondary to a variety of systemic causes as listed in *Table 1.1*. Patients with secondary mania usually do not have any family history of affective disorder and often manifest a later than usual age of onset. In all cases of mania, particularly those arising in later years of life and with a negative family history of affective disorder, a careful search should be made for a systemic aetiology. This includes obtaining a good clinical history, doing a thorough physical and neurological examination, evaluating for metabolic and haematological abnormalities, and performing electroencephalographic, neuropsychological and neuroradiological studies.

Kraepelin's observation that manic depressive disease runs in families was subsequently confirmed by later investigators. It is generally agreed that about 15% of the first degree relatives of manic patients have a history of affective disorder. No specific familial pattern of transmission has been identified. Similarly, no consistent association has been discovered between the transmission of mania and any other genetic markers. The available data do not support the hypothesis that there is a single gene which is responsible for the illness. The model most commonly presented nowadays is that affective disorder results from a combination of many factors including genetic predisposition and environmental causes, with the illness appearing when the sum of these factors crosses a certain threshold. Some investigators have suggested that unipolar illness has a familial pattern that is different from bipolar disorder, but this suggestion is not universally accepted.

Figures 1.1 and *1.2* illustrate the numerous theories, chemical as well as structural, currently proposed as the biological mechanisms responsible for mania. The multiplicity of these theories, all of them needing substantiation, reflects the level of uncertainty rather than knowledge about the nature of mania.

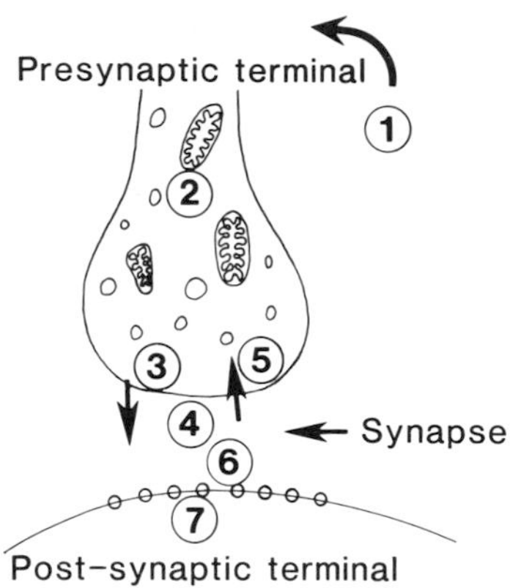

Figure 1.1 A schematic representation of neurochemical theories of mania. (**1**) Chemical events outside the neurotransmitter systems influence events at the neuronal junction (e.g. changes in cyclic AMP activity influencing noradrenergic pathways). (**2**) There is an increased amount of the neurotransmitter (noradrenaline, serotonin, GABA or even dopamine) available inside the presynaptic neuron. (**3**) Excessive amounts of the neurotransmitter are released into the neuronal junction. (**4**) Excessive amounts of the neurotransmitter are available at the synapse because the neurotransmitter cannot be broken down. (**5**) Excessive amounts of neurotransmitter are available at the synapse because the presynaptic neuron cannot adequately absorb (reuptake) the neurotransmitter. (**6**) There is an excess of one neurotransmitter at the synapse relative to another (e.g. one of the theories suggests that there is an excess of dopaminergic transmitters at the synapse relative to cholinergic transmitters). (**7**) The neurotransmitter has an aberrant action because of the altered sensitivity of the receptors on the post-synaptic neuron. The various neurochemical theories suggest that one or more of these events are responsible for the appearance of mania. The most well known of these theories, the catecholamine theory of Joseph Schildkraut, postulates an excess availability of noradrenergic transmitters at the synaptic junction as being responsible for the development of mania. This theory, however, like all others that followed it, almost certainly greatly oversimplified the actual situation, and conclusive evidence for it is still lacking.

Clinical Features

The first episode may be either manic or depressive, and about 10% of the patients may have only manic episodes without any depressive episodes. Current research suggests that these unipolar manics are not significantly different from bipolar manics, except for the difference in age of onset mentioned earlier. In a significant number of patients, there may be only one episode of mania. Manic attacks can recur at any age, and there is conflicting evidence as to whether the incidence of manic attacks increases with age.

An untreated manic episode may last from 6 months to a year before remitting spontaneously. A majority of patients can lead relatively normal lives between episodes. In an occasional patient, the episode may last for years as chronic mania. Some patients may exhibit significant residual social deficits (e.g. inability to hold a job) despite the absence of the manic syndrome.

Mania may occur rather suddenly or be preceded by a prolonged hypomanic episode or a mild depressive state. Hypomania refers to a clinical syndrome that is similar to, but not as severe as, mania. Some patients may have a long history of hypomania without ever experiencing a manic episode. The switch from

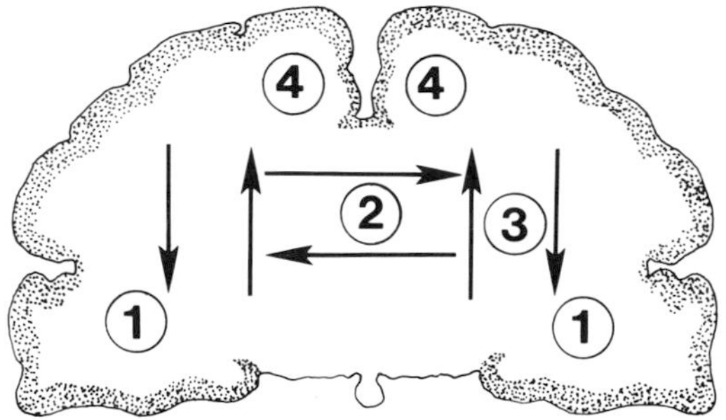

Figure 1.2 A schematic representation of structural theories of mania; the diagram shows a section through the two cerebral hemispheres. (**1**) Affective disorders result from a dysfunction of right or non-dominant hemisphere of the brain, and schizophrenia results from left hemispheric dysfunction. This theory originated from Pierre Flor Henry's observation that patients with an epileptic focus in the non-dominant temporal lobes sometimes presented with signs of affective disorders, whilst those with foci in the dominant temporal lobes presented with a picture of schizophrenia. This theory has later been modified several times. (**2**) Mania results from the overactivation of left hemisphere secondary to decreased inhibitory influences of the disabled right hemisphere. (**3**) Mania results from overactivation of subcortical structures secondary to cortical damage. (**4**) Mania results from a defect in the frontal lobes, the defect probably being in the medial and orbital areas. Like the neurochemical theories, the structural theories of mania also lack evidence to enable one to decide which, if any, offer fruitful possibilities for future research.

hypomania or depression to mania can be gradual or precipitous. Sometimes, the somatic treatments of depression may result in an abrupt switching of mood. The manic syndrome often progresses in stages, starting with a euphoric, happy state and moving on to an irritable, violent state. Then, the manic patient proceeds to exhibit 'psychotic' features of delusions, hallucinations, first rank symptoms and severe thought disorder. As the illness remits, the severe stages give way to the milder states.

Table 1.2 lists the phenomena often noted in manic patients. Aretaeus's description of mania, noted at the beginning of this section, is remarkably similar to modern descriptions of the syndrome. The hallmark, or the 'gestalt', of mania is a distinctly elevated or irritable mood in combination with stimulus-bound hyperactivity and rapid or pressured speech. The patients are often very happy and feel as if they are 'on top of the world', frequently mentioning that they are feeling 'high' or 'hyper'. They exhibit a cheerful, exuberant, infectious mood, often making the examiner laugh along with them. When the predominant mood is one of irritability, many patients are abusive and combative, with the slightest provocation evoking a fit

Table 1.2 *Phenomenology of mania*

Affect

- Intense
- Broad
- Labile
- Related

Mood

- Euphoric, elated, expansive
- Irritable, hostile, labile
- Transient depression

Thought and speech

- Rapid, pressured, flight-of-ideas
- Clang associations, rhyming, punning, joking, *Witzelsucht*, grandiosity

Dominant themes (content)

- Religion
- Sex
- Business/financial
- Persecution
- New theories/inventions

Cognitive

- Distractibility
- Stimulus-bound
- Short attention span
- Impaired concentration

Behaviour

- Hyperactive, hypergraphic, restless, agitated
- Intrusive, importunate, demanding
- Loud, vulgar, obscene, verbally abusive
- Aggressive/assaultive, threatening/menacing
- Sexually provocative/seductive
- Nudity, sexual exposure
- Incontinence of urine/faeces
- Faecal smearing
- Self-decoration, head decoration ('Mohawk' haircut, turban, earrings, wigs)
- Laughing, singing, dancing, gesticulating, saluting, military and sporting gestures, poses, postures

Social behaviour

- Extravagance
- Bad cheques
- Big bills
- Sudden trips
- Gifts
- Gambling

Vegetative signs

- Insomnia (feels less need for sleep)
- Increased libido
- Increased appetite

Based on a classification provided by Taylor,M.A., Sierles,F.S. and Abrams,R. (1985) *General Hospital Psychiatry*, The Free Press, New York.

of rage, and resulting in violent or destructive acts. Very often, the affect is labile with rapid shifting of intense moods. Manic patients may present with transient depressive states, with the happy, cheerful manic suddenly starting to cry for no apparent reason. Within minutes, this sadness may yield to extreme anger following a trivial occurrence.

In the initial phases of the illness, the patient takes on new projects and works excessively. As the illness progresses, the manic patient becomes more hyperactive, assuming several tasks simultaneously, but is unable to complete any of these. This is associated with a perception of limitless energy. Variations of hyperactivity include restlessness, intrusiveness, inquisitiveness and gregariousness. Manic patients are extremely distractible, with every stimulus in their sensory sphere demanding their immediate attention. Naturally, their concentration and the ability to attend to a task are usually severely impaired.

Manic patients are loud, talk rapidly, and their speech cannot be interrupted as they need to continue talking. The manic patient experiences 'racing thoughts', i.e. thoughts that rapidly succeed each other. Speech is often characterized by a breakdown of associations: themes with vague connections appear in succession, often the latter theme beginning before the first one ends. This 'flight of ideas' is often seen in mania, as are 'clang associations' (using words that sound similar, e.g. 'I fly, I fly, look at the sky!'). Other formal thought disorders may also occur, but much more rarely than in schizophrenics.

Manics are often very dramatic and exhibit a highly elevated self-concept. Grandiosity is very common and is considered by some as an essential feature of mania. Manic patients know everything and can do anything; they have special powers that other ordinary mortals cannot have. They may be extremely generous, conferring expensive gifts upon mere acquaintances or strangers. Deficits in judgment and lack of inhibition are common; manics engage in spending sprees or suddenly and whimsically embark on journeys. They engage in odd or dangerous activities without considering the consequences, such as directing traffic whilst standing in the middle of a heavily travelled highway, or walking around in a naked or half-naked state. They may dress in bizarre or gaudy clothes or wear eccentric headgear. They may be sexually promiscuous or engage in socially unacceptable erotic behaviour.

Sleep is much decreased, with manic patients often going for days without any sleep at all, or sleeping a couple of hours per day at most. The lack of sleep, however, does not disturb the patient, nor is the patient tired. Manic patients often state that they need no sleep at all, or else not as much as they used to. Some patients try to induce sleep by drinking alcohol or using sedative street drugs. Either for this reason, or for lack of good judgment, alcohol and other substances are often abused by these patients.

Delusions are common, with predominant themes of wealth, power, persecution and religion. Auditory hallucinations are not uncommon and even first rank symptoms such as thought broadcasting, experiences of influence and experiences of alienation are often seen. A significant proportion of patients may also exhibit the characteristic motor abnormalities of catatonia, though stupor and mutism are uncommon.

Unlike depression, there are no universally accepted rating instruments to quantify manic symptoms. As already described, manic symptoms can vary at different stages of the illness in the same person, and not all the symptoms are present in every patient. This poses a problem in quantifying manic symptoms, as a numerical sum of item scores in a scale may not give an accurate picture of severity. Of the several different scales available, the Manic State Rating Scale developed by Drs Alan Biegel and Dennis Murphy from the National Institute of Mental Health, Bethesda, MD, USA, and the modified version of Dr Ivy Blackburn and her associates, developed in Edinburgh, UK, are used frequently in mania research. For routine clinical management purposes, however, a rating scale is not necessary.

Diagnosis

There is wide variability among modern diagnostic systems as to the symptoms and signs required for a diagnosis of mania. Dr Michael Young and his associates examined the symptom patterns of successively admitted patients with a research diagnosis of mania. Using a statistical technique called latent class analysis, they suggested that if a person exhibits two out of the three features of (i) elevated, expansive or irritable mood, (ii) rapid or pressured speech and, (iii) hyperactivity, that person would also exhibit most of the other features of mania, and would be diagnosed as having mania by other diagnostic systems as well. If replicated, these findings would greatly simplify the diagnosis of mania.

Differential Diagnosis

Mania secondary to systemic illness

As already noted, systemic illnesses affecting the brain can mimic mania. For example, damage to the medial and orbital regions of the frontal lobes produces a syndrome closely resembling mania. The frontal lobe patient, however, often presents with a decreased intensity of affect with a superficial silly mood, and the hyperactivity and increased self-esteem commonly seen in mania are absent. Patients with partial complex seizures may also present with the clinical picture of mania, but the correct diagnosis can be made by paying close attention to the presence of ictal phenomena, the preictal and postictal confusional states, interictal personality changes, and characteristic electroencephalographic findings. Brain damage resulting from other causes (tumours, cerebrovascular accidents, etc.) can also produce a clinical picture which, at times, is indistinguishable from the manic syndrome except for the history of the antecedent factors.

Drug-induced manic-like behaviour

Some street drugs (e.g. amphetamines) can cause a manic-like syndrome by virtue of their cerebral toxic properties. Where acute intoxication from substances of abuse mimics mania, the diagnosis can be made from the presence of characteristic physical symptoms or from the presence of the drug and its metabolites in the patient's blood or urine. Sometimes patients with a long history of substance abuse present with a maniform syndrome in the absence of acute intoxication, and it is hard to decide whether the mania is primary or secondary to drug abuse.

Schizophrenia

The differential diagnosis of mania from schizophrenia continues to be controversial, and patients with affective disorder continue to be misdiagnosed as having schizophrenia. One reason is the decades-old misconception that certain symptoms—hallucinations, delusions, first rank symptoms, catatonia and formal thought disorder—are pathognomic of schizophrenia. This problem is compounded by the erroneous belief that manic patients are only euphoric, and when a manic patient has an irritable mood some clinicians do not look for or recognize mania. If an irritable manic patient also has ideas of persecution, that patient is often diagnosed as suffering from paranoid schizophrenia.

Several recent controlled investigations demonstrated that patients with an episodic illness, a good response to lithium, and a family history of affective disorder can at times present during the course of illness with symptoms of irritable mood, severe formal thought disorder, catatonic symptoms, delusions of a persecutory or jealous nature, auditory and other hallucinations and first rank symptoms. None of these symptoms were pathognomic of schizophrenia or any other psychiatric illness. This research also suggested that these purportedly schizophrenic symptoms were not helpful as prognostic indicators, while the affective symptoms seemed to predict a good outcome.

Elevated mood, rapid or pressured speech, and hyperactivity are rare in schizophrenia. Some schizophrenic patients present with a characteristic picture of apathy, lack of emotional response, volition and lack of ambition. Manic patients often give a history of prior manic or depressive episodes which completely remitted, allowing normal, or close to normal, functioning. In schizophrenia, a significant deterioration in social functioning is the rule. A family history of bipolar affective disorder suggests the presence of mania rather than schizophrenia.

Another problem in the differentiation of schizophrenia from mania is deciding which diagnosis should be made when both are possible but not certain (e.g. an irritable manic patient with delusions of persecution). The modern approach is to make the diagnosis of schizophrenia only when there is no evidence for an affective disorder. This is because a misdiagnosis in favour of schizophrenia exposes the patient to increased social stigma and potentially irreversible neurological damage (e.g. tardive dyskinesia) due to over-use of neuroleptic drugs. Moreover, the diagnosis of schizophrenia would augur a poor prognosis that might lead to a pessimistic attitude on the part of the treating professional. On the other hand, diagnosing mania in preference to schizophrenia would encourage a trial of relatively non-toxic medications (like lithium), and suggest a more optimistic approach from the treating professional. If the diagnosis of mania turns out to be erroneous, the patient would not respond to conventional treatments of mania and would show the progressive social deterioration characteristic of schizophrenia. At that point, the diagnosis can be revised with little, if any, harm done.

Schizoaffective disorder

Some investigators suggest that when a manic patient also exhibits symptoms of formal thought disorder, delusions, perceptual disturbances, first rank symptoms and catatonia, a diagnosis of schizoaffective disorder, a disorder hypothesized to be different from both schizophrenia and mania, should be made. Two groups of investigators, Drs Richard Abrams and Michael Alan Taylor from North Chicago, USA and Dr Harrison Pope and his associates from Boston, USA, compared manic patients with and without these schizophrenic symptoms and found that the two groups of patients did not differ from each other in treatment response, longitudinal course and family history of psychiatric illness. The only clinical feature to make any difference was the presence of emotional blunting. Manic patients with emotional blunting were similar to schizophrenics, and were more severely ill and had a poorer outcome than manics without blunting. It was suggested that patients exhibiting mania and emotional blunting together may be suffering from a variant of schizophrenia and not schizoaffective disorder. The diagnosis of schizoaffective disorder seems to have little clinical and heuristic value at the present time.

Cyclothymia

Cyclothymic disorder, in which mild depressive moods alternate with hypomanic states, is another condition that should be differentiated from mania. In cyclothymic disorder, however, neither the depressive states nor the hypomanic states are of sufficient severity or duration to be diagnosed as major depression or mania. Some investigators consider cyclothymic disorder to be a relatively benign variant of bipolar disorder, that responds to similar treatments.

Personality disorders

Various personality disorders (e.g. borderline, narcissistic) can present with some of the features associated with mania. The absence of the full manic syndrome, coupled with the presence of behaviours resulting in a lifelong pattern of significant characteristic interpersonal problems, would aid in identifying these conditions. In some patients mania may co-exist with a personality disorder, and both conditions should be diagnosed.

Treatment

In the acute phases of the illness, manic patients are very difficult to manage outside a hospital. They often lack insight into their condition, do not see themselves as being ill, and are likely to refuse treatment. As manic states can lead to behaviours resulting in irreparable harm, the patient should be hospitalized immediately (involuntarily, if necessary). Even in the hospital, manics can be extremely disruptive because of their hyperactivity, intrusiveness and impulsiveness. Strict limits should be placed on behaviour and explained to the patient. The dangers of violence and exhaustion from hyperactivity are ever present with inadequately treated manic patients, and should be addressed adequately by the ward staff. Restraints may be needed to prevent the patient harming himself or others. Once the severe manic syndrome is controlled, depending upon the resources and the compliance of the patient, treatment can be continued on an outpatient basis.

In the acute stages of the illness, psychotherapy is neither practical nor useful, and somatic treatments are imperative. Once the symptoms are controlled, the patient's personality and environmental factors may interfere with maintenance treatments, and appropriate psychological and behavioural interventions may be needed to assure compliance with medication and prevention of relapse.

Since the discovery in 1949 of the efficacy of lithium carbonate in mania (see Section 6), lithium has become the first choice of treatment in this condition. Lithium, a remarkably safe medication when taken properly under supervision, can be used both to treat an acute manic episode and to prevent recurrence of the illness. The principles and details of lithium therapy will be presented in the remainder of this volume.

However, lithium takes 1 week to 10 days before it has positive effects on acutely ill manic patients. In some irritable or psychotic patients it is impossible to wait that long: there is a risk of exhaustion or injury. Neuroleptics (e.g. chlorpromazine, haloperidol) are very effective in the treatment of the acute manic symptoms. These drugs, however, are not generally suitable for maintenance treatment of manic patients as they have toxic side effects with long-term use, and do not invariably prevent recurrence of mania. So, with few exceptions, lithium should be started as soon as possible and neuroleptics tapered off gradually once lithium reaches therapeutic concentrations in the blood.

Some manic patients do not respond either to lithium or to high doses of neuroleptics, and instead deteriorate quickly, as a result of a continuous state of manic excitement. In such cases, electroconvulsive therapy

(ECT) can be extremely effective. Published reports and clinical experience suggest that manic patients often need more treatments (eight or more) per course of ECT than do depressive patients. In cases of manic excitement, ECT is often given on two or three successive days, instead of the conventional method of alternate days. Once the excitement is controlled, the conventional timing is resumed. In some patients, it may even be necessary during the initial phase to induce seizures twice under the same anaesthesia. ECT has been demonstrated to be effective as a maintenance treatment for mania, but its relative efficacy *vis à vis* lithium has not been thoroughly investigated.

Several alternative treatments have been proposed for manic patients not responding to lithium, of which the anticonvulsant carbamazepine is the one best studied (see Section 13). Carbamazepine is useful in the treatment of the acute manic episodes, but its efficacy in the prophylaxis of manic disorders is not well demonstrated.

Lithium non-responsive patients who cannot tolerate carbamazepine, may be treated with another anticonvulsant sodium valproate (see p. 52). Several other medications, listed in *Table 1.3,* have been anecdotally reported to be useful in the treatment of mania. None of these treatments has been tested adequately for efficacy in the treatment of mania, but all of them may be considered in the treatment of manic patients that do not respond to conventional treatments.

We have come a long way from the days of treating manic patients by fasting or flogging as in ancient times, or with bromides and baths as in Kraepelin's time. The advent of lithium therapy has completely changed the management of mania. No longer suffering from the side effects of sedatives or neuroleptic drugs, properly treated manic patients can now lead full, productive lives free of any signs of illness.

Table 1.3 *Somatic treatments of mania*

Treatments with proven efficacy

- Lithium carbonate
- Neuroleptics
- Electroconvulsive therapy

Second line of treatments

- Carbamazepine
- Sodium valproate

Other treatments reported to be useful

- Ascorbic acid
- Choline, lecithin
- Clonazepam
- Clonidine
- Clorgyline
- Fenfluramine
- Methylene blue
- Physostigmine
- Propranolol
- Spironolactone
- Tryptophan
- Verapamil

Bibliography

Kraepelin,E. (1913) *Manic Depressive Insanity and Paranoia.* (Barclay,R.M., transl.) E.& S.Livingstone, Edinburgh, UK, 1921. Facsimile edition published by Arno Press, New York, USA, 1976.
This classic describes manic depressive illness in detail. The clinical descriptions are still valid and make for interesting reading.

Pope,H.G.,Jr and Lipinski,J.F. (1978) Diagnosis in schizophrenia and manic depressive illness. *Arch. Gen. Psychiatry,* **35**, 811–828.
A review looking at the differential diagnosis of schizophrenia and manic-depressive illness and the specificity of the so-called schizophrenic symptoms.

Winokur,G., Clayton,P.J. and Reich,T. (1969) *Manic-Depressive Illness.* C.V.Mosby Co., St Louis, USA.
This book, though somewhat outdated, should be read for its review of the literature and for the excellent chapter on the results from the authors' study describing the characteristics of manic and depressive episodes.

Young,M.A., Abrams,R., Taylor,M.A. and Meltzer,H.Y. (1983) Establishing diagnostic criteria for mania. *J. Nerv. Ment. Dis.,* **171**, 676–682.
The authors' use of latent class analysis, a novel statistical technique, permits them to conclude that the diagnosis of mania can be made with good validity, based on the presence of only two core symptoms.

2. Depression

P.J.McKenna

Perhaps nothing in psychiatry has aroused as much dispute as depression. On the one hand, the concept describes a universal human experience which may become severe and prolonged without ever deserving the designation of abnormal. On the other, it must encompass states of devastation of mood, accompanied by the wildest delusions and hallucinations, which are liable to give even the most experienced psychiatrist pause. To make matters worse, any formulation must accommodate the variable association of depression with mania.

Historically, clearly abnormal depressed mood states have been recognized from antiquity as 'melancholia'. It was not until the end of the nineteenth century, however, that Emil Kraepelin drew together a number of melancholic states, some simple and some complicated by delusions and hallucinations, and argued that they were all manifestations of a single disorder. He further incorporated these into a general category of manic depressive insanity, a disease characterized by the tendency to recurrent development of episodes of depressed and elated mood. Apart from replacement of the term 'insanity' by 'psychosis', Kraepelin's classifactory scheme stands essentially unchanged to the present day.

Interest in depressive states not immediately announcing their abnormal quality began towards the end of the last century, when the concept of psychiatric illnesses as reactions emerged. In the early part of this century attention began to focus on depressive states as prime examples of this, and the rise of psychodynamic psychiatry gave added impetus to this approach. The idea of depression as an understandable response to adverse experience became established, quickly achieved prominence, and the contemporary controversies over the number, classification and distinction of depressive states were ushered in.

Current views can be outlined as follows. It is recognized that some individuals develop depressive states that are independent of adverse experience, which may show grossly abnormal features, which resolve completely often with physical treatments, and which are prone to recur or be followed by episodes of mania. In short, a form of depression exists which is to all intents and purposes a medical illness; this is referred to variously as endogenous depression, major depression, or (as here) manic-depressive psychosis depressed type. It is also accepted that in some people under stress the normal response of unhappiness may become pronounced. These states are not accompanied by bizarre symptoms and respond poorly to medical treatments, though social measures can be effective. Such presentations, which are not illnesses in any meaningful sense, are generally referred to as reactive or neurotic depression. Finally, it is clear that significant numbers of depressed patients do not fit neatly into one or the other of these categories, thus raising important questions about the nature of manic-depressive psychosis depressed type and its relationship to reactive or neurotic depression.

Clinical Features of Manic-depressive Psychosis Depressed Type

The general illness characteristics of manic-depressive psychosis are well established. It occurs with a prevalence of 2–5% in the population and is about twice as common in women as in men. Some patients exhibit episodes of both depression and mania with, on average, depressive episodes outnumbering manic by about four to one. This is the bipolar form of manic-depressive psychosis. Other patients have a so-called unipolar illness, i.e. they experience periods of depression only. Cases of unipolar mania almost certainly also occur, but are rare. At least half of the patients who develop an attack of mania, and up to two-thirds of those with depression, will have no further episodes. Others suffer only occasional episodes separated by years or decades. Yet others will follow a regularly or erratically relapsing course; a small number experience more or less continuous affective illness with only brief periods of normality between—the rapid cycling variant of manic-depressive psychosis.

Manic-depressive psychosis depressed type may occur in childhood, though there are considerable difficulties in estimating its frequency. It is uncommon in early adult life but its prevalence increases steadily with age and becomes commonplace after the age of 40. Opinions differ as to whether a peak incidence is reached in middle age or whether the illness increases steadily in frequency throughout life.

The onset of an episode of manic-depressive psychosis depressed type is highly variable. Most typically it emerges gradually over a few months; occasionally it develops over days or weeks; there are undoubtedly cases where mood insidiously worsens over years. Once established, an episode lasts on average 6–9 months, but once again this is variable: remission may take place almost immediately; occasionally the illness will persist, despite aggressive treatment, for years. Perhaps the most reliable characteristic of manic-depressive psychosis depressed type is its tendency to recover. Even before the discovery of effective treatments, the rule was spontaneous remission with full recovery of function, even after months or years of illness. In a small percentage of cases, however, the abnormal state persists indefinitely, these patients showing a picture of chronic depression.

The symptom picture of manic-depressive psychosis

depressed type has been defined as a primary disturbance of mood from which all other symptoms can be more or less directly derived. In practice, the picture consists of an altered mood plus several other classes of symptom, any one of which can dominate the mental state to the virtual exclusion of all others.

Alteration of mood

The central abnormal mood state of manic-depressive psychosis depressed type is said to have a distinct quality and to bear only a superficial resemblance to that of ordinary unhappiness. Terms like 'loss of interest', 'vital inhibition' and 'anhedonia' (inability to experience pleasure) have been used to try to capture the quality of the change, which patients themselves quite commonly contrast with their usual experience of sadness. The mood state tends to be unreactive to circumstances, though it may fluctuate in intensity on a day-to-day basis.

It has to be said, however, that this distinctive mood is a far from universal finding. Sometimes the mood is merely reported as 'miserable' and no amount of questioning will elicit any exceptional features. In other cases, there are only nebulous complaints, or another mood state altogether, like irritability, dominates the picture. Occasionally, there is no subjective mood change whatsoever, although the accessory features of manic-depressive psychosis depressed type are plainly evident.

Psychomotor changes

There may be varying degrees of impairment in thinking, energy and motor activity. At the mildest these psychomotor changes may be represented only by vague subjective descriptions of reduced energy or slowness in thought and movement. When more severe, objective motor retardation can be discerned. Movements are slow, hesitant, poorly sustained; the posture is slumped, facial expression does not vary; expressive gestures all but disappear; speech becomes soft and monotonous; and replies are delayed and tend to trail off. In the most extreme expression of these symptoms, the patient sinks into depressive stupor: though conscious, all movement ceases and the patient lies mute and incontinent with a peculiar vacant, strained, disturbed facial expression.

A few patients with manic-depressive psychosis depressed type, instead of developing retardation, show the inverse abnormality—agitation. This ranges from a minor, slightly unnatural, fidgetiness to a pronounced state of motor unrest, the patient standing up and sitting down, pacing back and forth, wringing his hands and pulling at his hair. Sometimes retardation and agitation seem simultaneously present.

Abnormal experiential phenomena

Changes in judgment, belief and perception are characteristically present in manic-depressive psychosis depressed type, even if they have to be sought. Commonly they take the form of unfounded ideas of hopelessness, self depreciation and self blame: the patient will feel that he may never recover, that he is a failure, that he has let his family down and that he is a burden to them. Alternatively, there may be an unreasonable concern with health, the patient believing he has syphilis, cancer and so on. In some cases, via various transitions, these ideas give way to clear-cut depressive delusions. The patient expresses floridly abnormal fixed beliefs; that he is the worst sinner in the world, that he deserves the death penalty, that his insides are rotting, even that he is dead! These delusions can be accompanied by hallucinations which also betray a pronounced depressive quality—examples include hearing gallows being erected outside, seeing corpses, empty coffins and crowds of monsters, and hearing the screams of children being tortured.

Delusions and hallucinations are, by definition, psychotic phenomena and their presence as a complication of manic-depressive psychosis depressed type sometimes blurs the boundary with the other main psychotic illness, schizophrenia. It has traditionally been maintained that the delusions and hallucinations of manic-depressive psychosis should be 'congruent' with the mood state, i.e. their content should express depressive themes. It is, however, clear that this is not always the case; largely for this reason, the issue of whether manic-depressive psychosis and schizophrenia are distinct conditions is a long-standing area of dispute in psychiatry.

Neurotic symptoms

It is not disputed that manic-depressive psychosis depressed type appears in some way to be able to release various symptoms which, when they occur in isolation, are termed neurotic. The most notable of these is anxiety. The majority of episodes of manic-depressive psychosis depressed type are accompanied by some increase in general anxiety level; not uncommonly this becomes a prominent feature; in a minority of cases there are clear-cut phobias or panic attacks. In much the same way, obsessive-compulsive symptoms, particularly obsessional ruminations, may complicate otherwise unremarkable cases of manic-depressive psychosis depressed type. Rarely, hysterical conversion symptoms present for the first time in the same setting.

It is the occurrence of these neurotic symptoms, above all, which raises conceptual and diagnostic difficulties for manic-depressive psychosis depressed type. Anxiety, obsessional or other neurotic symptoms may occasionally dominate the clinical picture with the depressive syndrome being barely detectable in the background. Consequently, it can be impossible to decide whether the patient has a primary neurotic disorder or is suffering from a 'masked' depression. Conceptually, the relationship between anxiety and depression, in particular, is intimate, far from fully understood, and has yet to be adequately encompassed in any theoretical model.

Miscellaneous features

In many cases of manic-depressive psychosis depressed type there is a cluster of quasi-physiological changes or biological symptoms. These include poor appetite, weight loss, sleep disturbance, with early morning wakening, diurnal variation in mood and loss of libido. As with other classes of depressive symptom, there is no necessity for biological symptoms to be present; they tend, for instance, to be absent in younger patients. Their major importance is diagnostic – such symptoms are only seen in reactive or neurotic depression when this is severe and even then are usually not full-blown.

A group of ill-defined cognitive changes are also recognized in manic-depressive psychosis depressed type. Usually they are evidenced by subjective poor concentration and memory difficulties. Less commonly, there is an objectively discernible narrowing, stereotypy and impoverishment of thought, the patient constantly rehearsing a small repertoire of depressive themes. Very rarely cognitive symptoms overwhelm all others and give rise to a picture resembling that of organic intellectual impairment, the so-called depressive pseudo-dementia.

In manic-depressive psychosis depressed type all kinds of non-specific aches and pains are common; occasionally somatic symptoms dominate the picture, and lead to fruitless physical investigations. Anti-social and aggressive behaviour is occasionally seen; this is usually, but not always, minor and in general is inextricably bound up with a desire for punishment. Also well recognized are the frequent suicidal and self harming thoughts. Suicide is, in fact, a real risk, and may be extremely violent.

The Relationship with Reactive or Neurotic Depression

The greatest controversy in manic-depressive psychosis depressed type surrounds not its existence, which is undisputed, but its separability from the state of understandable unhappiness designated reactive or neurotic depression. There are essentially two schools of thought. The first, deriving from Kraepelin and influenced by the striking picture of severe depressive states, maintains that manic-depressive psychosis depressed type and reactive or neurotic depression are entirely separate conditions. Any similarities between their symptoms are superficial, and the former is an endogenous illness while the latter is the response of an intact nervous system to environmental stress. The second view, first formally articulated by the British psychiatrist Aubrey Lewis, takes account of clinical experience with large numbers of depressed patients. It argues that manic-depressive psychosis depressed type and reactive or neurotic depression are in some sense on a continuum with each other: a spectrum of presentations of depression is apparent, there is no clear point of demarcation along this, and the relationship to precipitating stress in any particular case is not simple. Conflict over these views has generated a great deal of experimental investigation, and this has proceeded along two main lines – analysis of depressive symptom patterns and examination of the role of antecedent stress.

The symptoms displayed by patients complaining of depression are amenable to investigation by statistical techniques like factor, cluster and discriminant function analysis. On theoretical grounds, in a large, unselected population of depressed patients, the symptoms should segregate in two patterns if there are two kinds of depression, or fail to do so if there is only one. With only one important exception, the results of such investigations are in agreement: a symptom complex conforming closely to the conventional picture of manic-depressive psychosis depressed type can be isolated as a coherent syndrome, distinct from one or more other categories.

Such studies provide strong justification for the existence of an entity of manic-depressive psychosis depressed type. Unfortunately, the same studies make its conceptualization difficult. The disorder is not easily understood as a discrete *category* of illness with a unique set of symptoms or signs. It seems rather to represent a *dimension* of suffering, along which certain symptoms tend to cluster, producing a progressively more distinctive state as severity increases. Adding further complexities, some studies have found no single corresponding symptom complex of reactive or neurotic depression, but instead two or three different forms of this. The concept of a single entity of reactive or neurotic depression clearly does not do justice to the diversity of non-psychotic depressive states.

The other avenue of investigation into the relationship between manic-depressive psychosis depressed type and reactive or neurotic depression has been to look for the presence of precipitating stressful events. Traditionally, manic-depressive psychosis has been characterized as an innate illness arising *de novo*, whereas in reactive or neurotic depression there is the obvious implication of response to adverse experience. Although the assessment of stressful life events is fraught with methodological pitfalls, a number of studies have been undertaken and a reliable conclusion has been reached: life events do significantly predispose to the development of a clinically depressed state and this holds true to the same extent in manic-depressive psychosis depressed type as in reactive or neurotic depression.

In terms of its reactiveness, then, manic-depressive psychosis depressed type is not distinct from reactive or neurotic depression. Nevertheless, there is a qualification to this conclusion. Though established beyond reasonable doubt, the association between depression and preceding stress is not strong. Half of all depressions develop in the absence of any identifiable life events, this applying equally to cases of manic-depressive psychosis depressed type and reactive or neurotic depression. Even following the powerful stress of bereavement, the incidence of clinical depressive states is only about 5%.

In summary, manic-depressive psychosis depressed type and reactive or neurotic depression are distinct in terms of the clinical features they show. Even though the two constellations of symptoms overlap to an uncomfortable degree, and may be better understood in some way as 'dimensions' rather than 'categories' of illness, the available evidence points to a fundamental distinction between them. On the other hand, manic-depressive psychosis depressed type is not distinguishable from reactive or neurotic depression on the basis of the part played by antecedent stress —the 'reactiveness' of the two conditions. Nevertheless, the role of stress in both disorders is small and it is at least as difficult to understand why it plays so little a role in reactive or neurotic depression as it is to understand why it should contribute to the development of manic-depressive psychosis depressed type.

The Aetiology of Depression

As with most psychiatric disorders, the cause of manic-depressive psychosis depressed type is unknown. At present, all that can be said is that a number of general aetiological factors have been identified, and that a large body of evidence points to a specific pathogenesis of the depressive state in the shape of abnormal monoamine neurotransmitter function.

General aetiological factors

Heredity. It is common psychiatric knowledge that affective psychosis, bipolar and unipolar, shows a familial tendency, and the evidence for a genetic component to the disorder is strong. To move beyond this broad statement, however, has proved difficult, and the many family history studies have faced considerable methodological obstacles. The state of the evidence can be outlined as follows. The risk of the identical twin of a patient with manic-depressive psychosis depressed type developing the same illness is of the order of 30–50%. The risk in other first degree relatives is in the range of 5–15%. However, at least half of all patients who develop manic-depressive psychosis depressed type will have no demonstrable family history of the condition. No simple model of inheritance can be made to fit these data; clearly, genetic factors are not all-important and it is widely believed that in manic-depressive psychosis genetic predisposition interacts with ill-defined or unknown environmental influences.

Personality. This is traditionally given particular scrutiny in psychiatric illness. In the case of manic-depressive psychosis depressed type it has emerged that while, broadly speaking, the disorder may strike anyone, it shows a mild preference for certain personality types. Individuals showing a life-long affective colouring to their temperament, either hypomanic (hyperthymic), depressive (dysthymic), or alternating between the two (cyclothymic), have been regularly observed to be prone to develop episodes of manic-depressive psychosis. Kraepelin, in fact, considered that such individuals were merely suffering from a sub-clinical 'constitutional' form of the illness. Formal evidence supports this association, particularly that between depressive personality style and unipolar manic-depressive psychosis depressed type. Somewhat more tenuously, the obsessional personality trait, with love of orderliness, meticulousness, rigidity and indecisiveness has been claimed to predipose towards manic-depressive psychosis depressed type. This view continues to figure in the literature but systematic investigation has yielded only conflicting results.

Loss. Loss is the most contentious aetiological factor postulated for manic-depressive psychosis depressed type. Deriving ultimately from psychoanalytic views, it maintains that experience of particular classes of stress increases the individual's later vulnerability to depression. The relevant stresses typically involve an element of loss, either overt, as in bereavement or parental separation, or more covert, as in loss of status, self-esteem and so on. Some versions of the hypothesis emphasize the immediate impact of loss events; others argue that their occurrence at critical periods in childhood increases susceptibility to depression in adult life. While, as described above, there is good evidence that stress is a significant factor in the precipitation of manic-depressive psychosis depressed type, attempts to implicate loss events in particular have not met with any great success. Whether loss in early life is a significant risk factor for adult depression is even more contentious, with studies finding an association and those failing to do so being equally divided.

Pathogenesis: the neurotransmitter hypothesis

When Kraepelin originated the concept of manic-depressive psychosis, he believed the disorder to have an essentially organic basis. Subsequently, there was a progressive recognition that states more or less indistinguishable from manic-depressive psychosis depressed type could occur as a complication of various physical illnesses affecting brain function. In the 1950s, this aetiological tradition received renewed impetus following three fortuitous observations. Reserpine, a drug introduced to lower blood pressure, was noted to induce depressive states in a significant proportion of patients. Another drug, iproniazid, undergoing evaluation as an anti-tuberculosis agent, was found to elevate mood quite regularly. A few years later imipramine, an experimental analogue of the anti-schizophrenic drug chlorpromazine, though ineffective in schizophrenia, appeared to have dramatic effects on depression. These three drugs were all shown to exert their principle pharmacological effects on monoamine (noradrenaline, dopamine and serotonin) systems in the brain, and the neurotransmitter hypothesis of manic-depressive psychosis was born.

Three decades later, despite massive advances in understanding, the role of monoamine neurotransmitters in manic-depressive psychosis depressed type is far from clearly understood. No monoamine abnormality has been conclusively demonstrated, and the actions of antidepressant drugs on these systems is more complex than originally thought. Nevertheless, too much evidence has accumulated to dismiss their importance in the pathogenesis of depression and mania. For example, when the effects of a wide variety of psychotropic drugs are examined, clear correlations emerge between their mood altering properties and their ability to induce changes in monoamine transmitter function. Broadly, drugs which elevate mood either clinically (e.g. tricyclic antidepressants) or experimentally (e.g. amphetamine) tend to enhance noradrenaline, dopamine and serotonin function. On the other hand, those which have depressant effects (e.g. reserpine) tend to impair function in these systems. There are, however, many inconsistencies in this simple model. The direct relationship between mood and monoamine function is perhaps best substantiated for noradrenaline; it holds true only equivocally for dopamine, and in the case of serotonin the evidence is highly contradictory.

There has been some direct examination of monoamine function in patients with manic-depressive psychosis depressed type. It is possible to examine the metabolic products of monoamine metabolism in urine and cerebrospinal fluid. Also, in patients who die coincidentally or by suicide whilst depressed, brain monoamine levels can also be measured directly. The results of many studies have revealed no unequivocal abnormalities; the findings can perhaps be best described as intriguing. There is a degree of support for reduced noradrenergic function in depression; analogous changes in dopamine function have not been convincingly demonstrated; the data on serotonin suggest that levels may be low in both mania and depression (and remain low between episodes). A few recent studies

Table 2.1 *Findings of abnormal monoamine function in depression*

	Monoamine		
	Noradrenaline	Serotonin	Dopamine
Urinary metabolites	Some difficulties in interpretation; levels low, but only significantly so in bipolar cases	Serious difficulties in interpretation; some studies report reduced levels	Cannot be determined because of difficulties in interpretation
Cerebrospinal fluid metabolites	Conflicting findings of normal or reduced function	More consistent findings of reduced fuction, but not all studies in agreement. Function may be reduced in mania as well	No marked alteration; a few studies suggest minor reduced function
Post mortem brain	No alteration in most indices of function. Recent studies raise possibility of reduced function	Initial studies suggested reduced function. More recent studies point to unaltered function or increase in some indices	No alteration in function a consistent finding
Overall views	Strong suggestions of abnormal function. Recent shift of emphasis from simple reduction to more complex alterations	Original view was reduced function predisposing to episodes of both depression and mania. Recent findings challenge this and suggest normal, increased or complex changes in function	Normal function, or reduced function plays only accessory role in some cases

have challenged all these findings and have pointed instead to increased serotonin function in depression (*Table 2.1*).

In short, converging lines of evidence make it difficult to resist the conclusion that monoamine function is disturbed in manic-depressive psychosis depressed type. At the same time, however, it has become increasingly clear that the relevant changes are not simple. Some authors, attempting to resolve the contradictions in the data, have proposed there may be different subgroups of depressed patients—those with altered noradrenaline or those with altered serotonin function, for instance. Others have argued that only one transmitter abnormality is primary, and the changes seen in the other systems are secondary consequences of this. But perhaps the most plausible view is that manic-depressive psychosis depressed type, rather than representing a *fixed* alteration in monoamine levels, is in fact the expression of a *dynamic* dysregulation: an underlying abnormality in homeostatic regulation makes one or more monoamine systems vulnerable to unstable function under stress. This unstable function may result in overall high, normal or low transmitter levels, but, more importantly, in their erratic, uncoordinated and desynchronized function.

The Treatment of Depression

To a considerable extent, the treatment of manic-depressive psychosis depressed type reflects prevailing views on its causation and nosological status. When a patient presents with a depressive complaint, the diagnostic aim is to determine whether he shows the set of symptoms characteristic of the disorder. If so, the major therapeutic approach is pharmacological, to correct the presumed underlying monoamine transmitter abnormalities. Psychological treatment is not entirely disregarded, however, and may assume particular importance after recovery.

In an acute episode of manic-depressive psychosis depressed type, the first line of treatment is to use tricyclic antidepressants or related drugs. These act to enhance noradrenaline and serotonin function, but probably exert their main effects by initiating a complex sequence of alterations in neurotransmitter regulation, the net result of which is to move function towards normality. They show a delayed mode of onset, and treatment fails in a significant proportion of places for reasons which remain unclear. Electroconvulsive therapy (ECT) is the usual second line of treatment, being given when tricyclic antidepressants fail or when severity of the episode precludes any delay in treatment. ECT induces a generalized epileptic seizure, and this in turn gives rise to various changes in monoamine function. The effectiveness and safety of this treatment has been established beyond reasonable doubt in well controlled studies. Monoamine oxidase inhibitors find only occasional usage; although they elevate monoamine levels they have been found generally to be less effective than tricyclic antidepressants.

When manic-depressive psychosis depressed type follows a relapsing course there is need for maintenance or prophylactic treatment. Both tricyclic antidepressants and lithium have been shown to exert significant protection against development of further episodes (Section 13), and broadly speaking they are probably of about equal effectiveness. Patients with bipolar illnesses may, however, respond better to lithium than those with unipolar manic-depressive psychosis depressed type (see Section 9).

Psychotherapy also finds its major application during the maintenance stage of treatment. Its goal is to modify the patient's attitudes, habitual responses, or basic personality in the hope that this will prevent the stresses which can trigger off future episodes of depression.

Occasionally, despite aggressive treatment, patients with manic-depressive psychosis depressed type either fail to improve or follow a rapidly relapsing course. In such cases combination drug treatments may be tried: a number of 'cocktails' have been devised, combining lithium, tricyclic antidepressants and monoamine oxidase inhibitors or other drugs. In a few cases, maintenance ECT, given, for instance, monthly, may be effective.

Finally, there is the psychosurgical procedure of prefrontal leucotomy. This operation disconnects certain pathways in the frontal lobes of the brain and in the past was carried out indiscriminately or even gratuitously on large numbers of chronically ill patients. This practice has rightly been condemned; nevertheless, it leaves the legacy that in selected cases of manic-depressive psychosis depressed type it can bring about dramatic improvement.

Acknowlegement

This work was funded, in part, by the Veterans Administration General Medical Research Program.

Thanks are due to Professors Egill Snorrason and the late Erik Jacobsen, both of Copenhagen, and to Dr Neil Johnson of Lancaster, for their interest in my work on the first era of lithium therapy.

Bibliography

Kendall,R.E. (1976) The classification of depression: a review of contemporary confusion. *Br. J. Psychiatry,* **129**, 15–28.
The definitive article on the relationship between manic-depressive psychosis depressed type and reactive or neurotic depression.

Siever,L.J. and Davis,K.L. (1985) Overview: toward a dysregulation hypothesis of depression. *Am. J. Psychiatry,* **142**, 1017–1031.
A model for understanding affective disorders as failures in monoamine transmitter regulation, rather than as simple increases or decreases in their activity is presented in this paper. This model is likely to be influential in determining the direction of future research.

Snaith,P. (1981) *Clinical Neurosis*. Oxford University Press, Oxford.
Contains an authoritative account of depression, from the standpoint of reactive or neurotic depression.

Willner,P. (1985) *Depression: A Psychobiological Synthesis*. Wiley Interscience, New York.
An exhaustive review of all aspects of the aetiology of depression.

3. Manic-depressive Illness

Ming T.Tsuang and Michael J.Lyons

Although there are written descriptions from as early as the second century AD of individuals who experienced alternating periods of euphoria and depression it is Emil Kraepelin, who worked around the turn of the century, who is usually given credit for the modern conception of manic-depressive illness. However, a French psychiatrist, Jean Pierre Falret, described 'circular insanity' in 1854 in terms that bear a striking similarity to the current diagnosis of manic-depressive illness or bipolar disorder.

The term bipolar disorder refers to individuals who have experienced at least one manic episode, though as the word 'bipolar' suggests, there is an implicit assumption that a depressive episode has occurred or will occur. A semantically consistent diagnostic system would reserve the designation 'bipolar' for individuals with both manic and depressive episodes and 'unipolar' for individuals with only one type. In what follows here, the convention is adopted of using the term 'bipolar' for individuals who have experienced at least one manic episode, and 'nonbipolar' for individuals who have experienced one or more depressive episodes and no manic episodes. 'Nonbipolar' is preferred to 'unipolar' because some authors reserve 'unipolar' to describe individuals with recurrent depressions. The category of 'nonbipolar' also includes individuals with only one depressive episode. While there are some individuals with a history of only manic episodes, experience suggests that the large majority will eventually suffer a depressive episode.

A number of sub-categories within the overall category of bipolar disorder have been suggested. The term 'bipolar I' is commonly used to describe individuals who have experienced at least one full-fledged manic episode, while 'bipolar II' refers to individuals who have experienced a major depressive episode as well as at least one hypomanic episode, (a period of elevated mood and associated features that is not as extreme or incapacitating as a full manic episode). 'Cyclothymia' refers to a chronic, alternating pattern of hypomanic periods and depressive periods not severe enough to be considered major depression with periods of normal mood being relatively brief.

Epidemiology

Epidemiological research indicates that bipolar disorder is the least common of the principal psychotic conditions, probably occurring less than half as often as schizophrenia. Available information from a survey of several areas in the USA suggests that approximately 1% of the population has ever had a manic episode; nonbipolar depression is about four or five times more common. Women are about twice as likely as men to experience nonbipolar depression; female rates of bipolar disorder also exceed male rates but the differences are not as great.

Unlike schizophrenia, there are no striking associations of demographic characteristics with bipolar disorder other than the sex difference in rates. While many major psychiatric disorders are more common in the lowest social classes, bipolar disorder is not, and there is some suggestion that it may be more common in groups of above average socio-economic status. Individuals with bipolar disorder are less likely to be married than unaffected individuals but it is unclear whether bipolar disorder is a cause or an effect.

So far, one of the most productive strategies for identifying risk factors for bipolar disorder has been genetic-family research. Evidence from the three major types of psychiatric genetic research (family, twin and adoption studies) supports the role of genetic factors in bipolar disorder. However, the existence of identical twin pairs discordant for bipolar disorder suggests that non-genetic factors are also important.

Once the role of genetic factors is demonstrated, genetic research seeks to identify the mode of transmission. There is evidence suggesting that there may be at least two genetically distinct subtypes of bipolar disorder. One subtype seems to be transmitted by a gene on the X-chromosome, but cases of father-son transmission indicate that this is not the only form of inheritance. It has been estimated that X-linked transmission may account for about one third of bipolar disorder. Evidence has also been adduced to support the possibility that the genetic liability to develop bipolar disorder may lie on a continuum with nonbipolar depression.

Age at Onset

The researchers Frederick Goodwin and Kay Jamison from the US National Institute of Mental Health reviewed 15 studies that provided information about the age of onset of bipolar disorder. Combining the studies yielded an average age of onset for males of 33.2 years and for females 31.7 years. Unfortunately, most of these studies reported the *average* age of onset, which can be misleading because the 'average' may be inflated by a relatively small number of individuals with very late onset. These figures are also difficult to interpret unambiguously because some investigators consider 'onset' to be the first symptoms, others the first episode, and still others the first treatment. The range of ages of onset is quite broad, with one study reporting a range of 8–74 years for the occurrence of the first symptoms. There is equivocal evidence suggesting two peaks in the distribution of ages, with one peak before age 30 and another during the mid to late 40s. The onset of bipolar disorder usually occurs at an earlier age than nonbipolar depression.

Number of Episodes

The number of episodes that an individual with bipolar disorder will experience is quite variable. Some studies have found that 50% of such individuals will experience only one episode while other studies found no subject with fewer than two episodes. Conflicting findings are difficult to reconcile, due at least in part to differing definitions of an episode. For example, some studies classify a hospital stay of several years as one episode.

One consistent finding has been that bipolar disorder is associated with a greater number of episodes than nonbipolar disorder. In a study conducted at the US National Institute of Mental Health, Kathleen Squillace and her colleagues found an average of 30.9 previous affective episodes among their bipolar patients and 2.6 among the nonbipolar, although there were no significant differences between the groups in the number of weeks the patients were symptomatic or the number of hospitalizations per year. These researchers also found that the number of episodes during the preceding year was a good predictor of the number during the subsequent year and that there was a high correlation between the number of manic and depressive episodes.

Duration of Episodes

Since the development of effective treatment, it is no longer feasible to study the natural or untreated course of bipolar disorder. Fortunately, relevant data are available from the period before the advent of lithium therapy. The average length of episodes reported in these early studies ranges from 3 to 12 months. Professor F.Wertham working at Johns Hopkins Medical School, for example, reported that most untreated first episodes of mania lasted from 60 to 180 days and several lasted more than 5 years. There are conflicting findings with regard to the relationship between duration of illness and length of episode, with some authorities asserting that episode length increases, others saying that it decreases, and yet others reporting a relatively consistent length. Manic episodes begin more abruptly than depressive episodes and bipolar individuals have a more rapid onset of depressive episodes than do nonbipolars.

Cycle or Period Length

Cycle length refers to the length of time between the onset of one episode and the onset of the next. Thus, a cycle includes an episode and the time from the end of the episode until the beginning of the next episode (called the 'free period'). Frederick Goodwin and Kay Jamison have conducted a thorough review of findings regarding cycle length. There is a consistent finding that the first several cycles typically become successively shorter. The longest cycle length is usually found between the first and second episodes, especially in individuals with an onset before age 30. The Swiss psychiatrist Jules Angst found that 17% of his bipolar patients had an initial cycle length of more than 5 years. Later age of onset has been reported to be associated with shorter cycle length. It also seems that increasing age, independent of age of onset, predicts shorter cycle length.

Outcome

The absence of a chronic, deteriorating course was central to Kraepelin's differentiation of manic-depressive illness from dementia praecox (or schizophrenia). Subsequent research has confirmed his assertion that affective disorder has a more favourable outcome than schizophrenia. However, there is evidence that bipolar disorder may have adverse effects on long term functioning relative to individuals without psychiatric disorder. In a study conducted in Iowa it was found that in the areas of marital, residential, and occupational status and psychiatric symptoms, individuals who had been hospitalized with bipolar disorder had an outcome intermediate between schizophrenics and non-psychiatric, surgical patients. Specifically, 30–40 years after their hospitalization, bipolar patients were functioning better than schizophrenics, less well than surgical patients, and about the same as nonbipolar depressives in the four domains examined. In the area of marital status 70% were married at the time of follow-up, 8% were divorced or separated and 22% had never married. In the area of residential status almost 69% lived in their own or their families' home, 17% lived in a nursing or country home and 14% were in mental hospitals. About 68% of the sample received a rating of 'good' for occupational status because they were either working, retired or functioning as a housewife or student. Some 8% were incapacitated by physical illness and 24% were incapacitated by mental illness. At the time of the follow-up evaluation 50% of the sample were free of psychiatric symptoms, 21% had some symptoms, and 29% had incapacitating symptoms. These data are cross-sectional, that is, they represent a 'snapshot' of how people were functioning at the particular time they were evaluated 30 or 40 years after their hospitalization. We do not have information about how people came to be in these categories or how stable a given level of functioning is. It may be that at any given time about 50% of the sample will be symptom free, but the individuals comprising this group may change over time. It is worth noting that at least half of the bipolar subjects had a 'good' outcome in each domain. This underscores the variability in prognosis; some individuals recover fully and others may progress to rapid cycling or nearly continuous episodes. Factors contributing to negative outcomes probably include chronic symptoms as well as the social consequences of behaviour during episodes and identification as a psychiatric patient. Bipolar disorder is associated with an elevation of mortality risk. Death from other than natural causes, most often suicide, is primarily responsible.

The information reviewed above reflects some of what has been learned about bipolar illness. Much, however, remains to be learned. Future research in areas such as treatment, genetics and outcome offers the promise of providing the knowledge we will need to reduce the suffering associated wtih bipolar illness and other psychiatric disorders. Resources expended for research now are a wise investment that will pay off in the future through savings in the area of treatment expenses and losses in productivity.

Acknowledgement

Work funded in part by the Veterans Administration General Medical Research Program.

Bibliography

Belmaker,R.H. and Van Praag,H.M. (eds) (1980) *Mania: An Evolving Concept.* Spectrum Publications, New York.
Considers mania from biological, psychological and social perspectives. Written for professionals, it has interesting chapters on creativity and the subjective experience of mania.

Post,R.M. and Ballenger,J.C. (eds) (1984) *Neurobiology of Mood Disorders.* Williams and Wilkins, Baltimore, USA.
A comprehensive collection of papers for a professional readership with an emphasis on biological, neurological and biochemical factors.

Shopsin,B. (ed.) (1979) *Manic Illness.* Raven Press, New York.
Deals with a wide range of topics, ranging from psychoanalytic aspects of mania to biological treatments. It is suitable for readers with a background in psychiatry.

Winokur,G., Clayton,P.M. and Reich,T. (1969) *Manic-Depressive Illness.* C.V.Mosby Co., St Louis, USA.
The authors review the major findings in the field, present the results of their own clinical and genetic-family research and discuss possible aetiologies and treatments.

4. The Chemical Nature of Lithium

Teresita C.Frianeza-Kullberg

Lithium, with an atomic number of 3, is the first member of the family of alkali metals, designated as Group IA in the periodic table of elements illustrated in *Figure 4.1*.

The Bohr atomic model for lithium (*Figure 4.2*) represents a single *s* electron outside a noble gas core, which is characteristic of alkali metals. This electron is so heavily shielded from the nuclear attractive force that the first ionization energy (i.e. the energy required to remove an electron from the lithium atom against the attraction of the nuclear charge) is very low, while the second ionization energy is ten times greater than the first. As a consequence, the chemistry of the alkali metals is essentially that of the +1 ion (Li^+), as exemplified by lithium carbonate in *Figure 4.3*.

The unique properties of lithium amongst the alkali metals, namely the fact that it has the highest melting point, the highest boiling point, the smallest ionic radius, and the highest ionic charge density, differentiate lithium from the other alkali metals in its chemical behaviour. Moreover, lithium exhibits a similarity to magnesium, a Group IIA metal, to which it bears a diagonal relationship in the periodic table (*Figure 4.1*).

In general, the reactivity of the Group IA metals increases as one proceeds down the group. With oxygen and the halogens, lithium is the least reactive and caesium the most reactive; however, with hydrogen, carbon and nitrogen, the trend is reversed. A schematic diagram of lithium reactions is given in *Figure 4.4*.

The three major bulk lithium chemicals are: lithium sulphate, Li_2SO_4; lithium carbonate, Li_2CO_3; and lithium hydroxide, LiOH. The first of these, lithium sulphate, the product from the spodumene ore-leaching process, is otherwise obtained from the reaction of sulphuric acid with lithium carbonate or lithium hydroxide. Industrially, lithium carbonate is prepared from lithium sulphate and sodium carbonate, and lithium hydroxide is manufactured from lithium carbonate and calcium hydroxide. Lithium halides are synthesized from lithium hydroxide or lithium carbonate (except for LiF) and the corresponding acid halide. Their molten salt chemistries are especially useful as, for example, the eutectic composition (the composition of an alloy or solution of two or more

Period	Group																	
	Ia	IIa	IIIa	IVa	Va	VIa	VIIa	VIII	VIII	VIII	Ib	IIb	IIIb	IVb	Vb	VIb	VIIb	O
1	H																H	He
2	**Li**	Be											B	C	N	O	F	Ne
3	Na	Mg											Al	Si	P	S	Cl	Ar
4	K	Ca	Sc	Ti	V	Cr	Mn	Fe	Co	Ni	Cu	Zn	Ga	Ge	As	Se	Br	Kr
5	Rb	Sr	Y	Zr	Nb	Mo	Tc	Ru	Rh	Pd	Ag	Cd	In	Sn	Sb	Te	I	Xe
6	Cs	Ba	La*	Hf	Ta	W	Re	Os	Ir	Pt	Au	Hg	Tl	Pb	Bi	Po	At	Rn
7	Fr	Ra	Ac**															
** Lanthanide series*			Ce	Pr	Nd	Pm	Sm	Eu	Gd	Tb	Dy	Ho	Er	Tm	Yb	Lu		
*** Actinide series*			Th	Pa	U	Np	Pu	Am	Cm	Bk	Cf	Es	Fm	Md	No	Lr		

Figure 4.1 Periodic table of the elements.

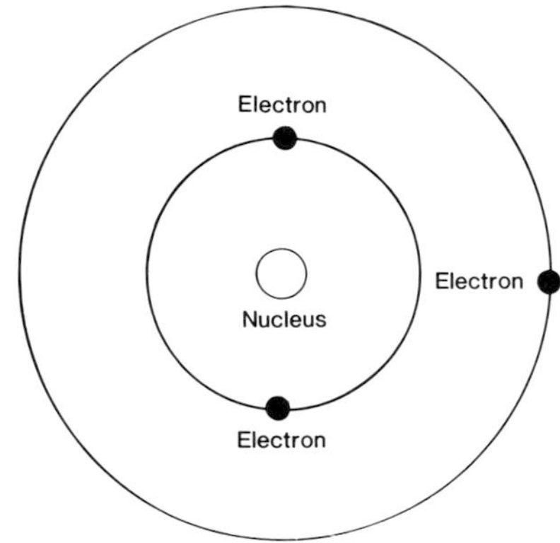

Figure 4.2 Bohr atomic model of lithium.

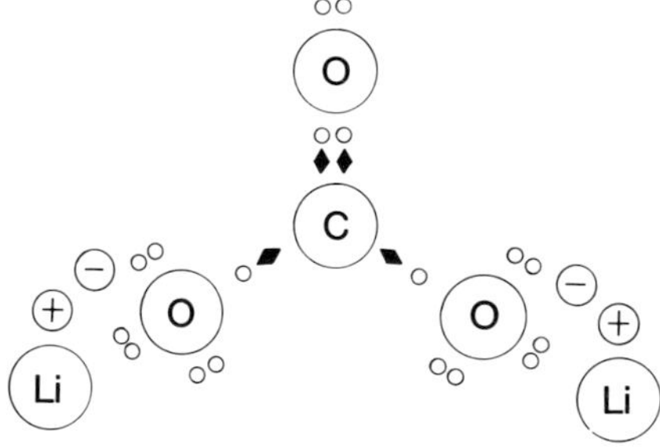

Figure 4.3 Lewis structure of lithium carbonate.

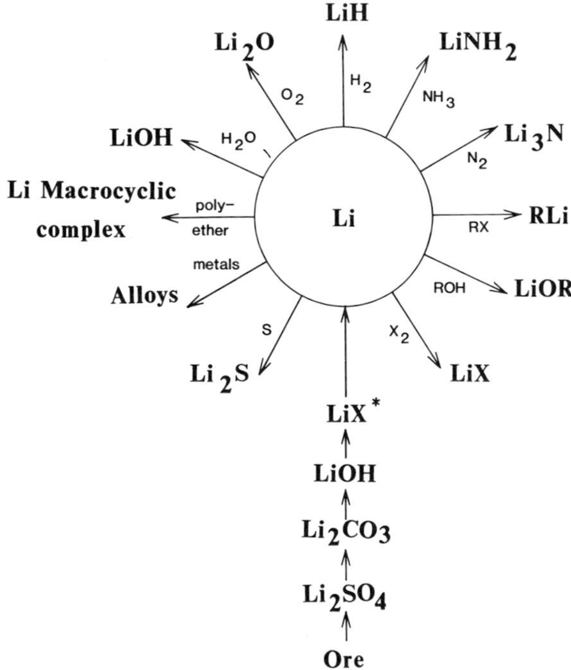

Figure 4.4 Schematic diagram of lithium reactions.

metals, at the lowest melting point) of 55% LiCl to 45% KCl (by weight) used in the electrolytic production of lithium metal.

Lithium metal is a major component in high energy batteries due to its high electrochemical equivalent which is exceeded only by beryllium, and to the fact that its standard oxidation potential is the highest of all elements. It is available commercially in ingots, special shapes, shots and dispersions. Other applications of the metal are in the preparation of the amide, nitride, hydride, alloys, and organolithium compounds. Lithium metal reacts more slowly with water at ambient temperatures than either sodium or potassium. It requires special handling under dry conditions or inert atmospheres, since the metal tarnishes readily by forming an oxide-nitride surface film when exposed to moist air.

The abnormally strong affinity of lithium for nitrogen is a behaviour manifested uniquely by lithium. Crystalline lithium nitride is ruby-red and has a high ionic conductivity, excellent for use as a solid electrolyte in batteries. Other nitrogen compounds are the amide, $LiNH_2$, and the imide, Li_2NH. Of the alkali metals, only lithium forms the imide. Alkali metals exhibit an unusual phenomenon in liquid ammonia as shown by the reaction:

$$M + (x + y)\ NH_3 \rightleftharpoons M(NH_3)_x^{+} + e^{-}(NH_3)_y$$

where the metal atom is in equilibrium with the metal ion and the solvated electron. These ammoniated solutions have very strong reducing properties, are highly conductive, strongly paramagnetic, and are either blue or bronze in colour depending upon the metal concentration.

Lithium hydride is produced by the reaction of lithium metal with hydrogen at 700°C or, under mild conditions (25−50°C at atmospheric pressure), in the presence of a catalyst such as $TiCl_4$-naphthalene. The hydride is a reducing agent and an excellent source of hydrogen. Other hydrides are lithium aluminum hydride and lithium borohydride.

Another unusual behaviour of lithium is its reactivity with oxygen to form lithium oxide, other alkali metals forming a peroxide or a superoxide. Lithium oxide, otherwise called 'lithia', can also be obtained by decomposing lithium hydroxide, lithium carbonate or lithium peroxide.

Oxyhalogen compounds of lithium are prepared from the reaction of lithium hydroxide with the halogen. Lithium hypochlorite is used as a disinfectant, especially in swimming pools.

Lithium alloys with other elements of the periodic table, namely: Be, Mg and Ca in Group IIa; B, Al, Ga and Tl in Group IIIA; Si, Ge, Sn and Pb in Group IVA; As and Sb in Group VA; Cu and Ag in Group IB; and Zn and Cd in Group IIB. The lithium-aluminium alloy has gained considerable importance recently for its use in the aircraft industry. Rapid progress is being made towards improvement of its physical properties, such as corrosion resistance and strength.

Extensive research is also currently being focused on mixed metal oxides of lithium such as $LiAlO_2$, $Li_2B_4O_7$, $LiCoO_2$, $LiFeO_2$, Li_2MnO_3, $LiMnO_2$, Li_2MoO_4, Li_2SiO_3, Li_4SiO_4, Li_2TiO_3, $Li_2FeV_3O_8$, and Li_2ZrO_3, as a result of the need for new ceramic composite materials and new fast-ion conductors for batteries.

Organolithium compounds, the most important organoalkali compounds, are industrially prepared from metallic lithium and the corresponding alkyl or aryl halides. Other synthetic routes are by metal-hydrogen exchange, metal-halogen exchange, or metal-metal exchange. Organolithium compounds are air-sensitive liquids or low-melting solids, highly reactive with water, and soluble in hydrocarbons or other non-polar solvents. They resemble Grignard reagents in their reactions but are more reactive, have fewer side reactions, are easily separated from the products, and are available in any desired concentration. Alkyllithiums, such as *n*-butyllithium, are used in polymerization and other organic synthetic reactions.

Complexes of alkali metals with macrocyclic polyethers [crown ethers, having a cyclic arrangement of $(ROR)_n$ groups] and cryptates (bicyclic compounds containing atoms other than oxygen) are attracting much interest because of their potential utilization in transporting alkali ions across membranes in living systems. The formation of these complexes depends largely upon the size of the ion, the size of the cavity, and the solvent. Lithium benzo-13-crown-4, dibenzo-14-crown-4, and 2″,4″-dinitro-6″-trifluoromethylpentyl-4′-aminobenzo-14-crown-4 complexes have been found to be useful for the analytical extraction of lithium. The need to minimize the side effects of lithium toxicity by administering lower doses of lithium has stimulated the preparation of a new series of acyclic dioxa diamide lithium carriers with a higher rate of lithium transport. Other potential applications are in lithium extraction from sea water and brines, in lithium batteries, and in the manufacture of a lithium selective test paper and electrode.

Other lithium compounds are presently being studied for cancer chemotherapy and herpes virus infections. Indeed, the field of lithium chemistry offers many opportunities for investigation and technological advancement.

Bibliography

Bach,R.O. (ed.) (1985) *Lithium: Current Applications in Science, Medicine and Technology*. John Wiley & Sons, New York.

An updated reference on recent developments in the areas of lithium metallurgy and electrochemistry, organolithium chemistry and lithium in medicine. It is addressed to research and development managers, scientists, engineers, psychiatrists, toxicologists and virologists.

Hart,W.A. and Beumel,O.F.,Jr (1973) Lithium and its compounds. In *Comprehensive Inorganic Chemistry*, Bailar,J.C., Eméléus, H.J., Nyholm,R. and Trotman-Dickenson,A.F. (eds). Pergamon Press, Oxford, pp. 331−368.

This article is an excellent review of lithium chemistry for scientists as well as readers with a fundamental background in chemistry.

Pascal,R. (ed.) (1966) *Nouveau Traité de Chimie Minérale*. Masson et Cie, Paris, Vol. 2. Part 1 (Lithium, Sodium), pp. 21–165. Gives a detailed description of lithium compounds. It contains thermodynamic data such as phase diagrams, solubility data, etc. and also lists numerous references.

Wakefield,B.J. (1974) *The Chemistry of Organolithium*. Pergamon Press, Oxford.
A comprehensive review of organolithium chemistry is presented. The versatility of organolithium compounds in organic synthetic reactions is emphasized.

5. Natural Occurrence, Production and Reserves

Ihor A.Kunasz

Occurrence

In 1817 young August Arfwedson, working so diligently in the laboratory of the famous Swedish scientist Baron Jons Berzelius, probably never imagined what his new discovery (Section 6) would mean to the future industrial and medical worlds. At first an analytical headache (he was trying, unsuccessfully, to achieve a full oxide analysis) it resulted in the discovery of a new element. Berzelius named it 'lithion' and it later became the third element in the periodic table – lithium. The sample given to Arfwedson was a specimen of petalite found in a pegmatite body on Utö Island off the coast of Sweden. Pegmatites are coarse-grained igneous rocks in which lithium and other rare elements may have been concentrated during the crystallization sequence of a magma.

Among approximately 2750 minerals described in the literature, about 250 contain more than 0.0001% lithium. Although 27 minerals contain more than 1% lithium, only about six (spodumene, petalite, amblygonite, lepidolite, zinnwaldite and eucryptite) have been considered as lithium ores and used in further upgrading or as feed for the production of lithium chemicals.

Lithium is a pronounced lithophile element which occurs in the predominant silicate-bearing solid portion of the earth's crust, where it will occur in an average concentration of about 20 p.p.m. Li. The process of sequential crystallization of a magma, which begins with the formation of basic rocks (such as gabbros) and ends with acidic rocks (such as granite), produces a progressive enrichment of lithium in these rocks as shown in *Table 5.1*.

Table 5.1 *Progressive enrichment of rocks with lithium in the sequential crystallization of a magma*

Rock type	% Li
Ultrabasic	0.0001
Gabbros, basalts	0.0004–0.0007
Syenites, diorites, andesites	0.0004–0.0010
Granites	0.0033–0.0130

Since the lithium concentration is too low to form lithium minerals during the progressive crystallization of a magma, the residual fluids are left enriched in this and other elements. These fluids, still saturated with respect to silica and also loaded with volatiles, are often forcibly injected into the surrounding rocks, where they crystallize into rocks characterized by very large crystals and very exotic mineralogy. Often, the cooling process will lead to the formation of various zones within the pegmatites, each zone being characterized by a specific mineral assemblage. Pegmatites are fascinating rocks because it is in them that some of the most beautiful gem-quality minerals have been discovered, tourmalines in particular. Since they could be vulgarly described as the 'garbage dumps' of the Earth, it is easy to comprehend the assiduity of both professional mineralogists, who try to unravel the formational history of the pegmatites, and the mineral collector, who hopes to discover some of nature's masterpieces. From a lithium standpoint pegmatites have yielded some two dozen unique lithium-bearing specimens, as well as the gem varieties of spodumene: hiddenite (green), triphane (yellow) and kunzite (lavender).

From the latter portion of the 19th century up to the beginning of World War II, lithium ores and chemicals were produced only from pegmatites. The first commercially mined lithium ore was zinnwaldite — a lithium-bearing mica obtained as a by-product of tin-mining in the Harz Mountains in Southern Germany. The centre of production passed to France with its lithium deposits located in the Massif Central. At the turn of the 20th century, the United States became, and still is, the largest producer of lithium ores, chemical compounds and lithium metal. The most significant change in the structure of the lithium producing industry has concerned the source of the raw material. While lithium minerals found in pegmatites at first constituted the main source of raw materials

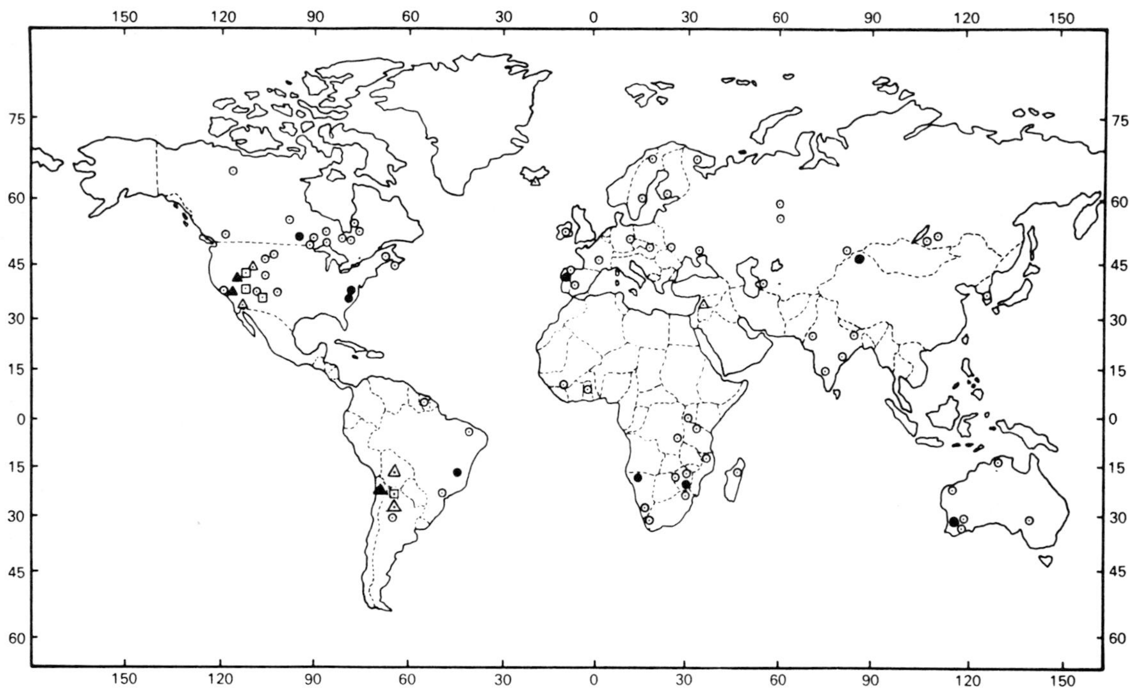

Figure 5.1 Lithium occurrence in various geographical regions. Open symbols indicate regions of occurrence; filled symbols denote producing districts (note that in the USSR areas of production are not known and so the areas are shown only as regions of occurrence). Circles indicate occurrence as pegmatite, triangles as brine and squares as clay.

for conversion into lithium chemical and compounds, the 1960s saw a significant shift towards the production of lithium compounds from brines associated with volcanic activity and aridity. Today, two major areas produce a significant proportion of the lithium compounds: Silver Peak, Nevada, USA and the Salar de Atacama, Chile. Lithium carbonate produced from these brine deposits represents about 30% of the total world supply. *Figure 5.1* indicates the geographical distribution of lithium deposits.

Production

Although some lithium is used as a medicament to aid certain psychiatric ailments, the majority of it is used in industrial applications.

Lithium is produced in three basic forms: mineral concentrates, chemical compounds and metal.

Lithium ores, following some upgrading techniques, can be used directly in certain applications, such as glass and pyroceramics. The lithium ions cause glass and ceramics to crystallize from within the structure and, in so doing, increase the physical and chemical durability of the glass. In pyroceramics, the addition of lithium actually results in a negative coefficient of expansion (though very small) which permits transfer from the refrigerator to the oven without experiencing breakage. Corningware® is based on the addition of lithium ores to achieve this performance. Petalite from Zimbabwe and Brazil, and upgraded spodumene from Australia, Canada and Zimbabwe, are used directly in such applications.

The bulk of lithium is sold as chemical compounds. Although there are some seventy such compounds commercialized in amounts varying from trial quantities to several million pounds, four compounds are significant in terms of market importance: lithium carbonate, Li_2CO_3; lithium hydroxide monohydrate, $LiOH.H_2O$; butyllithium; and lithium chloride, LiCl.

Lithium carbonate is used as an energy saver and pollution control chemical in the conversion of alumina, Al_2O_3, to primary aluminium. It is also used in the manufacture of certain glasses and pyroceramics. Further purified it provides a pharmaceutical product used in the treatment of certain psychiatric disorders, to which this book is dedicated. Lithium carbonate is also used in the production of a number of other chemicals.

Lithium hydroxide monohydrate is the basic constituent of lubrication greases, to which lithium imparts great stability under extreme temperature conditions. In its anhydrous form, lithium hydroxide exhibits a high absorbance for gases such as carbon dioxide and is currently being used in rescue breathing equipment.

Butyllithium acts as a catalyst in the production of synthetic rubber and as a reagent in organic chemical synthesis.

Lithium chloride is becoming more and more important as it is the required chemical for the production of lithium metal. Lithium metal exhibits a high energy density per unit weight (or volume) which reduces space requirements — an important advantage with the current trends towards miniaturization. Superior low temperature performance and a shelf life 2–10 times greater than conventional cells make lithium systems quite attractive. Uses for lithium batteries range from pacemakers to electronic equipment, to military support systems. The future may see aircraft constructed with lithium-aluminium alloys, resulting in lighter planes, and thermonuclear fusion reactors, in which non-radioactive lithium will be the primary fuel.

At the present time, about 60 million pounds per year of lithium carbonate is used to produce all the lithium chemicals and lithium metal in the world. By comparison, the amount used in lithium therapy is very small, constituting less than 1% of the total.

Reserves

In the 1970s, concern began to be expressed regarding the availability of sufficient reserves of lithium ores to satisfy future requirements for secondary batteries and thermonuclear power generation. The National Academies of Sciences and Engineering of the USA commissioned a study of the reserves of lithium available in the world. The results of the evaluation indicated that nearly eleven million tons of elemental lithium are available to industry, while the present usage represents only about 6000 tons of elemental lithium. Although projections of secondary batteries based on lithium did not materialize, the world lithium reserves known to date were found to be adequate for such a usage as well as for the anticipated future requirements of thermonuclear fusion reactors. Since reserves of lithium are many times any conceivable market demand, there is little active exploration for new lithium reserves. Our present knowledge indicates that there are large new reserves to be discovered should there be a quantum surge in lithium demand.

Bibliography

Hammond,A.L. (1976) Lithium: will short supply constrain energy technologies? *Science*, **191**, 1037–1038.
A useful analysis of lithium availability as the situation was seen in 1976.

Kunasz,I.A. (1980) Lithium — how much? *Foote Prints*, **43**, 23–27.
A discussion of the availability of lithium reserves under various demand conditions, such as batteries and thermonuclear fusion energy production.

Kunasz,I.A. (1983) Lithium raw materials. In *Industrial Minerals and Rocks*. Lefond,S.J. (ed.), AIME, New York, pp. 869–880.
A helpful review of lithium minerals, their occurrence, production and uses.

6. Historical Origins

Amdi Amdisen

The First Lithium Era

Soranus of Ephesus, who lived in the 2nd century AD, recommended in his main work *On Acute and Chronic Diseases* the use of natural waters, e.g. alkaline waters, in the treatment of mania. It has recently been suggested that he specifically meant waters from the ancient Greek (now Turkish) town of Ephesus. The content of lithium salts in these waters is comparatively high, but compared to the lithium doses used in modern therapy they do no contain more than a tiny fraction of the amount needed to obtain a therapeutic or prophylactic effect against mania. It should also be borne in mind that, although Soranus probably came from Ephesus, he was trained as a physician in Alexandria and lived as a doctor in Rome – and that he only mentions the natural alkaline waters in one brief passage out of a much larger context:

> Utendum quoque naturalibus aquis, ut sunt nitrosae, et magis si odoris non fuerint tetri, quo membranae capitis quatiantur.

(...Use should also be made of natural waters, such as alkaline springs, particularly those free from any pungent odour which might injure the membranes of the brain) so the idea of Soranus' unwitting use of 'lithium waters' in mania should be discarded.

Lithium was discovered as an element around 1815 and was given its chemical symbol, Li, by the Swedish scientist Baron Jacob Berzelius, originator of the modern system of chemical symbols. It was called lithium, because his assistant, August Arfwedson, had found it in stone (Greek: *lithos*).

James Parkinson, the author of *An Essay of the Shaking Palsy* (Parkinson's Disease), wrote, around 1805, another work, *The Nature and Cure of Gout* in which he drew attention to the current concepts of the 'uric acid diathesis' and 'irregular gout' and proposed the treatment of gravel, gout and irregular gout with 'alkaline salts'. The main pathogenetic idea was that certain individuals had an inherited proneness (a 'diathesis') to periodic circulation of excess uric acid in the blood, which led to periodic uric acid formation precipitated as the sodium salt. Precipitation in thc urinary system resulted in urate gravel; gout stemmed from precipitation on tendons or ligaments or in the joints, especially the more peripheral ones, of the limbs. Precipitation in other organs led to 'irregular gout'. The most important treatment was the use of 'caustic fixed alkalis', which were thought to prevent the formation of 'animal acids' in the stomach, and to detoxify the absorbed uric acid through enhanced illumination by making it less insoluble.

At that time the ill-defined theory of affinity of one chemical for another was prevailing (it was based on the mutual reactivity of substances but failed to pay due regard to their concentrations): under its influence, in the years 1845 – 1860, lithium salts got the reputation of being the most efficient and indispensable alkaline salts in the prophylactic treatment of gravel, gout and 'irregular gout', a notion championed by Sir Alfred Baring Garrod, a noted authority on gout and gout-related conditions (*Table 6.1*).

From about 1865 to 1880 first mania and later melancholia were incorporated into the group of gouty diseases, which meant that they were both acutely and prophylactically treated with lithium-containing mixtures of 'alkaline salts'. William Hammond, for example, in 1871 recommended lithium bromide in tremendously high doses (at least as far as lithium is concerned—45 mmol six times within the first 12 – 18 h, followed by small daily doses only—against acute mania and acute melancholia. About 1880, the Danish neurologist Carl Lange claimed to have discovered a new, hitherto overlooked gouty disease, which he named 'periodic depression' (undoubtedly what we would today call a masked, recurrent, unipolar, endogenous, slight depression). He treated his patients prophylactically for years with 'alkaline salts' which meant in practice that they often took 5 – 25 mmol of lithium per day. However, he never attached any special importance to the lithium salt, as such, apart from what had been the general attitude for decades towards alkaline salts in general and their use against the uric acid diathesis.

Table 6.1 *A few selected examples of disorders which might have been caused by uric acid deposition, according to Garrod (1876)*

Body region	Disorder
Brain	Mania, depression, hysteria, hypochondriasis, headache, epilepsy, apoplexy
Spinal cord	Pain and tenderness in the lumbar spine and pain in the legs
Muscular and nervous system	Neuralgia, cramps
Digestive organs	Dyspepsia, constipation, diarrhoea
Skin	Prurigo, pityriasis, psoriasis, eczema, acne
Heart	Palpitations, irregular rhythm
Lungs	Coughing, asthma, dry pleurisy
Kidneys	Interstitial nephritis, concretions
Eyes	Conjunctivitis, sclerotitis

The notion of the gouty diathesis as the pathogenetic factor in gravel, gout and irregular gout was rejected by the world of medical science shortly after World War I. In Denmark, the homeland of Carl Lange and the condition of 'periodic depression', a psychiatrist by the name of H.J.Schou came out strongly for the existence of a special slight depression identical with that described by C.Lange and essentially different from the depressive phase of Emil Kraepelin's concept, the manic-depressive psychosis. H.J.Schou was, however, against C.Lange's prophylactic therapy, which mainly consisted of preventative diets, daily exercise and first of all daily prophylactic intake of alkaline salts; he was especially against the daily exercise in depressed patients. Thereby, H.J.Schou also brought about the abandonment of long-term prophylactic therapy of recurrent masked, unipolar depression with lithium (a particular irony in view of the later emergence of his son, Mogens Schou, as a

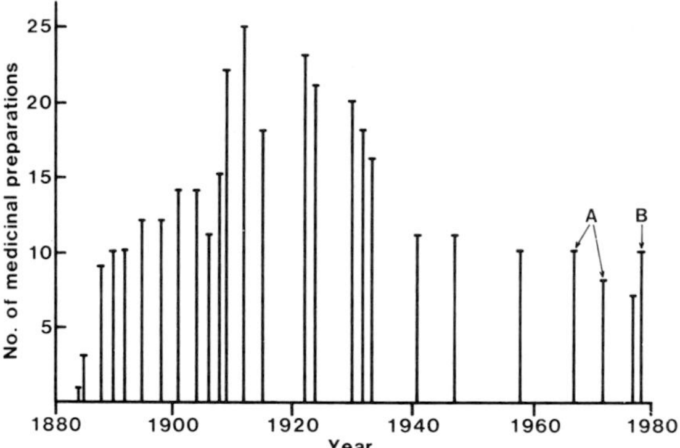

Figure 6.1 The number of lithium preparations available according to 'Martindale' (*The Extra Pharmacopoeia*): **A**. lithium carbonate introduced against mania, and the use of lithium citrate against gout and rheumatism still maintained; **B**. both lithium carbonate and lithium citrate advocated for use against manic-depressive illness. From Amdisen,A. (1984) In *Current Trends in Lithium and Rubidium Therapy*, Corsini,G.U. (ed.), pp. 11–26, MTP Press, Lancaster, with permission.

major proponent of lithium therapy). Nevertheless, the idea of the uric acid diathesis remained partly alive until recently, and lithium salts may still, in some countries, be available over the counter as anti-rheumatic drugs — a legacy of the one-time inclusion of rheumatic conditions amongst the illnesses related to the uric acid diathesis.

Lithium, in the form of the carbonate, has also been used in antacid powders and tablets for several decades. Lithium acts as a diuretic drug and lithium citrate was recommended for this purpose in 1874 by Garrod; in the late 1960s the *Extra Pharmacopoeia* (known familiarly as 'Martindale') still mentioned this use. The number of lithium preparations made available over the years for a variety of medical uses, according to the various editions of Martindale are shown in *Figure 6.1*.

Lithium salts were at first expensive and not easily available for the treatment of the gouty diseases, but in 1876 Garrod mentioned that this had been remedied when the German scientist Robert Bunsen (inventor of the Bunsen burner) constructed the first flame spectrophotoscope in the 1850s, thereby stimulating interest in the study of lithium salts. In 1864 lithium salts were first entered in the *British Pharmacopoeia*.

Intermezzo: Lithium as a Salt Substitute

Shortly after World War II, watery solutions of lithium chloride (25%) were marketed in the United States as a substitute for ordinary table salt for persons on salt-free diets (mostly patients with heart disease). In the first few months of 1949, several of these persons died from lithium intoxication. The United States Food and Drug Administration (FDA) looked into the matter and warned against the 'dangerous substances' through newspapers and radio broadcasts. The use of lithium salts was banned and an FDA working group very quickly conducted a series of extensive and excellent animal experiments which disclosed lithium's renal toxicity, especially during sodium depletion.

For about 20 years the FDA remained reticent about releasing any lithium drug for general use. In other countries the American lithium scare was recorded but generated no formal intervention against the drug.

At about the same time as the salt substitute furore was erupting in the USA, John Frederick Joseph Cade, an Australian psychiatrist, published the results of his retrial of lithium in the treatment of psychotic excitement.

In the USA in 1950 Dr John F.Talbott made an unsuccessful attempt to defend the use of lithium chloride as a salt substitute when he claimed that about only 12 mmol daily would be enough for this purpose. He also stimulated a new wave of clinical research by his use of the now commercially available flame photometer to estimate the concentration of Li^+ in serum; Talbott found that the use of lithium chloride could be both efficient and safe provided that the serum lithium concentration never exceeded 1.00 mmol/l. He did not, however, take into account the pronounced fluctuations of the serum concentration in relation to the time of each lithium intake; neither did some of the other early investigators who carried out trials on lithium therapy.

The Psychiatric Era of Lithium

Shortly after World War II the Australian psychiatrist John Cade (*Figure 6.2*) repeated Hammonds trial of lithium in high doses in severely psychotic patients (ten manics, seven excited schizophrenics and three severe depressives). He noted a very positive response in all the manic patients; the schizophrenic patients responded to some degree, but there was no effect in the depressed patients. It is worth noting that the clinical trial which Cade conducted would not be permitted in most countries under the legislation which prevails today governing medical experimentation.

Figure 6.2 John Cade (centre), Mogens Schou (right) and P.C.Baastrup (left) photographed together at the time that investigations of the prophylactic efficacy of lithium against depression were still being undertaken. From Johnson,F.N. (1984) *The History of Lithium Therapy*, Macmillan, London, with permission.

In his search for appropriate dosages Cade consulted the seventh edition (1927) of *A Manual of Materia Medica and Pharmacology* by Culbreth, in which five anti-rheumatic or diuretic lithium preparations were still mentioned (the carbonate, bromide, benzoate, citrate and salicylate). Cade chose a dose schedule which was in some respects similar to that of Hammond who, in 1871, started with a high dose on the first day followed by reduced daily dosages. Today, it is common knowledge that even extremely high single acute overdosages may not give rise to toxic reactions. Cade used high dosages, although much lower than Hammond's 45 mmol six times on the first day of treatment, but he continued treatment with the high dosages until the mania disappeared—even if this took several weeks—and often the dosage was not reduced at all. This implied an enhanced risk of acute intoxication and is probably why one of Cade's first lithium patients died in a state of typical lithium intoxication 2 years after successful periodic lithium treatment had been started.

Cade's high and near-toxic doses were adopted by Drs C.M.Noack and Edward M.Trautner when they re-examined Cade's results in a greater number of patients. In 1951 they discarded treatment monitoring which made use of serum lithium (SLi) concentrations, but even when this procedure was re-introduced in 1954, similarly high and arbitrary SLi concentrations were also adopted—with no consideration being taken of the complexity of the pharmacokinetics of drugs with fast elimination. It was not until the late 1960s and early 1970s that this aspect became increasingly recognized, culminating in the introduction of the '12-h standardized serum lithium' (12h-stSLi) (see Section 21, pp. 88–91).

For several obvious reasons lithium treatment spread only slowly from Australia to general use elsewhere in the world. In the first place, lithium was not a new drug; it was, moreover, cheap and no medical firm could hope for either patent or economic profit. A few years later the first neuroleptic drug, chlorpromazine, appeared as a competitor to lithium in the treatment of mania: this had strong support from the pharmaceutical industry. During the next few years still more neuroleptics were marketed. Lithium's slow spread followed two main geographical routes during the first decade after Cade's 1949 publication. The one to Great Britain was based on close cultural connections between the two countries and was directly influenced by Cade's work. The other route was started when Professor Erik Strömgren in Aarhus, Denmark, became strongly impressed by Noack and Trautner's work from 1951. A local, partly double-blind, re-examination was initiated in Aarhus by Strömgren in cooperation with Mogens Schou (*Figure 6.2*) and two other colleagues. Samuel Gershon moved from Australia to the USA where he conducted the first trial of lithium in mania in the late fifties and Mogens Schou met Ronald R.Fieve in the USA. These three persons devoted the greater part of their professional years to the study of lithium therapy and one may well wonder what would have become of it without them.

Similar digressions appeared on each of the two routes. On that to Great Britain, G.P. Hartigan, working in Canterbury, rediscovered the forgotten preventive treatment of Lange's 'periodic depression' with lithium-containing anti-rheumatic drugs. Probably without knowing of the early idea that manic-depression was a gouty disease he presented his findings in a lecture in 1959 and Mogens Schou encouraged their publication in 1963.

On the route via Aarhus, P.C.Baastrup (*Figure 6.2*), simultaneously but quite independently, made the same discovery and, again at Mogens Schou's instigation, published the results in 1964. Some data from the primary 1954-investigation had indicated antidepressive effects of lithium (in fact preventive antidepression): an unsuccessful trial on acute antidepressive effects was subsequently conducted in Aarhus, but the results were never published. The credit for the rediscovery—which was made in in-patients who undoubtedly were more severely depressed than Lange's out-patients—was accorded to Hartigan and Baastrup. Like Hartigan Baastrup also knew nothing about the old connection between affective disorders and the rheumatic diathesis or about Lange's periodically depressed patients and, at that time, in the early 1960s, he was not aware of the preventive antidepressive effect seen in the Danish patients from 1954, nor was this ever discussed during his close cooperation with Mogens Schou in the following years.

Baastrup's and Schou's collaborative work resulted in a joint publication of an open study which showed a prophylactic effect of long-term lithium treatment in both bipolar manic-depressive and recurrent depressive patients ('unipolar' manic depressives).

The demand for double blindness in clinical investigations was at its most uncompromising peak in the late 1960s, and Baastrup's work was severely criticized on methodological grounds. In spite of Schou's defence and counterattack, Baastrup felt himself obliged to carry out a double-blind discontinuation study on his well-responding long-term lithium patients in order to answer the critics of his methodology and to establish firmly the efficacy of lithium prophylaxis. This rewarding study was published in 1970.

Although lithium-induced polyuria had been known for a hundred years and kidney damage had been demonstrated by the FDA working group in 1950 and in later animal studies, the alarm bell was set ringing when, in 1977, a paper was published which indicated that long-term lithium treatment might induce slight chronic irreversible kidney damage with accompanying reduction of the renal concentrating ability. This has gradually been recognized as a fact and adequate control procedures and preventive reduction of the lithium dose have been suggested (see Section 57).

The later part of the history of lithium is concerned mainly with similar refinements of the practical management of lithium therapy, with the twin aims in mind of reducing the unwanted side effects of lithium whilst maximizing therapeutic benefits. The outcome of that story is the subject of the remainder of this book.

Acknowledgements

Thanks are due to Professors Egill Snorrason and the late Erik Jacobsen, both of Copenhagen, and to Dr Neil Johnson of Lancaster, for their interest in my work on the first era of lithium therapy.

Bibliography

Amdisen,A. (1984) Lithium treatment of mania and depression over one hundred years. In *Current Trends in Lithium and Rubidium Therapy*, Corsini,G.U. (ed.), MTP Press, Lancaster, pp. 11–26.
A concise survey of the main historical trends in the development of lithium therapy, with special emphasis on the pre-Cade era.

Johnson,F.N. (1984) *The History of Lithium Therapy*. Macmillan, London.
A book presenting in comprehensive detail the historical facts from about 1775 to 1984.

Part II

MEDICAL APPLICATIONS

7. The Acute Treatment of Mania

Neil Coxhead and Trevor Silverstone

It was some 40 years ago that John Cade (see Section 6) introduced lithium into modern psychiatry by presenting ten case histories showing impressive results in the treatment of mania. Yet, despite the relatively venerable history of the use of lithium in mania there have been remarkably few clinical trials of its efficacy on this indication. Those that have been done have been lacking in uniformity; they have varied considerably in the range of severity of mania treated, the dosages of lithium employed and the doses of neuroleptic given as a comparison. Nevertheless, it is possible to draw some broad conclusions from them.

Clinical Trials

Double-blind placebo-controlled trials

In 1954 a group of research workers at Aarhus University Institute of Psychiatry in Denmark, headed by Dr (now Professor) Mogens Schou reported on 38 patients treated over a period of several years, utilizing a double-blind placebo-controlled technique for part of the time. As with all the early trials, diagnostic criteria were not standardized, with eight patients showing atypical features. After a short drug-free period, lithium (in the form of the carbonate, citrate or chloride) was given at a dose of 24–48 mmol/day (equivalent to 0.9–1.8 g/day of lithium carbonate), resulting in serum levels of 0.5–2.0 mmol/l, although higher dosages and serum levels were achieved in some cases. The treatment period was approximately 2 weeks and was alternated with placebo administration. Of the 30 atypical cases, a definite improvement was seen in 12 and a possible improvement in a further 15. The lack of a clear distinction between the therapeutic and prophylactic usage of lithium in this study and the difficulty in discovering whether a particular treatment was carried out in a blind or open fashion, make the results difficult to interpret.

Some 15 years later, Dr F.K.Goodwin and his colleagues in the USA treated 12 manic patients over several months with lithium carbonate at an initial dose of 900–1800 mg/day according to the patients' age and weight, in order to achieve a serum level of 0.8–1.3 mmol/l. Placebo treatment periods of various lengths were substituted according to a decision by the non-blind investigator and were generally timed to occur 4–6 weeks after starting lithium. The majority of these patients were severely ill, and eight required seclusions prior to treatment. Eight patients remitted completely on lithium, four of these subsequently relapsing during placebo substitution. In addition, one other patient had a partial response; the remaining three developed schizophrenic features and may have been misdiagnosed initially. Thus this trial produced very favourable results for lithium, but contained only a small number of patients and did not assign patients to different treatment groups in a random manner.

One of the first (uncontrolled) trials of lithium in the treatment of affective disorders to be carried out in the UK was published in 1956 by Dr David Rice. When Rice subsequently took up a post at Hellingly Hospital in Sussex, UK, he communicated his ideas to a new colleague, Dr Ronald Maggs. Maggs took up the investigation and compared 2 weeks of treatment on lithium with 2 weeks on placebo in 28 patients, using a cross-over design with an intervening 2-week treatment-free period. The dose of lithium carbonate was 1.5 g/day for 6 days per week, and serum levels up to 2.0 mmol/l were allowed. Ten patients did not complete the 6-week study period. The results from the remaining 18 showed a significant decrease in the mean rating score during the lithium treatment period, with a non-significant decrease in the mean rating score during the placebo treatment period. Amongst the dropouts, two showed signs of toxicity and five became more disturbed in their behaviour. A pilot study before the main trial had shown that a third of manic patients otherwise suitable for inclusion in the study would have to be eliminated because they would be unable to co-operate in taking oral medication. This suggests a bias against the inclusion of more severely ill patients. Working in the USA, Dr Peter Stokes and his co-workers in 1971 used four consecutive treatment periods of 7–10 days in 38 patients, 34 of whom showed more than a defined minimum severity of mania at the start of each treatment period. Patients were assigned alternatively to receive either lithium or placebo, with later crossover to the other treatment. Lithium chloride solution was given at a constant dose of 0.5 mmol/kg/day, the maximum serum level being planned to be 1.5 mmol/l, though in practice the mean serum level after 7–10 days was 0.93 mmol/l with a maximum level of 1.63 mmol/l. No direct comment on the proportion of severely ill patients was made in the report of this study but eight patients also required chlorpromazine, and intramuscular lithium chloride was given when there were problems with oral compliance. In total there were 56 lithium treatment periods during which 75% of patients improved compared to 41% of patients improving during the 42 placebo treatment periods. This difference was statistically significant and remained so after account was taken of the fact that median mania ratings were often higher at the start of lithium treatment than at the start of placebo treatment, due to the influence of the immediately preceding treatment. Although mania ratings worsened during placebo treatment, the striking relapse which had been seen within 24 h of crossover by Frederick Goodwin and his group was not observed. This is the only report in which a placebo response rate was given; the improvement on lithium was considered by the investigators to be 'disappointingly low' in relation to this.

All four of these trials used some form of multiple crossover, increasing the number of treatment periods that could be compared and allowing within-patient comparisons on the different effects of lithium and placebo. In other ways, however, the trials are not comparable: treatment period varied; treatment response was expressed in different ways; diagnostic criteria and initial illness severity varied. In only one were serum lithium levels used as a basis for adjusting the dosage to a given range; in the other three, the initial dosage was adhered to unless resulting in excessively high serum levels, and the attained minimum levels were not given.

Double-blind trials of lithium against antipsychotic drugs

The first comparative trial of lithium with chlorpromazine was carried out in 1968 by Dr Gordon Johnson and colleagues. The trial included schizo-affective patients (not discussed here) as well as 27 manic patients diagnosed according to current criteria (one manic patient was later reclassified as schizo-affective). After a 5-day placebo period either lithium carbonate 1–2 g/day or chlorpromazine 200–400 mg/day (assigned randomly) was given for 3 weeks and dosage was increased until signs of therapeutic response or toxicity were seen. The serum lithium levels were above 1.0 mmol/l in all cases and the final dose range of lithium was 1.5–3.5 g/day. The chlorpromazine dose range was 200–1800 mg/day. Out of the 18 patients treated with lithium, 14 showed definite signs of remission as compared to four out of the 11 chlorpromazine treated patients. In the lithium-responsive patients remission occurred after 2–14 days with a mean of 8 days. Lithium was considered to be particularly effective in producing what was referred to as the 'normalization of affect and ideation' whereas chlorpromazine had an early effect on hyperactivity. The highest serum lithium level obtained was 2.55 mmol/l and toxic effects such as anorexia, nausea, diarrhoea and vomiting were common at levels over 2.0. In a study reported 3 years later the same investigators, using a similar design, noted that both lithium and chlorpromazine produced significant improvement, but again there was a tendency for lithium to produce greater and more consistent improvement whereas chlorpromazine, although it had an earlier effect on hyperactivity, was less effective against euphoria and excitability.

Dr Gottfried Spring, in collaboration with four colleagues, treated 14 patients for 3 weeks with either lithium or chlorpromazine, with crossover after this period to the other treatment if complete, or nearly complete, remission had not been achieved. The results of this study appeared in 1970. Lithium carbonate was given at a dose of 1.8 g/day for the first week, increasing to 3 g/day if there was no response. Chlorpromazine was increased as necessary up to 1600 mg/day. Two patients left the trial in the first 3 weeks because of physical illness unlikely to be related to their trial medication. Seven patients on lithium and five on chlorpromazine completed the first 3 weeks. Six of the seven on lithium and three of the five on chlorpromazine who completed 3 weeks treatment responded. On crossover the two chlorpromazine failures responded to lithium but the lithium failure did not respond to chlorpromazine. Thus eight of nine patients treated with lithium were responsive. All patients responding to lithium did so at serum levels not exceeding 1.3 mmol/l. The numbers were not large enough, however, to reveal a statistically significant difference between the two treatments. Nevertheless, an interesting additional observation made was that responsiveness to lithium in acute mania on one occasion did not necessarily predict response on another occasion, a finding that had also been noted the previous year (1969) by Frederick Goodwin and his team.

In the same year that Spring and his colleagues reported their study, Dr S.R.Platman gave details of thirty patients entered into a lithium–chlorpromazine comparative trial. Seven dropped out leaving 13 patients who received lithium and 10 receiving chlorpromazine for the whole 3-week period. Initial dosages were 1200 mg daily for lithium and 400 mg daily for chlorpromazine with mean maximum doses of 1823 mg/day and 870 mg/day, respectively. Serum lithium levels were above 0.8 mmol/l in all cases. Weekly ratings were made of six broad categories of symptoms and behaviour. Although no statistical differences had emerged between the two treatments by the third week of treatment, the authors' impression was that lithium was superior in producing a general improvement, and the majority were discharged on this therapy.

In a multicentre trial comparing 3 weeks treatment with lithium (200–300 mg/day) and chlorpromazine (500–4000 mg/day) 255 patients participated. This large-scale study was coordinated by Dr Robert Prien and his colleagues Drs E.M.Caffey and C.J.Klett and although it was reported earlier in mimeographed form, the version in the scientific journals appeared in 1972. It was noted that 22% of lithium patients and 14% of chlorpromazine patients failed to complete; significantly more terminations of lithium treatment occurred in the highly active group. Thus chlorpromazine was more effective overall in the highly active group when treatment dropouts were taken into account, but the treatments were equal in the mildly active group. It was noted that chlorpromazine exerted its effect more quickly (4–7 days) in the highly active group. As in previous trials lithium took about one and a half weeks to be fully effective. Amongst the highly active patients, significantly more of these treated with lithium complained of side effects, mainly gastro-intestinal symptoms, confusion and tremor, whereas more side effects such as somnolence and dry mouth occurred on chlorpromazine in the mildly active group. Prien and his colleagues concluded that chlorpromazine was clearly a better treatment than lithium for highly active manic patients, but that for mildly active patients lithium produced fewer side effects and was just as effective. Another multicentre study, this time by a Japanese group led by Takahashi, and reported in 1975, involved 80 manic patients with a wide range of severity of illness. Diagnostic criteria were vague. The treatment period of 21–35 days followed a 7-day drug-free period. Starting doses were 600 mg/day of lithium carbonate or 150 mg/day of chlorpromazine for 3 days, then medication was altered according to symptoms and side effects up to a maximum of 1800 mg/day lithium or 450 mg/day chlorpromazine. No other psychotropic medication was allowed. Of the 80 patients, 77 completed 3 weeks on trial medication; two dropouts suffered side effects on chlorpromazine and one dropout received a non-trial neuroleptic. Six other patients were also excluded from statistical analysis because they shifted to a depressive phase during treatment (five of these had been on chlorpromazine). Improvement was noted in 67.6% of the lithium patients compared to 47.1% of those on chlorpromazine, with the improvement occurring earlier on lithium. The mean serum lithium concentration was 0.57 mmol/l with a maximum level of 1.50 mmol/l and the mean chlorpromazine dose was 256 mg/day. The authors stated that Japanese patients appeared to be more sensitive to both lithium and chlorpromazine, especially the latter. The doses and serum level do seem low by Western standards and this difference makes comparison with other trials difficult.

In a trial published in 1973, comparing haloperidol, chlorpromazine and lithium, involving 30 inpatients, Dr Baron Shopsin and co-workers reported that haloperidol was most effective in the first week but that lithium was more effective in the longer term. Seven out of the ten lithium patients were discharged improved, compared to one of the ten chlorpromazine patients and two of the ten on haloperidol. While the two antipsychotic drugs were better at reducing hyperactivity, they had less effect on manic ideation and mood. This finding is in contrast to that of Prien and his colleagues, but the earlier study included more disturbed manic patients and its multicentre nature may have resulted in variations in diagnosis and level of expertise in the use of lithium.

However, two more recent trials have tended to support the suggestion that lithium may be less effective against more severely ill patients. In 1980 a group headed by Dr Garfinkel carried out a 3-week trial comparing lithium + placebo, haloperidol + placebo and lithium + haloperidol in 21 severely ill manic patients. By the eighth day, significant improvement had occurred among the patients receiving haloperidol, whether or not in conjunction with lithium, but not in those receiving lithium alone, resulting in many of the latter group being withdrawn. It was apparent that lithium took 6–10 days to exert its full effect and that this was too long for severely disturbed patients. Two years later Dr Braden and colleagues compared lithium with chlorpromazine in 78 psychotic patients with at least two manic symptoms (such patients might have a diagnosis of schizophrenia, schizoaffective psychosis, mania or 'other psychosis'). Of these, 43 completed at least 10 days of the 21 days of the trial. The early dropouts were equally distributed between the two drug groups, but the reasons were different. Early termination on chlorpromazine was due to side effects, whereas many terminations on lithium were due to failure to improve. Lithium appeared to be a less effective treatment for overactive psychotic patients regardless of diagnosis. Some schizophrenics did appear to respond to lithium, whereas overactive manics did not. Thus lithium responsivity may be more state dependent than diagnosis dependent, with the possibility that a patient may respond to lithium on one occasion but not on another. There is very little information available on whether the approximately 30% of acute manic patients who fail to respond to lithium are consistent in this regard in subsequent episodes.

It is difficult to make any broad generalization from these nine comparative trials, largely because of the variations in diagnostic criteria and in the information given about severity of illness, as well as differences in the doses of both lithium and the antipsychotic drugs. Nevertheless, it does appear that in mild to moderate mania, when rapid behavioural control is not necessary, lithium may be as efficacious as chlorpromazine or haloperidol and is, moreover, accompanied by fewer side effects. In severe mania lithium is less effective, even when adequate blood levels are attained.

Clinical Management

Lithium is recommended in the management of acute mania in the following situations: (i) in the mildly manic patient who is co-operative and aware of his condition, and who may have previously been on prophylactic lithium; (ii) in the patient who has not responded to antipsychotic medication; and (iii) in the patient for whom antipsychotic medication does not give a complete response, or who cannot tolerate persistent side effects from such medication. Such adjunctive treatment may be particularly useful when the antipsychotic alone has not produced a complete remission, especially if the patient has previously been on prophylactic lithium and the relapse was due to non-compliance. Lithium may also be useful in patients who tend to have a depressive episode immediately after mania, and in those who are going to proceed to a prophylactic trial of lithium.

Lithium is likely to be less useful in acute mania when: (i) the patient is hyperactive or otherwise severely disturbed; (ii) there is any doubt concerning renal function or state of hydration; (iii) there is a possibility of acute confusional state; (iv) the patient is not co-operative with oral medication or venepuncture; or (v) there is any possibility of pregnancy. The presence of already diagnosed hypothyroidism is not a bar to the use of lithium although the dose of thyroxine may need to be adjusted. Providing that the normal precautions are observed, elderly patients cope very well with lithium and it may be preferable to antipsychotics with this age group because of the high incidence of Parkinsonian side effects which attends the use of antipsychotic drugs.

All patients selected for lithium therapy should have a physical examination (see Section 15) but it is very difficult to measure creatinine clearance in the manic patient and other investigations may also be difficult to perform in the severely disturbed patient, providing a further reason why lithium is often not suitable as the first line of treatment.

Many of the patients admitted in acute mania are re-admissions and many will be on prophylactic lithium. It is often noted that the serum lithium is low at this stage and this is usually assumed to be due to non-compliance, whether as a cause or as a result of the manic episode. However, there has long been a controversy as to whether the brain (and some other tissues) retain more lithium during mania, thus reducing the serum level and the renal excretion; with the resolution of the episode the serum level is said to increase, thus reducing the lithium requirement (see Section 9). Drs Athanasio Kukopulos and Daniela Reginaldi indeed found in Italy in a survey of 37 bipolar patients that 31 showed an increase in serum lithium during depression and a decrease during mania with constant dosage. Thus it may be appropriate to reduce the dosage of lithium as the manic symptoms resolve, but this will not be necessary in all cases.

If the patient has not shown a substantial improvement in mental state after two weeks on lithium with a serum level of 1.5 mmol/l in the latter part of the treatment, then he or she can be considered to be effectively non-responsive to lithium and an alternative form of treatment will be necessary.

Related issues, such as the combined use of lithium and other agents in treating mania, and the prediction of therapeutic dose levels from an initial loading dose, are dealt with elsewhere in this book (Sections 17 and 46, pp. 67–73 and 167–171, respectively).

Bibliography

Kocsis,H. (1980) Lithium in the acute treatment of mania. In *The Handbook of Lithium Therapy*. Johnson,F.N. (ed.), MTP Press, Lancaster, UK, pp. 9–16.

In this chapter and in that by Peet the reader will find some discussion, and full bibliographic details, of the studies referred to in the present section.

Peet,M. (1975) Lithium in the acute treatment of mania. In *Lithium Research Therapy*. Johnson,F.N. (ed.), Academic Press, London, pp. 25–42.

This highly competent review deals in some detail with the earliest clinical trials of lithium against mania.

8. Acute Treatment of Depression

Ernest P.Worrall

Originally lithium was not thought to have any significant short term antidepressant effects. This was surprising in the face of the claims made for the drug in treating acute manic phases and in reducing both manic and depressive episodes in the longer term; surprising, too, because the simplest explanation of the long term useful effects of the drug in reducing manic episodes was that all that one was doing was continuing effective active treatment. Equally, the most likely explanation for any long term reduction in depression was that one was continuing what should have been effective acute treatment. However, since the main early question about the usefulness of lithium as a treatment was in whether it did in fact reduce long term morbidity, the inherent paradox in the prophylactic antidepressant claim was not a subject of great interest. Nevertheless, by the early 1970s, especially in the USA, the belief that the drug had no significant acute antidepressant effects was being changed to the view that its effects were 'uncertain'. Since then considerable evidence has been produced both from controlled trials and other sources, that the drug has major acute antidepressant effects.

Evidence for an Antidepressant Action

There are two accepted methods for establishing whether or not a drug has an antidepressant effect. In the first the drug is compared to a placebo and in the second the drug is compared to another known antidepressant. The first method is the more exact and requires fewer patients to settle the issue, but with the increasing availability of safe and effective treatments this becomes a more difficult procedure to justify. The second method requires more patients to get a clear-cut answer, but can also answer questions other than simply 'Does this new drug have an antidepressant effect?'

Placebo comparisons can be made in different ways. Individual patients can be given the putative antidepressant for part of the study period and a placebo for the other, with a comparison then being made of the degree of depression in the two periods in each patient. This technique is sometimes called 'placebo substitution'. Although there can at times be difficulties in the interpretation of placebo substitution studies, in some ways this is the technique which is the most convincing in demonstrating that a drug has a particular effect as it is the method which is nearest to good conditions of ordinary clinical practice: it can convince the doctor that that drug has an effect on that particular patient, but it does not give any information as to how many patients would demonstrate that effect. The other way a placebo study can be made is by 'group comparisons' where one group of patients is given a placebo and another group is given the putative antidepressant. At the end of the trial either the average level of symptoms is compared in both groups or a comparison made between the numbers in each group who have recovered.

In 1971 Dr Peter Stokes and colleagues from New York, USA, reported in the *Lancet* a placebo substitution study of lithium in the acute phases of mania and depression. They failed to show any significant benefit from lithium in treating acute depressive episodes in 18 patients. That trial has been fairly criticized for only observing the effects of the drug over the course of 10 days—too short a time to expect a clear effect from lithium. Despite this shortcoming this study was widely accepted at the time as it fitted in with earlier views about the lack of useful acute antidepressant effects of lithium.

In 1976, however, Professor Joe Mendels in Philadelphia, USA, reported a controlled placebo substitution study which showed a very clear-cut acute antidepressant effect of lithium. By that time four other previous American controlled placebo substitution studies had shown similar results.

Although no controlled placebo group study had at that time been carried out, one of two trials conducted by a group of investigators in Dundee, UK, and reported in the *British Journal of Psychiatry* in 1979, came as near to that as was felt ethically feasible. Over a 5-year period two controlled studies of the acute antidepressant effects of lithium were conducted. One of these studies looked at the acute antidepressant effects of lithium in patients who had failed to respond to a standard tricyclic antidepressant: in these patients, the substance tryptophan, which was believed to have at best weak antidepressant effects, was compared with a combination of lithium and tryptophan. The group given tryptophan alone showed no significant change over the 3 weeks of the trial whereas the group given tryptophan and lithium together showed a clear major antidepressant effect over those 3 weeks.

In fact, since the negative (or, more correctly, inconclusive) report of Stokes in 1971, all of the controlled studies reported subsequently (including a very recent placebo-controlled double-blind study by M.C.Khan of Hartlepool, UK, and his colleagues, which managed to overcome the ethical problems of controlled placebo group studies) have shown lithium to have acute antidepressant effects.

One of the problems in this area is that reviews of the use of lithium have tended simply to repeat the earlier views about the lack of acute antidepressant effects and have generally not taken into account the evidence of the controlled studies since 1971. Because of that, when lithium has been used at all in the treatment of depression it has tended to be in conjunction with an agent of known antidepressant potential. This actually provides us with a third piece of evidence which can be interpreted as being a further demonstration of lithium's acute antidepressant effects. Nearly all of an increasing number of reports which make the claim that lithium augments the effects of other standard antidepressant drugs (in particular, tricyclic antidepressants) seem to be describing the same phenomenon, i.e. that some severely depressed patients who have completely failed to respond to a first-line antidepressant dramatically respond within anything from a few days to a couple of weeks to the addition of lithium. The simplest and most economical explanation of most, but not all, of the cases reported has been that lithium has itself produced the acute antidepressant effect and that, in the absence of any discernible effect from the first drug, the same antidepressant effect would have occurred with lithium even in the absence of the first drug. Despite that being the most logical explanation, the fact that those reporting this observation have not first tried giving lithium on its own to these patients seems to be the result of the influence of the general reviews of lithium which, as already argued, are based on negative results obtained prior to 1971 and which had been prematurely accepted and not corrected in the light of later work.

Comparison with Other Antidepressants

An individual depressed patient's main concern is what effect a particular antidepressant will have on his or her own illness. A psychiatrist's advice to a new patient will be stated in terms of the probability of a particular antidepressant being effective. That estimate will be based on results from drug trials involving group comparisons. Put more starkly, a psychiatrist would be delighted with an antidepressant which gave a 90% probability of response, but the one in ten of the patients who do not obtain this effect would be disappointed to say the least. The overall result of standard antidepressant drugs such as tricyclics in controlled drug trials is that around 60% of patients find that they have a useful effect. Drug trials which involve group comparisons can give two sorts of answer to the question of how potent one antidepressant is compared to another. Comparing the average level of symptoms in one group given one treatment with the average level in another group can give a guide to the psychiatrist as to which drug would most reduce the overall level of symptoms in a group of patients. By the nature of averages, however, that figure could conceal wide differences in individual patient responses between the two groups. Although there are statistical techniques which can highlight such a situation, it would be fair to say that these are not always adequately reported in drug trials. The other sort of answer which can be obtained from a group comparison is that X% of patients recover with one treatment compared to Y% with another treatment. Because of the nature of the statistical techniques used to analyse drug trials this second type of answer requires a larger number of patients than the first. As a result, many drug trials are able only to give answers in terms of average level of symptoms for the group as a whole.

In those patients subject to repeated episodes of depression, careful observation of the results of different sorts of antidepressant drugs for a particular patient can give a much more exact prediction for the treatment of future episodes for that patient than can ever be derived from inferences from drug trials.

Apart from looking at the overall level of symptoms, drug trials may also be able to show whether there are differences in the speed with which the effects of different antidepressant drugs are expressed. There is no evidence that standard antidepressant drugs differ in their speed of effect. In the group comparisons of lithium and other antidepressants reported since 1971 there is no obvious difference in either the overall reduction in average symptoms with lithium compared to a standard tricyclic antidepressant, in the numbers of patients responding to one rather than the other, or in the time scale of these effects. However, the two trials reported from Dundee indicated that, in the particular group of depressed patients studied, lithium was slower to act than a tricyclic antidepressant (imipramine), that the overall reduction in the average level of symptoms was no different in the lithium group from the tricyclic group, but that more patients had a beneficial effect from lithium than did from the tricyclic.

What is of more interest to patients might be the question of whether they would respond to lithium if they fell into the group who failed to respond to a standard tricyclic. The second of the Dundee trials in which the effects of lithium were examined in a group of patients the majority of whom were tricyclic non-responders, suggested that, for a proportion of patients at least, that would be the case. As has been hinted earlier, the reports of combined treatment where lithium was added to the treatment of patients who had failed to respond to a first-line antidepressant, also strongly suggest that some patients in the acute stage of a serious depressive illness would respond to lithium when a tricyclic had failed.

Responders to Lithium

Many of the controlled studies which have reported a positive effect of lithium in the acute treatment of depression have looked at the factors which might predict which patients would show this effect. The only consistent finding has been that those patients with a previous history of hypomania or even a family history of bipolar illness are more likely to have a useful acute antidepressant effect. Nevertheless, nearly all of the studies have shown numbers of patients with histories of treatment for purely depressive episodes also showing a clear-cut response. One explanation of this may be that, both because of the short time span of an acute antidepressant drug trial and the rigorous unequivocal criteria needed to classify previous hypomania episodes for the purposes of research, many mild hypomanic episodes may be missed. It is the common experience of psychiatrists who deal with large numbers of endogenously depressed patients, and who offer long term follow-up and support to these patients, to find that a surprising number of patients whose presenting problem was depression in fact have mild hypomanic episodes which would otherwise never come to the attention of doctors and do not present problems to the patient or the relatives. In view of the overall findings from the clinical trials it remains probable that the only patients who are helped are those with bipolar illness but they may include patients who only ever require actual treatment for their depressive episodes.

Practical Implications

The majority of patients complaining of depressive symptoms and who are seen by general practitioners are not going to be suffering from bipolar affective disorder. Studies have shown that around 1 in 1300 of the population are being prescribed lithium. On average, therefore, in the UK each general practitioner will have two patients on his own list on lithium. The vast majority of these patients up to now will have been on long term treatment with lithium. Even if one considers prescribing lithium as a relatively short term acute treatment in patients whose previous history would not indicate continuing the drug in the long term, each general practitioner would only have a handful of patients complaining of depressive symptoms where the drug would likely to be effective. That would suggest that the initiation of lithium even as an acute treatment should remain a specialist procedure.

The question arises as to which patients presenting with acute depressive episodes should the psychiatrist consider suitable for using lithium as the treatment of first choice. From what has already been said, it would seem that these will be patients who clearly have a bipolar illness and where the previous history suggests that long term treatment would be desirable. It would be reasonable under such circumstances to use lithium as an acute treatment for the current depressive episode rather than starting another antidepressant and changing treatment to lithium once the patient is over the acute episode. On the evidence presented earlier, lithium would be likely to be at least as effective as a standard antidepressant and it seems only common sense not to expose a patient to the different risks of two drugs, however small, when one drug might suffice.

In a similar situation with a unipolar depressed patient, no such clear advice can be given. Psychiatrists use lithium as a long term preventive treatment in unipolar patients. That use is based on the results of trials comparing lithium and tricyclic antidepressants in long term prevention. These trials have not examined the degree to which the long term lithium and tricyclic responders overlap or whether, in a particular patient, acute response to one drug predicts long term response to that same drug. A coherent prescribing policy for the acutely depressed unipolar patient anticipating long term preventive lithium treatment depends on those questions being answered.

In acutely depressed bipolar patients and seriously depressed patients with a family history of hypomania where the past history would not indicate long term preventive treatment, lithium may still be the acute treatment of choice. In such patients, tricyclic antidepressants can precipitate hypomania and in some can produce rapid swings between hypomania and depression (rapid cycling). Lithium does not carry this risk and in these patients is otherwise as effective an antidepressant as a tricyclic.

The other group of patients where lithium might be tried would be in those seriously depressed patients where a standard antidepressant has failed. Lithium should be considered as an option. As many patients in that situation will require to remain on antidepressants for at least some months after they have improved, it is undesirable that such a patient should be treated with a combination of antidepressants, with neither the patient nor the psychiatrist knowing whether one drug alone would have been effective or whether the combination is needed. In those situations it is preferable that the drugs should be tried individually before combined treatment is started.

Bibliography

Khan,M.C., Wickham,E.A. and Reed,J.V. (1987) Lithium versus placebo in acute depression: a clinical trial. *Int. Clin. Psychopharmacol.*, **2**, 47–54.

The most recent report of an acute antidepressant effect of lithium.

Mendels,J. (1976) Lithium in the treatment of depression. *Am. J. Psychiatry*, **133**, 373–378.

One of the first papers to report that lithium might have an antidepressant effect in a defined subgroup of patients.

Worrall,E.P., Moody,J.P., Peet,M., Dick,P., Smith,A., Chambers,C., Adams,M. and Naylor,G.J. (1979) Controlled studies of the acute antidepressant effects of lithium. *Br. J. Psychiatry*, **135**, 255–262.

Give details of controlled trials carried out in Dundee.

9. Prophylaxis of Recurrent Mood Disorders

M.T.Abou-Saleh

The discovery of the prophylactic effects of lithium salts opened a new era in the management of affective disorders. Lithium, in a number of controlled investigations of variable methodological stringency, has been shown to reduce substantially the long-term morbidity of recurrent affective disorders. Dr G.P.Hartigan, from St. Augustine's Hospital in Canterbury, UK, was the first to report on the usefulness of prophylactic lithium in the management of recurrent affective disorders (see Section 6, pp. 24–28). He gave lithium to 32 bipolar and eight unipolar patients, and to five patients with cyclothymic personality disturbance over three to four years and found that the majority had responded favourably to the treatment.

An early study by Drs Poul-Christian Baastrup and Mogens Schou in 1967, showed that in a group of 88 patients with recurrent affective disorders who had received lithium for periods of up to five years, affective morbidity was reduced from an average of 13 weeks a year before lithium to 2 weeks a year on lithium therapy.

There followed a European collaborative study led by Dr Jules Angst, involving 244 patients with unipolar, bipolar and schizoaffective disorders. This study established that lithium treatment led to a substantial reduction in the number of episodes and hospital admissions in the patients. Moreover, lithium also led to elongation of cycles in bipolar and unipolar illnesses, and to shortening of episodes in bipolar patients during lithium treatment. Dr Roy Hullin from Leeds, UK, obtained similar results using this design of study.

The second phase of evaluation was the discontinuation trial. Dr Baastrup and his co-workers in Denmark, carried out the first discontinuation study. Patients who had been well controlled on lithium for years were randomly allocated to receive placebo or to continue with lithium. Discontinuation of lithium therapy for five months was associated with a relapse in 54% of the patients, compared with no relapses in patients who continued on it.

The third phase of study was the prospective double-blind trial. Dr Alec Coppen and his co-workers at Epsom in Surrey, UK, carried out a multi-centre collaborative trial involving 65 patients who had lithium or placebo for a period of two and a quarter years. Patients who had received placebo and who had also received *ad hoc* conventional treatment, including antidepressants, ECT and neuroleptics, spent 27% of their time as in-patients and a further 19% of their time with an out-patient episode. By contrast, patients treated with lithium spent only 5% of their time as in-patients and 7% of their time with an out-patient episode and their need for conventional treatment was greatly reduced.

Two studies by Dr Robert Prien in the USA followed: the first study as a placebo-controlled study of lithium for a period of two years whilst the second was a comparative study of placebo, lithium and imipramine. A total of 205 bipolar patients were studied in the first trial and 44 bipolar and 78 unipolar patients in the second trial. In the bipolar patients, the incidence of both depressive and manic episodes during the two year trial period was three times greater in the placebo group than in the lithium group. In the unipolar patients, 92% of the patients suffered depressive episodes whilst taking placebo, compared to only 44% of patients who had lithium. It was noted that in bipolar patients, imipramine failed to reduce manic episodes.

Dr Coppen and his colleagues then carried out double-blind studies of mianserin and maprotiline in comparison with lithium in the prophylaxis of unipolar illness. These studies involved patients who had responded to prophylactic lithium and who were then randomly allocated to continue with lithium or receive mianserin or maprotiline. They found that over a year of the trial, patients who had received lithium suffered significantly less morbidity than those who had mianserin and maprotiline.

The UK Medical Research Council's latest multi-centre trial found lithium to be as effective as amitriptyline in prophylaxis of unipolar illness. This trial involved two studies. In the first, a high risk group of unipolars were included (they had had three or more episodes of depression) and were randomly allocated to lithium or amitriptyline. In the second study, patients who had had either one or two episodes were studied and were randomly allocated to lithium, amitriptyline or placebo. It was shown in both studies that lithium was as effective as amitriptyline, and in the second study that both were superior to placebo.

Doubts have been cast on the usefulness of lithium in the prophylaxis of unipolar illness. Schou, however, in a review of the results of nine studies on lithium and five studies on antidepressants reaffirmed the usefulness of lithium in the prophylaxis of unipolar illness: he estimated that prophylactic treatment with lithium reduced the mean percentage of patients falling ill during the first year from 67% to 22% and that prophylactic antidepressants reduced the relapse rate from 67% to 35%.

Prien and co-workers have recently reported the results of the National Institute of Mental Health's multi-centre collaborative study comparing lithium, imipramine and their combination in the prophylaxis of unipolar and bipolar illnesses. With bipolar patients, lithium and the combination were superior to imipramine in preventing manic recurrences and were as effective as imipramine in preventing depressive episodes. With unipolar patients, imipramine and the combination treatment were more effective than lithium carbonate and placebo in preventing depressive recurrences. Lithium was superior to placebo in the moderately ill unipolar and as effective as placebo in the severely ill unipolar patients. The patients involved in the investigation were, however, described as atypical with a few clear-cut periods in which they were well, and this may account for the finding that lithium was only as useful as placebo in the severely ill unipolar patients.

There has been only one study in which the usefulness of lithium was compared with that of long-acting neuroleptic medication in patients with bipolar illness. Dr U.G.Ahlfors has led a Scandinavian multi-centre investigation in which the efficacy of flupenthixol decanoate in preventing manic and depressive relapses was compared with that of lithium. They found that flupenthixol was as effective as lithium in reducing the frequency of manic episodes, but not as effective in preventing depressive episodes, and they suggested that flupenthixol might therefore be used with patients who have failed to respond to lithium or have not tolerated it.

Indications for Prophylactic Treatment

A crucial decision for the clinician to make is when to start prophylactic lithium. A detailed and profound discussion of this topic was forwarded by Professor Jules Angst who analysed the course of illness in 159 unipolar patients, in 95 bipolar patients and 150 schizoaffective patients over 19 to 27 years. He found that only 37% of unipolars, 15% of bipolars and 18% of schizoaffective patients had suffered one episode of illness during that period. He decided that it would be desirable to start prophylaxis if a patient was likely to suffer two further episodes in addition to the present one in the subsequent five years. Angst examined numerous criteria to see which identified those patients at risk. His conclusions were surprisingly simple: the presence of one episode in the previous five years in unipolars, in the previous four years in bipolars, and in the previous three years in schizoaffectives fulfilled this criterion for starting prophylactic treatment.

The World Health Organization has recently provided guidelines based on these findings: prophylactic treatment should be started in unipolar depression after three episodes, particularly if one discrete episode has occurred within the last five years, apart from the present episode. In bipolar illness, prophylactic treatment should be given after the second episode.

The Lithium Clinic

The complexities of the management of patients with affective disorders demand the expertise of a team which includes psychiatrists, nurses and social workers. These complexities are partly related to the nature of lithium therapy as the main long-term treatment. Plasma lithium concentrations have to be monitored regularly and thyroid and renal functions checked (see pp. 59–62 and 105–107). Lithium clinics have emerged in the UK and USA out of psychiatric out-patient clinics. These are out-patient sessions held regularly during which clinical progress is ascertained, plasma lithium concentrations monitored and daily dosages adjusted. Patients find this milieu supportive and encouraging as they realise that they are not alone in their predicament. The topic of lithium clinics is dealt with more fully in Section 34, pp. 127–129. Some patients may prefer to attend their general practitioners or would be more willing to be attended by a community psychiatric nurse in their own homes.

Who Responds to Prophylactic Lithium?

Response to prophylactic lithium varies considerably (see Section 14, pp. 57–59) and studies suggest that two thirds to three quarters of patients with recurrent affective disorders show favourable responses. Response varies from complete, when no further morbidity is observed, through partial, when the severity and the duration of episodes is ameliorated or modified, to failure to respond, when morbidity continues unabated. It is of utmost importance that clinicians are able to make estimates or predictions of the likelihood of favourable responses to lithium: this would spare the potentially unresponsive patient exposure to a long-term treatment that is not without hazards.

Among bipolar patients, those with frequent episodes (rapid cycling patients who suffer four episodes or more per year) show a greater incidence of prophylaxis failure than those with non-rapid cycling illness. Studies carried out at the Medical Research Council's Brain Metabolism Unit in Edinburgh, UK, and at the Medical Research Council Neuropsychiatry Laboratory in Epsom, Surrey, UK, have indicated a few clinical and psychological predictors of response to prophylactic lithium. Among unipolar patients, those with endogenous and psychotic features had an excellent response compared with those with non-endogenous illness. Moreover, patients wth pure familial depressive disease (with family history of depression) had comparatively better response than those with sporadic depressive (no family history of depression) and depression spectrum disease (family history of alcoholism and sociopathy). In both bipolar and unipolar patients, those with greater disturbance in their personality characteristics, including neuroticism, introversion, less drive and less self-confidence responded less well than those with less personality disturbance. The most powerful predictor of long-term response, however, was an empirical one: a trial of lithium for 6–12 months predicted response over many years. These results were confirmed in a later study by Dr Alec Coppen, which indicated that lithium in lower doses, and at serum levels of 0.45–0.6 mmol/l was highly effective (no, or only slight morbidity) in 78% of unipolar and 73% of bipolar and schizoaffective patients studied for the duration of one year. Moreover, lithium was as effective in the elderly with recurrent affective disorders (aged more than 70 years) as in young and middle-aged patients. Unipolar patients rated as endogenous on the Newcastle scale showed significantly less morbidity than the non-endogenous patients.

Professor Mogens Schou has argued that complete response to lithium occurs in 30–60% of patients, partial response in 30–50% and lack of response in 10–20% of patients. Response should be evaluated in relation to previous morbidity prior to starting lithium, e.g. a patient who has many relapses during lithium might still be a relatively good responder as he might have had more frequent relapses if lithium had not been started.

Professor Schou has suggested that incomplete or unsatisfactory response to lithium may have many causes, including non-compliance and discontinuation against medical advice (see pp. 117–121), gradual onset of the prophylactic action, non-adjustment of dosage, hypothyroidism, and the need for supplementary or alternative treatment. The clinician confronted with a patient with incomplete response should bear all these factors in mind before discontinuing lithium.

Dr A.Coppen has recently suggested that folic acid may enhance the effects of prophylactic lithium. In a double-blind trial, folic acid given in physiological doses (0.2 mg per day) was evaluated in comparison with placebo in a group of 75 patients receiving prophylactic lithium. It was found that patients with the highest plasma folate concentrations during the trial showed a significant reduction in their affective morbidity and patients who had their folate levels increased to 13 mg/ml or above had 40% reduction in their morbidity.

Concluding Remarks

Affective disorders are by nature recurrent and are associated with enormous distress to patients and their families. Whilst these illnesses are recoverable, they often pose a life-long liability that requires a long-term, if not indefinite treatment. The usefulness of lithium in the prophylactic control of recurrent affective disorders has been firmly established. The majority of patients with bipolar and unipolar illness should experience no or little morbidity and disability whilst receiving prophylactic lithium.

The usefulness of the lithium clinic cannot be over emphasised. It enables patients to be regularly supervised and any deterioration of their mental state to be observed and treated early. Regular assessment and on-the-spot estimation of plasma lithium levels also greatly encourage compliance.

Bibliography

Baastrup,P.C. (1980) Lithium in the prophylactic treatment of recurrent affective disorders. In *Handbook of Lithium Therapy*. Johnson,F.N. (ed.), MTP Press, Lancaster, UK, pp. 26–38.
This very readable chapter provides guidelines on the use of prophylactic lithium including the importance of weighing the risks and benefits of the treatment, the value of a short course of treatment to determine future response and other practical aspects of treatment such as setting, monitoring, preparation and dosage.

Schou,M. and Thomsen,K. (1975) Lithium prophylaxis of recurrent endogenous affective disorders. In *Lithium Research and Therapy*. Johnson,F.N. (ed.), Academic Press, London, pp. 63–84.
An early survey of the evidence for lithium prophylaxis, this chapter is neverthless still well worth reading for its assessment of technical and methodological issues.

10. Schizophrenia

Frederic J.Sautter and
David L.Garver

At a symptomatic level there is a good deal of similarity between the more florid types of mania in which hallucinations and thought disorder may appear, and certain forms of schizophrenia. There are also retarded schizophrenic states in which the patient, appearing withdrawn and unresponsive, seems very much like a patient in a deep depression. All this has led some to wonder whether there may be more than a superficial resemblance between schizophrenia and the affective disorders and whether, indeed, the two types of disorder may share certain fundamental underlying mechanisms. If this were so, then psychopharmacological agents effective against schizophrenia might also be expected to be useful in mood disorders, and *vice versa*. To some extent, confirmation of this expectation is to be found in drugs such as chlorpromazine and haloperidol, both of which are not only effective in handling schizophrenic symptoms but are also used to bring about rapid control of mania. It is not, therefore, surprising that lithium, having proved its worth in the treatment of manic-depressive illness, should have been tried in schizophrenic patients too.

The results of double-blind studies of lithium in the treatment of schizophrenia have been equivocal, with some positive outcomes but many negative ones. In trials comparing lithium and chlorpromazine, it is the latter which has been found the more effective agent, though lithium did have a degree of therapeutic action. At the present time, the status of lithium as an anti-schizophrenic drug remains unresolved.

The reasons for the failure to resolve the standing of lithium in this regard are two-fold. In the first place it is generally recognized that there is a group of patients who suffer from a condition which appears to combine features of both schizophrenia and affective dysfunction—the so-called schizoaffective disorder. Whether this is a true 'borderline' condition lying midway between the states of schizophrenia and manic-depressive illness, or whether it is more appropriately conceived of as a combination of the two, is open to dispute. What is clear, however, is that the affective component often appears responsive to lithium therapy, though the schizophrenic element is usually more resistant: combined lithium-neuroleptic treatment is frequently employed to produce effective relief.

The differential diagnosis of mania and schizophrenia is not always easy, despite the introduction of more rigorous criteria following DSM-III, and when one adds to this the existence of schizoaffective disorder it is easy to see that those trials which showed lithium to be effective against schizophrenia may well have included in the patient group a large number of individuals whose symptoms owed more to affective dysfunction than to schizophrenia.

The second reason for the confusion about the anti-schizophrenic potential of lithium is the growing consensus among psychiatric researchers that schizophrenic disorders actually consist of a number of genetically and biologically distinct illnesses. In the process of identifying schizophrenic subtypes there has been a great deal of interest in a group of patients who exhibit symptoms that are similar to that of schizophrenia, but do not follow the deteriorating course that typifies the bulk of the schizophrenias. The term 'good prognosis' schizophrenia has been used to describe these patients. More specifically, these good prognosis schizophrenics have an illness that is characterized by schizophrenic-like psychotic episodes of less than 6 months duration with subsequent return to baseline functioning. Further studies indicate that the first degree relatives (i.e. parents, siblings, offspring) of these good prognosis schizophrenics evidence a high incidence of affective disorder and a paucity of classic schizophrenic illness.

Lithium-responsive Schizophrenia

Research efforts at the University of Cincinnati College of Medicine, USA, have focused upon investigating a group of psychotic patients that respond favourably to treatment with lithium. Most of these lithium-responsive schizophrenic-like psychotics have an episodic (rather than chronic, deteriorating) illness course; they meet the criteria for DMS-III schizophreniform disorder and for good prognosis schizophrenia. In one recent study, the psychiatric life histories of first degree family members of 16 patients drawn from the lithium-responsive group were compared with those of first degree family members of 33 lithium non-responsive psychotic (mood incongruent) patients. It was found that the two groups of relatives did not differ in the incidence of schizophreniform disorder, unipolar major depressive disorder, or bipolar disorder. The most robust finding in this study, however, was that while just under 8% of the relatives of the lithium non-responsive patients suffered from a schizophrenic spectrum disorder, *none* of the relatives of the lithium-responsive patients had an illness within the schizophrenic spectrum, a result which appears to indicate that this lithium-responsive schizophrenic-like illness is familially distinct from the deteriorating schizophrenias.

Lithium-responsive Psychotic Illness and the Affective Disorders

In an attempt to answer the important question of the relationship between lithium-responsive psychotic illness and the affective disorders, the family patterns of illness of the lithium-responsive psychotics were compared with the family patterns of illness of patients suffering from DSM-III bipolar disorder, and of psy-

Table 10.1 *Psychiatric illness (DSM-III) in first degree relatives of lithium-responsive and lithium non-responsive schizophrenic-like psychotic patients and in relatives of (manic-depressive) bipolar patients*

Patient (proband)		Relatives			
n	Diagnosis	*n*	Diagnosis	*n*	Morbid risk[a](%)
18	Li-responsive schizophrenic-like psychotic	79	Schizophrenia	1	1.7*
			Schizophreniform	1	2.1
			Unipolar disorder	8	18.6
			Bipolar disorder	2	4.1
			No illness	67	–
51	Li-nonresponsive schizophrenic-like psychotic	195	Schizophrenia	14	9.9*
			Schizophreniform	2	1.8
			Unipolar disorder	10	9.8
			Bipolar disorder	3	2.7
			No illness	166	–
16	Bipolar (manic-depressive) disorder	75	Schizophrenic	3	5.7*
			Schizophreniform	1	2.3
			Unipolar disorder	4	9.6
			Bipolar disorder	4	9.1
			No illness	63	–

[a]Morbid risk = $N_S/[N_T - (n_o - 0.5n_w)]$ where: N_S = number of schizophrenics observed; N_T = total sample size; n_o = total number who have not reached the period of susceptibility; n_w = number of schizophrenics who are within the period of susceptibility (15–39 years). The morbid risk is the probability that a person who survives through the period of susceptibility will develop a specific illness. For example, the period of susceptibility for schizophrenia is 15–39 years of age. If the morbid risk for schizophrenia is 10%, it means that the probability of a person 40 years of age or older having schizophrenia is one in ten. $^*P < 0.001$.

chotic patients who were lithium non-responsive. The three groups of relatives differed in the overall incidence of DSM-III schizophrenia, schizophreniform disorder, unipolar disorder and bipolar disorder (*Table 10.1*); the most important finding, however, was that the three groups of relatives were markedly different in terms of the morbid risk for DSM-III schizophrenia, this being especially low among relatives of patients with a lithium-responsive schizophrenic-like disorder.

Two other findings were of considerable interest. First, the morbid risk for DSM-III bipolar disorder was lower among relatives of the lithium-responsive schizophrenic-like patients than it was among relatives of the bipolar patients. This may indicate that this lithium-responsive illness is relatively distinct from the bipolar disorders. Second, there was a distinct trend toward morbid risk for unipolar disorders being higher in the relatives of the lithium-responsive patients than it was in the relatives of the patients with bipolar disorder or lithium non-responsive psychotics.

Implications of Research Findings

These data would seem to indicate that there is a lithium-responsive schizophrenic-like illness that is familially and probably genetically distinct from the bulk of the deteriorating schizophrenias and the lithium-responsive illness may also be relatively distinct from the bipolar affective disorders as well. Further investigations of the family patterns of illness in this group of patients should help researchers to develop a better understanding of the relationship between schizophrenic and affective disorders. These findings have implications for the attending physician: psychotic (mood incongruent) patients that have an episodic illness with full recovery between episodes and who do not present with a family history of schizophrenia may well be responsive to lithium. This is a further indication of the value of taking a full and detailed psychiatric history and one which extends to first degree relatives, too.

Bibliography

McCabe,M.S., Fowler,R.C., Caderet,R.J. and Winokur,G. (1971) Familial differences in schizophrenia with good or poor prognosis. *Psychol. Med.*, **1**, 326–332.
Provides a background of the concept of 'good prognosis' schizophrenia and shows how family studies may be used as a method of validation of diagnosis. It is suitable for sophisticated non-medical readership.

Sautter,F.J. and Garver,D.L. (1984) Familial differences in lithium responsive versus lithium nonresponsive psychosis. *J. Psychiatr. Res.*, **19**, 1–8.
This article provides a more detailed presentation of some of the data briefly presented in this chapter. It is fairly technical and may not be suitable for non-medical readership.

11. Use in Other Psychiatric Conditions

Mogens Schou

It is not, perhaps, unexpected that a treatment modality of simple chemical structure which, through mechanisms as yet unknown, exerts marked action on a major psychosis should also have been tried on other psychiatric indications. When available therapeutic options are few and ineffective, even odd chances may be worth taking, and if the condition treated is one involving changes of mood or a periodic course or both a certain rationale can be claimed for trying lithium.

Some of the trials have had success, and positive casuistic observations have subsequently been substantiated by systematic trials of rigid design. Others showed initial promise, but did not stand up to proper placebo-controlled checking. Most remain in the realm of positive experiences with one or a few patients. The indications have nevertheless been included in *Table 11.1* of suggested uses. Additional observations may be sufficiently promising to justify systematic testing on larger patient groups.

Table 11.1 *Suggested uses for lithium on psychiatric indications other than the endogenous psychoses*

Deviant behaviour
- Episodic pathological aggressiveness and assaultive behaviour
- Self-mutilation
- Hyperactivity in children
- Explosive behaviour in adolescents
- Deviant sexual behaviour
- Child abuse

Dependence
- Alcoholism
- Opiate abuse
- Cocaine abuse
- Amphetamine abuse

Drug-induced psychoses
- Prednisone-induced psychosis
- Corticotropin-induced psychosis
- L-DOPA-induced psychosis
- Cocaine-induced psychosis

Psychopathological conditions with known or presumed organic origin
- Organic brain syndrome
- Minimal brain dysfunction and attention deficit syndrome
- Post-traumatic stress syndrome with amnesia
- Emotional sequelae of herpes encephalitis
- Behavioural disturbances or affective symptoms in dementia
- Epileptic psychosis
- Maniform symptoms in multiple sclerosis
- Emotional disturbances secondary to metastases in the brain
- Psychotic symptoms in Fahr's disease

Other
- Obsessive-compulsive neurosis
- Compulsive gambling
- Premenstrual tension syndrome
- Anorexia nervosa and bulimia
- De Clerembault's syndrome
- Central pain
- Periodic hypersomnia, e.g. as part of the Kleine-Levin syndrome

Aggressiveness

It is among the deviant behaviour indications that we find some of the best documented lithium effects outside manic-depressive illness. Foremost among them is episodic pathological aggressiveness and assaultive behaviour. Positive effects have been seen in patients with unstable character disorder, in violent sociopaths, in children, and in mentally retarded persons, and the responders were not thought to be suffering from manic-depressive illness. In oligophrenics the calming and stabilizing effect could be seen when the aggressiveness took the form of self-mutilation as well as when others were attacked. It is not clear whether the effect of lithium in such instances is exerted primarily on the assaultiveness as such or on the—usually irregular—periodicity of the explosive behaviour.

Documentation of lithium effects on periodic aggressiveness is so solid, based on double-blind as well as on single-blind studies with large numbers of treated subjects, that one would expect lithium to be used rather widely on this indication. This has not, however, been the case, and a reason may be general hesitation about administering drugs to children and to inmates of penal and ward institutions. Perhaps the prevailing anti-drug attitude prevents some of the afflicted persons from obtaining valuable help. It seems worth noting that many of those given lithium reported substantial subjective relief from their previously uncontrollable bouts of rage and violence. There was increased capacity to reflect on the consequences of aggressive behaviour: 'Now I can take time to think before I hit him!'.

Lithium doses, serum lithium concentrations, and general treatment guidelines are the same when lithium is used for periodic aggressiveness as when the indication is recurrent manic-depressive illness. Since children have more active kidneys than adults, they require relatively higher lithium doses (higher in relation to body weight) to achieve the same serum lithium concentrations. Usually children have few side effects. In the treatment of children it is of particular value that lithium is without sedative action which might interfere with school performance and intellectual development.

Drug Abuse

Even long-term lithium treatment does not lead to addiction, and lithium does not induce euphoria. On the contrary, a few manic-depressive drug addicts complained that they had difficulty becoming 'high' when on lithium. This has led to lithium treatment of drug dependence, but positive single case experiences are outweighed by negative treatment outcome with larger groups.

Alcohol Abuse

Some manic-depressive patients drink overmuch alcohol while manic or depressed; as lithium controls the affective illness, their alcohol problem disappears. Positive reports about lithium effects in alcoholism not secondary to manic-depressive illness are counterbalanced by clearly negative studies, and the subject clearly merits further investigation. Possible effects of lithium include fewer drinking bouts, reduced craving for alcohol, and amelioration of the symptoms of alcohol intoxication. Some caution seems indicated in prescribing lithium to a group of persons notoriously unreliable as regards the intake of not only drugs but also food and fluid.

Drug-induced Psychoses

Drug-induced psychoses often show affective symptomatology (mood disturbance), but their duration is usually so short and their development and course so unpredictable that systematic treatment trials are next to impossible.

Organic Brain Syndromes

Organic illness of the brain may lead to mental symptoms of various kinds, and changes of mood are not rare among patients suffering from these diseases. Depression is most frequent and easiest to understand, the seriousness of the underlying illness taken into consideration. Manic symptoms—more paradoxical under the circumstances—arouse speculation about the cerebral origin of, or regulatory influence on, our emotions. Lithium treatment of psychopathological conditions with known or presumed organic origin has occasionally had good effects on abnormal emotions or mood instability, but systematic documentation is lacking. In view of the often protracted course of these diseases such treatment trials must be encouraged, but it should be noted that patients with organic brain damage, especially those with temporal lobe epilepsy, are apt to develop neurotoxic side-effects of lithium.

Personality Problems

Lithium is prophylactically as effective against recurrent endogenous depression as against the bipolar form of manic-depressive illness (pp. 38–41), and some of the unipolar patients report an effect not only on their depressive episodes but also on their personality during the intervals between episodes. Habitually anxious and obsessive of nature, they feel, when under the influence of lithium, freer and more self-confident. One does not know whether this is a result of new safeness under the protection of lithium, or whether lithium may exert more direct effects on certain personality features. Observations such as these naturally led to lithium treatment trials, some of them double-blind, in patients with obsessive-compulsive neurosis; their outcome has been negative.

Premenstrual Syndrome

If affective symptomatology and periodic occurrence are targets for the long-term effects of lithium then the premenstrual tension or dysphoria syndrome ought to be an obvious candidate for lithium treatment. Uncontrolled trials have indicated positive effects of lithium; placebo-controlled studies on larger patient groups have not.

Anorexia and Bulimia

Anorexia nervosa and bulimia are presumably among the pathological conditions that have been subjected to treatment trials with the widest variety of agents and procedures; none has revealed striking and sustained effect. Lithium is no exception, even though increased mood stability and better weight control have been seen in some cases.

Periodic Hypersomnia

Publications from recent years have reported marked response to lithium of periodic hypersomnia, e.g. as part of the Kleine-Levin syndrome, and it has been suggested that lithium may be the treatment of choice for this uncommon and often misdiagnosed disease.

Concluding Remarks

No doubt there will continue to be reports in the literature regarding the effective use of lithium in conditions which one would not have had any good reason to expect to be lithium-responsive. The suspicion must always be entertained in such cases that the underlying pathology is one of affective dysfunction, manifesting itself in an aberrant manner. Recommendations for the use of lithium as the treatment of choice for new indications should, in principle, always be supported by adequate clinical trials, though where the condition concerned is of rare occurrence it may not, in practice, be feasible to carry out such studies with any degree of methodological rigour. It must often be left to the psychiatrist's judgement as to whether in any individual patient a trial with lithium may be warranted, having regard to the reports in the literature (negative and positive), the failure of other medications, and the special characteristics—mental and physical—of the patient.

Bibliography

Campbell,M., Perry,R. and Green,W.H. (1984) Use of lithium in children and adolescents. *Psychosomatics,* **25**, 95–106.
Gives a survey of the evidence for lithium's efficacy in child psychiatry, based on literature studies and personal clinical experience, and provides practical guidelines.

Fawcett,J., Clark,D.C., Gibbons,R.D., Aagesen,C.A., Pisani,V.D., Tilkin,J.M., Sellers,D. and Stutzman,D. (1983) Evaluation of lithium therapy for alcoholism. *J. Clin. Psychiatry,* **45**, 494–499.
Special emphasis is placed on compliance problems in this report of a double-blind placebo trial on 84 alcoholic volunteers

Kline,N.S. and Simpson,G. (1975) Lithium in the treatment of conditions other than the affective disorders. In *Lithium Research and Therapy*. Johnson,F.N. (ed.), Academic Press, London, pp. 85–98.
This summarizes what was known about the range of indications for lithium up to the mid 1970s, and classifies the conditions into episodic and non-episodic disorders. It is a useful starting-point for a consideration of later developments.

Schou,M. (1980) The psychiatric uses of lithium outside manic-depressive illness. In *Handbook of Lithium Therapy*. Johnson,F.N. (ed.), MTP Press, Lancaster, UK, pp. 68–72.
A shorter, but more recent account than that given by Kline and Simpson, this article also provides a useful reference list.

Sheard,M.H. (1984) Clinical pharmacology of aggressive behavior. *Clin. Neuropharmacol.,* **7**, 173–183.
In addition to lithium therapy, the uses of propranolol and carbamazepine in pathological aggression are discussed, together with reflections on the neurobiology of aggressive behaviour.

12. Use in Non-psychiatric Conditions

Mogens Schou

During the first century after its introduction into medicine lithium was used on many non-psychiatric

Table 12.1 *Suggested uses of lithium in non-psychiatric conditions*

Thyroid disease
- Hyperthyroidism (Graves' disease, Basedow's disease)
- Thyrotoxic crisis (thyroid storm)
- Thyroid cancer (conjointly with radioiodine)

Other endocrine disease
- Addison's disease
- Inappropriate secretion of antidiuretic hormone
- Diabetes mellitus

Blood disease
- Congenital neutropenia
- Cyclic neutropenia
- Neutropenia as part of Felty's syndrome
- Neutropenia caused by cancer chemotherapy
- Thromobocytopenia
- Functional thrombocyte incompetence
- Acute myeloid leukaemia
- Non-Hodgkin lymphoma
- Agranulocytosis
- Aplastic anaemia
- Fanconi's anaemia
- Sickle cell anaemia

Headache and pain
- Migraine
- Cyclic migraine
- Cluster headache
- Central pain
- Trigeminal neuralgia
- Painful shoulder syndrome

Movement disease
- Blepharospasm and orofacial dystonia, torsion dystonia
- Spasmodic torticollis
- Tardive dyskinesia
- Huntington's chorea
- Parkinsonism
- On-off syndrome in Parkinsonism
- L-DOPA induced hyperkinesia
- Organic brain syndrome
- Tic, e.g. as part of Gilles de la Tourette's syndrome

Other neurological disease
- Epilepsy
- Hyperkalaemic periodic paralysis
- Hypokalaemic periodic paralysis
- Hypermagnesaemic periodic paralysis
- Engelberg-Welander's spinal amyotrophy
- Menière's disease
- Myotonia

Disturbance of fluid and electrolyte metabolism
- Hyperkalaemic periodic paralysis
- Hypokalaemic periodic paralysis
- Hypermagnesaemic periodic paralysis
- Inappropriate secretion of antidiuretic hormone
- Water intoxication
- Idiopathic oedema

Cardiac disease
- Congestive heart failure
- Variant angina pectoris

Intestinal disease
- Chronic secretory diarrhoea
- Familial Mediterranean fever
- Pancreatic cholera
- Ulcerative colitis

Various
- Asthma
- Cancer chemotherapy (conjointly with slow neutron capture treatment)
- Dental caries
- Peptic ulcer
- Periodic vomiting
- Periodic fever
- Recurrent herpes infection
- Seborrhoeic dermatitis
- Vitiligo

Non-therapeutic use
- Indicator of delivery of water and sodium from the proximal kidney tubes

indications, but the treatments were based on erroneous theoretical assumptions, and efficacy was in no instance proven. These early indications have not been included in *Table 12.1*, which shows non-psychiatric uses of lithium suggested since 1950. The newer indications have usually an empirical background. Some are based on side effects observed during lithium treatment in psychiatry, some on the particular physical properties of the lithium ion, and some derive from incidental observations. A few are purely speculative.

As with the use of lithium on psychiatric indications other than endogenous psychoses (Section 11, pp. 44–46), substantiation of therapeutic value on non-psychiatric indications ranges from rigidly controlled trials to clinical anecdotes. The more solidly documented uses are mentioned below; if an indication is left unmentioned, this means that the evidence permits neither positive nor negative conclusions.

Thyroid-related conditions

Within the first decade of prophylactic lithium treatment of manic-depressive illness some of the patients developed goitre and a few were subjected to subtotal thyroidectomy. Cases of myxoedema were also observed. We now know that these adverse reactions can be treated effectively by administration of thyroxine concurrently with lithium.

Lithium exerts at least five distinct effects on the thyroid gland (see Section 60, pp. 220–226). One of them is to inhibit release of one of the thyroid hormones, thyroxine, and hypothyroidism may develop. There is a compensatory rise of thyroid stimulating hormone (TSH) and the overstimulated gland tissue may proliferate.

This effect of lithium has been put to use in the treatment of hyperthyroidism. Administration of lithium leads to reduction of the output of thyroxine and a lessening of general tissue exposure. There is also inhibition of the conversion of thyroxine to triiodothyronine in the periphery. The effect of lithium administration is well documented through clinical trials, but the value of the treatment is diminished by the occurrence of lithium-induced side effects and the fact that other effective therapies are available. Lithium treatment of hyperthyroidism has not become an established procedure, but thyrotoxic crises may respond better to a combination of lithium and an anti-thyroid agent (thiamazole, carbimazole) than to either drug given alone.

Lithium inhibits escape of thyroxine, and hence of iodine, from the gland. This means that when lithium is given in combination with radioiodine for thyroid cancer, the ratio of thyroid tissue irradiation exposure to total body irradiation exposure is increased favourably.

Inappropriate Secretion of ADH

During lithium treatment some patients develop a condition resembling renal diabetes insipidus with increased production of dilute urine and augmented fluid consumption (see Section 57, pp. 206–213). This is caused by an inhibitory effect of lithium on the distal kidney tubules and collecting ducts, which are rendered less responsive to the action of the antidiuretic hormone (vasopressin, or ADH). This effect of lithium has been put to therapeutic use outside psychiatry. In the condition known as inappropriate secretion of ADH the pituitary produces too much vasopressin. The patient consequently reabsorbs too much water, the extracellular space expands, and signs of hyponatraemia develop. Under these circumstances, a lowering of the renal response to the antidiuretic hormone is desirable, and lithium treatment has been used with at least temporary effect in such cases. The same mechanism may have been involved in a few cases where lithium was used to treat water intoxication.

Neutropenia and Leukaemia

During prophylactic lithium treatment a number of patients develop an increase in the number of circulating white blood cells (leukocytosis). This has led to experimental use of lithium for treatment of neutropenia (a fall in the count of certain white cells) whether spontaneous or induced by cancer chemotherapy (see also Section 59, pp. 218–220). The rise in the number of circulating leukocytes is evident, and according to some reports there are fewer infectious complications and febrile episodes. Lithium stimulates granulopoiesis by increasing the number of granulocyte-macrophage colony forming stem cells, but other mechanisms may also be involved.

There have been reports about development of leukaemia during prophylactic lithium treatment, but the frequency is so low that coincidence cannot be excluded, and lithium has in fact been used for the treatment of leukaemia, both acute and chronic. The results have not, however, been convincing. The effect of lithium on haematopoiesis may not be limited to stimulation of neutrophil production. Attempts at treating other haematological diseases with lithium have in some cases given clearly negative results but have in other instances led to observations which require further investigation.

Headache

Several forms of headache show a more or less recurrent pattern, and it was therefore natural to investigate whether long-term lithium administration might exert a prophylactic action upon them. Ordinary migraine responds poorly in most cases, cyclic migraine possibly better, and cluster headache has become one of the established non-psychiatric indications for lithium treatment. The chronic form of cluster headache seems to respond better than the episodic form. General treatment guidelines are the same as with other long-term lithium treatments, though required doses and serum levels may be slightly lower.

The use of lithium for treatment of other forms of pain is based on the observation of single cases, and no systematic studies have been carried out.

Movement Disorders

Apart from sometimes producing tremor (not of the Parkinsonian type) lithium in non-toxic doses has very few effects on posture, movement or coordination (see Section 66, pp. 240–246). Treatment with lithium has nevertheless been tried in a number of movement diseases and other neurological diseases. Positive experiences with single patients or small groups of patients alternate with negative reports. Systematic studies have been carried out with a few of the suggested indications (e.g. Huntington's chorea and Menière's disease); the results were negative.

Periodic Paralysis

Since lithium is a cation, chemically and biologically related to sodium and potassium and also to calcium and magnesium, treatment effects might be anticipated in diseases which directly involve fluid and electrolyte metabolism, and perhaps particularly in those with a periodic course. Periodic hyperkalaemic paralysis and periodic hypokalaemic paralysis did not, however, respond to lithium, but in one case lithium in combination with digitalis lowered the frequency of paralytic attacks in hypermagnesaemic periodic paralysis.

Congestive Heart Failure

Lithium got a bad name in medicine when, in the 1940s, lithium chloride was used as a taste substitute for sodium chloride by patients who, owing to cardiac or renal disease, had to live on a salt-free diet (see Section 6, pp. 24–28). This led to several severe intoxications and a few deaths, and we now know that uncontrolled lithium intake under these circumstances is particularly dangerous. It may therefore at first sight come as a surprise that lithium has been used for the treatment of congestive heart failure and, according to some reports, with good effect. The patients' oedema disappeared, and there was subjective relief. This has presumably two explanations. One is that increased knowledge about lithium as a drug permits treatment under appropriate dosage and laboratory control. The other is that one property of lithium is the exertion of a rather pronounced diuretic action which sets in more quickly than, and is distinct from, the previously mentioned inhibitory action on response to the antidiuretic hormone.

Gastrointestinal Problems

Use of lithium for the treatment of intestinal diseases, especially those with diarrhoea, is also surprising, since loose stools is a rather frequent early side effect of lithium treatment (see pp. 196–202). The reports about lithium therapy on this indication do not permit definitive conclusions. The same can be said about the use of lithium on the indications grouped in *Table 12.1* under the term 'Various'. Supplementary casuistic observations may encourage systematic trials.

Viral Infections

In 1980 it was first reported that lithium salts could inhibit the replication of the herpes simplex virus and it has been suggested that an ointment containing lithium succinate might bring about symptomatic relief and lowered virus excretion in genital herpes. The potential of lithium for the control of herpes simplex and other DNA viruses, either applied topically or given in oral doses, has yet to be fully explored.

Research on Renal Functions

This section has dealt with therapeutic uses of lithium. A non-therapeutic use should finally be mentioned, because it is an important one, and because its discovery has been a direct result of the use of lithium as a prophylactic agent in manic-depressive illness.

The risk of lithium treatment is not that it will eventually ruin the patients' brains or thyroids or kidneys; it will not. The main danger is development of lithium intoxication. Severe intoxication can lead to permanent brain damage or to death. Prevention of intoxication is therefore a major responsibility for the treating physician, and exploration of mechanisms involved, and measures called for, has been a major enterprise for lithium researchers.

Since lithium is eliminated almost exclusively with the urine, this has led to a close and detailed examination of how lithium affects the kidneys and the manner in which lithium is handled by the kidneys (see Section 57, pp. 206–213). These questions have to a large extent been answered through a combination of animal experiments and investigation of lithium-treated humans, under ordinary circumstances and during intoxication. Caveats for the avoidance of lithium intoxication, as deduced from these studies, are spelled out in full elsewhere in this book.

With the knowledge thus gained it has, in addition, been possible to give a valuable tool to those who have the kidneys as their main research area or medical responsibility, namely the so-called lithium clearance method for determination of the output of water and sodium from the proximal tubules, a value referred to as Vprox. Lithium is filtered freely through the glomerular membrane and is reabsorbed in the proximal tubules together with, and to the same extent as, water and sodium. However, under almost all circumstances lithium passes unreabsorbed through the loop of Henle, the distal tubules and the collecting ducts, so that the renal lithium clearance is identical with and can be used as a measure of Vprox. The lithium clearance method consists in determining the lithium clearance after administration of a small test dose of lithium to the animals or human subjects under investigation, a dose so small that it does not affect kidney function.

It is accordingly now possible, for the first time, to determine Vprox without performing micropuncture, without the use of anaesthesia and surgery, and repeatedly in the same subject under varying dietary conditions. It is also possible to investigate the influence of different agents on kidney function. The technique is equally applicable to normal subjects and to patients suffering from various diseases. The method has, after some initial hesitation about accepting something that came from psychiatry, been greeted enthusiastically by kidney physiologists, internists and nephrologists. It is now being used extensively and with interesting results.

Concluding Remarks

The use of lithium in medical conditions additional to the psychiatric illnesses which constitute its primary indication has already led to a number of useful insights into the mechanisms underlying certain types of pathology. Given its extraordinary ability to penetrate into virtually all recesses of the body, the lithium ion is able to produce effects on a wide variety of processes and systems and, as a secondary consequence of these effects, is also able to modify still other bodily functions. It is therefore likely that lithium treatment will be tried in conditions for which, at the moment, it is not indicated: from its success (or, indeed, even from its failure) in such uses we may expect to learn more about the ways in which physiological functions are interrelated.

Bibliography

Rossoff,A.H. and Robinson,W.A. (eds) (1980) *Effects on Granulopoiesis and Immune Function*. Plenum Press, New York.
A useful, but technical, survey of what was known about lithium and its actions at the level of the white blood cells in 1980.

Savoldi,F., Boro,G., Manzoni,G.C., Micieli,G., Lanfranchi,M. and Nappi,G. (1983) Lithium salts in cluster headache treatment. *Cephalalgia*, **3**, 109–114.
Carries a helpful review and evaluation of work done on lithium treatment of cluster headache and other forms of headache.

Schou,M. (1980) The range of non-psychiatric uses of lithium. In *Handbook of Lithium Therapy*. Johnson,F.N. (ed.), MTP Press, Lancaster, UK, pp. 73–79.
An account of medical uses outside psychiatry with a useful table classifying these applications according to the presumed mechanism of action of lithium.

13. Prophylactic Alternatives to Lithium

A.G.Oswald and R.H.S.Mindham

A significant number of manic depressives seem to gain little benefit from lithium prophylaxis despite the maintenance of adequate plasma levels over prolonged periods. In a study conducted by Dr Athanasio Kukopulos and his colleagues in Italy, it was reported that amongst one group of 213 bipolar patients maintained on lithium for an average of 3.5 years, with a plasma level of at least 0.8 mmol/l, 41% showed a complete remission of illness, 31% showed shorter and less severe episodes, and 28% appeared unchanged in terms of the frequency, duration and severity of their illness episodes. Rapid cyclers, who had three or more affective episodes per year, were particularly likely to respond poorly to lithium prophylaxis and this has since been confirmed in a number of other studies.

It is not only in the prophylaxis of lithium non-responders, however, that alternatives to lithium are of interest. Persistent side-effects (e.g. polyuria or loss of libido), fears regarding possible complications (e.g. thyroid or renal) and the consequences of overdose, either accidental or deliberate, may all encourage the patient or his doctor to seek alternative methods of prophylaxis. In addition, lithium is known to carry a slight—but to the patient significant—risk of being teratogenic and to be secreted in breast milk with a risk of adverse effects on the breast feeding infant (see Section 38, pp. 139–146 for a detailed assessment of the risk involved). It is thus not recommended for women who are planning a pregnancy, in the first trimester of pregnancy, or breast feeding, and if relapse represents a serious possibility, alternative treatment needs seriously to be considered.

The drugs which have been considered as possible prophylactic alternatives to lithium are listed in *Table 13.1*. These drugs and other treatments may also be combined with lithium and some of these combinations are considered in Part VII of this book.

Carbamazepine

Carbamazepine is an iminodibenzyl derivative structurally related to the tricyclics and some neuroleptics. It is a potent antiepileptic and in the 1960s was noted also to reduce the severity and frequency of psychiatric symptoms associated with temporal lobe epilepsy. Since that time attention has been paid to its value in the treatment and prophylaxis of affective illness not associated with epilepsy.

A number of trials, both uncontrolled and double-blind controlled, have suggested that carbamazepine has an antimanic action considerably greater than placebo and somewhat similar, in efficacy, to that of chlorpromazine. Although it is certainly less effective than tricyclic medication, it may also have an anti-depressant effect in some patients.

The first open, uncontrolled study of carbamazepine as a prophylactic in bipolar illness was by Dr T.Okuma and his colleagues in Japan who found that it was completely or partially effective in 34 out of 51 patients. This and other uncontrolled trials have suffered from small sample size, a variety of methodological problems, combining of carbamazepine with lithium, neuroleptics or tricyclics, and short duration of follow-up, as well as the problem of assessing prophylaxis. One such trial however, in which carbamazepine was prescribed in addition to the patient's usual psychotropic medication, followed up 32 bipolar patients for mean of 6 years; complete or partial prevention of manic episodes was observed in 75% of patients and of depressive episodes in 62% of patients. The introduction of carbamazepine appeared particularly beneficial in the rapid cycling bipolar patients, i.e. the sub-group which often tends to be least responsive to lithium therapy. Another open study showed that when carbamazepine was added to the medication of eight lithium-resistant rapid cycling bipolar patients, four showed a good prophylactic response over 3 years.

A controlled double-blind study was reported by Okuma and his associates in 1981 and in it carbamazepine was found to be significantly better than placebo in preventing the recurrence of manic and depressive illnesses over the period of 1 year, prophylaxis being deemed effective in 60% of the carbamazepine group but in only 22% of the placebo group. Subsequent work on the use of carbamazepine in the treatment of affective disorders and on its adjunctive use with lithium to treat patients who have proved to be resistant to lithium alone, is outlined in Section 47, pp. 171–176. It is not known how the long-term risks of carbamazepine compare with those of lithium.

Table 13.1 *Some possible prophylactic alternatives to lithium*

Anticonvulsants
- Carbamazepine
- Sodium valproate

Neuroleptics
- Flupenthixol

Tricyclics
- Imipramine

Other drugs
- Bupropion
- Clorgyline
- Levothyroxine

Sodium Valproate

Sodium valproate may also have a prophylactic action in bipolar patients not responsive to lithium. In an open uncontrolled study seven such patients who were maintained on sodium valproate (800 – 1800 mg/day) suffered no relapses during an 18 – 36 months period. Six of the seven patients were also on lithium (0.5 – 0.8 mmol/l), however, and it is thus not clear whether the prophylactic effect was a consequence of the lithium, the valproate or some synergistic action between the two (see Section 47, pp. 171 – 176).

Imipramine

Robert Prien and his colleagues in 1973 published a now well-known study comparing the prophylactic efficacy of imipramine, lithium and placebo in both unipolar and bipolar patients. The patients, who had been successfully treated for depressive illness, were given one of the three drugs for a 2-year period following discharge from hospital. The results were as shown in *Table 13.2*.

Thus in unipolar patients, imipramine and lithium appeared equally effective prophylactics, but in bipolar patients lithium seemed clearly superior, imipramine tending to precipitate manic episodes. Other studies, including some quite recent ones, have produced similar results. Where lithium has failed as a prophylactic in unipolar patients, a tricyclic antidepressant may be regarded as a prophylactic alternative, though the clinician must always be alert to the possibility of causing a new manic episode and of producing a state of rapid cycling.

A single maintenance dose of 75 – 100 mg of imipramine at night is normally thought to be adequate. The side effects of imipramine are well known and the physical hazards resulting from overdose are probably no greater than with lithium.

Table 13.2 *Results of a study comparing lithium and imipramine in the prophylactic treatment of affective disorders*

Illness	Lithium	Imipramine	Placebo
Bipolar group			
Manic relapses	12%	67%	33%
Depressive relapses	12%	0%	55%
Unipolar group			
Depressive relapses	33%	29%	85%

Flupenthixol

Flupenthixol is a neuroleptic of the thioxanthene group. Although its antidepressive and antimanic properties are unproven it may nevertheless have prophylactic effects which make it an alternative to lithium. One open study showed that flupenthixol decanoate was as effective prophylactically as lithium; this work involved a 2-year follow-up of 30 manic-depressive patients, most of whom were unipolar. In another open study carried out over 14 months it was reported that although flupenthixol reduced the frequency of manic episodes in a group of lithium-resistant unipolar and bipolar patients, it increased the duration and frequency of depressions. This increase in depressive morbidity was seen only in patients who had been on lithium prior to the onset of the trial and was therefore suggested to be a consequence of lithium discontinuation rather than of flupenthixol decanoate treatment. However, a double-blind cross-over trial by Dr I.Esparon and his colleagues from Dundee found that the use of flupenthixol in lithium-maintained patients had no additional prophylactic effect in 11 bipolar patients who had responded poorly to lithium prophylaxis alone.

Although further controlled trials are needed to assess the prophylactic potential of flupenthixol decanoate it would seem reasonable to consider it as a prophylactic alternative to lithium in those bipolar patients with mainly manic episodes who comply poorly with oral medication or who have gained little benefit from lithium and carbamazepine, alone or in combination. A dose of 20 – 40 mg of flupenthixol decanoate may be given intramuscularly every 2 weeks. The side effects of neuroleptic medication are well known and in long-term use the possible onset of tardive dyskinesia might give particular cause for concern. The drug is not thought to be teratogenic, however, and although it is secreted in breast milk in small quantities it has not been shown to have any adverse effect on breast-fed babies.

Bupropion

Bupropion is an aminoacetone antidepressant which

has not yet been reported to precipitate manic episodes and there is growing evidence that it is an effective prophylactic in bipolar patients.

Several uncontrolled studies support the usefulness of bupropion in prophylaxis: three bipolar patients who had remained well for a year on the drug, relapsed within 8 weeks of stopping it; a mixture of 40 unipolar and bipolar manic-depressive patients showed significantly fewer depressive and manic episodes during an average period of 336 days on the drug; and an equally good result was found when bupropion, alone or in combination with low dose neuroleptics, was used in 11 bipolar or schizoaffective lithium non-responders over 1 year. These results are interesting, not least because of the few side effects reported.

To clarify the prophylactic potential of bupropion, a controlled trial is required, comparing it with lithium in bipolar patients over a 2 or 3 year period. At present, however, it might be used as an alternative to flupenthixol in those bipolar patients who have gained little from lithium and carbamazepine, alone or in combination.

Clorgyline

Clorgyline is a type A monoamine oxidase inhibitor. Used in combination with lithium and or carbamazepine, it was reported in a study published in 1982 by Dr W.Z.Potter and coworkers to be an effective prophylactic in rapid cycling bipolar illness refractory to both lithium and carbamazepine alone, although the number of patients involved in the study was small and other workers have found monoamine oxidase inhibitors to induce mania in a substantial minority of patients.

L-Thyroxine

L-Thyroxine (0.3–0.5 mg/day) has been reported by Drs H.C.Stancer and E.Persad to have a strong prophylactic action in five out of ten refractory rapid cycling bipolar patients. These five patients were all women, three of them having the onset of their illness in the postpartum period and one in the involutional period. The significance of these findings remains unclear.

Concluding Comments

Before lithium failure is accepted it must be considered whether the trial of lithium has been adequate, and in particular whether sufficiently high serum levels of the drug have been maintained for long enough. There is good evidence that even where lithium does not prevent relapses it can reduce their frequency and severity and therefore a failure to respond to lithium should not be accepted uncritically.

Where unipolar patients have gained little from lithium prophylaxis, the first choice alternative is a tricyclic antidepressant. In bipolar patients refractory to lithium the choice of a prophylactic alternative lies mainly between carbamazepine, neuroleptics and bupropion and there is a great need for the prophylactic efficacy of these drugs to be tested in a controlled fashion, against lithium and against each other. At present, however, the first choice alternative for prophylaxis of lithium-resistant bipolar patients in most circumstances is probably carbamazepine, alone or in combination. Flupenthixol by depot injection may be preferred for those bipolar patients who comply poorly with oral medication or who have gained little from lithium and carbamazepine. It may also be useful for those women who are planning a pregnancy, or who are currently pregnant or breast feeding.

Bibliography

Esparon,I., Killoori,I., Naylor,G.J., McHarg,A.M., Smith,A.H.W. and Hopwood,S.E. (1986) Comparison of the prophylactic action of flupenthixol with placebo in lithium-treated manic-depressive patients. *Br. J. Psychiatry*, **148**, 723–725.

This article contains details of earlier work on flupenthixol but the results differed from the previous studies in finding no additional benefit conferred by flupenthixol in lithium-treated patients.

Okuma,T., Inanaga,K., Otsuki,S., Sarai,K., Takahashi,R., Hazama, H., Mori,A. and Watanabe,S. (1981) A preliminary double blind study on the efficacy of carbamazepine in the prophylaxis of manic-depressive illness. *Psychopharmacology*, **73**, 95–96.

Dr Okuma and his group were the first to report on the use of carbamazepine for treating manic-depressive illness. This article is an example of their work on this important topic.

Potter,W.Z., Murphy,D.L., Wehr,T.A., Linnoila,M. and Goodwin,F.K. (1982) Clorgylline: a new treatment for patients with refractory rapid-cycling disorder. *Arch. Gen. Psychiatry*, **39**, 505–510.

Dr Potter and his group report on the effectiveness of clorgyline in patients refractory to lithium. This paper is interesting as an example of an increasing number of reports on alternative treatments for patients for whom lithium does not appear to work.

Prien,R.F., Klett,C.J. and Caffey,E.M. (1973) Lithium carbonate and imipramine in prevention of affective disorders. *Arch. Gen. Psychiatry,* **29**, 420–425.

A classic study showing lithium and imipramine to be of equal effectiveness in unipolar patients, with lithium the more effective of the two in the prophylactic treatment of bipolar patients.

Stancer,H.C. and Persad,E. (1982) Treatment of intractable rapid-cycling manic-depressive disorder with levothyroxine. *Arch. Gen. Psychiatry,* **39**, 311–312.

Rapid cycling is a problem which is increasingly being reported in the literature. Sometimes it is resistant to treatment. This report showing the effectiveness of levothyroxine in such conditions is especially interesting in view of the thyroidal effects of lithium.

Part III

CLINICAL PRACTICE: THE DECISION TO TREAT

14. Patient Selection and Response Prediction

Peter R.Joyce

The most clear-cut indication for lithium therapy is in the prophylactic treatment of patients with bipolar affective disorder. The selection of patients for lithium prophylaxis depends upon assessing the risk of future affective episodes by considering a patient's past history in terms of severity and frequency of affective episodes. Lithium should be considered on a prophylactic basis when a bipolar patient has suffered two or more affective depressions within a limited period of time (often 2–4 years), or occasionally after just one severe manic episode, especially in a young patient with a family history of bipolar disorder. Lithium therapy prophylaxis also needs to be considered in recurrent depressive illness; probably after three or more depressive episodes. However, the decision in unipolar depression involves both the question of prophylactic treatment and whether to use lithium or another antidepressant.

To use lithium successfully as prophylaxis requires the patient to know and understand the rationale for use and the possible problems; otherwise long term treatment is unlikely to be successful. Thus, the consideration of patients for lithium prophylaxis requires a full assessment, not only of the illness, but also of relevant psychological and social factors. There is evidence that better lithium prophylaxis occurs in patients with a good pre-morbid personality, low 'neuroticism', and good inter-episode functioning, and in those with satisfactory social support (from members of the immediate family, close friends, and so on).

The use of lithium also needs to be considered in the acute treatment of depression, in mania, and in some psychotic patients who would probably be diagnosed as having 'schizophrenia' on most clinical criteria. In these situations, with the possible exception of mania, lithium is not the usual first line of treatment. In mild to moderate mania lithium could be the acute treatment of choice, although, if mania is severe, a neuroleptic is likely to be required alone or in conjunction with lithium (see Section 46, pp. 167–171).

Clinical Predictors of Lithium Response

With most psychotropic drugs, and lithium is no exception, a past history or family history of drug response is a favourable predictor of outcome. Non-response to lithium on previous occasions, however, should not weigh heavily against the current use of lithium until it is certain that the patient or relative has an adequate trial of lithium, both in terms of blood levels and of duration of treatment. An adequate trial of lithium for prophylaxis probably requires a number of months or a year, and early failure should not deter the patient from continuing with treatment. A good response over the first 12 months is a very favourable prognostic sign.

In addition to a family history of lithium response, a family history of bipolar affective disorder should count in favour of considering lithium therapy in all clinical situations (e.g. prophylaxis of unipolar depression and in the acute treatment of schizophrenia).

Among bipolar patients being considered for prophylaxis thc bcst prcdictor of a poor prophylactic response is in patients with a rapid cycling disorder (i.e. four or more affective episodes within the past 12 months). Although the presence of rapid cycling predicts a poor response, lithium may still need to be considered as there are no other really satisfactory treatments for rapid cycling bipolar disorder, although carbamazepine may have a place (see Section 13, pp. 50–54), and there are some patients who do show a therapeutic response to lithium even though they are rapid cyclers. In the non-rapid cycling bipolar patients prophylaxis tends to be better in those recovering from a manic rather than from a depressive episode. In the prophylaxis of unipolar depression the severity of the last depressive episode may influence the likelihood of successful prophylaxis, with a very severe depressive episode predicting a poorer outcome with lithium.

In the acute treatment of mania, the presence of a mixed mood suggests a poor outcome with lithium therapy. It has been suggested that those manics who

Table 14.1 *Clinical predictors of response to lithium prophylaxis*

Good pre-morbid personality
Low neuroticism
Good inter-episode functioning
Adequate social support
Family history or past history of lithium response
Family history of bipolar affective disorder
Recovering from a manic rather than depressive episode
Less than four affective episodes in the past year (i.e. not a rapid cycler)

are elated and grandiose respond better to lithium than those who are paranoid and destructive, but other investigators have been unable to substantiate this suggestion.

In the acute treatment of depression, bipolar patients are more likely to respond to lithium than are unipolar patients. However, lithium augmentation in depressed patients on antidepressants can be considered in both bipolar and unipolar patients (see also Section 45, pp. 161 – 166). *Table 14.1* lists the most important clinical predictors of lithium response.

Possible Biological Predictors of Lithium Response

Although at the present time there are no established biological predictors of lithium response for general clinical use, a number of interesting and potentially important predictors have been reported in research studies (*Table 14.2*). Among the most interesting studies in progress are those being carried out in the USA by Dr David Garver and his colleagues at the University of Cincinnati College of Medicine, USA, in which patients with a variety of psychotic disorders (manic, schizoaffective, schizophreniform and schizophrenic) are being treated with lithium alone. In these studies the criteria for lithium response are relatively stringent and include not only short term improvement in psychosis but also the requirement that patients can be discharged from hospital on lithium alone. Clinically the lithium responsive patients include most manic patients including those with mood-congruent psychotic features. However, there is also another group of psychotic patients who respond to lithium: these patients tend to have better premorbid and inter-episode functioning, to have family histories of affective disorder and to lack family histories of schizophrenia, but occasional lithium-responsive patients meet clinical criteria for chronic schizophrenia.

Table 14.2 *Possible biological predictors of lithium response*

Intracellular/extracellular lithium ratio
Calcium/magnesium ratio and increasing levels with lithium
Blood antigens
Growth hormone response to apomorphine
Response to physostigmine
Response to stimulant drugs
Visual average evoked response
Plasma folate
Subclinical hypothyroidism

One of the biological markers being studied by this research team is the growth hormone (GH) response to apomorphine, which is presumed to reflect dopaminergic neurotransmission. Like other research groups, they have found an increased GH response in 'schizophrenic' patients, while manic patients with mood-congruent psychotic features have a low GH response. However, those patients with 'schizophrenia' who responded to lithium had an even greater GH response than those who did not respond to lithium. Further, within their psychotic patients, a combination of both the GH response and the ratio of intracellular to extracellular lithium was a better predictor of lithium response than either variable alone. Another intriguing finding, in the light of evidence that physostigmine temporarily relieves manic symptoms, was that improvement in thought disorder with a physostigmine infusion was a subsequent predictor of lithium response in a group of psychotic patients. Although the numbers of patients in these samples are small, and drug-free management of psychotic patients requires special staffing, these studies are important both for clearly documenting the lithium responsiveness of some patients with 'schizophrenia' and for providing useful leads to predictors of lithium response.

The intracellular/extracellular lithium ratio in bipolar patients has also been found as a predictor of lithium response by others, but there are conflicting results. Similarly, suggestions that certain HLA antigens (e.g. HLA-A3) predict lithium response have not been supported by other workers. It has been suggested that a positive M antigen predicts lithium responsiveness, although this awaits independent confirmation.

In patients commenced on a prophylactic lithium regimen after recovering from an affective episode, it has been reported that responders show an increase in serum calcium over the first 4 months of treatment, while non-responders show no change in serum calcium. In depressed subjects the calcium/magnesium ratio has been described as a predictor of antidepressant response to lithium, and it has been reported that responders show an increase in calcium and magnesium over the first 5 days of treatment which is not shown by non-responders.

Other reported predictors in depressed patients of a response to lithium include an augmenting visual average evoked response and a mood brightening following a test dose of amphetamine. This latter finding is of interest in that mood brightening with a test dose of stimulant drug may predict both antipsychotic and antidepressant responses to lithium in 'schizophrenic' patients, and response to lithium augmentation in depressed patients not responding to antidepressants.

A further finding of note is that low plasma folate is associated with a higher affective morbidity during lithium prophylaxis, and the addition of folate to lithium therapy appears to decrease the affective morbidity.

Finally, although thyroid function has not been directly implicated as a factor in lithium responsiveness, subclinical hypothyroidism is increasingly associated with rapid cycling bipolar disorder, which in turn has a poor response to lithium. Only future studies may elucidate whether thyroid function directly predicts lithium response.

Summary

At the present stage of development in our understanding of lithium responsiveness, the characteristics of a patient likely to have a good prophylactic response to lithium include a good pre-morbid personality, good inter-episode functioning, a family history of primary affective disorder and a frequency of recurrences of less than four per year. Biological predictors of lithium response are still in the research arena and have not yet been developed to the point where they are clinically useful. However, the biological predictors are potentially important in that they could well give clues to the underlying biological mechanisms of lithium response.

Bibliography

Consensus Development Panel (1985) Mood disorders: pharmacological prevention of recurrences. *Am. J. Psychiatry,* **142**, 469–476.

This review article summarizes the consensus views of a panel of American professionals on the pharmacological prevention of recurrences in affective disorders.

Garver,D.L., Hitzemann,R. and Hirschowitz,J. (1984) Lithium ratio *in vitro*: diagnosis and lithium carbonate response in psychotic patients. *Arch. Gen. Psychiatry,* **41**, 497–505.

A recent paper from Garver's group on biological and clinical predictors of response to lithium in psychotic patients.

Grof,P., Hux,M., Grof,E. and Arato,M. (1983) Prediction of response to stabilizing lithium treatment. *Pharmacopsychiatry,* **16**, 195–200.

This review summarizes a Canadian group's extensive experience with predicting lithium response to prophylactic treatment.

15. Preliminary Tests

Roy Hullin

Whenever any new form of treatment is instituted, the question naturally arises as to its possible ill effects upon the patient. To some extent these will be known in advance if they are of general or widespread occurrence amongst those receiving the treatment. There will, however, be certain effects which depend upon the susceptibilities of the particular patient; one person may be more predisposed than another to develop thyroid problems, skin rashes, cardiac arrhythmia and so on. By a careful and appropriate choice of pre-treatment screening tests, the likelihood of side effects happening, their nature, and perhaps some indication of their degree, may be obtained. This procedure is good clinical practice and is not specific to lithium therapy but applies equally to the use of other major psychotropic drugs.

Such knowledge may be used in various ways. Most obviously, it alerts the physician to the need to keep a close watch on certain functions and possibly to take measures either to prevent or to correct the more serious side effects. Secondly, the patient can be given advance information as to what side effects may occur; this may prevent the patient from terminating treatment without first seeking medical advice should such symptoms actually develop, and medical advice is likely to be sought sooner than might otherwise be the case. Thirdly, family members and friends of the patient, and paramedical or social services personnel who have contact with the patient, can be asked to be vigilant for certain types of side effects.

The Choice of Preliminary Tests

Pre-treatment screening tests fall into a number of categories. There are those tests which would be regarded as absolutely essential and without which the commencement of therapy would be unwise, if not indeed irresponsible. Other tests might be considered highly desirable and still others quite useful provided that the testing facilities were readily available. A final category would include tests of no currently established predictive value but which might, if performed on a sufficiently large population of patients, be seen to detect subgroups with special monitoring needs in pro-

Table 15.1 *Preliminary tests recommended to be used before lithium treatment is commenced*

Test	Normal range (2 SD)[a]
Whole blood	
Haemoglobin	13.5–18.0 (men); 11.5–16.5 (women) g/dl
White cell count	4.0–11.0 × 10^9/l
Sedimentation rate	0–5 (men); 0–7 (women) mm/h
Plasma	
Sodium	135–145 mmol/l
Potassium	3.6–5.0 mmol/l
Urea	2.5–7.1 mmol/l
Creatinine	50–140 μmol/l
Serum	
Total T4 (thyroxine)	60–140 nmol/l
Total T3 (triiodothyronine)	1.6–3.0 nmol/l
Free thyroxine index (FTI)	1.1–2.7
Thyrotrophin (TSH)	<8 mU/l
Urine	
Qualitative tests	
Protein, sugar, casts	
Creatinine clearance[b]	70–140 ml/min
Lithium clearance (3 or 4 h)[b]	10–40 ml/min
Pregnancy test	
Cardiovascular	
Electrocardiogram	
Blood pressure	
Body weight	

[a]The normal range values are, to some extent, dependent upon the laboratory; the ranges given are those for the laboratories at Leeds General Infirmary, UK.
[b]The normal range of creatinine and lithium clearances are lower in the very elderly and hence the values given must be interpreted accordingly.

phylactic treatment.

Disagreement between clinicians may be expected in regard to what tests are properly included in all these categories, but in general the consensus will be greater for tests regarded as essential than for those with potential, but unproven, value.

In countries where, for economic or other reasons, routine testing procedures are not readily available, the criteria determining the need for preliminary tests will be particularly stringent. In fact, such tests may be dispensed with altogether if the alternative is to withhold the treatment.

Specific tests

The two most important areas of physiological functioning, as far as lithium therapy is concerned, relate to renal and cardiovascular systems. If there is any suggestion that a patient is at renal or cardiovascular risk, the case for commencing lithium therapy must be strong. The clinician has to balance the risks inherent in therapy, against the benefit of increased quality of life and reduced danger of suicide during depressive phases of the illness. However, using the lower 12-h plasma lithium range of 0.5–0.7 mmol/l which is effective prophylactically for most patients, the risks are much less than when higher plasma levels are employed. Absolute contraindications for lithium treatment at these lower levels must now be very rare. *Table 15.1* gives a list of special tests recommended to precede therapy and in this list are several tests related to renal and cardiovascular functioning.

Creatinine clearance

Creatinine clearance provides a useful index of glomerular filtration rate; it is calculated as $(v \times u)/(t \times b)$ where v is the volume of urine passed in t minutes, u is urine concentration of creatinine and b is its mean blood concentration. The value is subject to certain instabilities and fluctuations, and whilst these are not likely to be very important clinically their effect can be minimized by taking the urine sample over a full 24 h; if this is not possible one may substitute 3- or 4-h clearance (although the timing of the collection is then critical and the results are liable to greater error). Short-term creatinine clearance tests can usefully be accompanied by tests of lithium clearance; for this, a loading dose of 600–800 mg of lithium carbonate is administered some 12–16 h before the clearance test is commenced.

Electrocardiogram

If specific abnormalities are evident following an electrocardiogram (ECG or EKG) it would be wise to enquire into the patient's family history to establish whether or not there is likely to be a genetic predisposition to cardiovascular problems which could be exacerbated by lithium.

Blood tests

Tests to establish haemoglobin levels, white cell count and sedimentation rate may reveal problems hitherto unsuspected. A low haemoglobin level, for example, may lead to the suspicion that, in a female patient, the depressive episodes could be linked to an anaemic condition, particularly if the episodes were associated with heavy menstrual flow. Elevated sedimentation rate might lead one to suspect infection or other organic problems which also need to be investigated for a possible aetiological link with affective dysfunction.

Thyroid tests

Endocrine changes associated with lithium therapy are well documented (see Section 60, pp. 220–226).

Pre-existing thyroid dysfunction could well be exacerbated by lithium and thyroid function should be examined before a decision is taken to start treatment. Hypothyroidism, whilst not a contraindication since it can be treated with L-thyroxine, might constitute an additional reason for not commencing lithium therapy if combined with other negative pointers. A raised serum thyrotrophin (TSH) is the best indicator of hypothyroidism.

Other tests

The patient should be weighed. Obese individuals should be given advice on a healthy (though not sodium-free) diet. Very underweight individuals need to be informed that lithium in some patients may lead to a fairly rapid increase in body weight which will need to be controlled: low compliance is often associated with weight gain in individuals who have made a point of keeping their weight down.

Female patients of child-bearing age need to be questioned about the likelihood of their being pregnant. If necessary, a pregnancy test should be performed.

Testing and Dose Regimes

There is now a tendency for dose (and hence serum) levels to be kept lower during lithium prophylaxis than was once the case (this is especially so with elderly patients; increasingly, psychogeriatricians are finding it beneficial to use lithium for the treatment of recurrent depression which often develops in later life and which has a marked effect on the quality of life enjoyed, and the use of lower dosages and blood levels is recommended for these patients since the risk of unwanted side effects is correspondingly greater). This raises the question of whether too assiduous pre-treatment screening is really necessary, given that the side effect pattern would certainly become less evident with such administration regimens. This is a question which can only be answered when we have developed much more experience with different dosage regimes.

Testing and Combination Treatment

There is a move to try lithium in combination with other psychoactive agents, particularly in cases which have proved refractory to lithium. If this practice continues and develops, we will need to face the possibility that new pre-treatment tests may be occasioned by special requirements of the agent being combined with lithium, and also by the combination having side effects not shown by either agent used separately. So far, there is no indication that this is likely to be a major problem, but it is one of which we need to remain aware.

Bibliography

Hullin,R.P. (1980) Physiological functions monitored in association with lithium therapy. In *Handbook of Lithium Therapy*. Johnson,F.N. (ed.), MTP Press, Lancaster, UK, pp. 159–168. Gives a detailed discussion of the rationale for various tests to be carried out before and during lithium therapy.

16. Preparation of the Patient

F.Neil Johnson

Once a decision has been taken to institute lithium therapy, the question arises as to how (or, indeed, whether) to prepare the patient. There are those who would argue that no special preparation is really necessary, that lithium is in principle and practice just like any other medication, and that its administration ought not to be attended by any special support measures. However, since the likelihood is that lithium therapy, once commenced, will be continued for several, perhaps many, years, and since, too, the patient's rigorous compliance with a predetermined medication regime is of particular importance, it surely makes good clinical sense to spare some time to ensure that therapy is started under the most favourable circumstances that can be arranged.

Informing the Patient

By the time that lithium therapy is decided upon, the patient will almost certainly have been subjected to a variety of other medications and may well have developed a distrust of all drugs. To overcome this, lithium therapy has to be introduced on a note of optimism and presented to the patient as a well-tried and established treatment of proven effectiveness.

There are several short pamphlets which can be given to those patients thought suitable, in which the basic facts about lithium therapy are clearly laid out; there is a danger here that the emphasis which such documents often place on side effects and toxicity may lead the patient to become overanxious about possible dangers, and thus encourage non-compliance with treatment. Of course, the psychiatrist has an obligation and duty to alert the patient to such matters, but this should be done in such a way as to emphasize the balance of benefits of treatment over the costs in terms of unwanted effects. Indeed, it can be stated quite clearly that, properly administered, lithium is one of the safest available treatments for any psychiatric condition.

Inevitably, the patient will have questions. The manner of framing replies will depend upon the clinician's judgement of the effect likely to be produced on the patient. Thus if asked whether lithium therapy will have to be continued indefinitely, the psychiatrist may feel that some circumspection is necessary in replying. Whilst certain patients might readily accept an affirmative answer made quite bluntly, others would instantly react by rejecting a medication which appeared to be a life sentence. Comparisons with other long-term medications, such as insulin treatment for diabetes mellitus, are often used to set lithium therapy into a suitable context. Other psychiatrists talk in terms of a trial period of one or two years, followed by the possibility of a test withdrawal.

Informing the Patient's Family

Compliance with medication is so important an aspect of successful lithium therapy that special attention paid in the early stages to achieving it will be amply repaid in terms of therapeutic outcome. In this respect, enlisting the help of a patient's immediate circle of acquaintances — usually family members — can be a great asset. It is sometimes useful to introduce the subject of lithium therapy to the patient and family together, so that emphasis can be placed on the need for tolerance and understanding of the patient's problems, and the need for strict adherence to the medication schedule can be outlined. The tendency of family members to dissuade a patient from continuing to take lithium, once stability has been achieved, is well-known, and needs to be headed off, if possible, at an early stage.

The Treatment Schedule

Details of the treatment schedule, serum lithium estimations, attendance at regular lithium clinics, and follow-up physiological function tests (pp. 105–107), can be given to the patient. One should be aware,

17. Dosage and Serum Levels

Paul J.Perry and Bruce Alexander

Serum Lithium Concentrations

Lithium dosing requirements vary depending on the phase of the patient's affective illness. Current data suggest that the amount of lithium required to control an acute manic episode is significantly greater than the amount of lithium necessary to prevent subsequent episodes of either depression or mania.

Acute mania

It has been observed that patients with lithium levels exceeding 1.4 mmol/l experience no greater improvement in their manic symptoms than do patients with lower serum lithium concentrations. Although a few of the most ill patients will show either improvement or complete remission with serum concentrations above 1.4 mmol/l, a similar proportion of very ill patients respond to serum concentrations below 1.4 mmol/l while experiencing considerably fewer adverse effects. Additionally, it is relatively rare for patients to experience complete remission of the manic symptoms with serum lithium concentrations below 0.9 mmol/l. Thus a serum concentration ranging between 0.9 to 1.4 mmol/l is required for treating acute mania, and experience shows that lithium carbonate doses anywhere between 150 and 4200 mg/day are required to achieve this level. Since such a wide dosage range is required to achieve such a narrow therapeutic blood level range, it is not surprising that measurements of lithium levels in the blood are necessary to monitor and adjust the dose which patients receive. Depending on the severity of the manic symptoms, control of the attack is usually obtained within 4–10 days after the start of drug treatment. Relapse occurs within as few as 2 days if the lithium is abruptly discontinued during the manic cycle.

Manic patients in the midst of an acute episode require and tolerate higher lithium doses than the doses tolerated by the same patients once the manic attack begins to abate. This is because of increased rates of lithium clearance through the kidney in manic patients. Therefore, frequent assessments of serum lithium levels, with samples being drawn twice weekly, are required in the treatment of acute manic episodes because of the possibility of a rapid rise in lithium levels as an episode begins to resolve.

Prophylaxis

Until recently, most clinicians recommended a serum lithium concentration of 0.8–1.2 mmol/l for prophylaxis of recurrent affective illness. However, more recent data suggest that lower serum lithium concentrations are as effective (see pp. 38–41), and that serum lithium concentrations of 0.4–0.6 mmol/l on a divided daily dose schedule, or 0.45–0.59 mmol/l on single daily dose schedule, are appropriate in the prophylactic treatment of some affectively ill patients.

Serum Lithium Concentration Sampling

The serum lithium concentration recommended for the treatment of acute mania or the prophylactic treatment of affective illness is based on the steady-state lithium concentration drawn 12 h after the last dose. To understand the clinical significance of this recommendation, one must be cognizant of several lithium pharmacokinetic parameters, i.e absorption rate, tissue distribution rate and elimination half-life. The serum lithium concentration versus time curve presented in *Figure 17.1* demonstrates all three pharmacokinetic parameters. For any given dose, absorption is represented by the initial ascending portion of the curve; distribution is represented by the terminal ascending and initial descending portion of the curve; and the elimination half-life is represented by the terminal descending portion of the exponential curve. Practically speaking the most obvious method to determine the ideal time to sample a drug's concentration in the serum

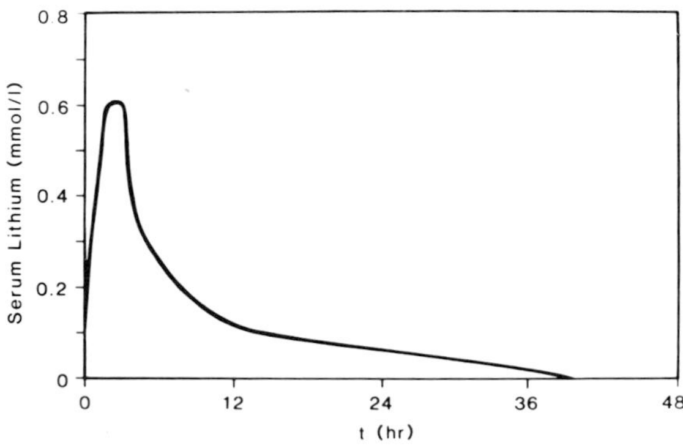

Figure 17.1 Serum concentration versus time curve for lithium.

is to inspect a curve such as that shown in *Figure 17.1* and determine the most stable area of the curve, i.e. the area of the curve where the serum concentration changes at the slowest rate. Obviously the least dynamic area of the curve in *Figure 17.1* is during the terminal elimination portion. Generally, following rapid absorption, lithium is distributed at a slower rate such that distribution is complete within 6–10 h. Thus, in the case of lithium, serum sampling should not be drawn prior to 10 h after the last dose. Therefore, 12 h has been selected as the ideal time to draw serum lithium concentrations. A fuller discussion of the value of the 12-h standard serum lithium level is given later (pp. 88–91).

Steady-state conditions for lithium require that the patients not have their serum lithium concentration measured until at least four to five half-lives have elapsed. Four half-lives indicates that the patient has reached a serum lithium concentration of 93.75% of its maximum whereas five half-lives implies that the serum concentration is 96.88% of its maximal attainable concentration for a particular maintenance dose. Assuming the individual patient's lithium half-life is unknown and that lithium half-lives range from 10 to 40 h for patients with normal renal function, approximately (4 × 40) = 160 h, i.e. 7 days, ought to elapse before measuring a steady-state lithium level.

Dose Regimen

Table 17.1 demonstrates the effect of the dosage schedule on a standard (i.e. not slow or sustained release) dosage formulation on the 12-h steady-state serum lithium concentration. Three dose regimens are illustrated; in the first, lithium is given three times a day, i.e. every 8 h (the q8h schedule); in the second the lithium is given twice a day, i.e., 12-hourly (the q12h schedule); and in the third (q24h) a single daily dose is used. This table illustrates two points. First, there is a relatively small difference between the 12-h serum lithium steady-state concentrations for the q8h and q12h schedules but a considerably larger difference between these two schedules and the q24h schedule. Thus, the greater the increase in the dosing schedule interval the greater the disparity between the 12-h steady-state concentrations. Second, as the half-life increases, the percentage increase in the 12-h steady-state concentration decreases. This information is important in clinical situations where a patient on a divided daily dosing schedule is being converted to a single daily dosing schedule. If the clinician assumes a 24 h half-life for the patient, then an approximately 20% increase in the 12-h steady-state lithium concentration ought to be anticipated. However, as an examination of the data in *Table 17.1* suggests, in practice this figure can range from 12% to 33%.

Figure 17.2 presents a computer simulation model of a serum lithium concentration *versus* time curve for a slow-release lithium product. The single daily dosing schedule, although producing a higher 12-h steady-state concentration, results in a significantly lower serum lithium trough concentration. Because of the clinically significant polyuria caused by lithium in at least 40% of patients (pp. 206–213), this is an extremely important observation. Investigators have found that 24-h urine output volume positively correlates with the trough or minimum serum lithium concentration, but that it does not correlate with lithium dose, patient age, length of treatment, maximum serum lithium concen-

Table 17.1 *The effects of three different dosage schedules on 12-h steady-state lithium concentration (mmol/l) for a maintenance dose of 1200 mg/day of lithium carbonate (standard release)*

Half-life (h)	Schedule q8h	q12h	q24h
12	0.54	0.60	0.80
18	0.75	0.81	1.00
24	0.96	1.02	1.20
30	1.18	1.24	1.41
36	1.41	1.46	1.63

q8h = divided doses given every 8 h; q12h = every 12 h, q24h = a single daily dose.

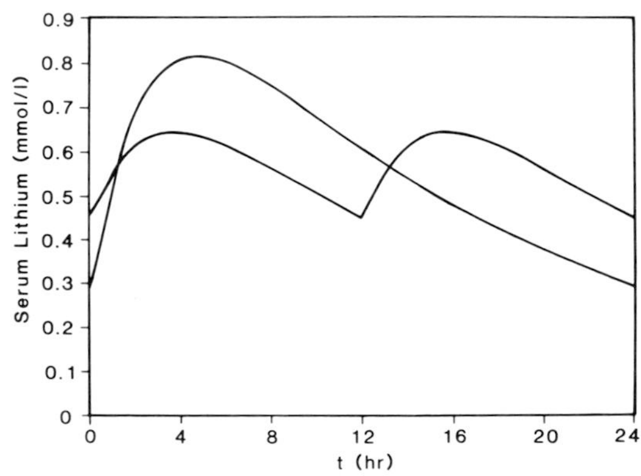

Figure 17.2 Effect of dosing on 12-h and 24-h steady-state serum lithium concentration.

tration, or 12-h serum lithium concentration. This finding implies that the only direct change in lithium therapy that can result in a decrease in lithium-induced polyuria is switching from a divided daily dosing schedule to a single daily dosing schedule.

Product Formulations

The lithium product formulation may influence the risk of lithium adverse effects. *Figure 17.3* presents computer-simulated curves for lithium carbonate 600 mg p.o. q24h dose for both a standard-release (Lithotabs®) and slow-release dosage form (Lithobid®). Because of its rapid absorption, a single oral dose of regular-release lithium carbonate results in a peak serum level usually within 90 min. However, the peak serum lithium concentration for the slow-release formulation occurs between 4 and 6 h following ingestion. The peak serum lithium concentration at steady-state for the regular-release formulation is 0.76 ± 0.14 mmol/l whereas the peak concentration for the slow-release formulation was 0.42 ± 0.09 mmol/l, a 45% decrease in peak level.

The slow-absorption lithium formulations were developed in an attempt to decrease the adverse effects associated with peak and rapidly rising serum concentrations as well as to increase compliance. Products in which absorption is slowed to the greatest extent, such as Quilonum Retard®, Lithionit Duretter® and Lipett C®, do indeed seem to produce the lowest incidence of tremor and nausea, but they can cause diarrhoea when ingested on an empty stomach due to lithium reaching the large intestine and acting as an osmotic cathartic. Additionally, it has been noted that the urine concentrating ability of the kidneys is significantly better with slow-release lithium than with

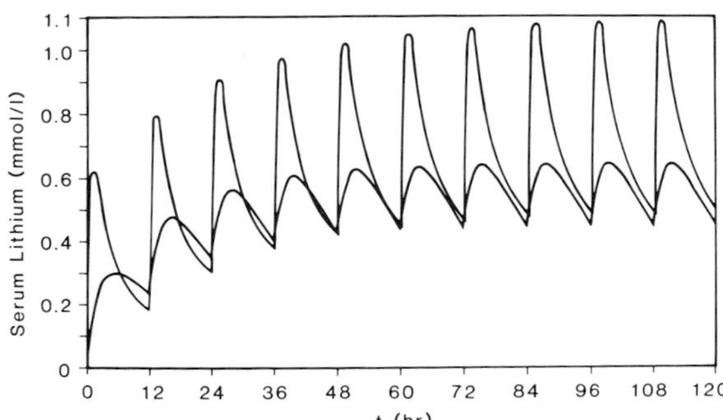

Figure 17.3 Serum concentration versus time curve for standard-release and slow-release lithium dosage formulations.

the regular-release formulation. On the other hand, another study was unable to elicit any differences in the adverse effect profiles of patients given both regular-release and slow release, i.e. Lithobid®. Thus if slow-release lithium preparations do cause fewer adverse effects, the difference is not large and it is restricted to a minority of patients.

Adjustment of Lithium Dosage: Pharmacokinetic Approaches

Retrospective dose adjustments

Lithium obeys first-order linear pharmacokinetics. The following formula describes the pharmacokinetic behaviour of a first-order drug.

$$C^{ss}_{av} = F.DM/Cl.t \qquad (1)$$

where C^{ss}_{av} is the mean blood level at steady-state, F is the fraction of dose absorbed, t is the dosing interval, Cl is the renal clearance and DM is the maintenance dose.

In normal clinical situations, the only terms in the equation that change with an increase or decrease in dose are the maintenance dose and the lithium steady-state concentration. Thus, with all other terms being constant, the equation can be rearranged to read:

$$C^{ss}_{av} = \text{K}.DM \qquad (2)$$

where K is a constant. This means that as the dose increases or decreases, the steady-state serum lithium concentration must increase or decrease proportionally. Thus a patient with a steady-state concentration of 1.0 mmol/l at 1200 mg/day will have a steady-state level of 1.25 mmol/l if the dose is increased to 1500 mg/day, whereas if the dose is decreased to 900 mg/day, the concentration should be 0.75 mmol/l. It must be remembered that the concentration term in this equation is the mean serum level, not the peak, 12-h or trough level. However, clinically this method can be utilized as a reasonable prediction of the 12-h steady-state lithium concentration. Further details of lithium kinetics are given in Section 18, pp. 73–75.

Prospective dose adjustments

Single point method—dose predictions. The first dosage prediction schedule described in the literature was a method whereby an individual daily lithium dose

Table 17.2 *Dosages required to attain a serum lithium level in the range 0.41–0.89 mmol/l for prophylaxis or in the range 0.9–1.3 mmol/l for the acute treatment of mania, as related to the 24-h serum lithium level noted 24 h after a single test dose of 1200 mg lithium carbonate (standard preparation)*

24-h serum lithium level after 1200-mg test dose (mmol/l)	Daily dose (mg)
Prophylaxis	
0.12–0.14	2400
0.15–0.16	2100
0.17–0.20	1800
0.21–0.25	1500
0.26–0.34	1200
0.35–0.49	900
0.50–0.85	600
Acute anti-manic	
0.15–0.18	2400
0.19–0.23	2100
0.24–0.30	1800
0.31–0.40	1500
0.41–0.56	1200

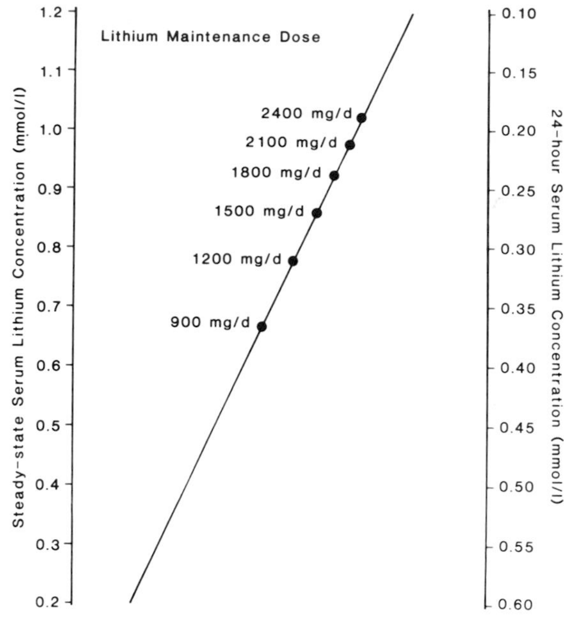

Figure 17.4 Lithium dosing nomogram for predicting steady-state serum lithium concentrations for 900–2400 mg/day maintenance doses following a 1200-mg lithium carbonate test dose and then measuring the 24-h serum lithium concentration.

could be predicted from a serum sample collected 24 h after a single 600 mg test dose of lithium carbonate. The recommended maintenance dose is supposed to result in a steady-state serum lithium concentration between 0.6 and 1.2 mmol/l. This method requires the patient be lithium-free prior to the test and the laboratory to be capable of accurate, reproducible lithium analyses. The practicality of the dosing schedule was evaluated independently. In one study 31% of the patients failed to achieve the defined steady-state range. It was postulated that factors such as a lack of research laboratory facilities and drug interactions make the use of this dosing protocol impractical for the clinical psychiatrist. However, a second study found the 0.6–1.2-mmol/l range was achieved in 23 of 24 patients dosed with this schedule.

Because of the two above conflicting reports, the method for deriving the schedule was re-examined and two new more precise dosing schedules were recommended, i.e. a schedule for lithium prophylaxis (0.41–0.89 mmol/l) and a schedule for the treatment of acute mania (0.9–1.27 mmol/l). The dose schedules are presented in *Table 17.2*. The clinical usefulness of the new relationships was subjected to prospective testing and it was found that 83% of the prophylactically dosed patients fell within the therapeutic range while 85% of the acutely manic patients were within the therapeutic range.

Single point method—steady-state level prediction. A mathematical relationship exists between drug concentration in serum or plasma at steady-state and a single drug concentration at some time after a test dose has been administered. Investigation of this mathematical model led to the derivation of the following linear equation:

$$C^{ss}_{12h} = 0.131 + 3.29\,(C^{*}_{24h}) \tag{3}$$

where C^{ss}_{12h} is the steady-state lithium concentration at 12 h post dose for a 1800 mg/day dose and C^{*}_{24h} is the 24-h serum lithium concentration following an initial 1200 mg dose. The dosing nomogram presented in *Figure 17.4* can be utilized in place of the equation. The larger the range of half-lives for the population the poorer the correlation between the steady state and single dose concentrations. However, a 4-fold variation in half-life introduces relatively little error. If one assumes a range of 10–40 h for lithium half-lives it is obvious that patients with significantly reduced renal function should not have their dose determined by the use of this equation because of their extended lithium half-lives which can quite easily exceed 40 h.

Multiple point method—steady-state level prediction. A pharmacokinetic method that keeps the number of serum lithium samples to a minimum and more accurately predicts steady-state lithium levels would be useful in facilitating the treatment of manic-depressive patients. Using standard pharmacokinetic equations, a method has been established whereby the steady-state serum lithium concentration can be predicted with somewhat greater precision than is possible with the single-point method. The patient is administered a 1200-mg test dose of lithium carbonate. Serum lithium samples are obtained over a 24-h period, usually beginning at 12 h following the dose. Normally only 12 and 36 h samples are necessary. These two data points allow for the calculation of the patient's lithium elimination half-life. *Figure 17.5* illustrates the information that the equations allow the clinician to generate. By knowing the patient's serum lithium half-life and serum lithium level at 12 h after the 1200-mg test dose, the clinician can predict the 12-h steady-state serum lithium concentration for any dose of lithium.

The maintenance dose protocols noted earlier guarantee serum lithium concentrations only over rather widely spaced ranges. The multiple point serum lithium concentration prediction protocol offers greater flexibility in that the clinician can administer any dose to achieve any desired therapeutic serum lithium level with 77–90% confidence that the observed serum lithium level will be within 0.1 mmol/l of the predicted serum lithium level. Although not as precise, the single-point serum lithium concentration prediction nomogram described above yields predictions that are within +0.15 mmol/l for 73% of the predictions.

Although the multiple point serum lithium concentration prediction protocol is the most efficient means of predicting steady-state serum lithium concentrations it is also the most difficult system to use. With this drawback in mind, a pharmacokinetic interactive computer program has been developed; written in BASIC, it is run on either an IBM personal computer, an Apple 2E computer, or any IBM PC compatible computer. The clinician who does not have access to either minicomputers or programmable calculators can still utilize the multiple point method employing a handheld calculator with a natural log function. The user enters the patient's name, the serum levels and times plus the number of hours after the dose that

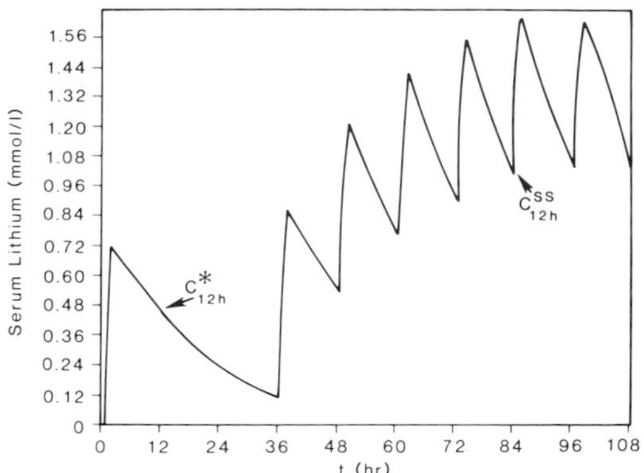

Figure 17.5 The 12-h steady-state lithium concentration measured by multiplying the 12-h serum lithium concentration after the test dose by the accumulation factor (a function of the half-life).

future blood level measurement will be drawn; a hardcopy output states the half-life, the number of days necessary to reach steady-state and the correlation coefficient for the fit of the one-compartment pharmacokinetic model. This is followed by a table of steady-state blood levels that would be expected to result from various doses and dosing schedules. The table is especially helpful in giving the clinician a feel for the interaction between dose, schedule and half-life. It can also transform steady-state serum lithium concentrations not drawn at 12 h after the dose into 12-h levels. These data outputs give the user useful information for treating the specific patient and as well as for understanding the kinetics of lithium in general. Clinicians can obtain the program software or a listing of the computer program by writing to Dr Paul Perry or Dr Bruce Alexander at the College of Pharmacy, University of Iowa, Iowa City, IA 52242, USA.

Prospective dosing caveat

A potential source of error in the prospective dosing protocol is intraindividual variability in lithium clearance. The relationship between steady-state drug concentration and clearance for first order linear kinetic models is demonstrated by Equation 1 (p. 69). In that equation, the value of F (the fraction of dose absorbed) can be assumed to be 1.0, while the maintenance dose (DM) and dosing interval (t) are constant during the dosing period. Thus, the relationship between a steady-state lithium concentration and lithium clearance is given by Equation 4.

$$C^{ss}_{av} = X/Cl \qquad (4)$$

where X is the constant $F.DM/t$.

During the night, lithium clearances are approximately 22% less than daytime lithium clearances. It is thought that the mechanism for diurnal variation in lithium clearance results from the glomerular filtration rate being significantly lower at night when the patients are in a supine position, and being higher during the day because the patients are then erect. Thus the primary source of error in lithium prospective dosing methods originates from dynamic glomerular filtration rate changes stemming from changes in the hyperactivity of the manic patient. Thus, if a patient is administered a lithium test dose in a hyperactive state (i.e. sleeping and supine only 2 h per night) and then the 12-h steady-state lithium level is measured a week later when the patient is no longer hyperactive (i.e. sleeping 8 h per night), a significantly higher than expected steady-state lithium level is quite likely. The reverse situation should also hold true. Thus, the hyperactive manic patient will have the serum lithium level rise significantly once activity levels and sleep normalize, while the euthymic patient will have the lithium concentration decrease significantly if mania recurs.

Because of the dynamic relationship of steady-state serum lithium concentrations between manic and euthymic state, the utility of dosing schedules and nomograms is questionable in manic patients. The only means by which the clinician can recognize this dynamic state is by being aware of the patient's lithium half-life. Manic patients with short half-lives will eventually develop longer half-lives once they become euthymic.

Adjustment of Lithium Dosage: Non-pharmacokinetic Approaches

A mathematical formula for determining lithium dose, based on a number of dependent variables, has been derived:

$$\text{Dose} = 6.215\,(C_{\text{Li}}) - 1.926(\text{form}) - 2.844(\text{TCA}) - 0.070(\text{age}) + 1.885(\text{sex}) + 0.082(\text{weight}) + 5.143 \quad (5)$$

where dose is expressed in hundreds of milligrams per day, C_{Li} is the desired lithium concentration in mmol/l, form is 0 for standard preparations of lithium carbonate or citrate and 1 for a sustained release preparation (e.g. Lithobid), TCA is 1 for concomitant antidepressant (tricyclic) use or 0 for no antidepressant usage, age is in years, sex is 0 for females and 1 for males, and weight is in kg. Validation of the dose predictions of the model were correct within +300 mg/day in 64% cases and +600 mg/day in 92% cases of over 100 cases studied. An independent evaluation of the equation found accurate predictions in 26% of patients dosed according to this method. The equation tended to overpredict the dose.

Another investigator, using the same mathematical approach, was able to improve somewhat on the clinical utility of this approach. The maintenance dose is defined by Equation 6:

$$\text{Dose} = 9.56 - 1.19(\text{sex}) + 0.064(\text{weight}) - 0.021(\text{age}) - 2.73(\text{depression}) + 2.26(\text{state}) + 0.035(CL_{\text{CR}}) \quad (6)$$

where the sex is 1 for males and 2 for females, depression is 1 for absence and 2 for presence and/or tricyclic antidepressant use, state is coded 1 for acute and 2 for non-acute symptoms, and CL_{CR} is the creatinine clearance calculated by the Cockroft–Gault equation, presented in Equation 7:

$$CL_{\text{CR}} = (140 - \text{age})(\text{weight})/(72)(\text{serum creatinine}) \quad (7)$$

Equation 5 is limited to use in patients with creatinine clearances greater than 45 ml/min. It is assumed that this is not a problem with Equation 6 since creatinine clearance is accounted for in the equation.

Adjustments of Lithium Dosage: Conclusions

Comparing and contrasting the utility of the pharmacokinetic and non-pharmacokinetic approaches to lithium dosing leads one to the conclusion that as the complexity of the dosing approach increases so too does the accuracy and sensitivity of the dosing method. Thus the most accurate means of determining the dose is by using the two-point pharmacokinetic method, followed by the one-point pharmacokinetic method. Although the other remaining lithium dosing approaches are considerably easier to utilize, the clinician does sacrifice a considerable degree of accuracy and sensitivity in dosing.

Bibliography

Lesar,T.S., Tollesfson,G.K. and Koch,M. (1985) Relationship between patient variables and lithium dosage requirements. *J. Clin.*

Psychiatry, **46**, 133–136.
This discussion is suitable for clinicians wth some knowledge of multiple regression analysis.

Perry,P.J., Prince,R.A., Alexander,B. and Dunner,F.J. (1983) Prediction of lithium maintenance doses using a single point prediction protocol. *J. Clin. Psychopharmacol.*, **3**, 13–17.
A useful discussion of the dose prediction issue.

Perry,P.J., Alexander,B., Prince,R.A. and Dunner,F.J. (1984) Evaluation of two prospective lithium maintenance dose schedules. *J. Clin. Psychopharmacol.*, **4**, 242–246.
An interesting comparison which illustrates several conceptual issues and is aimed at the psychiatrist.

Perry,P.J., Alexander,B., Prince,R.A. and Dunner,F.J. (1986) A single point dosing protocol for predicting steady state lithium levels. *Br. J. Psychiatry*, **148**, 401–405.
Some rudimental knowledge of pharmacokinetics is needed for a full appreciation of this article.

Perry,P.J., Alexander,B., Dunner,F.J., Schoenwald,R.D., Pfohlt, B.M. and Miller,D. (1982) Pharmacokinetic protocol for predicting serum lithium levels. *J. Clin. Psychopharmacol.*, **2**, 114–118.
Again, this discussion of serum level prediction assumes some basic statistical knowledge and familiarity with the concepts of pharmacokinetics.

18. Kinetics and Tissue Distribution

Rolland I.Poust

The pharmacokinetics of lithium provide the basis for the size and frequency of dosing (see Section 17, pp. 67–73) and the rationale for monitoring plasma levels as an adjunct in the evaluation of patient response and progress.

Whilst lithium is generally well-absorbed upon oral administration, absorption can be markedly affected by the formulation, especially in the case of sustained release products (see pp. 94–98). Once absorbed, lithium is subsequently distributed into most body tissues, especially those consisting of a large proportion of water. Lithium is not protein bound and thus distributes throughout body water, both intra- and extracellularly; as a result, its apparent volume of distribution is about 50–90% of body weight. Lithium concentration in lung, kidney, muscle and heart is about the same as in the plasma. Concentrations in the bones and white matter of the brain are somewhat higher.

Peak plasma concentrations are generally achieved within 1–2 h of oral administration of lithium, regardless of the salt given. These levels occur later, at 3–6 h, when sustained-release forms are administered. Beyond the peak, concentrations fall quite rapidly (especially if a conventional dosage form has been administered) for 4–6 h followed by a slower decline. Measurable amounts of drug remain in the plasma for at least 24 h after administration. Mathematical analysis of plasma concentration-time curves has given rise to quantitative information on the absorption, distribution, and excretion of lithium.

Input–Output Balance

Lithium excretion occurs almost exclusively through the kidney, renal lithium clearance being generally between 10 and 40 ml/min. Thus, any disease or drug which adversely affects the kidney's ability to function will affect the excretion of lithium, particularly its rate. In turn, alteration of the excretion rate of lithium will affect the plasma concentration and subsequently tissue distribution and retention of the drug. About 50% of a dose of lithium is excreted in the urine during the first 24 h after administration, and another 40% in the next 24 h. However, these values vary considerably among individuals. Small amounts can be found in the urine 1–2 weeks after administration of a single oral dose.

A Pharmacokinetic Model

The rate of influx and efflux of lithium is not uniform for all body tissues, a kinetic phenomenon which has led to the view that the body acts as a two-compartment system in the way in which it handles lithium. The pharmacokinetics of lithium are therefore usually described in terms of a two-compartment mathematical model (see *Figure 18.1*). This model assumes that the

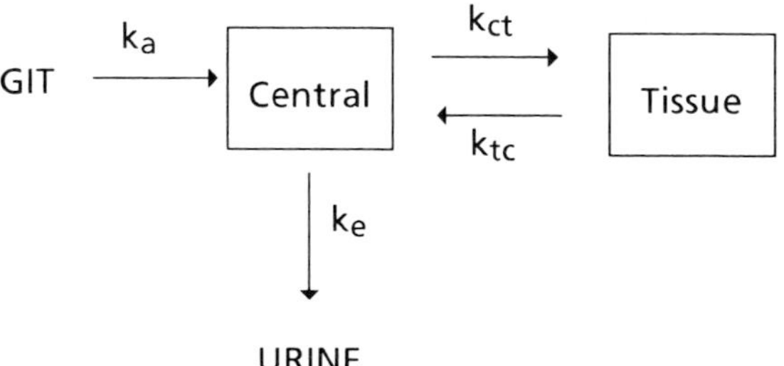

Figure 18.1 Schematic diagram of two-compartment mathematical model used to describe the pharmacokinetics of lithium. The symbols k_a, k_{ct}, k_{tc}, and k_e illustrate the absorption, distribution between central and tissue compartments, and excretion of lithium, respectively. GIT = gastro-intestinal tract.

rates of transfer between compartments (organ and tissue groups) are dependent on the lithium concentration at any given time. Generally, the first, or central, compartment is assumed to consist of blood excluding the erythrocytes or red blood cells (RBCs), highly perfused organs and tissues, and the kidneys. Concentration changes in these organs and tissues can be expected to parallel those in the plasma. The second, or tissue, compartment is thought to consist of the RBCs and less well-perfused organs and tissues such as bone and brain matter.

The model describes the biphasic plasma concentration-time curve obtained beyond the peak of a plot of logarithm of concentration *versus* time (see *Figure 18.2*). The first portion of this bi-exponential curve has a distribution half-life of about 4–6 h while the terminal elimination portion has a half-life of about 24 h. Concentrations in the second compartment generally increase up to the time corresponding to the beginning of the slower decline in plasma concentrations, i.e. the end of the distribution phase (*Figure 18.3*). These concentrations then decline at a rate parallel to the decline in plasma concentration. Mathematical analysis of plasma concentration-time curves reveals that the absorption of lithium is quite rapid and that model parameters are predictive of plasma half-life. Values of rate constants derived from such analyses have little clinical significance other than in quantitating the effect of another drug or a disease state on the elimination rate of lithium from the body. The most important pharmacokinetic parameter is the biological half-life which is derived from the terminal portion of the curve. The model predicts that it will be a constant regardless of dose. This terminal portion usually begins beyond 8–10 h after dosing. Because correlations between plasma concentration and response (and toxicity) are based on the plasma concentrations in this portion of the curve, it is important to draw plasma samples for monitoring purposes during this phase and not prior to absorption cessation or to the establishment of distribution equilibrium.

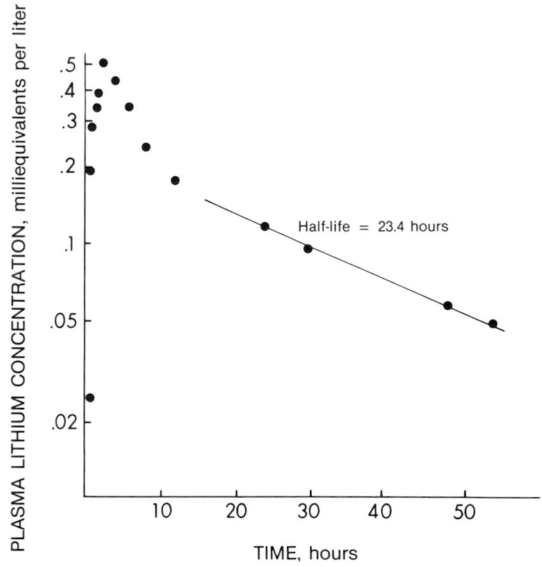

Figure 18.2 Semilogarithmic plot of plasma lithium concentration as a function of time following the administration of a single, 600-mg dose of lithium carbonate to a normal volunteer. The last four points were used to calculate a biological half-life of 23.4 h.

Biological Half-life

Biological half-life values for lithium appear to vary considerably among individuals. Some of this variation can be explained on the basis of physiological differences (renal function, age and so on), concomitant administration of other drugs (such as thiazide diuretics) and disease (especially of the kidney). Other

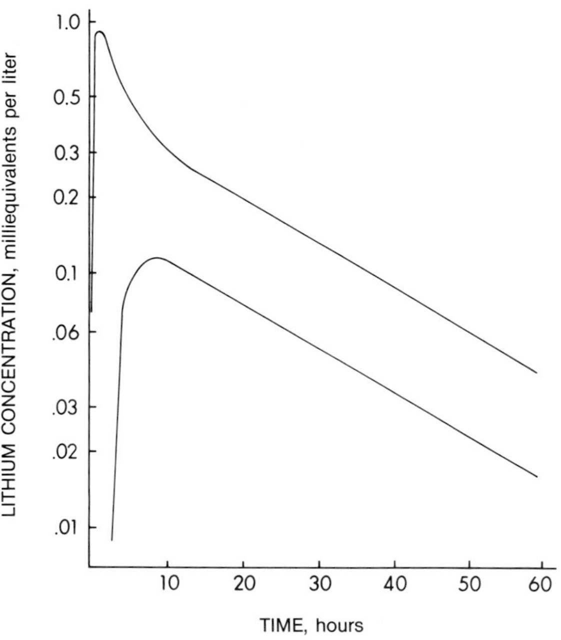

Figure 18.3 Semilogarithmic plot of relative amounts of lithium in the central and tissue compartments of a normal volunteer following administration of a single, 900-mg dose of lithium carbonate. This plot shows the temporal relationship between plasma (central compartment) and tissue levels.

sources of variation may lie in the premature cessation of plasma level sampling or in the use of plasma levels determined during the distribution phase. Half-life values as low as 12 h and as high as 41 h have been reported following adminstration of a single dose or during the early stages of therapy. Generally, the half-life of lithium is considered to be approximately 24 h. Equilibrium plasma levels occur within about 5–7 half-lives, or within 1 week. However, one report in the literature indicates that lithium half-life may increase significantly during long-term therapy. In this study, lithium half-lives were measured in three groups of patients following termination of therapy. The first group had just begun therapy, the second had been taking the drug for less than one year and the third had been taking the drug for more than one year. Half-lives increased from a mean of 28.8 (±9.12) h in the first group to 39.6 (±13.20) h in the second, and to 58.32 (±21.84) h in the third. The investigators did not discuss the relationship between dose, plasma concentration and therapeutic response among the three groups of patients. However, these differences in half-life, especially between the first and third groups, are sufficient to indicate the need for dosage regimens to be tailored for individual patients.

Summary

In brief, lithium is well absorbed, is distributed widely in the body, and is described kinetically by a two-compartment system. Its biological half-life varies among individuals and can be used for tailoring dosage regimens for individual patients. However, the half-life may increase significantly during long-term therapy. Because of the variation in half-life and its potential for change, monitoring of lithium plasma levels is clearly a necessary adjunct to rational lithium therapy.

Bibliography

Amdisen,A. (1977) Serum level monitoring and clinical pharmacokinetics of lithium. *Clin. Pharmacokinet.*, **2**, 73–92.
This review provides a comprehensive guide to the relationships among dosing, pharmacokinetics and plasma levels.

Goodnick,P.J., Fieve,R.R., Meltzer,H.L. and Dunner,D.L. (1981) Lithium elimination half-life and duration of therapy. *Clin. Pharmacol. Ther.*, **29**, 47–50.
The authors report that the biological half-life increases significantly in patients who have been on the drug for one year or longer.

Thornhill,D.P. (1981) The biological disposition and kinetics of lithium. *Biopharm. Drug Dispos.*, **2**, 305–322.
Describes in detail the absorption, distribution, excretion, pharmacokinetic models, plasma level measurement, intoxication and interactions of lithium.

19. Excretion

Klaus Thomsen

Lithium is excreted almost exclusively through the kidneys, excretion through sweat and faeces normally amounting to less than 5%. The renal excretion plays an important role as a major determinant of the serum lithium concentration. If the excretion is lower than the intake, lithium accumulates in the organism with a consequent risk of intoxication. If it is higher than the intake, the serum lithium concentration decreases with the risk of ineffective treatment and relapses.

The Renal Lithium Clearance

During maintenance treatment lithium excretion equals lithium intake and lithium excretion varies proportionally with the serum lithium concentration. When lithium treatment is started, both concentration and excretion are initially zero, but soon lithium accumulates in the body and concentration and excretion rise. After about 5 days the excretion reaches a level which equals the intake and it then remains at this level. Intake, excretion, and serum lithium concentration are now linked together according to the following expression:

$$\text{daily intake} = \text{daily excretion} = \text{serum concentration} \times \text{clearance} \times 1.44 \qquad (8)$$

where the daily intake and excretion of lithium are expressed in mmol/day, the serum concentration is the average lithium concentration during the 24-h day expressed in mmol/l, and clearance is the average lithium clearance during the 24-h day expressed in ml/min. Lithium clearance is the amount of lithium which is excreted per minute when the serum concentration is 1.0 mmol/l: it differs from one person to another and is a measure of the excretion speed. Patients with a high clearance excrete high amounts of lithium at a given serum lithium concentration and therefore need high doses to obtain proper serum concentrations. The multiplier 1.44 is included in the formula because the left-hand side of the formula is expressed as mmol/day and the right-hand side is expressed as ml/min. The 24 h of the day contain 1440 min.

It appears from Equation 8 that in principle the dose needed to obtain a certain serum concentration can be calculated from the lithium clearance. But in practice it is better to give a small daily dose during the first week and to measure the serum lithium concentration when equilibrium has been achieved after about one week. Since this concentration varies proportionally with the intake the dose can now be adjusted. A fuller discussion of ways of predicting the maintenance dose is given on pp. 67–73. The expression shows also that at a given dose the serum lithium concentration depends entirely on the lithium clearance. A decrease in the clearance will, for example, lead to an increase in the serum concentration. The concentration will therefore remain constant at a given dose only if the clearance is constant. If, on the other hand, the serum concentration is constant, it can be concluded that the clearance is also constant.

From clinical experience of the lithium treatment of patients it is known that the serum concentration usually remains fairly constant day after day, week after week, and month after month. This indicates that the average clearance usually remains constant. But that is not always so. Drugs, diseases, food and environment may influence the lithium clearance and lead to increase or decrease of the serum concentration.

The Renal Handling of Lithium

Lithium is not bound to plasma proteins and is therefore filtered freely through the glomerular membrane. It is re-absorbed in the proximal tubules in the same percentage of the glomerular filtration rate as sodium and water, whereas it is neither re-absorbed nor secreted in the more distal tubular segments, i.e. the loop of Henle, the distal tubules and the collecting ducts. The fraction of the filtered lithium load which is excreted in the urine is accordingly identical with that delivered from the proximal tubules to the loop of Henle, and this fraction is equal to that of filtered sodium and water which is delivered out of the proximal tubules. That fraction, Vprox/GFR, is about 25% in both humans and rats (*Figure 19.1*).

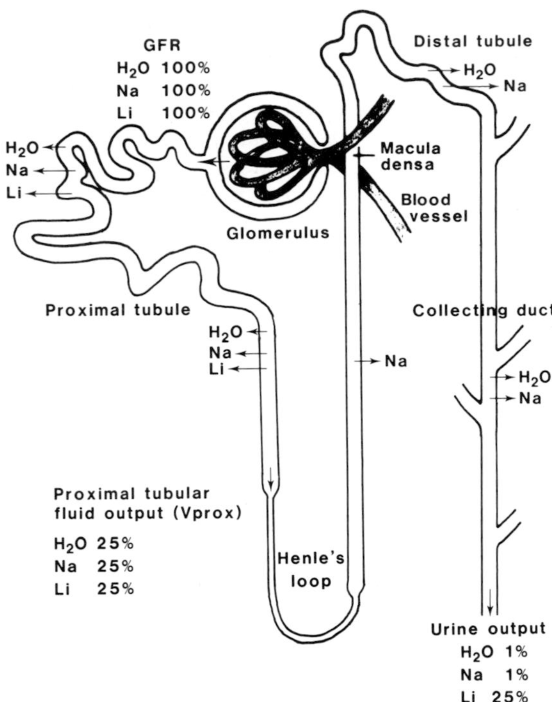

Figure 19.1 Diagram showing a nephron with its different segments. For water, sodium and lithium are shown the percentages of the filtered load which is delivered from the proximal tubules to the loop of Henle. The percentages which are excreted in the urine are also shown. The glomerulus is the anatomical arrangement where the blood vessels come into contact with the tubules. The tubules are long pipes of which the kidneys contain many thousands. Fluid containing various electrolytes and other substances from the blood is pressed into the pipe at one end through the glomerular membrane. The fluid then passes along the tubules and all substances which are needed by the organism are reabsorbed in appropriate amounts while what is not needed or is harmful is excreted in the urine. The tubules are divided into sections according to anatomical and functional characteristics. The one nearest to the glomerulus is called the proximal tubule, the next is the loop of Henle, followed by the distal tubule, and finally the collecting duct. The macula densa (MD) is a region of the tubule which is sensitive to the flow to the distal tubules and which is involved in its regulation. Glomerular filtration rate (GFR) is the amount of fluid which passes through the glomerular membrane per minute. Proximal tubular fluid output (Vprox) is the amount of tubular fluid which passes from the proximal tubules to the loop of Henle per minute. Vprox is equal to lithium clearance (CLi), which is a measure of the rate at which lithium is excreted in the urine.

For freely filtered substances which are neither reabsorbed nor secreted the renal clearance is equal to the glomerular filtration rate (GFR), whereas for partly re-absorbed substances the fraction of the filtered load which is excreted in the urine can be calculated as their clearance divided by GFR. The excreted fraction of the filtered lithium is CLi/GFR. Since CLi/GFR is equal to Vprox/GFR, CLi is equal to Vprox. The lithium clearance is accordingly equal to a distinct physiological variable, namely the very important flow of tubular fluid which leaves the proximal tubules and enters the loop of Henle.

Cations other than lithium, such as sodium, potassium and calcium, are re-absorbed in the distal part of the nephron, each of them with its own specific transport system with specific regulating hormones. But lithium does not occur normally in the organism except in extremely minute quantities and does not have a transport system of its own. This explains its unique treatment in the kidneys.

Knowledge about the renal handling of lithium has come from studies in humans and rats. In experiments involving rats, small samples of tubular fluid have been removed from various segments of the kidney tubules by micropuncture and their lithium content analysed. The proximal tubular fluid output has also been measured by micropuncture and the results have been compared with the lithium clearance measured in the urine. It was found that lithium clearance was closely correlated with the micropuncture data. The micropuncture technique cannot be used experimentally in humans because it requires exposure of the kidneys to surgical intervention. The only way to study human lithium excretion has therefore been to compare lithium clearance with other indirect methods of estimating the proximal tubular fluid output such as the urine flow during maximal water load. Studies in humans have also been carried out with diuretic drugs affecting various parts of the nephron and in patients with various kidney diseases. In all these cases, lithium clearance appeared to be influenced as was to be expected if CLi equals Vprox.

Lithium Clearance and Tubular Fluid Output

The fact that the lithium clearance is linked to the proximal tubular fluid output means that it is not always constant. The proximal tubular fluid output increases during expansion of the extracellular volume and decreases when the organism is sodium- or water-depleted, for example during intake of a low sodium diet, after sweating in a sauna, or when patients with lithium-induced polyuria do not drink sufficiently (*Table 19.1*). It also explains why the lithium clearance may decrease during illness when intake of food and possibly of water is insufficient and where loss of water may be increased due to sweating or electrolytes may be lost due to vomiting.

Table 19.1 *Factors influencing renal lithium clearance*

Changes in glomerular filtration rate
Kidney disease
Age
Pregnancy
Lithium intoxication
Changes in tubular re-absorption of sodium
Changes in sodium intake
Extrarenal loss of sodium
Diuretic drugs
Water deficiency

The link between lithium clearance and proximal tubular fluid output also explains the effect of various diuretics which lead to loss of sodium and water and therefore also to a compensatory reduction of proximal tubular fluid output and lithium clearance. This applies to the most commonly used group of diuretics, the thiazides.

The effect of another loop diuretic, furosemide, is a little more complicated because it also affects the proximal tubules, leading first to an increase of lithium clearance and later on, when volume depletion has developed, to a decrease. Over a period of 24 h little or no effect is seen on lithium clearance. The only diuretics which lead to an increase of lithium clearance are the less commonly used aminophylline and acetazolamide which inhibit re-absorption mainly in the proximal tubules.

The concatenation of lithium clearance and proximal tubular fluid output also explains why the lithium clearance often follows changes in the glomerular filtration rate. In conditions where the number of functioning nephrons decreases, for example in old age, during kidney disease with pyelonephritis or glomerulonephritis, or after removal of one kidney, GFR decreases but Vprox/GFR tends to remain unaltered, which means that the total output decreases proportionally with GFR. The lithium clearance is influenced in the same way. This means that the lithium clearance decreases with age and during kidney disease.

Lithium Clearance as a Tool

The proximal tubular fluid output plays an important role for kidney function. It determines the amount of electrolytes delivered to the distal tubules and it takes part in the regulation of the extracellular fluid volume. The flow is carefully regulated by its own hormonal system which is located in the region known as the macula densa at the borderline between the ascending limb of Henle's loop and the distal tubules (*Figure 19.1*). The regulation has been the subject of numerous investigations but our present knowledge is nevertheless limited, because no appropriate method has been available for determination of the proximal tubular fluid output in unanaesthetized, unoperated animals or in humans. However, along with the establishment of the lithium clearance as a measure of this variable, the situation has changed radically, and the lithium clearance has become a valuable tool in studying the role played by the proximal tubular fluid output under a variety of circumstances.

The lithium clearance method has already been put to many uses, both in humans and in animals. In humans it has been found that the lithium clearance is related to sex, age, and body surface because it is correlated with the glomerular filtration rate. It increases only slightly with increasing sodium intake, whereas it increases much in response to infusion of saline, presumably because this leads to an increase of the extracellular volume, while intake of sodium with the food does not. The lithium clearance is unaffected by intake of both potassium and water, provided that variations in the latter do not affect the extracellular fluid volume. Although the average lithium clearance is constant from day to day, it varies during the day, and these variations are associated with variations in urine flow, sodium excretion and potassium excretion. It is the changes in the proximal tubular fluid output which lead to the relationship between lithium clearance and urine flow, sodium clearance, and potassium clearance. It is not the changes in urine flow, sodium excretion, or potassium excretion which lead to the changes in CLi. The variation of Vprox during the day probably plays a role in homeostasis. Studies in humans have also shown that lithium clearance increases during pregnancy. It is unaltered in patients with essential hypertension and in patients with diabetes mellitus. It is unaffected by administration of neuroleptic and antidepressant drugs. During lithium intoxication the lithium clearance may be severely depressed together with the GFR, due to a toxic effect of lithium on the kidneys. Other nephrotoxic drugs may also influence the lithium clearance and studies are in progress to use changes in CLi as an early warning of the toxic effect of such drugs.

The discovery of the lithium clearance as a tool in kidney research and much of the underlying scientific work were made in a psychiatric research laboratory. The method has now been adopted by other research areas and important information is coming back to psychiatry, to the benefit of psychiatric patients. The use of lithium as a test substance in somatic diseases and under different experimental conditions provides helpful information about the lithium clearance, so that lithium treatment of manic-depressive patients can be made safer and more effective.

Bibliography

Thomsen,K. (1978) Renal handling of lithium at non-toxic and toxic serum lithium levels. A review. *Dan. Med. Bull.*, **25**, 106–115.
A fairly technical survey of the way in which lithium is excreted by the kidney, establishing the basic principles and concepts.

Thomsen,K. (1984) Lithium clearance: a new method for determining proximal and distal tubular reabsorption of sodium and water. *Nephron*, **37**, 217–223.
An account of a technique which has wide application in areas beyond lithium therapy.

Thomsen,K. and Schou,M. (1986) Lithium clearance: a new research area. *News Physiol. Sci.*, **1**, 126–128.
A further account of the applications of this simple, non-invasive method of measuring the delivery of water and sodium from the proximal kidney tubules.

20. Measurement of Serum Lithium Levels

Robert Y.Xie and Gary D.Christian

While all psychiatrists know, or should know, that the safe conduct of lithium therapy involves the measurement of serum lithium levels, the methods which are currently available (and others which are in the process of being developed) for carrying out such measurement are not always a matter of common knowledge or understanding. This is partly due to the fact that psychiatrists do not really need to know how the serum level is determined: they merely require the information about the value which is obtained. Another factor which deters enquiry about methods of lithium estimation is the use of terminology which is unfamiliar. The following account attempts to minimize this latter difficulty. It is never an entirely satisfactory situation that an important aspect of medical technology should remain a mystery to patient and clinician alike, both of whom have their actions determined by its findings, and it is hoped that this outline of serum lithium measurement techniques will go some way to correcting this situation.

Atomic Absorption and Flame Emission Methods

Atomic absorption spectrometry (AAS) and flame emission spectrometry (FES) are the two most widely used analytical chemistry instruments for the determination of metals. Currently, serum samples are exclusively analysed for lithium by these two methods in clinical laboratories. FES was commercialized about 5 years before the first lithium treatment of manic-depressive patients. AAS, which is based on very similar principles, was commercialized about 10 years later. Because AAS is a very reliable and versatile technique, more and more clinical laboratories are now equipped with it. In the sense of monitoring, lithium therapy has been fortunate from the very beginning, because chemists have provided the powerful tools needed and these have been subjected to continuous improvement.

Theory

An atom is composed of a nucleus and electrons. The electrons around the nucleus occupy various energy orbits. An atom can absorb discrete units of energy to transfer an electron to a higher energy orbit. The energy can be in the form of heat or light, the thermal energy (heat) being proportional to the temperature and photo energy (light) being proportional to the wave frequency and inversely proportional to the wavelength (consequently, light at different energy levels will disperse on a scale of wavelengths). When the electron is at a higher energy orbit, i.e. higher electronic energy level, we say that the atom is in an excited state; when the electron is in its normal orbit, i.e. lower electronic energy level, we say that it is at ground state. Atoms in an excited state will automatically return to the ground state and, in so doing, will emit light to release their excess energy.

The emission of light by atoms in an excited state returning to thc ground state is the basis for FES, and the absorption of light by ground state atoms to reach the excited state represents AAS (*Figure 20.1*). Because there are discrete electron orbits in the atoms, the emitted light shows discrete lines on a wavelength scale (*Figure 20.2*), called a spectrum. These spectra serve as 'fingerprints' of elements; the occurrence of a spectrum line indicates the presence of an element and the intensity of the line gives quantitative information about the amount of the element.

Flame emission spectrometry

Flame emission spectrometry is so named because of the use of a flame to provide the energy of excitation

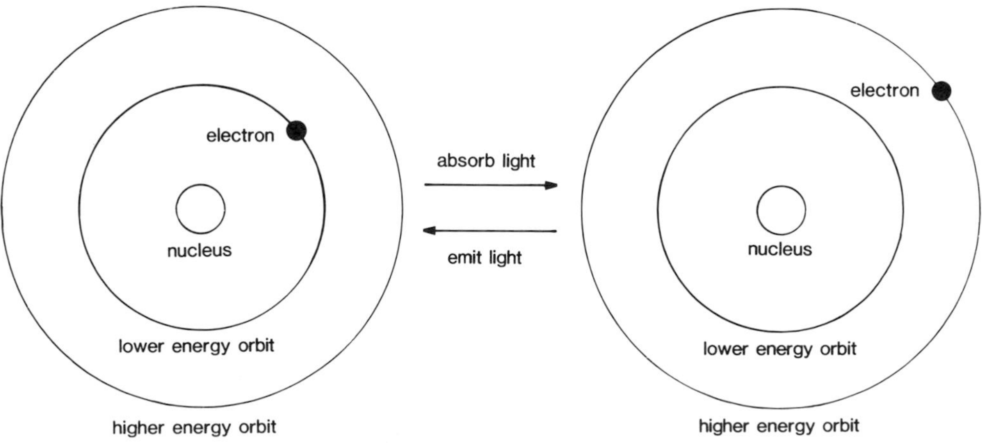

Figure 20.1 Relation of atomic absorption and atomic emission.

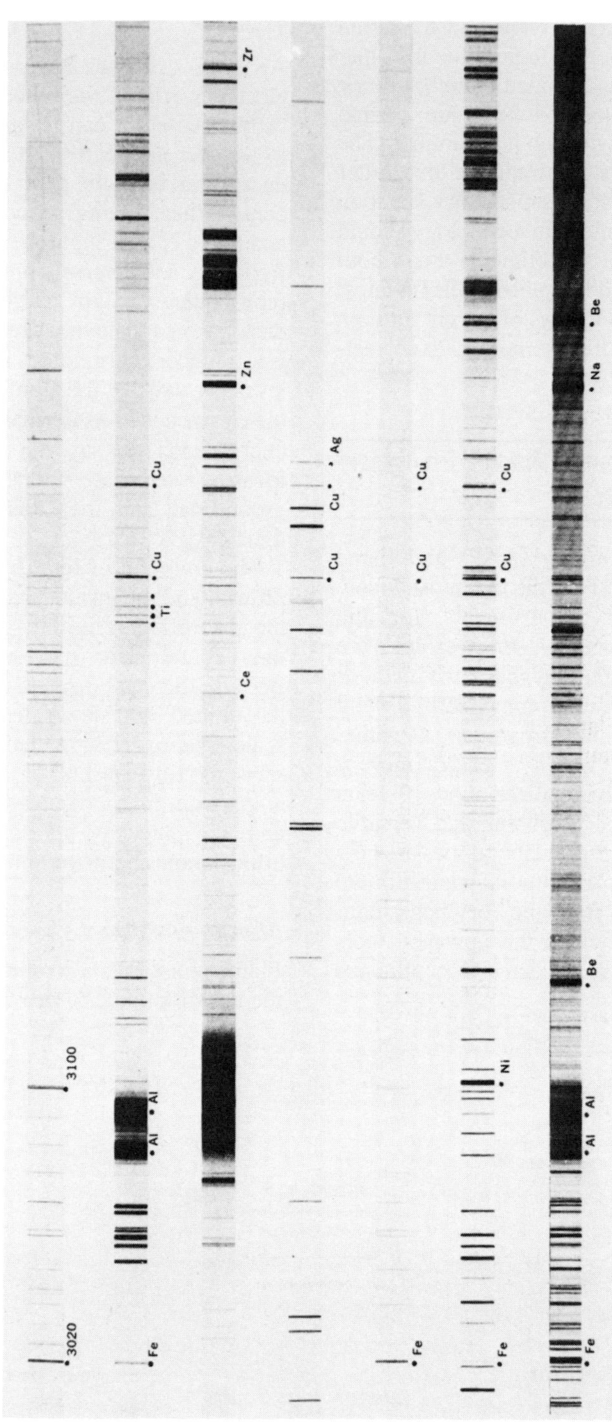

Figure 20.2 Typical atomic spectra. [From Christian,G.D. and O'Reilley,J.E. (1986) *Instrumental Analysis* 2nd Edition. Allyn and Bacon, London, reproduced with permission.]

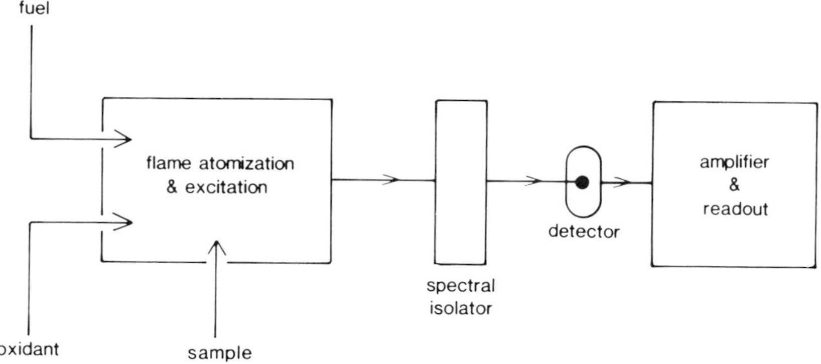

Figure 20.3 Flame emission spectrometer design.

for atoms introduced into the flame. Combustion flames also provide a remarkably simple means for converting ionic analytes in a sample solution into free atoms. When a sample solution of fine mist is introduced into a flame, a series of events and reactions rapidly occur. One is that of the sample being desolvated and vaporized into gaseous salt molecules, which upon further heating dissociate into free atoms. A small proportion of these free atoms will absorb additional energy from the flame and become excited. However, atoms can only remain in excited states for a very short period of time (of the order of 10^{-8} second) and they return to the ground state, emitting light of discrete wavelengths. Only one of the characteristic spectrum lines is measured. The intensity of emitted radiation is proportional to the quantity, or concentration, of the sample analyte.

The instrumentation for a flame emission spectrometer is relatively simple. It is composed of the following major parts: a burner for sample introduction, atom formation and excitation; a device to isolate the desired spectral region; a light intensity detector; and an amplifier plus read-out device (*Figure 20.3*).

Atomic absorption spectrometry

Atomic absorption spectrometry in some respects is the reverse of FES. Free ground state atoms can absorb radiation (light) at various discrete wavelengths, corresponding to transitions from a lower to a higher energy level. The free ground state atoms can be provided by a flame, as in FES. As previously stated, only a small proportion of the free atoms is excited in a flame, and therefore if a beam of light of specific wavelength is passed through this cloud of unexcited atoms, this large proportion of atoms can absorb part of the light. This absorption phenomenon of atoms (the reverse process of atomic emission) is the basic principle of AAS.

The sample atoms absorb light only at their own characteristic wavelengths. It is therefore essential that the light source emits at exactly the same wavelength. This can be achieved by using a hollow cathode lamp in which the cathode is made of the same element as the element being determined. In application, this has been found to be very advantageous, since it has led to a high degree of freedom from interference from absorption by other elements in the sample (such as sodium and potassium in serum lithium analysis) because they absorb at other characteristic wavelengths. A disadvantage, however, is that for each element to be determined, a separate light source must be used. One has, therefore, to be aware that a clinical chemistry laboratory which is equipped with AAS instrumentation might not be able to analyse serum lithium because of the lack of a lithium lamp. However, AAS instruments are sometimes equipped to perform FES measurements as well.

After the radiation from the hollow cathode lamp passes through the sample in the flame, the intensity of the radiation is measured. The more atoms in the flame, the more radiation is absorbed. Thus, in contrast to FES, the measured intensity is inversely proportional to the concentration of the analyte (the fraction of light absorbed is proportional to the concentration).

Like flame emission spectrometry, AAS also uses a device to isolate the desired spectral region; a detector for light intensity measurement; and an amplifier plus read-out device (*Figure 20.4*).

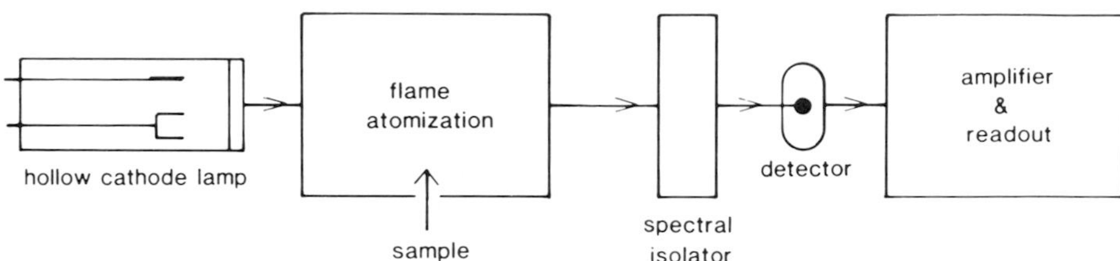

Figure 20.4 Atomic absorption spectrometer design.

FES and AAS serum lithium analysis

Blood samples are collected in glass tubes, and the collected blood sample will clot within 1 h. The fibrinogen-free plasma, the serum, can then be isolated and analysed after centrifuging. It is found that the serum lithium level is stable over a 1-year period under frozen storage conditions. Thus, serum samples can be analysed when they are received or can be held for a more convenient time for analysis. However, in practice hospital samples are almost always analysed as they are received. Samples are generally diluted with an appropriate solution to minimize effects of other sample constituents.

All samples are compared with standards to determine their concentration values. Like the scales on a ruler, standards are scales of concentration. Standards are made of a series of solutions of known lithium concentration in a similar matrix to the sample solution. They are often made in a bovine albumin matrix to match the serum protein level and other serum components. In FES, often an internal standard element is added to samples and standards at a fixed concentration, and the ratio of the FES signals from the lithium and internal standard element is measured. This compensates for variations in rate of sample aspiration into the flame and so forth.

Comparison of FES and AAS

In the search for a better understanding of human body conditions and mechanisms, the task of analysis of more and more elements is placed on clinical laboratories. Thus, AAS, being an extremely versatile and specific analytic technique, is often the choice. With the development of modern technology, AAS has become a common tool in many hospitals in the USA and Europe. Recent advances in AAS have resulted in a vast increase in its capabilities. However, FES *per se* has not been improved much since its early age, and the limitations of FES cannot be eliminated by means of simple instrument improvement. Nevertheless, because alkali metals are excited at a temperature lower than most elements and the characteristic wavelengths of the spectra of alkali metals are widely separated from each other, FES remains more than adequate for serum lithium analysis.

Much work has been done to compare the results of serum lithium analysis by the two methods. Generally, both have been found to give satisfactory results, and when applied to the same samples the results are very comparable.

New Developments of AAS and FES

Although the flame AAS and FES methods are currently in use and the analytical results are reliable, modifications—particularly in the atomization source—have been made, which improve the sensitivity or versatility of measurements. Among them, electrothermal atomization AAS and inductively coupled plasma emission spectrometry (ICP) are the two most important ones.

Electrothermal atomization AAS

Electrothermal atomization, AAS, using a graphite furnace as an atomization source, is a simple modification of flame AAS. Any commercially available flame AAS instrument can be easily switched to an electrothermal atomization mode by installing a graphite furnace at the burner position. The graphite furnace, which performs the same function as the flame, is an electrically heated graphite sample cell. It is usually 100−1000 times more efficient than a flame, due to the controlled inert gas environment and avoidance of the dilution and expansion effects that occur in the flame. Normally, the graphite furnace method only utilizes 1−50 μl of the sample solution (which is added with a micropipette), compared with 1−3 ml in flame AAS. The temperature of the graphite furnace can be controlled, or programmed, according to the atomization and excitation temperatures of the elements under study. The organic matter (proteins) in the sample must be burned off at a lower temperature before atomizing the analyte (lithium). Electrothermal atomization AAS has been successfully used for serum lithium analysis. However, because of the convenience and sufficient sensitivity for serum lithium analysis, flame AAS is mostly used for routine analysis in clinical laboratories.

Inductively coupled plasma emission spectrometry

ICP has gained great popularity in recent years because of its outstanding performance. Commercial ICP systems became available only in 1974, and now there are more than 5000 instruments in operation in the world. Since ICP and FES are both based on measurements of the emission radiation from the analyte, ICP has been called the second generation FES. However, in terms of instrumentation and performance, ICP revolutionizes FES.

A plasma is a flowing gas in which a significant portion of the gas molecules is ionized. The plasma is coupled (i.e. interacts) with a magnetic field around it. ICP is so called because of the use of an inductively coupled plasma discharge as the energy source for atomization and excitation. The plasma discharge is generated by electrical induction of a flowing conductive gas, which is often argon. At room temperature, argon is not a conductor, but it can be made electrically conductive if it is heated. To start the ICP discharge, a pilot spark is applied to the argon. This pilot discharge absorbs energy from the magnetic field around it and turns rapidly into a stable discharge plasma. The temperature of the ICP discharge is very high, in the region of 9000 – 10 000K. Because of the high temperatures and inert atmosphere (argon), atomization and excitation are both very efficient in the ICP discharge. Thus, it is most favoured for the analytes which require high excitation energy. Serum lithium samples have been analysed by ICP. Due to the low excitation and ionization energies of lithium atoms, the ICP method is not superior to the FES method, and in practice, ICP is hardly used to analyse serum lithium samples, because the instrumentation is very expensive in terms of capital cost and operational cost (see *Table 20.1*).

In conclusion, both electrothermal atomization AAS and ICP can readily measure serum lithium levels. But, due to some practical reasons such as technological

Table 20.1 *Practical aspects of serum lithium analysis methods*

Methods	Capital cost	Operational cost	Development stage	Future
FES	Medium	High	Well developed	Will be continuously used in the clinical laboratory
AAS	High	High	Well developed	Will be continuously used in the clinical laboratory
ETAAS	High	Medium	Developed	Will be used in the laboratory as a reference method or for limited sample size
ICP	Very high	High	Developed	Will be used in the laboratory as a reference method
Spectrophotometry	Low	Low	In development	Will be used in the laboratory; doctor's office
Fluorometry	High	Low	Need to be improved	Will only be used in laboratories
ISE	Low	Low	Not far from commercialization	Will be widely used in the laboratory; doctor's office

maturity and economic considerations, traditional FES and AAS are still preferred over electrothermal AAS and ICP. However, there are other areas of analytical chemistry, especially in spectrophotometry, fluorometry and electrochemistry, which have demonstrated promising methods for serum lithium measurements.

Spectrophotometric Method

Spectrophotometry is perhaps the most frequently used of all spectroscopic methods, and it is important in the quantitative analysis of biological samples. Serum lithium has been successfully measured by various spectrophotometric methods, and in the future we will probably see more developments in this field.

Theory

A molecule is composed of various numbers of atoms, and the energy levels of a molecule are far more complicated than those of an atom, which has only electronic energy levels. The energy levels of a molecule are determined by the sum of the contributions from electronic, vibrational and rotational energies. For each electronic energy state of a molecule, there normally are several possible vibrational states and for each of these, in turn, numerous rotational states. Consequently, the number of possible energy levels for a molecule is much larger than for an atom. A molecule may be excited from any of the vibrational and rotational levels in the ground state to any of a large number of possible vibrational and rotational states, by absorption of light. Because light of slightly different energy corresponds to each of the many possible transitions, photometric spectra of molecular absorption consist of hundreds or thousands of lines so closely spaced that they appear as continuous absorption bands in contrast to the sharp lines that characterize atomic spectra. A continuous radiation source is used, such as a tungsten bulb.

The lifetimes of the excited states of molecules are rather short. When molecules return to their ground state, rather than emitting this energy as light most of them will be deactivated by molecular collisional processes in which the energy is lost as heat, and the heat will be too small to be detected in most cases. This is the reason for colouration of the solution. The relation between colour and absorption is listed in *Table 20.2*. Colorimetry, in its simplest form, refers to a method in which visual matching of the colour intensity of the sample with that of a series of standards is conducted to estimate the sample concentration.

Visual colorimetry suffers from poor precision since the eye is not sensitive enough to identify the small colour differences. However, photoelectric devices can precisely measure the light intensity before and after the light passes through the sample solution and so the absorbed light can be easily determined. Beer's law states that the fraction of absorbed light is logarithmically proportional to the concentration of the absorbing substance in a solution.

Spectrophotometric serum lithium analysis

Lithium itself is not a molecule and so it is not directly applicable in spectrophotometry. However, if there is a foreign molecule that can complex (associate) with lithium to give a compound that absorbs the light, then we can indirectly measure the lithium spectrophotometrically. As a matter of fact, this concept opened a whole field of analytical chemistry and many elements are readily measured by this method. The solution of the foreign molecule is called a reagent, the compound of the foreign molecule associated with metal is called a metal complex and the foreign molecule part of the metal complex is called a ligand.

It is a long recognized fact that to form a well-defined metal complex, the ligand must possess two or more complexing groups on the molecule. Furthermore, coloured substances owe their colour to absorption of light due to several special kinds of molecular groups. Therefore, a useful spectrophotometric reagent must have these features.

Finding a lithium reagent is by no means a small job. Besides having to meet the above requirements,

Table 20.2 *Colours of different wavelength regions*

Wavelength absorbed (nm)	Absorbed colour	Visualized (transmitted) colour
380–450	Violet	Yellow-green
450–495	Blue	Yellow
495–570	Green	Violet
570–590	Yellow	Blue
590–620	Orange	Green-blue
620–750	Red	Blue-green

the reagent should be very selective towards lithium because the concentrations of a number of elements (especially sodium) in the serum are much greater than that of lithium. The sodium concentration is 140 times greater than a commonly encountered serum lithium level of around 1.0 mmol/l, and its chemical properties are very similar. Investigators have designed and synthesized a number of lithium reagents, two of which have been successfully used for serum lithium analysis, although the sodium interferences of these two compounds are relatively large compared to that of a newly developed compound called crown azophenol 5. The applications of this new compound are currently under study; however, based on its performance in aqueous solution (*Figure 20.5*), we can predict that it has a potential future in spectrophotometric serum lithium analysis.

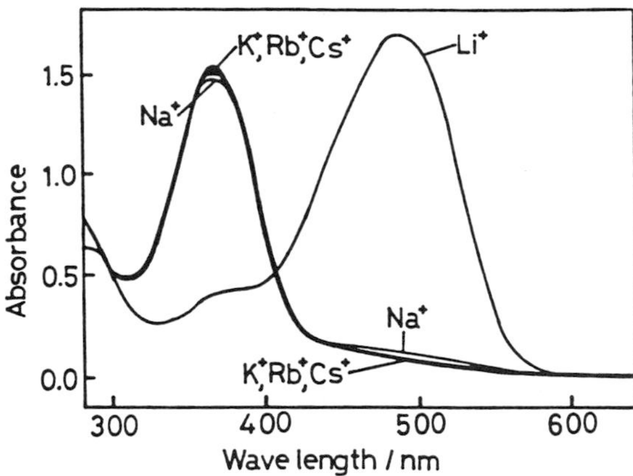

Figure 20.5 Spectra of alkali metal ions with crown azophenol *5*. [From Kimura, K. (1985) *Chemistry Lett.*, **1239**, reproduced with permission.]

Instrumentation

A spectrophotometer, which is composed of a white light source, a sample cell, a wavelength dispersion device and a detector, is a relatively inexpensive instrument. The beauty of this instrument is its simplicity. Some spectrophotometers are as small as less than half the size of this book. Because of this feature, the spectrophotometric method could be used in doctor's offices or even in patients' homes.

Application

The results of spectrophotometric serum lithium analysis are in good agreement with results obtained by AAS and FES. However, this method has not yet been routinely used in clinical laboratories. This is not surprising when we consider that these developments are relatively new and that some of the compounds are still not commercially available. Moreover, synthesis of these compounds is generally very complex, and research on serum lithium application is limited. Therefore, commercialization of the spectrophotometric serum lithium analysis method still needs a period of time. However, it is probable that spectrophotometry will be an important method in the future for serum lithium analysis.

Molecular Fluorescence Method

Molecular fluorometry has become an important method in clinical chemistry because of the associated parameters that can be exploited to achieve additional sensitivity and specificity. Samples of serum from lithium-treated patients which have been analysed by this method are very comparable with results of the other methods.

Theory

During the process of absorbing electromagnetic radiation (light), molecules are elevated to an excited electronic state. Most molecules will dissipate this excess energy as heat by collision with other molecules. With certain molecules, however, particularly when absorbing high energy radiation such as ultraviolet (u.v.) radiation (invisible light, wavelengths 200 − 380 nm), only part of the energy is lost via collisions, and the electrons return to the ground state, emitting radiation of lower energy than was absorbed. Because fluorescence occurs from the lowest excited state, the wavelengths of emitted radiation are independent of the wavelength of the excitation, and the fluorescence spectrum is a continuous band due to closely spaced energy levels in the molecules. The intensity of emitted radiation, however, is dependent on the excitation wavelength and proportional to the intensity of incident radiation. Therefore, in practice, a very stable excitation source, adjusted at optimum wavelength, is commonly applied.

Fluorescence intensity is directly proportional to the analyte concentration. The limit of detection is very low with a high intensity excitation source and a sensitive fluorescence detector.

Fluorometric serum lithium analysis

Similar to spectrophotometric serum lithium analysis, in fluorometry we need a reagent to react with lithium to form a lithium complex which, when excited, can fluoresce. Several such reagents have been synthesized and reported recently. Among them, only 1,8-dihydroxyanthraquinone was actually applied to serum lithium analysis, although some other reagents seemed to be superior to 1,8-dihydroxyanthraquinone in terms of specificity and sensitivity. Fluorometric serum lithium analysis generally suffers from a high emission background of serum protein. Consequently, it is necessary to remove sample proteins before analysis. This is carried out by adding acetone to the serum samples and then centrifuging, because the lithium complexes are formed in the organic solvent. The deproteinization step adds complexity in the analytical process and requires extra time and labour. The solution lies in automation. A flow-through dialysis system could be a perfect design for the automation, since the dialysis process can remove proteins and reduce the lithium concentration of the sample at the same time. These are exactly the sample preparation needs for fluorometric serum lithium analysis.

Instrumentation

For fluorescence measurements, it is necessary to separate the emitted radiation from the incident radiation. This is most easily done by measuring the fluorescence at right angles to the incident radiation (*Figure 20.6*). The fluorescence radiation is emitted in all directions, but the incident radiation passes straight through the sample solution. A spectrofluorometer is composed of a u.v. source, a wavelength dispersion device to select the wavelength of excitation from the source, a sample cell, a second wavelength dispersion device to select the wavelength of fluorescence, and a detector (*Figure 20.6*).

Application

The results of fluorometric serum lithium analysis are in good agreement with those of AAS and FES methods. However, additional work has to be done before it can be routinely used in clinical laboratories. Automation deserves priority in optimization of the method. Since fluorometry is a very sensitive method, it is probably suitable not only for serum lithium analysis, but also for analysis of even lower lithium concentration levels of other bio-organic fluids.

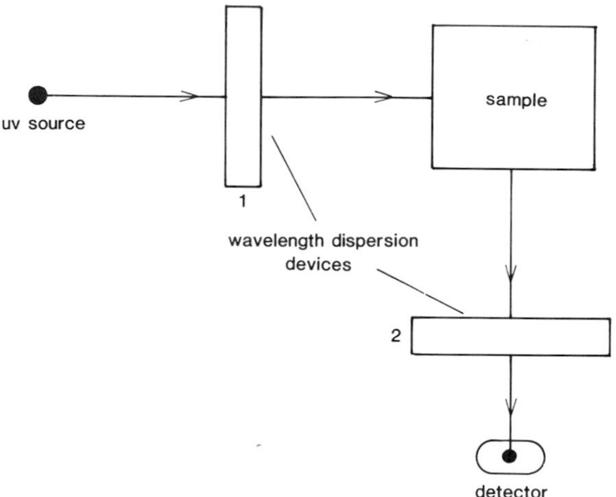

Figure 20.6 Simple design of a spectrofluorometer.

Lithium Ion-selective Electrode Method

Clinical analysers based on ion-selective electrodes are available for the potentiometric analysis of sodium, potassium, calcium and pH in blood serum. These instruments have the advantages of compactness, low sample volume consumption, short analysis time and minimal operational cost without the necessity of a flame, compressed gasses or other complicated instrumental requirements. It has been long desired to incorporate a lithium ion-selective electrode into these instruments. Until very recently, there has not been a satisfactory lithium ion-selective electrode available. Work has proceeded over a number of years to develop a lithium ion-selective electrode system for application to serum lithium analysis, and lately this work has been attended by success.

Theory

Relatively successful lithium ion-selective electrodes are liquid-membrane type electrodes. The liquid-membrane is a layer of polymer film in which a lithium complexing reagent similar to the reagent discussed in spectrophotometry is added. The membrane is either assembled on a glass tube with an internal salt solution electrical contact or directly cast on a conductive wire to form an ion-selective electrode. When an appropriate electrode membrane is in contact with an analyte solution, an electric field is built across the membrane. Consequently, the potential of the electric field changes with changes of the solution concentration. Thus, the quantity of the analyte can be measured *via* the membrane potential, which is proportional to the logarithm of the analyte concentration.

Ion-selective electrode serum lithium analysis method

The key of the lithium selectivity of the electrode is the complexation specificity of the reagent in the membrane. Much effort has been devoted to the design and synthesis of such a lithium complexing reagent. Recently, a major breakthrough has taken place in this area. The new reagent has greatly improved the electrode performance so that it can readily detect the clinical levels of lithium. This electrode has been constructed and incorporated in a semi-automatic analysis system (flow injection system). Both diluted serum samples and undiluted samples can be measured. When the undiluted sample is applied, a dialysis module is placed before the ion-selective electrode module. With this arrangement, electrodes avoid direct contact with serum samples. Consequently, it thoroughly solves the problems commonly associated with the clinical analysers such as protein interferences and electrode poisoning from degenerated serum samples. However, the trade-offs of this method are the relatively slow sampling speed and reduced lithium selectivity due to the dialysis process. On the other hand, diluted serum samples can be directly measured with the ion-selective electrode module. This method has the advantage of fast sampling speed and higher lithium selectivity, but the lifetime of the electrode probably is not as long as that in the dialysis system. In either case, lithium ion selective electrodes can accurately measure serum lithium samples and the results are in good agreement with those of the AAS method.

Instrumentation

Clinical analysers based on ion-selective electrodes vary from multi-element to single element capabilities. Besides the indicator electrode that senses the analyte ion, a second reference electrode, whose potential is constant, is needed to complete the electrochemical cell. This is usually a saturated calomel electrode (SCE) or a silver/silver chloride electrode, and all potentials are measured relative to this reference electrode. The basic measuring unit is a simple voltage meter which measures the potential difference between the two electrodes (*Figure 20.7*), but in the computer age most analysers are equipped with electronic microprocessors. The analysis process is reduced to pushing a few buttons. Thus, the users of the analyser do not need to be well trained technicians. Although the lithium analyser is still a bench model, it can be predicted that a commercial model will not be too different from currently used analysers.

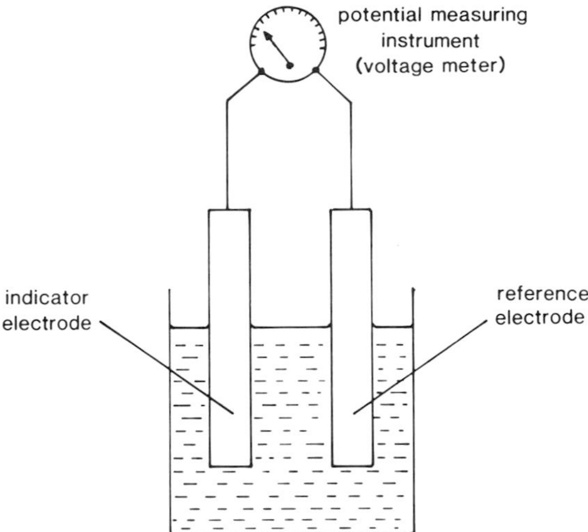

Figure 20.7 Potentiometric measurement set-up.

Application

The lithium analyser based on an ion-selective electrode is still in a developmental stage, but it is likely that a commercial lithium analyser based on an ion-selective electrode will soon be born and have a great impact on routine serum lithium analysis. Since this kind of analyser is inexpensive and simple to operate, it is likely that the analyser will not only be used in clinical laboratories, but also in doctors' offices and potentially even in patients' homes.

Summary

The above discussions include the most important methods and developments for serum lithium analysis. Some practical aspects of these methods are summarized in *Table 20.1*. Whilst there appears to be a future in the spectrophotometric and lithium ion-selective electrode methods for serum lithium analysis, other serum analysis methods are still important because any analytical chemistry method has its own unique advantages.

Bibliography

Blijenberg,B.G. and Leijinse,B. (1968) The determination of lithium in serum by atomic absorption spectroscopy and flame emission spectroscopy. *Clin. Chim. Acta,* **19**, 97–99.
One of the first articles to compare atomic absorption and flame emission techniques in lithium estimation, this paper is still well worth reading.

Barnes,R.M. (1978) Recent advances in emission spectroscopy: inductively coupled plasma discharges for spectrochemical analysis. *CRC Crit. Rev. Anal. Chem.*, **7**, 203–296.
A useful review of technical issues in emission spectroscopy.

Wheeling,K. and Christian,G.D. (1984) Spectrofluorometric determination of serum lithium using 1,8-dihydroxyanthraquinone. *Anal. Lett.*, **17**, 217–227.
An account of the application of molecular fluorometry to lithium estimation. It is necessarily written at a level which would be difficult for those without the appropriate background.

Xie,R.Y. and Christian,G.D. (1986) Serum lithium analysis by coated wire lithium ion selective electrodes in a flow injection analysis dialysis system. *Anal. Chem.*, **58**, 1806–1810.
Ion-selective electrode analysers of lithium may be of great practical use in the future. This article considers one system which incorporates such an analytical device.

21. The 12-hour Standardized Serum Lithium (12h-stSLi)

Amdi Amdisen

The term 'serum lithium (SLi) level' is still often confusedly used without specification, i.e. without consideration of the conditions under which the measurement was obtained and which crucially determine its value—for example, the time of blood drawing, the dose regimen, etc. This is often the case, not only in daily clinical work, but also under research conditions and even in experimental animal work. The concept 'SLi-level' when used in this way is ambiguous, and unless details of all relevant determining variables are given the serum level data are essentially incomprehensible.

It should be recognized that a patient, who has a half-life ($t_{1/2}$) of around 20 h in the elimination phase of SLi (normal interindividual distribution about 10–50 h; right skewed; mode close to 20 h; arithmetic mean around 24 h), even with three lithium doses per day may typically show variations of SLi during the 24-h day from 0.70 mmol/l to 1.60 mmol/l when conventional tablets and dose regimens are used (*Figure 21.1*). Consideration of data such as that presented in *Figure 21.1* suggested the possibility of obtaining approximate reproduciblity of SLi for any

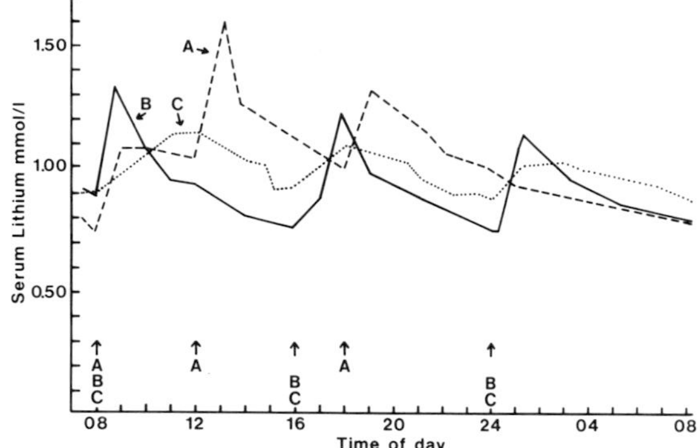

Figure 21.1 The 24-h concentration profile of Li^+ in serum of the same person ($t_{1/2}$ = 19.8 h) in steady-state with an equal dosage (36 mmol/day), but with three different dose regimens. **A**, standard release, twice daily; **B**, standard release, three times daily; **C**, sustained release, three times daily. Patients with differing $t_{1/2}$ would be placed on different mean levels and show different SLi-profiles. From Amdisen,A. and Sjögren,J. (1968) *Acta Pharm. Suecica,* **5**, 465–472.

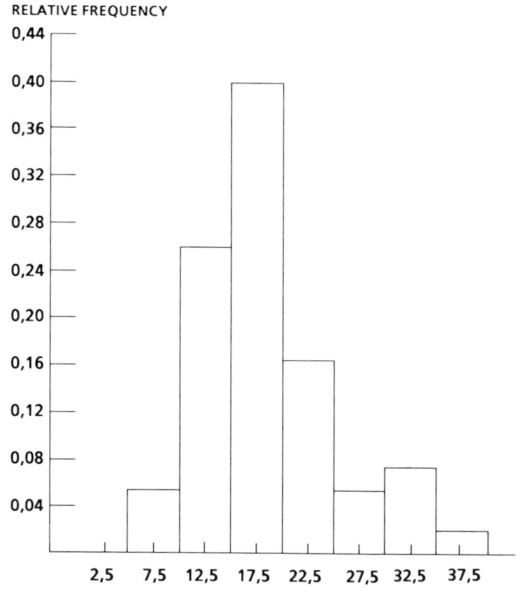

Figure 21.2 Inaccuracy (%) of the 12h-stSLi as a control instrument in daily clinical treatment monitoring. 57 long-term lithium patients provided 10–30 values each, to allow calculation of the individual coefficient of variation (CV). From Müller-Oerlinghausen,B. (1981) *Bibliotheca Psychiatr.*, **161**, 224–236, with permission.

individual, in blood samples drawn about 12 h after the evening dose.

Figure 21.1 also reveals the extent of the variation of the 24-h-day SLi, which may amount to about three times the so-called 'therapeutic interval' of 0.50–0.80 mmol/l, and if a single dose per day regimen were to be used the 24-h-day variation would be much larger. This 'therapeutic interval' of 0.50–0.80 mmol/l has recently been recommended instead of the 0.80–1.00 mmol/l range which was held to be desirable in the early stages of therapy and also instead of the range 0.35–1.25 mmol/l for the prophylactic maintenance level. However, the 0.50–0.80 mmol/l range is still an arbitrary choice reflecting the rather large lithium doses which were introduced in the early 1950s and does not take into account the question of interindividual variability. It is essentially based mainly on somewhat unreliable anecdotal data or retrospective and approximate estimates.

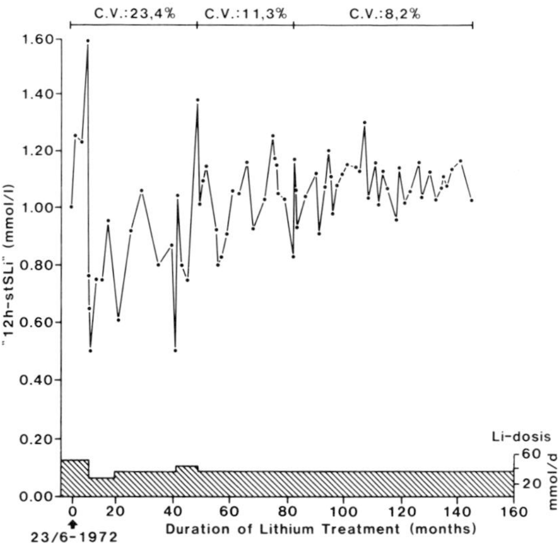

Figure 21.3 Inaccuracy (%) of the 12h-stSLi in a male patient with bipolar manic-depressive psychosis. The coefficient of variation (CV) was retrospectively calculated after dosage normalization to 36 mmol/day. Several severe and moderate relapses occurred during period I (CV 23.4%) with conventional lithium carbonate tablets and little information given to the patient. Before and during period II (CV 11.3%) that patient was given more thorough information and switched to slow controlled-release tablets and had milder, but still disturbing, relapses. Before and during period III (CV 8.2%) he received intensive and often repeated information and had no relapses. From Amdisen,A. (1985) *Lithium as a Pharmacological Agent.* Dissertation, University of Göteborg, 1985, with permission.

Individual Reproducibility

The 12-h standardized serum lithium (12h-stSLi) was conceived as a means of providing a clinical control measure for monitoring the individual patient under normal conditions, and of providing an index of serum level which would be reproducible from one determination to the next. The choice of a 12-h interval also took into consideration the practicalities of the everyday clinical situation.

The 12h-stSLi has detailed specifications: 12 h (± 1/2 h) elapse between the evening dose of lithium and blood-taking in the morning before the first lithium dose of the day; a multiple dose per day regimen is usually implied, but the concept can be intraindividually extended to a once-a-day regime; the patient is in a steady-state between lithium intake and elimination; a high-quality preparation of lithium has to be used (i.e. high bioavailability and consistency of formulation between batches); a laboratory analysis with a precision of better than 2% is obtainable and may therefore fairly be demanded of the laboratory; and the patient must comply strictly with the prescribed dose and the time of administration especially during the last few days before the assessment of the 12h-stSLi.

Provided that all these demands can be fulfilled, the 12h-stSLi represents an extremely valuable instrument in the supervision of the treatment status of the individual patient. However, if one or more of the demands are not fulfilled, the reproducibility of the 12h-stSLi is compromised. In practice this means that monitoring the variation in the value of the dose-normalized 12h-stSLi over a period of treatment may disclose partial non-compliance by the patient (see *Figures 21.2* and *21.3*). Especially, provided that it is possible to exclude changes in the pharmacokinetics of lithium in the individual for other reasons.

Reliability of the Intraindividual 12h-stSLi

Several single-patient examples showing the satisfactory individual reproducibility of the 12h-stSLi of selected patients mainly during clinical research have been published. On the other hand, a pronounced dominance of partial patient non-compliance is indicated in non-selected patients showing poorer reproducibility. A recent study of the 12h-stSLi values routinely obtained in a lithium clinic in West Berlin, involving well-informed lithium patients in long-term treatment, revealed in several patients a rather high frequency of inaccuracies (the coefficient of variation interindividually varying from 20 to 35%). In those patients, the 12h-stSLi was clearly a control instrument of limited, or no, practical use (*Figure 21.2*).

However, an improvement of the precision may be achieved by providing the patient with more thorough and detailed information, and by trying to ensure intensified cooperation by the patient with the drug administration schedule, especially concerning the 12-h time interval, time of day of blood drawing, and adherence to the time points of the dose regimen in the last few days before the blood taking (*Figure 21.3*). Some improvements in reliability may also be obtained by switching to a lithium preparation with more consistency from dose to dose.

Re-establishment of Patient Compliance

Figures 21.2 and *21.3* suggest that provided inaccuracies of laboratory analysis, variations in the lithium preparation, and exceptional individual changes of lithium pharmacokinetics, can all be excluded, an inaccuracy of 12h-stSLi greater than 10% between successive evaluations should warrant a discussion with the patient about non-compliance. This early warning of a problem with compliance may be a major factor in determining a successful therapeutic outcome (see also Section 31, pp. 117–121).

The 'Therapeutic Interval' Based on the 12h-stSLi

Beyond the limited goal of making the 12h-stSLi an instrument for long-term monitoring of lithium therapy in the individual patient, following dosage adjustment on the basis of clinical signs and symptoms, an attempt has been made to use the 12h-stSLi as a universally valid guide to treatment efficacy by stating a 'therapeutic interval' in terms of the 12h-stSLi value in lithium treated patients by showing how this value relates to clinical experience concerning both therapeutic effect and toxic reactions.

Before the recognition of the importance of serum pharmacokinetics a 'therapeutic interval' of 0.5–2.0 mmol/l was recommended based on experience with about 50 patients, among whom, however, was a severely intoxicated patient, who showed a serum lithium level as low as 0.6 mmol/l. After the introduction of a partly specified serum level (as the level in a blood sample drawn in the morning before the first lithium dose of the day) a therapeutic interval of 0.6–1.6 mmol/l was recommended. Following the introduction of the 12h-stSLi in about 1970, a therapeutic interval of 0.35–1.25 mmol/l was proposed, although an interval of around 0.80–1.00 mmol/l was recommended initially when commencing therapy. All these intervals were based solely on anecdotal data or retrospective and approximate estimates.

The most recent recommendation is a therapeutic interval on a somewhat lower level of 0.50–0.80 mmol, based upon evidence that lower serum levels lead to less impairment of the kidneys (pp. 206–213). This evidence related to a claimed close relationship between the 12h-stSLi and the rate delivery of fluid from the proximal tubules. It has, however, to be said that since the correlation coefficient, whilst statistically significant, is only of the order of about 0.20, care must be exercised in attaching too much clinical relevance to it; we may be in danger of having set up yet another quite arbitrary, and in several cases probably unreliable, therapeutic interval.

Interindividual Variability of the 12h-stSLi

Both the anti-manic and prophylactic effects of lithium show quite long latency periods between the start of medication and onset of the desired action of the agent. It therefore seems reasonable to assume that the achievement of an appropriate 'drug load' is decisive for the therapeutic effect. One representative index of drug load is the mean serum lithium concentration over the full 24-h day (MSLi), when equal daily doses are administered. It is important to note that MSLi and 12-stSLi are not identical, the principal difference between the two depending on the wide interindividual variations which occur in the half-life of lithium. Since the time course of serum lithium levels can be described by a pharmacokinetic two-compartment model (pp. 73–75), the trend of this relationship can be revealed by pharmacokinetic simulation. *Table 21.1* shows the daily doses and the values of the 12h-stSLi needed to give a modest MSLi of 0.75 mmol/l in the case of a fast-releasing conventional tablet in a one-dose per day regimen, and also in the case of a slow-release

Table 21.1 *The relationship between elimination half-life of serum lithium and the daily dose or 12h-stSLi*

Half-life (h)	Daily dose (mmol/75 kg)	12h-stSLi	
		1 dose/day (conventional release)	2 doses/day (sustained release)
10	82	0.51	0.43
15	50	0.62	0.53
20	36	0.66	0.59
30	23	0.70	0.64
50	13	0.72	0.68

Data from Amdisen,A. and Nielsen-Kudsk,F. (1986) *Pharmacopsychiatry*, **19**, 416–419.
Mean 24-h serum lithium, 0.75 mmol/l.

tablet in a twice-a-day regimen. The table indicates how the 12h-stSLi and the daily dose depends non-linearly on the half-life, a range of such values being chosen which corresponds approximately to the inter-individual biological range of 10–50 h. From this table it can immediately be seen that, in principle, each patient has his or her personal therapeutic interval for the 12h-stSLi, and that consequently an interindividual and universally valid therapeutic interval of clinical relevance cannot be specified.

It is furthermore noteworthy that a patient with a lithium dosage adjusted to give a 12h-stSLi averaging 0.50 mmol/l would have almost to double the dosage to reach a 12h-stSLi averaging 0/80 mmol/l (i.e. still within the modern therapeutic range). It is a common experience that doubling the lithium dosage of a patient can lead to incipient subacute renal toxicity. Even the currently accepted therapeutic interval of 0.50–0.80 mmol/l may not always be a safe guarantee of the avoidance of the vicious circle of lithium toxicity.

It is possible that certain patients (especially those with a long lithium half-life, and therefore with a need for proportionally lower dosage), would not get the full benefit of the lithium therapy because their 12h-stSLi level would be too low if the therapeutic interval of 0.50–0.80 mmol/l were to be too strictly adhered to.

Contrarily, it is worth observing that patients with a short lithium half-life are characterized by the need for a proportionally higher lithium dosage to reach a modest level of the 12h-stSLi. Such patients should, in principle, be kept on a comparatively low 12h-stSLi (and *vice versa* for patients with longer half lives). Recognition of this prevent the use of an individually and biologically incorrect mean 12h-stSLi as an index to guide the clinician in adjusting oral dosage.

Clinical Implications

The message which emerges from these considerations is that the serum lithium level, even when assessed as the strictly standardized 12h-stSLi, is not by itself necessarily a sufficient guide to the safety or otherwise of the treatment. Rational lithium therapy requires the recognition that individuals vary widely in their elimination rate of lithium and thereby in their lithium half-life characteristics, and that the elimination rate is a determinant of the 12h-stSLi level which would be most likely to produce a therapeutic effect with a minimum of problems.

Bibliography

Amdisen,A. and Carsson,S.W. (1986) Lithium. In *Applied Pharmacokinetics*. Evans,W.E., Schentag,J.J., Jusko,W.J. and Harrison,H. (eds), Applied Therapeutics, Inc., Spokane, WA, pp. 97B–1:B.
An account of the present status of applied clinical pharmacokinetics of the lithium ion.

Amdisen,A. and Nielsen-Kudsk,F. (1986) Relationship between standardized 12-h serum lithium, mean serum lithium of the 24-hour day, dose regimen and therapeutic interval: an evaluation based on pharmacokinetic simulations. *Pharmacopsychiatry*, **19**, 416–419.
An indication of the non-existence of a generally valid 'therapeutic interval' of any single time-specified serum lithium concentration and indirectly an indication of the inapplicability of the serum/plasma concentration of adjustment of any drug dosage when the individual biological terminal half-life of the active agent is below 30 h.

22. Estimation in Saliva and Tears

Hannah Ben-Aryeh

The drawing of blood samples in order to monitor serum lithium levels is experienced by many patients as physically uncomfortable and its necessity may lead in some cases to diminished compliance with medication. This, and the fact that lithium therapy, being a long-term treatment, will require many such blood samplings, justifies the consideration of alternative body fluids for dosage monitoring purposes.

Urine would, on the face of it, seem to be a likely candidate for such a role, but a variety of factors (such as unpredictable variations in urine concentration) essentially rule it out as a viable indicator of tissue lithium levels.

The two other body fluids which can be easily collected by non-invasive methods are saliva and tears.

Saliva

Saliva can be collected by the patients themselves; it can be done at home and the sample mailed for analysis so that the results can be available to the psychiatrist at the time of the patient's next visit. Many studies have been published in which saliva has been used to monitor various drugs and hormone levels; and excellent results have sometimes been obtained, e.g. with steroid hormones such as cortisol. Drugs such as diphenylhydantoin, theophylline and digoxin have been measured in saliva with varying results, and opinion is divided on the usefulness of saliva measurements in these cases.

To date, something in excess of 60 studies have been published in which the monitoring of lithium levels in saliva has been examined. It is not possible to make simple comparisons between such studies, however, since the subjects have sometimes been healthy volunteers and at other times patients; in addition, the length of treatment and time elapsing since the last medication have both varied widely. The mode of collection of saliva has also differed: some investigators have examined resting whole saliva; some have obtained saliva by mechanical or taste stimulation; still others have collected stimulated saliva from the parotid gland. All these factors influence the saliva lithium concentration value which is obtained, and could explain the differences in results between various laboratories.

Saliva and serum lithium levels

In order to keep to a minimum the variability stemming from sources such as those noted above, it is necessary to adhere to a standard procedure (as, indeed, is also the case with serum lithium measurements; see pp. 88–91).

A standard, reproducible procedure whereby the patient produces a sample of saliva by spitting, needs to be instituted 2 h after a meal and then only in patients who have been at least 3 months on lithium therapy. This last point is actually very important, since in the early stages of lithium therapy the saliva lithium concentration varies markedly and does not correlate with serum lithium concentration. Unstimulated whole saliva is preferable to stimulated saliva.

Provided that these precautions are observed, a significant correlation ($r = 0.87$) is found between saliva and serum lithium concentrations, the relationship by which the serum level can be calculated from that in saliva being:

$$\text{Li(serum)} = 0.36\ \text{Li(saliva)} + 0.13$$

The results of the study from which this relationship was derived are shown graphically in *Figure 22.1*. It can be seen that the saliva lithium concentration is higher than in serum, though the mechanism whereby lithium is transported into the saliva, is not yet fully understood.

The results of different studies on saliva lithium levels tend to be somewhat contradictory in certain details. In work carried out in the Rambam Medical Center, Haifa, Israel, it was found that psychotropic drugs did not influence the saliva lithium concentration. In a follow-up study a significant correlation between saliva and lithium levels in 13 out of 18 patients was found. Studies performed in other centres, however, have given different results, ranging from significant relationships in seven out of 23 patients, to varying relationships or none at all in three out of three patients.

The practical usefulness of saliva levels

Given the inter- and intra-subject variability in saliva lithium levels, the practical utility of such values in monitoring lithium therapy is questionable. It has, however, been suggested that it may be possible to make effective clinical use of such measurements if a saliva/serum ratio can first of all be established for each patient. This, of course, ignores the possibility of such a ratio varying with the clinical state of the patient, an issue about which there is so far no information.

Saliva levels may provide a useful monitoring index in children, in elderly patients, and in circumstances

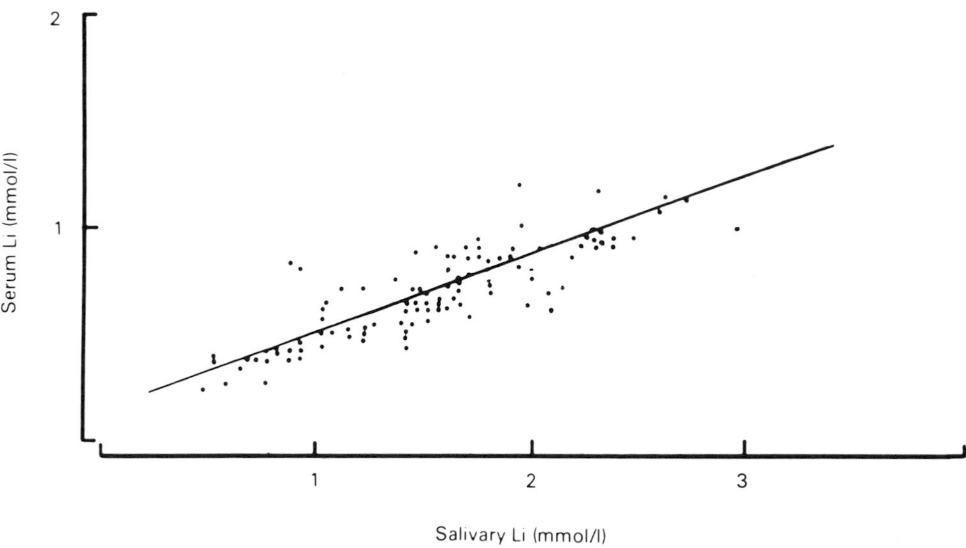

Figure 22.1 The correlation between serum and saliva levels in 118 manic-depressive patients treated wtih lithium over a period of at least 3 months. Redrawn from Ben-Aryeh,H., Naon,H., Szargel,R., Gutman,D. and Hefetz,A. (1980) *Oral Surg. Oral Med. Oral Pathol.*, **50**, 127–129.

which make the collection of blood samples difficult, though it seems unlikely that they will ever be used routinely where serum levels can be obtained. In view of the discrepancy between various laboratories further research is still needed.

Tears

The possibility of using tears as a biological fluid in which to assess levels of lithium, has recently sparked some controversy, with some research workers holding that this may be feasible, whilst others deny it.

In a study on healthy volunteers reported in 1982, it was stated that the tear/serum lithium ratio was very close to unity, and had this been confirmed in subsequent work it would have meant that tears would have been a viable alternative to serum as a fluid for tissue level monitoring. Such confirmation has not, however, been forthcoming: indeed, tear/serum ratios ranging from 0.70 to 0.88 have been found in different patients. There has been some discussion of the point in the recent literature, with some investigators maintaining that tears could well be useful in a minority of patients who cannot or will not tolerate blood sampling, but other investigators remain unpersuaded.

In work done at Haifa, information has been obtained on the effect of long-term lithium on the rate of tear secretion, showing that such rates were lowered. This may be an interfering factor in any attempt to use tears for lithium monitoring.

Bibliography

Ben-Aryeh,H., Naon,H., Horovitz,G., Szargel,R. and Gutman,D. (1984) Salivary and lacrimal secretions in patients on lithium therapy. *J. Psychiat. Res.*, **18**, 299–306.
A useful account of lithium effects on saliva and tears, presenting data on the correlation between salivary and serum lithium levels and a discussion of the usefulness of unstimulated saliva for lithium monitoring.

23. Other Fluids

F.Neil Johnson

In addition to serum, saliva and tears, a number of other body fluids contain measurable quantities of lithium and could, in principle at least, be used to assess tissue lithium levels. In practice the difficulties are such as to preclude such use.

Since by far the greater part of ingested lithium is excreted in the urine it might be thought that urine levels would give a useful indication of tissue levels, but in fact there are quite considerable 24-h variations in urinary output of lithium which do not relate to serum levels. In addition, urine contains various other substances which need to be removed or which require special precautions to be taken prior to assessing the lithium content, if serious interference with the lithium determination is to be avoided. Urine is, for these and several other reasons, never used in the routine monitoring of tissue levels of lithium.

Lithium is found in cerebro-spinal fluid, though in concentrations somewhat lower than in serum. The problems of obtaining cerebro-spinal fluid samples preclude the use of this fluid for monitoring purposes.

In males, lithium appears in ejaculate in concentrations greater than in serum – about twice the serum level, in fact. It goes without saying that the use of ejaculate levels for monitoring purposes is virtually inconceivable.

Glandular secretion of lithium tends to produce fluid concentrations greater than those occurring in serum. This is particularly true of parotid salivary secretion (Section 22, pp. 91–93) and also of secretion in sweat in which the concentration can be up to four or five times that of the serum concentration. Sweat has not been used for monitoring serum levels and there is no reason to presume that it could ever really be used for such purposes. The diurnal variation, if any, of sweat levels has not been investigated.

Breast milk in nursing mothers contains lithium if the mother is receiving lithium treatment, and this, indeed, is the reason why breast-feeding is almost always contraindicated. It would not be appropriate to consider breast milk as a fluid for monitoring general tissue levels of lithum.

Faecal material often contains lithium, but could not be used for tissue level monitoring since the source of the expelled lithium is two-fold. A small proportion comes from transfer from serum into the gut. By far the greater proportion, however, represents the unabsorbed residuum of ingested tablets and is greatest in preparations of low bioavailability characteristics; this source of lithium owes nothing to general tissue levels.

One has to conclude that, with the possible exception of saliva, and the even more dubious exception of tears, serum represents the only really viable fluid for tissue lithium level monitoring.

Bibliography

Jefferson,J.W. (1984) Lithium monitoring. In *Handbook of Diagnostic Procedures*. Hall,R.C.W. and Beresford,T.P. (eds), Spectrum Publications, New York, pp. 161–181.
A clearly written and authoritative account of the various aspects of tissue level monitoring using different body fluids.

24. Lithium Preparations

Roderick Shelley and
Trevor Silverstone

When choosing a lithium preparation for clinical use in a given patient it is necessary to have a thorough knowledge of its pharmacokinetics. This is because, unlike other psychotropic drugs, lithium has a narrow therapeutic range, extending from serum levels of 0.4 mmol/l, the minimum required for clinical efficacy, to 1.5 mmol/l, above which acute toxic side effects may begin to be evident. Furthermore, if blood levels are sampled 12 h after lithium ingestion (see pp. 88–91) serum values obtained towards the upper normal range at this time may, with some formulations, have been preceded by levels above 1.5 mmol/l. The characteristic serum profile resulting from a single lithium administration, as shown in *Figure 24.1* can be modified by slowing the rate of lithium release from orally administered preparations.

The rate of absorption for any lithium formulation will govern the steepness and the magnitude of the

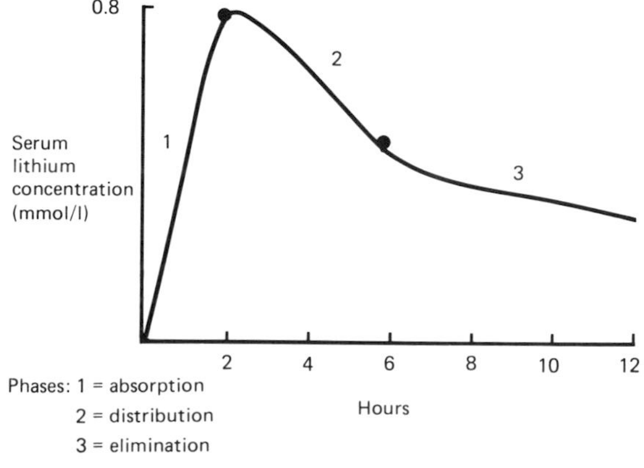

Figure 24.1 The three phases of the lithium serum profile.

serum peak, both of which parameters may influence the nature and severity of certain side effects. If absorption rate is too rapid, then changing to a slow-release formulation may produce a suitable adjustment of the rate. As the absorption rate declines the serum profile becomes flattened, leading to a serum plateau, rather than a peak followed by a trough. The elimination phase of the decay curve is thereby altered, causing an increase in the half-life of the preparation. This reduces the dosage frequency and improves compliance. Furthermore, the chances of survival after an overdose are increased since there is more time to wash out stomach contents before peak serum levels are reached. Slow release may, however, lead to lithium accumulation, especially in those with compromised renal clearance, as a longer half-life means that more of the drug is present in the body when the next dose is ingested.

The relationship between rate of lithium release and side-effects has been studied. There is a general tendency for gastrointestinal side effects such as nausea to be associated with rapid absorption, whereas diarrhoea and loose bowel motions appear associated with slower rates of absorption. Tremor, and other central nervous system complications, are more likely with faster rates of release (and hence absorption) which produce steep serum gradients and higher serum levels. The implications of altered rates of lithium absorption for renal function is more controversial; this is dealt with in detail elsewhere in this book (see Section 26, pp. 99–105). Over many years it has been assumed that reducing peak serum levels would protect against long-term renal side-effects. Recent investigations suggest that, on the other hand, the serum trough succeeding the peak may be important in a way not previously considered: such a trough is most likely to occur when a standard lithium preparation is administered once daily. It may allow renal tubular cells which have been damaged by high levels of lithium to regenerate; this may not be possible with the more constant serum levels associated with slow-release preparations.

In a recent study, however, in which a single dose high-peak/low-trough regimen was compared to a twice daily steady-state regimen over a 1-year period, no difference in renal function was found between the two regimes. Clearly this issue is one which needs further investigations.

Types of Lithium Formulations

'Standard' lithium preparations are those which conform to the British Pharmacopoeia criteria. Whilst they are not intended to have altered release characteristics, not all BP formulations will necessarily have the same bioavailability, because the criteria permit some latitude. The *in vitro* tests used to assess the rate of release do not allow for all the factors likely to influence bioavailability *in vivo*. Furthermore, a 10–11% difference in bioavailability characteristics between batches of the same preparation has been demonstrated.

In order to modify the rate of release, a number of different lithium formulations have been devised. The terms used to describe these have included 'slow-release', 'delayed-release', 'controlled release', or 'sustained release'. What is meant by these terms is not usually defined. In general it could be said that 'slow-release' means that the rate of release is slower than for standard BP formulations, resulting in a more gradual slope with a postponed and smaller serum peak. 'Delayed-release' means that the onset of release is postponed but that thereafter the serum profile is similar to a standard BP formulation. 'Controlled release' means that an attempt has been made to formulate the preparation so as to deliver lithium in a preplanned way with particular reference to the slope of the serum increase and the size and timing of the peak value. 'Sustained release' means that the rate of release is very slow but constant, resulting in a plateau-like serum curve.

The lithium formulations currently available in the British Isles include Priadel®, Camcolit®, Liskonum®, Phasal® and Litarex®. They all contain lithium carbonate, with the exception of Litarex which contains lithium citrate (see *Table 24.1*).

Table 24.1. *Lithium preparations available in the British Isles*

Name of preparation	Salt	Lithium content	
		mg	mmol
Camcolit-250	Carbonate	250	6.8
Camcolit-400	Carbonate	400	10.8
Priadel	Carbonate	400	10.8
Priadel-200	Carbonate	200	5.4
Liskonum	Carbonate	450	12.2
Phasal	Carbonate	300	8.1
Litarex	Citrate	564	6.0

Of these, Priadel has been the most studied. An initial clinical investigation indicated that it had slow-release characteristics, though subsequent comparison with the standard BP formulation, Camcolit, resulted in some conflicting findings. Dr S.Tyrer reported in 1976 that he had found Priadel to be equivalent to Camcolit, a finding which was supported by Dr Roy Hullin a year later. However, other investigators and even Tyrer himself in a later study, have reported differences between Priadel and Camcolit, showing Priadel as having slow-release characteristics. Similar properties have also been observed when Priadel was compared with other standard formulations.

The rate of release of Phasal appears to be slower than that of Priadel, but the serum levels achieved with Phasal are less reliable. In some subjects the drug liberation is too slow, resulting in incomplete absorption and excessive faecal excretion of lithium from Phasal compared with Priadel or Camcolit.

Litarex showed the slowest rate of absorption when compared to Priadel and Camcolit; this was characterized by a flatter serum curve and less lithium excreted in the urine. The serum levels obtained also appear consistent with this preparation.

There is apparently only one published report on the pharmacokinetic profile of Liskonum. This was produced by Drs Mengech and Ojwang in 1984, and suggests that this product may have slow-release characteristics, but because no other reference preparation was included in the study this remains unproven. Furthermore, the small dose used (450 mg) makes comparison with other formulations difficult.

Methodological Issues

Some methodological criticisms can be levelled at the studies which have been carried out in order to compare lithium formulations.

The design has, for example, often been such that not all subjects were given all preparations. Where two preparations were compared four reported studies did use a cross-over design, but when more preparations were investigated only one study has used a balanced cross-over design.

The usual schedule of blood sampling has been 1–2 hourly which means that pharmacokinetic values such as the maximum serum concentration, or the time taken to reach maximum serum concentration, may not be pinpointed accurately.

The populations studied were often mixed, including both patients and normal volunteers. Where patients only were involved, not all were suffering from affective disorders; with mood disorder patients only, three reports have stated the nature of the affective state of the patients, and in only one of these were the patients all at the same mood level. Until such time as the issues regarding the effect of mood or diagnosis on lithium pharmacokinetics are resolved it is important to recognize, when designing such studies, that these influences may be important.

Similarly, cognisance has not been taken of the effects of age, food, weight and concomitant medication on lithium bioavailability, distribution and excretion.

The number of subjects in many studies have been inadequate for appropriate statistical analysis; in only three studies did the number equal or exceed ten, and not all of these studies were of a balanced cross-over design.

Serum data have often not been complemented by assessment of urinary excretion, and only one study made reference to whether or not all the tablets came from the same production batch (and in that case the tablets came from two batches).

A Recent Study

In order to resolve some of these questions a study has recently been completed which was designed to compare the single-dose pharmacokinetics of Priadel, Camcolit-400, Liskonum and Litarex. This work was carried out at the Academic Unit of Human Psychopharmacology, based at the German Hospital, London, UK, and was reported in 1986.

Twelve normal male volunteer subjects (mean age 32 years), none of whom was taking any other medication, participated in the trial. They were assigned in random order to take each of the four preparations in turn according to a balanced cross-over design under single blind conditions. For each preparation the tablets were taken from the same production batch.

The subjects having fasted overnight, a dose of 27.0 mmol (30.5 mmol in the case of Liskonum) of lithium was administered orally to each with 200 ml of cold water. A standard breakfast was allowed 30 min later.

Blood for lithium estimation by flame photometry was sampled before lithium administration, half-hourly for 8 h after administration, hourly for the following 4 h, and then a further sample was taken by venipuncture 24 h after administration. Urine was collected prior to administration and on each subsequent mic-

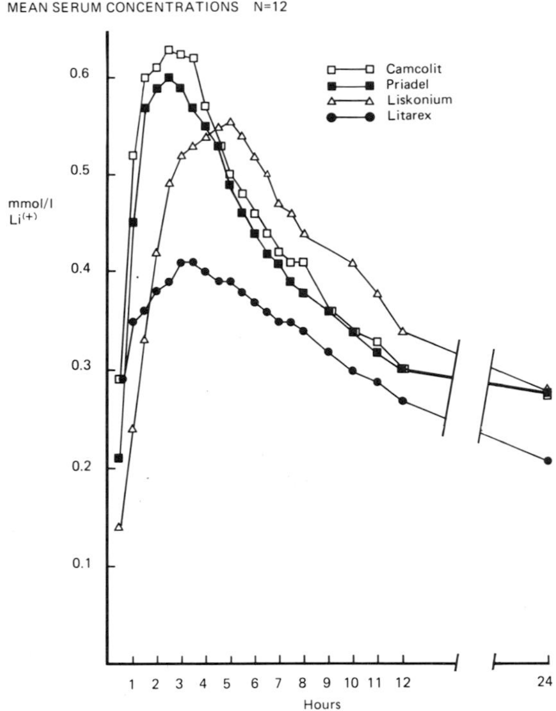

Figure 24.2 Mean serum concentrations of 12 volunteer male subjects given a single dose of four available lithium preparations; each subject was tested once on each preparation. % lithium recovered in the urine fell and the elimination half-life value rose, in the order: Camcolit, Priadel, Liskonium, Litarex.

turition during the study day. The volume of urine voided was recorded and an aliquot removed for lithium estimation. From these measurements were estimated the mean serum concentrations, areas under the 24-h serum curve, and elimination half-lives.

The relevant results are contained in *Figure 24.2*, and confirm that it is possible to formulate lithium preparations which demonstrate slow-release characteristics. The resulting reduced rate of absorption was shown by smaller, postponed serum peaks and longer half-lives. The areas under the serum curves and the percentages recovered in the urine were, however, reduced, suggesting that slow release was achieved at the expense of bioavailability.

If a clinician requires a lithium preparation which avoids a high serum peak, then Litarex would appear to be the most appropriate. Its rate of absorption is consistent, and with a half-life of 22 h it need only be administered once daily (this is contrary to what has been previously recommended).

The differences between Priadel and Camcolit-400 were not significant. In view of the fact that Priadel has been shown to be slow-release when compared with other standard formulations, it is possible that Camcolit-400 may also be slow-release. This is supported by the unpublished *in vitro* finding that the dissolution rate of Camcolit-400 is slower than that of Camcolit-250. Both Priadel and Camcolit-400 are rapidly absorbed and provide reliable serum levels. The 24-h serum profile is that of a peak followed by a trough. These preparations are worth considering particularly where the clinical judgement is that the serum trough is indicated in order to protect against renal side-effects.

Liskonum lies between these two preparations and Litarex. It has genuine slow-release properties yet is not sustained-release. Similar to the other three, it reliably produces consistent serum levels. The slightly higher dose administered needs to be allowed for when interpreting the data further.

Clinical Implications

Whilst there is now a reasonable body of pharmacokinetic evidence concerning the lithium preparations available within the British Isles, the transfer of this kind of information to the clinical situation must be done with circumspection.

In the first place, studies carried out on volunteers may not necessarily be applicable to patients with affective disorders. Secondly, lithium pharmacokinetics may alter with changes in mood. Thirdly, the pharmacokinetic profile is only one factor which has to be taken into account in choosing an appropriate lithium formulation: this is highlighted by recent work on *in vitro* dissolution rates, using improved testing techniques, which indicates that there may be substantial variations in dissolution according to gastric pH (of the British products, Priadel in its 200 and 400 mg form appears to be least affected by this variable). In addition, where a product exists in two dosage sizes (e.g., Camcolit 400 and Camcolit 250, and Priadel 400 and Priadel 200) it is important that the pharmacokinetic profile and other properties of the one form are matched by those of the other form. This is certainly true for Priadel, according to recent *in vitro* evidence, whereas Camcolit 400 may differ in its release characteristics from Camcolit 250. This is an important factor to be borne in mind when changing dosage regimes.

The choice of the most appropriate lithium formulation depends upon the solution of a complex clinical equation, in which the most important factors are pharmacokinetic profile, bioavailability, stability of lithium release under conditions of varying gastric pH, interchangeability of different dosage forms, and a multitude of patient characteristics.

Bibliography

Amdisen,A. (1975) Sustained release preparations of lithium. In *Lithium Research and Therapy*. Johnson,F.N. (ed.), Academic Press, London, pp. 197–210.
This early account of the principles underlying sustained release lithium preparations still has much to offer. It contains useful accounts of pharmacokinetics and acute overdosage in relation to sustained release.

Johnson,F.N. (1980) The choice of an appropriate lithium preparation. In *The Handbook of Lithium Therapy*. Johnson,F.N. (ed.), MTP Press, Lancaster, UK, pp. 225–236.
Issues dealt with include side effects and intoxication, bioavailability, variations in serum levels and a number of metholodogical issues.

25. Gastrointestinal Absorption

Stephen Partridge

The small intestine is the main site of lithium absorption. The uptake of lithium from the stomach and the large intestine may be regarded as negligible in the normal state.

The wall of the small intestine is essentially composed of three layers, the absorptive cell layer (epithelium), the sub mucosa and the muscle layers. The absorptive epithelium is a single layer of cells. These cells are mainly columnar absorptive cells although other types are present. The luminal membrane of the absorptive cell is specialized for absorption, and is called the brush border membrane (see *Figure 25.1*). The surface of the brush border membrane is covered in a layer of glycoprotein, called the glycocalyx, which serves as a support for the mucus layer protecting the intestinal surface and provides a beneficial environment for the enzymes involved in food digestion at the intestinal surface. The epithelial cells are joined together at the brush border. These junctions are called zonulae occludens or tight junctions (see *Figure 25.1*). The tight junctions are in fact small absorptive pores and together with the spaces between the absorptive cells (lateral intercellular spaces) form the main absorptive pathway for water and electrolytes in the small intestine.

The sub mucosa contains nervous and connective tissue and also the intestinal blood supply responsible for the removal of absorbed substances into the body.

Transport Routes

There are two possible mechanisms of lithium absorption, each involving a different route, the transcellular and paracellular routes (see *Figure 25.1*).

Transcellular transport

This route of absorption involves the movement of lithium into the absorptive cells via the sodium channels in the brush border membrane or by its being

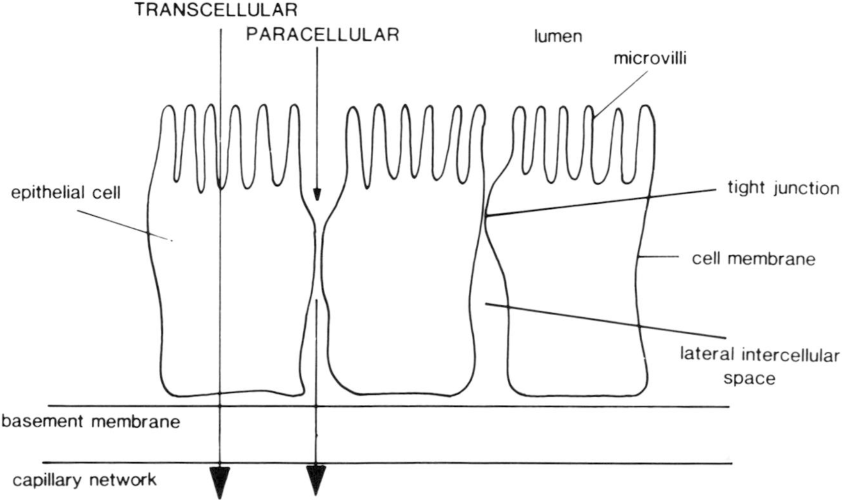

Figure 25.1 Possible transport routes for lithium across the intestinal epithelium.

taken up into the cell by either the sugar or amino acid cotransport system in which lithium replaces sodium. In both of these forms of transcellular transport, lithium replaces sodium as the transported ion. Once inside the absorptive cell lithium is then pumped out of the cell across the basolateral membrane by the sodium pump.

Paracellular transport

The paracellular transport route for lithium is anatomically composed of the tight junctions and lateral intercellular spaces (see *Figure 25.1*). When absorbed by this route, lithium simply diffuses across the tight junctions and lateral intercellular spaces. This mode of absorption is passive (i.e. no carrier protein is involved).

Lithium Absorption in Man

The relative contributions of the paracellular and transcellular transport pathways have been determined using both animal and human absorption kinetics. The data indicate that whilst the primary absorptive mechanism is by a simple diffusion of lithium into the body by a paracellular route, it is likely that some lithium is absorbed by the transcellular route. The amount of lithium absorbed will be determined by the amount of lithium present in the intestinal lumen.

Bibliography

Diamond,J.M., Ehrlich,B.E., Morawski,S.G., Santa Ana,C.A. and Fordtran,J.S. (1983) Lithium absorption in tight and leaky segments of intestine. *J. Membr. Biol.*, **72**, 159–183,

A useful survey of the primary transport routes of lithium in the intestine.

Ehrlich,B.E. and Diamond,J.M. (1980) Lithium membranes and manic depressive illness. *J. Membr. Biol.*, **52**, 187–200.

An excellent review of lithium transport.

26. The Dosage Regimen

M.T.Abou-Saleh

Whilst the introduction of lithium salts for the management of affective disorders has provided one of the most rewarding therapeutic advances in psychiatric practice, lithium's wanted effects have to be set against its unwanted effects and a crucial notion is the optimal dosage/serum level for achieving maximal clinical and minimal unwanted effects. This concept has recently become the concern of health professionals and patients in view of the finding that lower dosages/serum levels of lithium are as effective as the previously recommended rather higher ones, and of the emergence of the controversy over the least hazardous dosage regime, particularly in relation to kidney function.

Dosage/Serum Level and Clinical Response

The adequacy of a particular lithium dosage for the individual patient is best determined by the serum level achieved by the daily dosage. The dosage level *per se* is, however, also important as it relates to serum level achieved: they are closely linked and changes of level are determined by the size of the individual dose administered and the timing of subsequent doses, as explained in more detail earlier (pp. 67–73).

The widely accepted therapeutic range of serum lithium levels of 0.8–1.2 mmol/l 12 h after the last dose, has been empirically determined from the earlier studies of its use in the treatment of mania. Put in its historical context, the question has been more one of deciding what was the non-toxic dosage or range of serum levels than of establishing a therapeutic range, in view of the narrow therapeutic–toxic margin: whilst there is disagreement as to what is the minimum effective 12 h serum level there is full agreement on the minimum serum toxic level (1.5 mmol/l).

Since lithium is mainly used in the prophylaxis of recurrent affective disorders it is in this context that studies of the relationship between dosage/serum level and clinical response have been undertaken. The first study, carried out in the USA and reported in 1972, was by Robert Prien. In that investigation, 32 patients were classified as either treatment failures or successes on the basis of the presence or the absence of an attack of illness during the 2 years of the trial. It was found that treatment successes had received higher doses and had higher serum lithium levels than treatment failures. 53% of the patients receiving daily doses of 1000 mg or less were failures compared with only 20% of the patients receiving doses exceeding 1000 mg. Fifty-five percent of patients with levels of 0.7 mmol/l or less were failures compared with only 14% of patients with higher levels, and there was no difference in treatment outcome between patients with levels of 0.8–1.0 mmol/l and those with levels exceeding 1.00 mmol/l.

The failure rate for 13 patients who had received the placebo in the study was 69%.

The findings of this study concurred with the views of Professor Mogens Schou of Aarhus University, Denmark, who had contended that levels below 0.8 mmol/l are often ineffective. The study was, however, a retrospective one, and was not specifically designed to address the question of dosage and serum level in relation to clinical response. Moreover, the patients included in the study were a relatively high risk group: 60% of the patients had been hospitalized two or more times in the previous 5 years.

The next important study was directed by Dr Roy Hullin, Director of the Regional Metabolic Research Unit at High Royds Hospital in West Yorkshire, UK, and was first reported in 1978 by Drs T.C.Jerram and R.McDonald. These workers carried out an open prospective study over 1 year in which they investigated the efficacy (relapse rates) in groups of bipolar and unipolar patients maintained at three different lithium levels: below 0.49, between 0.5 and 0.69, and above 0.7 mmol/l. Relapse rates of these groups were 18%, 13% and 20%, respectively. To determine the minimum effective levels, they carried out a further study over 1 year and allocated patients to one of three groups with ranges of 0.25–0.39, 0.4–0.59, and 0.6–1.0 mmol/l. Relapse rates for the latter three groups were 62%, 15% and 18% respectively, a marked increase in the group maintained at levels between 0.25 and 0.39 mmol/l, indicating that a lithium level of 0.4 mmol/l is probably the minimum effective level. The study had the advantage of being a prospective study that included a representative sample of the population of patients attending a lithium clinic. Its disadvantages, however, were three-fold. Firstly it was an open and a not a double blind study and thus subject, in principle, to the unintentional bias of the clinicians involved. Secondly, in the evaluation of outcome the investigators had not considered the subclinical morbidity experienced by patients in the form of lithium modified episodes (episodes that have been modified in their severity and/or duration) during the trial period. Thirdly, 70% of the patients included in the study had a bipolar illness and its findings therefore may not apply to the unipolar group of patients.

There followed a series of reports of retrospective studies from the USA and the UK. Drs Democritis Sarantidis and Brent Waters from the University of Ottawa in Canada reported in 1981 their findings in a retrospective study in which they observed a group of bipolar and schizo-affective patients over a period of 12 months. They found that patients maintained at serum levels below 0.7 mmol/l had suffered less illness than they had experienced prior to starting lithium, and that lithium levels were highest in the patients in the non-responder group who had suffered the same or greater illness on lithium than before it had been started.

Dr Paolo Decina and Professor Ronald Fieve from the New York State Psychiatric Institute, USA, reported in 1981 their review of the follow-up charts of 14 unipolar patients on prophylactic lithium: they found that seven patients who had responded well had significantly lower serum lithium levels (mean 0.59 mmol/l) than the seven patients who failed to respond (mean 0.99 mmol/l). The following year, Dr S.P.Sashidharan and colleagues from the Royal Edinburgh Hospital, UK, reported their observations on 53 bipolar and unipolar patients studied retrospectively over 4 years. They found that responders spent significantly more time at lithium levels below 0.9 mmol/l than did non-responders.

The latter three retrospective studies clearly indicate an unexpected, if not paradoxical, association between poor clinical response and higher lithium levels. This may be related to the recognition by the treating physicians of high-risk patients and the prescription of high lithium doses in an attempt to prevent relapses.

The first double-blind study was reported by Dr Waters in 1982 in which he and his colleagues studied the relapse rates of bipolar patients who were randomly assigned to lower levels (0.3–0.8 mmol/l) and higher levels (0.8–1.4 mmol/l) of lithium. Patients in each group were followed up for 6 months before being switched over to the other group for another 6 months. They found that significantly more of the relapses (83%) occurred during the low level phase (mean 0.51 mmol/l), with only 17% occurring during the high level phase (mean 0.99 mmol/l) of the trial.

The second double-blind study was reported by Dr Alec Coppen, Director of the Medical Research Council Neuropsychiatry Research Laboratory in Epsom, UK, in 1983. The study assessed changes in morbidity and side effects in 72 patients with recurrent affective disorders under double-blind conditions over a period of 1 year. The patients had been previously maintained on lithium dosages to give 12-h serum lithium levels of 0.8–1.2 mmol/l. The patients were randomly allocated either to remain on their previous dosage or to receive a 25% or 50% reduction in dose. Different amounts of lithium carbonate (controlled release preparation: Priadel®; Delandale Laboratories, Canterbury, UK) were packed into identical looking capsules to maintain the double-blind nature of the trial. The research co-ordinator (who was not involved in the clinical assessment of patients) monitored the plasma levels of lithium and ensured that no patient had a 12-h serum lithium level of less than 0.45 mmol/l. Morbidity was assessed by a composite index which included measures of severity and duration of symptoms. For each group, changes in morbidity were determined for the year of the trial in comparison with morbidity in the year preceding the trial. The patients were classified in terms of their serum levels during the trial and divided into groups with the following ranges: 0.45–0.59 mmol/l, 0.6–0.79 mmol/l and 0.80 mmol/l and above. It was found that patients who were maintained at lower serum levels below 0.79 mmol/l had significant reduction in their morbidity (34%) whilst those who remained at levels of 0.8 mmol/l and above had a slight increase in morbidity. Similar results were found for both the unipolar and bipolar patients except that, in the former group, those with the less severe illnesses (i.e. those with depressions which were understandable in terms of personality, early life experiences and social circumstances) had a more substantial reduction in their morbidity (58%), whilst those with more severe illnesses of the biological type had a smaller reduction in morbidity (28%). These changes in morbidity were not related to changes in unwanted effects experienced by the patients or to the prescription of extra medication including major tranquilizers for those who had manic symptoms and antidepressants for those who suffered from depression. Whilst this study had the several advantages of the double-blind design, the use of a representative sample of lithium clinic patients, and the employment of what was probably a more valid measure of morbidity over time, it had the disadvantages of including patients who were not maintained solely on lithium and of its results being analysed in terms of the serum lithium level rather than dosage status. Its findings, however, were provocative: lower serum levels had been shown to be more effective than levels within the previously recommended therapeutic range. Moreover, there appeared to be a relationship between the type of depression and optimal dosage/serum levels of lithium.

In conclusion, and from the evidence marshalled above, it appears that dosages and serum levels previously recommended (0.8 mmol/l and above) may well be too high for satisfactory prophylaxis, the minimum effective serum level being around 0.4 mmol/l 12 h after the last dose. This notion has significant implications for the use of lithium therapy and its unwanted effects, particularly for elderly patients.

Optimum Dosage/Serum Level and Unwanted Effects

There have been fewer studies of the relationship between lithium dosage/serum levels and unwanted effects. It is, however, not unreasonable to suppose that lower dosages/serum levels are likely to be associated with fewer unwanted effects: certainly, peak levels of lithium have been shown to be associated with nausea and tremor. A distinction, however, ought to be made between unwanted effects experienced by patients (i.e. complaints of side effects) and those assessed more objectively (including physiological measures). Lithium's specific unwanted effects, including excessive thirst, excessive urination, trembling hands, poor memory and weight gain are also commonly complained of by patients with anxiety and/or depressive symptoms on no medication. These observations prompted a study of the relationship of these subjective side effects to illness and personality factors. The prevalence and magnitude of subjective side effects were compared between depressive patients on no medication, lithium treated patients, and a large group of normal subjects. It was found that depressed patients who were drug-free complained more of these subjective side effects than the other two groups. Moreover, the frequency of the side effects in the lithium treated group of patients was strongly related to their personality characteristics such as neuroticism (proneness to anxiety), lack of confidence and drive. These side effects, however, were not related to their lithium dosage or serum levels.

Lithium's specific subjective side effects have also been studied in the context of a trial of lithium as a continuation treatment over 1 year, in comparison with placebo, in patients who had recovered as a result of electroconvulsive therapy. It was noted that patients who had received placebo showed more depressive symptoms and more side effects than those who had received lithium. It is therefore important to consider the contribution of the illness *per se* and of personality characteristics to the experience of side effects before they are solely attributed to lithium or any other psychotropic medication. None of the studies reviewed earlier on the relationship between dosage/serum level and clinical response had specifically studied side effects except for the study by Dr Coppen in which it was shown that patients who were maintained on serum levels between 0.45 and 0.79 mmol/l following a 25–50% reduction of dosage experienced fewer side effects, most notably in their complaints of tremor. In the placebo-controlled one-year study, measurements were also made of the patients' plasma thyrotropin (TSH) levels and their 24-h urinary volumes before and after starting the trial. It was found that patients who were maintained on lower serum levels during the trial had significant reductions in both measures during the trial, indicating a reduction in adverse effects on thyroid and renal functions. Dr Hullin, in his studies, had also assessed renal and thyroid functions, looking at glomerular and tubular function (creatinine clearance and urine osmolality after water deprivation, respectively) in patients attending his lithium clinic in comparison with an age- and sex-matched group of psychiatric patients taking other psychotropic drugs. He found no differences between these two groups in either of these renal functions, a finding which is not in harmony with the results of many other investigations of renal function in relation to lithium therapy (pp. 206–213). He has explained this discrepancy by his method of lithium management: in his studies lithium was administered in divided daily dosages to produce serum levels which are lower (0.4–0.6 mmol/l) than those generally used elsewhere. In this context he also noted his finding of a relatively lower rate of hypothyroidism as determined by TSH levels: he has found that only 10% of his patients are biochemically hypothyroid in comparison with rates reported by other investigators (20–30%).

In summary it can be confidently stated that lower dosages/serum levels of lithium are not only clinically effective, but are also associated with fewer unwanted effects, including ones of a subjective nature and, more importantly, fewer adverse effects on thyroid and renal functions.

The Dosage Regimen

Lithium, like most other psychotropic drugs, has tended to be routinely prescribed in a divided daily dosage regime of two to three doses per day. This regime has been advocated to avoid peak serum and tissue concentrations assumed to be conducive to greater adverse effects, and to provide a reasonably uniform, if not constant, concentration assumed to be necessary for a favourable clinical response. Slow or sustained-release preparations were introduced with the specific aim of meeting these two conditions. However, neither of the two assumptions has been backed by experimental evidence and the routine practice of dividing the daily dose has recently given way to more informed prescribing habits for lithium and other psychotropic medication.

It has been shown that lithium has a long elimination half-life (12–24 h) (pp. 88–91) indicating that it need not be prescribed in more than one single dose per day. A few clinicians adopted this single daily dosage regimen from an early stage in the belief that it would encourage better compliance, an important and often overlooked aspect of treatment, particularly in chronic and relapsing conditions like affective disorders (see pp. 117–121). Dr Coppen, for example, adopted this dosage regimen from the late 1960s, using a sustained release preparation (Priadel®), whereas Dr Hullin has adhered to a divided dosage regimen using a conventional preparation. In Denmark an interesting situation has prevailed. Professor Schou, at Aarhus University Institute of Psychiatry, Risskov, has consistently advocated a multiple dose regime, but psychiatrists at the other leading centre for lithium research in Denmark, the Psychochemistry Institute at the Rigshospitalet in Copenhagen, converted to a single daily dosage regimen in the early seventies and have subsequently produced most of the original research relating to the advantages of this dosage schedule. These studies have focused on the merits and the disadvantages of a single daily *versus* a divided daily dosage regime on kidney function. A more detailed exposition of the toxic effects of lithium on kidney function is provided in Section 57 (pp. 206–213).

Profile of Serum Lithium Levels and the Dosage Regimen

Earlier studies by Dr Amdi Amdisen from Professor Schou's department had shown that a single daily and divided daily dosage regimes produced quite different profiles of serum lithium levels over 24 h. More recently, Dr B.J.Lauritsen from the Copenhagen group has led an investigation in collaboration with Professor

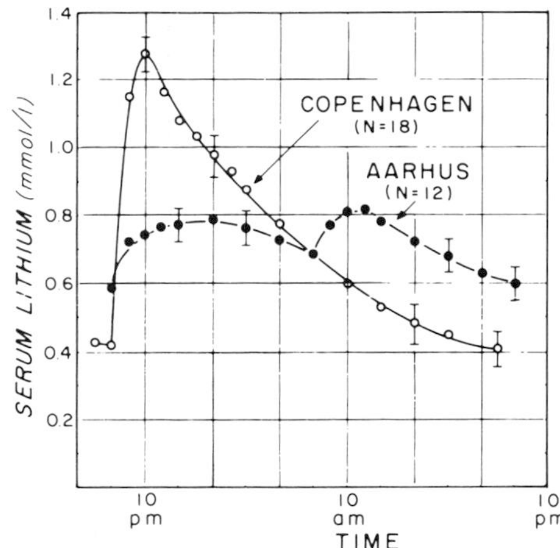

Figure 26.1 Variations in serum lithium concentration throughout a 24-h period in 18 patients receiving a standard-release lithium preparation once a day, compared with data from 12 patients receiving a sustained release preparation twice a day in divided doses (means ± SEM). From Schou,M., Amdisen,A., Thomsen,K., Vestegaard,P., Hetmar,O., Mellerup,E.T., Plenge,P. and Rafaelsen,O.J. (1982) *Psychopharmacology,* **77**, 387–390, with permission.

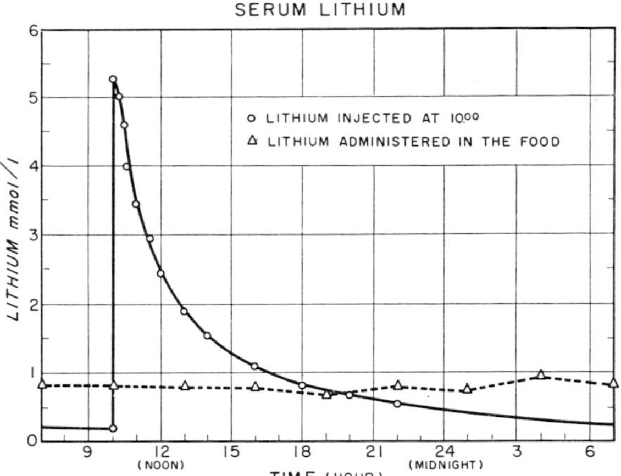

Figure 26.2 Serum lithium concentrations in rats receiving single daily intraperitoneal injections of 800 mmol lithium chloride (continuous line) or 60 mmol/kg lithium chloride in the food (broken line). From Plenge,P., Mellerup,E.T. and Norgaard,T. (1981) *Acta Psychiatr. Scand,* **63**, 303–313, with permission.

Schou's group at Aarhus into profiles of serum lithium levels around the clock with different treatment regimens. They compared the profiles in 18 patients receiving a conventional preparation in a once daily dose regimen (Copenhagen) with those in 12 patients receiving a slow-release preparation in a twice daily dosage regime (Aarhus). The two groups of patients had similar mean daily doses of lithium, though, as shown in *Figure 26.1*, the two groups had substantially different curves of serum lithium levels over 24 h. It is evident that patients who had been maintained on a single daily dosage regimen had early sharp peak lithium levels within 2–4 h of ingestion of the drug but had lower levels in the second 12 h of the day. Patients who had received a divided daily dosage regimen, however, showed smaller peaks and had a relatively constant level throughout the 24 h. The two groups had identical mean 12-h and mean average levels over 24 h. Other administration schedules, however, will give different profiles and a 12-h serum lithium level in a divided dosage regimen using conventional preparation would be an underestimate of the amount of lithium to which the patient has been exposed, whilst a 12-h serum lithium level in a single daily dosage regimen with a sustained release preparation would be an overestimate of such exposure. Moreover, the use of a sustained release preparation in a single daily dosage regimen is likely to be contentious.

The Dosage Regimen and Kidney Function

The adverse effects of lithium on renal functions have been recognized from an early stage. Patients are often troubled by excessive thirst (polydipsia) and excessive urination (polyuria). It was only in the late 1970s, however, that reports started appearing to indicate that lithium could cause irreversible kidney damage. The topic is covered in detail later (pp. 206–213).

It was Drs Per Plenge and Erling Mellerup from the Copenhagen group who undertook most of the research work on the relationship between the dosage regimen and renal function. Their first study was one involving animals in which they evaluated the toxic effects of two administration schedules analogous to the single daily and the divided dosage regimens. One group of rats received a fixed amount of lithium in food pellets (divided dosage regimen) and another group had it injected intraperitoneally once a day (single daily regimen). Lithium was administered for 5 months. The two schedules produced strikingly different serum/lithium profiles. As shown in *Figure 26.2* the injected rats showed an extremely high peak of 5.0 mmol/l shortly after the injection, thereafter lithium levels dropped to below 0.5 mmol/l. Rats which had consumed their lithium in their food showed a very smooth serum lithium profile, with levels varying between 0.6 mmol/l in the evening and 0.9 mmol/l in the morning, a range that is well within the therapeutic range in the human situation. Water consumption, and consequently urine excretion, were significantly increased in the group given lithium in their food. At the end of the study the kidneys were examined. Half of the rats who had received lithium in their food showed severe kidney damage whilst none of the rats who had been injected showed such damage. Moreover, there was an association between the functional and structural changes: rats which showed severe kidney damage had the greatest water consumption. In explanation of their findings, Plenge and Mellerup suggested that kidney damage may only occur if tissue lithium levels do not drop below a minimum level and they speculated about the implications of their findings for the clinical situation *vis à vis* the single daily or the divided daily dosage regimens. These findings prompted them to re-analyse the results of their previous investigation of the relationship between lithium effects, lithium dose and maximal serum levels. They found that 24-h urinary volume showed no association with maximum or 12-h lithium levels, but was associated with minimal serum levels: patients who had the greatest 24-h urine volumes had the highest minimum serum levels. They concluded that to avoid kidney damage during long-term lithium treatment, it may be more important to have regular periods with low levels than it is to avoid peaks and they have accordingly strongly advocated a single daily dosage regimen.

They confirmed these preliminary findings in their clinical study in which they examined functional and structural changes in patients who had been given lithium in a single daily dosage regimen in comparison with patients who received it in a divided dosage regimen. They found that the functional and structural changes were most pronounced in the group of patients who received their lithium in divided doses. They noted that the serum lithium profiles were markedly different between the two groups: those who had a single daily dosage regimen had the peak around 1.5 mmol/l within 4 h of injection, and 12-h lithium levels around 1.0 mmol/l with a minimum level of 0.5 mmol/l before next dose of lithium was given. For the group who had the divided dosage regimen, serum lithium levels never dropped below the 12-h serum level of 0.7 – 1.0 mmol/l. A criticism that could be levelled at this study is that the group of patients who had the divided dosage regimen were patients who had been started on this regimen since the early 1970s or had come from other clinics and preferred to stay on it; treatment regimens were not, therefore, randomly allocated. Moreover the two groups received different doses, with the group on the divided regimen receiving higher doses of lithium which may have contributed to the greater functional and morphological changes in these patients.

Dr Paul Perry from the University of Iowa in the USA has studied the pharmacokinetics of a single daily dosage regime in comparison with a divided one (see pp. 67 – 73). Eight patients who had been maintained on a divided dosage schedule were converted to a single daily dosage schedule. He found no significant changes in either serum half-lives or renal lithium clearance levels following the change of dosage regimen. There was, however, a significant decrease in the 24-h urine output during the single daily dosage regimen. Dr Perry has, however, noted that his findings were preliminary and that no firm conclusions could be drawn from the small group of patients studied.

Prompted by these findings, Professor Schou's group instigated a similar study in collaboration with the Copenhagen group, to compare patients who had throughout received a slow-release preparation in a divided dosage regimen, with patients treated by the Copenhagen group with a conventional preparation in a single daily dosage regimen. It was noted that the Copenhagen group of patients were on average older, and had been on lithium for longer and had slightly higher mean serum concentrations. The results indicated that the dosage regimen had no effect on glomerular function (creatinine clearance) but did influence tubular function as indexed by the 24-h urinary volume which was lower in the Copenhagen group. These findings were discussed separately by the two groups. The Copenhagen group considered them a further confirmation of their suggestion that a single daily dosage regime is safer than a divided dosage regime. Professor Schou's group, however, deferred judgement on the matter awaiting the results of further and better designed investigations, ideally carried out within the same clinic with random allocation of treatment regimen in conjunction with the assessment of clinical and unwanted effects.

Drs Plenge and Mellerup have extended their arguments to suggest that a dosage regimen with even longer intervals between doses, i.e. every second or third day, may be as effective as a daily regimen and less harmful on the kidney. They have further speculated that lithium given every second or third day may be particularly beneficial in non-responding patients who require higher doses which they would not tolerate on a daily dosage regimen. The efficacy of such an unorthodox regimen remains to be shown. Moreover, such a departure from a daily dosage regimen may lead to less compliance, unless, of course, dummy tablets were to be given on the non-dosage days.

Summary

The use of lithium salts in the management of affective disorders has provided one of the most rewarding therapeutic advances in medical practice. Lithium's efficacy, however, must be set against its hazards, particularly on kidney functions. This has provoked clinical scientists to determine the optimal conditions for lithium therapy including the minimum effective dose/serum level and the safest dosage regimen. There is a body of evidence which indicates that lithium is effective in considerably lower dosages than previously recommended and serum levels of 0.4–0.5 mmol/l may, in some circumstances, be as therapeutic as the previously recommended levels of 0.6 mmol/l and above. These lower dosages/serum levels are associated with fewer unwanted effects. The routine of prescribing lithium in a divided dosage regimen has been advocated to avoid peaks and ensure constant levels. This has been recently challenged: there is a substantial body of evidence to indicate that a single daily dosage regimen is associated with fewer unwanted effects, specifically on kidney function. A divided dosage regimen may, however, be favoured with certain patients (particularly the elderly) who experience unwanted effects related to peaks of serum lithium.

Bibliography

Coppen,A., Abou-Saleh,M.T., Milln,P., Bailey,J. and Wood,K. (1983) Reducing lithium dose reduces morbidity and side effects in affective disorders. *J. Affect. Dis.*, **6**, 53–66.
This paper reports the results of the first double-blind study of the efficacy and safety of lower doses/serum levels of lithium in the prophylaxis of recurrent affective disorders.

Schou,M., Amdisen,A., Thomsen,K., Vestergaard,P., Hetmar,O., Mellerup,E.T., Plenge,P. and Rafaelsen,O.J. (1982) Lithium treatment regimen and renal water handling: the significance of dosage pattern and tablet type examined through comparison of results from two clinics with different treatment regimens. *Psychopharmacology*, **77**, 387–390.
This paper provides an excellent review of the literature on the advantages of the single daily dose regimen in comparison with a divided dosage regimen. It also reports the results of a comparative study of kidney functions in patients maintained on these dosage regimens drawn from the two famous Danish clinics, complemented by the views of clinical scientists from these clinics.

27. Laboratory Monitoring

Mogens Schou

When lithium therapy of mania was first used by John Cade (see pp. 24–28), he did not monitor the treatment through laboratory examinations. The dosage was raised until side effects appeared or became intolerable and was then reduced somewhat for continued treatment.

This procedure would hardly be considered good treatment practice today. Laboratory tests carried out before and during the treatment are considered mandatory and are in general use in the industrialized countries. In developing countries even strongly indicated lithium treatment is often not instituted because facilities for laboratory monitoring are unavailable, and in countries without a socialized health system poor patients usually do not receive treatment with lithium (in itself a relatively inexpensive drug) because they cannot afford the cost of regular laboratory examinations.

Is laboratory monitoring in fact under all circumstances necessary for the execution of lithium treatment? Is extensive testing required, or can responsible lithium treatment be based on the monitoring of a few variables? How often and under what circumstances should laboratory monitoring take place? The following is an attempt at answering, or at least at commenting on, these questions.

Developing Countries

Recurrent manic-depressive illness is such a devastating and dangerous disease and lithium administration exerts such effective relapse prevention, that physicians must be justified in exposing the patients to a certain risk if the alternative is that the illness remains untreated. This situation may prevail in some of the developing countries. Since ordinarily dosage adjustment is based on the outcome of serum lithium determinations, alternative guidelines for choice of dosage are required if, for reasons of finance or availability of laboratory facilities, serum monitoring is not readily available. Experience from systematic surveillance of a large group of lithium-treated patients indicates that lithium doses of the following magnitudes may be appropriate in most cases: for patients up to 40 years of age, 25−35 mmol/day; for patients aged 40−60 years, 20−25 mmol/day; and for patients older than 60 years, 15−20 mmol/day. The development of troublesome side effects or the occurrence of relapses may necessitate adjustment to dosages that are respectively lower and higher than these standard levels.

Industrialized Countries

In the industrialized countries laboratory facilities are usually available, and even if the local laboratory is not equipped for serum lithium determinations, blood or serum samples can be sent by mail and results reported by mail or by telephone. Lithium determinations do not require the samples to be kept cold, lithium does not deteriorate in the sample, and a limited degree of haemolysis does not interfere with the analysis. It is of course necessary to ensure that evaporation from the samples does not take place.

During lithium treatment the serum lithium concentration may be determined once a week during the first 2−3 weeks while dosage adjustment takes place. Thereafter, the patients may be followed with regular laboratory examinations at intervals of, for example, 4−6 months. The serum lithium concentration should be determined under standardized circumstances, namely in blood samples drawn 11−13 h after the last intake of lithium and under steady-state conditions, that is at least 4−5 days after start of treatment and after dosage changes. If a shorter or longer time than about 12 h has elapsed since the last intake of lithium, the patients should report this, because the information is of importance for the assessment of the serum lithium value. This issue is dealt with in more detail in Section 21, pp. 88−91. The patients need not be fasting.

Serum lithium levels of 0.5−0.8 mmol/l are appropriate for most patients, but adjustment to levels lower or higher than this standard range may become necessary if the patient develops troublesome side effects or suffers relapses. Attention should be directed particularly towards unexpected changes of the lithium concentration. A consistent rise of the concentration with unchanged dosage, or a disproportionate rise after dosage increase, may indicate that lithium is excreted less effectively by the kidneys, and it may be necessary to subject the patient's kidney function, general health, drug intake, and dietary habits to closer examination.

The serum creatinine concentration may be determined at the same time as the serum lithium concentration as an extra safeguard against the development of otherwise unrecognized kidney disease. However, such determinations can hardly be considered strictly necessary, since constancy of serum lithium levels with unchanged lithium dosage is an equally sensitive, and more directly relevant, indicator of unaltered kidney function. If creatinine determinations are carried out, attention should again be focused on changes rather than on absolute values; a consistent rise of serum creatinine may indicate lowering of kidney function even if the concentration is below the upper limit of the normal range.

In some hospitals the concentration of thyroid stimulating hormone (TSH) in serum is determined at intervals. The purpose is to aid early detection of lowered thyroid function. Lithium-induced hypothyroidism may develop so insidiously that diagnosis on clinical grounds alone is difficult, and it is important not to overlook, and hence leave untreated, even slight underfunctioning. Prescription of thyroxine on the basis of clinical suspicion supported by consistent elevation of TSH has occasionally markedly improved the patient's quality of life.

Some patients develop polyuria and polydipsia during lithium treatment as a result of lithium-induced lowering of renal concentrating ability. It has been suggested that determination of concentrating ability through measurement of urinary osmolality after thirst or after administration of the vasopressin analogue, DDAVP, should be part of the routine checkup. Issue must, however, be taken with this suggestion because a fall of maximum osmolality might tempt psychiatrists and, in particular, consulting nephrologists to discontinue lithium without proper reason. Even if in some patients the osmolality may fall to a low value, this does not mean that the patients are going to develop renal insufficiency, and it does not constitute grounds for discontinuing prophylactically effective and otherwise well-tolerated lithium treatment. The finding merely signifies that the patients should respond readily to feelings of thirst and avoid situations that may lead to dehydration.

It was suggested above that laboratory examinations might be carried out at intervals of 4–6 months, but the frequency of the control visits is usually determined by considerations other than the laboratory checkup. It is important for confident cooperation between patient and physician that they meet at intervals to discuss treatment progress, side effects, and dosage adjustment as well as possible social and personal problems associated with the illness and the treatment (pp. 121–124). The main importance of the laboratory visits may lie in the provision of a structured framework for these contacts rather than in the laboratory answers themselves.

There are, however, situations when laboratory examination is important, and this is particularly so if the patient develops one or more of the symptoms that may herald incipient lithium intoxication. The signs and symptoms are generally unspecific (apathy, sleepiness, heaviness of the limbs, slight muscle twitches, uncertain gait, indistinct speech, nausea, vomiting), and a serum lithium determination may reveal whether the complaints are in fact due to lithium accumulation or whether another cause should be sought.

There are a number of additional laboratory examinations which it might be interesting, and on occasion helpful, to carry out during lithium treatment. They may include, for example, assessment of serum thyroxine and triiodothyronine, thyroid antibody titre, serum calcium, the haematological picture, urine volume, glomerular filtration rate, and renal concentrating ability. Interest and facilities as well as time and money may determine what is considered worthwhile laboratory supplement to clinical observation. Some of these tests may be required in case of complications, but under ordinary circumstances their execution is determined by scientific curiosity rather than clinical need.

Bibliography

Schou,M. (1986) *Lithium Treatment of Manic-depressive Illness: a Practical Guide*, 3rd Edition, Karger, Basel.
Written specifically for patients and relatives this book deals in non-technical language but considerable detail with questions that may arise before and during lithium treatment. The book is available also in German, French, Danish, Swedish, Italian and Japanese.

Vestergaard,P., Schou,M. and Thomsen,K. (1982) Monitoring of patients in prophylactic lithium treatment: an assessment based on recent kidney studies. *Br. J. Psychiatry,* **140**, 185–187.
A brief, but useful, survey of tests and procedures for keeping a check on progress during maintenance treatment.

Part V

CLINICAL PRACTICE: TREATMENT IN PROGRESS

28. Monitoring Progress

F.Neil Johnson

It is in the nature of lithium therapy that the patient should be kept under surveillance throughout the full period of treatment. In general, the treatment may be divided into a number of phases, each carrying its own special surveillance requirements.

Phase I

The first phase is the period of institution of treatment. Here the tissue levels of lithium are rising rapidly and the body is having to adjust to the presence of a new substance suddenly introduced into the metabolism. Monitoring in this phase is primarily the province of hospital medical and paramedical staff and is directed mainly towards the observation of physiological and biochemical functions (See Section 27, pp. 105–107).

Phase II

Phase II covers the first 2–4 months (the period may vary from patient to patient) when one is looking for a distinct therapeutic effect, usually the alleviation of an ongoing manic or hypomanic phase. During this phase the patient is usually seen regularly and frequently by a number of individuals, including the prescribing clinician or other senior members of the medical team, the personnel running the out-patient clinic, and the family practitioner.

Serum lithium level tests are performed (the frequency depends on the particular clinician's feelings about such matters, and also upon how the patient's levels seem to be stabilizing), and various physiological function tests may be done if there is any reason to suspect that disturbances are possible of endocrine, renal, or other systems. The main emphasis, however, is on symptomatic presentation and the patient's subjective response to treatment.

Any family, business, or other problems which the illness may have caused will hopefully also be resolving in this phase, and such matters will be the province of medical social workers and similar agencies.

Phase III

The third phase represents the period of long-term maintenance treatment. Its duration depends essentially upon the age at which the patient was started on lithium. This phase is characterized by a number of features as regards the monitoring or progress.

Clinical surveillance

The frequency with which the patient attends the lithium clinic becomes much reduced, and may be as infrequent as once a year or even less. Clinical monitoring passes into the hands of the patient himself who has to be aware of the kinds of problems which may occur and alert to their appearance. Relatives and other close acquaintances can help in this respect, provided that they are well-briefed about the nature of lithium side-effects. The family practitioner (Section 33, pp. 124–127) clearly has a major role to play here, both in keeping a check on physiological functions (and advising on any changes in the treatment regime when illness or injury intervenes) and in ensuring continued compliance with medication (Section 31, pp. 117–121).

Treatment regimen

Since it is now standard practice to try to reduce lithium dosage to the lowest compatible with continued prophylactic efficacy, Phase III may be a time for experimenting with dosage reduction. There are all kinds of issues raised by such a suggestion, of course. In the first place, one wonders whether to leave well alone if the patient seems to be stable, both psychiatrically and physiologically. Secondly, since any adjustment to treatment will necessarily entail increased clinical activity, more frequent serum levels taken, more visits to the clinic, and so on, one risks reawakening in the patient the fears and anxieties associated with the original severe form of the illness. Thirdly, one risks the re-appearance of the illness if dose levels drop too far.

Against such arguments one might set the dangers of long-term side effects, particularly renal, occurring as a result of too-high dose levels. In the final analysis the decision must be left to the clinician and patient to reach after full discussion. There are no simple guidelines which can be laid down.

If the patient expresses any concern about remain-

PRIADEL CHART
(SLOW LITHIUM CARBONATE)

HOSPITAL ....
PATIENT NUMBER ....
UNIT/WARD ....
....
CONSULTANT ....

PATIENT INFORMATION

NAME ....
ADDRESS ....
....
TEL. No. .... DATE OF BIRTH ....
DIAGNOSIS ....

DATE	SERUM LITHIUM (in mmol/l)	TIME OF DAILY DOSE	TIME OF BLOOD SAMPLE	DAILY DOSE	NEXT TEST DUE AT ON	SIGNATURE OF DOCTOR

PRIADEL controlled release tablets each contain 400 mg. lithium carbonate B.P.

DELANDALE LABORATORIES LTD., DELANDALE HOUSE, OLD DOVER ROAD, CANTERBURY, KENT.

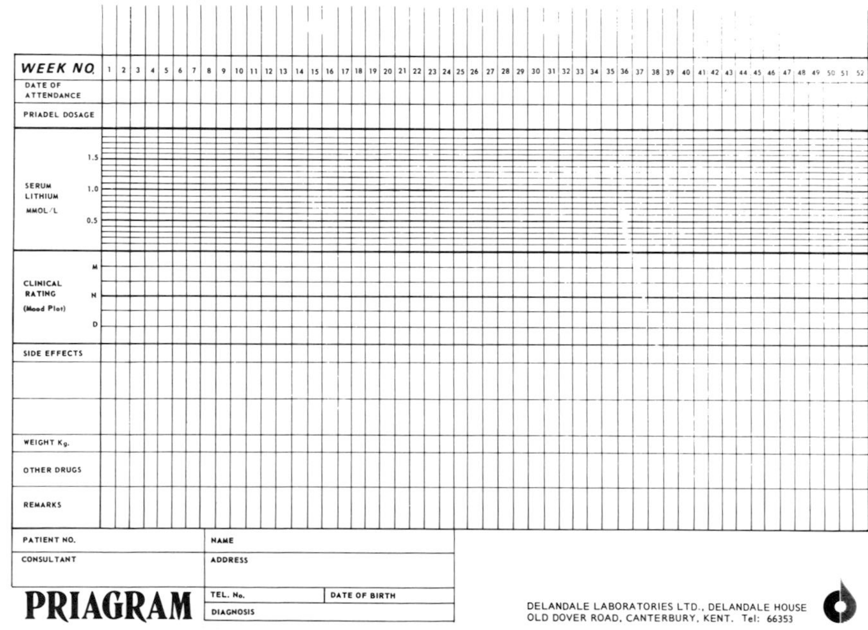

WEEK NO.	1	2	3	4	5	6	7	8	9	10	11	12	13	14	15	16	17	18	19	20	21	22	23	24	25	26	27	28	29	30	31	32	33	34	35	36	37	38	39	40	41	42	43	44	45	46	47	48	49	50	51	52
DATE OF ATTENDANCE																																																					
PRIADEL DOSAGE																																																					
SERUM LITHIUM MMOL/L 1.5 1.0 0.5																																																					
CLINICAL RATING (Mood Plot) M N D																																																					
SIDE EFFECTS																																																					
WEIGHT Kg.																																																					
OTHER DRUGS																																																					
REMARKS																																																					

PATIENT NO.	NAME	
CONSULTANT	ADDRESS	
PRIAGRAM	TEL. No.	DATE OF BIRTH
	DIAGNOSIS	

DELANDALE LABORATORIES LTD., DELANDALE HOUSE
OLD DOVER ROAD, CANTERBURY, KENT. Tel: 66353

Figure 28.1 An example of a patient record form.

ing on lithium for an indefinite period, Phase III is the time when one might consider a supervised withdrawal of treatment. All the provisos noted previously with regard to dosage reduction apply again. Treatment withdrawal has a very high chance of being followed by relapse, and all precautions need to be taken to spot this in its early stages. Relatives, family practitioner, social workers, and others have to be aware of what is going on.

Phase IV

The final phase of treatment comes when the patient enters the period of advanced years when various physiological functions may not be operating quite as efficiently as they ought or once did. The issue of the elderly patient is covered in detail in Section 36, pp. 135–138.

Documentation

Very many different kinds of document have been designed for the purpose of keeping a detailed record of a patient's progress. *Figure 28.1* shows an example of a double-sided record card which allows a comprehensive record to be maintained in a concise manner. By recording serum lithium levels in parallel with clinical ratings, the psychiatrist can see at a glance how clinical status is related to the lithium intake and can make a judgement as to the optimum serum level to be aimed for in a given patient.

Bibliography

Johnson,F.N. (1975) Lithium and the psychiatric social worker. *Social Work Today,* **5**, 344–346.
The role of social workers as agents in monitoring the progress of lithium therapy is considered in detail.

Kerry,R.J. (1975) The management of patients receiving lithium treatment. In Johnson,F.N. (ed.), *Lithium Research and Therapy.* Academic Press, London, pp. 143–164.
A classic account of progress monitoring procedures which has not dated.

29. Relapse

Marco Catalano, Mariangela Gasperini, Adelio Lucca and Enrico Smeraldi

A proper evaluation of, and interpretation of the reasons for, relapses which may occur under prophylaxis with lithium salts, is one of the main problems which arises in the proper management of lithium therapy. The occurrence of clinical relapses can cause the appearance of pessimistic or rejecting attitudes on the part of the patient, the patient's relatives and by the practitioner himself. The psychiatrist must be in a position to provide all these individuals with an exhaustive explanation for the occurrence of relapse in order to ensure a proper continuation of lithium therapy. It may be unwise to stop prophylaxis because of the risk of further, and possibly more serious, relapses, and the psychiatrist must be able to explain as much in a clear and persuasive way.

Unfortunately, it is not always easy to recognize or to evaluate exactly what the factors are which are involved in the occurrence of a relapse. For one thing, the definition of what constitutes a relapse depends upon the diagnostic criteria which are used and these may differ from one psychiatrist to another. Similarly, assessing the severity of a relapse implies the possibility of quantifying symptoms and this is seldom a simple matter. Comparisons between patients are confounded by factors which are not always very easy to check (e.g. compliance by patients with their treatment programme), or which are related to methodological differences (e.g. dosages of lithium, time interval between the last lithium dose and drawing of the serum sample, and so on).

Factors Determining Relapse

A recent study carried out in the Institute of Clinical Psychiatry of the University of Milan, Italy, has attempted to examine the question of relapse under conditions which permitted close control of relevant variables. Strict diagnostic criteria (DSM-III) were applied, and lithium levels in plasma and red blood cells were determined under carefully standardized conditions. Relapses were rated according to their severity as 'major' or 'minor'.

The results of the study were intriguing but inconclusive. In the whole group of 44 patients the lithium ratio (i.e. the ratio of the lithium level in the red blood cells to that in the serum) was unrelated to the major variables in the study, though it did seem to be associated with the polarity of the illness taken in combination with the presence or absence of relapse. In a subset of 27 patients who had more than one relapse the lithium ratio was lower just before and during a relapse than it was during the normothymic phase; in the relapsed unipolar patients lithium ratios were higher than the median, and they had a greater incidence of minor relapses. This work clearly hinted at some connection between relapse and an objectively determinable biological index—the lithium ratio.

In subsequent follow-up work at the same centre, patients were selected who had a well-documented family history in terms of the presence or absence of affective disorders.

Contrary to the finding of the earlier study, the lithium ratio was not found to be closely linked to the occurrence of relapses, but there were methodological differences between the two investigations which could account for this. Moreover, the second study did not involve the comparison of the lithium ratios in the pre-relapse and relapse periods, a distinction which the earlier work had suggested might be important.

Age was found to be related to relapse frequency, relapses becoming more common as age increased. This could be explained by the action of age-related factors such as pharmacokinetic change, compliance with treatment, etc.

Particularly important, however, was the relationship between relapse probability and the presence or absence of affected relatives (i.e. relatives known to have had some form of affective disorder). The greater the genetic and familial incidence of affective disorders, the lower the risk of relapses in the patient. Such a result is in accord with other reports in the literature indicating a better response to lithium treatment in patients with a higher frequency of affective illness amongst their relatives.

The age of the patient at which the affective disorder was first detected seemed also to be related to relapse probability, with an early onset (12−19 years) being associated with a lower relapse rate than seen in other age groups. There had been earlier indications of this in the literature, and so the finding was not out of line with expectations.

Less easy to understand in the results of the Milan study was the conclusion that the polarity status (unipolar *versus* bipolar) did not seem to affect relapse frequency, particularly in view of several reports that polarity was a factor closely related to clinical outcome on lithium therapy. There are, however, other reports in which such an association was not found and it is possible that the bipolar/unipolar distinction is not sufficiently specific an index in studies of this kind.

Clearly, this work has to be considered preliminary, but it is representative of the kind of studies which are presently being pursued in an attempt to understand why it is that some patients seem to improve permanently once lithium therapy has been stabilized, whilst others have occasional relapses.

Preliminary though it is, this work and other investigations of a similar nature do give rise to a few guiding principles as far as the management of relapses is concerned.

The Management of Relapse

The first important principle is that the practitioner should not rush to stop lithium as a consequence of relapses, even if they frequently occur, but he should follow the course of the illness before deciding. The possibility has to be taken into account that, in these patients, lithium may be useful simply by effecting a decrease in the clinical severity of relapses.

Secondly, the practitioner needs to know his patient very well, with particular regard to family history, age of onset of the illness and the patient's actual age, since these are the factors which appears to be indicative of likely relapse frequency and may stimulate the patient and practitioner to greater vigilance.

Of course, attention to all the various other factors which are dealt with elsewhere in this volume and which are linked to effective therapeutic outcome, the avoidance of side effects, and increased compliance with the medication regime, will help to ensure that relapse frequency is kept to a minimum.

Bibliography

Catalano,M., Gasperini,M., Lucca,A., Brancato,V. and Smeraldi,E. (1987) Red blood cell:plasma Li ratio variability in affective patients. *Neuropsychobiology,* **18**, 5−8.

A preliminary report of work in progress concerning possible relationships between the lithium ratio and other factors of clinical relevance. It is fairly simple to understand, requiring only some knowledge of statistics and laboratory methods.

Smeraldi,E., Petroccione,A., Gasperini,M., Macciardi,F., Orsini,A. and Kidd,K.K. (1984) Outcome on lithium treatment as a tool for genetic studies in affective disorders. *J. Affect. Dis.*, **6**, 139–151.
This article concerns relationships between family history of illness, morbidity risk and good or bad outcome under lithium therapy. Technically it is sophisticated and requires knowledge of statistics and genetics.

30. Terminating Treatment

P.J.Goodnick

A clinician is frequently asked by his patients if he must take lithium for his entire life, and, if not, when he can stop taking lithium. Most practitioners are at a loss for a response, since there have not been any established guidelines. Further, if a physician permits a patient to stop lithium, he often cannot answer questions such as: Am I at a risk of quickly relapsing into either mania or depression if I stop my lithium?; Is there a lithium withdrawal syndrome?; Will my lithium-related side effects clear up?; and Will I still need to take my medicine for low-functioning thyroid? In addition, a practitioner often cannot tell an inquisitive patient how it comes about that lithium works and then reverses itself when it is stopped.

This section is aimed at answering these questions and related ones to the degree permitted by current evidence, and suggests guidelines for termination of lithium therapy.

Relapse after Terminating Treatment

A frequent worry of both physicians and patients on stopping lithium is that of relapse into either mania or depression. Furthermore, reports of Dr Joyce Small of Indiana University, Indianapolis, Indiana, USA, in 1971 and of Dr Andrew Margo of the Institute of Psychiatry, De Crespigny Park, London, UK, in 1982 alerted physicians of possible 'rebound mania' after stopping lithium. However, the results from a series of studies clearly show that the rate of recurrence of either mania or depression averages only about 12.5%, given the following conditions: (i) that the patient has been without any major symptoms for at least 1 year; and (ii) that the patient has been able to maintain that stability on lithium alone, without, in particular, any antidepressants or neuroleptics.

A related question is whether this rate of recurrence is particularly higher after stopping lithium, or is simply part of the pattern of recurrence of manic-depressive disorder in general. Dr Poul C.Baastrup of the Glostrup Psychiatric Hospital, Denmark, reported in 1970 that approximately 50% of patients experienced recurrences within 6 months of stopping lithium. This double-blind study followed his initial open one that found 22 of 25 patients relapsing in the first year after discontinuation, with the mean onset of relapse occurrence being 3 months following termination of lithium. Three other long-term studies found that between 33% and 100% of patients relapsed in 6–9 months off lithium. One of these pinpointed the mean onset of mania after 12.5 weeks and of depression after 7 weeks off lithium. Drs S.Sashidharan and R.McGuire of the University of Edinburgh in UK reviewed results, in 1983, of their own and previous studies on relapse during lithium discontinuation. They presented convincing evidence that relapses occurring in the first weeks after stopping lithium were simply part of a pattern of recurrence occurring gradually over a period of months, and they emphatically stated that they could discover no evidence supporting the possibility of rebound psychosis. Results of the work of Dr Paul Grof of the Department of Psychiatry at McMaster University in Hamilton, Ontario, Canada in 1985 further supported these conclusions.

When and How to Discontinue Lithium

Unfortunately, simple long-term duration of treatment with lithium is not, in itself, necessarily preventative of relapse. Dr Baastrup's 1970 work showed that 12 of 21 relapsing patients had received lithium for 4–7 years, whilst two of the four patients having recurrences in the work of Drs George Christodoulou and Eleftherios Lykouras of the Department of Psychiatry of Athens University, Greece, in 1982, had been in a programme of lithium prophylaxis for 3.5–5 years.

Based on his own experience at McMaster University, Canada, Dr Paul Grof stated in 1985 that early relapses appeared to be related to:

(i) poor stability in the year before lithium discontinuation;
(ii) discontinuation at a time of high risk for relapse (generally late spring and early autumn);
(iii) discontinuation by the patient, not under the suggestion of the physician (this may occur when a patient is slightly hypomanic);

(iv) a history of many previous episodes of mania and depression—in particular, rapid-cyclers who have had at least four episodes per year;
(v) a history of manias superimposed on chronic psychosis.

Work by Dr Greil of the Psychiatrische Universitätsklinik München in West Germany led him, in 1981, to conclude that patients requiring medication in addition to lithium to maintain stabilization of mood (e.g. antidepressants and neuroleptics) are much more likely to relapse on stopping lithium. The rate of relapse in these patients was 83% (6 of 7) in contrast to 27% (3 of 11) who had been maintained on lithium alone.

Thus, Dr Paul Grof suggests that patients being considered for even short-term discontinuation should have been stable on lithium for at least 2 years, should have a clear diagnosis of manic-depressive disorder without any background history of chronic psychiatric disorder and should preferably have had a past history of seasonal regularity of episodes of mania and depression.

'Lithium holidays' have been suggested as a way of reducing lithium-induced side effects, e.g. impairment of urinary concentration and weight gain, and early investigators suggested withholding lithium intake for one day every 7–14 days. In 1981, Dr Frank Ayd Jr of the West Virginia School of Medicine, USA, presented results of a study which involved stopping lithium for one week of every four; he was encouraged by the lack of relapse in patients in this program. However, in view of the maintained tissue lithium concentration and the length of half-life of elimination, Dr Grof insists that to alter the metabolic and enzymatic impact of lithium, the minimum duration of lithium discontinuation should be 3–4 weeks. Unfortunately, little evidence is available to demonstrate potential benefits and/or risks of this procedure; Dr Grof reports that, on following this procedure, he has had only seven relapses on 72 discontinuations, and he then goes on to suggest longer term discontinuation once a short-term trial of lithium withdrawal has been completed without relapse, concluding that lithium holidays should be attempted only in specialized setups such as lithium clinics.

Some further guidelines can be provided for the clinical procedures being used for short- and long-term discontinuation. Preferably, the patient should be living with a responsible other person, relative or friend, who can also monitor the patient's mood during discontinuation of treatment, and who should be involved in planning the lithium withdrawal and instructed as to early warning signs of relapse. Although these signs vary somewhat from individual to individual the best ones are changes in the need for sleep (mania) or insomnia (depression) changes in appetite (depression) and changes in future plans (either mania or depression). A patient should be seen initially once per week for the first month, and thereafter once per month for at least a year. If a sudden new stress develops during the first year off lithium, the patient should again be seen weekly for 1 month. If 1 year is completed without difficulty, the patient may then be discharged and be seen again only as needed.

Some investigators have at times suggested intermittent lithium treatment with episodes alone being treated, or with treatment being re-instituted at earliest signs of relapse. The difficulty in this plan is, as stated by Dr Grof, that one cannot always correctly anticipate the timing of future episodes for a particular patient. Furthermore, one does not really know the period of lithium treatment which is sufficient to prevent a relapse, or at least to stop the early symptoms from developing into full-blown recurrence of mania or depression. This clinical research has not been done.

Effect of Lithium Withdrawal on Side Effects

As expected, lithium-induced side effects fade away with cessation of therapy. As outlined in *Table 30.1*, there is close to a 100% fall in reported side effects over short-term discontinuation. Furthermore, although not quite as dramatic, urinary concentrating ability is gradually increased, despite lack of change in serum creatinine. Lithium-induced thyroid suppression is reversed significantly within a few weeks, with free T_4 increasing by 25%. Other substantial decreases have been found in white blood count (44%) and triglycerides (35%) within a few weeks of lithium discontinuation.

Is There a Lithium Withdrawal Syndrome?

A withdrawal syndrome usually develops within days of sudden cessation of treatment with the following symptoms: anxiety, restlessness, tremor, irritability, fatigue, nausea, sweating, headache, insomnia, excessive sleep, diarrhoea, blurred vision. Whilst some clinicians have presented individual case reports of possible withdrawal symptoms, closer examination

Table 30.1 *Changes in side effects, clinical indices and neurochemistry following discontinuation of lithium treatment (based on findings of a number of studies reported between 1981 and 1986)*

	Increase	Decrease
Overall side effects		− − − −
Renal side effects (total)		− − −
Polydipsia		− − − −
Polyuria		− − − −
Renal indices		
Urinary concentrating ability	+	
Urine specific gravity	+	
BUN	+	
Creatinine	0	
Tremor		− − −
Dry mouth		− − − −
Muscle weakness		− − − −
Thyroid indices		
T_4 Thyroxine	+	
T_3	l	
Free T_4	+ +	
T_4/TBG	+	
TSH		− −
Other clinical indices		−
Calcium		−
Magnesium		−
Cholesterol		−
Triglycerides		− −
White blood count		− −
Red blood count		−

+ or −, 0−24%; + + or − −, 25−49%; + + + or − − − 50−74%; + + + + or − − − − 75−100%; 0, no change.

suggests that these may be simply a recurrence of symptoms of mood change.

Uncontrolled studies of withdrawal symptoms have raised the possibility of a lithium withdrawal state, but controlled studies have been convincingly negative. Dr Waldemar Greil and his associates in 1981 reported symptoms consistent with a withdrawal state spontaneously reported by six of ten patients who did not relapse during lithium discontinuation. Drs J.King and Roy Hullin of the University of Leeds, UK, conducted a questionnaire survey in 1983 of possible withdrawal symptoms after cessation of lithium. Only 27 of 110 completed the questionnaire; five of these 27 (19%) reported temporary anxiety on stopping lithium 1−9 years earlier (mean was approximately 4.5 years). In contrast, Drs George Christodoulou and Eleftherios Lykouras in 1983 and Dr Arthur Rifkin at Mount Sinai Hospital in New York, USA in 1980, conducted controlled studies of lithium discontinuation which looked for psychological and physical symptoms of lithium withdrawal: none were found and it is probably safe to conclude that there is, in fact, no specific lithium withdrawal state. However, because of ever-present concerns on possible relapse, it is probably better to reduce gradually the lithium dosage over a period of weeks, rather than to stop a dose as high as 1500 mg/day abruptly.

Bibliography

Baastrup,P.C. and Schou,M. (1967) Lithium as a prophylactic agent: its effect against recurrent depression and manic-depressive psychosis. *Arch. Gen. Psychiatry,* **16**, 162−172.
This is of special historical interest, being the first paper discussing discontinuation of lithium prophylaxis.

Goodnick,P.J. (1985) Clinical and laboratory effects of discontinuation of lithium prophylaxis. *Acta Psychiatr. Scand.,* **7**, 608−614.
Presents results of a controlled week-by-week study of lithium withdrawal and discusses parameters of mood change, side effects, and biochemistry.

Greil,W., Broucek,B., Klein,H.E. and Engel-Sittenfeld,P. (1982) Discontinuation of lithium maintenance therapy: Reversibility of clinical, psychological, and neuroendocrinological changes. In *Basic Mechanisms in the Action of Lithium.* Emrich,H.M., Aldendorf,J.B. and Lux,H.D. (eds), Excerpta Medica, Amsterdam, pp. 235−248.
Reviews effects of lithium discontinuation on clinical state, psychological testing, multiple neuroendocrine measures and in particular, examines those factors that lead to increased risk of relapse.

Sashidharan,S.P. and McGuire,R.J. (1983) Recurrence of affective illness after withdrawal of long-term lithium treatment. *Acta Psychiatr. Scand.,* **68**, 126−133.
Reviews in detail previous work on short-term and long-term lithium discontinuation and discusses the need to interpret effects of short-term withdrawal in terms of long-term results.

31. Compliance with Medication

Kay Redfield Jamison

... The endless questioning finally ended. My psychiatrist looked at me, there was no uncertainty in his voice. 'Manic-depressive illness'. I admired his bluntness. I wished him locusts on his lands and a pox on his house. Silent unbelievable rage. I smiled pleasantly. He smiled back. The war had just begun. ...

Patient with manic-depressive illness

Literature and history bear witness to the tendency for some individuals to resist with passion when cornered by fate, to 'rage against the dying of the light'. Others more readily submit to what may, or may not, have been inevitable. Some differences occur also in the expression of resistance to confronting serious illnesses such as manic-depressive illness. Some patients for years resist accepting their diagnosis, their physicians, and lithium. Others accept the illness and lithium with remarkable alacrity and seeming equanimity. Most fall within these extremes. For every patient who follows the treatment course, there is at least another who does not—who resists, protests, objects, takes too little, takes too much, or does not take at all.

The consequences of untreated or inadequately treated bipolar illness are well-known: recurrence and intensification of affective episodes, often accompanied by interpersonal chaos, alchohol and drug abuse, personal anguish and family disruption, financial crises, marital failure, psychiatric hospitalization, suicide and violence. The effects of lithium non-compliance are, in practical terms, equivalent to those of lithium non-responsiveness. The two are equivalent in their clinical consequences in that the patient continues to experience unstable moods. If the patient refuses to take lithium, or takes it on an ineffectual basis, then lithium's therapeutic efficacy is negated. This is an obvious point, although frequently ignored. There is one difference between lithium non-responsiveness and non-compliance: the latter is reversible and carries with it the possibility of change through education and learning.

The first-reported instance of lithium non-compliance in a manic-depressive patient was, in fact, the first patient ever treated with lithium by Dr John Cade (see pp. 24–28). Several anecdotal reports of lithium non-compliance have subsequently been published, along with proposed explanations for the phenomenon. Among the reasons given by investigators in early reports were decreases in creativity and productivity, denial, intolerance of reality-based depressions, preference for a hypomanic lifestyle, lithium-induced relapses, and provocation by family members who missed the patient's hypomanias.

Bipolar patients, like other patients with chronic relapsing illness, are often bothered by the idea of having a lifetime disorder symbolized by the necessity of taking daily medication. Hence the need to be non-compliant to facilitate denial of the illness. More specifically, patients often feel 'flattened' in emotions—missing the subjective 'high' of hypomanic periods. This is further testified to by the fact that patients experiencing the predominantly manic form of the illness (more commonly in men) are least likely to adhere to a lithium regimen. This finding also suggests that a greater degree of loss of insight—most characteristic of the manic forms of the illness—may be a factor in non-compliance.

Table 31.1 *Risk factors for lithium non-compliance*

Younger
Fewer episodes
Male
Complaints of 'missing highs'
History of grandiose, euphoric manias
Elevated mood
History of non-compliance

Table 31.2 *Reasons most frequently given by patients for discontinuing lithium*

Lithium side effects
Miss 'highs'
Bothered by idea that moods are controlled by medication
Feel well, see no need to take lithium
Feel less creative, less productive
Feel depressed

Many patients not only miss the subjective experience of their 'highs', but the vocational, interpersonal, sexual and artistic advantages of hypomanic indefatigability and inspiration. Clinical observations suggest that many patients develop a relative decline from their baseline (pre-lithium) behaviour in becoming less outgoing, less ambitious, less confident, and less sexually aggressive. Such changes can have profound effects on established relationships.

Risk factors for lithium non-compliance, summarized from several studies, are presented in *Table 31.1*. Generally, compliance appears to increase with age which, in turn, coincides with an increasing risk period for affective recurrences. Importantly, and not surprisingly, better compliance is associated with a larger number of affective episodes requiring treatment.

An interesting pattern evolves for the one rather consistent patient predictor of non-compliance, a constellation of elevated mood variables (these include missing of 'highs', elevated mood in its own right and a history of grandiose delusions). There is some evidence that patients experiencing proportionately more manic than depressive episodes are more likely to be non-compliant. *Table 31.2* presents a summary (based on

Table 31.3 *Lithium side effects cited most frequently by patients as reasons for discontinuing lithium*

Weight gain
Cognitive impairment
Tremor
Increased thirst
Lethargy/tiredness

the research literature) of reasons most frequently given by patients for discontinuing lithium.

Medication Factors

Patients consider weight gain, cognitive impairment, tremor, increased thirst and lethargy as the major reasons for stopping lithium (*Table 31.3*). Gastric irritation, nausea, vomiting and diarrhoea are less often mentioned by patients. The failure of studies to correlate such effects with compliance is intriguing. It is likely that the importance of these factors differs from patient to patient and is cancelled out in the overall data. For instance, tremor would be a greater problem in a typist or a tennis player, gastric symptoms in a patient with ulcer disease, and weight gain in women. Weight gain can result from water retention, decreased physical activity relative to baseline and increased consumption of high-calorie beverages to quench the increased thirst induced by lithium.

Accordingly, it is necessary to warn patients about high-calorie carbonated drinks and to prescribe regular exercise. In general, gastrointestinal side effects are minimized when lithium is taken with meals, or in four divided daily doses (rather than two), or by changing from tablet to capsule. When functionally disruptive, tremor may respond to reduction in dosage or intermittent use of propranolol.

It is important to recognize that lithium may precipitate—or fail to protect against—'atypical' retarded depressive relapses (without vegetative signs), which may respond to a brief course of tricyclics. Conceivably, some of what are considered 'lethargic' and 'memory' side effects of lithium can be accounted for by such unrecognized depressive relapses. Sometimes rapid-cycling is induced by concomitant chronic use of heterocyclic antidepressants; because the emergence of manic episodes is prevented by lithium this may evolve into recurrent and frequent episodes of depression. If this is suspected, the heterocyclic drug should be suspended. These episodes are important to recognize and treat appropriately, because patients may stop lithium out of discouragement from their emergence. Conceivably, some of the 'emotional blunting' ascribed to lithium may be due to unrecognized mini-episodes of this nature.

Some misunderstanding between patients and physicians occurs because of the strong emphasis placed by many psychiatrists on the more 'medical' side effects of lithium (thyroid and kidney functioning, polyuria, tremor). This was a natural emphasis, particularly in earlier clinical studies where there was considerable concern about the long-term somatic effects of lithium. In the midst of investigating these problems, however, relatively little attention was paid to side effects which many patients find more distressing: decreased energy, slowing of cognition, decreased memory and concentration, and lessened enthusiasm. The overlap between the symptoms of affective illness and these lithium-induced changes in cognitive functioning and energy levels has led to a tendency to dismiss many patient complaints as being due to breakthrough depressions or other manifestations of affective illness. Indeed, it is often a difficult differential diagnosis, but several studies have observed cognitive side effects of lithium in normals, as well as in patients with affective disorders. The effect of lithium on personality is of relevance to compliance, as research indicates that many patients are less sociable, outgoing, active and elated when on lithium.

Some of the cognitive effects may be unavoidable and, as yet, untreatable; certainly not all patients on lithium experience them. It is, however, important that they be taken seriously and corrected to the extent possible. In some instances decreased energy and slowed intellectual functioning are due to lithium induced hypothyroidism. This can be easily treated. In other cases, the problems can be due to too little lithium, leading to breakthrough depressions or too much lithium, leading to mild neurotoxicities. Subtle titration of the lithium dosage can substantially improve the problem.

Treatment Factors

Guidelines for maximizing lithium compliance are summarized in *Table 31.4*. It is important to order regular lithium levels and enquire frequently about possible problems with compliance and concerns about the medication. Physician attitudes toward lithium are critical, as are those held by psychotherapists involv-

Table 31.4 *Guidelines for maximizing lithium compliance*

Monitor compliance
Regular lithium levels
Enquire frequently
Encourage queries and concerns from patients
Side effects
Forewarn
Treat aggressively, especially lithium-induced hypothyroidism
Minimize lithium level
Education
Early symptoms of mania and depression
Unremitting and worsening course of (untreated) manic-depressive illness
Medication
Minimize number of daily doses
Pillboxes, especially if on two or more medications
Involve family members in administering, if appropriate
Written information about lithium and side-effects
(Limited) patient-titration of lithium level
Adjunctive psychotherapy
Self-help groups

ed in the patient's care. In general, physicians who are ambivalent about the role of biological factors in the causation and treatment of affective disorders will convey their ambivalence to their patients and possibly contribute to unsatisfactory compliance. The problem is further compounded by a large number of mental health workers who are antagonistic to lithium and other psychoactive medications; they may, in subtle or overt fashion, sabotage drug compliance. By contrast, clinicians with extreme biological persuasions may 'oversell' lithium and thereby pave the way to patient disillusionment (when minor relapses occur) or they may underestimate the role of psychological factors in this illness and its treatment. Thus, physicians may emphasize 'objective' somatic manifestations of bipolar illness under treatment and overlook 'subjective' symptoms like dulling of emotions or memory disturbances, which are extremely important for many patients. The evidence from studies in general medical settings and lithium clinics suggests that by failing to educate the patient and his family, physicians may inadvertently contribute to lithium non-compliance. Thus, as in other illnesses, compliance is enhanced when the patient and his family have a clear understanding of manic-depressive disease (and its course without treatment) and the role of lithium in attenuating this.

Patients often express resentment at how little information they have received about manic-depressive illness and lithium. Although most lithium clinics and affective disorders clinics routinely provide formal and informal education to patients and families—through lectures, books, articles, pamphlets, discussion groups and ongoing communication between clinicians and patients—this is not always practical in private practices or community mental health centres. It is vitally important, however, that physicians in whatever setting participate in a continuing process of informed consent. The ability to assimilate information about medication and illness varies enormously from time to time, and patients need to be made an active part of the treatment process. Too often a physician is made to feel an unyielding advocate of lithium, which often leads to an adversarial, rather than collaborative situation.

Finally, it is important to stress the role of psychotherapy in the treatment of manic-depressive illness (see Section 32, pp. 121 – 124) and specifically in the area of encouraging lithium compliance. Lithium patients tend to place a far higher value on adjunctive psychotherapy than do clinicians and non-compliant patients have been shown to regard psychotherapy as highly useful in helping them adhere to a regimen of lithium treatment. This is consistent with recent findings that patients treated with cognitive therapy were more lithium compliant than patients who did not receive psychotherapy. The psychotherapy patients also had, derivatively, fewer affective episodes and fewer hospitalizations. Self-help groups, such as those organized by the National Depressive and Manic-Depressive Association, are extremely helpful to many patients and their families (see pp. 129 – 132).

The natural tendency for many clinicians is to assume, having once diagnosed the disease and prescribed an enormously effective drug, that the difficult part is over. On the contrary, as the patient quoted at the beginning of the chapter said:—the war has just begun.

Bibliography

Bech,B., Vendsborg,P.D. and Rafaelsen,O.J. (1976) Lithium maintenance treatment of manic-melancholic patients: its role in the daily routine. *Acta Psychiatr. Scand.*, **53**, 70 – 81.

Goodwin,F.K. and Jamison,K.R. (1988) *Manic Depressive Illness.* Oxford University Press, New York.

Jamison,K.R. and Akiskal,H.S. (1983) Medication compliance in

patients with bipolar disorder. *Psychiatr. Clin. N. Am.*, **6**, 175–193.
Kropf,D. and Müller-Oerlinghausen,B. (1985) The influence of lithium long-term medication on personality and mood. *Pharmacopsychiatry,* **18**, 104–105.

32. Psychological Aspects of Treatment

Kay Redfield Jamison

Manic-depressive illness is a complicated, unpredictable, serious and fiercely recurrent illness. It is destructive, often life-threatening and unbelievably frightening to those who experience it. Yet, in its milder forms, it can be an asset to productivity, creativity and sociability. Severe mania and depression are debilitating, but hypomanias are often desired and sought-after states. Moods are such an essential part of the substance of life, of individuality and identity, that few patients find it an easy task to distinguish normal moods from mild and moderate expressions of the disorder. Even under the best of circumstances treatment is, or ought to be, complicated; the expectation of a straightforward therapy, due to the availability of an effective medication, is clearly unrealistic.

The Need for Psychotherapy

Characteristics of manic-depressive illness create certain problems which invite psychotherapeutic intervention. The personal, interpersonal and social sequelae of manic-depressive illness are usually severe, and they can create catastrophic reactions in patients experiencing recurrent manic and depressive episodes. Suicide, violence, alcoholism and hospitalization are but a few of the well-established correlates of the illness. Denial is a natural response. Although biological variables predominate in aetiology and in much of the symptomatic presentation, the primary manifestations are behavioural and psychological, with profound changes in perception, attitudes, personality, mood and cognition. Psychological interventions can be of unique value to the patient undergoing such devastating changes in self-perception and in the perceptions of others.

The fact that manic-depressive illness is so effectively controlled by medication makes certain problems particularly difficult to manage without psychological interventions. Medication is the central treatment, not an adjunctive one and from time to time lithium noncompliance becomes a major theme in the therapy of many patients. Confusion often arises because both lithium and the illness itself can affect cognition, perception, mood and behaviour. Concerns about being on medication in general, and specific concerns about lithium, are substantive psychotherapeutic issues. These concerns about lithium derive both from the direct effects of lithium on the illness (depriving some patients of much sought-after 'highs' and energy) and from the side effects of the drug. These issues are addressed in detail in Section 31, pp. 117–120.

Because lithium is such a highly effective medication there is a tendency for many clinicians to minimize the value of their role, and the role of psychotherapy, in the treatment of manic-depressive illness. Many patients find psychotherapy a highly useful adjunct to lithium treatment and, in the one study in which patients were actually asked their opinions on the matter, twice as many patients as therapists thought psychotherapy was helpful to them in remaining compliant with medication.

The Appropriate Psychotherapeutic Style

The psychotherapy of manic-depressive illness requires considerable flexibility in style and technique. This flexibility is necessitated by the changing moods, cognitions, and behaviours, as well as the fluctuating levels of dependency intrinsic to the illness. In the therapeutic relationship a permissive approach is often useful in maximizing the patient's sense of control over his illness. It is important not to overcontrol the patient and not to allow lithium to become the focus of a power struggle. A thin line exists between overly extensive therapeutic control (which can lead to increased dependency, decreased self-esteem, decreased compliance and increased acting-out) and too little control (occasionally leading to feelings of insecurity, unnecessarily tenuous holds on reality and feelings of abandonment). Thus, firmness and consistency in ordering routine lithium levels or tests of thyroid and kidney functioning may be interpreted as caring, but undue emphasis on precise medication patterns (for example, not allowing for some degree of self-titration) may result in unnecessary power struggles and problems in lithium compliance. Collaborative aspects of management—self-ratings, chartings, patient and family education (through films, lectures, books, handouts)—are also an integral part of good clinical care.

Focal Issues in Psychotherapy

In manic-depressive illness, psychotherapy is often centered on issues involving losses, as well as those involving general concerns about the illness and its effect on the patient and his life.

Losses are those regretted alterations of prior functioning which derive from the effects of lithium on the symptoms of the illness. These changes can include decreases in energy level, loss of euphoric states, increased need for sleep, possible decreases in productivity and creativity, and decreased sexuality.

Studies of patient attributions suggest that many patients feel their manic-depressive illness makes positive contributions to their lives in one or more important ways, specifically through increased sexuality, productivity, creativity and sociability. Attributions of such kinds are important for several reasons. From a clinical perspective it is important to realize the meaning, nature and value of positive behaviour and mood changes (as well as negative ones) for an individual patient. From a learning theory point of view, such altered states of consciousness can be highly potent re-inforcers which create in some patients a potentially strong, variable reinforcement schedule with significant benefits on the one hand, and the risk of severe emotional and pragmatic problems on the other.

Treatment management under such circumstances is not an altogether straightforward matter. For example, compliance with a therapeutic lithium regimen—which, at best, has a tenuous and delayed relationship with the alleviation of dysphoric features of manic-depressive illness—competes with a highly positive, intermittent reinforcement schedule, an exceedingly difficult behaviour pattern to modify. In some ways it is analogous to a drug self-administration paradigm in which a highly pleasurable, and occasionally immediate, state can be obtained. Thus, for some patients the illness may represent, in effect, an endogenous stimulant addiction. Clinical experience suggests that patients may attempt to induce mania by discontinuing lithium, not just at times when they are depressed, but also when they have to face problematic decisions and life events. Because the negative consequences accrue only later, it is not always clear to the patient that the costs outweigh the benefits.

Thus, it is important that the clinician be aware of the positive features of mood swings in order better to understand, and thereby treat, affective disorders. The subtle and powerful clinician–patient alliance possible in lithium therapy is predicated on a thorough understanding of not only the benefits of lithium to the patient but also the realistic, and unrealistic, fantasies of loss that many patients have during lithium treatment.

Therapeutic issues of general concern involve many areas of patients' adjustment to having manic-depressive illness: fears of recurrence, denial of the illness, discrimination of normal from pathological moods, effects of the illness on normal developmental tasks and others.

Fears of recurrence

These are almost ubiquitous in patients with manic-depressive illness. Some patients become preoccupied with such fears and may almost be described as illness-phobic; they become unduly self-protective and hyperalert for signs of an impending episode. These concerns are often reflected in the process of learning to differentiate normal from abnormal moods and states. A related concern is a perceived decreasing tolerance for affective episodes. This is usually secondary to the stress of the illness, and to the large amount of psychological energy consumed by earlier bouts of depression and mania. Patients often express fears about the decreasing tolerance by families and friends for such recurrences. Bipolar illness also takes a severe toll in its cumulative effects on relationships and professional activities.

Denial

Denial of the illness, of its severity, and occasionally even of its existence, as well as denial of the possibility of recurrence, are frequent clinical themes in bipolar illness. In some instances, the cognitive impairments in depression and mania are sufficiently pronounced that they alone account for some problems in recollection. More often, repression and psychological and temporal distance cause the depression to pale into relative insignificance for a certain proportion of patients. Frequently, the severity and nature of the manic episode is minimized or forgotten. Again, this can be due to several factors: the relatively clearer perception for the earlier and more enjoyable stages of mania, amnesia secondary to the organic features of manic psychosis and repression. In addition, the sheer volume of cognitions, perceptions, and behaviours during mania makes detailed recall of the manic episode unlikely.

Mood discrimination

Problems in learning to discriminate normal from abnormal moods are common throughout the psychotherapy of bipolar patients maintained on a lithium regimen. Many manic-depressives, because of the intensity of their emotional responses, fear the escalation of a normal depressive reaction into a major depressive episode and, somewhat less commonly, fear the escalation of a state of well-being into hypomania or mania. Many common emotions, of course, range across several mood states, spanning euthymia, depression and hypomania. For example, irritability and anger can be part of normal human existence or can be symptoms of both depression and hypomania. Tiredness, sadness and lethargy can be due to normal circumstances, medical causes or clinical depression. Feeling good, being productive and enthusiastic, and working hard can be either normal or pathognomonic of hypomania. These overlapping emotions can be confusing and arouse anxiety in many patients; patients may then question their own judgement and become unduly concerned about recurrences of their affective illness.

Therapy often consists of helping the patient to discriminate normal from abnormal affect and of teaching him to live within a narrow range of emotions while learning to use those emotions with greater subtlety and discretion. Closely related to the discrimination of moods is the slow, steady process involved in patients' learning to unravel what is normal personality from what has been superimposed upon it in terms of turbulence, impulsiveness, lack of predictability and depression.

Developmental issues

Developmental tasks, previously overshadowed by the manic-depressive illness, often become issues for the euthymic patient. In an ironic sense, manic-depressive illness can act in some ways as a protection against many of the slings and arrows of fortune encountered in normal life. Because late adolescence and early adulthood are the highest risk periods for the onset of the illness, many of the developmental tasks of these periods—individuation, interpersonal intimacy, romantic involvements, hurts, rejections and career developments—are impaired or temporarily halted. Once the illness is in remission and/or under control, patients often have to deal with these problems—as well as those of a more general existential nature—within the therapeutic situation.

Illness effects

Concerns about effects of the illness on a family system can be profound. Patients report feeling guilty about things done while manic and those left undone while depressed. The most frequently voiced concerns centre on the interpersonal sequelae of the illness, effects strongly felt by spouses, family members and friends as well.

Genetic aspects of the illness

Concerns about the genetic component of manic-depressive illness are considerable for many patients. Such concerns relate to worries about possible transmission of the disorder to children; over-identification when a close family member, particularly a parent, has the illness; and, occasionally, guilt over receiving an effective treatment (lithium) which was not available to an afflicted parent. This latter phenomenon, although not common, is particularly striking in those patients whose parents committed suicide or were hospitalized for long periods of time. A similar guilt is sometimes seen in those patients successfully treated with lithium whose siblings or parents refuse treatment.

Psychological Support

Types of psychological support for the treatment of lithium patients range from none at all to combined use of individual and group psychotherapy. Most commonly, however, a general physician or psychopharmacologist is the one who treats lithium patients, usually within a limited time frame of 20–30 min, every several weeks. Clearly, very little in-depth psychotherapeutic work takes place in such a context; however, the doctor can still provide an emotionally supportive atmosphere, be aware of the general psychological issues involved in being on lithium and having an affective illness, and encourage patients to express their concerns. Providing a therapeutic relationship of this kind increases the likelihood of lithium compliance and makes it more probable that the patient will be referred for formal psychotherapy if there is a need for it.

The encouragement of patients' participation in self-help groups is also important and most major American cities now have, or are starting, branches of the National Depressive and Manic-Depressive Association. The issue of self-help groups is considered in detail in Section 35, pp. 129–132.

Bibliography

Cochran,S.D. (1984) Preventing medical noncompliance in the outpatient treatment of bipolar affective disorders. *J. Consult. Clin. Psychol.*, **52**, 387–878.
Reports the finding that cognitive therapy, in conjunction with lithium treatment, resulted in fewer episodes of affective illness and hospitalizations than did lithium alone.

Jamison,K.R., Gerner,R.H., Hammen,C. and Padesky,C. (1980) Clouds and silver linings: positive experiences associated with the primary affective disorders. *Am. J. Psychiatry*, **137**, 198–202.
An account of positive experiences associated with bipolar affective illness and perceived long- and short-term effects of the illness on sexual behaviour, productivity and social ease.

Jamison,K.R. and Goodwin,F.K. (1983) Psychotherapeutic treatment of manic-depressive patients on lithium. In *Psychopharmacology and Psychotherapy*. Greenhill,M.H. and Gralnick,A. (eds), The Free Press, New York, pp. 53–77.
A review of the literature and a general clinical discussion of the role of psychotherapy in the treatment of manic-depressive illness.

33. The Role of Primary Care Physicians

M.K.Hasan and F.Joseph Whelan

It is estimated that at any given time approximately 20% of a given population in an industrialized world are suffering from some form of emotional illness. Increased recognition of emotional illness by society at large and by the medical profession in particular, combined with a shortage of psychiatrists all over the world, makes it not only desirable but imperative that primary care physicians (general or family practitioners) should be actively involved in the outpatient management of the emotionally ill patients. The stigma associated with psychiatric referral results either in a large number of patients not seeking treatment or, when the need is recognized, in treatment not being initiated. The primary care physician (especially in the UK and Europe) with his closeness to the patient and family is in the best position to carry out this role. It therefore behoves our educationalists and planners to ensure that better undergraduate education in psychiatry be imparted and continued in primary care training. Emphasis on early recognition by the primary care physician, coupled with education of the patient and family in a non-psychiatric friendly atmosphere, not only activates the therapeutic process, but also results in greater patient compliance with treatment, decreased recidivism or relapses, and increased productivity. Therefore it is necessary for the primary care physician to develop a basic knowledge of lithium, and of the indications and principles of treatment, unwanted effects on various organs and systems, and the management of this drug.

Knowledge Required by the Primary Care Physician

When to refer for lithium therapy

In order to have any chance of working, lithium therapy must be prescribed. Since, in general, primary care physicians do not usually undertake the initiation of lithium treatment, this means that a decision must be made, sooner or later, to refer the patient to an appropriate centre—usually a hospital—where the treatment may be commenced under all necessary supervisory conditions. It is, of course, better that this referal should be sooner rather than later and this means that the diagnosis of the existence of a lithium-responsive illness should be made quickly and accurately. To the experienced family practitioner this should present few problems.

Epidemiological evidence. The practitioner should be aware of the fact that depressive conditions are more common among women than men (pp. 9–16), especially in divorced or separated women, and this should act as a first-line clue that a depressive state may exist, even though it may be masked by other symptoms.

Diagnosis with rating scales. Various rating scales have been devised and widely used to diagnose mania and depression, and to make distinctions between these affective conditions and other states (anxiety, schizophrenia, etc.). It is, however, seldom necessary for the family practitioner to resort to such measures; attention to symptom patterns (see pp. 3–9 and 9–19) is usually sufficient, particularly if the physician has intimate knowledge of the family. As a general rule, if any doubt exists as to whether a patient presents with anxiety or depression, less danger is entailed by assuming that it is the latter, since erroneous diagnosis of anxiety as depression can lead to prescription of depressant drugs, thus worsening the condition and perhaps triggering a suicide attempt.

Indications. It is important that the family practitioner should be clear that lithium is classically indicated in unipolar mania, bipolar affective disorders (mania and depression), recurrent depression (unipolar), and rapid cycling affective disorders, and also that lithium is effective in a subgroup of depressed patients with a positive family history of bipolar illness, when the affective states occur more than once every 2 years and where the attacks are disabling with increased frequency and intensity with passage of time. Lithium is also effective in those depressed patients with high incidence of manic episodes and/or cyclothymic personalities in the first or second degree relatives. The use of lithium in experimental conditions should be avoided by the primary care physician.

If these conditions are satisfied by any particular patient and it is felt that a trial with lithium carbonate is warranted, it is best not to prescribe any other treatment but to refer the patient immediately to a psychiatrist so that lithium can be initiated without fear of any interfering drug interactions occurring.

Pretreatment tests

These have been discussed elsewhere (see pp. 59–62), but it may be noted there that the primary care physician may expect to see certain tests carried out on any patient referred for possible lithium therapy, and he should prepare the patient for this. Such tests may include haematological examination, thyroid function tests, tests of nitrogen metabolism, renal clearance, and cardiac electrical activity. It may be that the family practitioner already possesses knowledge of certain medical characteristics of the patient (significant renal disease, cardiovascular disease, need for thiazide diuretics, etc.) which might preclude lithium therapy, or render it inadvisable, and such information should be passed to the psychiatrist charged with looking into the possibility of instituting lithium therapy.

If preliminary tests are not done, or if not enough are done, the family practitioner should exert his right to know why. He should also see to it that suitable tests are performed at intervals, in accordance with the general principles of good clinical manangement.

Dosage levels

One of the main tasks of the family practitioner will be to act as the first line of professional support and information to the patient during maintenance therapy, and he must, therefore, be able to give advice on such matters as dose levels, dose regime and serum levels (pp. 67–73, 88–91 and 99–105). In this regard it has to be remembered that elderly patients may require lower doses and often respond at lower therapeutic levels than do younger patients, and once the dosage has been stabilized lithium should be given as a single bedtime dose (slow release form) (pp. 94–98) as it facilitates compliance (pp. 117–121). Capsules tend to cause less nausea than do tablets. It should never be given on an empty stomach, as this tends to increase nausea and abdominal discomfort. The primary care physician should encourage the patients and families to maintain a 'lithium diary' noting when lithium is taken and what changes are noted in mood or other aspects of bodily functions. Arrangements can, if it is felt desirable, be made with the local laboratory that patients be allowed to call and know their lithium level. This allows the patient and the family to have some control over the illness. It also allows the patient and the family to determine the therapeutic level at which the patient functions best, since individual variations do occur.

Side effects

Since side effects of lithium are varied, and can occasionally masquerade as physical illnesses unrelated to lithium therapy or mood disorder, the family practitioner must be trained to recognize them, and also to advise the patient on how to minimize the risk that they will occur.

Should the patient take an overdose of lithium, either deliberately or inadvertently, or should serum levels rise for any other reason (sodium loss, etc.), it is likely to be the family practitioner who is first called in to deal with matters, and he must know at once what measures to take and in what order (pp. 154–158).

Drug interactions

In a patient's lifetime, most of the medications he receives will be prescribed by the family practitioner. It is virtually inevitable that while a patient is receiving lithium a wide variety of other medications will also be prescribed for common ailments, operations, and so on. The family practitioner must keep abreast of current information on likely interactions between lithium and other drugs, particularly in those cases where a rise in serum lithium levels has been reported or might be expected to occur (pp. 161–191). This is even more important as more and more drugs become available without prescription.

Supporting the Patient and Aiding Compliance

It is not unknown for some primary care physicians to be rather antagonistic towards lithium therapy. In purely medical terms, it is difficult to understand why this should be, but one or two possible reasons suggest themselves. In the first place, by having to refer the patient to someone else for treatment, the family practitioner may feel that somehow he has lost control of the treatment situation. There are relatively few other psychiatric drugs which need to be initiated in the hospital setting. Secondly, the need for close serum monitoring, at least in the early stages of treatment, may lead the family practitioner to believe that lithium therapy is too potentially dangerous and that is should be replaced as soon as possible by a less hazardous form of treatment.

This attitude, which can convey itself to the patient and lead to reduced compliance with the medication regimen, has somehow to be reversed and converted into one of the positive regard and support for lithium therapy. A proper programme of training will clearly be of benefit in this direction.

If the family practitioner is persuaded of the efficacy of lithium and the need for administration to be sustained in accordance with a strict regimen, there are several ways in which he can act to enhance compliance and offer positive support during therapy.

Contact with patient and family

It is essential that the family practitioner should educate both patient and family about lithium therapy, taking up information provided by the prescribing psychiatrist and amplifying and, if necessary, extending it. Family members and others likely to be able to support the patient should also be involved. The patient will be making frequent visits to the hospital for serum monitoring, etc., in the early stages of therapy, but the family physician should not allow this to interfere with his own contacts with the patient. Initial bimonthly visits may be needed. Once the patient has become stabilized, the interval can be prolonged. Group counselling, either by the primary care physician or by his nurse (or both), on a monthly basis has been found to be effective in increasing compliance by increasing involvement. Sessions of 50 min with ten to twelve patients, which focus on feelings, likes, dislikes, and reasons for taking lithium, discourage discontinuation of drug therapy and have been found to be effective (see also pp. 121–124). Family members should be involved in these sessions. Six to ten sessions are usually recommended, and attendance at further (reinforcing) sessions may be reinstituted if compliance is poor. Further discussion of patient compliance is given elsewhere (pp. 117–121).

Lithium clinics

Lithium clinics in rural and urban areas could be established by family practitioners, especially where laboratory facilities are not readily available. In such places blood can be centrifuged as soon as possible and allowed to clot for at least 30 min, and the serum can then be transported or mailed to a local laboratory the following day. Telephone conversations with a psychiatrist (specialist), especially in rural areas, are not only desirable but highly recommended, as they increase confidence on the part of the primary care physician in treating such patients.

An Increased Role for the Family Practitioner

Whilst lithium therapy is almost always currently instituted by a psychiatrist based in a hospital, and with the patient frequently (though not always) hospitalized whilst serum levels are being stabilized, there is increasing pressure being brought to bear for the family practitioner to initiate and supervise the treatment when this can be done on an outpatient basis. There seems, in principle, little objection to this, provided that the following safeguards are applied:

(i) The family practitioner has access to laboratory facilities so that serum lithium levels can be established.

(ii) There is good liaison with a psychiatrist in a local hospital, enabling the family practitioner to obtain advice and to discuss the case where necessary.

(iii) The family practitioner is familiar with all aspects of lithium therapy, and particularly with such issues as contraindications, side effects and possible adverse interactions.

If a once-a-day administration regime is used, the likelihood of long-term toxicity is reduced (pp. 99–105), and, if the 12-h serum level is kept as low as is compatible with therapeutic success, short-term side effects may also be minimized. Under these circumstances, it may be possible to envisage lithium therapy becoming a treatment offered and maintained, in suitable cases, by the family practitioner.

Bibliography

Hasan,M.K. and Mooney,R.P. (1983) Indications for lithium therapy of the mentally ill in general practice. *Compr. Ther.*, **9**, 48–52. A short but useful and very readable article which sets down the major features of lithium therapy which must be known by any primary care physician.

34. The Lithium Clinic

Ronald R.Fieve and Eric D.Peselow

The emergence of lithium as the treatment of choice for recurrent bipolar affective illness and its efficacy in preventing recurrent unipolar episodes have contributed to a need for specialized outpatient psychiatric clinics. The first lithium clinics, established in the late 1960s, were Dr Ronald R.Fieve's New York State Lithium Clinic, USA and Dr Ray Kerry's Lithium Clinic in the UK. According to a report published by the Laboratories of Smith, Kline and French in 1978, there were, at that time, 122 lithium clinics in the USA, and some increase has taken place in the ensuing years.

The lithium clinics in the USA widely vary in terms of composition and goals of treatment. In some, the emphasis is on affective disorder rather than on any particular treatment, so that patients may be receiving either lithium alone or lithium in conjunction with other therapies. In other clinics the emphasis is on the lithium therapy itself rather than the diagnosis. This section will describe a model lithium clinic, The Foundation for Depression–Manic Depression established in New York by Ronald R.Fieve in 1975, and will pay special attention to organization, procedures, and manpower utilization. The issue of economics of lithium clinics is dealt with in Section 70, pp. 257–259.

Organization and Procedures

Unlike traditional outpatient psychiatric clinics which offer treatment for a heterogeneity of psychiatric diagnostic groups (along with heterogeneous treatment), the rationale behind a specialized clinic is to supervise long-term treatment of large numbers of affectively ill patients and to help educate these patients about their medications and illness. By focusing on affective illness and pharmacological treatment, the staff members of these clinics develop expertise in clinical evaluation and psychopharmacological drug monitoring.

For the past 11 years, Dr Fieve and his associates have not only developed research, training, and clinical treatment programmes in the Foundation for Depression–Manic Depression, but have evaluated the manpower and cost/benefit efficacy of this approach. Approximately 750 bipolar and unipolar patients have been accepted and treated in this setting since 1975 and as of May 1st 1986 this facility was treating approximately 240 individuals on an ongoing basis. This particular clinic, with its research focus, has the added benefit of studying characteristics of lithium responders and non-responders in addition to pursuing a wide variety of pharmacological and non-pharmacological approaches to acute and recurrent unipolar and bipolar illness.

The criteria for acceptance of a patient rests on meeting the diagnostic requirements outlined by J.P.Feighner and his associates in 1972 for primary affective disorder. The patient is then further subclassified according to Fieve–Dunner criteria as bipolar I (a history of hospitalization to mania), bipolar II (a history of hospitalization for depression with a history of hypomania), bipolar other (a history of mild hypomania and mild depression) or unipolar (a history of hospitalization or out-patient treatment for depression only). In order to make these diagnoses, all staff (nurses, psychologists and MDs) are trained and supervised in the administration of a structured SADS interview supervised by a senior psychologist or psychiatrist.

If the patient fulfills the diagnostic criteria, he or she is offered the opportunity to be treated at the clinic, and is then asked to give informed consent for initial treatment, the maintenance of confidential records, and initial medical work-up. Prior to receiving pharmacological treatment, all patients undergo a comprehensive medical examination including complete blood count, comprehensive blood chemistry screening, thyroid testing, urinalysis and, if lithium is considered, 24-h urine for creatinine clearance (see pp. 59–62). Other tests, such as the dexamethasone suppression test, thyroid stimulation test, and 24-h urine for MHPG, are available and given if felt to be clinically appropriate.

The initiation of treatment usually depends upon the symptoms and manner of presentation to the clinic. Approximately 60% of bipolar patients and 50% of unipolar patients are found to be already receiving medication following either a hospitalization or outpatient treatment for acute manic or depressive episodes. Such patients are either receiving lithium alone (approximately 50–55%) or lithium plus other medications (neuroleptics, antidepressants, carbamazepine) and tend to be referred either euthymic or with mild hypomanic or depressive symptoms for the purpose of close medical and psychiatric supervision and continued stabilization of their affective disorder. The remaining patients present, many for the first time, with acute mild, moderate or severe depressive symptoms or mild or moderate hypomania (severe manic patients are generally referred immediately for hospitalization).

All new patients, regardless of their initial symptoms, are seen weekly until they are stabilized on lithium or lithium plus concomitant medication until they are clinically well. This usually occurs over a 3- to 8-week course. Once stabilized in this manner, the patients are seen bi-weekly over a 4- to 6-week course and then every 4 weeks for clinical evaluation, behaviour and mood ratings, and serum lithium and in some instances antidepressant monitoring. Patients who have been stable for greater than one year are seen on a 4- to 6-week basis.

At all visits to the lithium affective disorder clinic, patients are rated as to whether or not they exhibit affective symptoms and/or side effects. This information, along with patient medication, serum lithium or antidepressant monitoring, and global mood ratings by the patient, doctor and nurse is recorded on computerized research forms. Patients' ratings consist of 26 depressive items rated on a 0–3 point scale based on DSM III criteria (from which a Hamilton depression score can be extracted and nine manic/hypomanic symptoms rated on a 0–3 point scale based on DSM III criteria for mania. Side effects are also rated on a 0–3 point scale with 21 common listed side effects and space for the patient to list any other adverse experience. This method not only allows for adequate documentation of clinical care, but has permitted retrospective research analysis of the efficacy of these agents in recurrent affective disorders, as well as the correlation of serum lithium and/or antidepressant levels with acute and recurrent illness, and of serum levels with side effects.

Manpower Utilization

The patient load is handled by one supervising psychiatrist, one nurse and two or three paramedical personnel. The rating team personnel consist of a psychiatric nurse and one or two aides who generally vary from week to week. The supervising physician works closely with the patient during initial presentation, when changes in medication dosage are required, when there are signs of toxicity, or during an affective episode. When the patient, however, is stable (as is the case for more than half of the time), the physicians's contact with the patient is usually brief and generally limited to corroborating mood and side effect ratings and to dispensing medication.

The lithium affective disorder clinic is held twice weekly for 5 h on each day, and 2–3 h periods are set aside on two other days to handle emergency situations. The clinic is attended by virtually the entire group of 240 patients each month. The clinic model makes optimal use of its small medical staff by maximum utilization of paramedicals, enabling a large outpatient population to be managed quickly and inexpensively. The traditional psychiatric model (patient problem and direct patient–psychiatrist interaction) has been shifted to patient-rating team interaction with consultations by a supervisory psychiatrist. The primary focus in the lithium clinic is on the presence or absence of an affective episode. Care during the symptom-free period has resulted in decreased psychiatric contact, and increased emphasis on the use of non-physician ratings team.

Until recently, no attempt was made to deal with the intrapsychic or interpersonal problems of the patients except as they related to mood. Recently, however, there has been increasing awareness and research into non-biological therapies for affective disorders. There is some evidence for the effectiveness of both interpersonal therapy and cognitive therapy in the treatment and prevention of outpatient depressive episodes. In addition, there is anecdotal evidence that the use of supportive psychotherapy and group therapy might diminish recurrence for unipolar and bipolar patients. Generally, the focus of group therapy allows patients to gain support from others who have similar problems resulting from their affective illness. There is some evidence that group and supportive therapy improve compliance, with consequent reduction in relapse (see pp. 117–121). The affective disorder clinic described here employs a psychologist and two therapists for patients who require the above approaches, either as a consequence of their illness or as a result of their difficulty in handling real life stresses regarding their vocation or interpersonal relationships. Approximately 20% of patients receive one or more of these non-biological approaches in addition to pharmacotherapy.

Specialization in Medical Services

The lithium clinic specializes in the treatment of affective disorders. This is important because it offers many affective disorder patients specialized diagnostic and treatment benefits, unique to their illness. This is in opposition to the general psychiatric model which still predominates in the United States today, whereby a mixed diagnostic patient population is treated and given lithium along with all other forms of treatment.

An analogy to the specialized lithium clinic is the existence of specialized medical clinics, i.e. diabetes clinics, arthritis clinics, cardiology clinics and hypertension clinics. Forty years ago, these medical problems were treated by the same physician in one general medical clinic in a hospital center. With the discovery of specific treatments for these illnesses, the need for specialization developed and thus specific clinics all side by side in the medical section of hospital centers, but separate and distinct, came into existence. Such specialization made for improved care for patients.

Specialized clinics have been slow in coming to psychiatry, but have risen rapidly in recent years. Since the initial lithium clinics of Fieve in New York, USA, and Kerry in the UK, it is estimated that there are approximately 200 such clinics in the USA today. In addition, the 1980s have seen the rise of specialized alcohol, substance abuse, anxiety, tardive dyskinesia and geriatric psychiatric clinics. With specific treatments for psychiatric illnesses (lithium for affective disorders), specialization is possible and such specialization can provide optimum and cost-effective care for the mentally ill.

Bibliography

Daley,R.M. (1978) Lithium responsive affective disorders. Model comprehensive plan for treatment. *N.Y. State J. Med.*, **78**, 594–601.
This article fully explains the economic feasibility of the specialized lithium clinic.

Ellenberg,J., Salamon,I. and Meaney,C. (1980) A lithium clinic in a community mental health center. *Hosp. Community Psychiatry*, **31**, 834–836.
Describes the advantages and practicality of a specialized clinic existing separately within a community mental health center.

Fieve,R.R. (1977) The lithium clinic: A new model for the delivery of psychiatric services. *Curr. Psychiatr. Ther.*, **17**, 189–200.
An early description of the concept of the lithium clinic.

Kerry,R.J. (1969) A special lithium clinic. *Dis. Nerv. Syst.*, **30**, 490–492.
Dr Kerry details the structure and functions of a lithium clinic established in the UK.

Shelley,E.M. and Fieve,R.R. (1974) The use of non-physicians in a health maintenance program for affective disorder. *Hosp. Community Psychiatry*, **25**, 303–305.
Gives a comprehensive understanding of how paramedical personnel can be utilized inexpensively and efficiently in the care of psychiatric outpatients.

35. Lithium Self-help Groups

John A.J.Rook

Even as little as 20 years ago it was considered bad form, upsetting to others and embarrassing to mention manic-depressive illness or other mental illnesses in public. Nowadays, however, the stigma of mental illness is dwindling and most patients and relatives want to share their experiences openly with each other. Expressions such as ‘manic-depressive insanity’ or ‘recurrent insanity’ are thankfully obsolete. Lithium treatment itself has helped open discussion to become possible. The administration of a carbonate salt can be discussed more easily than some other treatments such as abreaction, narcosis treatment, months in a mental hospital or the well-known electro-convulsive therapy.

So, in other words, lithium, as well as being an effective form of control therapy for most manic-depressive patients, also has the considerable bonus of being a clear chemical treatment for what is after all now widely seen as a chemical illness. The assumption of the past that manic-depressive illness or cyclothymia were something that the patient and relatives should be ashamed of, has gone. Now patients are not inhibited and want the chance to talk freely about the problems and to exchange views and ideas.

In the last 10 years the number of patients being treated with lithium has increased dramatically. There were over 35 000 in the British Isles in 1985 and the pressure from many of them, and just as importantly from their relatives too, to start or join a self-help group has been, and is, considerable. The Lithium Club, founded in 1983 in the UK is now trying to fulfil this need.

The pressure to establish a self-help group arises from the understandable desire to talk to and befriend other patients, and from the frustration of needing help to meet another patient. Clearly, members of the medical profession are unable to pass on information about their patients or to help contacts to be made. The self-help groups which have started in several parts of the UK are successfully filling the lines of communication that are so badly needed. Indeed, it is a not uncommon experience to meet new members of such groups who, despite having been on lithium for more than 15 years, have never knowingly met another patient. In all cases they proclaim their loneliness, frustration and isolation. They deeply regret that, other than their doctor, they have had few understanding people to talk to, and they express a wish that a self-help group had been available many years earlier. The closest members of their families have exactly the same feelings.

At the present time there are not enough self-help groups to cater for the nationwide needs of lithium patients. This problem could be solved by the efforts of the patients and relatives who do not live near an existing group.

How to Start a Group

Starting any kind of organization, however limited its membership, is not a task to be taken on lightly in view of the considerable commitment of time and energy that it will inevitably involve. However, there are some simple guidelines which may be followed for those in the UK who feel that the enterprise is worthwhile and these guidelines, suitably modified, may also be adopted by individuals in other countries wishing to establish similar groups.

(i) Contact The Lithium Club at Birdbrook Hall, Birdbrook, Halstead, Essex CO9 4BJ, UK, for names of patients in your area.

(ii) See the psychiatric nurse at your local hospital and ask for his or her friendly support in contacting local patients and arranging a first meeting.

(iii) Hold the inaugural meeting in a room with a comfortable atmosphere and adequate seating.

(iv) See the object of the first meeting as being to elect a committee and establish your self-help group.

(v) Ask patients' spouses or closest relatives whether they wish to attend, but the numbers of this first meeting need not exceed ten people.

(vi) Make, if you wish, a small charge for light refreshments. The time of the meeting will probably be early evening. Lapel badges can be worn by all, with the addition of 'Li' for lithium patients.

(vii) At the meeting, you, or perhaps the psychiatric nurse, should explain the purpose of the new group and listen to suggestions from the others present.

(viii) You need formally to elect a Chairman, Treasurer and Secretary. To be formally established you must have a constitution to enable you to open a bank account. You can either become a branch of the main Lithium Club and use its constitution, or have one of your own drawn up. Each member would pay a small annual subscription, plus an entrance fee to any expensive function that you might hold. The kinds of function that are appropriate for a lithium self-help group are basically decided by the demands of the members of that group.

(ix) From the experience of other lithium self-help groups, it is advisable to limit your membership to one county or other defined geographical region—otherwise it can become geographically very difficult for some members to attend meetings.

Aims and Objectives of the Lithium Club

The Lithium Club was founded by patients for patients and their spouses, and has the following as its main objectives:

(i) To provide opportunities for lithium patients and their spouses to meet for discussion of all aspects of lithium treatment, and of those disorders for which the drug can be used.

(ii) To support the medical profession in its work with lithium patients, and to encourage medical practitioners and psychiatrists to think in terms of prescribing lithium treatment in all appropriate cases at an earlier stage.

(iii) To achieve a sufficiently high membership, spread throughout the country, to enable every member to have a local branch with friendly, helpful contacts.

Many patients have already found meeting other patients an invaluable experience. There is now no need for any lithium patient to feel alone.

Amongst the successful activities that the Club runs are social evenings organized by the executive committee which often include a medical expert as a guest speaker. An up-to-date list of lithium contacts is made available to members once they have agreed that their own names be included. Recently published information is circulated, together with a quarterly newsletter. A pen-friendship scheme is encouraged and any local social activities are supported.

One of the most important functions of The Lithium Club came about by accident; namely an advice service from officers of the Club to members needing help. Confidence has been given to many worried new patients. For example, they have been advised as to what to say at job interviews about their illness, which will be honest without alarming the interviewer. One or two patients have shown bouts of mania and in these cases another member has usually been able to see them, control their actions, and get them to their doctor as soon as possible.

Concerned friends and relatives of patients can get forgotten by a busy doctor and members of the Lithium Club do their best to inform them about lithium therapy and put their minds at ease, though it should be emphasized that when such advice is given to patients an attempt is always made to work alongside the medical profession and, if in doubt, the patient or the problem is always referred back to the doctor.

It should be noted that it is part of the objective of the Lithium Club to educate the public, as well as the patients and relatives, about the disorder as a biochemical imbalance, its manifestations, course and therapy. Knowledge of the disorder helps to erase the fears and stigmas associated with it.

How Members of the Group Keep in Contact

This is one of the most important functions of the Club. Initially, a list of members, their addresses and telephone numbers, within the patient's area, are supplied to the new member. Some members are too timid to make contacts through the list, but nonetheless the list reassures the patient that he or she is not alone. Chance meetings at social evenings seem to be the most successful first point of contact. Due to the tremendous empathy between patients and spouses speaking a 'common language', friendships are quickly formed. Certainly, the members of the Club's committee, who tend to meet more often than ordinary members, form strong friendships very rapidly.

Once initial contacts have been made, they can be continued by patients attending regular club meetings; but better still, when patients find they live near one another, they may periodically visit each others' homes, go out for tea or a drink together, etc.

If a patient is ill, or needs particular help, then the committee tries to inform members living nearby. For patients who are abroad the pen-friendship scheme enables people to write very openly and helpfully to one another. The newsletter is also a useful means of contact; its contents include a list of future club activities, together with articles from fellow members and from experts on lithium therapy.

The Economics of Setting up and Maintaining a Group

When a group of lithium patients and their spouses come together to form a new self-help group in their area they may be worried about financing the project. It has been found that, after an introductory sum of say £50 – 100 from a well-wisher or the main branch of the Lithium Club, a new club is soon self-financing. A membership fee of about £4 should be charged annually and increased with inflation. Any would-be member who genuinely cannot afford the membership fee is usually allowed membership on a reduced or even no fee basis. In addition, an entrance fee can be charged to any functions that are too expensive for the club to subsidize totally. Secretarial work is best carried out by an unpaid volunteer and stationery expenses, etc., should lie within the club's income.

Obtaining charitable status for a self-help group of this kind is difficult because much of the Club's income is spent on social functions for the benefit of members. The Lithium Club at the present time is, however, seeking charitable status for a Lithium Trust, with the sole aim that any money raised would be used to help doctors and research workers increase their understanding of all aspects of lithium therapy.

An additional source of financial support can come from one of the several pharmaceutical companies that manufacture preparations of lithium carbonate. The manufacturers are seeking goodwill amongst patients and doctors. If money is going to be sought in this way, however, it should be for a particular project and not be relied on as a fundamental part of a club's economic structure.

The Future of the Lithium Club

The Lithium Club considers that its long term aim is to be a nationwide organization to ensure that every patient in the country has the opportunity of having a friendly contact. At the moment the Club has members in parts of the country where there is no branch available. It is hoped that, county by county, with the help of the main committee, people will find the strength to start new groups which will be of direct and positive help to their local patients and their families.

Relationship to Doctors and Research Workers

Doctors have an important role to play in helping self-help groups to be successful in their aims. Their main contribution is in recognizing the usefulness of self-help groups and then being prepared to introduce their patients to their local group. Leaflets and other material are always available at the headquarters of the Lithium Club, indeed many thousands have been distributed to the medical profession.

The other valued contribution which doctors and research workers can make is in being prepared to talk at local branch meetings, and particularly in answering members' questions on lithium therapy. Up-to-date articles on common patient problems for the Club's journal are also very worthwhile. It is not suggested that doctors become members of a self-help group, but rather that they should provide support. Ideally, doctors, research workers and the committees of lithium self-help groups should work together in the best interests of the patients, to try to improve the quality of their lives and enable them to come to terms with both their illness and their therapy.

Related Organizations

There are ways in which self-help groups can draw upon assistance from established medical and social services. The Lithium Club does not work on its own in its attempts to improve the quality of life of cyclothymic and manic-depressive patients. The main comparable self-help group is The Manic Depression Fellowship of Great Britain, Richmond Council for Voluntary Services, 51 Sheen Road, Richmond upon Thames, Surrey, UK. The aims of that organization are similar to those of the Lithium Club, but they do not limit their membership to lithium patients and their spouses. There are several patients who are members of both groups. The major difference between the groups is that the Lithium Club is a more specialized organization and is able to concentrate on enabling members on similar therapy to meet, share their problems and make lasting friends.

The Scottish Association for Mental Health, 40 Shandwick Place, Edinburgh, EH2 4RT, UK and The Mental Health Association of Ireland, 2 Herbert Place, Merrion Road, Dublin 4, Eire, both keep literature available to members of the public; in this literature are the names and addresses of self-help groups appropriate to the illness. The Citizens' Advice Bureaux should also be able to give information on all local groups and services.

Counselling and advisory services can be helpful, particularly if a patient's family matters are in a confused state and if relatives are unable to discuss their associated problems with the doctor. In this context there is The National Association of Young People's Counselling and Advisory Services, 17–23 Albion Street, Leicester, LE1 6GD, UK and, for all needing counselling with family problems, The Marriage Guidance Council, Little Church Street, Rugby, Warwickshire, UK.

Part VI

CLINICAL PRACTICE: PATIENT FACTORS

36. Young and Elderly Patients

Stephan Schmidt and Waldemar Greil

The typical lithium-treated patient, both in the clinic and in private psychiatric practice, is middle-aged (between 35 and 60 years) and shows a history of several episodes of recurrent affective disorder (unipolar depression, bipolar or schizoaffective psychosis). The average age of long-term lithium-treated patients still undergoing therapy in the Psychiatric Hospital of Berlin University, West Germany, has been calculated to be about 51 years; in the Psychiatric Hospital in Aarhus, Denmark, it is 44 years (±12). Most patients with affective psychoses treated by private practitioners will receive their first administration of lithium at an age of between 40 and 50 years, though about 18% of these patients will be between 50 and 60 and 12% between 60 and 80 years.

Usually, affective disorders have their first appearance between 30 and 40 years of age, but they can also begin in childhood as well as in the elderly. The likely course of the illness and the risk of a relapse seem to change depending on the patient's age at the beginning of the disorder: patients with the first episode of a unipolar depression before their 20th year will, on average, have the second episode 6 years later; patients with the first episode when they are between 20 and 30 years will get a second episode about 5 years later, and so on. If the first manifestation of the disorder comes after the 60th year, the second episode

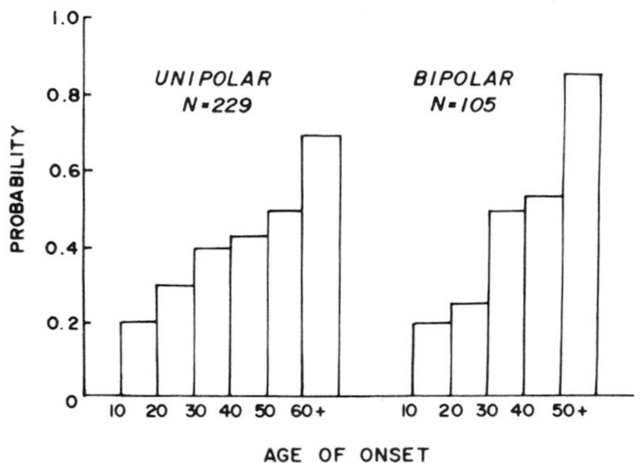

Figure 36.1 Risk of a relapse within 2 years, as related to the patient's age at onset of a unipolar or bipolar disorder. From Zis,A.P., Grof,P., Webster,M. and Goodwin,F.K., (1980) *Psychopharmacol. Bull.*, **16**, 47–49.

will tend to appear shortly afterwards (one and a half years, on average). *Figure 36.1* demonstrates this relationship between the age at onset of unipolar or bipolar psychosis and the risk of a relapse within 24 months. The probability of a recurrence following the first episode grows with increasing age at onset. It is not unusual for affective disorders to display a late beginning and this may be the case in about 10–15% of patients. An early beginning on the other hand, and especially the occurrence of a first episode of a recurrent affective disorder in childhood, seems to be relatively rare and creates diagnostic problems.

Children

Affective psychoses in childhood

It is actually quite difficult to describe a characteristic picture of affective psychoses in children: only observation over several years and the nature of the long-term course of the disease with recurrent episodes can strengthen the diagnosis of an affective psychosis. The famous German psychiatrist Kraepelin, 1913, produced an estimate, based on reviews of the charts of about 900 patients, that 0.4% of all patients with affective psychoses had their first episode before their 10th year. Other authors confirmed this result but Dr Jules Angst, Research Director of the Psychiatric Hospital of Zurich University, Switzerland, and his co-workers, were unable to establish any case of such an early manifestation of affective psychoses before the 12th year in a total of 2369 inpatients.

Often, the symptoms of depressive or manic states in children are quite similar to those found in adults (see pp. 3–19) but sometimes the clinical picture will be atypical: manic symptoms in children can, for example, be similar to schizophrenia. The main symptom of depression may be hyperactivity, aggressiveness or social withdrawal (i.e. symptoms that can be mistaken for conduct disorder), sleep problems, poor school performance, headache and anxiety. Frequently, the main characteristic is the prominence of somatic symptoms and antisocial behaviour. The differential diagnostic procedures are, therefore, of great importance and have to consider a depressive reaction, a depressive personality disorder, a conduct disorder, a somatic depression, early stages of incipient schizophrenia or depressive symptoms of an epileptic disorder. An accurate diagnosis is a prerequisite for a precise determination of the risk of recurrence of the affective symptoms and of the indication for long-term prophylactic lithium treatment.

Indication for lithium treatment in children

Although lithium is now established in adult psychiatric care, its place in child and adolescent psychiatric treatment is not yet clear.

In the first report of the use of lithium in the younger age group, published in 1959, a description was given of the successful treatment of a 14-year-old boy who suffered from what was described as periodic psychosis with longer manic and shorter depressive phases. This patient appeared to have been suffering from manic-depressive illness. But despite that report and subsequent ones detailing observations and case histories of children suffering from an affective psychosis, it has remained a matter of controversy as to whether recurrent affective psychoses exist in children.

In children and adolescents the indication for prophylactic long-term lithium treatment has to be rigorously established. After 2 or 3 major affective episodes within a period of 1–2 years it might be useful to start prophylactic treatment in children or (more often) in adolescents. Close adherence to the dose schedule, and regular monitoring of serum lithium levels, are prerequisites for successful treatment and therefore the patient and his family have to be able to understand and to cooperate with the treatment (pp. 111–113).

Possible further indications for lithium therapy in children may be acute manic or aggressive states, or states of loss of impulse control. In aggressive states, especially in association with affective disturbances, lithium seems to have a therapeutic as well as a prophylactic effect, possibly because of a specific anti-aggressive efficacy. In 1984, an extensive study was carried out, involving 61 children, aged 6–13 years, who showed severe symptoms of irritability and aggressive conduct disorder, and who had been resistant to other therapeutic procedures. In that study, lithium was compared with the neuroleptic drug haloperidol. Both substances had significant therapeutic effects, but lithium produced fewer side effects on motor behaviour as well as on cognitive and psychomotor processes.

Management

Lithium treatment in children and adolescence can, in general, follow the same procedures as those described for adults, though special attention has to be paid to compliance with the medication regimen. Sometimes, long-term lithium treatment will not be feasible because of a lack of cooperation on the part of the patient or his parents.

If children do not tolerate periodic determination of the lithium serum level by venipuncture, lithium concentration can be determined in the saliva, provided that due regard is paid to the possible sources of inaccuracy involved in such a technique (pp. 91–93).

Side effects in children

There are only a few reports concerning the immediate side effects of lithium treatment in children and little information about its long term effects, especially on the kidneys, but the majority of reports published to date have not indicated any serious side effects or toxic reactions of lithium in the younger age group. It may be that children and adolescents are much less prone to side effects, possibly because their high renal lithium clearance enables them to tolerate relatively high lithium doses without severe side effects. If side effects such as nausea, vomiting or tremor develop, they are transient in most cases.

However, particular attention should be paid to the suppressant effects of lithium on the thyroid gland and to possible lithium-induced changes in calcium metabolism. Considering some of the recent evidence about possible harmful effects of lithium on calcium metabolism in children, the use of lithium in children should be considered only under special circumstances. Children and adolescents of any age receiving lithium therapy should be screened to eliminate any disturbances of their calcium metabolism prior to the start of treatment, and it is preferable that this should be monitored during the course of lithium therapy. In children, body size and body weight should be monitored regularly and X-rays (e.g. hand radiographs) should be taken every 1–2 years to exclude lithium-induced changes of growth of bone.

Concerning the long-term effects, there is a report of five children, aged 13–15 years treated with lithium for 3–5 (mean, 4) years. None of these children exhibited clinical or laboratory signs of impaired renal function.

In view of the present state of knowledge regarding the clinical efficacy, and in view of possible biochemical and endocrinological sequelae of lithium therapy, long-term lithium treatment is indicated, even in older children, only in severe degrees of psychiatric disturbance not amenable to other forms of therapy.

The Elderly

Affective psychoses in the elderly

Although common, depressive states are not at all easily diagnosed in older patients, who may normally be expected to show varying degrees of intellectual, as well as motor, retardation and a reduction of emotional responsiveness and intensity. Furthermore, older patients are more apt to have medical problems and it may be difficult to distinguish between symptoms of an affective disorder and symptoms of somatic disturbances. Depressed old people rarely complain of depression but instead describe a multitude of other symptoms such as insomnia, dizziness, anorexia, constipation and other signs, which together suggest physical rather than mental disorder. Furthermore, older patients may appear to be confused, they complain of changes in memory and concentration and can, therefore, be misdiagnosed of having a senile dementia. But in some of these patients, who are in fact suffering from depressive disorder, treatment with antidepressants or lithium is able to reduce the symptoms and to normalize mental function. Also, manic episodes in the elderly can often lack the characteristic elated mood; instead they can be experienced as nonspecific irritability, typically associated with other (often less pronounced) symptoms of increased psychomotor activity, and sleep or appetite disturbances.

Indication for lithium treatment in the elderly

In the majority of older patients the main indication for lithium treatment is the need to continue prophylaxis initiated when the patient was younger. In the elderly there is high risk of further affective episodes, especially in bipolar affective psychoses. Since unipolar depression can stop in some patients according to the natural course of the disease, a withdrawal trial of lithium may be convenient in patients who have been symptom-free for several years.

In unipolar as well as in bipolar or schizo-affective psychoses the risk of further recurrences is higher in patients who continue to present with minor mood disturbances even during lithium treatment (the so-called 'partial responders').

Indications for the initiation of prophylactic lithium treatment in the elderly are generally analogous to the criteria used in younger patients. In affective psychoses prophylactic treatment is useful after at least two episodes within 3–5 years. In older patients it is

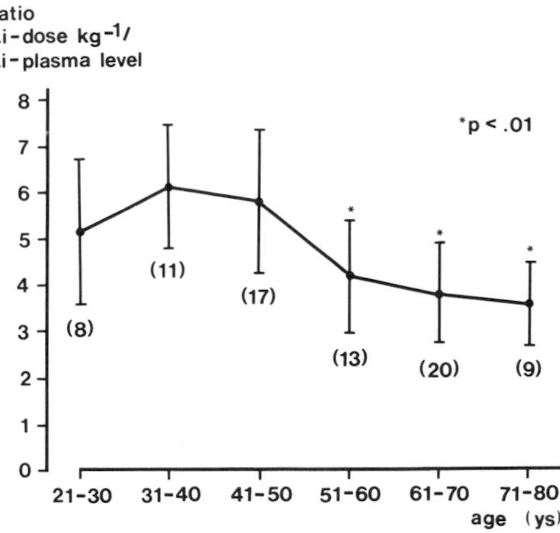

Figure 36.2 Change in the ratio of body weight-related doses to serum lithium levels at different ages (in parentheses: number of subjects). From Greil,W., Stoltzenburg,M.C., Mairhofer,M.L. and Haag,M. (1985) *J. Affect. Dis.*, **9**, 1–4.

necessary to pay special attention to a number of points. In the first place, the frequency, duration and intensity of major affective episodes have to justify the decision to embark upon a continuous pharmacological treatment. Secondly, for every patient the possible risks must be estimated (e.g. pre-existing somatic disorders and contraindications); older patients are more prone to develop impairing side effects and individual predisposition to somatic disturbance must be considered. Thirdly, the therapeutic efficacy of lithium demands the regular intake of the drug, and therefore the patient's intellectual and social condition should be such as to enable him to understand the treatment regimen and to follow it. This can be difficult in patients taking several different drugs because of concomitant somatic disorders.

Management of lithium treatment in the elderly

Lithium treatment in older patients has to be undertaken in full consideration of the physiological changes which occur in cardiac, metabolic, renal and neurological functions in the elderly. Renal clearance is reduced and the volume of distribution of water-soluble drugs such as lithium is diminished. This is very important for lithium dosing in the elderly: several studies have shown a strong relation between lithium serum levels and age. *Figure 36.2* compares the ratio of weight-related dosages to plasma levels in different age decades and shows a highly significant decrease with age, despite marked inter-individual

Table 36.1 *Mean daily dose needed for a plasma lithium level of 0.8 mmol/l in patients of different age groups*

Age (years)	Li^+ (mmol)	Lithium carbonate (mg)
≤45	29.4	1085
46–64	23.7	873
≥65	19.0	699

variability. The decline appears to set in at 50 years of age and seems to be less pronounced in the following decades. In clinical practice it is therefore usual to give lower lithium doses to older patients. *Table 36.1* gives the mean daily lithium dose in 78 patients and demonstrates the necessity of reducing lithium dose in the elderly to exclude toxic lithium serum concentrations.

The main parameter used in controlling lithium-therapy is the 12-h lithium serum level (see pp. 88–91). In the elderly, this level should be lower than usual, e.g. between 0.4 and 0.6 mmol/l, and it is generally held that the serum level should be kept as constant as possible (achieved in some cases by a multiple dose schedule) to avoid unwanted side effects. However, in view of recent discussion of the advisability of less frequent dosing, such as once per day, or even once every two or three days (see pp. 99–105) there is clearly a need to examine in more detail the relative efficacy of different administration schedules in the elderly.

Side effects in the elderly

In older patients, side effects can manifest themselves even in the lower range of lithium doses, and certainly at lower lithium serum levels than they do in younger patients. These side effects can include states of confusion, neurological symptoms and gastro-intestinal complaints.

Special precautions are necessary in the case of elderly patients taking diuretic drugs because of hypertension (pp. 180–183) or anti-rheumatic drugs because of arthrosis (pp. 183–186); specific agents within both groups of substances can diminish renal lithium clearance and thereby induce high serum lithium concentrations, elevating the risk of lithium toxicity. It is very important to instruct elderly lithium-treated patients that they should have regular water intake.

Whilst cardiac disturbances under lithium therapy seem to be rare, underlying cardiac problems may be exacerbated. It is not clear whether lithium can induce bradycardia especially in patients simultaneously taking digitalis, but if an elderly patient is suspected of having any degree of cardiac insufficiency, regular ECG monitoring becomes essential.

If lithium-treated older patients appear to have discrete confusional states, or rapid changes in cognitive functions and memory, these should be considered as possible symptoms of lithium overdose or toxicity and should lead to complete somatic and neurologic examinations including determination of lithium serum levels.

Conclusion

Up to now, the main emphasis in clinical practice as well as in research has been the long term treatment of middle-aged patients with recurrent affective disorders. But children and older patients can be treated with lithium successfully as well provided that the special age-related problems concerning diagnosis, indication and management are regarded carefully.

Bibliography

Foster,J.R., Gershell,W.J. and Goldfarb,A.I. (1977) Lithium treatment in the elderly. I. Clinical use. *J. Gerontol.*, **32**, 299–302.
A review is presented of the clinical use of lithium in manic states in the elderly with special regard to toxicity.

Greil,W., Stoltzenburg,M.C., Mairhofer,M.L. and Haag,M. (1985) Lithium dosage in the elderly. A study with matched age groups. *J. Affect. Dis.*, **9**, 1–4.
This study on lithium dosage in different age groups demonstrates that mean daily lithium doses are significantly lower in the elderly.

Youngerman,J. and Canino,I.A. (1978) Lithium carbonate use in children and adolescents. A survey of the literature. *Arch. Gen. Psychiatry*, **35**, 216–224.
A review of 190 cases of lithium use in children and adolescents reported in the literature and a discussion of the indications for the use of lithium in the younger age group.

37. Sex Differences

Stephan Schmidt and Waldemar Greil

In general the number of lithium-treated women is considerably higher than that of men. That is because unipolar depression occurs more frequently than bipolar psychoses and women seem to suffer more often from unipolar depression, whereas no difference can be found in the incidence of bipolar psychoses in men and women.

Up to now there have been only a few hints that special problems may be associated with the sex of the patient. In general it may be said that in both sexes the indication for, and management of, lithium treatment can follow essentially the same principles.

In a couple of reports, however, the effectiveness of lithium in preventing affective recurrences was found to be greater in men than in women, and a higher incidence of relapses occurred in women during prophylactic lithium therapy, especially when lithium was administered in doses towards the lower end of the therapeutic range. It is not, however, possible to determine from such slender evidence whether or not there is really a difference in lithium responsiveness in women and men.

There are, in fact, several possible explanations of these isolated reports.

In the first place, the often observed greater effectiveness of lithium in preventing bipolar recurrences rather than unipolar depressions may provide an explanation of the findings in view of the greater incidence of bipolar psychoses in men than in women.

Secondly, the manner of renal handling of lithium appears to be, to some extent, sex-related, lithium clearance being greater in males than in females. Sex is a factor which is included in empirically derived equations used to predict the therapeutic dose level to achieve a desired serum level (see pp. 67–73).

An increase in body weight consequent upon lithium treatment is a well-known effect of lithium (pp. 195–196); this, too, has been shown, in rats and in humans, to be sex-related, with a series of reports from a group of investigators in Brazil suggesting that the susceptibility to weight increase is greater in females than in males.

Lithium side effects may be of differential importance to the two sexes: because of cosmetic ideas, lithium-induced weight gain, goitre or skin problems may be of greater importance to women. Lithium-induced sexual dysfunction in men (loss of potency and libido) are quite uncommon, at least in terms of their frequency of reporting in the literature (pp. 252–254), and the causal relationship with lithium treatment when such effects do occur is not yet clear, but in individual cases a brief trial off lithium may be useful to evaluate the role of lithium in causing the disturbances.

A special problem concerns young women who desire to become pregnant: this issue is dealt with in full elsewhere in the following section.

38. Pregnancy, Delivery and Lactation

Jean-Michel Lemoine

Prophylactic lithium treatment is more and more often given to women in their child-bearing years, exposing them to the risk of a possible confrontation between lithium and motherhood, and giving rise to questions of possible teratogenicity and toxicity. The trend towards increased prescription to women of this age group may be related to the fact that there is a relative tendency for women to develop manic-depressive illness more often than men, the age of maximum risk coinciding with procreative potential years. A secondary factor may be that lithium treatment has undoubtedly resulted in the preservation of relationships that might otherwise have been disrupted by untreated manic-depressive illness, and as a result the lithium therapy may have increased a little the birth rates in these families. With the possible exception of reported (but still not confirmed) adverse effects on sexuality and fertility, many factors seem to be converging to increase the risk that fecund and pregnant women will be exposed to lithium.

The physician is consequently confronted with four parameters whose interests and requirements do not always coincide: viz. the drug, the illness, the mother and the fetus. Of all the drugs which have been suspected of having some degree of teratogenicity, i.e. harmful effects upon the developing fetus and embryo, lithium is perhaps the only one which must be given continuously over a long period of time. Against any possible dangers posed by the drug, however, one has to weigh the potential seriousness of withdrawal which might lead to relapse. The treatment may need to be continued to protect the health of the mother but, in so doing, there is an increased risk of exposing the fetus to possible teratogenic influences.

These aspects of lithium treatment certainly represent a subject about which the most queries are raised by female patients and by medical practitioners.

Sexual Functions

Data on the repercussion of lithium treatment on the psychoneuro-endocrine axis controlling the sexual functions are still uncertain. In handling the patient's complaints about possible lithium-related impairment of sexual activity, the responsibility of associated drugs and of the psychosocial dimension of the illness must more often be contemplated. While there have been occasional reports of loss of libido and potency in assocation with lithium use, the drug generally does not impair male sexual function or have any adverse sexual effects in women. A fuller discussion of this matter is to be found on pp. 252–254.

Fertility

It is known that lithium may affect *in vitro* sperm mobility and/or viability. While there have been few reports suggesting that lithium may interfere with male fertility and conception, and while clinical data on the matter are contradictory, it may be said that lithium treatment does not appear to alter human fertility under the usual conditions, though there is a possible decrease of fertility brought about by alteration of the parental chromosomal potential, or by a very early and direct toxicity on the pre- or just-implanted egg. While in certain species lithium can induce a decrease in the size of the litter, this theoretical possibility is more difficult to identify under clinical conditions.

Chromosomes

Experimental data from both *in vivo* and *in vitro* studies are inconclusive and sometimes contradictory: the effects of lithium on chromosomes vary widely according to the specifics of the experimental conditions. It is, however, generally agreed that lithium has no significant effect on human chromosomes, at least when administered in therapeutic concentrations.

In the same way, there is a theoretical possibility, but not so far any evidence, that certain anomalies reported in the offspring of lithium-treated animals might occur by the alteration of the genetic characteristics of parental gametes; it has, however, never been established that lithium can alter the genetic material or produce malformations in children conceived by fathers taking this drug at the time of conception.

Teratogenic Risks

Animal studies

The effects of lithium on development and morphogenesis have been demonstrated in many species of invertebrate animals (studies on sea urchins, for example, were begun before 1900) and non-mammalian vertebrates. In such work it was found that exposing eggs to lithium produces essentially different anomalies in the differentiation of the primary tissue layers according to the species being studied. Experiments on sea urchin eggs showed that exposure to lithium salts could produce developmental anomalies., Similar effects of lithium, though of a less marked kind, have been confirmed in isolated vertebrate systems, in amphibia, and in developing chick embryos (abnormal anatomy of head, neck, brain and sensory organs).

The direct extrapolation of such findings to mammalian and human systems is not, however, possible for at least four reasons. In the first place, the range of doses used in such laboratory studies has been extremely wide, often lying well outside the human therapeutic dose range. Secondly, in mammalian species, there is a limit to the exposure to which the fetus can be subjected and which cannot be passed because of the advent of toxic effects upon the mother. Thirdly, the experimentation on lower species has concerned only the direct action of lithium ions on the eggs, which is a very different situation from that occurring under clinical conditions. Finally, the evaluation of the importance of the experimental findings is made difficult because there are almost no data on baseline frequencies of malformations in many of the pre-mammalian forms studied.

In studies performed on mammalian species, effects such as decreased litter size (resulting from fetal resorption and/or infertility), development defects, and maternal or fetal toxicity or mortality, have often been reported, especially with excessive doses and large 'pulses' (serum peaks) of lithium; the results are, however, much more conflicting and inconclusive as far as fetal malformations are concerned. Some studies suggest a strong pathomorphic influence in higher vertebrates and especially in laboratory rodents, whilst others fail to confirm these teratogenic effects in the same species, even with very elevated doses.

A number of variables need to be considered in the interpretation of these studies: doses and concentrations, route and schedule of administration, timing of serum concentrations, species used, quality and 'susceptibility' of the genotype, embryonic stage at time of exposure, and other factors which may crucially determine the outcome. Therefore, the literature wavers between reports of the most disquieting teratogenic potentialities and the total innocuousness of lithium salts.

It seems very likely that at least three major animal species (monkeys, rabbits and, perhaps, rats) can receive lithium by mouth and at clinical doses during pregnancy without the drug having any pathomorphic influence, though doubt exists in some rodents—and especially in mice: in the latter, different anomalies have been reported (cleft palate, malformations of eyes and external ears), as well as embryo-fetal toxicity. Analysis of these studies indicates, however, that when fetal damage was massive, the mothers had most often been exposed to lithium doses far in excess of those used in human treatment. Often the schedules used also exposed the fetus and the mother to large 'pulses' of lithium (and even, sometimes, involved intensely hypertonic lithium solutions being placed directly in the peritoneal cavity). The likelihood of fetal malformations increases generally as the dose increases and is higher when the drug is given in a single daily dose and by parenteral routes.

Lithium salts, therefore, can be both toxic and teratogenic at least to some rodents and at least under some experimental conditions: the data are, however, inconclusive in terms of their implications for treatment in humans, though clearly they suggest that the greatest caution should be exercised.

Human studies

Up to 1969–70, there was only a very poor and inconclusive literature about the possible hazards of lithium use in pregnancy. Subsequent to that date, the late Dr Morton Weinstein of the Langley Porter Institute, San Francisco, USA, undertook to establish, in collaboration with a colleague, Dr M.D.Goldfield, an American Register of pregnancies in which the mother had been exposed to lithium at least in the first trimester and regardless of outcome. Later, at the suggestion of Dr Mogens Schou of Denmark this register was combined with the Scandinavian Register, begun earlier, and also with the Canadian Register, started somewhat later by Dr Andre Villeneuve of Quebec: data from these three sources were combined in the International Register of Lithium Babies. Unfortunately, in 1973 the Canadian and Scandinavian branches of the International Register ceased collecting these data but the American Register continued to solicit reports about lithium treatment in pregnancy until the death of its compiler in 1979. Despite this interruption in data gathering there is no reason to believe that the data which Dr Weinstein presented relating to about 225 cases would have changed substantially over recent years.

A 'lithium baby' was defined, for the purpose of the register, as a child born to a mother who was given lithium during at least the first 3 months of pregnancy, the trimester when morphogenesis takes place; another criterion was that the conceptus had to be available for morphological examination. Congenital malformations were defined as macroscopic abnormalities of structure attributable to faulty development and present at birth.

The operation of the Register was retrospective: its existence and its interest was announced and reiterated through notices in psychiatric, obstetric, paediatric and general medical journals and requests at professional meetings; physicians in all countries were urged to submit reports about all pregnancies, complicated or uncomplicated, and all babies, normal and abnormal, which might come to their attention and in which lithium had been used at any point of the first trimester.

The Register workers themselves were well aware of the many problems inherent in this method, regarding the collection of data on lithium babies and the interpretation of such information.

The chief defect of a retrospective study is the tendency for the sample to be incomplete and selective. The principal source of error is therefore the risk of over-reporting the pathology; the mother of a malformed child is more likely to be questioned about drug intake during pregnancy than is the mother of a child born without malformations, and physicians are probably more motivated to send reports of children with malformations than of normal children. A prospective procedure with entry of the children into the register before delivery would certainly have been preferable but not easily arranged. The method which the Register used will, therefore, have tended to exaggerate both the pathology and the frequency of the most evident and serious malformations, and it is difficult to assess by how much. Data from Scandinavia are, for a variety of reasons, probably more inclusive and less selective, and almost certainly come closer to a 100% sample of all pregnancies exposed to lithium; this information may be used to estimate and partially control the distortions of the retrospective study. In any case, there is bound to be a high degree of uncertainty involved in calculating frequencies from only 225 cases and the possibility of random errors is considerable.

Another criticism is the lack of a suitable control-group: the incidence of malformations in babies of untreated mothers with affective disorders is insufficiently known.

Other problems relate to the frequent lack of information about the associated use of psychoactive drugs (or other drugs), about possible complications of pregnancy such as gestational diabetes or hypertension, or about different antecedents or predisposing conditions (obstetric, teratogenic, infectious and chromosomal). Lastly, the Register takes no account of certain data that would perhaps merit better exploration (spontaneous abortions, perinatal mortality, prematurity and/or delayed intra-uterine growth, prolonged pregnancies, etc.).

Results of the Register of Lithium Babies

The last published report on the Register (1980) includes 225 cases of lithium babies. Of these, seven were stillborn (one of these was malformed—tricuspid valve atresia—and appears also in that group), two had trisomy 21 (but both mothers were in their late 30s) and 25 (11.1%) were malformed (the proportion in the Scandinavian Register is less, being 3.6% in 1974).

Of the 25 malformed babies, 18 (representing 72% of all reported malformed infants) had significant anomalies of the cardiovascular system: coarctation of the aorta, patent ductus arteriosus, ventricular septal defect, mitral atresia, tricuspid atresia, single umbilical artery and six cases of Ebstein's anomaly. The remaining seven malformed babies had anomalies of the central nervous system, the external ear, the endocrine system and the ureters (the rate in the general population being about 3%).

In such a retrospective study, there is only a suggestion that pregnancies exposed to lithium have somewhat increased risk of an anomalous outcome. If there is an increase in total abnormalities due to lithium, it must be small and far less than the alarming results of at least some early animal studies seemed to portend. It is certainly interesting to notice that the estimated rate of malformation has tended to increase with the years, with the likely falling off of methodological rigour and perhaps especially after the Scandinavian Register stopped.

The situation changes when the *types* of malformations in the lithium-babies are analysed: there is a marked over-representation of severe, often fatal, cardiovascular malformations and more especially of the Ebstein's anomaly. Moreover, other case reports have been published describing such malformations.

Another large study of the babies of lithium-treated mothers has been published by Professor B.Kallen and A.Tandberg of the University of Lund, Sweden. This was also a retrospective study by record linkage of three national registries. Among manic-depressive women who had given birth to a child between 1973 and 1979, the total delivery outcome was poorer than expected, with a high rate of perinatal deaths and/or congenital malformations. A higher rate was revealed among infants born to women who had used drugs in early pregnancy and this phenomenon appeared more especially related both to women who had used lithium and to heart defects. Even if open to argument on statistical grounds, this study supports the idea that there is a link between the use of lithium in early pregnancy and the birth of an infant with a serious heart defect (though it does not confirm the prevalence of Ebstein's anomaly).

Maternal, Fetal and Neonatal Toxicity

During pregnancy, lithium readily equilibrates across the placenta so that the concentration in fetal serum nearly equals that in maternal serum.

It is well known that pregnancy interferes with many physiological functions, such as renal glomerular filtration rate, fluid balance, endocrine regulation, and in the second half of pregnancy lithium clearance rises gradually by 30–50% until delivery, in parallel with creatinine clearance, and falls abruptly at this time to the pre-pregnancy value. So lithium level has a tendency to decrease with an unchanged dose as delivery approaches and the physician could be tempted to increase the dose: lithium toxicity has occasionally been reported in mothers and/or (more often) in the newborns of mothers taking lithium at term. These data are nevertheless debated and opposite effects have been noted.

Maternal toxicity

When intoxication begins, for one reason or another,

before the delivery, during the last weeks of pregnancy, the chief danger is the lack of recognition of the role of lithium, because early lithium toxicity in the pregnant woman may masquerade as one of the ordinary physiological upsets of the pregnancy (nausea and vomiting, weight gain, fluid retention and oedema, changes in the frequency of urination, etc.). The subsequent danger is that 'corrective measures' applied (such as sodium restriction and/or the prescription of diuretics) may seriously worsen the toxic state. Case reports of maternal and/or fetal lithium toxicity often have such complicating factors (oedema, hypertension, etc.) since these conditions and their treatment may further disrupt fluid-electrolyte balance.

More often, signs of maternal intoxication begin within a few hours of delivery and are the same as classical features of lithium toxicity; even with prompt withdrawal of the drug, recovery is typically slow and may require several weeks.

Fetal and neonatal toxicity

Because the placenta provides no protection for the fetus against lithium, all factors which predispose to maternal intoxication likewise predispose to fetal and neonatal intoxication; therefore, avoiding maternal toxicity is essential for avoiding fetal toxicity. But it is not always sufficient, and neonatal lithium toxicity has been described with both non-toxic and toxic lithium levels in the mother, and with or without evidence of maternal intoxication at the time of delivery.

The symptoms are not specific indicators and the neonatal toxicity may be very difficult to differentiate from other causes of fetal distress. Clinical features are generally manifested as hypotonia, lethargy and duskiness or cyanosis—the so-called 'floppy baby syndrome'. Many other symptoms have also been reported, including bradycardia or tachycardia (often with different arrhythmias), heart murmur, shallow respiration, hypotension, hypoglycaemia, hypothermia, stupor and neurological depression with poor sucking reflex and absent Moro reflex, low Apgar score, etc.

Even in the absence of such acute distress, different functional anomalies of the cardiovascular, renal and neuromuscular systems, without structural lesions, have occasionally been reported. Because the clearance of lithium is known to be considerably prolonged into the neonatal period, the disappearance of those signs may take up to 10 days, generally without sequelae.

Maternal lithium therapy has also been associated with a few cases of thyroid abnormalities (large goitres, generally euthyroid), essentially in the newborns of 'susceptible' women; they gradually disappeared over several months. It would be prudent to monitor closely, and possibly adjust, the thyroid status of such women.

Breast feeding

Lithium passes easily from blood into breast milk. Its concentration in the milk is about half that of maternal serum (nearly 100% in the colostrum, then gradually decreasing to 30%) and the nursing infant's serum lithium concentration is very close to the concentration of the ingested breast milk.

Despite such rather low serum levels there are some reports of lithium toxicity in breast-fed babies with the same clinical features as in the affected neonate. Such a risk must not be underestimated for many reasons, especially in view of the immaturity of the renal functions and susceptibility to alterations in fluid-electrolyte balance the causes of which are common at this age (transitory disturbances of fluid and electrolytes balance, dehydration or sodium loss by vomiting, diarrhoea or reduced fluid intake, unstable thermoregulation, pronounced febrile responses to minor infections, and other stresses).

Lithium-exposed Children

Additional concerns include the theoretical possibility that lithium exposure could cause subtle abnormalities even in the absence of obvious malformations at birth: it has, for example, been contemplated that lithium may be a behavioural or physiological teratogenic agent, causing alterations in the developing nervous, endocrine and/or skeletal system during prenatal (and perhaps post-natal, if breast feeding) exposure, even with non-toxic concentrations. The only study of this possibility has been carried out by Mogens Schou in a follow-up of Scandinavian lithium babies who had been born without malformations and who were at least 5 years old: this study failed to reveal any statistically significant increase in the frequency of physical or mental disturbances among these children. Effects of early exposure on the later development of chromosomes are unknown.

Guidelines for Responsible Clinical Practice

The following recommendations are closely prompted

by the very sensible guidelines prepared by Morton Weinstein shortly before his death and are based on the preceding data.

Lithium and fecund women

Even if the data from various studies are inconclusive, it must be admitted that there is, at least, a theoretical risk, and so lithium must be considered as 'likely to be' teratogenic in human, especially with respect to the cardiovascular system. In view of this, four main principles should be operated.

(i) Women in their childbearing years should be treated with lithium only if there are very strong indications for its use: the most unequivocal indication is certainly the continuing prophylaxis of manic-depressive illness characterized by frequent and severe relapses (but the treatment decision must always be individualized). More exceptionally these indications may include the treatment of acute episodes when they are not effectively controlled by conventional therapies. It is rarely found necessary to *initiate* a lithium treatment in a pregnant woman.
(ii) These lithium-treated women should be informed of the possible risks and encouraged to avoid pregnancy and to maintain an effective contraception.
(iii) They should be urged to inform their physicians if they decide to become pregnant or as soon as they discover that they are pregnant.
(iv) Before initiating lithium treatment, it is necessary to do a pregnancy test.

Desire for, or early discovery of, pregnancy

Because of the potential teratogenic risks and the potential for toxicity, the use of lithium should theoretically and ideally be avoided for a few days before conception and throughout the pregnancy. There are, however, certain qualifications to be made of this general principle.

In the first place, the risks of potential harm to the fetus must be considered in relation to the mother's interests; the risk of an affective relapse if lithium is withdrawn may outweigh the risk of lithium damaging the fetus during early pregnancy, particularly since alternative treatments which may become necessary are seldom as effective. The risk of affective relapse occurring in the drug-free state during pregnancy will vary greatly among women.

Cross-over studies, carried out over the period of a year, on patients given lithium prophylactically have showed that among those stopping lithium treatment, 70% suffered one or more relapse, while among those continuing lithium treatment only 20% relapsed; by extrapolation, it can be estimated that, over the 4–5 month period of withdrawal that would be involved in pregnant women, relapse might be expected in 40% as against only 10% of those who continued lithium prophylaxis.

In individual pregnant women, risk frequencies may, of course, differ considerably from this. Pregnancy may even sometimes appear to 'protect' the manic-depressive woman, at least during the first 6 months. The decision to continue or discontinue always requires a fully informed and individualized preliminary conversation between the patient and her physician.

There is a general consensus amongst authorities in the field of lithium therapy that early unplanned pregnancy discovery does not routinely justify therapeutic abortion; such a decision could be debated in individual situations.

Lithium maintenance during pregnancy

Lithium should, in general, be continued only if judged clinically obligatory because, for example, of convincing evidence based on past experience that withdrawal would seriously endanger the mother or the pregnancy.

In the majority of cases it may be advisable to stop lithium treatment a few days before conception or as soon as possible after an unplanned pregnancy has been discovered, and possibly to start treatment again only after the third or half of the pregnancy has passed if clinically necessary (it is indeed debated whether teratogenic changes can still occur during the later stages of the fetal period given that organogenesis is largely complete at this stage). The risk of the mother's relapse is perhaps greater towards the end of pregnancy and after delivery.

The risks of continued prophylaxis have been considered as minor when the pregnancy and lithium treatment are both carefully supervised and as being far greater if lithium is discontinued. However that may be, if lithium is continued or restarted during pregnancy, the guiding principle should always be to reduce all risks, of whatever kind, to a minimum.

Special considerations relate essentially to dosage and fluctuations in serum lithium level. While there is no evidence from human studies, some animal studies do show a relationship between increased teratogenic risk and higher maternal serum lithium levels; moreover, maternal and/or fetal toxicity are often very obviously related to excessive serum lithium concentrations. These concentrations should be kept as low as possible but they must remain compatible with desired effects (see pp. 67–73). It will be necessary to carry out frequent clinical and laboratory evaluations to ensure the safe and effective use of lithium: of lithium treatment is continued, serum levels should be monitored at least once a month in the first half of pregnancy, and preferably more often if this is feasible and up to once a week towards the end of uncomplicated pregnancies.

Dosage adjustments are sometimes necessary on account of an increase in renal lithium clearance (and consequent increased lithium elimination) during the course of pregnancy, to avoid the patient's 'escaping' from lithium control.

In addition to using the smallest amount of lithium adequate for clinical effectiveness, fluctuations and 'pulses' in maternal serum concentrations should be minimized particularly since they are transmitted directly to the fetus. To avoid these fluctuations, lithium may need to be given, if possible, in a more divided dosage regimen: three, four or even five times a day.

All physiological disturbances which may disrupt fluid-electrolyte balance should also be avoided.

Early lithium toxicity in the pregnant woman may, as noted earlier, be mistaken for one of the ordinary physiological upsets of pregnancy. Lithium toxicity should be considered in the differential diagnosis of all such events, and lithium level systematically measured. If a rapid check of the serum lithium concentration is not possible, it would usually be wise to discontinue lithium until the nature of the problem is clear.

Pregnant women often develop complications such as weight gain, oedema, hypertension, and so on: these conditions and their treatments may further disrupt fluid-electrolyte balance, leading to difficulties with lithium treatment.

Labour and delivery

During pregnancy a progressively greater intake of lithium is sometimes necessary to maintain a given effective serum level because of increasing renal clearance; at delivery, lithium clearance falls abruptly in many cases to pre-pregnancy values and, as a consequence, maternal serum lithium levels can rise quickly and substantially, exposing the mother and/or newborn to intoxication.

It is necessary to monitor serum levels more and more frequently and to make adjustments of the lithium dosage during late pregnancy and around delivery. It is advisable to reduce the daily dose by 50% (or to the pre-pregnancy value) in the last expected week of gestation, to discontinue lithium as soon as the onset of labour is noted, and to re-institute treatment gradually at the pre-pregnancy dose once the mother has stabilized in the post-partum period. The baby should have an early serum level determination and electrocardiogram.

Breast feeding

Because of the toxic risks and the possible unknown long-term effects, breast-feeding should be discouraged: it is the mother and not the child who needs the drug and exposure to lithium may be harmful to the infant. Moreover, at this age, renal lithium clearance cannot be assumed to be as effective as in adults and transitory disturbances in water and electrolyte balance are common.

Having said that, however, it is only right to point out that there have been very few reports of lithium toxicity in breast-fed babies, and there are more and more physicians who disagree that lithium treatment of the mother is an absolute contraindication to breast-feeding. It is, for example, pointed out that the child has been exposed to lithium during many months of fetal life: further exposure to a lower concentration through breast-feeding for a few months may not, under such circumstances, seem unduly risky. Also, breast feeding offers immunological, nutritional and other benefits to the child and its psychological and emotional significance for mother and child should not be underestimated. It is held by some that bottle feeding is not always desirable or even possible and several mothers taking lithium have nursed without difficulties. As with all aspects of lithium treatment in pregnancy a decision on breast feeding should be reached through a fully informed discussion between physician and parents.

Those who choose to breast feed should be instructed to watch for signs of toxicity in their babies; these are the same signs as described for newborns (hypotonia, lethargy, cyanosis, etc.). If a breast-fed baby develops restlessness, fever, vomiting, diarrhoea, sluggishness or a general picture of being unwell, bottle feeding should be substituted until the nature of the disturbance is clarified and lithium intoxication is ruled out; serum lithium levels should be quickly and systematically measured if there is any doubt. Elevated dosage and serum level fluctuations should be particularly avoided in breast feeding mothers; it seems advisable, from this point of view, to recommend them to breast feed, as far as possible, just before the lithium intake so as to minimize the milk's lithium level and the risk of a 'pulse' of lithium.

Bibliography

Lemoine,J.M. and Edou,D. (1985) Lithium et grossesse. *Gaz. Med. France,* **92**, 57–60.

A brief, but readable and up-to-date account of the practicalities of lithium therapy during pregnancy.

Weinstein,M.R. (1980) Lithium treatment of women during pregnancy and in the post-delivery period. In *Handbook of Lithium Therapy*. Johnson,F.N. (ed.), MTP Press, Lancaster, UK, pp. 421–429.

The last survey written by Morton Weinstein before his untimely death, giving the most recent details of the figures for morphological abnormalities in lithium babies.

Weinstein,M.R. and Goldfield,M.D. (1975) Administration of lithium during pregnancy. In *Lithium Research and Therapy*. Johnson,F.N. (ed.), Academic Press, London, pp. 237–264.

A detailed account of results from animal studies, as well as a description of data available at that time in the International Register of Lithium Babies.

39. Concomitant Physical Illness

Henri Lôo, C.Gay and A.Galinowski

There are two aspects of the problem of lithium and concomitant physical illness: the occurrence of physical illness during lithium treatment and the prescription of lithium to a patient with a pre-existing physical illness (*Table 39.1*). Concomitant illnesses may change the pharmacokinetics of lithium as do some treatments prescribed in the course of these illnesses. Lithium use can also have an effect upon the course of an illness.

Table 39.1 *Illnesses likely to worsen with lithium treatment*

Cardiovascular disease
repolarization defects
rhythm and conduction defects
cardiac insufficiency and myocarditis
Neurological disease
abnormal movements
Parkinson's disease
organic brain syndrome
cerebellar syndrome
Huntington's chorea (+ baclofen)
Kidney failure
Thyroid disease
hypothyroidism
thyroiditis
hyperthyroidism
Metabolic imbalance
excessive weight
hyperparathyroidism
Gastrointestinal disease
irritable colon
ulcerative colitis
Skin disease
psoriasis
acne
hair loss
Systemic disease
Systemic lupus erythematosus
Eye disease
senile cataract
exophthalmos
Myeloproliferative disorders

Cardiovascular Disease

Some cardiac conditions, either pre-existing or occurring for the first time during treatment with lithium, will be contraindications to the commencement or continuation of lithium therapy; other conditions require only clinical and EKG monitoring. An account of lithium effect on normal cardiac functioning is given on pp. 213–218.

Lithium may worsen repolarization defects secondary to various cardiac affections. Actually, lithium rarely worsens pre-existing repolarization defects except in cases of hypokalaemia. Lithium may aggravate a sinus bradycardia as it slows down the frequency of sinus node cells. Any type of sinus node dysfunction (sinus node abnormality, sinoatrial block and atrioventricular block) and any type of sinus arrhythmia can be aggravated by lithium or occur during treatment. Only ventricular arrhythmias and sinus rhythm dysfunctions associated with a cardiac lesion (infarct, heart failure) are contraindications to lithium use. Other rhythm defects require close monitoring.

Atrioventricular or intraventricular blocks do not seem to be influenced by therapeutic doses of lithium.

Bundle branch blocks existing before lithium treatment or occuring during lithium use require only regular EKG monitoring. However, conduction defects associated with a cardiac lesion can be aggravated by lithium. Lithium may favour the occurrence of severe arrythmia: in that case, conduction defect is a contraindication to lithium use.

Cardiac insufficiency and myocarditis are two conditions which are contraindications to lithium use. Should they occur during treatment lithium must be discontinued. Indeed lithium may facilitate the occurrence of conduction and rhythm dysfunction and aggravate cardiac failure owing to its anti-inotropic action. Besides, treatments such as a low-sodium diet and certain types of diuretics which may be prescribed under such circumstances cannot be combined with lithium.

Coronary insufficiency may require the interruption of treatment: some types of coronary insufficiencies are not contraindications to lithium use. Lithium-induced hypothyroidism may aggravate a pre-existing coronary insufficiency.

Prescription of lithium in the weeks following a myocardial infarct is forbidden. Lithium may favour conduction and rhythm dysfunction as well as cardiac insufficiency. Besides, some treatments prescribed after infarct cannot be combined with lithium. Myocardial infarct is a temporary contraindication to lithium use. Future prescription of lithium will depend upon the course and the cardiac sequelae of the disease.

Lithium can be prescribed to hypertensive patients. It has no effect on blood pressure in man. However, some treatments for hypertension should not be combined with lithium, such as low-sodium diet, many kinds of diuretics and alpha-methyl-DOPA. No toxic accidents have been reported with clonidine and beta-adrenoreceptor blocking agents.

Neurological Disease

Abnormal movements

Any type of tremor may worsen with lithium, especially essential and extrapyramidal tremor. Lithium also causes tremors in subjects with a family history of tremors. Lithium-induced tremors may appear at moderate plasma lithium levels. Treatment consists in using minimal yet effective doses of lithium, in prescribing beta-adrenoreceptor blocking agents and/or diazepam. There is no interaction between these compounds and lithium. Lithium increases ataxic movements in cerebellar syndromes. Tardive dyskinesia is known to improve with lithium. However, at times lithium seems to aggravate it. Lithium has no direct effect on Huntington's chorea; however, the combination of lithium with baclofen might increase hyperkinetic movements.

Parkinson's disease

Lithium increases muscular rigidity and tremor in patients with Parkinson's disease. Therefore lithium should be used in L-DOPA-induced mania only for a short time. Long-term use of lithium in Parkinsonism is contraindicated. Besides, patients with Parkinson's disease seem to be very sensitive to the neurotoxic effects of lithium. The Parkinsonian syndrome may occur while patients are on lithium. The causative role of lithium has been considered, but a combined neuroleptic treatment should be taken into account.

Organic brain syndrome

Generalized or focal EEG irregularities, without any concomitant epileptic symptoms, are often aggravated by lithium. On the whole, lithium increases the amplitude and decreases the frequency of EEG waves. It favours the occurrence of paroxysmal spiking. Lithium-induced EEG irregularities are not a contraindication to continuing lithium treatment, though lithium may induce epileptic fits when altered EEG recordings pre-exist and EEG irregularities are predictive of a risk of neurotoxicity, even though serum lithium levels remain within the normal range. Despite all this, they are not a contraindication; but they do require carefully administered doses and frequent EEG monitoring.

The influence of lithium on epilepsy varies. Sometimes, lithium seems to decrease the frequency of fits, whilst on other occasions it aggravates epilepsy, especially the temporal lobe variety. It may on occasion alter only the EEG recordings without inducing an increase in the number of fits. Pre-existing epilepsy, or epilepsy occuring during treatment, is not a contraindication to lithium use: it demands, however, that the frequency of fits and the EEG be controlled at the beginning of treatment and, if necessary, that an anti-epileptic treatment be started or adjusted, though there are reports that some toxic effects of hydantoins may be increased with lithium (see pp. 171 – 176).

Patients with cognitive impairment are oversensitive to several effects of lithium. Lithium often induces a slowing down of thought processes and may be reported to impair memory and cognition. However, it does not accelerate the organic process of impairment. In cognitively impaired patients, lithium may cause neurotoxic effects, particularly clouding of consciousness, even at normal serum lithium levels. If this is observed, lithium usually must be discontinued. Cognitive impairment is a relative contraindication, all the more so because lithium is sometimes less effective in that kind of pathology.

Muscle Disease

Lithium may aggravate myasthenia by interfering with the synthesis and the release of acetylcholine. Myasthenia gravis is a contraindication to lithium. Besides, lithium potentiates the effects of myorelaxant drugs (see also pp. 190–191).

Kidney Disease

Kidney insufficiency resulting from nephropathy is a contraindication to lithium use. When the insufficiency is only moderate and stable, and lithium is absolutely necessary, serum lithium levels and creatinine clearance should be monitored. Some nephrotoxic drugs increase the risk of kidney toxicity when combined with lithium (see pp. 206–213 for a full discussion of lithium effects on the healthy kidney).

Thyroid Disease

Lithium should be used with caution in the presence of thyroid disease for it may induce a hormonal imbalance, usually hypothyroidism (pp. 220–226). Several cases of hyperthyroidism have been reported in patients taking lithium but the mechanism of the phenomenon remains unknown. There are two kinds of risks when giving lithium to patients with hyperthyroidism: worsening of the hyperthyroidism and occurrence of hypothyroidism in a patient stabilized by an anti-thyroid treatment. The incidence of lithium-induced hypothyroidism is rated between 3% and 30%. Such a percentage warrants regular controls of T3, T4, TSH and free thyroxine index in a patient with hypothyroidism who has been successfully treated by substitution therapy and who is taking lithium. Lithium may induce anti-thyroid antibodies and aggravate thyroiditis. Screening for anti-microsomal antibodies before initiating lithium therapy appears to be justified in patients with possible thyroiditis. See pp. 220–226 for further details of thyroidal effects of lithium.

Metabolic Imbalance

Carbohydrate metabolism: weight gain and diabetes mellitus

Weight gain is a frequent side effect during lithium treatment (see pp. 195–196). Previous obesity is not a contraindication to lithium use but may lead to further weight gain should no preventive measures be taken. A low-carbohydrate diet is suggested. A low-sodium diet is strictly forbidden (see pp. 151–152).

The effects of lithium on glucose and insulin are not clear but are certainly relatively minor. In the beginning of lithium treatment of patients with diabetes mellitus there might be an insulin-like effect of lithium with a trend towards low blood glucose levels. During long-term administration lithium may cause hyperglycemia by inhibiting insulin secretion and increasing glucagon secretion. On the whole, glucose metabolism is minimally affected by lithium in diabetic patients. Blood glucose levels should be checked at the beginning of the treatment in a diabetic patient and then, if necessary, doses of insulin or oral anti-diabetics should be adjusted accordingly. The occurence of hyperglycemia during lithium treatment is not a contraindication to maintaining the treatment but may require therapeutic measures (a low carbohydrate diet, anti-diabetic medications).

Metabolism of calcium and phosphorus

Lithium may aggravate some dysfunction of calcium and phosphorus metabolism as in parathyroid pathology. It may cause or facilitate hyperparathyroidism, which always remains moderately severe. However, should hyperparathyroidism occur, it is preferable to discontinue lithium. The development of parathyroid adenomas has been attributed to lithium: in this case surgery must be undertaken and lithium discontinued. Lithium might possibly favour the occurrence of moderate osteoporosis, or at least accelerate its course.

Gastrointestinal Disease

Sodium-losing enteropathies often lead to lithium overdosage and cause accidents. They are a contraindication to lithium use. Lithium, which favours diarrhoea, may aggravate irritable colon and ulcerative colitis. These pathologies require specific treatment. On the other hand, some types of psychosomatic ulcerative colitis may improve. Lithium may aggravate gastrointestinal troubles secondly to gastrectomy, intestinal resection and ileostomy. A major functional discomfort may become a contraindication to lithium use. Lithium may aggravate gastritis or gastroduodenal ulcers, perhaps by the local phenomenon of irritation. This drawback is reported mainly when patients are fasting. Usually it disappears when lithium is taken during meals. The risk is minimized with liquid forms of lithium salts (gluconate), or by employing a preparation with confirmed high bioavailability which allows lithium to be absorbed in the upper part of the gastric tract, leaving little, if any, lithium to descend to the lower tract where it is not absorbed and causes osmotic inflow of water into the gut, to produce loose stools.

Any episodes of diarrhoea or vomiting tend to create the conditions under which high serum lithium levels may develop because of the loss of water and sodium, especially in some diarrhoeas of great severity (salmonellosis) or duration (amoebiasis). In acute vomiting or diarrhoea, patients should temporarily discontinue their treatment. At the same time, the loss of sodium and water should be compensated for and the aetiological treatment undertaken.

In case of gastroesophageal reflux, metoclopramide is often prescribed. It can facilitate the digestive absorption of lithium and increase serum lithium levels. Prescription of gastric antacid gels and of sodium bicarbonate may, on the other hand, favour a decrease in serum lithium levels.

Infection and Fever

Any infection with concomitant fever during lithium treatment may favour the occurrence of an intoxication with high serum lithium levels because of the loss of sodium and water secondary to perspiration induced by high body temperature. Patients should be required to increase their water and sodium intake during fever episodes. If lithium is to be maintained during that episode, serum lithium levels and blood electrolytes should be monitored daily. Temporary discontinuation of lithium may be advisable in cases of fever. Actually, patients with fever often eat reluctantly. Moreover, the concept of 'high' intake of water and sodium is often underestimated by patients. Infection requiring antibiotics should not lead to the prescription of tetracyclines, which tend to increase serum lithium levels, or of antibiotics of known nephrotoxicity, which would add to lithium nephrotoxicity (see pp. 206–213).

Some drugs (metronidazole, spectinomycin, tetracyclines) may increase serum lithium levels. When their prescription is justified, serum lithium levels should be monitored regularly. Use of non-steroidal anti-inflammatory drugs (for instance in the treatment of dental infections) may also increase the risk of toxicity because they may diminish renal clearance of lithium and cause an increase in serum lithium levels (see pp. 183–186).

Skin Disease

Two dermatological diseases may occur during, or be aggravated by, lithium therapy. For the first of these, psoriasis, specific therapeutic measures should be taken but the severity of the eruption and resistance to treatment may require that lithium be discontinued. Lithium may worsen acne and acneiform reactions observed in seborrheic patients. Treatment by tetracyclines demands that serum lithium levels be controlled regularly because they may elevate serum levels and cause intoxication. Hair loss in some patients may be accelerated by lithium use. A subclinical lithium-induced hypothyroidism should be ruled out. Further details of the cutaneous effects of lithium are given on pp. 232–234.

Alcoholism

Lithium may cause major side effects if somatic complications occur in alcoholic patients, such as cognitive impairment, cerebellar syndrome, myocarditis, epilepsy and peripheral neuropathy. Lithium use should be avoided in such cases. Somatic complications of alcoholism have to be diagnosed by pre-lithium screening.

The combination of lithium and alcohol has been noted to reduce diuresis and may be responsible for disturbed serum lithium levels, whereas taken separately these compounds increase diuresis. Experimental studies in animals suggest a possible toxic interaction between lithium and disulfiram. This last interaction has not been reported in man.

Rheumatic Disease

Rheumatic diseases are not a contraindication to lithium use. However there are risks in combining lithium to compounds used in rheumatology. Non-steroidal anti-inflammatory drugs sometimes increase serum lithium levels and favour the occurrence of toxic overload. In contrast, steroids increase the renal clearance of lithium decreasing serum lithium levels. A low-sodium diet accompanying steroid therapy is an absolute contraindication to lithium use. See pp. 151–152 for a discussion of this issue.

Haematological Disease

Lithium causes reversible granulocytosis of a benign nature, which should not be confused with the same type of effect caused by a concomitant infectious disorder. Although lithium *in vitro* seems to affect platelet aggregation and blood coagulation there are no reports of aggregation or coagulation problems in patients treated by lithium (pp. 218–220).

Lithium has proved effective in some neutropenic states. In view of the stimulatory effect of lithium on granulocyte proliferation, established myeloproliferative disorders, especially chronic myeloid leukaemia and cases at high risk of developing leukaemia, are contraindications to lithium use. Apart from special indications, such as infection or blood disorder, haematological tests are not required.

Systemic Disease

Lithium may favour the occurrence of systemic diseases of a systemic lupus erythematosus-like kind but without identified anti-DNA antibodies. Lithium should be used with caution in a patient with systemic lupus erythematosus, because it may aggravate the illness and interfere with other treatments.

Eye Disease

Cases of aggravation of a senile cataract, of decreased visual acuity and of other eye problems have been reported during lithium use. Lithium may disrupt the hydroelectrolytic balance in the lens. Also, cases of exophthalmos have been reported in the absence of obvious Graves' disease. No aggravation of pre-existing exophthalmos has been reported. The causative role of lithium has to be confirmed in such cases. Prescription of carbonic anhydrase inhibiting diuretics is frequent in cases of elevated intraocular pressure. Combination with lithium requires regular monitoring of serum lithium levels in order to prevent any lithium overload.

Bibliography

Jefferson,J.W., Greist,J.H. and Ackerman,D.L. (1983) *Lithium Encyclopedia for Clinical Practice*, American Psychiatric Press, Washington DC.

This generally useful reference text has brief sections devoted to lithium treatment in certain physical illness states.

40. Surgery Under Lithium

T.Pottecher, B.Ludes,
M.Lichnewsky and B.Calon

Risks Associated with Surgery

When a patient under lithium therapy has to undergo surgery three types of complication may occur: interference between lithium and anaesthetic agents; post-operative increase of blood lithium levels as a result of electrolyte and fluid imbalance; and relapse of psychiatric disease if lithium treatment is discontinued whilst surgery takes place.

Pre-operative treatment with lithium can have a number of effects which may cause problems for the patient. It may, for example, increase the activity duration of anaesthetic agents (barbiturates, benzodiazepines), modify opiate-induced catalepsy, cause nephrogenic diabetes insipidus if neuroleptic agents are also used; and potentiate the action of non-depolarizing as well as depolarizing muscle relaxants.

In fact, reports in the literature which deal with these matters tend to overestimate the consequences of lithium therapy. In most of the experimental studies, the blood levels of lithium salts were higher than is usually the case in clinical practice; moreover, most of the complications which have been observed in man have been related to a relative or absolute overdose.

In the immediate post-operative period, the high risk

of hyperlithaemia is usually related to a decrease in urinary elimination. This may be due to a decrease in sodium excretion in the proximal tubule secondary to dehydration, to the use of diuretics which have their site of action in the distal convoluted tubule (see pp. 180–183), or to the administration of certain non-steroidal anti-inflammatory agents for analgesia (pp. 183–186).

The risk of relapse of the psychiatric disease cannot be precisely evaluated but the evidence is that early post-operative reintroduction of lithium therapy is usually wise. Indeed, the risk of suicide may be present. When resumed administration of lithium is not possible, an effective sedation should be seriously contemplated: at the very least, the patient needs to be kept under close surveillance.

Clinical Management of a Surgical Patient Under Lithium

In clinical practice, lithium therapy should be maintained at normal dosage until the day before surgery, unless there are features of the condition for which lithium withdrawal is required, or aspects of pre-operative treatment which pre-dispose to lithium toxicity. During the pre-operative period, clinical and electrocardiographic signs of lithium overload should be looked for, and a decision taken as to the advisability of continuing or terminating treatment, or reducing the daily intake of lithium. Daily determinations of the lithium blood level are mandatory before and after surgery; the serum level should not exceed 0.9 mmol/l, and levels of 0.5–0.8 mmol/l would be preferable. During recovery, respiratory monitoring will detect signs of residual curarisation.

In the post-operative period, dehydration should be avoided by adequate water and electrolyte supply. Loop and distal action diuretics are contraindicated; only osmotic diuretics (urea, mannitol) and certain anti-aldosterone analogues (triamterene, amiloride) can be used (see also Section 49, pp. 180–183). Dopaminergic doses of dopamine (2–5 mg/kg/min) are recommended when required. If non-steroidal anti-inflammatory drugs are indicated, only salicylates should be administered (see pp. 183–186).

As soon as possible after surgery lithium therapy should be recommenced; it is not wise to let such a patient leave the hospital without adequate therapeutic blood levels of lithium.

Concluding Remarks

When considering the actions to take when a lithium-treated patient requires surgery, it is important to keep in mind that, in clinical practice, the risks of hyperlithaemia are usually overestimated and those of lithium therapy discontinuation underestimated.

Bibliography

Pottecher,T., Gallani,M. and Otteni,J.C. (1982) Lithium et intervention chirurgicale. *J. Méd. Strasbourg,* **13**, 363–364.
A brief, but useful, survey of surgical complications with lithium.

41. Diet

F.Neil Johnson

Very little has been written about the need for special attention to be paid to the diet of patients on lithium therapy, and no systematic study has been undertaken to determine whether the effectiveness of lithium is in any way determined by the nature or quantity of foodstuffs consumed, or the frequency with which eating activity occurs. There are, however, a number of important points which can and should be made.

Calorific Value of the Diet

An increase in body weight is a well-known and not uncommon side effect of lithium (see Section 53, pp. 195–196), and this may cause secondary problems. It can, for example, lead to reduced compliance with medication, particularly in women who are concerned about losing their slim appearance, and it can add to the health risks of any patient who is already, or has a tendency towards, overweight even without lithium. In such cases it is appropriate to advise patients to follow a calorie-controlled diet, and advice on the matter can be sought from a dietician if necessary. It is usually sufficient for a patient to eat less of everything, rather than to make a point of avoiding particular dietary elements.

Sodium Content

There is a tendency for low-sodium diets to be regarded as more healthy than diets with moderate or high sodium content. Whilst this may well be true in cases where there is a predisposition to hypertension there are also dangers associated with a dietary intake of sodium which is too low. Since the renal handling of lithium in the proximal tubules is linked to that of sodium, and since sodium reabsorption occurs when dietary sodium intake is low, there is a danger of reduced lithium excretion under such circumstances, and a consequent rise in serum levels. Patients on lithium should be warned not to make special attempts to reduce their sodium intake, and to use table salt sparingly but not to cut it out altogether.

Fluid Intake

Because lithium treatment is often associated with a nephrogenic diabetes insipidus-like syndrome, characterized by polyuria and polydipsia, many patients drink large quantities of sweetened soft drinks. This can have the two-fold consequence of increasing the body weight and of inducing tooth decay. It is best to advise patients to accompany their meals with water or sugar-free beverages.

Timing of Meals Relative to Lithium

There is no particular advantage in taking lithium before, with, after, or between main meals as far as therapeutic effects or absorption into the blood are concerned, but compliance may be enhanced by an association of tablet taking with a specific mealtime. A few patients also claim that the occasional nausea noted in the early days of therapy can be reduced by taking lithium with, or just before, a main meal. There is, however, no hard evidence on this matter.

Special Diets for Gastric Problems

If gastric problems occur during lithium therapy—particularly if this happens in the first week or so of treatment being initiated—the possibility should be seriously considered that it is the lithium which is the causal agent. If, for example, a sustained release preparation is employed which achieves its sustained release properties at the expense of low bioavailability, there may be a substantial portion of unabsorbed tablet which finds its way to the colon where, by stimulating osmotic transfer of fluid into the gut lumen, it causes diarrhoea. It would be inappropriate to attempt to deal with the problem by dietary adjustment or by the use of a dietary binding agent; far better is to change the medication for one with high bioavailability.

Bibliography

Thomsen,K. and Leyssac,P.P. (1986) Effect of dietary sodium content on renal handling of lithium. *Pflugers Arch.*, **407**, 55–58. An elegant paper which gives detailed experimental evidence for the effects of dietary sodium on lithium excretion.

42. Life Style

Jonathan M.Himmelhoch and Alan G.Mallinger

The effects which, in principle, lithium therapy may have upon the life style of a patient are of two kinds. Firstly there are effects stemming directly from the actions of lithium upon the organs and systems of the body; and secondly there are changes which the patient has to make in order to accommodate the demands of the therapeutic regime and to optimize the conditions for successful treatment. Whether, or to what extent, any particular patient's life style is in practice significantly altered will depend in large measure on how disruptive the affective disorder has been on normal functioning, on how effective lithium is in alleviating the disorder, and on how well the therapeutic regimen is managed.

Direct Effects of Lithium

Since John Cade first demonstrated lithium's effectiveness in manic excitement (pp. 24–28), understanding of its optimal use in the other phases of manic-depressive illness has developed slowly, and most of lithium's negative effects on daily activity and on life-style are probably derived from poorly designed treatment regimen for both the depressive and the maintenance phases of bipolar disease.

There are still some psychiatrists who conceptualize

lithium purely as an anti-manic agent. The most persistent derivative notion of such a view is that the lithium level therapeutic in the treatment of mania (0.8−1.5 mmol/l) must be therapeutic in all phases of manic-depressive illness. Such levels, however, are not sacrosanct. Bipolar depressives who present with decreased motor activity and with normal or increased sleep, often respond to merely 600−900 mg lithium daily, with modest blood levels of 0.45−0.65 mEq/l. Paradoxically, more traditional doses and blood levels often fail. In elderly patients lower levels are clearly preferable (see Section 36, pp. 135−138). Moreover, recent experience in many lithium research clinics suggests that commonly accepted maintenance lithium levels are often simply too high. The results are, on occasion, oedema; thirst and excessive urinary output; carbohydrate craving and weight gain; sluggishness and decreased sex-drive; or, finally, impaired creativity. All of these may have important consequences for life-style and activity.

Most of the time these nagging and insidious impediments to a normal life are produced by low-grade lithium toxicity born of heavy handed lithium administration. There are, however, theoreticians, such as Judd and Shaw, who hypothesize that the therapeutic actions of lithium salts actually consist of subtle toxicity, so that the negative impact of lithium on life-style is intrinsic to its use and can at best be minimized, but never completely avoided. However, experience in over 2000 patients at the Western Psychiatric Institute and Clinic suggests that in most cases the lithium regimen can be adjusted to avoid negative effects on life-style and to permit that productively hypomanic mood level that most bipolar subjects prefer. The respected lithium researcher, Mogens Schou, described a similar experience in relationship to artistic creativity when he found that approximately one-third of his artistically creative subjects actually reported improved creative powers, one-third stayed the same on lithium treatment and only one third reported lessened creative powers.

Although Judd found lithium-induced cognitive and motor deficits in normal volunteers, it does not logically follow that these deficits explain the therapeutic efficacy of lithium treatment. Indeed, the critical neuropsychological observation by J.H.Court that seemingly accelerated hypomanic patients show greater deficits in reaction time and other measures of psychomotor function than do even the most severe depressives, implies that the sum of lithium effects in most bipolar patients should be in the direction of normalization and/or improvement of life-style and activity. This does, indeed often seem to be the case, even though in the early stages of lithium therapy there may be performance decrements. For example, a star professional basketball player referred to the Western Psychiatric Institute and Clinic because of weight gain, sluggishness and loss of star quality 'moves' on the basketball floor, as a consequence of lithium treatment, watched his weight normalize and his points per game (p.p.g.) average, which had dropped to 6.9 p.p.g. early on lithium therapy, rebound to 16.7 p.p.g.—identical to his original performance level; his assists per game, which had declined to 2.1, gradually climbed back to the expected 6.9. This recovery took place without any intervention, except watchful waiting.

Still there is a sub-group of manic-depressive patients who suffer difficult problems in life-style on lithium therapy. These patients' mood swings may overwhelm the 'fine-tuning' of their low dose lithium; they therefore require higher doses, which actually impairs the membrane transport mechanism that removes lithium from cells, so that linear increments in dosage lead to more than linear increases of intracellular lithium. The sub-group includes patients with brittle, rapidly developing, psychotic manic phases; rapid cyclers; and subjects who pay dearly for each 'productive hypomania' with painful, refractory and prolonged depressive episodes. Sometimes such patients benefit from recently discovered adjunctive therapies, such as carbamazepine, a temporal lobe anticonvulsant with mood-stabilizing effect. The rest must simply live with their lithium-induced restructuring of life-style. In the end, many are entirely lost to treatment, preferring an existence which is a painful mixture of excess, rebellion, depression, creativity and freedom, to a numbed, boring and unspontaneous life.

Demands of the Treatment Regimen

Even when the therapy is adjusted so as to minimize side effects and to maximize clinical benefit, there remain some costs associated with the treatment procedure. In order to ensure the continuation of the therapy's effectiveness, the patient must come to terms with the need for continued supplies of lithium and for periodic serum lithium monitoring, for example. This means that to some extent the patient's life has to be geared to the availability of prescribing and monitoring facilities; that presumably precludes taking up residence for long periods in remote parts of the world. It is unlikely that this would be a serious matter for the majority of individuals, of course, but for those whose work or vocation is such that these considerations are important, the effects on life style may be profound.

It is well know that serum lithium levels rise as body sodium becomes depleted (see Section 19, pp. 75–78). As a consequence, the successfully treated patient must maintain a life style which is unlikely to lead to sudden or marked fluctuations in sodium loss. Strenuous physical activity, excessive use of the sauna, or exposure to other circumstances producing excessive sweating (visiting hot climates, for example) must be avoided, and diet has to be adjusted to maintain moderate salt content. Again these are not serious problems for the great majority of patients.

Probably the most marked feature of the lithium patient's life style which differs from that of the non-patient, is the need to adhere to a self-administration regimen, i.e. to take tablets once or twice a day. Whilst this seems a small price to pay for freedom from the tyranny of a recurrent affective disorder, for some patients it is a tyranny of another kind—a constant reminder of the continuing underlying illness and of their vulnerability to relapse. To the extent that the patient needs the social support of family and friends to support the maintenance of lithium prophylaxis in the face of such feelings, there must inevitably occur subtle, but pervasive, changes of life style.

These are matters which are not peculiar to lithium therapy, of course; they occur with all medications, but are particularly prominent where lithium treatment is concerned. They have not been subjected to close experimental scrutiny, but they would clearly repay such examination by suggesting ways of improving both the quality of life of the lithium patient and compliance with medication.

Bibliography

Johnson,F.N. (ed.) (1980) *The Handbook of Lithium Therapy*. MTP Press, Lancaster.

The various facets of lithium therapy which impinge upon life style are covered in this book, written primarily for psychiatrists.

Schou,M. (1979) Artistic productivity and lithium prophylaxis in manic-depressive illness. *Br. J. Psychiatry*, **135**, 97–103.

A classic paper in which the effects of lithium on the life style of highly creative individuals are closely examined. It is eminently readable.

43. Coping with Excessive Doses

Irving H.Gomolin

The treatment of lithium intoxication requires:

(i) assessment of the severity of intoxication;
(ii) identification and treatment of any predisposing condition which has preciptated intoxication;
(iii) institution of appropriate supportive and corrective measures for the complications of intoxication; and
(iv) the elimination of the lithium ion from the body, i.e. reduction of the serum lithium concentration.

Assessment of the severity of intoxication requires a thorough history and physical examination for the signs and symptoms of intoxication, and measurement of the serum lithium level. The laboratory evaluation should also include determination of serum electrolytes, blood urea nitrogen (BUN) and creatinine. Except for very mild intoxication, a complete blood count and urinalysis should be obtained. An elevated white count may result from lithium therapy but the practitioner must maintain a high index of suspicion of infection as a precipitating condition. Precipitating events such as a febrile illness should be sought and treated. Similarly, the recent use of a concomitant drug and/or low salt diet which can reduce lithium excretion must be identified. Complications of an altered mental state, such as aspiration pneumonia, or pressure sores, should be identified and treated. Treatment should include measures to prevent these complications.

Acute Overdose

In cases of acute overdose, one must attempt to remove lithium from the stomach prior to its absorption. In patients who are alert, emesis induced by syrup of ipecac is preferred to gastric lavage. Although lithium intoxication may be associated with vomiting, spontaneous vomiting is, in general, ineffective in removing large quantities of toxic material from the stomach and does not constitute effective gastric emptying. In patients who are obtunded, lavage with a large bore gastric tube should be performed following insertion of a cuffed endotracheal tube to protect the airway from vomitus. Both emesis and lavage are probably of little benefit unless performed within 2–3 h of ingestion of a toxic amount. Some investigators have recommended repeated gastric lavage as lithium may be present in gastric fluid for extended periods of time. In this regard, it may be useful to measure the lithium concentration in the gastric fluid. Unless there is visualization of tablet pieces, or if the concentration is exceedingly high, i.e. indicating continued presence of dissolving tablets or slow release capsules, this measure is probably not worthwhile as relatively small amounts of lithium will be removed. Furthermore, the patient is subjected to the risk of fluid and electrolyte disturbances, and possibly unnecessary intubation and/or aspiration.

Emesis should be induced regardless of the presence or absence of symptoms of intoxication since the goal here is to prevent absorption of potentially toxic amounts of lithium. The potentially toxic dose of lithium carbonate is approximately 40 mg/kg, equivalent to 7.5 mg/kg or 1.1 mmol/kg of elemental lithium, but this does not consider the lithium level prior to acute overdose. Furthermore, the history of acute overdose is notoriously unreliable with regard to actual amount or other drugs ingested. It is, therefore, also important to suspect a polydrug overdose among these patients and to attempt to ascertain whether there has been access to other drugs. Some of these patients may have been treated with other neuroleptic agents and many overdoses involve concomitant alcohol ingestion.

The use of activated charcoal and cathartics following emesis or lavage is probably not beneficial in preventing lithium absorption. However, these measures are indicated when polydrug intoxication cannot be ruled out. In these situations, toxicological screens on samples of gastric fluid, blood and urine may be helpful. The practitioner should be aware that many of these screens involve a search for only a limited number of toxic substances. Therapy then becomes directed as described below.

Insidious Intoxication

Lithium poisoning develops gradually in most cases and the interventions described above will not be required. Besides identifying and treating precipitating causes, and the institution of supportive measures, the goal of therapy is to reduce the serum lithium level. Lithium intoxication is usually accompanied by levels greater than 1.5–2 mmol/l. The finding of a lower lithium concentration, however, does not exclude lithium toxicity. For example, the patient may be seen at a time when the serum level has fallen but damage to tissues has already occurred. This probably relates to the slower removal of lithium from tissues such as the brain.

In general, patients with lithium toxicity will remain toxic at least until the serum level has been reduced to within the therapeutic range. Since lithium is almost exclusively excreted by the kidney, acceleration of lithium removal from the body relies either on an increase in renal excretion or on removal by artificial means, i.e. haemodialysis or the less efficient means of peritoneal dialysis.

Many patients with lithium toxicity will be found to have renal dysfunction as evidenced by an elevated serum BUN and creatinine. The clinician must determine whether this represents chronic or acute renal failure. If it has been determined that acute renal failure exists, the clinician must then determine whether this is pre-renal in origin, i.e. due to volume depletion, or due to an acute intrinsic renal injury (acute tubular necrosis) which has complicated the intoxication. Some patients may have acute, superimposed on chronic, renal failure.

Patients with pre-renal failure will have, by definition, a reversible reduction in glomerular filtration rate. Unless this is corrected, renal lithium clearance can be expected to be slower than normal for that particular patient. In patients with otherwise normal renal function, the renal lithium clearance is 10–40 ml/min, but clearances as low as 5 ml/min have been observed during intoxication. Therefore, restoration of renal function in these patients by volume repletion will increase renal lithium clearance towards normal and accelerate the elimination of the lithium ion by the kidney. On the other hand, for patients with relatively fixed renal failure, i.e. chronic or acute tubular necrosis, and without evidence for significant volume depletion, fluid therapy alone will not significantly increase renal lithium clearance.

Another way of expressing the elimination of lithium from the body is the half-life, which is the time required for a given serum level to become reduced by 50% assuming no further lithium is administered. The half-life varies inversely with renal lithium clearance and is between 7 and 20 h for most individuals. In patients with renal dysfunction, it will be prolonged.

It must be emphasized that there are no controlled clinical studies which determine the optimal therapy for lithium intoxication. The choice of therapy depends on the severity and complications of intoxication, the potential for complications of various therapies, the extent to which abnormalities in renal function are reversible, and the serum lithium level.

Saline Therapy

For patients with mild to moderate toxicity, most authorities recommend the relatively rapid intravenous infusion of isotonic saline, e.g. 1–2 litres within 6 h. Some refer to this therapy as forced diuresis. This intervention will be most beneficial to patients with volume depletion since the glomerular filtration rate will rise and hasten the otherwise reduced clearance of lithium. Also, patients with hyponatraemia will benefit because hyponatraemia otherwise encourages the renal tubular reabsorption of lithium. A large urine output during volume repletion may partly be due to the lithium induced impairment of renal concentrating capacity and not the infusion of saline *per se*. This concentrating defect predisposes the patient to hypernatraemia. Fluid balance and serum electrolytes must, therefore, be strictly monitored.

If the patient's clinical condition is stable or improving, and the serum lithium level has fallen at 6 h, continued therapy with normal saline is indicated until recovery is evident and lithium levels are close to 1 mmol/l. It is desirable to infuse saline at a rate which is associated with a decline of 20% or more in successive lithium levels drawn at 6-h intervals. This approximates to a half-life of 18 h and corresponds to a renal lithium clearance which is within the normal range. Infusions of 7 or more litres of saline in the initial 24 h are reported in the literature when more serious intoxications (associated with levels of 3 mmol/l or greater) have been treated in this manner. As the glomerular filtration rate is restored to normal, and fluid losses due to polyuria are replaced, lithium concentrations can be expected to fall fairly quickly. For instance, a patient with an initial level of 2.5–3 mmol/l, will achieve levels close to 1 mmol/l within 24 h, assuming a half-life of about 18 h. For patients with chronic renal disease, acute renal injury, and the elderly, the half-life may be longer and levels will fall less rapidly.

The renal lithium clearance can be increased with the administration of osmotic diuretic agents such as urea or mannitol. Aminophylline and urinary alkalinizing agents such as acetazolamide and sodium bicarbonate also increase clearance. The potential for complications of some of these therapies and the relatively minimal salutary effects demonstrated in some studies have led authorities such as Thomsen and Schou no longer to recommend their use. Saline infusion appears most rational for patients with reversible lowering of lithium clearance. Some authorities recommend alkalinization of the urine. Acetazolamide should be avoided because of its potential for acidaemia. The use of sodium bicarbonate requires extreme caution because of the potential for hypernatraemia. Nevertheless, isotonic infusion with sodium bicarbonate can be accomplished by appropriately mixing the former with half normal saline solutions.

Dialysis

Most authorities recommend dialysis for patients with severe intoxication such as those with serious central nervous system dysfunction or cardiovascular collapse, as well as for all patients with levels greater than 4 mmol/l regardless of symptoms. Dialysis may also be indicated for patients who would otherwise be treated with saline infusion but for whom the required fluid volumes cannot be tolerated because of complications such as pulmonary oedema or anuria due to acute tubular necrosis. Some investigators, however, have successfully treated serious intoxications with fluid therapy alone.

The principle of dialysis is the creation of a concentration gradient between one compartment, i.e. the blood, and a second, i.e. the dialysis fluid (dialysate). Lithium ions will passively diffuse from the plasma, where the concentration is high, to the dialysate where the concentration is lower. As the concentration in the dialysate rises, the net diffusion of lithium from plasma will decrease. The extent of contact between these two compartments will also determine the amount of lithium which may be cleared from plasma.

Peritoneal dialysis

Peritoneal dialysis involves instillation of (lithium free) dialysate into the peritoneal (abdominal) cavity. Lithium in the plasma of the peritoneal blood vessels can then diffuse into the dialysate. The dialysate must be drained, discarded, and replaced with fresh dialysate at frequent intervals, since removal of lithium from plasma will decrease as the lithium concentration in the dialysate rises. Lithium clearance by this method is approximately 15 ml/min.

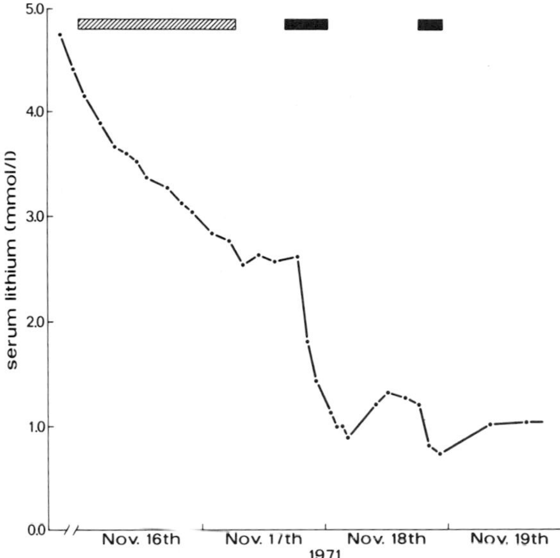

Figure 43.1 Changes in serum lithium levels in a 45-year-old female suffering from severe intoxication and subjected to peritoneal dialysis (hatched bar) and haemodialysis (black bars). Reproduced from Hansen,H.E. and Amdisen,A. (1978) *Q.J.Med.*, **47**, 123–144; with permission of Oxford University Press.

Haemodialysis

Haemodialysis is much more efficient than peritoneal dialysis and is the recommended method of choice when dialysis is indicated. The clearance of lithium with this procedure is said to be 50 ml/min but one report has demonstrated a clearance of 187 ml/min. Haemodialysis is more efficient than peritoneal dialysis because it brings a large volume of the patient's blood directly to the dialysis machine. Haemodialysis may cause hypotension, among other complications, and must be performed under the supervision of an appropriate consultant. Volume depletion must be corrected prior to, or in association with, this procedure. The recommended duration of this procedure is 8–12 h. During haemodialysis, serum lithium concentrations fall rapidly. Since this procedure clears lithium from the blood more rapidly relative to the diffusion of lithium out of tissues, the serum level may rise when dialysis is terminated. Haemodialysis may be repeated depending on the patient's clinical condition and serum lithium level. *Figure 43.1* demonstrates this phenomenon and also the relative efficacy of peritoneal versus haemodialysis in one particular patient.

It is important to note that dialysis is of greatest benefit when serum levels are high, since the actual amount of lithium removed will be greater than when levels are low:

Amount removed/unit time = total clearance × mean plasma concentration
= (renal + dialysis) clearance × mean plasma concentration

The above equation also demonstrates that the relative efficacy of dialysis is increased when patients have a low renal lithium clearance, e.g. as a result of chronic renal failure or acute tubular necrosis. It would also appear that dialysis for low serum concentrations of lithium may not be worthwhile as relatively little lithium will be removed, as, for example, in the case of a severely intoxicated patient who is found relatively late following intoxication, when levels have fallen slowly spontaneously. Nevertheless, dialysis may be required to treat acute renal failure (tubular necrosis) *per se*.

Summary

Lithium intoxication may be severe and life-threatening. Knowledge of the precipitants of intoxication and prompt intervention will identify most intoxications prior to their progression to more serious poisoning. Many clinically important intoxications can be managed with saline infusion although haemodialysis is the most efficient mechanism for the removal of lithium from the body. Rigid guidelines for the use of dialysis require controlled clinical studies which identify the characteristics of those patients most likely to benefit from this procedure.

Acknowledgement

The author wishes to thank Dennis J.Chapron for reviewing the manuscript.

Bibliography

Parfrey,P.S., Ikeman,R., Anglin,D. and Cole,C. (1983) Severe lithium intoxication treated by forced diuresis. *Can. Med. Assoc. J.*, **129**, 979–980.
A brief account of the forced diuresis technique, but one which provides some useful technical details.

Thomsen,K. and Schou,M. (1975) The treatment of lithium poison-

ing. In *Lithium Research and Therapy*. Johnson,F.N. (ed.), Academic Press, London, pp. 227–236.
Presents useful guidelines for determining whether or not to use dialysis. It is a good review of the general area of intoxication treatment.

44. Risk Factors

F.Neil Johnson and Mogens Schou

In the following list (*Table 44.1*) an attempt has been made to classify and weight some of the factors that might be taken into account when lithium treatment is considered. It also indicates circumstances under which it may be advisable to stop treatment or reduce the dosage. This list is hardly exhaustive, and it should not be taken as a substitute for clinical judgement.

The weightings range from 1 to 4, where 1 indicates that the problem is slight or infrequent; 2 means that side effects occasionally are substantial, but they are not life threatening and can be dealt with by dosage reduction or other measures; 3 implies that lithium treatment should be given only on weighty indication and under close monitoring; 4 is used to indicate that lithium is absolutely contraindicated under all but exceptional circumstances and under rigorous supervision.

The list is at best a summary and should be regarded merely as a memory aid. One should not attempt to add up risk factor weights in order to provide an overall 'risk score', because each risk factor should be assessed in relation to the individual patient's medical and psychiatric situation.

For further details, reference should be made to other parts of this book.

Table 44.1 *Risk factors and their relative importance in lithium therapy*

Factor	Problem area	Weighting
Kidney disease with variable glomerular filtration rate, e.g. glomerulonephritis or pyelonephritis	Variable elimination	4
Cardiovascular disease with disturbance of fluid and salt balance	Variable elimination	4
Physical illness with fever	Lowered elimination	4
Other conditions with risk of dehydration or sodium deficiency, e.g. low sodium diet, rigorous slimming regimes, gastrointestinal disturbance, heaving sweating	Lowered elimination	3
Surgery and anaesthesia	Variable elimination	3
Unconscious for many hours	Risk of dehydration with lowered elimination	3
Pregnancy	Teratogenic risk	3
Delivery	Abrupt fall of elimination	3
Breast feeding	Effects on the child	2
Pre-existing acne or psoriasis	Exacerbation	3
Pre-existing organic brain damage	Neurological side effects	2
Pre-existing overweight	Further weight gain	1
High age	Lowered elimination	1
Concomitant medication:		
Diuretics	Lowered elimination	4
Nonsteroidal antirheumatics	Lowered elimination	4
Neuroleptics	Neurological side effects	2

Part VII

CLINICAL PRACTICE: TREATMENT COMBINATIONS

45. Antidepressants

Lawrence H.Price

Since the primary use of lithium is in treating mood disorder, it should not be surprising that lithium is often given in conjunction with antidepressant drugs. This practice developed not out of any particular theoretical rationale, but rather in response to clinical necessity. Typically, a bipolar patient whose mania had been successfully controlled with lithium might require an antidepressant to treat a new depressive episode. Alternatively, the emergence of manic symptoms in a depressed patient who had responded to antidepressant might necessitate lithium treatment. Only in the last few years have researchers begun to investigate systematically the possibility that, under certain circumstances, lithium might uniquely interact with some antidepressants to produce a greater antidepressant effect.

Acute Depressive Episodes

Acute bipolar depression

Many bipolar patients are chronically maintained on lithium to prevent recurrence of both manic and depressive episodes. Despite this, up to one-third of such patients will have recurrent depression within 2 years of a successfully-treated acute affective episode. The usual practice is to treat the emerging depression by adding an antidepressant to the ongoing lithium. The major reason for continuing the lithium is to prevent the development of antidepressant-induced mania, a kind of 'overshoot' phenomenon often seen when bipolar patients are treated for depression. For the same reason, some clinicians initiate lithium and antidepressant treatment simultaneously in bipolar depressed patients who are not already on lithium maintenance.

A secondary reason for giving lithium and an antidepressant concurrently is to take advantage of lithium's own antidepressant effects. Interestingly, early investigators thought that lithium was devoid of antidepressant actions (pp. 35–38). Although subsequent studies contradicted this belief (at least in certain patients), the suspicion lingered that lithium might impair the action of other antidepressant drugs. Conversely, some investigators speculated that lithium plus an antidepressant might actually be more effective than the antidepressant alone.

Of the few controlled studies of this issue, the best designed was carried out in 1974 by Professor Otto Lingjaerde, of Oslo University, and his colleagues at several other Norwegian hospitals. They randomly assigned 45 endogenously depressed inpatients to 6 weeks of double-blind treatment with tricyclic plus lithium or plus placebo. Both drugs were initiated simultaneously. In the total sample, depression ratings were lower in the lithium group after 4 weeks, but the same in both groups after 6 weeks. However, when results from the one hospital which enrolled the largest number of patients were analysed separately, the lithium group had lower depression ratings after just 1 week, a difference which continued through the fourth week but was lost at the sixth week. Thus, there was no evidence that lithium interfered with response to tricyclics, and some evidence that it might accelerate improvement. Although the authors reported no differences in response between the eight bipolar and 37 unipolar patients in this study, the proportion of bipolar patients was too small to permit any definitive statement about diagnostic differences.

Several studies, though none as carefully controlled as the Norwegian trial, have described the successful use of lithium in conjunction with a monoamine oxidase inhibitor (MAOI). The largest number of patients reported have received tranylcypromine, but phenelzine and isocarboxazid have also been employed. In general, MAOIs are used less commonly than tricyclics and related drugs in treating depression, primarily because of the special dietary constraints they impose and their greater potential for serious toxicity. The rationale for using an MAOI in lieu of a tricyclic in bipolar depressed patients receiving lithium is three-fold: firstly, MAOIs are often effective in patients who fail to respond to tricyclics; secondly, bipolar depression, in particular, might be more responsive to MAOIs than to tricyclics; and thirdly, there might exist a synergistic interaction between MAOIs and lithium that does not exist between tricyclics and lithium.

Unfortunately, the studies supporting these rationales have not been methodologically rigorous. While many uncontrolled reports have described tricyclic-refractory patients who subsequently responded to an MAOI, there has been no careful examination of whether an equal proportion of MAOI-refractory patients might improve on tricyclic medication. Thus, it is unclear whether different subtypes of depression respond preferentially to tricyclics or MAOIs, as often suggested, or whether MAOIs might simply be more effective than tricyclics. Similarly, although reports have documented the efficacy of MAOIs in bipolar patients, many previously unresponsive to tricyclics, there have been no controlled studies directly comparing MAOIs and tricyclics in bipolar depression. The evidence for a unique interaction of MAOIs with lithium should be considered equally tenuous. It is based primarily on the efficacy of this combination in patients unimproved on tricyclics plus lithium, although some studies in laboratory animals lend further support.

In addition to these investigations of lithium combined with standard antidepressants, two studies have examined the efficacy of lithium combined with tryptophan. Tryptophan, the amino acid precursor of the neurotransmitter serotonin, is believed by some researchers to possess antidepressant properties of its own. The studies of lithium plus tryptophan have shown significant antidepressant effects for this combination, in one study superior to those of tryptophan alone and in the other equivalent to those of amitriptyline. Unfortunately, these studies do not clarify whether the combination is superior to lithium alone, or whether bipolar depressed patients respond differently from unipolars.

It is worth returning to the question whether lithium might impede the effects of other antidepressants, particularly tricyclics. The few studies of this issue have never demonstrated such an action, although most of the patients in those studies were unipolar. Even in bipolar patients, however, it seems unlikely that this is a robust or common phenomenon. Nonetheless, occasionally bipolar depressed patients who have been very treatment-resistant will respond to a new tricyclic trial given after ongoing lithium treatment has been stopped. Although these patients are at higher risk for tricyclic-induced mania, this may be easier to treat than the preceding depression. One study has suggested that refractory rapid-cycling bipolar disorder may respond to lithium combined with low doses of the selective Type A MAOI, clorgyline.

Acute unipolar depression

Since lithium is not generally used in the USA (though the situation is different in other countries) for maintenance treatment in unipolar depression, most episodes of recurrence in unipolar patients will not involve a decision about continuation of lithium during acute treatment with another antidepressant. Similarly, the low likelihood of antidepressant-induced mania in patients with recurrent unipolar illness eliminates this rationale for combined treatment. If a unipolar patient is receiving lithium maintenance, the available evidence indicates no major contraindication to adding an antidepressant for acute treatment.

Given the fact of lithium's own antidepressant properties (pp. 35–38), the question arises whether any therapeutic advantage might be gained from administering lithium and an antidepressant together from the outset of treatment of an acute unipolar depression. As already discussed, there is inconclusive but suggestive evidence that an increase in efficacy or an acceleration in the rapidity of response might result from combinations of tricyclics or MAOIs with lithium. Although lithium alone seems to have greater antidepressant effects in bipolar than in unipolar patients, the combination treatment studies show no difference in response between the two subtypes, perhaps suggesting that different mechanisms are responsible for lithium's effects when used in combination and when used alone. In any case, the response rate to standard antidepressants alone is sufficiently high, and the evidence favouring lithium–antidepressant combinations sufficiently weak, that combination treatment cannot presently be recommended as a first-line approach.

Refractory depression

In 1981, Professor Claude de Montigny and his associates at the University of Montreal, Canada, described eight unipolar depressed patients who improved dramatically within 48 h of having lithium added to a previously unsuccessful tricyclic regimen. Professor de Montigny's rationale for this approach was based on a specific neurochemical hypothesis positing synergistic effects of long-term tricyclic and short-term lithium treatments on the neurotransmitter serotonin. In 1983, Professor George Heninger and his colleagues at Yale University, USA, reported a study confirming the initial clinical finding. In the Yale study, 15 depressed patients (14 unipolar) who had not responded to adequate tricyclic or tetracyclic treatment were alternately assigned to receive 12 days of either lithium or placebo in addition to their ongoing antidepressant. All treatment was double-blind. The lithium group did significantly better than the placebo group, with transient superiority in the first 2 days and sustained superiority after day 6. When the placebo group was subsequently crossed over to lithium, they responded as well as the group originally given lithium. Of the 15 patients in the study, 12 were judged responders.

The strategy of adding lithium to an ongoing course of antidepressant drug in order to obtain a more robust antidepressant effect has been called 'lithium augmentation'. Although this term has generally come to imply a specific sequence of drug administration, it originally derived from the assumption that lithium interacts in a uniquely synergistic way with the antidepressant so as to magnify the antidepressant's effects. Since it is this neurochemical interaction which is believed to underlie the clinical phenomenon, there is no assumption that lithium will exert significant antidepressant effects independently of the other drug.

To date, over 200 trials of lithium augmentation have been reported, with an overall response rate of 60–70%. Some of these trials were reported as anecdotal observations, which tends falsely to inflate the cumulative response rate, but three placebo-controlled studies and a larger number of extended case series utilizing some form of objective assessment constitute the major bulk of the data. In the most recent larger studies, the response rate has averaged 50%.

Lithium augmentation appears to be effective in both unipolar and bipolar depression, although some studies have inconsistently suggested that efficacy may be greater in one subtype than the other. Successful results have been observed with all major antidepressant classes, including tricyclics, MAOIs, unicyclics, bicyclics, tetracyclics, triazolopyridines, aminoketones, triazolobenzodiazepines and tricyclic–neuroleptic combinations. The majority of trials have involved tricyclics, and there are preliminary data which suggest that triazolopyridines and triazolobenzodiazepines may be inferior. The relationship between serum lithium level and clinical response is unclear, but positive results have been obtained with very low lithium levels (e.g. 0.15–0.40 mmol/l). The pattern of clinical response seems variable: in a study of 84 patients at Yale 31% were judged to be full responders, 25% partial responders, 39% unchanged and 5% adverse responders. Precipitation of mania has also been reported. The time course of response is similarly variable, ranging from 48 h to 3 weeks.

Important questions about lithium augmentation remain to be answered, particularly whether sequential addition is really superior to concurrent initiation of lithium and antidepressant. The use of this approach in other illnesses, such as obsessive–compulsive disorder, is still in its infancy. In any case, lithium augmentation in refractory depression is presently one of the best substantiated uses of lithium–antidepressant combination treatment.

Treatment guidelines for acute depressive episodes

Table 45.1 presents recommendations for the pharmacological management of acute depression. In drug-free bipolar patients, response rates are sufficiently high to warrant an initial trial of lithium alone. Some studies suggest that concurrent treatment with tryptophan may be beneficial, although this practice is not presently widespread. If lithium proves ineffective, or if the patient has relapsed while on maintenance lithium, sequential trials of tricyclic, MAOI, or newer heterocyclic agents may be added to ongoing lithium. Continued non-response would justify discontinuation of lithium and administration of a tricyclic alone, followed, if necessary, by lithium augmentation.

Drug-free unipolar patients should usually be treated first with a tricyclic. Failure to respond, or occurrence of a relapse while on maintenance tricyclic, can be managed either by sequential trials of MAOI or newer

Table 45.1 *Treatment guidelines for acute depressive episodes*

A. *Bipolar*
- (i) Drug-free
  - a. Lithium (+/− tryptophan)
- (ii) On lithium (acute or maintenance)
  - a. Lithium + tricyclic
  - b. Lithium + MAOI
  - c. Lithium + newer heterocyclic
  - d. Discontinue lithium; give tricyclic alone
  - e. Consider 'Refractory' (C)

B. *Unipolar*
- (i) Drug-free
  - a. Tricyclic
- (ii) On tricyclic (acute or maintenance)
  - a. MAOI or consider 'Refractory' (C)
  - b. Newer heterocyclic or consider 'Refractory' (C)
  - c. Consider 'Refractory' (C)

C. *Refractory*
- (i) Add lithium to ongoing antidepressant ('lithium augmentation')

heterocyclic agents, or by lithium augmentation of any of these drugs.

It should be emphasized that these guidelines, based on the available data and clinical experience, are by no means exhaustive. They must be considered in the light of the unique needs and circumstances of each individual patient. Decisions to proceed in a different sequence from that outlined, or to use treatments that have not been discussed here (e.g. ECT, stimulants, neuroleptics), will frequently be made by experienced clinicians based on such needs and circumstances.

Recurrent Depressive Episodes (Maintenance)

Recurrent bipolar depression

Maintenance of lithium treatment is clearly effective in preventing recurrent mania. It is also effective against recurrent bipolar depression, although this has been more difficult to show in placebo-controlled studies, since placebo-treated bipolar patients are more likely to have manic than depressive relapses. Maintenance imipramine treatment confers no protection against mania, but is as effective as lithium against recurrent bipolar depression. As noted earlier, however, the rate of depressive relapse is considerable even in bipolar patients receiving single-drug prophylaxis, raising the question as to whether lithium–antidepressant combinations might offer additional protection.

The most comprehensive study of this issue was carried out by the NIMH Collaborative Study Group, headed by Dr Robert Prien. They randomly assigned 117 bipolar patients to double-blind maintenance with lithium, imipramine, or lithium–imipramine. Patients were followed prospectively at five centres over a 2-year period. The findings, reported in 1984, were that 22% of patients treated with lithium–imipramine suffered depressive relapses, compared with 29% of the lithium and 28% of the imipramine groups. These differences were not statistically significant, whereas the rates for manic relapse (lithium–imipramine, 28%; lithium, 26%; imipramine, 53%) were clearly different.

The failure of this study to show any advantage of lithium–imipramine over lithium alone in the prophylaxis of bipolar depression is consistent with other evidence showing no advantage to the combination in bipolar II disorder (depression with hypomania). These findings argue against the routine use of lithium–antidepressant combination treatment for prevention of recurrent bipolar depression. It should be noted, however, that these studies have examined only one antidepressant (imipramine) and have used relatively low doses (75–150 mg/day). It is possible that other antidepressants, tricyclics or non-tricyclics, or even higher doses of imipramine itself might be useful in the combination treatment of selected patients.

Recurrent unipolar depression

Well-controlled studies have shown maintenance lithium to be better than placebo, and equal or superior to imipramine, amitriptyline, maprotiline, or mianserin, in preventing recurrent unipolar depression. As in the case of bipolar depression, however, relapse rates in unipolar illness remain high despite maintenance treatment with a single drug.

Again, the multicentre trial reported in 1984 by the NIMH Collaborative Study Group provides the best evidence regarding the efficacy of combined lithium–antidepressant in this situation. One hundred and fifty unipolar patients were randomly assigned to 2 years of double-blind maintenance on one of four treatment regimens. Depressive relapse rates were 26% for lithium plus imipramine, 33% for imipramine, 57% for lithium, and 65% for placebo. The combination and imipramine-alone regimens did not show statistically significant differences from each other, but both were superior to lithium and placebo. Interestingly, no patient receiving lithium alone experienced a manic episode, while rates ranged from 5 to 8% in the lithium–imipramine, imipramine and placebo groups. This suggests that imipramine alone did not predispose to mania in these previously unipolar patients, but it did eliminate the prophylactic properties of lithium when the two were given in combination, an effect not seen in combination-treated bipolar patients.

The NIMH findings are consistent with data from smaller studies in failing to show a clear advantage to combined lithium–antidepressant prophylaxis against recurrent unipolar illness. However, while some studies have found lithium equal or superior to tricyclics and tetracyclics, the NIMH group found imipramine superior to lithium. These investigators noted that there is substantial heterogeneity in unipolar patients across studies, and that lithium does seem to possess prophylactic efficacy in less severely-ill unipolar patients. In any case, the limitations of the evidence discussed with respect to recurrent bipolar depression apply here as well: although routine use of lithium–antidepressant maintenance does not seem justified, some unipolar patients may benefit from it.

Recurrent refractory depression

Patients who respond to lithium augmentation pose a somewhat different problem in terms of long-term treatment. In the previously discussed situations, combination treatment was considered in terms of enhancing preventive efficacy in patients who had responded acutely to a single drug. In contrast, lithium augmentation responders have, by definition, been refractory to single-drug treatment, but have derived acute benefit from combination therapy. The question then arises whether combination treatment should be continued or, if not, which drug should be stopped first.

Professor de Montigny and his associates described the only systematic prospective study of this issue in 1983. In nine unipolar patients who had rapidly responded to lithium augmentation, lithium was discontinued after 48 h while the tricyclic was maintained at its previous dose. When evaluated by non-blind raters 5 days later, five patients had relapsed and four had continued in remission. Other investigators have anecdotally reported sustained remission in patients maintained on both drugs for up to several months.

These preliminary observations suggest that while patients responding to lithium augmentation may be successfully maintained on the combination for extended periods, perhaps half of the unipolar patients can be maintained on tricyclic alone. It is interesting to speculate whether this finding is related to the NIMH group's demonstration of imipramine's equivalence with lithium–imipramine in preventing unipolar relapses. By analogy, it might be possible to maintain a subgroup of bipolar patients responding to lithium augmentation on lithium alone. At this point, however, there is no way of predicting which patients will relapse without two-drug maintenance.

Treatment guidelines for recurrent depressive episodes (maintenance treatment)

Table 45.2 suggests strategies for the pharmacological prophylaxis of recurrent depression. Lithium alone is the maintenance treatment of first choice in bipolar disorder. In patients who are poorly controlled on this regimen, a trial of lithium combined with a tricyclic, MAOI or newer heterocyclic drug would be warranted. Available evidence indicates that tricyclic doses lower than the equivalent of imipramine 150 mg/day are unlikely to be effective.

Table 45.2 *Treatment guidelines for recurrent depressive episodes (maintenance treatment)*

A. *Bipolar*
1. Lithium
2. Lithium + tricyclic (daily dose greater than equivalent of imipramine 150 mg),
   + MAOI, or
   + newer heterocyclic

B. *Unipolar*
1. Tricyclic, MAOI, or newer heterocyclic
2. Lithium (mild depressive episodes)
3. Lithium + tricyclic (daily dose greater than equivalent of imipramine 150 mg),
   + MAOI, or
   + newer heterocyclic

C *Refractory*
1. If positive response to lithium augmentation, continue lithium + preceding antidepressant

Unipolar patients should generally be maintained on a tricyclic, MAOI, or newer heterocyclic antidepressant, but lithium may be effective in patients whose episodes are relatively mild. Lithium–antidepressant treatment may be tried in poorly controlled patients, with the same caveats as above.

Patients responding to lithium augmentation should be maintained on the combination. Although half of unipolar responders may require only tricyclic maintenance, it is not yet possible to identify these patients in advance.

Again, these guidelines should be interpreted with flexibility as required by individual patients. It should be noted that, while these guidelines contain no specific suggestions as to duration of maintenance treatment, recent data indicate that relapse rates are high if drugs are discontinued before a 4–5 month symptom-free interval following resolution of an acute episode. Of course, many clinical situations will warrant longer or indefinite prophylaxis.

Adverse Effects

Since all psychotropic drugs have characteristic profiles of adverse medical effects, it might be expected that drug combinations would engender more side effects than treatment with a single agent. Indeed, this seems to be the case for the lithium–tricyclic combination: in the NIMH maintenance study mentioned earlier, the proportions of bipolar patients reporting some side effects were 95% for the combination, 81% for lithium and 61% for imipramine. The figures were 19%, 16% and 14%, respectively, when side effects were described as being of 'more than mild severity for at least two visits.' The proportions of unipolar patients reporting side effects were 84% for the combination, 79% for lithium, 78% for imipramine and 76% for placebo, with more significant side effects occurring at rates of 36%, 14%, 25% and 3%, respectively. In the combination-treated patients, the most common adverse effects were dry mouth, fine tremor, constipation, excessive sweating and polydipsia/polyuria. However, only two of the 74 patients in this group had side effects severe enough to require drug discontinuation. Similarly, Professor Lingjaerde and associates observed no major adverse reactions in the 20 patients they treated with lithium plus tricyclic.

Although systematic data are not as readily available for lithium–MAOI combinations, major problems have not been described by the several investigators who have studied this regimen. Some clinicians have noted the increased occurrence of myoclonic jerks, but this usually responds to dose reduction or addition of a low-dose benzodiazepine.

In addition to physical side effects, in the region of 5% of patients undergoing lithium augmentation experience an exacerbation of their depressive symptoms; paradoxical manic responses have also been observed to lithium augmentation, and rapid cycling has been reported in bipolar patients as a consequence of lithium–tricyclic combinations. While uncommon, these adverse psychiatric effects must also be considered possible complications of combination treatment.

In summary, although minor side effects are frequent with lithium–tricyclic and lithium–MAOI combinations, major adverse reactions are uncommon. The extensive clinical experience with these combinations supports the impression gained from published reports that they are generally safe. There are presently insufficient data to know whether equivalent safety can be assumed for combinations involving lithium and the newer heterocyclic antidepressants.

Conclusions

Given the widespread clinical use of lithium–antidepressant combinations, it is surprising how few methodologically rigorous studies have been performed to evaluate their efficacy. Much of our current knowledge still derives from the relatively uncontrolled observations of experienced clinicians. Available data suggest that lithium–antidepressant combinations, while safe, do not warrant use as first-line or initial treatments. There is clear evidence, however, that selected patients are likely to benefit from combination treatment under specific circumstances. The recent upsurge of interest in lithium augmentation as a treatment for refractory depression will undoubtedly help to clarify many lingering questions about lithium–antidepressant combinations in general. Similarly, preliminary success in using lithium augmentation to treat obsessive–compulsive disorder promises to help broaden the indications for combination treatment. Research stimulated by these developments should help clinicians to utilize lithium–antidepressant combinations to greater effect in the future.

Bibliography

Johnson,F.N. (ed.) (1987) *Lithium Combination Treatment.* Karger, Basel.

A technical monograph with detailed accounts of lithium used in combination with a wide variety of antidepressants.

Lingjaerd,O., Edlund,A.H., Gormsen,C.A., Gottfries,C.G., Haugstad,A., Hermann,I.L., Hollnagel,P., Makimattila,A., Rasmussen,K.E., Remvig,J. and Robak,O.H. (1974) The effect of lithium carbonate in combination with tricyclic antidepressants in endogenous depression. *Acta Psychiatr. Scand.*, **50**, 233–242.

The best study to date on the concurent use of lithium and tricyclic antidepressants in treating acute depression.

Price,L.H., Charney,D.S., Heninger,G.R. (1985) Efficacy of lithium–tranylcypromine treatment in refractory depression. *Am. J. Psychiatry*, **142**, 619–623.

The most recent study describing lithium–MAOI combination treatment in highly refractory patients.

Price,L.H. (1987) Lithium augmentation of tricyclic-resistant depression. In *Treatment of Tricyclic-Resistant Depression.* Extein,I. (ed.), American Psychiatric Association Press, Washington DC.

A comprehensive review of the clinical and preclinical literature on lithium augmentation of tricyclic treatment.

Prien,R.F., Kupfer,D.J., Mansky,P.A., Small,J.G., Tuason,V.B., Voss,C.B. and Johnson,W.E. (1984) Drug therapy in the prevention of recurrences in unipolar and bipolar affective disorders: Report of the NIMH Collaborative Study Group comparing lithium carbonate, imipramine, and a lithium carbonate–imipramine combination. *Arch. Gen. Psychiatry*, **41**, 1096–1104.

The most comprehensive study on the use of lithium–tricyclic combination treatment for preventing recurrent depression.

46. Neuroleptics and Antianxiety Agents

Donald R.Ross and
C.Edward Coffey

Neuroleptics, or antipsychotic agents as they are sometimes called, are used in the control of schizophrenia and mania. Two main groups of compounds are subsumed under the general heading of neuroleptics — the phenothiazines, including chlorpromazine and fluphenazine, and the butyrophenones, exemplified by haloperidol — though other types of psychoactive agents are sometimes also included. The neuroleptics act quickly to suppress the hyperactivity and agitation characteristic of mania and are the agents which are inicated when it is necessary to bring a manic episode rapidly under control until lithium can start to exert its therapeutic effects. Whilst the neuroleptics are also effective antianxiety agents they are nowadays seldom used on that indication alone; they tend to be associated with too great a degree of sedation and to have long-term side effects (such as the production of tardive dyskinesia) which preclude their prescription for all but the most serious psychiatric conditions.

For anxiety, the drugs of first choice are the benzodiazepines, of which chlordiazepoxide and diazepam are the best known, though there are others such as oxazepam and lorazepam which have special indications which make them the preferred choice under certain circumstances. The antianxiety agents have also been shown to have antimanic potential, though they tend not to be employed in such a capacity except when, for some reason, the neuroleptics cannot be tolerated by the patient.

Given this degree of overlap in their therapeutic effects, it is appropriate to consider the neuroleptics together with the antianxiety agents in this section.

Neuroleptics

Indications for combined use

The practice of combining lithium and neuroleptic medication is generally considered efficacious and safe in the treatment of several conditions. The most common use for this combination is in the treatment of the acute phases of mania. It normally takes 4–15 days before the antimanic properties of lithium take effect, and often one cannot wait that long to gain control of the manic patient's behaviour. A neuroleptic is quite effective in quieting and calming the agitated manic patient. After the lithium treatment has been established for 2 weeks and the manic episode is under control, the neuroleptic may be tapered and discontinued. Lithium and neuroleptics may also be used together to treat rapid cycling bipolar patients. Lithium alone is only moderately effective for many of these patients, and the addition of a neuroleptic may be required to reduce further the frequency and severity of manic episodes. Lithium and neuroleptic combinations are effectively used in the treatment of many patients with schizoaffective disorders and even (though more rarely) in schizophrenia.

Alterations in kinetics

Lithium interacts with many of the neuroleptics with subsequent alterations in the kinetics of lithium, the neuroleptic, or both. For example, lithium slows the absorption of chlorpromazine from the gut, potentially reducing serum chlorpromazine levels, and it increases the intracellular concentration of haloperidol as measured by the ratio of haloperidol in red blood cells to that in serum. This effect is less definite with other neuroleptics. When lithium is used in combination with phenothiazines (especially thioridazine), the concentration of intracellular lithium increases. It is suspected that the combination of lithium with a phenothiazine changes the diffusion properties of the cell membrane in such a way as to allow an increase in passive diffusion of lithium into the cell. This effect is not seen with the combination of lithium and haloperidol. Finally, lithium seems to potentiate the dopamine blocking effect of neuroleptics by a mechanism that is not understood. This may result in clinical manifestations of more severe Parkinsonian symptoms than might be expected in patients. A few patients may develop such severe muscle rigidity and motor slowing that they appear to age 75 years in the course of a few days. This has been dubbed the 'Methuselah Syndrome'. These symptoms abate with anticholinergic medications and reduction of the dose of neuroleptic.

Incompatibility of liquid preparations

Lithium citrate syrup is physically incompatible with

the liquid form of many neuroleptic medications. A precipitate forms and is unavailable for absorption when lithium citrate syrup is mixed with liquid preparations of chlorpromazine, haloperidol, thioridazine, trifluoperazine or fluphenazine. Administering these liquid preparations of lithium and neuroleptics together produces a definite risk of significant underdosage of each drug. If it is absolutely necessary to administer two liquid preparations, it may also be necessary to give one drug first, and then to allow 1–2 h to pass before giving the second drug, in order to prevent mixing in the stomach.

Neurotoxicity

Lithium/neuroleptic neurotoxicity is a rare entity but one that the clinician needs to recognize. There are about 40 cases reported in the literature. This syndrome is characterized by altered mental status (ranging from confusion to obtundation), cerebellar dysfunction (ataxia, nystagmus), tremor, and often extrapyramidal signs (motor slowing and rigidity). There may be a fever and the patient may develop seizures. The electroencephalogram shows diffuse slowing. There may or may not be alterations in serum chemistry including elevated glucose, blood urea nitrogen, serum enzymes (including creatinine phosphokinase), and an elevated white blood cell count. The proper treatment for lithium/neuroleptic neurotoxicity is the discontinuation of both medications. At times, intensive care supportive measures may be necessary. Approximately 10% of cases end in death or permanent neurological injury (dementia, dyskinesias): often, these are the cases in which the syndrome was not recognized sufficiently early and the lithium and neuroleptic were not discontinued.

There is controversy as to whether lithium and neuroleptics in combination produce any greater risk of a neurotoxic syndrome than do lithium or neuroleptic administered alone. Dr Poul-Christian Baastrup and colleagues from the Glostrup Psychiatric Hospital in Denmark reviewed hospital records of 425 patients who had been treated simultaneously with lithium and haloperidol. They found no increase in the incidence of side effects from the combined treatment and no additional side effects beyond those found with either drug alone. Richard Abrams and Michael Taylor from the Chicago Medical School, USA, obtained EEGs on 13 consecutive patients treated with both lithium and neuroleptics. They found no more EEG abnormalities when the two drugs were combined than with either drug given alone or with no drug at all. Despite this, reports of isolated cases of severe neurotoxic reactions to lithium–neuroleptic combinations occasionally appear in the medical journals.

There is also controversy over whether lithium–neuroleptic neurotoxicity is a distinct diagnostic entity or simply represents atypical cases of lithium toxicity or neuroleptic malignant syndrome. The characteristics of each of these conditions are compared in *Table 46.1*. Gottfried Spring and Mark Frankel from Case Western Reserve University, USA, have suggested that lithium–haloperidol neurotoxicity represents a form of neuroleptic malignant syndrome while lithium–phenothiazine (especially thioridazine) neurotoxicity represents a form of lithium neurotoxicity. This hypothesis fits nicely with the known drug–drug interactions that lithium and the different neuroleptics have on one another (see *Table 46.2*). Whether there are additional synergistic effects that might predispose to toxicity is unclear.

Perhaps the best that can be said is that if lithium–neuroleptic combinations do produce an increased risk of neurotoxicity, it is a very small risk. The clinician needs to be very aware of neurotoxic symptoms in his patients on this combination just as he does with patients on lithium or neuroleptic alone. If an early neurotoxic syndrome is suspected, EEG monitoring may be useful. Stopping both drugs at the first sign of neurotoxicity is the prudent course of action. It should be emphasized that there has been extensive clinical experience with the use of lithium and neuroleptics in combination, and this combination has been generally quite safe.

Somnambulism

Researchers at Yale University and Pennsylvania State University, USA, studied 114 patients treated with lithium–neuroleptic combinations and found 10 patients who developed sleep-walking episodes. These typically occurred shortly after starting combined therapy. The somnambulistic episodes were characterized by clumsy, uncoordinated walking, amnesia for the episode, and Stage 3 and Stage 4 sleep as recorded by EEG. The somnambulism ceased either spontaneously or after discontinuing the neuroleptic.

Lithium and dyskinesias

An area of recent interest has been the effect of lithium on movement disorders. This area may have implications for a potential beneficial effect of combined

Table 46.1 *Lithium/neuroleptic neurotoxicity compared with lithium neurotoxicity and the neuroleptic malignant syndrome*

	Lithium neurotoxicity	Lithium/neuroleptic neurotoxicity	Neuroleptic malignant syndrome
Clinical features	confusion, stupor, coma	confusion, motor slowing, posturing, stupor, coma	catatonia, stupor
	ataxia, dysarthria nystagmus	± cerebellar signs	dysphagia, drooling
	–	–	autonomic instability[a]
	tremor	tremor	–
	+choreoathetosis	–	–
	+Parkinsonian symptoms	±Parkinsonian symptoms	extreme rigidity
	muscle irritability, hyperactive reflexes	–	muscle necrosis
	seizures	±seizures	–
	+fever	±fever	high fever
Prognosis	death or permanent neurological damage 5–10%	death or permanent neurological damage 10%	death or permanent neurological damage 20%
EEG	diffuse slowing focal abnormalities	diffuse slowing	–
Laboratory results	glucose raised[b]	±glucose raised	–
	WBC count raised[b]	± WBC count raised	–
	–	±BUN raised	–
	–	± serum enzymes raised	CPK very much raised
Supportive care	ICU[c] dialysis	ICU	ICU
	–	–	dantrolene 1 mg/kg every 6 h
	–	–	bromocriptine 2.5–5 mg b.i.d.
	–	–	cool patient

[a]Raised heart rate, raised or lowered blood pressure, diaphoresis.
[b]Not due to toxicity *per se*.
[c]ICU = intensive care unit.

lithium–neuroleptic treatment. Tardive dyskinesia is a late occurring side effect of neuroleptic medication that is often very difficult to treat. It is thought to be caused by a post-synaptic dopamine receptor supersensitivity after chronic dopamine receptor blockade. Lithium has been used with a moderate degree of success in ameliorating tardive dyskinesia in some patients. However, more stringent, double-blind, placebo-controlled studies of lithium in the treatment of tardive dyskinesia have been less encouraging. There is some suggestion that lithium's benefit in tardive dyskinesia might require administrations of the lithium prior to the appearance of the dyskinetic movements. D.W.Gallager and her colleagues at the National Institute of Mental Health in Bethesda, Maryland, USA, in their experimental work with rats, demonstrated that lithium pre-treatment eliminated the rebound supersensitivity of post-synaptic dopamine receptors caused by chronic neuroleptic use. There have not been any studies comparing the incidence of

Table 46.2 *Summary of the indications, kinetic effects, toxicity and side effects associated with lithium in combination with neuroleptics or antianxiety agents*

Agent combined with	Indications	Kinetic effects	Toxicity/side effects
Neuroleptics			
Haloperidol (HPD)	Acute mania; rapid cycling bipolar disorder; schizoaffective disorder; schizophrenia (rare)	Intracellular HPD raised; DA blockade increased	Neurotoxicity (resembling neuroleptic malignant syndrome); somnambulism; Parkinsonian symptoms increased
Phenothiazines	As for HPD, above	Intracellular Li raised; DA blockade increased + reduced absorption of both agents	Neurotoxicity (resembling Li toxicity); somnambulism; Parkinsonian symptoms increased
Antianxiety agents			
Benzodiazepines	Acute mania	No significant effects	None
Barbiturates	None	No significant effects	None

tardive dyskinesia in human patients taking lithium and neuroleptics with that in patients taking neuroleptics alone.

Another related area of research has shown lithium to be an effective treatment for some patients with the 'on-off' syndrome of end-stage Parkinson's disease. Here, lithium produced an enhanced dopamine effect with a reduction in akinetic episodes and an increase in dyskinesias. C.Edward Coffey and collaborators at Duke University, USA, have speculated that this might be due to a stabilization of receptor sensitivity in the dopamine or acetylcholine tracts of the extrapyramidal system. This entire area still requires much more research, and the clinical usefulness of lithium in stabilizing dopamine receptors and preventing late occurring dyskinesias due to neuroleptics remains speculative.

Renal function

Lithium may eventually cause interstitial nephropathy in a small proportion of patients after chronic use (see pp. 206–213). This may produce a decrease in the ability of the kidney to concentrate urine and occasionally a subsequent reduction in glomerular filtration. Early reports suggested that neuroleptics used in combination with lithium produced a greater degree of renal impairment. However, subsequent studies have been unable to confirm those findings, and a review of the original studies reveals methodological errors that may explain the positive findings. At present, the clinical data do not show that neuroleptics in combination with lithium have any adverse influence on renal function.

Antianxiety Agents

Indications for combined use

There is relatively little literature on the combined use of lithium and antianxiety agents in a clinical setting. As mentioned above, manic patients started on lithium may require additional sedation for the first 5–14 days until the lithium takes effect. Although this is usually accomplished by the addition of a neuroleptic medication, an antianxiety agent such as lorazepam, given either by mouth or intramuscularly, may be added to lithium for sedation. In a carefully controlled study, this has been found to be a safe and effective combination. The combined use of lithium and antianxiety agents is more often a coincidence. A patient may be taking a barbiturate for a seizure disorder and subsequently require lithium, or a patient may be taking lithium and require an occasional benzodiazepine for sleep. Again, in these situations, the combination is considered safe.

Toxicity and side effects

There appears to be little in the way of demonstrable interaction between lithium and antianxiety agents. Lithium does not have any antianxiety effects itself, nor does it produce anxiety. A few patients experience a mild internal sense of uneasiness on lithium that they might confuse with anxiety. A larger group of patients develop a benign action tremor that can be socially embarrassing and lead to secondary anticipatory anxiety in social settings. The treatment of choice for lithium-induced tremor is propranolol rather than antianxiety agents.

There have been two single case reports of untoward effects of combining lithium and antianxiety agents. A 38-year-old, mentally retarded woman, who was given lithium and diazepam in an attempt to control aggressive outbursts, developed profound hypothermia. This reaction did not occur with lithium or diazepam alone, but did reoccur when the patient was again challenged with a lithium/diazepam combination. This seems to be an idiosyncratic reaction rather than a true drug–drug interaction. The second case report involved a 21-year-old man who developed a neuroleptic malignant syndrome while taking lithium and chlordiazepoxide. Discontinuation of lithium did not ameliorate the patient's condition. The meaning of the second case is not clear. In general, it is considered quite safe to use lithium and benzodiazepines in combination.

The use of lithium and barbiturates in combination is also safe. Studies with mice indicate that lithium might potentiate the sedative effects of barbiturates; however, there are no apparent significant interactions in humans.

Acknowledgement

This work was supported, in part, by grants from the NIMH (MH 30723, MH 40159 and MH 41803) and the North Carolina, USA, United Way.

Bibliography

Jefferson,J.W., Greist,J.H. and Baudhuin,M. (1981) Lithium: interactions with other drugs. *J. Clin. Psychopharm.*, **1**, 124–134.
A good reference paper with an excellent bibliography which covers all classes of drugs that interact with lithium.

Johnson,F.N. (ed.) (1987) *Lithium Combination Treatment.* Karger, Basel.
Contains separate chapters on lithium used with phenothiazines, butyrophenones, and antianxiety agents.

Levenson,J.L. (1985) Neuroleptic malignant syndrome. *Am. J. Psychiatry*, **142**, 1137–1145.
A comprehensive discussion of the neuroleptic malignant syndrome.

Spring,G. and Frankel,M. (1981) New data on lithium and haloperidol incompatibility. *Am. J. Psychiatry*, **138**, 818–821.
A good discussion of lithium–neuroleptic toxicity.

47. Antiepileptic Drugs

Robert M.Post

A series of anticonvulsant agents have emerged as alternative and/or adjunctive treatments for the patient who is inadequately responsive to lithium carbonate. Until recently, few options other than potentiation of lithium with tricyclic or monoamine oxidase inhibitor antidepressants for breakthrough depressions (pp. 161–166), and neuroleptics for breakthrough manias (pp. 167–171), had been available. These treatments each carried their own liabilities: the antidepressants for increasing the risk of manias or rapid cycling, and the neuroleptics for increasing psychomotor retardation and the risk of Parkinsonism or tardive dyskinesia. Among the other options now available, carbamazepine is prototypic of the anticonvulsants, and since it is the most well studied of these agents, most of the attention of this section will be directed to it. However, valproic acid has also been investigated in six different countries with evidence being obtained for positive acute antimanic and longer-term prophylactic effects in previously lithium-refractory patients. Clonazepam appears to have useful antimanic properties, and the anticonvulsant alprazolam may also have antidepressant properties, although these do not appear to be useful prophylactic treatments at this time. A special role for acetazolamide may emerge, and it is also noteworthy that electroconvulsive therapy, which will be discussed in the next section (Section 48, pp. 177–180), has potent anticonvulsant effects in both animal models and in man, and might also be considered among the anticonvulsant agents.

Carbamazepine

While this anticonvulsant now appears to have a range of clinical efficacy in mania and depression that parallels that of lithium carbonate, preliminary evidence suggests that there may be a differential profile of clinical predictors of response, side effects, and, possibly, mechanisms of action.

Interest arose in the possible clinical utility of carbamazepine because of: (i) its ability to dampen limbic system excitability in animals with kindled seizures and in patients with psychomotor seizures; (ii) the well documented relationship between limbic system dysfunction and affective dysregulation; (iii) reports of positive effects of carbamazepine on mood and behavior in epileptic patients; and (iv) the early uncontrolled experience in Japan with the use of carbamazepine in primary affective illness. Since the initial double-blind clinical trial published in 1978, there have been nine double-blind clinical trials and a larger series of uncontrolled studies that tend to reach the same conclusion, i.e. that carbamazepine has acute antimanic efficacy in approximately 60% of patients.

Antimanic effects

In the manic patients involved in trials at the Biological Psychiatry Branch of the National Institute of Mental Health, Bethesda, USA, double-blind treatment with carbamazepine produced a rapid onset of antimanic efficacy with a time course and magnitude that roughly paralleled that observed with neuroleptic agents (chlorpromazine, thioridazine or pimozide) in patients who were similarly diagnosed and rated (*Figure 47.1*). Similar findings were reported by Professor T.Okuma and his colleagues from Tohoku University in Japan, and by many other investigative groups in Europe. In the first 19 patients studied in a double-blind fashion, 12 robust responders were observed compared to seven non-responders: the responders, compared to non-responders, were significantly more manic during the placebo period prior to treatment, tended to be more dysphoric (i.e. had higher depression ratings during mania), and were more rapid cycling, as evidenced by the number of episodes in the year prior to NIMH admission or the number of episodes per year of illness. In addition, preliminary data suggested that, similar to the unpublished observations of Dr Paul Grof at Hamilton University in Ontario, Canada, carbamazepine responders tended to be overly represented in the group of patients who did not have a family history of affective illness in first degree relatives. Thus, preliminary data from NIMH and other laboratories suggest that many of the predictors of carbamazepine response may actually be just those clinical factors that tend to predict poor response to lithium carbonate; that is, patients with more severe mania, more dysphoric mania, more rapid cycling illness and a negative family history for affective illness (*Table 47.1*).

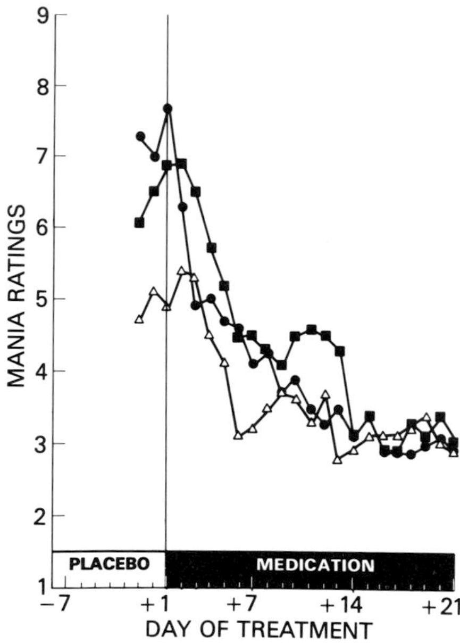

Figure 47.1 The time course of the antimanic effects of carbamazepine (■; n = 19) compared with those of neuroleptics (●; n = 17) and lithium (△; n = 19).

Antidepressant effects

The evidence for the acute antidepressant properties of carbamazepine is preliminary. Moderate to marked antidepressant response to carbamazepine was observed in 12 of the first 35 depressed patients (34%) entered into a double-blind clinical trial using an 'off-on-off' design. Patients with a greater initial severity of depression responded better to carbamazepine, as did those with a history of more discrete episodes of illness, less chronic depression and a positive acute antidepressant response to one night's sleep deprivation. Interestingly, neither minor EEG abnormalities nor a history of psychosensory symptoms (typical of those reported in epilepsy) were found to be predictive of response to carbamazepine.

While further clinical investigations are indicated, it would appear that, like lithium, the acute antidepressant efficacy of carbamazepine is less robust than its antimanic properties. It is of interest that sleep improved within the first week of treatment in both the manic and depressed patients, but the improvement in sleep antedated, and was not correlated with, the antidepressant response, which required several weeks or more. About 53% (eight of 15) of patients who did not respond to carbamazepine for treatment of their acute depression had a subsequent rapid onset and robust response to lithium potentiation.

Table 47.1 *Comparative, differential clinical, and side effects profile of lithium carbonate and carbamazepine*

	Lithium carbonate	Carbamazepine (CBZ)	Li + CBZ combination
Clinical profile			
Mania (M)	++	++	+++
Dysphoric	±	+	
Rapid cycling	±	++	
Severe	±	++	
Family history negative	+	+	
Depression (D)	±	+	+++
M D Prophylaxis	++	++	+++
Epilepsy	0	++	
Pain syndromes	0	++	
Side effects			
White blood cell count	↑	↓	−− Li*
Diabetes insipidus	↑	↓	↑ Li*
Thyroid hormones T_3, T_4	↓	↓	
TSH	↑	(−−)	↑ Li*
Serum calcium	(↑)	↓	(↑) (Li*)
Weight gain	(↑)	(−−)	
Tremor	(↑)	(−−)	
Memory disturbances	(↑)	?	
Diarrhoea	(↑)	−−	
Psoriasis	(↑)	(−−)	
Puritic rash (Allergy)	−−	↑	
Agranulocytosis	−−	(↑)	
Hepatitis	−−	(↑)	
Hyponatremia, water intoxication	−−	(↑)	
Dizziness, ataxia, diplopia	−−	(↑)	
Hypercortisolism, escape from dexamethasone suppression	−−	↑	
Teratogenesis	(↑)	(−−)	

Clinical efficacy: 0, none, ±, equivocal; +, effective; ++, very effective.
Side effects: ↑, increase; ↓, decrease; ( ), inconsistent or rare; −−, absent; +++, potentiation; Li*, effect of lithium predominates; ?, not known.

Time course of action

It is of interest that three different clinical effects of carbamazepine have very different time courses of onset. The anticonvulsant and antinociceptive effects of carbamazepine appear essentially immediately; the antimanic efficacy and improvement in sleep occurs within the first week of treatment, while there is a more protracted lag in onset and achievement of maximal antidepressant efficacy. These differential time courses are of considerable import in assessing whether or not carbamazepine is going to be effective in a given individual. This can be assessed rapidly, within the first week or two of treatment of the manic patient, but a longer period is required in order to assess the antidepressant effects of the compound.

Maintenance treatment

Both double-blind clinical trials and open clinical investigations are indicative that carbamazepine has a role in long-term maintenance treatment of affectively ill patients, particularly those who are inadequately responsive to lithium carbonate. Some 67% of patients reported in the literature (160 out of a total of 240) showed a moderate to marked decrease in the frequency and severity of both manic and depressive episodes when carbamazepine was used alongside, or added to, previously ineffective treatment regimens. It is of interest that a series of 17 patients studied by Dr A.Kishimoto in Yonago, Japan, were observed to have inadequate prophylactic responses to a clinical trial of either lithium or carbamazepine used alone, but showed excellent results when both drugs were used in combination.

Dosage

Individualization of dose, and titration of dose against side effects, are considerations of considerable import in initiating carbamazepine treatment. There is wide variability in the dose and the blood level at which individual patients will experience side effects. Typical anticonvulsant side effects of dizziness, ataxia, diplopia, or lethargy may be observed in some patients at very low doses of carbamazepine and blood levels of only 4–5 μg/ml, while other patients are able to tolerate much higher doses of carbamazepine (1600–2000 mg/day) and blood levels of 12–14 μg/ml or above with no side effects whatsoever. Thus, while blood levels of 4–12 μg/ml are usually considered as lying within the therapeutic range, it is much more important to increase dose very slowly, titrating increases against the appearance of even minor clinical side effects, and holding a given dose constant or reducing it until side effects abate. It is also of interest that carbamazepine induces its own hepatic metabolism and, after 3 or 4 weeks of treatment, blood levels will begin to decrease, even following the same dosage regimen. The anti-tuberculosis drug isoniazid and the antibiotic erythromycin, as well as some calcium channel antagonists (verapamil and diltiazem, but not nifedipine), have recently been reported to produce marked increases in carbamazepine blood levels and associated clinical toxicity; the physician should accordingly decrease the dose of carbamazepine and monitor blood levels closely if one of these agents is to be employed in conjunction with carbamazepine.

Toxicity and side effects

While there have been a series of case reports of CNS toxicity during the use of lithium and carbamazepine in combination, experience suggests that this is not a frequent side effect. It is noteworthy that both lithium and carbamazepine can individually produce these effects, even at blood levels that are considered to be within the therapeutic range of each agent. Thus, it is possible that the toxicity reported with the combination treatment may represent toxicities of either agent alone in many of the case reports. Initial evidence suggests that there are no pharmacokinetic interactions between lithium and carbamazepine, and for most patients the combination can be used with safety and clinical efficacy.

The side effects profile of carbamazeprine tends to be quite different from that of lithium carbonate (*Table 47.1*). There is also an interesting rule of thumb that, in many instances, the side effects of lithium carbonate override those of carbamazepine.

Haematological effects. Carbamazepine tends to suppress the white cell count, particularly neutrophils and other elements in the granulocytic series, without affecting lymphocytes or platelets. If other haematological indices are within normal limits (especially platelets) a total white count of 3000 might be considered the lower limit beyond which carbamazepine should be discontinued. The ability of lithium carbonate to increase the white count overrides the (uncomplicated) suppression of white count induced by carbamazepine. More problematic is the very rare idiosyncratic process of agranulocytosis or aplastic anaemia, which has been estimated to occur in between one in 20 000–40 000 patients treated with carbamazepine. The physician should warn the patient of the possibility of this side effect and emphasize that if a fever, sore throat, rash or petechiae develops, the patient should immediately return for blood-count testing. The need for, and frequency of, haematological monitoring in order to possibly detect this rare reaction is a subject of much debate in the literature. Some physicians suggest weekly monitoring for the first several months and monthly monitoring thereafter, while in many neurology clinics blood counts are monitored infrequently.

Endocrine effects. Carbamazepine decreases circulating levels of thyroid hormones T_3 and T_4 without substantially increasing TSH levels; when used in combination, lithium-induced increases in TSH levels predominate over those of carbamazepine.

Carbamazepine has been used to treat diabetes insipidus of central origin; however, it will not reverse the diabetes insipidus induced by lithium carbonate (since carbamazepine appears to act at the vasopressin receptor, while lithium appears to inhibit vasopressin effects below the receptor). Since carbamazepine produces a vasopressin effect opposite to that of lithium carbonate, there is some risk of the development of hyponatraemia and water intoxication. Serum sodium concentrations should be checked in any patient (particularly an older patient on high doses) who develops a confusional episode on this drug.

Cutaneous effects. Rashes appear to occur in approximately 15% of patients treated with carbamazepine and the drug is best discontinued when this occurs because of the risk of exfoliative dermatitis or the Stephens-Johnson syndrome. However, uncomplicated dermatologic reactions can be treated with prednisone in patients who have shown an initial positive response to carbamazepine and have not responded well to other agents.

Other Anticonvulsants

Valproic acid

A series of open and controlled studies spearheaded by Professor H.Emrich of the Max-Planck Institute of Psychiatry in Munich, FRG, suggests that valproic acid, when used in conjunction with lithium in previously non-responsive patients, may prove to be an effective acute antimanic agent or useful in long-term prophylaxis. Response in manic episodes appears better than in depressed episodes, and the more typical patient with bipolar illness, compared with those with schizoaffective or schizophrenic illness, is generally reported to do better on this regimen. Doses employed tend to range up to 1500 or 2000 mg/day in order to achieve blood levels between 50 and 100 μg/ml. These studies in psychiatric patients reported few side effects, although there have been reports of severe hepatotoxicity in some epileptics, particularly in children, and hepatic function should be monitored during treatment with valproic acid. Many patients appear to require lithium in conjunction with valproic acid; the combination appears well tolerated.

Clonazepam

Professor Chouinard in Montreal, Canada has reported acute antimanic efficacy of the anticonvulsant clonazepam in a double-blind comparison with lithium carbonate. Since clonazepam tends to have some sedative side effects, it might be used instead of a neuroleptic as a bedtime hypnotic as well as an antimanic in lithium-treated patients with breakthrough manias. It is also of interest that clonazepam exerts its anticonvulsant action at the level of the classical 'central-type' benzodiazepine receptor (modulating chloride fluxes) while carbamazepine appears to act through a different mechanism, that involving the so-called 'peripheral-type' benzodiazepine receptor which has a different distribution in the brain and has been thought to be linked to calcium channel fluxes. This differential mechanism of action of these two anticonvulsants could provide a rationale for differential clinical responsiveness in mania. Moreover, the possible effects of carbamazepine on calcium fluxes are of interest in relation to recent reports that some calcium channel antagonists may show some acute anti-manic and longer-term prophylactic efficacy in the treatment of manic-depressive illness. These preliminary findings are of considerable interest but require further systematic documentation. While most calcium channel antagonists do not appear to be potent anticonvulsants, flunarizine and nimodipine have been reported to exert anticonvulsant actions.

Alprazolam

The anti-panic agent alprazolam, which exerts its anticonvulsant efficacy through the 'central-type' benzodiazepine receptor, has been reported to have antidepressant effects. However, a series of case reports suggests that it may share the liability with tricyclic antidepressants of inducing manic episodes, and its use in the long-term prophylaxis of bipolar patients, either alone or in combination with lithium, would appear circumscribed at this time.

Phenytoin

While the initial clinical reports of efficacy of phenytoin in mania were positive, subsequent studies reported doubtful results, and double-blind clinical investigations remain to be performed. In a small series of patients administered phenytoin in a double-blind fashion in a study being conducted at NIH positive results have not been observed to date, although detailed case reports in the literature suggest that at least the occasional patient may show an unequivocal antimanic response to this anticonvulsant. The use of phenytoin in conjunction with lithium has not been reported.

Acetazolamide

A final anticonvulsant is worthy of mention. Inoue and colleagues at Tottori University in Japan reported a small series of patients with atypical dreamy confusional psychoses that tended to be associated with puerperal or premenstrual phases, who responded well to the anticonvulsant acetazolamide when they had not previously responded to either lithium or carbamazepine.

Table 47.2 *Effectiveness of anticonvulsants in manic-depressive illness*[a]

	Acute mania	Acute depression	Prophylaxis
Electroconvulsive[b] therapy (ECT)	++	++	±
Carbamazepine	++	+	++
Carbamazepine + lithium	++	++	++
Valproic acid	++		
Valproic acid + lithium	++		++
Clonazepam	++		
Acetazolamide	(+)		(+)
Alprazolam	−−	+	
Progabide		+	
Phenytoin	±	±	±

[a]Summary is based on preliminary data (up to July, 1986) and is likely to change as more evidence is gathered.
[b]ECT is paradoxically a potent anticonvulsant manipulation in animals and man. For symbols see *Table 47.1*.

Clinical Implications

As illustrated in *Table 47.2*, a series of anticonvulsants have emerged as possible alternatives or adjunctive treatments for the lithium-non-responsive patient. In addition to the possible differential clinical predictors of response to carbamazepine compared to lithium carbonate (manic severity, dysphoria, rapid cycling and negative family history), it is possible that patients treated late in the course of manic-depressive illness may be less responsive to lithium carbonate and require supplementation with anticonvulsants such as carbamazepine or valproic acid. In the patient who displays manic breakthroughs on lithium, carbamazepine would appear to be a first drug of choice (perhaps even in preference to neuroleptics). If a positive response to carbamazepine is observed, one might be more likely to continue with carbamazepine prophylaxis instead of neuroleptic maintenance. If a patient shows a good response to the combination treatment, lithium can always be cautiously withdrawn at a later date in order to assess whether carbamazepine alone is effective. The use of graphic representation of the life course of illness is strongly recommended in order to assess the impact of lithium carbonate and other treatments on the patient's illness.

Valproic acid might be the second anti-convulsant tried in the lithium-non-responsive patients, particularly since it has been noted that observed response to one anticonvulsant does not predict response to another. While good effects in acute mania have been reported, the utility of clonazepam in prophylaxis remains to be established, and one should be particularly cautious when employing alprazolam in the bipolar patient in light of reports of the induction of manic episodes even in some panic patients without a prior history. The calcium channel antagonists deserve further study.

Conclusions

While less than a decade ago lithium represented the only real treatment option for the bipolar patient, a series of alternative or adjunctive treatments are currently available and would appear to merit cautious clinical trials in the patient who is inadequately responsive to lithium carbonate. Given the range of treatments now available, there are grounds for considerable optimism in the treatment of even the most severely ill manic-depressive patient.

Bibliography

Johnson,F.N. (ed.) (1987) *Lithium Combination Treatment.* Karger, Basel.
In this detailed text there are chapters dealing with lithium used in combination with carbamazepine as well as with a range of other antiepileptic agents, including phenytoin, dipropylacetamide, valproate, and progabide.

Post,R.M., Uhde,T.W. and Ballenger,J.C. (1984) Efficacy of carbamazepine in affective disorders: implications for underlying physiological and biological substrates. In *Anticonvulsants in Affective Disorders*. Emrich,H.M., Okuma,T. and Muller,A. (eds), Excerpta Medica, Amsterdam, pp. 93–115.
Presents details of the possible mechanisms of action of carbamazepine and the rest of the book provides important information on the use and efficacy of various anti-convulsants.

Post,R.M. and Uhde,T.W. (1987) Clinical approaches to treatment-resistant bipolar illness. In *American Psychiatric Association Annual Review.* Wales,R.E. and Frances,A.J. (eds), American Psychiatric Association, Washington DC, Vol. 6, pp. 125–150.
Gives more details regarding clinical use, efficacy, and side effects of the anti-convulsants alone and in combination with lithium treatment.

48. Electroconvulsive Therapy

A.Kukopulos, A.Tundo, D.Foggia, G.Minnai, L.Toro and D.Reginaldi

Electroconvulsive therapy (or ECT as it is usually referred to) is used for the treatment of severe depressive (and sometimes — though more rarely — manic) conditions. The patient, anaesthetized and treated with muscle-relaxant drugs, has a pulse of direct current electricity briefly applied to the brain by means of external scalp electrodes. The result is an artificially produced epileptic-like seizure, the external manifestations of which are minimized by the muscle-relaxant medication.

A course of six to eight ECT administrations is often adequate to produce an alleviation of the ongoing affective dysfunction, though occasionally fewer are necessary whilst other patients may need an additional series, or even more.

There are several views as to the mechanisms by which ECT exerts its therapeutic action, though none receives unequivocal support from all quarters. It seems evident that release of neurotransmitters is crucially involved, though no simple model fits all the available facts.

Whilst ECT has been attended by considerable controversy, its effectiveness seems to be undeniable.

It is certain that ECT and lithium are often used in combination, either as a deliberate therapeutic measure or (more frequently, perhaps) in an unplanned way when a patient on lithium undergoes a sudden depressive relapse. For the most part, these instances of combined treatment pass unreported, since it is usually the case that only procedures which give rise to unwanted effects find an airing in the literature. The relatively few reports of combined lithium and ECT being associated with side effects not noted with either treatment used alone, have therefore to be viewed against the background of the unrecorded, but implicit, clinical experience indicating that the combination may be used with safety, provided that all necessary precautions are observed.

Evidence for ECT – Lithium Ill-Effects

In 1974 Drs G.Jephcott and R.J.Kerry first reported that one of their patients who was taking lithium carbonate could not be aroused for more than 2 h after ECT. This report was followed a year later by another of a patient who was receiving 1200 mg of lithium carbonate and had a serum lithium level of 0.46 mmol/l; 4 days after the last ECT a confusional state and epileptic seizures set in.

Once a few indications of a problem have appeared in the scientific journals, other investigators become motivated to give details of their own experiences, and over the next few years several instances were recorded of difficulties experienced with ECT in patients receiving lithium.

Thus in 1977 there was a report of transient subdelirium of two days' duration following ECT in a patient who was being treated with lithium carbonate. The day of the ECT the serum lithium level was 1.09 mmol/l. It was concluded that if ECT is to be given to a patient receiving lithium, the serum lithium concentration should be reduced to very low values.

In 1978 the occurrence was reported of an acute brain syndrome in a 41-year-old woman treated with lithium and ECT. An EEG revealed a diffuse slow wave dysrhythmia with posterior predominance. The serum lithium level was 1 mmol/l.

In 1980 Dr Richard D.Weiner and his colleagues reported the case of a 33-year-old woman who, after the fifth ECT, had lithium added to her treatment (300 mg twice a day). The next day she became disoriented and confused and the EEG showed evidence of status epilepticus. The same year Dr Arnold Mandel and co-workers presented two additional cases of persistent delirium following concurrent administration of ECT and lithium.

The accumulating evidence from these individual case reports led Dr Joyce Small and a group of her colleagues to undertake a retrospective study on the influence of the combination of lithium and ECT on side effects and outcome. Their results were published in 1980. They found that patients who received the combined treatment experienced more memory loss and atypical neurological findings than those receiving only ECT. They found no EEG difference between the two groups. Their data also suggested a possible interference with the therapeutic efficacy of ECT.

In 1983, a critical review of these reports stated that whilst both ECT and lithium could have untoward sequelae when used singly, there was inadequate evidence to support any suggestion that the two treatments interacted in such a way as to produce additional sequelae. It was, the review concluded, premature to advise avoidance of the lithium–ECT combination.

Indications for Lithium – ECT Combinations

Despite the lack of firm evidence against the use of lithium and ECT together, psychiatrists in general tend to avoid such a combination on the grounds that there is no particular indication for the combination. One can, however, point to four indications of this combined treatment.

Treatment-resistant mania

There is a certain number of manias which are particularly resistant to lithium and neuroleptics. These cases may also be resistant to ECT and, as a consequence, their hospitalization may last for more than a few months. In these cases the combination of lithium and ECT may significantly shorten the duration of the mania.

Treatment-induced mania

Some depressions tend to switch into mania, and this happens not only when they are treated with tricyclic antidepressants but (although probably less frequently) also when they are treated with ECT. This switch can be avoided only if lithium is used simultaneously with ECT. The only alternative to lithium would be a neuroleptic agent, since carbamazepine would act as an anticonvulsant.

Post-ECT hypomania

Many depressions are followed by hypomanic episodes which, if they last for some time, will be followed by another depression. These hypomanias could well be treated after the end of ECT, but at that time the patients will be out of hospital and his hypomania will keep him away from the doctor. It is best to prevent the onset of such hypomanias by giving lithium simultaneously with ECT.

Schizoaffective disorder

Mixed affective or schizoaffective states are quite frequent. In these cases ECT is often indicated and is very effective. At the same time the stabilizing action of a continuous treatment is required. This treatment may be a neuroleptic or carbamazepine, but in many cases lithium is the most strongly indicated.

A New Study of Lithium – ECT

Lithium in combination with ECT has been used over a number of years, for the four indications listed above, in the treatment of patients at the Belvedere Montello Clinic in Rome, Italy, and the clinical records of such cases have allowed a new assessment to be made of the clinical efficacy of the combined treatment procedure.

The data

The clinical records were examined of all the patients who had received ECT at the Belvedere Montello Clinic between January 1980 and December 1986, a total of 386 cases (224 women and 162 men); 256 patients had ECT and lithium at the same time, while 130 had ECT alone. The ECT treatments were modified by atropine, succinylcholine and thiopental sodium. The electrodes were placed on the non-dominant hemisphere, and the electrical stimulus was delivered by a constant current short square waves stimuli apparatus (Duopulse-Ectron).

Table 48.1 shows sex, age and diagnosis of the patients of the two groups. Both groups received other treatments, as is shown in *Table 48.2*.

The findings

Table 48.3 shows the number of ECT, the serum lithium concentration and the outcome of the ECT treatment. Of the 256 patients that had ECT and lithium, 203 (79%) responded well, while in 53 (21%) the treatment failed.

Table 48.1 *Details of patients involved in the most recent retrospective study of combined ECT and lithium*

Treatment group	Sex	Mean age (years)	Diagnosis			
			Affective	Schizoaffective	Schizophrenic	Other
ECT + Li	110(M); 146(F)	42	221	16	13	6
ECT	52(M); 78(F)	50	109	3	14	4

Of the 130 patients that received ECT alone, 97 (75%) responded well, while in 33 (25%) the treatment failed.

In order to examine the efficacy of the combined treatment versus ECT alone, an examination was carried out of the outcome of these treatments only in the cases of primary depression.

There were 176 cases of primary depression treated by ECT plus lithium (mean number of ECT, 8.05; mean serum lithium level, 0.53 mmol/l); 140 (80%) recovered, and 36 (20%) failed to respond (mean serum lithium level 0.51 mmol/l). Out of 101 primary depressions treated by ECT without lithium (mean number of ECT, 8.96), 20 (20%) failed to respond. The findings did not show that concomitant lithium decreased the efficacy of ECT; but did it cause unwanted effects?

Occurrences of acute brain syndrome in the study

Among the 256 cases that had ECT and lithium treatment, only three cases showed signs of acute brain syndrome. The first was a man of 57 who, after the second unilateral ECT, woke up in a state of severe agitation that lasted about 30 min and had to be calmed with 20 mg of intravenous diazepam. The patient had no recollection of the episode. His serum lithium level was 0.95 mmol/l, and he was receiving ECT because of a depression; apart from lithium he was receiving small doses of benzodiazepines.

Table 48.2 *Pharmacological treatment given in addition to ECT or ECT + Li to the patients in the retrospective study*

Pharmacological treatment	Treatment group	
	ECT + Li	ECT
Neuroleptics	65	16
Carbamazepine	74	13
Benzodiazepines	84	53
Antidepressants	23	41
Valproic acid	1	2
None	14	5

The second case was a woman of 41 who was hospitalized because of a mania. She developed mental confusion and disorientation for 3 days after the seventh ECT. Her serum lithium level was 0.75 mmol/l and at the same time she was receiving laevopromazine, haloperidol 12 mg and clotiapine 40 mg per day.

The third case was a woman of 59 who was hospitalized for a depression and who, after the second ECT, developed a confusional state. Her serum lithium level was 0.60 mmol/l. At the same time she was receiving 100 mg of maprotiline and 3 mg of lorazepam.

Of the 130 patients that received ECT without lithium, five showed confusion and agitation after ECT.

The first case was a man of 51, hospitalized for depression, who developed severe agitation after the second ECT. He was receiving small doses of benzodiazepam. The second case was a depressed man of 69 who, after the tenth ECT, developed confusion and delusions. With ECT he was receiving sulpiride 100 mg and amineptine 200 mg. The third case was a woman of 63, treated for depression, who developed mental confusion after the fourth ECT. The fourth case was a woman of 37, suffering from depression, who after the fourth ECT developed confusion that lasted four days. The fifth case was a woman of 57, suffering from depression, who developed confusion after the ninth ECT.

The greater proportion of cases that developed confusion in the group of ECT without lithium are likely to have reacted in this way due to the older age of this group in comparison to the group that had ECT and lithium together.

Table 48.3 *Response to ECT in patients receiving ECT alone or in combination with lithium*

Treatment group	Mean no. of ECT	Mean serum Li (mmol/l)	ECT response			
			All patients		Primary depressions	
			Good	Poor	Good	Poor
ECT + Li	8.3	0.76	203 (79%)	53 (21%)	140 (80%)	36 (20%)
ECT	8.6	–	97 (75%)	33 (25%)	81 (80%)	20 (20%)

Electroencephalogram (EEG)

In 30 cases an EEG test was carried out before the first and after the sixth ECT. In 10 cases an EEG was performed one month after the end of the treatment. Nineteen of these cases had been treated with ECT only, and 11 were treated with ECT plus lithium. At the second EEG, eight of the ECT only group and seven of the ECT plus lithium group had slow waves, 5–6 Hz in all leads, but predominantly on the right side; with hypernoea their amplitude increased and became slower, 3–4 Hz, with some spikes. In the other cases the slow waves were 6–7 Hz, while in three cases of the ECT-alone group there were found spikes on the right hemisphere both at rest and after hypernoea. Of the 10 EEG performed one month later, only two cases, both of which had received only ECT, showed some slow waves, but both of them had shown these changes also at the EEG before the treatment.

Conclusions

There is certainly no firm evidence in the literature that the combination of ECT and lithium is dangerous. The data from the most recent retrospective study, whilst not constituting a systematic trial, nevertheless point to the rarity and the mildness of the confusional states in 256 cases that had ECT and lithium simultaneously, in the combined treatment. Also, the equal efficacy of ECT alone and ECT plus lithium shown in the cases examined suggests that lithium in therapeutic doses does not interfere with the efficacy of ECT.

Acknowledgement

Grateful acknowledgement is made of the kind cooperation of Mrs Roberta Necci.

Bibliography

Jephcott,G. and Kerry,R.J. (1974) Lithium and anaesthetic risk. *J. Anaesthesiol.*, **46**, 389–390.
This was the first report of a possible adverse effect of combining ECT and lithium.

49. Diuretics

Enric Grau

The diuretics are a heterogeneous group of drugs which share the common property of increasing water excretion through the kidneys. The mechanisms by which this increased diuresis is brought about differ according to the type of diuretic agent used. Since approximately 95% of a single dose of lithium is eliminated in the urine it is not surprising that any drug which influences renal function should also have the potential to affect the elimination or retention of lithium. If a diuretic substance so affects the renal handling of lithium that blood levels do not fall as rapidly as they would be expected to do in the absence of the diuretic, the scene is set for a gradual rise in serum lithium levels with each consecutive dose, and hence the eventual appearance of unwanted effects and signs of lithium toxicity. If, on the other hand, the diuretic acts in such a way as to stimulate the rate of lithium excretion, the levels of lithium in the serum may fall to a point where the dose is not adequate to produce the desired therapeutic effect.

Since diuretic agents are not infrequently prescribed for a variety of conditions, it is inevitable that there should occur occasions when the simultaneous administration of lithium and diuretics is contemplated. When this occurs, it is essential that the physician should be fully aware of the possible implications of the diuretic for the concomitant lithium therapy.

The physiology of lithium excretion by the kidney is explained in Section 19, pp. 75–78. It is necessary here to note only that in the proximal tubule lithium is handled almost identically to sodium, whilst in the distal tubule sodium, but not lithium, is extensively absorbed. If anything occurs to produce a lack of sodium in the body, there is a compensatory attempt by the kidney to reabsorb sodium at the level of the proximal tubule: this inevitably means a corresponding reabsorption of lithium and hence a raised serum level and all that that entails for side effects and toxic reactions.

Diuretic agents fall into a number of quite separate classes, and these are considered below.

Osmotic Diuretics

These agents, the most commonly used of which is

mannitol, are freely filterable by the glomerulus but since they are not reabsorbed they act as osmotic solutes in the proximal tubular fluid.

In the proximal tubular fluid the major solutes are sodium salts; the sodium is reabsorbed at this level and water diffuses passively into the tubule. In the presence of osmotic diuretics, the concentration of sodium in the tubular fluid becomes abnormally low and the net reabsorption of sodium is diminished. As previously explained, the reabsorption of lithium and sodium in the proximal tubule is identical. Thus, when an osmotic diuretic is administered to patients taking lithium salts, there is a decrease of lithium reabsorption and a decrease of serum lithium levels.

Osmotic diuretics are sometimes used in cases of lithium overdosage due to their capacity to increase lithium excretion. Although long-term studies have not been carried out, when the association of lithium salts with osmotic diuretics is unavoidable, careful monitoring of blood levels should be done as a precautionary measure.

Carbonic Anhydrase Inhibitors

These diuretics are used currently in the treatment of glaucoma and may also be useful for reducing urine acidity. Acetazolamide is the prototype of this group. This drug is a reversible inhibitor of carbonic anhydrase and as a consequence is an inhibitor of hydrogen ion secretion by the renal tubule. The reabsorption of sodium in the nephron is accompanied by hydrogen ion and potassium ion transport in opposite directions to preserve the anion–cation equilibrium (*Figure 19.1*, p.76). Thus, the inhibition of hydrogen ion secretion by acetazolamide will lead to a decrease in sodium reabsorption in the renal tubule.

The inhibition of carbonic anhydrase by acetazolamide is greatest in the proximal tubule. Therefore, in patients taking lithium salts, it would lead to an increase of sodium and lithium excretion. This effect of acetazolamide has been well established when the drug has been administered in a single dose, but the clinical significance of a long-term association of acetazolamide and lithium salts is as yet unknown, so that careful monitoring of blood levels of lithium is advisable when this combination is used.

Due to its capacity for increasing lithium excretion, acetazolamide has been used in cases of lithium overdosage too.

Distal Tubule Diuretics

The thiazides are the diuretics of choice in the management of oedema and hypertension. Their action mechanism consists in the inhibition of sodium reabsorption in the distal tubule. They also increase the excretion of potassium. The nephron segments responsible for potassium secretion are distal to the site of action of thiazides and the drug-induced enhancement of flow through these distal segments acts a stimulant to potassium secretion.

The nature of the chemical interaction between thiazides and renal receptors is unknown. However, it is well established that, as a consequence of this interaction, there is an important increase of sodium excretion and a resultant negative sodium balance. In compensation there occurs an increase of sodium reabsorption in the proximal tubule and an increase of lithium reabsorption too in patients taking lithium salts, with a consequent high risk of lithium overdosage.

Although a single dose of thiazide (e.g. bendrofluazide) does not modify significantly the excretion of lithium, long term treatment with these diuretics produces a significant increase in serum lithium levels. For example, hydroflumethiazide 25 mg/day or bendrofluazide 2.5 mg/day over a 2-month period each produce a decrease of about 21–24% in lithium clearance. This is correlated with a rise in sodium excretion but not of creatinine clearance, the latter remaining essentially the same whether the patients are on thiazide treatment or not. Another type of thiazide, hydrochlorothiazide, administered in doses of 50 mg/day for 2 weeks produces a significant increase in serum lithium levels too. The administration of a single dose of thiazide does not produce a decrease in lithium excretion because the compensatory changes have not had time to happen (increase in proximal sodium, and hence lithium, reabsorption). However, after a week of treatment significant increases of serum lithium levels can occur.

The clinical importance of this interaction between lithium and thiazides is well established, and cases of lithium overdosage resulting from the concomitant use of the two have been described.

The concomitant use of lithium salts and thiazide diuretics should be undertaken with caution. Serum lithium determinations should be performed and the lithium dose reduced as needed. Some authors have provided guidelines which can be used for the initial reduction in daily lithium doses, based on averages obtained from several patients: according to these guidelines one would have to reduce the daily lithium dose by about 40% in patients given 500 mg chlorothiazide daily, with even greater reductions (about 60% or 70%) having to be made if 750 or 1000 mg of chlorothiazide was given on a daily basis. Monitoring of serum lithium levels should still be continued after such an initial modification, however, and additional refinements made based on the resulting serum level measurements and the clinical state of the patient.

Thiazide diuretics have been shown to reduce the polyuria and polidipsia (diabetes insipidus) induced by lithium. This is presumably because of inhibition of the action of the antidiuretic hormone produced by lithium. The reduction in extracellular volume that is required to treat diabetes insipidus with thiazide diuretics is of special concern in patients receiving lithium, because such a reduction causes a compensatory increase in sodium and lithium reabsorption in the proximal tubule. In addition, thiazide diuretics can aggravate the hypokalaemia which develops during diabetes insipidus induced by lithium.

Loop Diuretics

These are the strongest of all diuretics, and their action is the fastest. Ethacrynic acid, furosemide and bumetanide are the drugs used most frequently. Their diuretic mechanism is based on the inhibition of sodium reabsorption in the loop of Henle (*Figure 19.1*) and so its repeated administration produces an intense negative sodium balance. As a result, the association of lithium with loop diuretics might produce an increase in plasma lithium levels in some patients. Although several cases of lithium intoxication have been reported which seemed to be due to furosemide or ethacrynic acid plus dietary sodium restriction, experimental studies have failed to demonstrate an effect of furosemide or ethacrynic acid on lithium excretion. In five normal subjects stabilized on lithium, furosemide (40 mg/day for 2 weeks) did not affect serum lithium levels. Larger doses were not studied. Since furosemide has its major effects on the loop of Henle, it is possible that a balance is established between the decreased lithium reabsorption at this site and the compensatory increase in proximal tubular lithium reabsorption.

Although most patients are probably unaffected by this interaction, one should be alert for evidence of altered lithium levels if these diuretics are initiated or discontinued.

Aldosterone Antagonists

These compounds have a molecular structure similar to that of aldosterone and compete with aldosterone for the same receptors. Spironolactone is the aldosterone antagonist usually administered because it has the strongest action and greatest selectivity. Since the overall action of aldosterone is to enhance sodium reabsorption and potassium secretion in the distal tubule and collecting system, spironolactone will produce an increase of sodium excretion and an inhibition of potassium secretion (*Figure 19.1*).

It seems that spironolactone does not inhibit lithium reabsorption; thus continued administration of aldosterone antagonists in patients receiving lithium salts might lead to an increase of lithium reabsorption because of the negative sodium balance. In several patients with manic-depressive illness, spironolactone (100 mg/day) was noted to be associated with increasing serum lithium levels. Until this potential interaction is better described, one should be careful to monitor serum lithium levels if spironolactone is given continuously.

Other Potassium-sparing Diuretics

These agents interfere with transport in the most distal segments of the nephron (*Figure 19.1*). They induce a slight increase in the excretion of sodium and under ordinary circumstances there is little change in the excretion of potassium, although sometimes there is a slight increase. In many ways these effects resemble those of spironolactone, but it is clear that these drugs are not aldosterone antagonists. The greatest usefulness of these drugs is in conjunction with other diuretic agents. In general, the administration of a potassium-sparing diuretic with another natriuretic compound increases natriuresis and reduces potassium loss. The two drugs of this group which are frequently used are triamterene and amiloride.

Since these diuretic agents produce a discrete increase in the excretion of sodium, their continued administration in patients receiving lithium might produce a discrete decrease in lithium excretion. However, some authors have shown that triamterene may increase the excretion of lithium, suggesting that some reabsorption of lithium may occur in the distal nephron. Thus, the effect of these diuretic agents on serum lithium levels remains unclear. In nine patients with lithium-induced polyuria (diabetes insipidus), the administration of amiloride over a period of 18–30 days did not change urinary excretion of sodium or lithium, or the plasma levels of lithium. Further studies in normal subjects and patients are needed to assess the clinical importance of this interaction. The available data suggest the need for careful monitoring of blood levels if this combination is utilized.

On the other hand, amiloride mitigates lithium-induced polyuria at least, by blunting the inhibitory effect of lithium on water transport in the renal collecting tubule. Since amiloride reduces urinary output without decreasing lithium clearance to any great extent, and since its use does not need potassium supplementation, this agent may be the initial treatment of choice for lithium-induced polyuria.

Acknowledgement

Dr M.Franco is thanked for support and encouragement.

Bibliography

Thomsen,K. and Leyssac,P.P. (1986) Acute effects of various diuretics on lithium clearance. *Renal Physiol.*, **9**, 1–8.
A recent account of experimental studies on the way in which different diuretics affect the handling of lithium by the kidney.

50. Non-steroidal Anti-inflammatory Drugs

Malcolm M.Furnell

Amongst the most widely prescribed of all classes of drugs, the non-steroidal anti-inflammatory drugs (NSAIDs) are used for the treatment of a variety of inflammatory conditions ranging from the alleviation of minor aches, pains and fever to the amelioration of symptoms of chronic rheumatoid arthritis and osteoarthritis. A list of the NSAIDs currently available in the UK is given in *Table 50.1*. Aspirin is the oldest, and best known, of the NSAIDs and is perhaps the single most commonly taken of all drugs.

Table 50.1 *Non-steroidal anti-inflammatory drugs available in 1987 in Britain*

Aspirin	Indomethacin
Azapropazone	Ketoprofen
Benorylate	Mefenamic acid
Choline magnesium trisalicylate	Nabumetone
Diclofenac	Naproxen
Diflunisal	Phenylbutazone
Etodolac	Piroxicam
Fenbufen	Salsalate
Fenoprofen	Sulindac
Flurbiprofen	Tiaprofenic acid
Ibuprofen	Tolmetin

Some NSAIDs are known to affect the control of lithium treatment, by reducing the extent of the elimination of lithium from the body and thereby causing an increase in the serum lithium level. In view of the need to keep average serum levels low in order to avoid unwanted effects it can be seen that NSAIDs could contribute towards inducing a state of lithium toxicity by an unsuspecting GP who prescribes NSAIDs or by an unsuspecting lithium-controlled patient who may buy a NSAID for the treatment of minor aches and pains. The problem is compounded by the fact that the number of NSAIDs has increased markedly since the mid 1970s and the number of NSAIDs available without prescription is likely to increase in the next few years; currently, in the UK only aspirin and ibuprofen are available for purchase, without prescription, for the treatment of minor aches and pains. With increasing age and increasing longevity of the general population, arthritic illness may become more common and hence the greater the likelihood that lithium-treated patients will require a NSAID. It is therefore important to understand and appreciate the extent to which the NSAIDs can affect people who are taking lithium and with which NSAIDs this is most likely to occur.

NSAIDs and Serum Lithium Levels

Current knowledge of the extent to which NSAIDs interact with lithium treatment is limited. The effects which NSAIDs may have on controlled lithium treat-

Table 50.2 *Summary of findings reported in the scientific literature on the effect of NSAIDs given in normal therapeutic doses, on serum lithium levels*

Drug	Effect on serum lithium levels
Aspirin	1.5 g and 4 g (controlled-release aspirin) per day induced no changes; buffered aspirin (2.6–4 g per day) caused 30% increase (single case report).
Diclofenac	Increased by 26%
Ibuprofen	Inconsistent effects: up to 44% increase noted with doses of 1200–2400 mg per day; no change observed in a single case report with 600 mg per day.
Indomethacin	Increased by 30% to over 100%.
Ketoprofen	Increased by 100% (single case report).
Naproxen	Inconsistent effects: increased by up to 42% but no change noted in one patient (single study).
Phenylbutazone	Increased by 100% (single case report).
Piroxicam	Increased by over 100%.
Sulindac	No net change: two long-term case reports noted a sudden drop by 40–55%, gradually returning to normal (pre-sulindac) levels within a month; no changes observed in other studies.

ment have been examined and reported with less than one half of all NSAIDs currently on the market, in only a small number of people and, in most cases, for short periods of treatment. *Table 50.2* provides a summary of the information which is available to date on the concurrent administration of NSAIDs and lithium. It will be noted that different studies have given rise to results which are not always entirely consistent. What is clear, however, is that NSAID treatment may have various effects on serum lithium levels according to which particular product is administered. There may be an elevation in serum lithium levels (aspirin, diclofenac, ibuprofen, indomethacin, ketoprofen, naproxen, phenylbutazone and piroxicam), no change (aspirin, ibuprofen, naproxen and sulindac), or even a fall followed subsequently by a return to normal (sulindac). In most cases, the effect was measurable within a few days of starting the NSAID, necessitating the withdrawal of the NSAID in instances of elevation of serum lithium levels to prevent serious symptoms of toxicity. However, in one case of a 64-year-old man who was prescribed piroxicam 20 mg twice daily, signs of lithium toxicity were not recognized until 4 months after starting piroxicam although it was likely that his serum lithium levels had been gradually and insidiously rising throughout that time. In cases where a NSAID caused an increase in serum lithium levels, stopping the NSAID alone usually allowed the lithium to return to normal levels within a few days. In cases of more severe lithium intoxication, also stopping lithium administration produced a more rapid decline of serum lithium levels. No serious long term problems have been noted.

Studies with aspirin, ibuprofen and naproxen have shown inconsistent effects on the serum level of lithium. Only buffered aspirin (in doses of 2.6–4 g per day of aspirin) was shown in one case to cause an elevation in serum lithium levels, whereas in other reports aspirin (in similar doses) had no effect on lithium. Reports of the effects of ibuprofen are similarly variable. One 64-year-old women took ibuprofen 600 mg per day for 2 months without measurable change in serum lithium level, whereas this same patient showed marked elevation of serum lithium levels with piroxicam. However, other studies involving ibuprofen 1200–2400 mg per day showed variable degrees of elevation of serum lithium levels. In another study involving naproxen 750 mg per day for 6 days, only one patient showed no change in serum lithium levels, the others showing variable elevations up to 42% and exhibiting clinical signs of lithium toxicity during the short study period.

Alone among all NSAIDs, sulindac has consistently been shown to cause no net change in serum lithium levels. In two studies involving 10 patients aged 53–62 years, sulindac administration had no effect on serum lithium levels when the two drugs were given concurrently over 6 days. Although in two other case reports sulindac administration was followed by a temporary drop in serum lithium levels by 40–55%, there was no loss of therapeutic control. When no attempt was made to increase the lithium dose to compensate for the low serum lithium levels, the lithium levels returned to normal (i.e. pre-sulindac treatment level) within a few weeks and remained within the desired therapeutic range for several months subsequently.

Not only may lithium serum levels be affected in different ways with different NSAIDs, they may even be affected in different ways when the same NSAID is examined in different people (e.g. with aspirin, ibuprofen, naproxen and sulindac). It is therefore difficult to predict with any certainty how lithium treatment will interact with the other 13 NSAIDs. Indeed, doctors are not yet sure how these two drugs affect

Table 50.3 *Guidelines for combination treatment of NSAID with lithium*

Medical problem	Drug	Recommendations for use with lithium
i. mild occasional aches pains and fever	(a) paracetamol	(a) not a NSAID; preferred drug
	(b) aspirin 300 mg	(b) occasional doses only
ii. more severe rheumatoid conditions requiring medical care	(a) sulindac	(a) lithium dose adjustment may not be necessary
	(b) diclofenac, ibuprofen, indomethacin, ketoprofen, naproxen, phenylbutazone, piroxicam	(b) check serum lithium levels twice weekly until stabilized, then at regular intervals, reduce lithium dose when necessary, check renal function before and during combination treatment
	(c) other NSAIDs	(c) no information available—monitor as in ii(b)

each other in the body, although current evidence indicates that NSAIDs may inhibit prostaglandin systems in the kidney, which in turn may reduce the renal excretion of lithium. The way in which NSAIDs affect lithium elimination is almost certainly the key to understanding the mechanism of interaction, since lithium is almost entirely excreted from the body through the kidney and any NSAID-induced increase in serum lithium levels is accompanied by an associated decrease in the amount of lithium which is excreted in the urine.

Elderly people (who generally have reduced kidney function), people who are taking drugs which are known to affect kidney function, people who have pre-existing medical conditions which affect kidney function (e.g. congestive heart failure, hypertension), and some people who have been taking higher doses of lithium for many years, are most likely to show interaction between lithium and NSAIDs. Sulindac may be of particular advantage in this respect as it normally has no activity in the kidney and therefore it is the least likely of all NSAIDs to affect the renal handling of lithium.

Guidelines for Combination Treatment

Since the extent to which NSAIDs are known to affect lithium serum levels is variable, the concurrent administration of lithium and a NSAID must be regarded with care. For occasional headaches or mild fever, paracetamol would be preferred since this is not a NSAID. However, single doses of aspirin 300 mg may be more suitable for occasional use for mild aches and pains and should not affect lithium control. Rheumatic pains, however, which require the attention of a doctor, can be treated with NSAIDs, but with care. The doctor should first assess the patient's kidney function to ensure that lithium elimination is not already compromised.

The weight of current evidence indicates that sulindac is the safest alternative for NSAID administration in patients who are taking lithium. However, the doctor should watch for any early drop in serum lithium levels under the influence of sulindac treatment, and be prepared to use short-term adjunctive treatment until lithium levels restabilize. Initial lithium dose adjustment may not be required. Theoretical considerations may rule out adverse interaction between aspirin and lithium. The mechanisms of the effects of aspirin in the kidney are complex and may involve renal prostaglandins in a different way to other NSAIDs. Until more information is available, regular antirheumatic doses of aspirin should be given with care to lithium-controlled patients. Small daily doses of aspirin (when used for its anti-platelet activity) may prove to have no effect on lithium control.

Diclofenac, ibuprofen, indomethacin, ketoprofen, naproxen, phenylbutazone and piroxicam are known to cause a rapid increase in serum lithium levels and their concurrent use with lithium should be avoided. If it is necessary to use one of these NSAIDs, the maintenance dose of lithium should be reduced at the commencement of NSAID treatment to compensate for a potential rise in serum lithium levels. Patients should be advised not to buy ibuprofen from their community pharmacy. Serum lithium determinations must be carried out at regular intervals (twice weekly at first) and kidney function assessed periodically. With careful control, lithium levels should again stabilize within the required range and the patient should be successfully controlled for both conditions. Close biochemical and clinical supervision is essential throughout the period of concurrent administration of lithium and NSAID, especially during the first few weeks of treatment. If serum lithium levels are seen to rise above the safe range for lithium use, stopping the NSAID should cause lithium levels to fall within a few days. If serum lithium levels are markedly high, lithium should also be stopped to accelerate the fall to normal levels and the patient's progress closely monitored. *Table 50.3* summarizes the clinical guidelines of NSAID—lithium combination treatment.

Whilst no information is available on the interaction between lithium and other NSAIDs they should, perhaps, be regarded as having the potential to cause a rise in serum lithium levels. Again, the patient should be monitored closely and carefully during concurrent administration. All NSAIDs are known to have some idiosyncratic direct effect on kidney function in some people, which may therefore affect the ability of the kidneys to handle and excrete lithium. This idiosyncracy should therefore be borne in mind during the use of any NSAID. However, this effect on the kidney is usually reversible on stopping the NSAID with no resulting permanent damage.

Acknowledgement

Thanks are due to Mrs Judy Lehmann (Sussex Postgraduate Medical Centre, Brighton) for using her talents for literature search.

Bibliography

Clive,D.M. and Stoff,J.S. (1984) Renal syndromes associated with non-steroidal anti-inflammatory drugs. *New Engl. J.Med.*, **310**, 563–572.

A detailed summary of adverse effects of non-steroidal anti-inflammatory drugs on the kidney, with emphasis on biochemical mechanisms. This review should enable the reader to assess how lithium excretion may be affected by NSAIDs. An understanding of renal physiology is necessary.

Reimann,I.W., Golbs,E., Fischer,C. and Frolich,J.C. (1985) Influence of intravenous acetylsalicylic acid and sodium salicylate on human renal function and lithium clearance. *Eur. J. Clin. Pharmacol.*, **29**, 435–441.

This describes an experimental study of the effects of NSAID on lithium clearance, with comment on the current theory of NSAID–lithium interaction. An understanding of pharmacological principles is necessary.

51. The Social Drugs

Raymond F.Anton

Given lithium's success as a therapeutic agent in the treatment of affective disorders, it was inevitable that clinicians would begin wondering whether lithium would alter the behavioural effect of exogenously ingested psychoactive substances. In addition, since substances of both a licit (e.g. alcohol) and illicit (e.g. cocaine) type are used and abused by an increasing number of people, questions naturally arise about the safety and metabolism of lithium in patients who used these so-called 'social drugs'. Information directly related to this issue comes from the work of basic researchers eager to establish animal modes of mania, who initially reasoned that, if lithium could block the stimulatory effects of drugs like amphetamines in rodents, this would provide validity for the concept that the amphetamine-induced behavioural change might be a useful model of mania.

Lithium and Psychoactive Substances

The psychoactive substances (other than alcohol) most intensively studied in regard to lithium interaction have been the stimulants amphetamine, methylphenidate and cocaine. Some information is available on lithium's interaction with barbiturates and minimal information on its interaction with hallucinogens (phencyclidine). A summary of lithium's effect on the behavioural, cognitive, and emotional change caused by these substances is given in *Table 51.1*.

The ability of lithium to alter the stimulatory effect of amphetamine in rodents and man has perhaps been the most extensively studied interaction of all the substances except alcohol. The animal studies in this area are conflicting, with some investigators reporting an inhibition of amphetamine stimulation after chronic lithium treatment, while others report an enhancement of some of amphetamine's effects. It appears that some of the conflict arises from a species (mouse versus rat) or strain (mice) difference. In one of the more elegant studies in this area, Dr Rahel Hamburger-Bar and associates at the Jerusalem Mental Health Center, Israel, showed that there was an association between the ability of lithium to block

Table 51.1 *Summary of lithium's effect on behaviour induced by psychoactive substances*

Drug/substance	Species	Lithium effect
Amphetamine	Rodent	Decreases or no effect on hyperactivity (strain specific)
	Monkey	Decreases stimulant effect
	Man	Decreases euphoria
		Decreases activation
Methylphenidate	Man	Decreases activation
Cocaine	Rat	Decreases stimulant behaviour
	Monkey	Decreases stimulant effect
	Man	Antagonizes cocaine high (?)
		Reduces craving (?)
		Improves cocaine psychosis
Phencyclidine	Rat	Potentiates behavioural effects
Barbiturates	Rat	Potentiates sedation
	Man	Attenuates cognitive effects
		Enhances euphoric effect

amphetamine-induced activity and a specific chemical effect of lithium in the brains of mice. Both effects occurred only in certain strains of mice, while others were not affected. In reality, this finding may fit the clinical situation well, since it is clear that people experience amphetamines differently, some becoming dysphoric or unhappy, others becoming euphoric or stimulated. It would appear likely that lithium may actually have dissimilar effects on amphetamine stimulation depending on the underlying biology of the organism. In at least one well controlled human study, in agreement with the animal work, there was a variable inhibition by lithium of amphetamine-induced euphoria and stimulation in the same person and between different people. Nevertheless, in both the monkey and man, most studies suggest that lithium pre-treatment generally appears to inhibit the activating and euphorigenic effects of amphetamine.

In normal volunteers, the effects of methylphenidate, a stimulant drug having similar effects to amphetamine, were reduced after 2 weeks of treatment with clinically therapeutic levels of lithium. However, stabilized manic-depressive patients on lithium in another study showed marked activation and euphoriant responses to methylphenidate. It again appears that the underlying biological state of the organism will determine whether lithium will be effective in inhibiting the stimulatory and euphorigenic effects of these compounds.

Cocaine is fast becoming one of the most costly and dangerous drugs of abuse. Despite this, relatively few basic or clinical studies have been done on the interaction of lithium and cocaine. In the 1970s, Drs Arnold Mandell and Suzanne Knapp at the University of California at San Diego, USA, discovered, during some elegant studies, that cocaine affected one of the brain chemical transmitters (serotonin) in a specific manner and that lithium antagonized this effect. This provided evidence at the biochemical level that lithium may antagonize some of cocaine's effects in man. Additional support was derived from a study in rats in which lithium attenuated cocaine's behavioural effects. Indeed, the same authors reported on a few human cases where the effects of recreational cocaine use were reduced when the patients were treated with lithium for an underlying affective illness. More recently, Drs Gawin and Kleber at Yale University, USA, reported that only a subgroup of cocaine abusers, who had manic-depressive-like illnesses, seemed to reduce their cocaine craving and use during lithium treatment. Other cocaine abusers did not seem to obtain much long term benefit from lithium even though it may have antagonized the cocaine-induced high in some subjects. There is some additional evidence that lithium may be useful in treating the psychosis (which seems similar to mania or depression) induced by cocaine in some susceptible people. Clearly, more study is needed in this area.

Even less is known about the interaction of lithium with hallucinogens. One basic study in rats suggested that lithium, at serum levels equivalent to therapeutic levels in man, potentiated the effect of acute PCP (phencyclidine). Since other psychotropic drugs, such as antipsychotic agents, have been reported to enhance the PCP effect in some people, it is likely (given the meagre evidence available) that lithium has the potential to do the same.

The effect of lithium on barbiturate-induced behavioural effects has also not been extensively examined. In man, it appears that lithium may antagonize pentobarbital-induced decrease in awareness, enhance pentobarbital-induced euphoria, and have no effect on the calming or antianxiety effect of pentobarbital. It is not, however, clear what the implications of such findings might be for the administration of lithium to patients who abuse barbiturates.

Lithium and Alcohol-induced Behaviour

The most extensively studied interaction of lithium with another psychoactive substance is with acute alcohol ingestion and alcoholism. Almost all facets of

Table 51.2 *Summary of the effect of lithium on behaviours induced by acute or chronic alcohol intake*

Lithium	Alcohol	Species	Lithium effects
Chronic	Chronic	Rats	Decreases alcohol intake
Acute	Chronic	Rats	Decreases alcohol intake
Acute	Chronic	Rats	Increases alcohol withdrawal
Chronic	Acute	Rats	Decreases intoxication
Acute	Acute	Mice	Decreases activation
Chronic	Chronic	Goldfish	Increases alcohol tolerance
Chronic	Acute	Man (normal)	Decreases alcohol-induced mental acuity changes
Chronic	Acute	Man (alcoholic)	Decreases intoxication Decreases craving Increases mental acuity
Chronic	Chronic	Man (alcoholic)	Decreases withdrawal
Chronic	–	Man (alcoholic)	Improves abstinence

alcohol ingestion have been to some extent examined. These include acute sensitivity, tolerance, withdrawal, chronic intake, craving and abstinence. *Table 51.2* summarizes the findings in this area. Both animal and human studies add to our understanding of the lithium–alcohol interaction.

There is evidence that lithium may have a direct pharmacological effect which antagonizes some of alcohol's acute effects such as intoxication, decreased mental acuity and activation. This is independent of any 'mood stabilizing' effect of lithium. Additionally, however, lithium may provide a 'mood stabilizing' effect when given chronically to man, such that alcohol use and craving are diminished.

As *Table 51.2* suggests, the additive effects of lithium on many aspects of alcohol use and abuse seem to make it a very good choice for the treatment of at least some people with alcohol use control problems. A recent American study utilizing 84 alcoholic volunteers by Dr Jan Fawcett of Rush-Presbyterian-St. Lukes Medical Center, Chicago, USA seemed to confirm the suggestions of clinicians during the 1970s. Dr Fawcett reported that, in compliant alcoholic patients, lithium helped maintain abstinence over an 18-month period. Since the majority of these patients met criteria for major depression, it was not clear from this study (and controversial from previous studies) whether the presence of an affective illness in addition to alcoholism was needed to predict a good outcome. To answer this question and address other methodological issues, the United States' Veterans Administration is conducting a large scale (400 patients) study of lithium treatment for alcoholism, which is utilizing seven hospitals in various parts of the country. The results of this hopefully definitive study should be available in 1988. From clinical experience, however, it would appear that some chronic alcoholic patients, perhaps of the order of 20–40%, may benefit from lithium carbonate treatment: whether this estimate will be validated scientifically, and whether we will eventually be able to choose, beforehand, which patient may benefit will await further documentation.

Table 51.3 *Summary of the effects of psychoactive substances on serum lithium levels in man*

Drug/substance	Serum lithium level	
	Acute	Chronic
Alcohol	Increase	No change (?)
Methylxanthines (Theophylline, Caffeine)	Decrease	Decrease
Marijuana	Increase (?)	Increase

In general, it appears that most alcoholics tolerate 1200 mg daily of extended-release lithium carbonate quite well, both when sober and while drinking. Of note is recent evidence that lithium may, in fact, reduce the stomach irritation caused by alcohol, which would be of obvious added benefit to alcohol abusers since much morbidity is caused by bleeding from the upper gastrointestinal tract.

Psychoactive Substances and Serum Lithium Levels

Although lithium is a highly efficacious drug in the treatment of affective disorders, it has a low therapeutic index (i.e. causes toxicity at serum concentrations not too far above therapeutically effective serum concentrations). Therefore, serum lithium monitoring is done on patients treated with this compound. Since lithium is absorbed from the gut and excreted by the kidney, any substance which interferes with either of these two processes may potentially change the serum lithium level and hence cause therapeutic ineffectiveness or toxicity.

Despite the importance of reliable knowledge in this area, very little information is available regarding the effect of recreational and abused substances on lithium metabolism. *Table 51.3* summarizes what is known.

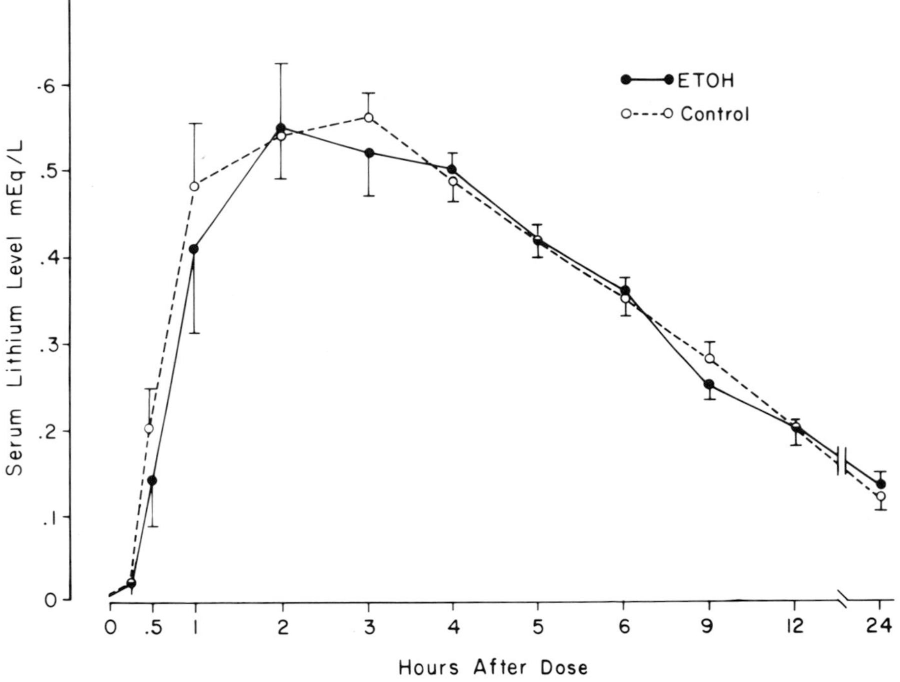

Figure 51.1 Serum lithium concentration–time curve for 600 mg lithium carbonate capsules at time 0 with either alcohol (0.5 gm/kg; ethanol) or a control non-alcoholic drink. Each point represents the mean serum lithium level of 10 subjects in both conditions, bars represent 1 SEM.

Alcohol

There is one study in rats and one in normal human volunteers that address the issue of the effect of alcohol on lithium metabolism. Both studies found that, when alcohol is taken in close temporal proximity to lithium carbonate, higher peak serum lithium levels than normal may occur. This may lead (depending on the dose of lithium, individual metabolic rates, and sensitivities) to increased acute toxicity. However, as depicted in *Figure 51.1* the overall lithium absorption and excretion curve is not appreciably affected by alcohol for a group of people averaged together. This suggests that, for the average person, there should be no chronic effect of acute alcohol on serum lithium levels. Chronic high levels of alcohol consumption during chronic lithium ingestion have not, however, been specifically studied, so any extrapolation to that condition needs to be done cautiously. Given the limited data, the best advice is for patients not to ingest lithium in close temporal proximity to alcohol, but alcohol in moderation (2–4 fluid ounces daily) should not appreciably affect steady state serum lithium levels.

Theophylline and caffeine

The methylxanthines are a class of drugs some of which (theophylline) are used to treat asthma and of which caffeine is a member. These drugs have a diuretic effect on the kidney, and the effects of this class of drugs on lithium excretion have been studied. The general finding both for theophylline and caffeine is that, although there is marked inter-individual variability, there is an increase in lithium excretion and a drop in serum lithium level after chronic use of these drugs. Since theophylline was most studied, it can be used as a model for caffeine. The excretion of lithium correlated with serum theophylline levels such that levels at the high end of the therapeutic range caused an increase in lithium excretion of over 30%, and a serum lithium decrease of over 20%. This reduction may put some patients at risk of a breakthrough manic or depressive episode. It would be wise, therefore, to use the least amount of theophylline that is therapeutically necessary and to check lithium levels frequently and adjust accordingly. By extension, it would appear that a large (undefined) daily intake of caffeine could decrease serum lithium levels and, therefore, that caffeine intake should be moderated.

Marijuana

There is scant information on the effect of marijuana on lithium metabolism. A report of a single human case suggested that, in a patient chronically maintained on lithium, the use of daily marijuana (3–4 marijuana cigarettes) caused an increase in serum lithium level. Since marijuana decreases intestinal motility, it is theoretically possible that more lithium would be absorbed, which would support the above observation. However, definitive control studies need to be done in order to establish a valid relationship between these compounds.

Summary

Lithium appears to affect the behavioural and psychological effects of many of the 'social drugs'. The effect appears clinically significant for stimulants and alcohol. On the other hand, these drugs may influence lithium metabolism to some degree. Given the immense importance of knowledge in this area, especially in light of the increasing number of people taking lithium for psychoactive conditions and using substances for recreational and abusive reasons, more emphasis should be placed on obtaining valid data with which to educate ourselves about the interaction of these compounds.

Acknowledgement

Angelica Thevos and Lucille von Kolnitz are thanked for their help in the preparation of this section.

Bibliography

Angrist,B. and Gershon,S. (1979) Variable attenuation of amphetamine effects by lithium *Am. J. Psychiatry*, **136**, 806–810.
Human volunteers were given amphetamine after pre-treatment with lithium. The results show variable effects of lithium. Not an extremely technical paper, this would be useful for both layman and clinician.

Anton,R.F., Paladino,J.A., Morton,A. and Thomas,R.W. (1985) Effect of acute alcohol consumption on lithium kinetics. *Clin. Pharmacol. Ther.*, **38**, 52–55.
Human volunteers were given acute lithium and alcohol. The main findings of this study have been given in the present book. For further technical detail, this paper may be consulted.

Fawcett,J., Clark,D.C., Gibbons,R.D., Aagesen,C.A., Pisani,V.D., Tilkin,J.M., Sellers,D. and Stutzman,D. (1984) Evaluation of lithium therapy for alcoholism. *J. Clin. Psychiatry*, **45**, 494–499.
Reports the largest controlled study to date on the use of lithium in a chronic alcoholic population. It is technical in parts, with sophisticated statistical techniques.

Gawin,F.H. and Kleber,H.D. (1984) Cocaine abuse treatment. *Arch. Gen. Psychiatry*, **41**, 903–909.
A practical report of non-controlled trials involving psychoactive drugs in the treatment of cocaine abuse. Although written for a psychiatric professional audience, it does include case reports which are illustrative reading for the clinician and layman alike.

52. Other Interactions

Ronald B.Salem

In view of the widespread use of lithium, it is inevitable that occasions should occur when it is administered simultaneously with drugs other than those considered above (pp. 161–190). In general, such combinations will be unplanned and, unless the prescribing physician is aware that the patient is already taking lithium or that potentially harmful interactions may occur between lithium and other agents, the combination may not be monitored and any untoward effects may either pass unrecorded or not be recognized as arising from an interaction with lithium.

It is only occasionally, when the effects of combination treatment are particularly noticeable, that they will be deemed of sufficient interest to warrant a report in the literature. As a consequence, information about interactions between lithium and a wide range of medications is sparse and scattered in the literature, and not infrequently is reported in a manner which lacks essential details.

It should go without saying that any clinician who knows that a patient is receiving lithium treatment should first check the available literature before initiating simultaneous treatment with another agent. Increased vigilance and more frequent serum monitoring are mandatory requirements of newly instituted combination treatment.

Some of the more important interactions between lithium and a variety of other agents which have not so far been considered in this book are listed in *Table 52.1*. If the evidence derives exclusively from case reports, the interaction is indicated with an 'A' and until further work has been done and reported, the combination should be used cautiously; 'B' indicates

Table 52.1 *Examples of a variety of interactions between lithium and other treatments*

Treatment	Effect on serum lithium level	Comments	Recommendation
Antibiotics			
Tetracyclines	↑	1 CR[a] ? secondary to nephrotoxic effect of tetracyclines	A
Spectinomycin	↑?	1 CR	A
Ticaracillin	?	1 CR	A
Cardiovascular drugs			
Digoxin	?	1 CR, but a recent report in six patients found no interaction	B
Dutiazem	↑?	1 CR: patient felt rigid, parkinsonized and stiff	A
Methyldopa	?	4 CR: toxicity for levels <1.5 mmol/l	B
	0	1 CR: toxicity in 3 volunteers	
Enalapril	↑	1 CR	B
CNS drugs			
Baclofen	?	Severe aggravation of hyperkinetic symptoms in two patients	A
Mazindol	↑	1 CR	A
Neuromuscular blocking agents			
Succinylcholine Pancuronium bromide	?	2 CR: prolongation of neuromuscular blockade. Other reports indicate the combination is compatible	B
Gastrointestinal drugs			
Antacids	0	No effects	–
Sodium bicarbonate	↓ (transient)	1 CR	C
Metoclopramide	?	1 CR: extrapyramidal effects	A
Magnesium sulphate	0	No effects	–
Bronchodilators			
Theophylline	↓	Several CR	C
Other drugs			
Cisplatin	↓ (transient)	1 CR	A
Caffeine	↓ or 0	Volunteer study	A

[a]CR, case reports.

that data are available which suggest that it would be wise to avoid the combination whenever possible; whilst 'C' is used when definitive data are available suggesting that blood levels should be monitored very carefully if the combination is to be utilized. For ease of reference the information is presented in tabular form (*Table 52.1*).

Bibliography

Salem,R.B. (1982) A pharmacist's guide to monitoring lithium drug-drug interaction. *Drug Intell. Clin. Pharm.*, **16**, 745–747.
A concise account of lithium interactions, giving many useful references to original reports in the literature.

PART VIII

EFFECTS ON ORGANS AND SYSTEMS

53. Body Weight

L.H.Storlien and G.A.Smythe

One of the well-known side effects of lithium is weight gain. Under some circumstances this can pose at least two serious difficulties. First, it may exacerbate problems of clinical management if it leads to discontinuation of the treatment (the patient can be faced with the choice of mood stabilization and concomitant weight gain, or of stopping treatment with the attendant risk of relapse). Second, there is the problem that the extent of weight gain seen in some lithium-treated patients could itself be detrimental to their general health. Studies with both humans and experimental animals have been helpful in elucidating some of the characteristics of lithium-induced weight gain and the possible mechanisms.

Extent: Sex Differences

The extent of weight increase with lithium therapy can sometimes be considerable, ranging to upwards of 15 kg in some cases. It should be said that weight gain does not occur in all those on lithium treatment, but, according to different reports, it is seen in between 20% and 75% of patients. This contrasts with very few complaints of weight increase over comparable time periods among control groups such as healthy non-patients, drug-free bipolar patients and bipolar patients treated with a placebo.

Lithium appears to induce weight gain in all age groups and in both sexes. Women are more often aware than men that they have gained weight while taking lithium. This could be related to possibly greater social pressure among women to remain slim. However, some animal studies suggest the greater susceptibility among females is a real phenomenon related to their physiology.

Mechanisms

Human and animal studies have both provided clues to the mechanisms involved in lithium-induced weight gain. One explanation follows from the finding that lithium brings about increased fluid intake. Lithium treated humans have repeatedly been found to complain of increased thirst, and in some studies they have been shown to drink significantly more fluid than untreated people. Likewise, in various studies lithium-treated animals have drunk from two to three times their normal intake. It has been suggested that lithium-treated patients satisfy their thirst by drinking fluids rich in calories, and that this could account for a significant part of the weight gain. As support for this, it has been found that when lithium-treated rats had access to sugar and sweet solutions as well as their normal food and water they drank significantly more total fluid than equivalently fed controls. A large part of this excess fluid intake was as the sugar solution and occurred without appropriate compensatory reduction in their normal food intake. Consequently, the lithium-treated rats had a higher total caloric intake and a faster rate of weight gain. Thus, lithium-induced weight gain could be at least partly due to increased thirst and therefore increased intake through high calorie fluids. This indicates the probable benefit of advising patients on lithium to satisfy their thirst with low or no-calorie drinks — water, diet soft drinks, tea and coffee with artificial sweeteners or unsweetened (see pp. 151 – 152). The one caution here is that if thirst is pronounced and fluid intake very high, care must be taken to see that over-consumption of artificial sweeteners (which can have their own difficulties, including effects on brain metabolism in very high doses) does not become problematical.

A second possibility put forward to account for lithium's effect on body weight is that weight gain is secondary to the therapeutic effects of lithium. That is, lithium-treated patients gain weight because they are feeling better and therefore eating more. However, in a number of studies the correlation between restoration of mood stability and weight change has been found to be poor. Further, in cases where placebo administration was successful in restoring euthymic mood no reports of excess gain were made. It therefore seems unlikely that merely improving mood control leads to excess weight gain.

The third notion which must be considered is that lithium indirectly increases body weight, not by increasing intake, but by decreasing energy expenditure (i.e. by lowering metabolic rate). As yet this hypothesis has not been rigorously tested; however, the available data suggest that lithium neither lowers basal metabolic rate nor inhibits weight loss when caloric restriction is imposed.

The final possibility revolves around the specifics of the increased appetite reported by some lithium-

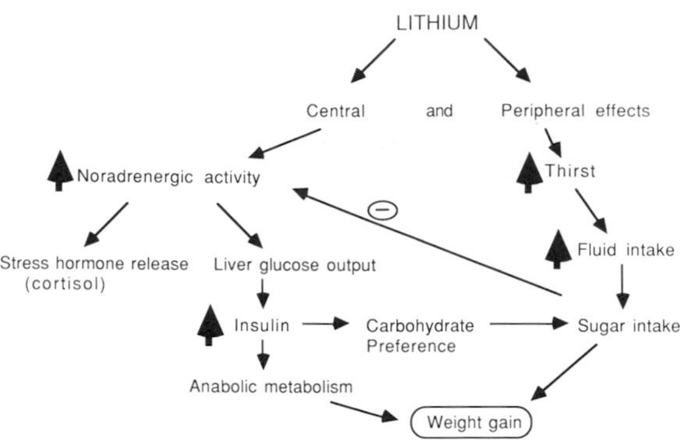

Figure 53.1 Theoretical scheme of how the combined central and peripheral effects of lithium might lead to weight gain. The ↑ symbol indicates increases in levels or activity. The core element of the scheme is the increase in brain noradrenaline activity which has the sequelae of increases in both stress hormones and glucose. This leads to greater production of the anabolic hormone insulin which, under experimental conditions, has also been shown to result in preferential carbohydrate intake. This combines with the effect of lithium to increase thirst, hence both carbohydrate craving and weight gain. An essential feature of this theoretical outline is the feedback effect of this sugar intake on brain noradrenergic activity (⊖). In this context, then, the carbohydrate craving acts as a brake to maintain equilibrium in the system. Unfortunately, if this is the case then advice to satisfy thirst from non-calorific sources may not provide the same feedback as carbohydrate-laden fluids.

treated patients and the relationship to changes in the body's hypothalamic-pituitary-adrenal (HPA) axis which mediates stress responses (*Figure 53.1*). There is evidence that lithium increases blood glucose. This hyperglycaemia may result either from a direct stimulation by lithium on glucose output or an indirect effect via the HPA stress axis, or both. Certainly, increases in the human adrenal hormone, cortisol and the equivalent hormone in the rat, corticosterone (the output of which is driven by ACTH from the pituitary, the release of ACTH in turn being under the control of hypothalamic noradrenergic activity), have both been reported following lithium treatment. Whatever the cause, a chronic drive to hyperglycemia will provoke both increasing levels of the body's major anabolic hormone, insulin, and over the long-term persistent hyperglycaemia and/or hyperinsulinaemia will be likely to lead to both weight gain and insulin resistance. Affective disorders are already associated with a higher than normal incidence of diabetes mellitus, and the potential of lithium to impair insulin action must be considered in the range of therapy side effects. Further, we have direct evidence from animal studies that lithium increases hypothalamic activity of the monoamine neurotransmitter noradrenaline. This is consistent with other work showing a clear relationship between noradrenergic activity in the brain and activation of the HPA axis (and hence increased corticosterone levels). However, blood glucose itself feeds back to reduce brain noradrenergic activity. Thus there is a physiological basis for the carbohydrate craving reported by many patients in reducing the activation of HPA stress axis (which is presumably aversive). Unfortunately, excess intake, progression to weight gain, glucose intolerance or even frank diabetes are obvious potential sequelae to the chronic ingestion of quantities of high sugar foods.

Clinical Management

The manner in which the issue of weight gain may be approached by the clinician is considered in more detail elsewhere (see p. 225).

Acknowledgement

This work was supported by the NH and MRC (Australia); thanks are also due to F.M.Higson for her assistance in the preparation of this section.

Bibliography

Stock,M. and Rothwell,N. (1982) *Obesity and Leanness*. John Libbey London.
This is a useful book for patients wishing to control a weight problem secondary to lithium treatment. It is not a diet book, but does discuss the principles of body weight regulation in relation to food intake and energy expenditure.

54. The Gastrointestinal System

L.Kersten

Whilst in animal experiments lithium may be administered by a variety of routes, in humans it is invariably given by mouth. The gastrointestinal tract is thus the first organ system to come into contact with lithium, and lithium concentrations will (at least in the period immediately after dosing) be higher in the gut than anywhere else in the body.

Once in the gut, two possible fates await the lithium. It may be absorbed, passing out of the gut into the blood and thence to the other organs and systems, or it may remain in the gut and eventually be eliminated in the faeces. By far the greater part is absorbed; the ratio of that absorbed to the total ingested is referred to as the 'bioavailability' of the preparation, a value which may vary according to a number of factors, the most important of which is the nature of the formulation, i.e. the kind of pill, capsule, or other medium used to package the lithium salt into dose-sized units.

Some lithium may actually pass back from the blood (via gastric juices, bile, saliva, etc.) into the gut, only to be re-absorbed at a later point. Thus the relationship between the level of lithium in the lumen of the gut and that in the rest of the body is one determined by quite complex kinetics.

Since the impact which lithium makes upon psychiatric disturbance depends upon its delivery to the rest of the body, the issue of absorption from the gastrointestinal tract is clearly of great practical importance.

Absorption and Elimination

Figure 54.1 demonstrates schematically the involvement of the various digestive organs in the absorption and elimination processes of lithium. Excretion, primarily by the kidney, occurs following lithium distribution via the systemic blood circulation. In the steady state, excretion processes are simultaneously counteracted by those of absorption; lithium bioavailability is found to be always in the region of 90%. Absorption of lithium by the epithelial tissue of the mouth is without practical significance. A relatively high amount of administered lithium is secreted via salivary glands each day, but its continuously rapid recycling into the digestive system means that total lithium absorption remains unaffected. The clinical utility of the measurement of salivary lithium concentrations in monitoring of therapy is controversial (see pp. 91–93).

The initial steep increase in serum concentrations after conventional lithium tablets provides evidence for a relatively high rate of lithium absorption in the stomach. Formulations of lithium salts which take the bulk of the tablet past the stomach lead to retarded rates of uptake into the serum. The amount of lithium returned to the stomach via the gastric juice is unimportant, particularly since it has been found that lithium has a potent gastric anti-secretory effect. Of practical importance is the fact that the concurrent administration of aluminium-containing antacids does not seem to change the extent of gastrointestinal lithium absorption.

Lithium transfer via the liver into the bile has been characterized as a facilitated diffusion process (i.e. a diffusion process which may be carrier-mediated but which needs no energy). Biliary lithium secretion, however, amounts to only 2–4% of the given dose.

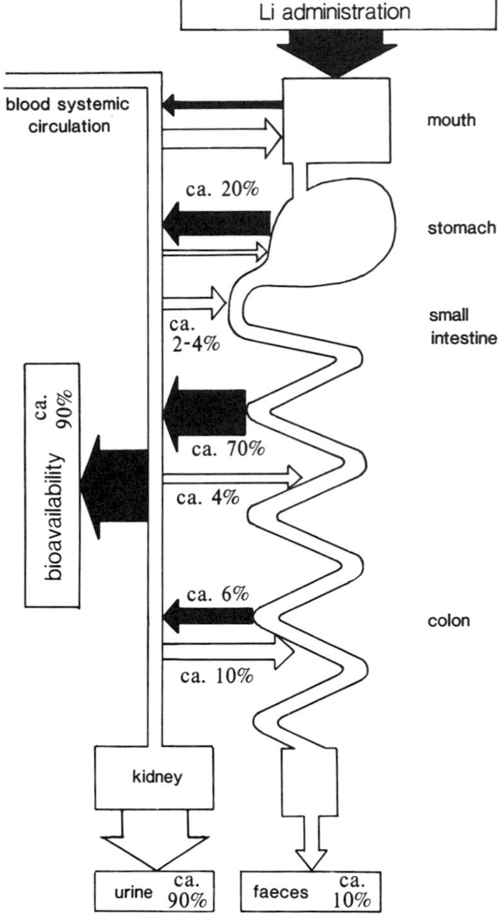

Figure 54.1 Importance of the various organs of the digestive system in the absorption (➡) and the elimination (⇨) processes of lithium after oral administration. Numbers indicate the approximate percentage of the administered dose.

Enterohepatic circulation of lithium is without importance, because only one fifth of the lithium eliminated with faeces is secreted via bile.

Since the pancreas has no concentrating ability, lithium concentrations in pancreatic secretions correspond to those in serum.

Without any doubt, the main portion of lithium is absorbed in the various segments of the small intestine by a trans- and paracellular route across the mucosa. Lithium-induced alterations of gastrointestinal hormonal regulation, especially an enhancement of aldosterone release, appear to stimulate the entry and transfer of lithium in intestinal epithelial cells. Some degree of colonic lithium absorption has been established, but is slight in comparison with that occurring in the small intestine.

There is evidence for an intestinal lithium excretion, too. Results from work done in rats indicate increased quantities of lithium in the segmental samples of faeces from the duodenum to the colon, and show, furthermore, that after ligation of the hilus of one or both kidneys a significant enhancement of faecal lithium output occurs. Increased faecal lithium excretion can, however, only partially compensate for the loss of the main elimination route which, via the kidney, normally amounts to about 90% of the administered lithium. For intestinal lithium excretion an active transport step must be postulated besides the possibility of a cation-selective paracellular transfer across the intestinal epithelia into the faeces. Under normal circumstances approximately 10% of the lithium administered is excreted in this way with the faeces. It must be taken into account that in all cases in which renal excretion capacity is reduced (e.g. in cases of renal insufficiency, in the elderly, etc.) or is not fully developed (e.g. in the postnatal period) a somewhat higher faecal lithium excretion is likely to take place.

Individual differences in absorption processes may contribute to the well-known interindividual variability of lithium bioavailability, and effectiveness, and of the incidence of lithium intoxication.

Although there are a number of different lithium salts, the one most commonly used for oral treatment is lithium carbonate. In principle, the different anions in other salt preparations are without importance for absorption, kinetics, effectiveness and side effects of lithium.

It must be emphasized that lithium accumulation rates, as well as rates of influx and efflux, are distinctly higher in secretory (so-called 'leaky') epithelia (kidney, intestine) than in other tissues, a fact which may have importance for lithium redistribution into the secretory organs.

Gastrointestinal Side Effects

Information about the manner in which lithium is absorbed by the gut at various levels goes some way towards helping to understand the gastrointestinal side-effects with which lithium therapy may sometimes be associated. The systemic effects which lithium produces are likely to be related to, amongst other things, interference by lithium with the binding sites of physiologically important ligands such as sodium, potassium, calcium, magnesium and imitations or inhibition of their effects. Alterations provoked by lithium in the water and electrolyte metabolism of the various organs of the digestive system are shown in *Table 54.1*.

The gastrointestinal side-effects most commonly seen with serum lithium concentrations in the usual therapeutic range and up to about 2 mmol/l are listed in *Table 54.2*, in which it is also indicated which of the side effects are transitory, occurring only in the initial stages, or persistent but harmless, and which of them are prodromal of an impending more general lithium intoxication.

Dr Per Vestergaard of the Psychopharmacology Research Unit of Aarhus University, Denmark reported in 1980 on the incidence of five common side-effects, including thirst and diarrhoea, in 235 patients on long-term treatment. He pointed out that about one in ten of the patients did not complain of side effects, two out of three had one or more complaints and one in four had three and more. Professor Mogens Schou of the same department had found in 1970 that one third of all patients reported mild abdominal discomfort at the beginning and during the first few weeks of treatment, but that none continued to manifest gastrointestinal distress after 1 year of treatment. Gastrointestinal symptoms are seldom encountered in those cases where intoxications have developed during long-term treatment, provided that a recent increase in the dosage has not taken place.

In another study it was reported that out of 21 patients who developed severe intoxications in maintenance treatment two developed gastrointestinal side effects.

The likely explanation of findings such as these is

Table 54.1 *Effect of lithium (serum levels 0.5 – 1 mmol/l) on water and electrolytes in organs and fluids of the gastrointestinal tract: a composite picture based on several selected reports*

Organ/fluid	Changes in Li levels (relative to serum)		Changes in water content or output	Changes in ionic concentration, etc.				Species used in study
	Acute administration	Chronic administration		Na^+	K^+	Ca^{2+}	Other changes	
Serum		–	0[a]	↓[b]	0	↑	Mg↑ Cu↑ Zn↓	man; rat
	–		0	↑	0	–	Cl↑	rat
Saliva	↑	–	↑	↓	↓	↓		man
Gastric	0	–	–	–	–	–	gastric acid↓	rat
Liver	↑	–	0	↑	↑	–		rat
Bile	↑	–	↑	↑	↑	↑	Cl↓ HCO_3↓ pH↓ Osm[c]↓ Bile acids↓	rat
Small intestine								
tissue	↑	–	0	↑	↓	–		rat
faeces	↑	–	0	↓	↑	–		rat
Colon								
tissue	↑	–	0	↑	↓	–		rat
faeces	↑	–	0	↓	↑	–		rat
faeces	–	↑	↓	↓	↓	–	Cl↓ HCO_3↓	rat
Total body	–		↑	↓	↓	↑	Mg↑ PO_4↑ HCO_3↑	man

[a]0 indicates that an effect was looked for, but not found; [b]↑ indicates an increase and ↓ a decrease compared to the corresponding control material (where Li levels are concerned, the comparison is relative to serum lithium levels); [c]Osm indicates osmolarity.

Table 54.2 *Gastrointestinal side effects during lithium treatment*

Symptom	Approximate frequency	Initial, harmless	Persistent, harmless	Prodromal of intoxication	Remarks
Anorexia	x	+	+	–	
Bad taste	x	+	+	–	
Constipation	x	+	+	–	increase after antidepressants
Diarrhoea	xx	+	–	+	slow-release preparations ↑; antidepressants ↓; SLi↓
Dry mouth	x	+	+	–	especially after Li + psychotropics ↑
Dyspepsia	r	+	+	–	
Dysphagia	r	+	+	–	
Haemorrhage, gastrointestinal	r	–	–	+	overdose, SLi ↓
Loose stool	xx	+	+	–	slow-release preparations ↑
Nausea	xx	–	–	+	Li + psychotropics ↓; SLi ↓
Pain, abdominal	x	+	+	–	
Pressure or bloating, epigastric	xx	+	+	–	
Salivation, increased	x	+	–	–	peripheral anticholinergic drugs ↓
Salivary glands enlargement	x	+	+	–	Li discontinuation ↓
Stomatitis	r	+	+	–	Li discontinuation ↓
Ulcer, peptic	r	+	+	–	Li may protect against peptic ulcer
Vomiting	xx	–	–	+	Li overdosage, SLi ↓; water and electrolyte substitution needed

Approximate frequencies are indicated by: xx, very commonly observed; x, relatively commonly seen; r, rarely seen; + yes; –, no; SLi, serum lithium concentration.

that the gastrointestinal side effects, when they occur at all, are indicative of adaptive changes taking place in the digestive tract to the presence of lithium and also to the build up of steady-state tissue levels. Following the initiation of treatment, the unwanted abdominal symptoms which appear seem to be related to the rapidity with which therapeutic serum lithium concentrations are attained. The steeper the rise, the more frequent and severe the gastrointestinal distress. In maintenance treatment, the use of a once-per-day dose leads to the occurrence of periodic rapid rises in serum lithium and to peak values, as well as to very low minimum levels, without a loss of effectiveness, and whilst such a regime may be desirable in terms of the reduced risk which it carries or renal functioning, it is nevertheless necessary to be aware that it may also carry an *increased* risk of gastrointestinal upset. This can be avoided by a number of strategies. In the first place a divided dose regimen may be used in the initial stages of treatment, reverting to a once-a-day schedule when gastrointestinal adaptation may be regarded as having occurred. Secondly, an initial once-a-day regimen may be put back temporarily to a divided dose regimen in those patients who prove susceptible to gastrointestinal symptoms. Thirdly, a once-a-day regime may be instituted *ab initio* using a controlled release preparation which delays the onset of the serum peak, thus resulting in a less rapid rise of serum level. This last procedure has the virtue of simplicity and stands less chance of confusing the patient as to the number of tablets to be taken each day.

Vomiting

The complex set of reactions involved in vomiting is controlled by the central nervous system and its appearance induced by lithium will be preceded by nausea, salivation and related central nervous symptoms. Acute lithium overdosage almost always leads to marked vomiting which has the attendant advantage that stomach contents of lithium are voided so that acute severe toxicity thus produced is rare. In most patients, high serum lithium concentrations are better tolerated following acute ingestion than as a result of cumulative overdose, because of the slow penetration of lithium across the blood–brain barrier into the central nervous system. In maintenance treatment the onset of nausea and vomiting is usually gradual and the manifestations are frequently not apparent until serum concentration is about 2 mmol/l. Persistent vomiting and diarrhoea provoke disorders of water and electrolyte metabolism: sodium depletion, in particular, should be prevented, because it is one of the primary exacerbating causes of lithium intoxication. In the majority of these patients in whom vomiting and diarrhoea occur lithium treatment must usually be discontinued, and water and electrolyte substitution is clinically indicated. Lithium-induced vomiting is poorly controlled by conventional anti-emetics.

Diarrhoea and associated symptoms

About 20% of patients treated with lithium experience diarrhoea, epigastric bloating and pain. Dr S.Bone of the New York State Psychiatric Institute, USA, and also Dr Per Vestergaard of Denmark both reported in 1980 that the incidence of diarrhoea was lower when the patients were taking tricyclic antidepressants concurrently with lithium (*Table 54.3*), suggesting that the anticholinergic constipatory effect of these drugs has an ameliorative influence.

Lithium-induced diarrhoea has been classified into two types: a persistent mild variety, associated with acceptable serum concentrations, and a severe form associated with lithium levels greater than 2 mmol/l. Most problems with this side effect are encountered during initial period of stabilization of the daily dose. Some authors have reported a lower incidence of various side-effects with sustained-release preparations, but if a substantial release of lithium occurs in the distal intestinal tract it results in an increased frequency of troublesome diarrhoea or loose stool: sustained or controlled release properties must be

Table 54.3 *Incidence (in percent) of the gastrointestinal side effects of lithium in relation to mood and presence or absence of concomitant tricyclic antidepressants (TCA)*

Symptom	Euthymic patients		Noneuthymic patients	
	Li (n = 69)	Li + TCA (n = 21)	Li (n = 14)	Li + TCA (n = 23)
Constipation	1.4	28.6[a]	28.6[b]	52.2[b]
Diarrhoea	10.1	14.3	21.4	21.7
Dry mouth	17.4	42.9[a]	14.3	78.3[a]
Nausea	8.7	0	28.6	30.4
Pain, abdominal	2.9	4.8	21.4[b]	17.4
Vomiting	2.9	0	7.3	4.3

[a]In comparison with the corresponding value for Li alone, $p < 0.05$; [b]In comparison with the corresponding value for euthymic patients, $p < 0.05$. Data from Bone,S., Roose,S.P., Dunner,D.L. and Fieve,R.R. (1980) *Am. J. Psychiatry*, **137**, 103–104.

combined with high bioavailability if this is to be avoided.

Both vomiting and diarrhoea can lead to an uncontrolled decrease of lithium absorption rate, because of the conversion of the small intestine and colon from absorbing into predominantly secreting organs. Such a functional change must be regarded as an early indicator of incipient damage to the intestinal epithelia.

Constipation

There is some disagreement in the literature regarding the incidence of constipation amongst patients on lithium therapy. Some reports indicate that it is rare and unimportant, whilst others have characterized constipation as a relatively common effect after taking lithium chronically. As shown in *Table 54.2*, a considerable number of patients questioned reported loose stools during lithium treatment, but most of them considered this rather a relief from previous constipation.

Stomatitis

It is important to remember that, in the case of the more rarely seen reactions (*Table 54.2*), cause and effect relationship have often not been clearly demonstrated, since they derive mostly from single case reports or studies with a very low number of patients. Thus, in the literature only three single case reports have described a non-specific stomatitis due to lithium. What is surprising, however, is that after lithium was discontinued the erosive and ulcerative lesions of the buccal mucosa disappeared, a second trial with lithium producing them again.

Salivation

A relatively frequent side-effect of lithium treatment seems to be dryness of mouth. In a study of 34 patients receiving lithium for up to 5 months, and 32 subjects receiving a placebo, this symptom was found in over 50% of the lithium subjects compared to 20% of the placebo treated subjects. Against this, however, must be set recent claims that in some patients, lithium may lead to increased salivation (sialorrhoea) rather than to a decrease. In a study involving the exact measurement of saliva volume, seven out of eight lithium patients were found to have increased salivation. If this is representative of the general patient population, sialorrhoea cannot really be classified as an unusual side effect. In each case sialorrhoea was associated with salivary gland enlargement and was reversed by lithium discontinuation. The concurrent administration of a peripheral anti-cholinergic drug brought relief from hypersalivation. The gland, however, remained enlarged, and lithium-induced changes in the electrolyte balance of the salivia also persisted (see *Table 54.1*), reflecting a direct effect of lithium on the glands, a phenomenon which is demonstrable in many other secretory organs.

To the extent that lithium does influence salivation, this is not to be regarded as a serious problem and no special treatment measures need to be advocated apart from advising the patient to drink plenty of water (a not unreasonable piece of advice anyway for any lithium-treated patient).

Importance of the Lithium Salt

It has been suggested that the nature of the anion in a lithium preparation may have some implications for the type and degree of gastric side effects. Of questionable value is the procedure advocated by some clinicians of substituting lithium citrate for lithium carbonate in treatment. Although in three patients intolerable gastrointestinal symptomatology was promptly relieved by lithium citrate, an open crossover study in 10 patients failed to confirm these results. The question also arises as to whether or not the daily quantities of lithium carbonate may raise the gastric pH up to values about 11 or more, which may induce irritation of the gastric mucosa with all the consequences which that would entail. However, clinical experience over many years suggests that this is not a problem in either short or long terms.

Are Gastrointestinal Effects Lithium-related?

Dr S.Bone and his colleagues, in an excellent study, reported in 1980, demonstrated a correlation between side-effects of lithium and the mood state in the patients. For 18 different symptoms their results indicated a tendency for patients' perceptions of side effects to vary with mood and with the concurrent use of psychotropic medications. So it is conceivable that some 'side-effects' are actually symptoms of the illness itself, because patients who were depressed or manic complained much more frequently of side effects than those who were euthymic. The results obtained by Dr Bone regarding the tendency of patients to report gastrointestinal side-effects are shown in *Table 54.3*.

Acknowledgement

This work was supported by Project HFR M30 of the Ministerium für Gesundheitswesen der DDR.

Bibliography

Bone,S., Roose,S.P., Dunner,D.L. and Fieve,R.R. (1980) Incidence of side effects in patients on long-term lithium therapy. *Am. J. Psychiatry*, **137**, 103–104.
The authors investigated 18 symptoms, including seven different gastrointestinal side effects, and found that mood and the concomitant use of other psychiatric medications such as antipsychotics and tricyclic antidepressants are positively correlated with the severity of reported side effects.

Schou,M., Baastrup,P.C., Grof,P., Weis,P. and Angst,J. (1970) Pharmacological and clinical problems of lithium prophylaxis. *Br. J. Psychiatry*, **116**, 615–619.
It was found that some of the common gastrointestinal side effects appear during the first weeks of lithium treatment, but they tend to be transitory.

Vestergaard,P., Amdisen,A. and Schou,M. (1980) Clinically significant side effects of lithium treatment. A survey of 237 patients in long-term treatment. *Acta Psychiat. Scand.*, **62**, 193–200.
The authors analysed the incidence of five common side effects (tremor, thirst, weight gain, diarrhoea, oedema) under the treatment regime used in their hospital.

55. Liver

Hans Kröger

Since lithium is eliminated from the body in exactly the same form, and in exactly the same quantity, as it is administered, the issue of its intermediary metabolism does not arise. For this reason, the effects of lithium on the liver have been largely ignored, the liver being the organ which carries a major share of the responsibility for breaking down and detoxifying intermediary metabolites.

However, it may well transpire that the lack of attention paid to the liver during lithium treatment has been a grave error, and that a number of hitherto puzzling aspects of the effects of lithium will be seen to be directly related to actions produced at the level of this organ.

It is clear that lithium enters the liver without difficulty, although one of the few studies on tissue levels of lithium in the liver—a postmortem report on a patient who had taken a fatal overdose of lithium—showed that the liver level (1.35 mmol/l) was appreciably lower than that of serum (1.93 mmol/l).

Direct effects of lithium on liver morphology are rarely reported. In 1983, Drs H.F.Sproat and F.S.Messiha, working in the Texas Tech University Health Sciences Center, Lubbock, Texas, USA, reported that lithium administered to mice resulted in histological changes in the liver, and specifically in variable liver lobular size with reduced cell definition. It is not clear what functional implications such changes might have, whether they are reversible, or whether similar changes might occur in patients receiving lithium treatment.

It is well established that lithium has effects upon a wide variety of enzymes and since the liver is a site of considerable enzyme activity one might reasonably expect to find lithium-related changes in liver enzymes and consequently in the metabolic pathways in which those enzymes are involved. This is indeed the case, though it has to be said that the studies conducted in this area have given rise to results which are highly variable and not always consistent or mutually compatible: this is almost certainly due to the use of different species, dose levels, and durations of lithium administration.

One area in particular where the issue of lithium effects on liver metabolism is of importance concerns the handling by the liver of various administered drugs. For example, after 7 days of lithium treatment in man, plasma levels of chlorpromazine are reduced, a fact which may reflect a stimulation by lithium of chlorpromazine metabolism in the liver. Since it is not unusual for lithium to be administered in combination with other therapeutic agents (haloperidol, tricyclic antidepressants, etc.), findings such as this have obvious practical relevance. It will, however, not be an easy task to make sense of all the varied experimental findings.

Lithium chloride increased the concentration, and prolonged the half-life of methamphetamine in the livers of mice, according to one study, suggesting an interference with methamphetamine detoxification mechanisms.

In man, lithium was found not to stimulate the metabolism of antipyrine or phenytoin, an unexpected finding in view of evidence from animal work that it increased aromatic hydroxylation, *O*-dealkylation and *N*-dealkylation and revealing once more the importance of species differences in this area of research.

The effects of *ad libitum* intake of lithium chloride on mouse liver ethanol aldehyde dehydrogenase were examined and it was reported that ethanol metabolism appeared to be enhanced, though another study claimed that lithium inhibited mitochondrial liver aldehyde dehydrogenase. Clearly this is an area which would repay further investigation.

Lithium is known to decrease the concentration of glycogen in the liver, suggesting an effect on hepatic glucose metabolism, though what the mechanism might be remains unclear: phosphofructokinase, the rate-limiting enzyme in glycolysis, is inhibited by lithium in brain and muscle but not, apparently, in the liver. The interference of lithium with glucose metabolism may help to explain the finding that when lithium was given continuously over a long period to mating pairs of mice, it delayed the postnatal growth and development of the pups, and though internal organs were relatively unaffected the liver was proportionately much reduced.

Recent work carried out at the Robert Koch Institute in Berlin has brought into prominence the far-ranging consequences of lithium effects on liver enzyme systems. Among numerous liver enzymes, one very important one is tyrosine aminotransferase (TAT); this is induced by glucocorticoids, by pancreatic hormones, and by some amino acids (such as tryptophan). The tryptophan induction of TAT appears to involve nicotine adenine dinucleotide (NAD) metabolism and this is important insofar as several psychoactive agents are also known to interfere with NAD metabolism. It was found that lithium induces this TAT in rat liver and that this was almost certainly connected with an alteration of NAD metabolism. It will be some time before the mechanisms of this kind of process can be fully determined, but it is clear that for a better insight into lithium treatment a close study of lithium effects on the liver will be extremely valuable.

Bibliography

Kröger,H. and Grätz,R. (1983) Influence of chlorpromazine, reserpine and lithium carbonate upon the induction of the tyrosine aminotransferase (TAT) in the rat liver. *Gen. Pharmacol.*, **14**, 649–655.

A fair degree of biochemical expertise is required for an understanding of this article. It is important in being one of the few reports concerning an action of lithium on liver-related processes.

56. Teeth

M.E.J.Curzon

A recent study by researchers J.F.Clarke and C.Kies at the University of Nebraska, USA, reported on an adult female who experienced rampant dental decay whilst on lithium therapy for 6 years. Although this study concerned only one subject, which is insufficient for definite conclusions, it nevertheless highlights a problem experienced by many patients on lithium therapy. Why this problem occurs and the relationship of lithium to dental decay has only been considered in recent years.

Trace Elements in Teeth

Trace elements, including lithium, may affect teeth in a number of ways. Lithium could be deposited in tooth enamel during development, could affect the metabolism of bacteria in the mouth, or act as part of the oral environment increasing or decreasing the prevalence of decay. By deposition in tooth enamel the subsequent ability of a tooth to resist dissolution may be affected, with possible consequences for the subsequent resistance of the tooth to decay. Fluoride is known to act by this mechanism, amongst a number of other trace elements. Analysis of tooth enamel for lithium consistently shows low concentrations of the element in teeth from whatever geographic source. The presence of this trace element in teeth has, therefore, prompted a number of researchers to look more carefully at the possible role of lithium on teeth.

Epidemiological Findings

The dental research on the relationship of lithium to dental decay has been going on in several countries. Studies in 1981 by Dr Rudi Schamchula of the Sydney Research Institute, Australia, indicated that children living in communities in South Australia with high lithium levels derived from artesian water, had significantly lower dental decay than a comparable group of children drinking surface or river water, which was significantly low in lithium (*Table 56.1*).

Other studies by the same Australian research group, but carried out in Papua-New Guinea, have also shown a low incidence of dental decay to be associated with

Table 56.1 *Caries prevalence in 10–11-year-old Australian children and in 12–14-year-old Texan children, related to the levels of lithium (Li) and fluoride (F) (mg/ml) in the drinking water; n = number of children examined*

Town	Water supply	Li	F	*n*	Mean number of decayed teeth or surfaces[c] ↓
Australia[a]					
Brewarrina	R	0.0002	0.20	129	3.8
Goodooga	W	0.1321	0.59	52	2.3
Texas[b]					
Farwell	W	0.049	1.9	46	2.9
Hereford	W	0.165	1.5	172	4.7
Wichita Falls	W	0.000	0.6	105	5.3
Lamesa	W	0.039	0.5	106	6.7
Levelland	W	0.039	0.5	127	6.5
Big Spring	W	0.015	0.2	102	6.9
Paducah	W	0.038	0.2	46	7.1

[a]Data from Schamscula,R.G., Cooper,M.H., Agus,M.M. and Un, P.S.H. (1981) *Community Dent. Oral Epidemiol.*, **9**, 27–31.
[b]Data from Curzon,M.E.J., Richardson,D.S. and Featherstone, J.D.B. (1986) *J. Dent. Res.*, **65**, 421–423.
[c]Australian data expressed as teeth affected; Texan data expressed as tooth surfaces affected.

lithium when present in saliva. In this case, the subject population was a tribe of New Guinea natives living mainly on a diet of sago. Analysis of many materials (teeth, saliva, urine, plaque, food, water and soils) revealed that high concentrations of lithium in enamel and saliva were related to low levels of tooth decay. It should be noted, however, that these people were also in the habit of chewing betel nut with lime, which would be full of many other elements also having an effect on decay.

In various parts of the world lithium occurs naturally in water supplies and is often associated with gypsum deposits. One such area is to be found in the Texas panhandle of the USA. Accordingly, following the Australian findings, a further dental study has recently been carried out using various Texas towns with high and low lithium levels (and high and low fluoride) in their water supplies. This project checked the dental decay status of 12–14-year-old children who were life-long residents. The results, as shown in *Table 56.1* revealed no beneficial effect of the lithium at all. Rather, any effect of the fluoride in the drinking water was offset by the lithium. The epidemiological findings on lithium and dental caries in humans are at present only equivocal with no clear causative effect.

Experimental Findings

Animal studies have similarly been unclear, with various studies showing no effect, reduction in decay and even an increase in decay. These various experiments have tried adding lithium to the food, to the drinking water, or have given it by injection. High doses of lithium when given to rats cause problems with salivation leading to an increase in dental decay. Low doses do not seem to give consistent results.

Possible mechanisms

The chemistry of lithium would not suggest any possible effect on tooth enamel. Those other elements that have been shown to affect dental decay, such as strontium or zinc, are generally those that can easily replace calcium in tooth enamel structure. Others, such as fluoride, can easily be fitted into the tooth enamel structure by replacing the -OH group in enamel apatite and so altering the chemistry of the tooth. Lithium is a very small atom and it is not logical that it could affect enamel in the same way. Indeed, being a highly reactive ion, lithium in enamel would not be stable.

Effects on bacteria

However, there is also the possibility that lithium might affect bacteria in the mouth and so indirectly affect dental decay. Nevertheless, Arthur Eisenberg of the Eastman Dental Center, Rochester, New York, USA reviewed all the available information up to 1983 and came to the conclusion that there was no evidence that lithium affects oral bacteria. Although there is a little experimental evidence that lithium could affect bacterial growth it only seems to occur with a few selected strains of oral bacteria under very defined conditions.

Effects on saliva

If, therefore, there is no scientific evidence that lithium affects dental decay on the basis of chemistry, epidemiology, animal or bacterial experiments, why do some people who take or consume large quantities of lithium develop high levels of dental decay? As shown in the diagram (*Figure 56.1*) the human tooth consists of enamel, dentine and cementum held into the jaws by a fibrous periodontal membrane. The crown of the tooth is bathed continually by saliva and at mealtimes

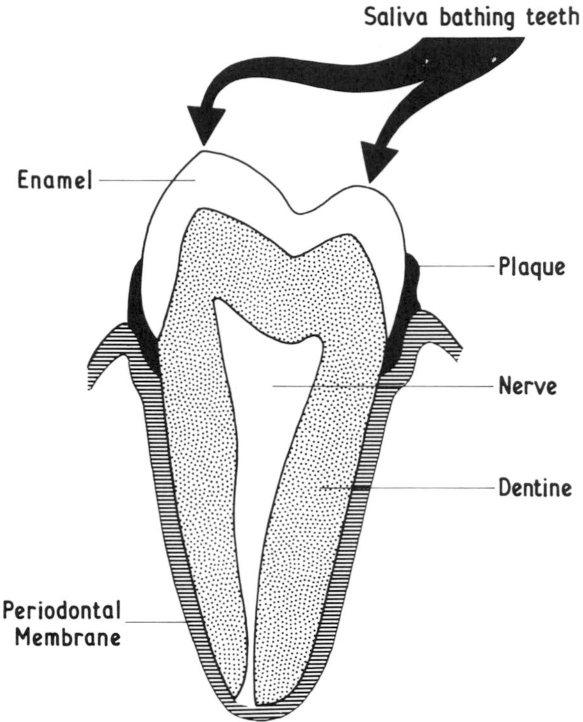

Figure 56.1 Structure of a tooth and its attachment in the jaw bone. Saliva continuously bathes the tooth crown cleaning the tooth and promoting remineralization.

by a slurry of food and saliva. Without saliva the self-cleansing action is lost, with the result that food debris, if containing any fermentable carbohydrates, stagnates around the teeth and a rapid, fulminating, type of dental decay results. Only rigorous oral hygiene with diet counselling can keep such a situation under control.

The effect of lithium on teeth is, therefore, an indirect one by bringing about a change in the natural mechanisms of oral cleansing. As the lithium intake to the body increases, as might occur in lithium therapy, so there comes about an effect on the salivary glands (see also pp. 91–93). The reduced salivary flow is not a sudden but a gradual one. The mouth becomes drier to the extent that the subject eventually complains of the condition, has difficulty eating and generally feels uncomfortable.

With the drying up of the salivary flow it becomes increasingly difficult to keep the teeth clean and to remove food debris. This also means that the antibacterial effect of the saliva, and also its ability to provide remineralization of the tooth surface, is removed. Without the protection of the saliva it is not surprising that cavities start up in teeth within only a few weeks. Part of this protection by the saliva is the provision of calcium and phosphorus ions to the tooth surface. These ions act to remineralize the tooth enamel as it becomes attacked by acids. The 1985 study by Jane Clarke in Nebraska, USA, noted that the metabolism of calcium and phosphorus were changed in her lithium therapy subject. Calcium depletion in saliva by lithium can, therefore, occur. Altered calcium and phosphorus secretion might also change the remineralizing potential of saliva.

Intake of soft drinks

A common reaction to the dry mouth effect of the lithium is to drink more (often sweet) soft drinks. But this habit, while relieving the dry mouth, enhances the increase in tooth decay. Instead of sweet soft drinks, water, sugar-free drinks or saliva substitutes should be used (see also pp. 151–152). The latter are specially formulated to have the slightly thicker consistency of natural saliva and, therefore, to stay in the mouth for a longer period than a drink.

Good dental care is essential and should be sought by anybody having lithium therapy. Visits to a dentist should occur as soon as, if not before, lithium therapy is started. A dentist with a knowledge and understanding of dry mouth, known as xerostomia, will be able to advise various regimes of oral hygiene and diet counselling for alleviating the problems of dry mouth. The routine use of fluoride mouth-rinses under the direction of a dentist will also prevent the rapid dental decay described above.

Concluding Remarks

In summary, therefore, the effect of lithium on the teeth is an indirect one. There is no evidence of any direct effects of the element on tooth structure or on oral bacteria. The major effect of lithium is by a reduction of salivary flow which can be easily offset by good dental care, the use of saliva substitutes and fluoride mouth-rinses.

Bibliography

Clarke,J.F. and Kies,C. (1985) *Nutritional/Dental Implications of Lithium Therapy.* M.S.Thesis, University of Nebraska, Lincoln, Nebraska, USA.

Curzon,M.E.J., Richardson,D.S. and Featherstone,J.D.B. (1986) Dental caries prevalence in Texas schoolchildren using water sup-

plies with high and low lithium and fluoride. *J. Dent. Res.*, **65**, 421–423.
Eisenberg,A.D. (1983) Lithium. In *Trace Elements and Dental Disease*. Curzon,M.E.J. and Cutress,T.W. (eds), John Wright, Bristol, pp. 311–323.
Schamscula,R.G., Cooper,M.H., Agus,H.M. and Un,P.S.H. (1981) Oral health of Australian schoolchildren using surface and Artesian water supplies. *Community Dent. Oral Epidemiol.*, **9**, 27–31.

57. Kidneys and the Fluid Regulatory System

Rowan G.Walker and
Priscilla Kincaid-Smith

Sir Alfred Garrod, the notable British physician who, as early as 1859, had advocated the therapeutic use of lithium carbonate 'in the cases of uric acid diathesis connected with gravel and likewise in chronic gout' (see Section 6, pp. 24–28) also recognized that lithium salts dramatically altered the urine output and caused nocturia; 'salts of lithium appear to be powerful diuretics increasing the flow of urine to an annoying extent, and I have known many instances in which a bottle of lithia water taken at bedtime would cause the patient to be disturbed during the night, whereas the same quantity of soda water would produce no such result'.

Despite noting the increased urine output (polyuria) due to lithium, Garrod nevertheless suggested that the use of lithium salts was quite safe. He also observed many other side effects of lithium and clearly recognized the importance of dosage and the role of the kidneys in the excretion of lithium from the body, reporting that 'in two cases I noted a trembling in one hand produced by this; in both patients there existed kidney mischief; and in the third case slight twitching of the arms occurred when the patient was taking very large doses'.

Occasional reports appeared subsequently in the literature, which hinted at possible kidney involvement in lithium toxicity, such as the finding in 1949 and 1950 of acute lithium intoxication in cardiac patients who were on low sodium diets—hence drawing attention to the importance of sodium in protecting against acute intoxication. It was not, however, until lithium became extensively used as a psychiatric treatment from the late 1950s onward that the issue of nephrotoxicity assumed real importance.

As the lithium ion was shown to be almost entirely excreted by the kidneys (pp. 75–78), the development of acute lithium intoxication was recognized as being usually due to a decrease in the renal elimination of lithium. The renal handling of lithium, the role of the kidneys in acute lithium intoxication and the well-recognized side effect of lithium in producing polyuria, gradually became the focus of increasing attention.

It is of special interest, but perhaps not surprising, that the first reports of chronic nephrotoxic effects of lithium emerged from Denmark and Australia. In these two countries lithium has clearly been used therapeutically for many more years than in any other country in the world. Only in 1969 for instance did the Food and Drug Administration (FDA) in the USA give approval for the use of lithium in psychiatric practice and even then approval was given only for the use of lithium in bipolar affective disorders.

In 1977, Jytte Hestbech and her colleagues in Denmark reported on 14 patients with either acute lithium toxicity and/or severe lithium induced polyuria and first suggested that long-term lithium treatment might also be associated with the development of chronic pathological lesions in the kidneys. The various implications of this finding created much apprehension amongst those physicians prescribing lithium, especially in the face of the widespread use of the drug. The same group of investigators later suggested that between 20% and 26% of patients on stable maintenance lithium therapy for more than 2 years developed a chronic focal interstitial nephropathy. About the same time, a case of progressive renal failure was attributed to lithium therapy.

Renal Effects

The handling of lithium excretion by the kidneys has been dealt with in detail in Section 19, pp. 75–78. This section therefore concentrates on describing the effects of lithium on kidney structure and function.

Polyuria/polydipsia and nephrogenic diabetes insipidus

Since 1876, when Garrod first described the diuretic properties of lithium salts, a wide body of literature has arisen describing symptoms of polyuria (increased urine output) and polydipsia (increased thirst) in patients taking lithium. It is perhaps surprising that at this time the exact incidence of lithium-induced polyuria is unknown although these symptoms are considered common side effects of lithium therapy. Various studies have indicated that the incidence of polyuria probably varies quite widely. The percentage of patients varies from as low as 4% in studies from the UK to as high as 50% in some Scandinavian studies.

Possible mechanisms for the polyuria/polydipsia syndrome in man were postulated between 1955 and the early 1970s. Initially, it was suggested that the polyuria might be due to excessive urinary potassium losses or sodium (solute diuresis) losses. Although it had been documented that both potassium and sodium loss might occur during lithium therapy, these phenomena tended to be transient and unlikely to be sufficient in degree to cause the polyuria. In rare instances, polyuria in patients taking lithium was shown to be due to glucose intolerance (i.e. diabetes mellitus).

In animal studies of acute lithium toxicity there was also a recognition of an increase in urine output. The lithium induced diuresis was gradual in onset and persisted until the pre-terminal phase of acute lithium toxicity, when polyuria and terminal renal failure occurred. Although it was noted in most experiments, that lithium produced a sodium loss, the diuresis observed could not be explained on the basis of an increased sodium excretion alone. The experiments of Mogens Schou in rats, reported in 1958, were particularly important: he noted that the addition of sodium to the rats' diet reduced dramatically the degree of polyuria produced by any dose of lithium even allowing for a slight osmotic diuresis induced by the added sodium. Sodium also protected against the development of acute lithium toxicity.

Despite the possibility that, in some instances, other factors may have influenced the degree of polyuria, the vast majority of patients on lithium therapy who develop polyuria and polydipsia appear to have nephrogenic diabetes insipidus; a disorder of the renal distal tubular cells (collecting ducts and distal portion of the distal convoluted tubule; see pp. 206–213) characterized by an insensitivity to vasopressin.

During the early and mid 1970s, a series of studies documented the inability of polyuric patients on maintenance lithium to concentrate their urine normally, either following water deprivation or after the administration of exogenous vasopressin. All the data confirmed that the origin of the polyuria was likely to be a lithium-induced urinary concentrating defect, i.e. lithium-induced nephrogenic diabetes insipidus. Moreover, there had been no real evidence in man that the polydipsia induced by lithium was of primary pituitary origin (i.e. primary diabetes insipidus due to lack of vasopressin). Patients exhibiting lithium-induced nephrogenic disturbances in water balance, have blood levels of vasopressin which are usually elevated.

The impaired urinary concentrating ability (as had been demonstrated in man) was also shown in animals to be due to an inhibition by lithium of vasopressin responsiveness in the distal portions of the nephron, and further this inhibition was likely to be (at least in part) at the level of vasopressin sensitive adenylcyclase activity. *Figure 57.1* shows the proposed cellular mechanisms of the action of vasopressin in distal tubular cells and the possible sites of lithium inhibition.

Although rats fed lithium were the traditional animal physiological models, much of the information on the mechanisms of lithium impairment of urinary concentrating ability came from the detailed studies on toad hemibladder. The bladder of the amphibian is the equivalent of the mammalian distal tubules. In more recent years, the mechanisms have been further elucidated using isolated rat papillae and micropuncture studies. However, the exact site of lithium interference with the action of vasopressin in the distal nephron remains not entirely clear. Evidence suggests that lithium acts both distal and proximal to the vasopressin-induced generation of adenosine 3′,5′-cyclic adenosine monophosphate (cyclic AMP); cyclic AMP is an important mediator step in the action of many hormones in various organs of the body.

Progressive impairment of urinary concentrating ability

To identify patients with the previously described lithium-induced nephrogenic diabetes insipidus syndrome, polyuria has generally been regarded as the screening test. Although urine volume is largely dependent on distal tubular function, it also varies with the glomerular filtration rate (GFR), with proximal tubular function, solute intake, psychogenic factors and drinking habits. Impaired urinary concentrating ability (demonstrated by fluid deprivation and/or non-responsiveness to the administration of exogenous vasopressin) has therefore been taken as the definitive maker of the distal tubular dysfunction in patients with lithium therapy, although the presence of polyuria is still widely accepted as a screening test of the defect.

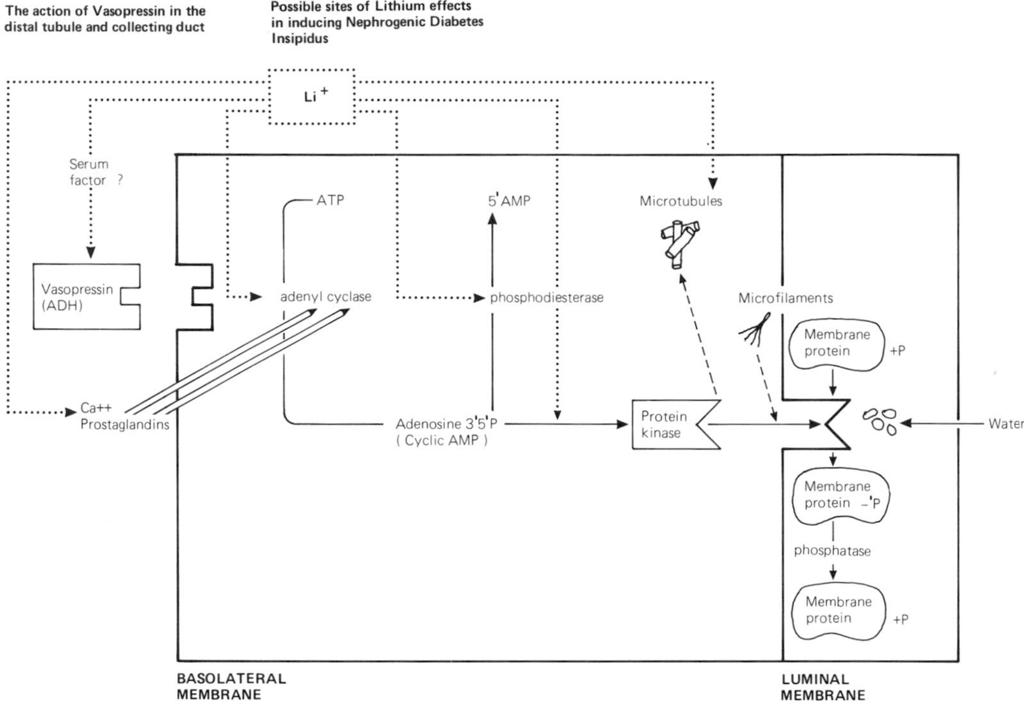

Figure 57.1 Detailed diagram of the action of vasopressin (ADH) in the cells lining the distal nephron (distal convoluted tubule and collecting duct). Note numerous postulated sites at which lithium has been implicated in producing nephrogenic diabetes insipidus.

Prior to 1977, the polyuria (and consequent polydipsia)/impaired urinary concentrating ability/nephrogenic diabetes insipidus syndrome, was regarded as a common side effect of lithium. It was assumed to be a manifestation of the therapy which was likely to be transient and not an indication of lithium toxicity. Numerous authors had commented that there was no evidence that the syndrome was irreversible.

However, between 1977 and 1979, several reports appeared documenting patients with persisting nephrogenic diabetes insipidus from periods of 4–20 months after the last exposure to lithium therapy. In 1978, two Scandinavian workers, Drs G.Bucht and A.Wahlin, first suggested that the impaired urinary concentrating ability in patients on lithium therapy was not always reversible. They demonstrated that defective urinary concentrating ability was present 2 months after discontinuation of lithium therapy and concluded that the demonstrated impaired urinary concentrating capacity indicated irreversible kidney damage rather than the reversible nephrogenic diabetes insipidus-like syndrome. Subsequently a series of publications appeared in the literature showing a correlation between the severity of the defect in urinary concentrating ability and the duration of lithium therapy, thus further suggesting a chronic change in the kidney.

Perhaps one of the most crucial studies addressing the effect of lithium on the kidney was that of Dr Jytte Hestbech and her colleagues in Denmark which was published in 1977. These Scandinavian workers demonstrated a clear correlation between the duration of lithium therapy and impaired urinary concentrating ability in 14 patients who were all on maintenance lithium therapy, but who had previously been either acutely lithium toxic and/or severely polyuric. In the same study, a correlation between urinary concentrating ability and observed renal histological changes (tubular atrophy) was demonstrated. It was the same group of workers who subsequently suggested that up to 26% of patients on maintenance lithium for more than 2 years would develop pathological renal histological changes, (chronic focal interstitial nephropathy) characterized functionally by progressive impairment of urinary concentrating ability.

Impaired distal urinary acidification

Although the defect in distal tubular function (impaired urinary concentrating ability) was the major renal function abnormality demonstrated in patients on lithium therapy, it was not the only lithium-induced functional lesion affecting the distal nephron. Lithium-induced impairment of distal urinary acidification was also documented in man and in animal species from the mid-1970s. As frank acidosis is not present, this distal renal tubular acidosis is regarded as incomplete. Prior to 1977, like impaired urinary concentrating ability, the partial distal tubular-renal acidosis induced by lithium was regarded as reversible.

GFR and proximal tubule function

Reports have appeared in the literature of lithium-induced acute renal failure requiring dialysis. The pathological basis of acute impairment of renal function (GFR) in such cases was thought to be secondary to reversible acute tubular necrosis.

When Jytte Hestbech and her colleagues (1977) described the pathological changes of chronic focal interstitial nephropathy in patients on lithium, marked impairment of GFR was not a feature and reference was made to the disproportionately large degree of renal pathological damage in relation to the relatively well preserved GFR. Although severe impairment of GFR was not present, 50% (seven out of the 14) of the patients studied had rises of serum creatinine (a marker of GFR) of more than 0.3 mg% over the period of lithium treatment.

Between 1977 and 1981, a series of reports (uncontrolled studies) of measurements of GFR in patients on lithium therapy appeared in the literature. Virtually all of these studies confirmed that some impairment in GFR was present in patients on lithium. However, none clearly documented any correlation between the duration of lithium and deterioration in any measurement of GFR. One very important cross-sectional study was that of Dr Gordon Johnson and his colleagues in Sydney, Australia, who showed that impaired GFR in lithium patients correlated with episodes of acute toxicity rather than duration of stable maintenance lithium therapy and in the few controlled studies of renal function that were available over this period, measurements of GFR were shown to be similar between patients on maintenance lithium therapy and other patients with affective psychiatric disorders not on maintenance lithium therapy.

There have been surprisingly few reports of the effect of lithium on GFR in animals. Virtually all studies have been of acute lithium toxicity in which impairment of GFR is likely to be secondary to acute tubular necrosis. There have been virtually no long-term animal studies of lithium effects on GFR.

Studies of urinary enzymes (e.g. *N*-acetyl-β-glucosaminidase and β_2-microglobulin), which are sensitive markers of proximal tubular damage, also have not shown differences between lithium treated patients and other psychiatric patients not treated with lithium, and studies on phosphate handling (proximal tubular function) in patients on lithium also appear to be normal.

Renal histology

Acute changes. The early descriptions of histological lesions in the kidneys associated with lithium therapy came either from necropsy specimens of patients who had died of acute lithium toxicity, or from renal biopsies of patients with lithium-induced acute renal failure. These descriptions frequently included changes in the tubules of the kidneys, but the pathological lesions of the tubules were wide ranging. Flattening of the epithelial cells of the distal tubule, proximal tubular necrosis, poorly differentiated tubular epithelial cells, vacuolation of the cytoplasm, distal convoluted tubules and collecting ducts featuring cellular polymorphism, pyknotic and hyperchromatic nuclei, granular cytoplasm and dysmorphic cells were changes all described in numerous single observations.

The findings of work performed in the Department of Nephrology at the Royal Melbourne Hospital, Australia, have been of some interest. These studies described the presence of ballooning, swelling and vacuolation of the cytoplasm in distal convoluted tubules and collecting ducts. In addition, strands and granules of periodic acid Schiff (PAS) positive staining material were observed in the cytoplasm of these cells of the distal nephron. The ultrastructural description of this lesion confirmed the granules to be composed of glycogen and the swelling of cytoplasm to be an increase in cell water. This type of lesion is thought to be acute and is only identified in patients on lithium. An example is shown in *Figure 57.2*.

That the tubules of the kidney were the principal site of lithium toxicity was also established in early animal studies of acute toxicity, although the histological descriptions were brief. Many of these studies described changes in proximal convoluted tubules but other reports documented changes in the distal tubular cells in cats, rats and dogs. In most of these reports,

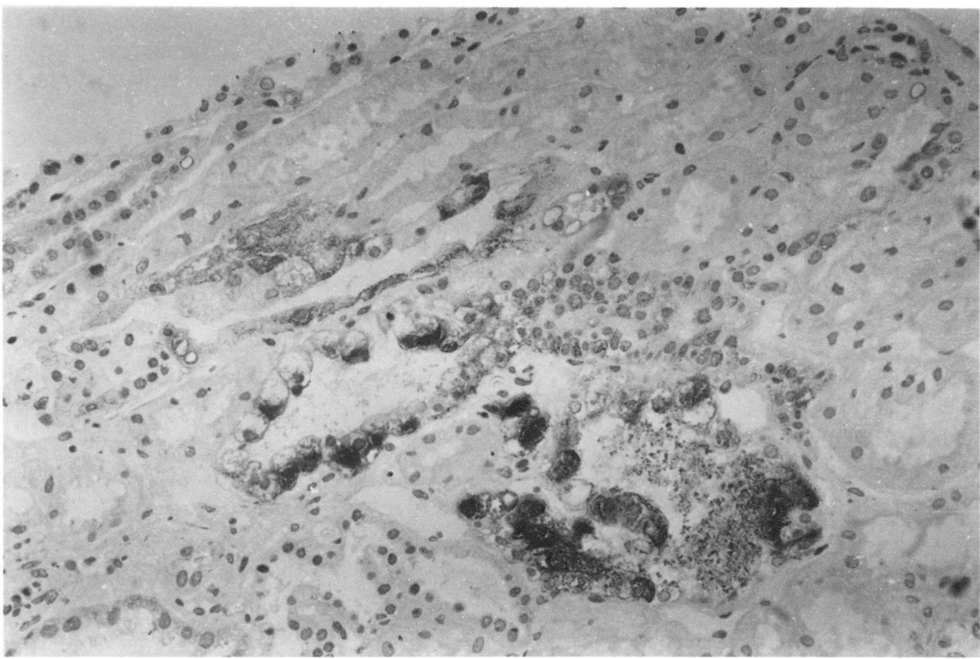

Figure 57.2 Photomicrograph of the acute specific lithium-induced lesion of cells lining the distal convoluted tubules and collecting ducts. Note dark staining (PAS-positive) granular material (glycogen) in the cytoplasm of the cells. Note also clear fluid-filled areas in the cells (vacuoles). The patient had been on lithium for 6 years and had had a recent episode of acute lithium toxicity although this lesion may be clearly seen in all patients on maintenance lithium. (PAS ×400).

the changes in the distal tubules were degenerative but other descriptions included dilatation of the distal nephron and flattening of distal tubular epithelial cells.

Chronic changes. Very few of the early histological descriptions contained evidence of chronic lesions, and indeed the first suggestion that lithium caused chronic progressive lesions of the kidney again came from the study of Jytte Hestbech and her colleagues in 1977. They described tubular atrophy, focal fibrosis and glomerular sclerosis (focal interstitial nephropathy) in 14 patients who had been on maintenance lithium therapy for more than 1 year, but in whom the renal biopsies had been undertaken in the study because of the presence of either acute lithium toxicity or because of severe impairment of urinary concentrating ability. These histological changes were quantitated and shown to be significantly greater than those observed in age-matched renal biopsy material obtained from renal cadaveric donors or from autopsy specimens. In a later study, Jytte Hestbech's co-workers noted that 50% of the renal biopsies also exhibited microcysts.

Hestbech and her co-workers concluded that impaired urinary concentrating ability should not, therefore, be regarded as a harmless condition in patients on maintenance lithium but rather as an indication of underlying lithium-induced chronic focal interstitial nephropathy. The same group later stated that up to 26% of patients on maintenance lithium for more than 2 years develop a chronic focal interstitial nephropathy characterized histologically by interstitial fibrosis and tubular atrophy (*Figure 57.3*). Amongst renal biopsies, 40% will show cystic formation (microcysts) in the cortex. These histological changes can be identified clinically by marked impairment of urinary concentrating ability which is progressive with the duration of lithium therapy.

Since the Scandinavian studies of 1977–1979, a number of other cross-sectional histological studies in patients on lithium therapy have been undertaken in centres around the world. Virtually all record the findings of non-specific chronic histological changes of varying degree similar to those described by Hestbech and her colleagues. As with renal function studies, renal biopsy findings of lithium-treated patients have been reported by most groups as part of cross-sectional

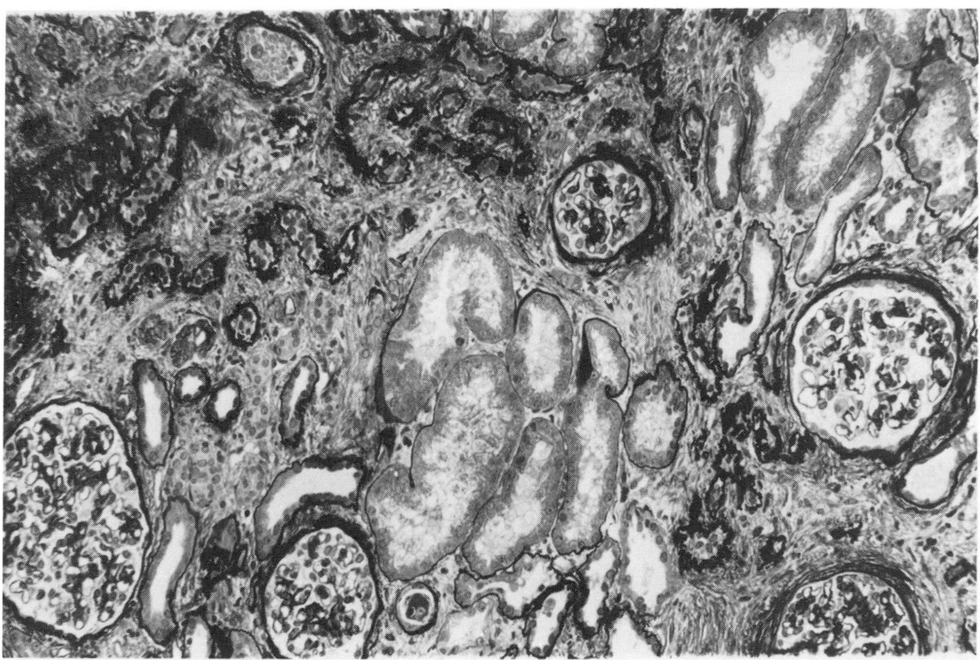

Figure 57.3 An area of focal interstitial nephropathy featuring particularly tubular atrophy and interstitial fibrosis (upper left). Note normal tubules (centre and upper right) and normal glomeruli. The patient had been on maintenance lithium for approximately 11 years with a history of more than one episode of acute lithium toxicity. (SM/MT ×200).

studies and either no controlled biopsies have been used or inappropriate controls have been used. Perhaps the most striking exception to this is again the work provided by the research group at the Royal Melbourne Hospital, Australia, which has used controlled renal biopsy material from other psychiatric patients not treated with lithium. The histological studies were completed just before commencing the patients on long-term lithium therapy. These studies have shown that the non-specific histological changes which were present in the patients taking lithium were also present in renal biopsies for other psychiatric patients never treated with lithium. This clearly has implications for defining the precise role of lithium in inducing chronic renal damage. However, one change that was clearly different between the lithium- and non-lithium-treated patients was the presence of distal tubular dilatation and microcyst formation.

There have been remarkably few long-term studies of lithium-induced nephrotoxicity in animals. In rats treated with lithium for periods of up to 4 months, histological changes were again evident at the level of the distal tubule, with distal tubule dilatation and epithelial cell flattening being prominent. In Scandinavian animal studies, early focal fibrosis and leucocyte infiltrations were also observed. A recent Australian long-term study in rabbits has confirmed that lithium in high doses produces the changes of focal interstitial nephropathy, distal tubular dilatation (*Figure 57.4*) and the distinctive glycogen-containing lesion in the distal nephron cells similar to that described in man.

Further interest has subsequently been focused on the dilatation of tubules in the distal nephron in animals, as this was considered to be the most consistent finding in the longer-term histological studies, particularly in rats. During the early 1980s the Scandinavian and American animal studies had suggested that the dilatation of the distal convoluted tubules was likely to be due to proliferation of tubular epithelial cells rather than just a consequence of lithium-induced polyuria. It was proposed that the proliferation of these cells made them unusually sensitive to the toxic effects of lithium. Subsequent cellular damage might lead to focal nephron and tubular atrophy and eventually focal interstitial fibrosis, i.e. those changes that had been identified in man as being due to maintenance long-term lithium. Others have suggested that distal tubular dilatation (microcysts)

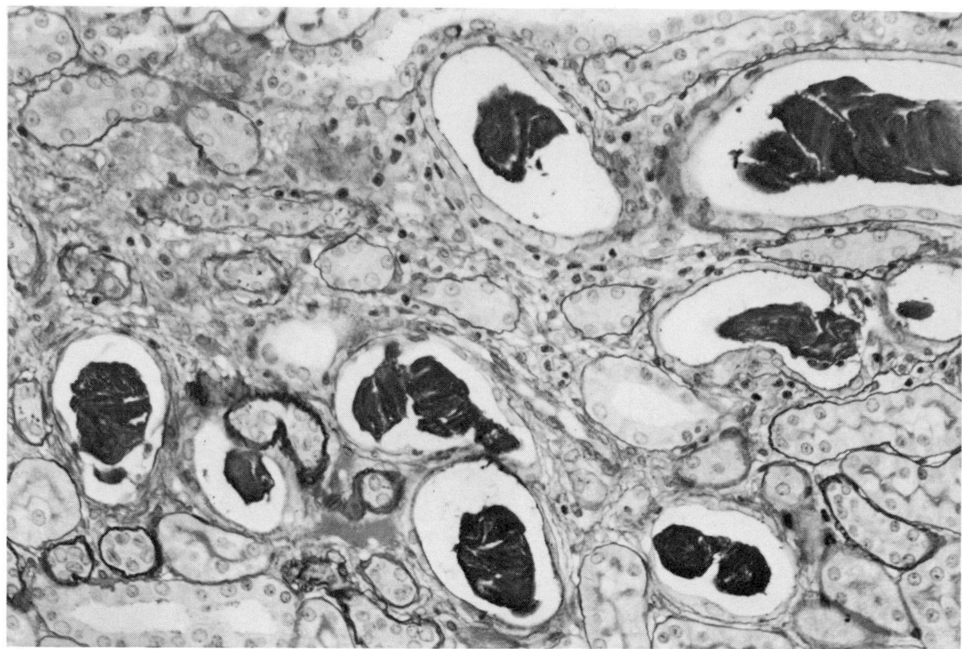

Figure 57.4 Dilated distal tubule from a rabbit given lithium in the diet for 3 months. Note amorphous material (PAS-positive staining) forming casts in the lumens of affected tubules. Note also that the cells lining the dilated tubules tend to be flattened. (PAS ×200).

may be secondary to tubular obstruction due either to cellular swelling or to cellular/proteinacious debris (casts) in the lumens of the tubules.

Some animal studies, particularly those from Scandinavia, have suggested that lithium given in constant dosage rather than single daily dosage accentuates these histological lesions in the kidneys. This has been used as an argument for single daily dosage rather than divided dosage in man. This aspect of maintenance lithium therapy remains highly controversial, particularly between UK and Scandinavian centres.

Concluding Remarks

In most animal species and man, lithium has been shown to be capable of causing major disturbance of water balance manifested as polyuria and polydipsia. These symptoms are associated with decreased urinary concentrating ability and are explained by a nephrogenic diabetes insipidus-like syndrome with disturbed responsiveness of the distal nephron tubule and collecting duct to the action of vasopressin. More specifically lithium appears to interfere with the action of the enzyme adenyl-cyclase and/or cyclic AMP produced in response to vasopressin-stimulated activity of adenyl cyclase. An additional effect of lithium in the distal tubule is to cause a partial distal tubular acidosis. Most of these effects are reversible on cessation of lithium therapy.

During acute lithium toxicity in animals, acute renal insufficiency (impairment of GFR) has been observed. There has been virtually no long-term study of the effects of maintenance lithium on GFR in animals. There have also been no long-term studies in man in which any observed histological changes can be related to progressive impairment of GFR. Impairment of GFR is, by and large, not a feature of stable long-term lithium therapy.

Short-term studies in animals indicate that a likely site of lithium toxicity showing histological changes is the renal distal tubule. Acute lithium toxicity studies have produced a wide range of tubular abnormalities. Longer term studies (up to 4 months) indicate that distal tubule dilatation is a consistent finding in most species given lithium. However, the clear development of chronic lesions (focal interstitial nephropathy) has only recently been established, but with doses and blood levels which would be considered to be in the 'toxic' range in man.

In man, non-specific histological lesions have been identified in patients particularly with a past history of acute lithium toxicity, but similar lesions have been identified in patients prior to lithium therapy. Distal tubular dilatation (microcysts) is a feature of lithium-treated patients' renal biopsies compared with other biopsy material and a highly distinctive lesion of the distal nephron cells, characterized by swelling and the accumulation of glycogen, has been identified only in lithium-treated patients. The precise relationship of these histological lesions to each other remains obscure.

Patients on long-term maintenance lithium therapy appear to be susceptible to the development of progressive impairment of urinary concentrating ability but this is most noticeable in patients with a history of acute lithium toxicity. The risk of acute lithium toxicity is increased in patients with extra-renal and renal losses of salt and water (e.g. impaired urinary concentrating ability). However, the risk of renal damage and impaired GFR appears to be extremely small in patients on stable maintenance lithium therapy without prior episodes of acute lithium intoxication. The minimal risk of renal damage should probably be compared to the risks of discontinuation of maintenance lithium therapy in patients with severe unipolar and bipolar affective disorders.

As suggested clinical guidelines, prior to commencement of lithium therapy it is appropriate to measure basic renal function (serum creatinine, blood urea, creatinine clearance) and to perform ward testing of the urine and urine microscopy to determine the presence of pre-existing renal disease. Patients with renal impairment (impairment of GFR) can be treated with lithium but the dose needs to be reduced in relation to the GFR. During lithium treatment, patients can be monitored by estimating urine volume (every 6 months) and renal function (serum creatinine and/or creatinine clearance, 12 monthly). Patients exhibiting polyuria/polydipsia and nocturia should be followed with great care. These symptoms should in the first instance be treated with reduction in lithium dosage aiming for lowest plasma lithium concentrations that have been shown to be normally effective — i.e. 0.4–0.6 mmol/l, and certainly below 0.8 mmol/l. It should be remembered that the avoidance of episodes of acute lithium toxicity is the most important factor in the long term preservation of renal structure and function.

Bibliography

Hansen,H.E. (1981) Renal toxicity of lithium. *Drugs*, **22**, 461–476.

A very useful overview of the area of renal toxicity, as it was known up to 1981; it remains relevant today.

Hestbech,J., Hansen,H.E., Amdisen,A. and Olsen,S. (1977) Chronic renal lesions following long-term treatment with lithium. *Kidney Int.*, **12**, 205–213.

This is well worth reading, primarily for its historical interest as one of the first reports of long-term renal lesions resulting from lithium therapy.

Johnson,G.F.S., Hunt,G.E., Duggin,G.G., Horvath,J.S. and Tiller, D.J. (1984) Renal function and lithium treatment: initial and follow-up tests in manic-depressive patients. *J. Affect. Dis.*, **6**, 249–263.

Acute renal toxic effects are compared in this report with effects appearing after long-term maintenance treatment.

Walker,R.G., Escott,M., Birchall,I., Dowling,J.P. and Kincaid-Smith,P. (1986) Chronic progressive renal lesions induced by lithium. *Kidney Int.*, **29**, 875–881.

Animal work has been particularly important in this area of research, and this paper gives details of the results of animal experiments. It is the most up-to-date account currently available.

58. Heart and Blood Vessels

Catherine A.Martin,
Lesley R.Dickson and Chien-Suu Kuo

The Cardiovascular System

In *Figure 58.1* the main features of the conduction mechanism of the heart are illustrated. The sinoatrial (SA) node is a group of specialized heart muscle cells which initiate the heartbeat: it represents the natural pacemaker. Impulses arising from this node spread out through both the atria, causing atrial contraction and eventually reach the atrioventricular (AV) node, another specialized group of cardiac cells which then spread the excitation throughout the muscular walls of the ventricle via the common bundle of His and the right and left bundle branches. Any effects of lithium upon the mechanisms of conduction may reveal themselves as changes in the electrical activity (and hence rhythm) of the heart.

The spread of electrical impulses through the conduction system and chambers of the heart is monitored by the electrocardiogram (ECG). The main features of the ECG are shown in *Figure 58.2*. The P wave reflects the depolarization of atria (the spread of the

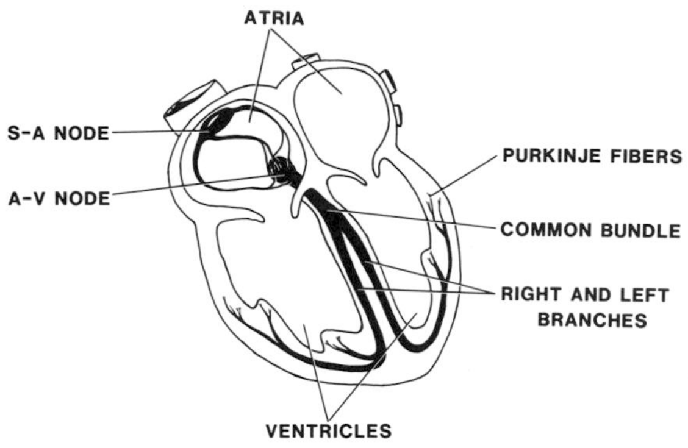

Figure 58.1 Anatomy of the cardiac conduction system.

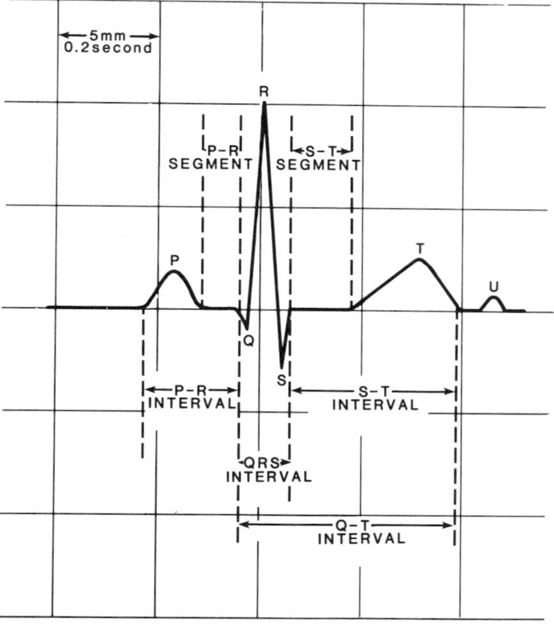

Figure 58.2 Main features of the electrocardiogram (ECG).

electrical impulse through the atria). The P–R interval is measured from the beginning of the P wave to the beginning of the QRS complex. This represents the time for the electrical impulse to travel from the SA node through the atrium, AV node, His bundle and bundle branches to the terminal branch of the Purkinje network. The QRS complex represents the spread of the electrical impulse through the ventricular muscle. The ST segment is the relatively isoelectric portion of the ECG between the end of the QRS complex and the beginning T wave. The T wave represents the recovery, or return to the resting state, of the ventricles.

Therapeutic Lithium Levels

In view of the fact that lithium has been in common use for manic-depressive illness since 1970 by many patients, including those who have other health problems and use other medications, it is remarkable that there have been so few reported cardiac difficulties. However, the following abnormalities have been noted in the medical literature.

Effects on the sinoatrial node

Several cases of abnormalities of conduction through the sinoatrial node have been described [see *Figure 58.3*(A)]. These include sinus node arrhythmias and block (sick sinus syndrome). Clinical manifestations have included dizziness, fainting, paroxysmal tachycardia (rapid heart rate) and shortness of breath on exertion. However, many patients have had no symptoms. It is important to note that several patients with these difficulties had other physical illnesses including thyroid abnormalities, coronary-artery disease and diphtheria in the past. It is thought that sinus node dysfunction may be secondary to a combination effect of lithium and a vulnerable conduction system. The sinus node abnormalities completely resolve after discontinuation of medication.

Effects on the atrio-ventricular node

Several cases of first degree AV block or slowing of the electrical conduction through the AV node have been noted with some authors reporting frequencies of near 40% [see *Figure 58.3*(B)]. Many of these patients were on other medications that could have had an additive effect on the conduction rate. For example, several patients were on antidepressants and/or major tranquilizers which could lead to a susceptibility to slowing of conduction through the AV node. One patient was on hydrochlorothiazide which may enhance the lithium–potassium shift in the cardiac cells and make the heart more vulnerable to lithium's effect on cardiac conduction. None of these patients had any clinical manifestations of the block.

Effects on the ventricle and His-Purkinje system

In 1979, Dr A.G.Tilkian and his associates reported a study in which they followed the ongoing electrocardiograms (ECGs) of 12 patients before and after starting on lithium. Some of these patients had pre-

A. **Sinus node arrythmias and block**

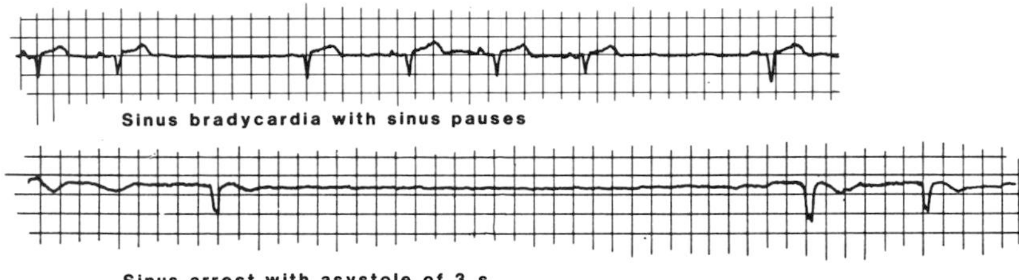

B. **First degree A-V block**

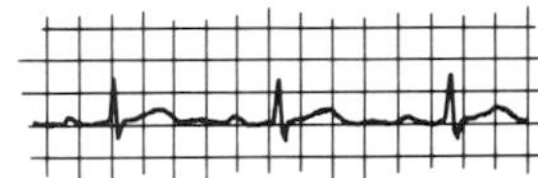

Figure 58.3 Supraventricular abnormalities.

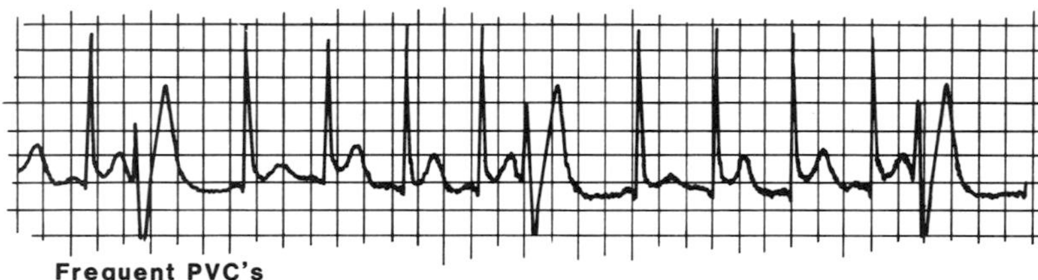

Figure 58.4 Ventricular abnormalities.

A. Before lithium **B. During lithium**

T wave flattening and inversion, small u waves

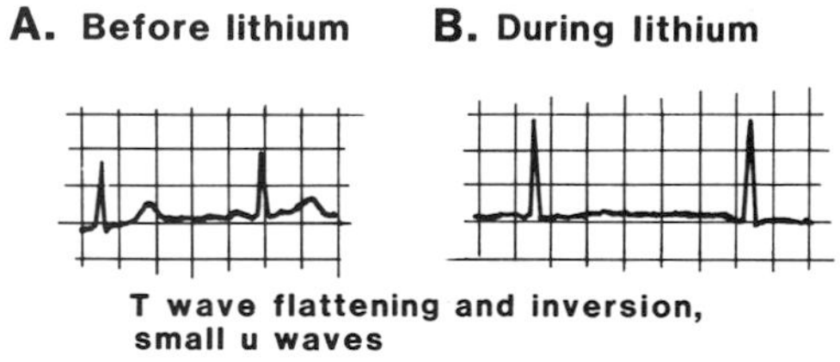

Figure 58.5 Repolarization abnormalities, showing T-wave flattening and inversion, and small U-waves.

existing heart disease. One patient had no ventricular arrhythmias and five had rare premature ventricular contractions (PVCs) and had no change when lithium was given. Five patients had frequent premature ventricular contractions (see *Figure 58.4*) and when lithium was started two had more frequent PVCs, two had no change and one had fewer PVCs. Some patients had complex ventricular arrhythmias and lithium had no effect on their frequency. No patients had any change in their symptoms while on lithium.

Only one case has ever been reported of multiple premature ventricular contractions, and that concerned a middle-aged man on lithium who presented with chest discomfort.

T-wave changes

The most commonly seen cardiovascular effect of lithium is T-wave notching, flattening or inversion (see *Figure 58.5*). This occurs in as many as 13–100% of any group of patients on lithium. There are no clinical symptoms related to these changes and they frequently disappear on continued medication and are reversible after drug withdrawal. T-wave changes may be potentiated by other psychotropic medications such as tricyclic antidepressants or neuroleptics.

Myocarditis

There is one reported case of myocarditis following therapeutic doses of lithium. This case was complicated by the fact that the patient also was hypothyroid and was simultaneously taking an antidepressant. A discussion of lithium effects on cardiac muscle is given in Section 64, pp. 236–239.

Clinical Guidelines at Therapeutic Levels

Because the frequency for cardiac-related difficulties is so low, there are very few restrictions on the use of lithium. However, as with any medication, a cautious approach is wise and the following guidelines are recommended.

Before starting lithium a standard evaluation of the patient's cardiac status should be obtained. The history and the physical and laboratory evaluations should focus on difficulties that may reveal the patient to be at increased risk for cardiac difficulties with lithium. Particular attention should be made to a history of cardiac difficulties and the use of diuretics and anticholinergic medication (antidepressants and neuroleptics). A baseline ECG, thyroid functions and potassium level and renal functions should be obtained (see pp. 59–62).

If a patient is in good health and no risk factors are identified it may be prudent to monitor the ECG on a periodic basis, perhaps yearly.

If risk factors are identified they should be dealt with in the following ways.

(i) If a patient's cardiac disease compromises the ability of the kidney to clear lithium, as in the case of heart failure, salt restriction or long-term diuretic use, lithium should be used cautiously with very frequent monitoring of lithium blood levels. It may be advisable to begin treatment in an inpatient setting. Outpatient follow-up with a check being kept on serum lithium levels should occur every few months.

(ii) Clinicians must be sensitive to the possibility that a normal serum potassium level may not truly reflect a normal cardiac cell potassium. Lithium may displace intracellular potassium thereby causing an intracellular depletion not accurately reflected in serum potassium level. However,this depletion is likely to be detected by the ECG. If the patient's ECG shows hypokalaemia changes, including generalized T-flattening and prominent U waves, obviously lithium and potassium levels should be obtained. Lithium dose and potassium supplement should be modified to obtain low normal lithium levels and upper normal potassium levels. Since hypokalaemia prolongs repolarization, the patient is at increased risk for ectopic beats and supraventricular and ventricular arrhythmias. If the ECG changes do not improve, the lithium should be discontinued for several months.

(iii) Frequent ECG monitoring is recommended in patients with ventricular arrhythmias or sinus node dysfunctions. Lithium should be started in low doses and gradually increased with frequent monitoring of lithium levels, pulse rate and cardiac symptoms. Ambulatory monitoring on a periodic basis in addition to intermittent standard ECGs is advisable. Treatment should begin in an inpatient setting. If arrhythmias do occur, the physician should consider: (a) discontinuing the lithium and initiating alternative treatment; (b) continuing lithium at lower serum levels; (c) continuing lithium with concurrent use of anti-arrhythmics; or (d) if lithium is the only effective treatment, then a pacemaker should be considered.

(iv) If patients on lithium present with the symptoms of palpitations, dizziness, fainting or breathlessness an ECG should be obtained. These symptoms may be intermittent, so care must be taken not simply to look for psychological explanations.

(v) In follow-up visits questions about palpitations and dizziness should be asked. The pulse should be monitored routinely.

(vi) Patients over 60 and on lithium for more than a year are at increased risk for ECG abnormalities and should receive more careful monitoring.

(vii) The following medications interact with lithium to produce cardiac effects and special guidelines are recommended.

Diuretics. Diuretics which deplete sodium and potassium such as thiazide, ethacrynic acid and furosemide contribute to lithium retention and increase the risk of cardiac intracellular potassium depletion. They should be used cautiously with lithium. When on such medication a minimal lithium dose should be started and gradually increased while frequent lithium levels are obtained. Frequent potassium levels and ECGs should be obtained to monitor cardiac hypokalaemia. Since there is some evidence that lithium levels are not affected by potassium sparing diuretics such as spironolactone and triamterene they may be preferable in the patient on lithium. A fuller discussion of lithium diuretic interactions is presented elsewhere (Section 49, pp. 180–183).

Hydroxyzine. Hydroxyzine reportedly potentiates the effect of lithium on cardiac repolarization and may precipitate cardiovascular toxicity. These medications should not be used simultaneously.

Methyldopa. Lithium toxicity has occurred with the simultaneous use of lithium and methyldopa. This combination should be avoided.

Tricyclic antidepressants. Tricyclic antidepressants can have the following cardiac effects: sinus tachycardia, atrioventricular blocks, intraventricular conduction disturbance, ventricular tachyarrhythmia, reduced contractility, and non-specific changes of repolarization. Since lithium potentially has similar toxicity, an additive effect may be possible (although this is not documented in the scientific literature). It may be prudent to be particularly alert to potential cardiac difficulties in patients on both tricyclics and lithium.

Toxic Lithium Levels

In contrast to therapeutic doses, lithium doses giving serum levels in excess of 1.5 mmol/l may have serious and potentially lethal cardiac effects. The following cardiovascular effects following toxic lithium levels have been reported (see *Figure 58.6*).

There have been a few reports of patients who developed sinus bradycardia, sinus arrhythmia or sinoatrial block on toxic lithium levels. The patients usually had symptoms of confusion, dizziness or fainting spells. One case was complicated by low potassium and another by the use of a neuroleptic. All abnormalities returned to normal following elimination of lithium.

Atrioventricular block with a junctional rhythm has been reported in a patient with a lithium level of 2.15 mmol/l and potassium of 2.5 mmol/l (normal = 3.5–5.4 mmol/l). This patient had symptoms of a heart attack and later fainting spells and required a pacemaker as bradyarrhythmias persisted.

Bundle branch block, ventricular tachycardia and ventricular fibrillation at toxic lithium levels have also been reported. Patients have presented with symptoms of confusion or fainting spells. The compromised neurological status had the biggest impact on the patient's symptoms. Those who survived the intoxication reverted to normal rhythms. However, ventricular fibrillation can also be part of the cardiovascular collapse at the terminal stage of fatal intoxication.

Other changes in ECG at toxic levels are similar to those of therapeutic levels and consist primarily of ST segment depression and T-wave flattening or inversion.

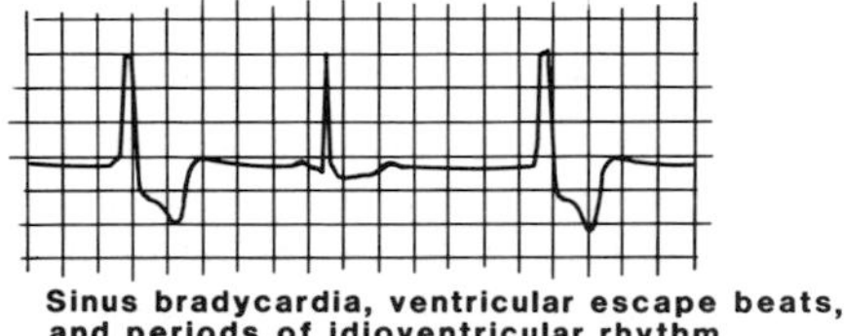

Figure 58.6 ECG abnormalities associated with toxic lithium levels.

There have been reports of myocarditis and heart failure in association with lithium intoxication, but some cases were complicated by hypothyroidism, low potassium or pre-existing heart disease.

In summary, toxic lithium levels lead to sick sinus syndrome, atrioventricular block, and potentially fatal ventricular arrythmias and myocarditis.

Clinical Guidelines at Toxic Lithium Levels

(i) Continuous monitoring of cardiac function should follow a serious episode of lithium intoxication. This should be done in an intensive care setting where fluid status can be monitored and dialysis initiated if necessary.

(ii) Lithium levels need to be monitored closely, as should sodium and potassium. Deficiencies such as low potassium need to be corrected and one needs to be aware that there may be shifts in potassium levels as the lithium level drops.

(iii) Evaluation of medications that could contribute to high lithium levels should be made and changes to alternatives considered.

(iv) Since the arrhythmias usually resolve as the lithium level falls to therapeutic levels and below, it will seldom be necessary to institute anti-arrhythmics.

Blood Pressure

The impact of lithium on blood pressure is not clear. One report, in 1985, stated that patients receiving lithium had lower blood pressures than the general population. What the patients' blood pressure was before lithium was started was not reported. In 1986, a large study (377 patients) by Drs Per Vestergaard and Mogens Schou of Aarhus University, Denmark, reported that neither diastolic nor systolic blood pressure was influenced by lithium treatment. It is interesting to note that Drs Vestergaard and Schou found that before lithium treatment patients had slightly lower blood pressure in the spring and autumn than in the winter and summer. On lithium these variations disappeared.

Further research is needed on the impact of lithium on blood pressure. However, it does appear that lithium does not have any adverse effects on blood pressure. Blood pressure should be monitored periodically. The main area of caution would be those patients who are on diuretics for hypertension.

Bibliography

Albrecht,J.W. and Muller-Oerlinghausen,B. (1980) Cardiovascular side-effects of lithium. In *Handbook of Lithium Therapy*. Johnson, F.N. (ed.), University Park Press, Baltimore, pp. 323–337.

Jefferson,J.W. and Greist,J.H. (1979) The cardiovascular effects and toxicity of lithium. In *Psychopharmacology Update: New and Neglected Areas*. David,J.M. (ed.), Grune and Stratton, New York, pp. 65–79.

The above two accounts are thorough reviews written primarily for the professional.

Jefferson,J.W., Greist,J.H. and Ackerman,D.L. (1983) *Lithium Encyclopedia for Clinical Practice*. American Psychiatric Press, Washington, DC, pp. 74–75, and 85–86.

A condensed and simplified account for the professional and sophisticated layman.

Tilkian,A.G., Schroeder,J.S., Kao,J.J. and Holtgren,N. (1976) The cardiovascular effects of lithium in man: review of the literature. *Am. J. Med.*, **61**, 665–670.

Another detailed review intended for the professional.

59. Blood

Rudra Prakash

The effects of lithium on blood were first reported in 1950. It is noteworthy that effects of lithium have been investigated more extensively on white blood cells (WBCs) than on any other constituents of the blood. It is equally true that beneficial effects of lithium on blood are much better known than the detrimental ones.

White Blood Cells

The WBC category includes granulocytes (neutrophils, eosinophils, basophils), lymphocytes and monocytes. With the exception of basophils, all WBCs are affected by lithium to a variable degree. An increase in WBC count occurs during both short- and long-term lithium therapy, though the long term effects may not be consistent or striking. A peak elevation of WBCs is usually seen after 1 week of lithium treatment. Though under experimental conditions outside the human body a rise in WBC count correlates positively with the lithium level, such a relationship has not been seen *in vivo* in clinical investigations. Indeed, in a recent case report, a stimulatory effective of lithium on WBCs was observed only at low lithium concentrations and the effect was reversed at higher levels of lithium. Age, sex and psychiatric diagnosis also do not appear to affect the WBC count.

The magnitude of increase in the WBC count induced by lithium is variable; a 30–45% rise is not infrequently seen. An increased WBC count is usually a reversible effect, a return to pre-treatment values occurs following 1–2 weeks of cessation of lithium therapy. These effects of lithium may be offset by those drugs which tend to reduce the WBC count (such as phenothiazines and carbamazepine). Recently, lithium has been used concomitantly with carbamazepine in order not only to potentiate the efficacy of treatment but also to offset any potential adverse effects of carbamazepine on WBCs.

The effects of lithium on other types of WBCs are less uniform. For example, a decrease, an increase, and a lack of change in the counts of eosinophils, monocytes and lymphocytes have been reported on different occasions. The mechanism by which lithium increases WBC count is incompletely understood. Several speculative explanations have, however, been offered: a facilitatory effect of lithium on colony stimulating factor (CSF) production; an inhibiting effect of lithium on cyclic AMP and suppressor T-lymphocytes; or a direct effect on granulocyte precursor or pluripotential stem cells (an increased production of granulocytes does actually occur; the effect is not due simply to a redistribution of the granulocyte pool).

The implications of the above findings are promising due mainly to the predictable and reversible nature of their occurrence. Thus, in 1974, researchers began to explore the usefulness of lithium in the treatment of blood disorders characterized by abnormally low WBC count (such as Felty's syndrome and blood changes caused by chemotherapy of leukaemia and cancer — due to the low WBC count, these patients are prone to developing infection and fever). Earlier investigations produced more encouraging results than later ones and a therapeutic or preventive role of lithium therapy in blood disorders has yet to be established. There is growing evidence that while lithium salts increase WBC count, the ability of WBC to fight against bacteria is compromised. It has also been suggested that lithium is more effective in raising WBC count in malignant diseases other than leukaemia; it must, however, be noted that, in non-leukaemic conditions, the initial WBC count may be normal with unaffected bone marrow.

Due to the predictable nature of its effects on WBCs, a lithium stimulation test has been used. A lack of response of WBC count to lithium dosing may represent a portentous sign, suggesting the possibility of an underlying blood disorder. Concern about the substantial risk of side effects of lithium in these cases has, of late, been expressed rather explicitly; the adverse effects which may attend lithium therapy may not make it as suitable an adjunctive treatment in blood disorders as was once hoped.

Another issue concerning lithium effects is whether the proliferation of WBCs may go unrestricted so as to induce leukaemia. This seems to be suggested by some ten or so anecdotal reports. Although in a study of 791 subjects treated with lithium, Drs Beverley Norton and Lawrence Whalley of the Royal Edinburgh Hospital, UK, reported only 33 deaths, with leukaemia not being overrepresented as a cause of death, it may nevertheless be wise, if only from legal, clinical and heuristic standpoints, to examine the complete blood count before, and periodically after, the initiation of lithium treatment.

Red Blood Cells

Unlike WBCs, red cells are not clinically affected by lithium salts. There have, however, been two case reports of anaemia. In 1973, Dr M.Z.Hussain and associates of Victoria Union Hospital, Prince Albert, Saskatchewan, Canada, reported the death of a 50-year-old woman as a result of aplastic anaemia, a rare type of blood disorder characterized by decreased or lack of production of various types of blood cells. In addition to lithium, the deceased had, however, received imipramine and thioridazine. It must be emphasized that the latter drugs may also cause similar blood disorder. Later, in 1981, from King George's Medical College, Lucknow, India, a report appeared of another case, this time of a different type of anaemia. The patient, then a 40-year-old man, developed anaemia secondary to folic acid deficiency following 5 months of treatment with lithium. His anaemia was, however, reversible and recurred whenever lithium was reinstituted.

It has been suggested that in the presence of lithium salts, granulocytes release vitamin (folic acid and B12) binding proteins. Theoretically, the release of these

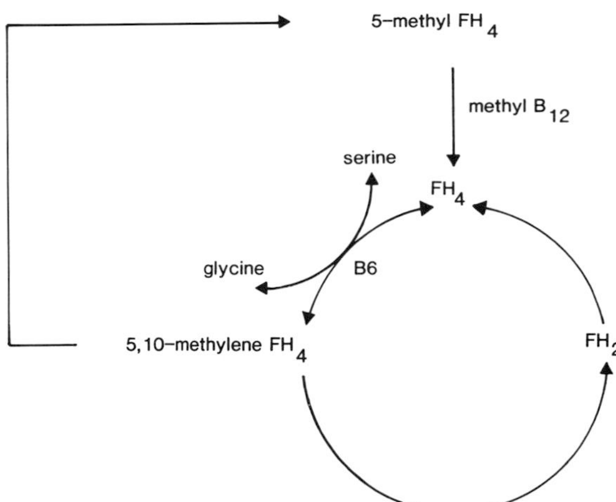

Figure 59.1 Metabolic interrelationship between vitamin B12 and folic acid. FH2, dihydrofolate; H4, tetrahydrofolate; B6, pyridoxine.

proteins could entrap the two vitamins, and thus render them unavailable for the production of blood. That lithium may affect the metabolism of folic acid is also indirectly suggested by the observation that the concentration of glycine, an inhibitory neurotransmitter, rises during lithium therapy. As illustrated in *Figure 59.1*, since folic acid deficiency, not necessarily of a clinical severity and caused by entrapping of binders released following lithium treatment, may block the conversion of glycine into serine, it may lead to accumulation of glycine. These assumptions are yet to be validated.

Platelets

There is a growing body of evidence that lithium increases platelet count (thrombocytosis). It has been speculated that lithium brings about this effect through its action on pluripotential stem cells or progenitor cells committed to megakaryocytic differentiation. The preliminary findings are encouraging, and further investigations are clearly indicated in order to exploit lithium to therapeutic advantage in bleeding disorders characterized by abnormally low platelet counts. As in conditions with low WBC counts, the toxicity of lithium may limit its use in bleeding disorders.

Concluding Remarks

The use of lithium in conjunction with anti-cancer

treatment may have a limited role in restoring WBC count. Similar effects on platelets warrant further investigations. That lithium may induce leukaemia is as yet unestablished, and the rare cases of anaemia in association of lithium treatment which have been reported may have had aetiologies unrelated to lithium. While both mental health professionals and patients must be aware of the effects of lithium therapy on blood, the rare nature of the more serious and potentially harmful ones cannot be overemphasized. It may, nevertheless, be prudent to evaluate complete blood count before, and periodically after, the commencement of lithium therapy.

Acknowledgement

Thanks are due to Drs R.S.Stein and Thomas A.Ban for their critical comments and suggestions.

Bibliography

Mant,M.J., Akabutu,J.J. and Herbert,A. (1986) Lithium carbonate therapy in severe Felty's syndrome: benefits, toxicity and granulocyte function. *Arch. Int. Med.*, **146**, 277–280.
A recent report of a clinical trial from University of Alberta, Edmonton, Canada. A useful reading for rheumatologists, haematologists and oncologists.

Prakash,R. (1985) A review of the hematologic side effects of lithium. *Hosp. Commun. Psychiatry*, **36**, 127–128.
A brief review for mental health professionals and paraprofessionals.

Rossof,A.H. and Robinson,W.A. (1980) *Lithium Effects on Granulopoiesis and Immune Function*. Plenum Press, New York.
A useful compilation of various papers presented at an international workshop on the effects of lithium on the haematopoietic and immune systems.

60. Hormone Systems

D.H.Myers and T.E.T.West

The endocrine glands comprise groups of cells whose function is to regulate other cells. Their regulatory products, hormones, have bloodborne access to every body cell, but an individual hormone will only affect those which bear specific receptors for it. The anatomical positions of the major endocrine glands are illustrated in *Figure 60.1* and their hormones, together

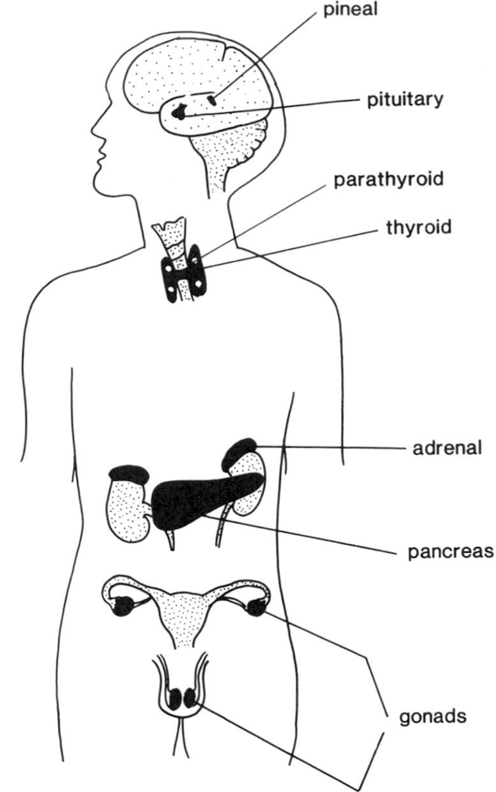

Figure 60.1 Position of endocrine glands discussed.

with accepted abbreviations, listed in *Table 60.1*. Lithium affects most of these glands, either directly or indirectly, though the clinical consequences vary considerably from one gland to another.

The Thyroid Gland

Thyroid hormones

The thyroid gland produces two hormones, T4 and T3, which stimulate metabolic processes in many tissues. Both contain a trace element, iodine, as an essential ingredient. The vagaries of iodine supply have undoubtedly been an important feature in the evolution of thyroid physiology. In particular, the thyroid is very efficient at trapping iodine from the blood, contains a large store of ready-made hormone (as thyroglobulin), and is capable in times of iodine deficiency of enormous compensatory enlargement, that is, of goitre formation.

Table 60.1 *Endocrine glands mentioned in the text*

Gland	Hormones	Abbreviation	Function
Thyroid	Thyroxine	T4[a]	See text
	Triiodothyronine	T3[a]	See text
Parathyroid	Parathyroid hormone	PTH	See text
Adrenal cortex	Cortisol		See text
	Aldosterone		
Testes	Testosterone		Stimulates growth of male sex organs and development of secondary sexual characteristics
Anterior pituitary	Growth hormone		Stimulates growth
	Prolactin		Stimulates female breast to manufacture milk
	Thyroid stimulating hormone (thyrotrophic hormone)	TSH	See text
	Adrenocorticotrophic hormone	ACTH	Stimulates adrenal cortex to manufacture and secrete cortisol
	Luteinizing hormone	LH	Stimulates testes to secrete testosterone and ovaries to secrete female hormones
Pancreas: islets of Langerhans	Insulin		Reduces blood glucose (liver output reduced; muscle, fat cell entry stimulated). Fat protein synthesis stimulated
Pineal	Melatonin		Function in man still speculative
Hypothalamus	Thyrotropin releasing hormone	TRH	Stimulates anterior pituitary to secrete TSH

[a]T4 and T3 refer to the total quantities of the respective hormones in the blood. FT4 and FT3 are used to refer to the concentrations of free hormone, i.e. to the fractions not bound to plasma protein.

T4 and T3 are released into the blood from the thyroglobulin store by the pituitary hormone TSH which, providentially, also stimulates the thyroid to make hormone to replenish the stock. The concentration of T4/3 in the blood is essentially self-regulating; thus a fall stimulates the pituitary to secrete more TSH but this effect is cancelled when the consequent rise in T4/T3 reaches a pre-determined value. When T4/T3 production falls, whether through thyroid disease or dietary iodine deficiency, the pituitary strives to restore the status quo by a continuously increased secretion of TSH. When thus stimulated, the thyroid enlarges to form a goitre. If, however, this compensatory measure is insufficient, or if thyroid disease is too advanced for it to occur at all, then not enough T4/3 is produced to meet the needs of the tissues, and a state called hypothyroidism results. In its fully developed form the features of hypothyroidism are dry skin, hoarse voice, hair loss, slow pulse rate, physical and mental sluggishness, constipation, excessive sensitivity to cold and puffiness around the eyes, and exceptionally, an organic psychosyndrome. Milder degrees of hypothyroidism present a less distinctive picture of malaise and mental dullness. The diagnosis is confirmed by finding low plasma concentrations of T4 and T3 (or of FT4 and FT3), accompanied by a high value of TSH if the gland itself has failed, but a low value if the failure is secondary to destruction of the pituitary gland.

Some disorders cause T4/3 to be secreted in excessive quantities. This excess, or hyperthyroidism, leads to weight loss, tremor, sweating, a rapid pulse, nervousness and irritability.

Lithium-induced Thyroid Effects

There is a small risk that patients taking lithium in therapeutic doses will develop clinical goitre, hypothyroidism or, rarely, both. The actual size of this risk is difficult to ascertain and we have to rely, for second best, on published prevalence figures. These range for hypothyroidism from 0% to 23%, but this wide variation is more apparent than real. It arises partly because investigators have not been able to compare like with like, have ascertained hypothyroidism in different ways, and have used differing criteria for diagnosing it. In addition, the samples studied have been small, and a small sample gives only a rough estimate of prevalence in the parent population. Nevertheless, it is reasonable to conclude from the prevalence data that the risk, although small, is definitely above the endemic one, and requires a number of precautionary measures referred to later.

Subtle changes in thyroid function are seen even in patients who do not develop thyroid disorder. After 4 months on lithium, there is a small but detectable fall in T4 (which remains nevertheless within the euthyroid range), accompanied by a rise in TSH; after a year, T4 is restored completely, and TSH almost, to their original values.

Collectively, these findings indicate that T4 secretion is slightly decreased by lithium but then restored by the self-regulating mechanism described earlier. The actual means by which lithium temporarily decreases T4/3 secretion is not yet clear, though there are many suggestions in the research literature. There is evidence that it impedes the release of hormone from the gland, and possibly also its manufacture.

Vulnerability of the thyroid to lithium

That, ordinarily, lithium has such a mild effect suggests that those who develop thyroid disorder must in some way be vulnerable. Autoimmune atrophic thyroiditis is now thought to be one important predisposing factor. This condition is characterized by an infiltration of the thyroid gland with lymphocytes, and by the circulation in the blood of antibodies to thyroid gland constituents — notably to cellular microsomes and to thyroglobulin. Some people so affected remain well, but others gradually become hypothyroid through an insidious destruction of the gland. The study of Dr W.M.Tunbridge and colleagues on a typical English urban community enables the course of the disorder to be pieced together. They showed that thyroid antibodies are fairly common in the adult population — 9% overall, and 12.7% in women — but that their frequency rises steeply in women after the age of 45. People with antibodies alone, or raised TSH values alone, showed no particular tendency to become hypothyroid in the following 4 years, but those with both these features became hypothyroid at the rate of 5% per annum. In this last group, women outnumbered men three to one. It is therefore clear that, on all counts, women over 40 are the group most susceptible to significant autoimmune thyroiditis. They, and more generally anyone with circulating thyroid antibodies, have an increased risk of becoming hypothyroid when treated with lithium. Before leaving the topic of antibodies, it should be mentioned that their link with lithium is a little less simple than at first supposed. On present evidence, lithium has no hand in causing autoimmune thyroiditis, but it may increase (and at other times possibly decrease) the rate of autoantibody formation, but is not known in this way to damage the thyroid.

As might be expected, the risk of lithium precipitating hypothyroidism is increased if the gland has already been partially destroyed for therapeutic reasons. Surgical removal is sometimes used to treat euthyroid goitre and hyperthyroidism; the radioactive isotope ^{131}I, which selectively destroys thyroid tissue, is sometimes used to treat hyperthyroidism.

Lithium and goitre

The other effect of lithium on the thyroid is to induce clinical goitre. Although the prevalence of this effect is low, the risk is definitely above the endemic one. Goitre is traditionally associated with diets deficient in iodine and used to occur, in the days before dietary iodine supplements, in the mountainous and glacier-swept regions of the world, whose soil contains little iodine. That reports of the highest prevalence of lithium-associated goitre come from two such regions — Bavaria and South Island, New Zealand — suggests complicity between lithium and iodine deficiency. However, Mogens Schou and his colleagues' original observation of lithium-induced goitre was made in Copenhagen, a maritime city where the diet is not notably iodine deficient, and with an endemic goitre rate estimated in women 28 years earlier as only 1.1%.

The reason why a minority of patients respond to lithium by goitre formation, and the role of dietary iodine in the process, is still a mystery. Fortunately, to quote Schou, 'Goitre is not a frequent side effect of lithium; nor a serious one'. Goitre induced in the fetus when a mother takes lithium is more serious and may cause death by asphyxiation. Although exceptionally rare — fewer than four cases have been reported — it adds to other congenital malformations, a compelling reason for avoiding lithium during pregnancy.

Precautions

Thyroid function should be assessed before lithium is started in any patient with goitre or previous thyroid disorder, and on all patients at regular intervals thereafter: a yearly FT4 or T4 (twice in the first year) is probably the minimum reasonable precaution. If the FT4 is borderline low, then a TSH estimation will resolve the uncertainty, values above 6 mU/l indicating that the thyroid is struggling. If the FT4 is definitely low, then a TSH estimation is still called for to exclude hypothyroidism secondary to pituitary failure which, although not caused by lithium, is nevertheless a rare naturally occurring endocrine disorder.

If a patient develops hypothyroidism or goitre while on lithium, one of two steps can be taken. Lithium can be stopped if its therapeutic value for that particular patient is in doubt. Early goitre and lithium-induced hypothyroidism are both reversible; the rare reports of permanent hypothyroidism are probably instances of the naturally occurring disorder. If stopping lithium is thought to be undesirable, the patient should be treated with T4. T4 reduces TSH secretion, thus allowing an early goitre to subside. When treating thyroid failure, it is a matter of judgement whether patients whose T4 is borderline low should be treated. If the TSH is above 35 mU/l, then it is probably better to do so. It is known that many of those whose TSH values lie between 6 and 35 mU/l do eventually overcome the effect of lithium and TSH values fall, but unless it is feasible to monitor thyroid function frequently, it is probably best to be safe and treat. It is possible for the patient on T4 therapy to be slightly undertreated yet have normal serum T4 values. It is, therefore, worth monitoring such treatment by estimating TSH, undertreatment being revealed by raised values.

Paradoxically, iodide in high doses inhibits the thyroid gland. This effect is only temporary if the thyroid is normal but may persist and induce hypothyroidism in patients taking lithium or with autoimmune thyroid disease; such patients should therefore avoid iodide-containing expectorants and cough mixtures.

There are reports of hyperthyroidism occurring in lithium treated patients. They are so rare (24 in all) as to suggest that the association is basically one of coincidence. It is likely, nevertheless, that lithium, with its complex effects on thyroid biochemistry and immunology, does influence the course of naturally occurring hyperthyroidism. The clinical importance of this association is that hyperthyroidism can precipitate mania and can itself be mistaken for an attack of mania.

The Parathyroid Glands

The concentration of plasma calcium (Ca) is, like the concentration of T4/T3, effectively self-regulating. A fall stimulates the parathyroid glands to secrete parathyroid hormone (PTH). PTH arrests and reverses the fall by liberating Ca from bone, by decreasing its loss through the kidney and, indirectly, by increasing its absorption from the gut. When consequently plasma Ca rises, PTH secretion is switched off at a predetermined value referred to as the 'set point'.

Clinical hyperparathyroidism results from the secretion of inappropriately large quantities of PTH. The consequences are severe: weakening of bone, damage to the kidneys, the deposition of stones in the urinary ducts and bladder, and a rise of Ca in the plasma to toxic levels. In recent years, extensive use of automated serum Ca estimation has revealed a mild variant of hyperparathyroidism taking the form of a slightly raised serum calcium and of PTH but without clinical evidence of disease. Some people with this condition, referred to as 'biochemical hyperparathyroidism', eventually develop the serious form of the disorder but others remain well.

Lithium-induced parathyroid effects

Information about the possible effects of lithium on parathyroid activity has come from two sources. Firstly, systematic investigation of unselected, but usually small, samples of patients have shown that lithium does cause a rise in serum PTH and calcium, together with a reduction in urinary calcium loss, findings which suggest primary parathyroid overactivity. However, the mean value of serum PTH, although raised, nevertheless remains within the physiological range, and the rise of serum calcium is similarly slight (1.8%, if protein adjusted). It is doubtful whether the term 'hyperparathyroidism', traditionally used to describe a severe illness, is entirely appropriate for these mild effects, and the more neutral term 'increased parathyroid activity' is probably more suitable. Dr E.M.Brown, using bovine parathyroid cells in tissue culture, found that lithium raised the set point at which calcium inhibited PTH secretion, and Drs F.Shen and D.J.Sherrard believe the same to be true for the human parathyroid: their elegant demonstration of a raised set point is, however, based on a single case study — perhaps too slight a basis to support any general conclusion.

The second source of information about the possible effect of lithium on parathyroid activity comes from a small special group of patients who have presented with hypercalcaemia while being treated with lithium. In fact, this group is so small — some twenty patients in all — as to suggest that its members are the minority who would have developed hyperparathyroidism anyway. The least presumptive view, therefore, is that lithium does not cause clinical hyperparathyroidism, but influences its course.

Lithium effect on hyperparathyroidism

There are two ways in which lithium might affect the course of hyperparathyroidism. Firstly, Dr T.M.Murray and colleagues have found that the pathologically overactive gland tissue associated with clinical hyperparathyroidism does have a raised set point. It might be, therefore, that lithium exacerbates this inherent set point defect. Such would happen (to make a speculative point) if lithium interfered with the ability of calcium to operate the defective 'PTH off' switches of the abnormal parathyroid tissue.

Secondly, lithium might magnify the effects of raised serum calcium levels. Those discovered by chance aside, many of the reported cases of lithium-associated hyperparathyroidism have presented with calcium neurotoxicity rather than with the later manifestations of the disorder such as bone disease, stones and renal damage. Chemically, lithium and calcium are very similar, and both are neurotoxic above critical blood concentrations, so it is possible that lithium reduces the threshold of calcium neurotoxicity.

Calcium and lithium toxicity have other features in common, such as thirst, polyuria, anorexia, nausea and, in extreme cases, vomiting. It would, therefore, be prudent to estimate serum calcium whenever a patient appears to be lithium intoxicated, to be suffering from an organic psychosyndrome, or to be showing any departure from their previous pattern of affective disturbance.

Hyperparathyroidism, once diagnosed, should be managed in the conventional way. Early operative removal of overactive parathyroid tissue is called for in severe cases, with careful follow up in those who have 'biochemical hyperparathyroidism'. Stopping lithium temporarily may cause the serum calcium to fall, disclosing a truer picture of the degree of intrinsic hyperparathyroidism; in mild cases, stopping it permanently may be the only definitive measure required.

The Adrenal Cortex

The two principal hormones of the adrenal cortex are aldosterone and cortisol. Lithium influences aldosterone secretion by its effect on the kidney, a topic discussed elsewhere (see Section 57, pp. 206–213).

Cortisol is secreted in response to a wide range of stressful stimuli. It provokes a breakdown of tissue protein to its constituent amino acids which are then rebuilt by the liver into protein and glucose. It is suspected that, by this means, protein of a type which is temporarily expendable is sacrificed, in times of stress, to make indispensable protein and fuel.

Some depressed patients have a raised plasma cortisol which then falls on recovery. Recovery from depression is thought to be the explanation for the decline in plasma cortisol seen in patients treated with lithium long-term. In aiding that recovery, lithium can be said to have an effect on cortisol secretion. Whether it also has direct effects is unclear. In high doses, it increases plasma cortisol, as do many other stresses. Reports on its short-term effects using therapeutic doses are scattered and inconsistent, but the best study failed to detect any at all.

The Testes

The testes secrete the male hormone, testosterone. One preliminary study, occasionally quoted, found that seven out of a group of ten patients treated with lithium had low plasma testosterone, but gave too little information to allow any conclusion as to the cause. A more comprehensive study on 16–24-year-olds failed to find any fall in plasma testosterone during the 13-week period of lithium treatment. There was, however, a slight but significant rise in the plasma concentration of the pituitary hormone LH (luteinizing hormone), leading to the suggestion that lithium might initially decrease plasma testosterone to an extent too small to be detected by assay, but sufficient to evoke a compensatory rise in pituitary LH secretion.

The Pituitary Gland

The pituitary gland lies at the base of the brain, and is divided into anterior and posterior portions. The posterior pituitary secretes a hormone, vasopressin, which stimulates the kidney to retain water, and which lithium may render less effective (see Section 57, pp. 206–213).

The anterior pituitary manufactures six hormones, five of which are listed in *Table 60.1*. Their secretion is controlled by a number of substances produced by the hypothalamus; those whose chemical identities are known are called 'releasing hormones'; the others are referred to as 'releasing factors'.

The effects of lithium on the anterior pituitary are far too small to endanger health. It has already been noted that, when lithium decreases the output of T4/3, the pituitary responds appropriately by secreting TSH, a secretion which can become quite brisk when the appropriate releasing hormone, TRH, is given intravenously. In addition (although here the information is sparse) the pituitary probably responds to a minute, lithium-induced decrease in blood testosterone concentration by a compensatory increase in LH secretion.

A wish to discover how lithium works, rather than concern about its safety, has motivated most of the studies of its effect on the pituitary. Their rationale, although intricate, starts from a simple assumption: that lithium acts at the site of the fault which underlies affective disorder. That site is thought by some (but doubts are growing) to be somewhere in the brain's network of monoaminergic neurones. These neurones are not accessible to direct study, but a group of them influences growth hormone and prolactin secretion. It is hoped, therefore, that the effect of lithium on the secretion of these two hormones might offer a fundamental, although indirect, insight into its mode of action. Such an expectation apart, there is an established link between affective disorder and pituitary function: dexamethasone, a synthetic corticosteroid, normally suppresses the pituitary secretion of ACTH, but fails to do so completely in some depressed patients. This dexamethasone suppression test has been used in an attempt to probe the nature of the relationship between affective disorder and lithium treatment, but results have so far been variable and difficult to interpret in any simple fashion.

In order to magnify the very mild effects of lithium on the pituitary, investigators have provoked the gland to increase its secretion artificially. Thus a group in Canada have used insulin hypoglycaemia to stimulate the secretion of growth hormone and prolactin. They find that lithium suppresses this provocative effect in manic depressive patients in remission, but does not do so in healthy controls.

The drug clonidine also increases growth hormone secretion. It does so by stimulating a particular type of monoaminergic receptor (the α_2-adrenergic postsynaptic receptor). A group in Italy find that lithium inhibits clonidine-provoked growth hormone secretion, from which they infer that it blocks α_2-receptors. Investigations of this type which appear to be breaking fresh ground need careful and extensive confirmation.

Obesity and Diabetes Mellitus

Patients treated with lithium often gain weight and a few become markedly obese (see Section 53, pp. 195–196). Part of the weight gain may be no more than restoration of weight lost during many previous manic-depressive relapses. Slaking the thirst, which is sometimes a side effect of lithium, with sweetened drinks is occasionally responsible (pp. 151–152). Stimulation of brain appetite centres and a direct effect on glucose metabolism have also been considered, more tentatively, as contributory factors.

Interest in the effect of lithium on glucose metabolism dates from 1924, well before the modern era of its use in psychiatry. It was originally claimed to be mildly beneficial in diabetes mellitus. Lithium enhances glucose uptake from the blood into muscle and brain, and in these respects resembles insulin, a resemblance which, given the complex and subtle properties of insulin, is probably only superficial. The widespread use of lithium in psychiatry has focused attention on the contrary possibility, that it might precipitate diabetes mellitus. Cases of diabetes mellitus developing in patients treated with lithium have been reported, but are probably instances of the naturally occurring disorder: the majority have been obese, middle-aged women, a group particularly prone to diabetes mellitus. Some presented with polyuria and thirst, a reminder that these symptoms should not be dismissed as a side effect of lithium unless the possibility of diabetes mellitus has been excluded.

Although knowledge of the effects of lithium on glucose metabolism is fragmentary and inconsistent, it is clear that those effects are small; they do not amount to a reason for avoiding lithium either in patients who already have diabetes mellitus or who develop it during the course of treatment.

The Pineal

The human pineal gland manufactures and stores several substances known to have a potent effect on other cells, though it has not been shown to secrete these substances in large enough quantities to have any significant physiological effect, and their presence may merely be a vestige of an ancestral endocrine function. The pineal interests psychiatrists because it contains a substance, melatonin, whose secretion varies with the season of the year and the time of day. Some affective symptoms likewise vary, though the resemblance may, of course, be purely accidental. A Swedish group reports that low nocturnal melatonin secretion is a marker for severe depressive illness, an important claim which needs confirmation. In rats, lithium delays the surge of melatonin secretion which normally occurs after dark. In man, it delays the decline normally seen with the coming of day. Whether these findings will help to elucidate the therapeutic effect of lithium remains to be seen.

Conclusion and Summary

The only known adverse effects of lithium on the endocrine glands are hypothyroidism and goitre: both are uncommon, easily detected and easily remedied. Lithium may complicate the presentation and possibly influence the course of naturally occurring endocrine disorders, namely of diabetes mellitus, hyperthyroidism and hyperparathyroidism. A number of investigations using sensitive assays and ingenious techniques take us beyond these familiar landmarks of clinical medicine. Lithium has been shown to have measurable, but small and sometimes contradictory, effects on a number of endocrine systems. But these systems, being part of a complex organism, are influenced by a host of other factors which cannot always be controlled or measured or, if the study is small-scale, given their full, representative scope. Together, therefore, such studies comprise not a comprehensive view but a set of snap-shots; it is reassuring, nevertheless, that they have probed so far beyond the clinical domain without revealing anything untoward.

Bibliography

Guyton,A.C. (1986) *Textbook of Medical Physiology* (7th edition). W.B.Saunders, London.
A clear, comprehensive account of the endocrine system, which does not require prior medical knowledge is to be found in this well-known text book.

Emerson,D.H., Dyson,W.L. and Utiger,R.D. (1973) Serum thyrotropin and thyroxine concentrations in patients receiving lithium carbonate. *J. Clin. Endocrinol. Metab.*, **36**, 338–346.
An account of an early prospective study of lithium and its thyroidal effects.

Smigan,L., Wahlin,A., Jacobsson,L. and von Knorring,L. (1984) Lithium therapy and thyroid function tests, *Neuropsychobiology*, **11**, 39–43.
Another of the few prospective studies of the effect of lithium on thyroid function, this article gives the clearest insight into the response of the thyroid to lithium.

Wilson,J.D. and Foster,D.W. (eds) (1985) *Williams' Textbook of Endocrinology* (7th edition). W.B.Saunders, London, UK.
An exhaustive, authoritative account, suitable for medically qualified readers, is given of disorders of the endocrine glands.

61. The Immune System

Freddie Ann Hoffman and
Philip A.Pizzo

Lithium salts are known to alter the immune system in both animals and man. Granulocytosis is a well-described side effect of chronic lithium therapy, but less well recognized are the effects of lithium on the lymphocyte and other aspects of immune function (*Table 61.1*). These effects may have important consequences for patients on chronic lithium therapy.

Types of Immune Mechanism

The immune system is a dual system which protects the body against foreign pathogens and malignant transformation of cells. This system is comprised of humoral and cellular components (see *Figure 61.1*). The cellular components of the immune system are derived from stem cells which arise from the yolk sac and reside successively in the fetal liver and then the bone marrow. Hormones and growth factors cause proliferation and differentiation of the stem cells into lymphocytes, monocytes and macrophages, granulocytes and erythrocytes. Immature lymphocytes subsequently travel either to the thymus gland, where they are further differentiated into T-cells (thymus-derived), or to the lymphoid tissue of the gastrointestinal tract (bursal equivalent), where they are differentiated into B-cells. The T- and B-cells when exposed to antigens, either in the form of foreign pathogens or foreign tissues, react to confer specific immunity against the antigenic stimulus.

Cell-mediated immunity is comprised of T-cells and the phagocytic cells. When stimulated by antigens, T-

Table 61.1 *Effects of lithium on the immune system*

Element of immune system	Effect	Element of immune system	Effect
Lympoid tissues		*Lymphocyte function*	
Thymus gland	Involution	Proliferation of T-cells by mitogens (lectins, alloantigens, etc.)	Increased
Lymphocytes		Proliferation of B-cells by mitogens	Somewhat increased
Peripheral blood		Natural killer cell activity	Enhanced
T-cells	No effect on number	Interferon inducers (e.g. poly I:C)	No increase in NK activity
B-cells	No effect on number	*Granulocytes*	
T-suppressor cell	Decreased function	Peripheral blood granulocytes	Increased
Lymphocyte macrophages products		Bone marrow precursors	Increased
Plasma-immunoglobulin levels		*Granulocyte function*	
IgM	Variable	Adherence	Decreased
IgG, IgA	No change/variable	Bactericidal activity	Decreased
Autoimmune antibodies	Increased	Phagocytosis	Increased
Cytokine production		Post-phagocytic metabolism	No effect
Interferon	Increased	Motility, chemotaxis	Increased
Interleukin-2	Increased	*Miscellaneous*	
Migration inhibitory factor	Decreased/inhibited	Viral plaque formation	Decreased
Colony stimulating factor	Increased	Viral shedding (herpes virus)	No effect
Thymosin	Decreased	Tumour growth and development in animals:	
Response to cytokine		Carcinogen-induced neoplasms	Enhancement (pre-treatment)
Interferon	Enhancement	Transplantable neoplasms	Inhibition (post-treatment)
Interleukin-2	Enhancement		
Colony stimulating factor	Enhancement		

cells produce cellular hormones, called lymphokines, that have immunoregulatory functions. The phagocytic cells, i.e. monocytes, macrophages and granulocytes, ingest foreign pathogens and substances, destroying them with intracellular enzymes and chemical processes. B-cells, in the presence of antigens, produce and secrete antigen-specific antibodies which bind specifically to the antigens. In addition to antibodies, the humoral immune system includes complement factors and other serum proteins, which have immunoregulatory and growth-promoting properties.

The immune system, besides protecting the body against infection, may also play a role in guarding against the development of malignancy. Immunodeficiency has been associated with a predisposition to the development of malignancies. Clearly, if lithium therapy is to be conducted in a manner which brings no harm to the patient, the effects of lithium on the various components of the immune system are of considerable importance in both short and long term therapy.

Effects on Cellular Immune Functions

The thymus gland

The fetal thymus gland is important for the normal development of the cellular immune system. Thymic hormones, or thymosins, influence immature lymphocytes, promoting their differentiation into T-cells. Congenital absence or malfunction of the thymus gland can result in an array of cellular immunodeficiency syndromes.

In 1977, Dr Jorge Perez-Cruet and his associates noted the occurrence of thymic involution in mice treated with lithium carbonate. These investigators explored the effects of chronic lithium ingestion on the thymus-dependent immune functions in both healthy volunteers and manic-depressive patients. Although no effects were observed in healthy individuals, abnormal *in vitro* T-cell function was noted in many of the psychiatric patients following long-term lithium therapy. These *in vitro* abnormalities were corrected

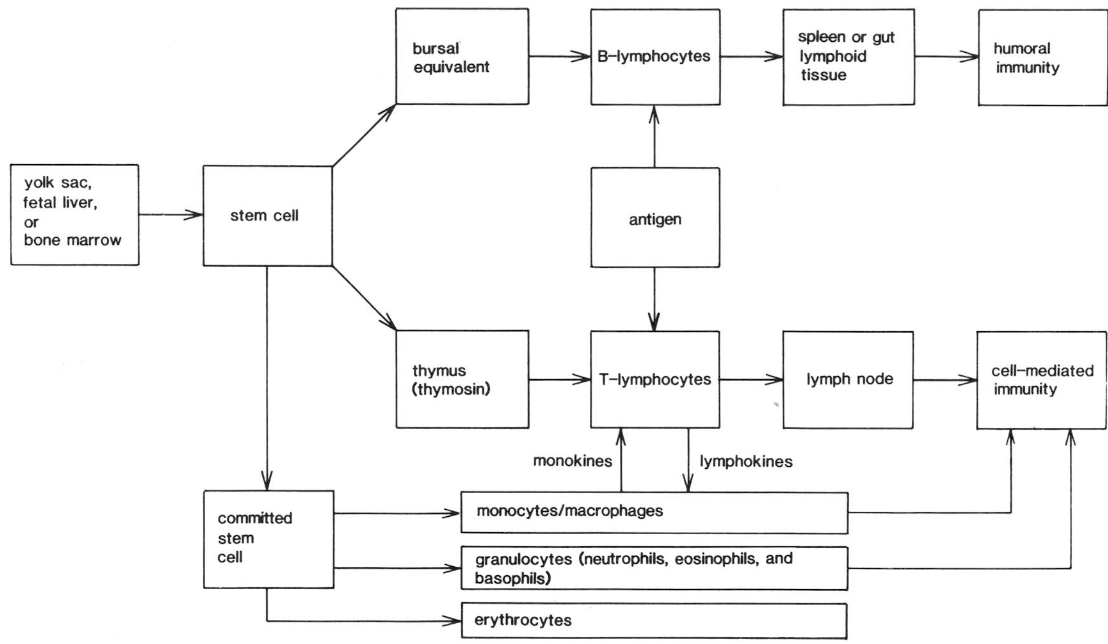

Figure 61.1 Representation of the main features of the immune system.

in the presence of thymosin, leading these investigators to conclude that lithium produces a thymosin-dependent immunodeficiency in man.

Lymphocytes

Although chronic lithium therapy has not been shown to alter the absolute numbers of lymphocytes, it does modify some of the functions of these immune cells.

Lithium therapy interferes with the activity of a population of T-cells, called suppressor T-cells. Suppressor T-cells are important for normal immunoregulation, protecting the body from unwanted immune responses. Lithium's interference with the inhibitory function of these cells may result in immune dysfunction. For example, the autoimmune diseases are thought to arise from a deficiency or an inhibition of T-suppressor cells. In autoimmune diseases, autoimmune antibodies, i.e. antibodies directed against the body's own antigenic determinants, may proliferate unchecked. Such antibodies may be directed against DNA (anti-nuclear antibodies, ANA), thyroid gland cells, gastric mucosa or other normal cells, producing tissue and organ destruction and dysfunction. Such autoimmune antibodies have been reported in patients on chronic lithium therapy, as discussed below.

Some immune deficiencies may arise from an over expression of T-suppressor cell activity. Enhanced T-suppressor activity may prohibit the normal development and function of the immune response. Serum from patients with certain kinds of immuno-deficiency syndromes exerts a suppressive effect on the mitogen-stimulated proliferation of lymphocytes from healthy individuals. Lithium added to these culture systems corrects this inhibitory effect, suggesting that abnormal suppressor T-cell activity may be responsible for the observed immune abnormalities in these patients.

Adjuvant-like effects

Both stimulatory and inhibitory receptors have been found on lymphocyte cell membranes. When stimulatory receptors are occupied by agents such as plant lectins, intracellular cyclic AMP levels rise, DNA synthesis is enhanced, as is cell proliferation, and a mitogenic response ensues. Although not mitogenic itself, lithium has been shown to augment the proliferation of lymphocytes in culture stimulated by T-cell mitogens. Lithium also enhances the stimulatory reaction of T-lymphocytes in the presence of foreign, or allogeneic, lymphocytes. It has been suggested that these effects may be mediated through the adenylate cyclase-cyclic AMP system.

Cytokines and lymphokines

Following stimulation by lectins or allogeneic cells, immune cells have been shown to produce a myriad of cellular hormones, generally referred to as cytokines. Lymphokines, produced by lymphocytes, and monokines, from monocytes or macrophages, are important regulators of cell growth and differentiation. Investigators from many laboratories have determined that lithium modulates the production and response of immune cells to cytokines. There are, for example, reports of a lithium-induced reduction of a lymphocyte migration stimulatory factor with a concomitant increase in migration inhibitory factor (MIF), and in cell culture therapeutic concentrations of lithium enhanced the production of interleukin-2 (or T-cell growth factor), when added to PHA-stimulated human T-cells; to a much lesser degree, lithium augmented the response of T-cells to exogenous interleukin-2. Lithium is also known to enhance colony stimulating factor (CSF) production, which stimulates bone marrow stem cell proliferation.

Peripheral blood mononuclear cells cultured with phytohaemagglutin A (PHA) or concanavalin A (ConA) in the presence of lithium ions were noted to produce an increase in the production of interferon and an enhancement of natural killer cell (NK) activity. When cells were similarly incubated with a double-stranded polyribonucleotide (poly I:C), which is a potent interferon-inducer, but without PHA, lithium did not enhance NK activity. One reason for the difference in the effect of lithium on NK activity in these two culture systems was thought possibly to be due to a difference in the mechanism by which PHA and poly I:C induce interferon production *in vitro*.

Granulocytes

Chronic ingestion of lithium has been shown to result in increased peripheral granulocyte counts in both humans and dogs. This increase in white blood cells is thought to be due largely to enhanced CSF production where CSF levels are suboptimal, resulting in increased stimulation of committed bone marrow stem cells.

Granulocytic cells (polymorphonuclear leukocytes, eosinophils, basophils) contain several kinds of digestive enzymes in cytoplasmic granules. Adequate numbers of granulocytes must be present in the circulation to maintain the body's defence against common pathogens (in particular, bacteria and fungi). Normal functions of these cells include mobility and migration to sites of inflammation, directed movement in response to particular stimuli (chemotaxis), adherence, ingestion (phagocytosis), and release of enzymes (degranulation). What effect, if any, chronic lithium therapy has on these functions of the phagocytic cells remains controversial.

Lithium, administered *in vitro*, may interfere with some functions of the granulocyte. While lithium appears to inhibit the adherence of granulocytes and may decrease the bactericidal capacity of these cells, it may enhance phagocytosis and increase the migration of granulocytes to sites of inflammation. Although granulocytes from healthy volunteers given an extended course of oral lithium showed a reduced capacity *in vitro* to kill bacteria in some studies, results of a similar study conducted by Dr Perez and associates demonstrated no changes in the granulocyte function of healthy controls. Lithium treatment, however, did result in the normalization of a chemotactic defect of granulocytes obtained from immunodeficient patients with recurrent infections. Other investigators who studied five patients with depressive disorders treated with lithium found no alterations in granulocyte motility, chemotaxis, phagocytosis or bactericidal activity.

In a patient with chronic benign neutropenia, it was reported that lithium treatment normalized the bone marrow granulocyte reserve and improved chemotaxis and phagocytosis of the granulocytes. An *in vitro* study was carried out on the effects of vinblastine, a chemotherapeutic drug known to disrupt the microtubule system of a cell, thereby inhibiting cellular replication and phagocytosis. When lithium was added to granulocytes from healthy donors incubated with vinblastine, phagocytosis, which was abrogated by the drug, returned to normal. Lithium did not augment the phagocytic capabilities of granulocytes which were not pre-treated with vinblastine. On the other hand, lithium was unable to correct the phagocytic defect produced by the agent, cytochalasin B, which disrupts the microfilament structures of cells, suggesting that lithium exerts a specific effect on the microtubular system.

Effects on Humoral Immune Functions

Plasma immunoglobulins

Patients with major depressive disorders have been reported to have abnormally low plasma concentrations of IgM, although IgA and IgG levels were not significantly different from normal control values. These results were subsequently confirmed in women receiving chronic lithium therapy as the sole treatment for their depressive disease. However, this abnormality appeared to be associated with unipolar disease and was not observed in bipolar disease.

In a study of healthy individuals no changes were found in serum IgG, IgA, IgM, complement factors C3 and C4, or total hemolytic complement levels, following ingestion of therapeutic doses of lithium carbonate over a 4-day period. *In vitro* incubation of human B-cells with lithium in the presence of mitogenic stimulation produced significant increases in IgG production at very low lithium concentrations ($\leq 10^{-2}$ mM). At therapeutic concentrations, IgG and IgM synthesis was increased in cultures incubated with lithium alone. The numbers of IgM-producing B-cells in the peripheral blood stream of patients receiving lithium carbonate therapy were significantly increased over those found in untreated healthy controls.

Autoimmune antibodies

Autoimmune antibodies are more commonly found in psychiatric patients than in healthy populations. Although not all studies agree, approximately 20% of psychiatric patients on chronic lithium therapy develop ANA. One mechanism by which lithium may stimulate the development of ANA is through its inhibitory effects on T-suppressor cell function (as previously noted). Since this T-cell population regulates B-cell production of antibodies, the reduction of suppressor function by lithium may allow antibodies directed against the body's own tissue to develop and proliferate unchecked.

In an evaluation of 54 patients on chronic lithium, no association was found between the development of ANA and age, sex, diagnosis, previous medication, histocompatibility antigens, blood group or other genetic marker, or the dose level or duration of lithium treatment. In another study, bipolar patients who had increased anti-thyroid antibody titres prior to lithium treatment, had a greater incidence of clinical autoimmune thyroiditis, which was accompanied by a significant increase in antibody titres following lithium. Only patients with latent thyroiditis developed autoimmune manifestations during lithium therapy, suggesting that low grade inflammation may disrupt the architecture of the thyroid gland, exposing and altering antigens which trigger an antibody response.

Miscellaneous Effects and Putative Mechanisms

Inhibition of adenyl cyclase

Cyclic nucleotides play an important role in the modulation of immune responses. While an increase in cyclic AMP (cAMP) is required for the initiation of lymphocyte proliferation, sustained increases in intracellular cAMP levels inhibit proliferation. Phagocytic cell function is also inhibited by elevated cAMP levels. Exogenous cAMP and agents such as theophylline and prostaglandin E1 (PGE1) which produce elevations in cAMP, have been shown to inhibit granulocyte adherence, phagocytosis, oxidative metabolism, release of lysosomal enzymes and chemotaxis.

Lithium has been found to enhance several functions of human blood mononuclear cells, reversing the *in vitro* inhibitory effects of agents which enhance cAMP, leading to the conclusion that lithium may interfere with the enzyme which converts AMP to cAMP.

Prostaglandin synthesis

Prostaglandins (PG) also modulate the immune system and appear to have immunoregulatory properties. In 1978, Dr David Horrobin proposed that PG perform a significant role in psychiatric disorders. He described the inhibitory effects of lithium on the synthesis of PGE1, which is synthesized by, and may regulate the activity of, T-suppressor cells. Although lithium does not have an effect on dihomo-γ-linolenic acid (DHLA), a precursor of PGE1, lithium appears to inhibit agents, such as prolactin and zinc, which mimic the effects of DHLA.

Effects on tumours and cell growth

Lithium's effects on the initiation, growth and development of tumours is a controversial subject on which little research has been conducted. In 1979, Dr F.Messiha and his co-workers noted that mice pretreated with lithium prior to administration of a carcinogen, methylcholanthrene, demonstrated an increased incidence and rate of growth of malignant sarcomas, over control animals which received saline injections. More recently, other investigators have noted that mice treated wtih lithium and cytotoxic drugs started on day *after* transplantation with murine melanoma cells, experienced a significant delay in the appearance of tumours, when compared to control groups which received lithium alone, chemotherapy alone, or saline. This combination group also demonstrated increased tumour necrosis and prolonged survival in comparison to the other groups, although animals that received lithium alone did no worse than the saline controls. Lithium may augment the distribution and transport of chemical agents into the cell, thereby enhancing the effects of both carcinogens and cytotoxic agents.

Lithium has been shown to mimic the effect of insulin in cultured tissues and *in vivo* in animals. In cultured normal mouse mammary epithelium, lithium at concentrations between 2 and 20 mM, has been shown to enhance DNA and RNA synthesis and cell proliferation. Although lithium cannot replace all of the hormone's actions, several studies suggest that lithium may act, like insulin, to alter the transport properties of the cell membrane, enhancing the intracellular transport of glucose and other molecules.

Anti-microbial activity

Dr G.Skinner and associates working at the University of Birmingham Medical School, UK, reported that lithium inhibits *in vitro* viral replication of herpes simplex viruses types I and II, pseudorabies and vaccinia at concentrations that did not effect the growth of host cells (see also pp. 46–50). The *in vivo* replication of herpes viruses in both animals and humans has been shown to be inhibited by lithium ingestion, which, it has been suggested, may be a result of lithium's effects on prostaglandin production. Lithium, however, does not prevent viral shedding following reactivation of latent virus, and its potential clinical benefit in herpetic infections remains to be determined.

Indirectly, lithium may enhance the body's defence against microbial pathogens through its enhancement of granulocyte numbers and effects on various immune functions. The use of lithium as an immunoadjuvant is discussed below.

Clinical Changes in the Immune System

The effects of lithium on the immune system have been studied in healthy individuals and patients undergoing treatment for psychiatric illnesses and other diseases. The clinical effects of lithium on the immune system appear to vary depending on the immune status of the individual. In a small study involving three healthy volunteers and five manic-depressive patients, no enhancement of immunological function was found. In another study, however, with patients with abnormal humoral immunity, in whom surface immunoglobulin (sIg)-bearing B-cells and plasma cells were either completely absent or variably reduced, lithium added *in vitro* to peripheral blood lymphocytes invariably produced immunoglobulin synthesis which was measurable, although lower than normal. Based on these *in vitro* findings, a phase I trial of low dose lithium (150 mg/day) therapy was carried out to determine whether lithium could induce sIg-bearing B-cells in patients with B-cell deficiencies. Serum lithium concentrations were maintained at $\leq$0.5 mM. Suppressor T-cell activity, which was positive before therapy, became negative after 2 weeks of lithium. Although serum immunoglobulin levels were difficult to assess, because patients continued to receive γ-globulin replacement, surface sIg-bearing B-cells were detectable in the peripheral blood following lithium treatment. These results support the theory that abnormal T-suppressor cell populations, which interfere with normal B-cell production of antibodies, may be responsible for some humoral immunodeficiency states.

Lithium's effects on the granulocytes and granulocytic precursors in the bone marrow has led to investigations regarding its usefulness as a modulator of bone marrow production in patients with various kinds of granulocytopenias and myelosuppression. Patients with severe and chronic myelosuppression are at high risk of developing bacterial and fungal infections. Although lithium has been reported to ameliorate the granulocytopenia associated with Felty's syndrome, aplastic anaemia, congenital neutropenias and cytotoxic cancer therapy, the results of various studies have not shown a consistent benefit. Lithium treatment may reduce the duration of severe bone marrow suppression; however, the extent of the depression of the peripheral granulocyte counts and the incidence of infection in immunocompromised populations appears not to be significantly altered.

In several studies, adult cancer patients tolerated lithium poorly, experiencing tremors, and nausea and vomiting even at non-toxic serum concentrations. An increased incidence of cardiovascular deaths has been noted in lung cancer patients with abnormal pretreatment cardiac examinations who received cardiotoxic chemotherapy and lithium. In a prospective randomized trial conducted by the Southeastern Cancer Study Group, 85 patients with acute myelogenous leukaemia were randomized to receive either chemotherapy alone or chemotherapy and lithium as an adjuvant; no significant differences in the depth or duration of myelosuppression were observed between the lithium-treated and untreated groups, nor did the lithium-treated patients experience any reduction in the incidence of febrile or infectious episodes. Although lithium may have specific effects on the immune system, its use as an immunoadjuvant in clinical treatment in cancer has not been consistently demonstrated.

Bibliography

Gelfand,E., Dosch,H., Hastings,D. and Shore,A. (1979) Lithium: a modulator of cyclic-AMP-dependent events in lymphocytes? *Science,* **203**, 365–367.
This article discusses a putative mechanism by which lithium may exert many of its effects in various systems. It will be accessible to someone with a general scientific background.

Horrobin,D. (1978) Lithium as a regulator of prostaglandin synthesis. In *Lithium: Controversies and Unresolved Issues.* Cooper,T.B., Gershon,S., Kline,N. and Schou,M. (eds), Excerpta Medica, Netherlands, pp. 854–880.
This chapter is a presentation from an international conference. It includes an extensive review of the literature and proposes a unifying hypothesis whereby lithium's effects may be explained and predicted in various clinical disease states. Although a scientific and/or clinical background may be necessary to comprehend the detailed discussion of biochemistry, the conclusions are simply stated.

Rossoff,A. and Robinson,W. (eds) (1980) *Lithium Effects on Granulopoiesis and Immune Function. Advances in Experimental Medicine and Biology, Vol. 27.* Plenum Press, New York.
This collection resulted from a scientific workshop held in 1979. Some of the entries are better organized than others. It represents an overview. A general scientific background is required, and a background in haematology and/or immunology would be helpful.

Shopsin,B., Friedmann,R. and Gershon,S. (1971) Lithium and leukocytosis. *Clin. Pharmacol. Ther.,* **12**, 923–928.
This journal article is a good example of a clinical trial. The discussion relates important findings to known effects of lithium on the various organ systems. A scientific and/or clinical background is required.

62. Skin, Hair and Nails

D.Lambert and S.Dalac

Changes occurring in the skin and hair, and (less commonly) in the nails, are sometimes associated with psychiatric conditions. The reason for this is unknown, though conceivably it may have to do with the fact that embryologically the nervous system develops from the same group of tissues that goes on to give rise to cutaneous structures, and close association between them is therefore understandable. It may not, therefore, be surprising that some drugs which affect psychiatric conditions, presumably via an effect on the nervous system, also affect the skin. This is certainly true of some anti-epileptic agents and it also happens occasionally during lithium therapy.

Cutaneous Eruptions

Cutaneous side effects in patients taking lithium carbonate have been reported by many investigators. The skin lesions first mentioned by C.L.Callaway in the USA in 1968, were pruritic maculopapular erythematous eruptions. Since that time a greater variety of skin problems have been described.

The occurrence of skin lesions is not infrequent in lithium toxicity. Approximately 1% of patients undergoing lithium therapy present with skin diseases of one kind or another, though not necessarily in a serious or severe form. The onset of dermatitis varies from 2 or 3 weeks to 7 or more years after the commencement of lithium. The majority of cases are reversible with the cessation of lithium, and re-institution is usually followed by a recurrence of the lesions.

Sometimes the eruption resolves spontaneously, or a gradual decrease in the dosage, and hence in the serum lithium, produces slight improvements. However, a great number of cutaneous lesions evolve with the optimal level of serum lithium. Jose Reiffers and Pierre Dick from Geneva, Switzerland, have found an accumulation of the metal in samples of epidermis, dermis and adipose tissue. Work carried out at the Dijon University School of Medicine, France, demonstrated that a vasculatis dermatitis induced by lithium evolved parallely with the skin lithium levels.

The mechanism of the effects of lithium carbonate on the skin is not known and may vary according to the types of disease.

Psoriasis

In those cases in which psoriasis has been reported to accompany lithium therapy, prolonged treatment with lithium could have induced the first manifestations of psoriasis or aggravated a pre-existing disease. All forms of psoriasis have been observed: rarely psoriasis vulgaris, more often general psoriasis, palmoplantar keratodermia and erythrodermia. In general, the psoriasis which was reported was severe, and conventional anti-psoriatic therapy showed no effect. The best therapy was etetrinate, 1 mg/kg/day, this allowed lithium therapy to be continued. In all other cases, the psoriasis represented a contraindication to the lithium therapy.

The disappearance of psoriasis after the withdrawal of lithium compounds and its recurrence on re-administration point towards an adverse skin reaction caused by the metal. However, therapy with lithium does not always exacerbate pre-existing psoriasis. The pathophysiological mechanism is not known. There is no relationship between changes of mood and psoriasis aggravation. A typical development of psoriasis occurs when mental improvement has already taken place. In psoriasis there is a genetically determined acceleration of epidermal cell proliferation. F.J.Bloomfield from the Department of Clinical Medicine, St James's Hospital, Dublin, Eire, used lithium salts to stimulate degranulation in order to assess neutrophil activity in psoriasis and was able to demonstrate that lithium salts can have a dramatic effect upon neutrophil activity in that condition. Lithium increases both the total mass of the circulating and marginal neutrophil pool and enhances their turnover in migration. Concurrently, lithium carbonate also inhibits the enzyme adenylate cyclase thereby lowering levels of cyclic adenosine monophosphate (cAMP) which could influence neutrophil chemotaxis, thereby permitting lithium carbonate to exacerbate psoriasis.

Seborrhoeic dermatitis

Seborrhoeic dermatitis is also encountered during lithium therapy. The general form can evolve into a characteristic psoriasis. Most often, the reports are of localized psoriaform or seborrhoeic keratosis of the scalp and the face. Histological examination is needed to confirm this diagnosis and to eliminate a psoriasis. The lesions can improve spontaneously or after discontinuation of treatment.

Follicular keratosis

Follicular keratosis develops first on the thighs, buttocks, upper arms, abdomen and later on the forearms. Small, grey, horny papules are centred by the ostium follicular. When localized at the knees and elbows they evoke a pityriasis rubra pilaris. The follicular orifices are distended by horny plugs and there may be mild inflammatory, nonspecific changes in the dermis with mononuclear cells. This eruption can improve spontaneously or after discontinuation of lithium compound therapy.

Acneiform eruptions

Acneiform eruptions are found in an area not usually affected by acne vulgaris, i.e. legs, upper part of the arms and forearms. In general, the face is unaffected or less severely so. The eruptions are preponderantly pustular and papular on erythematous bases without cysts or comedones. The lesions tend to persist for long periods and do not evolve in cycles as in acne vulgaris. The classical therapies for acne vulgaris are ineffective. Tetracycline should be avoided because in combination with lithium it may produce a nephrotoxic effect. The best therapy is isotretinoin which allows the continuation of the lithium treatment.

Other Cutaneous Manifestations

A great number of cutaneous diseases have been reported to be induced by lithium compound therapy, though in many cases only single case reports have been published. These conditions are listed in *Table 62.1*.

Hair loss

Hair loss (though not always of a severe nature) is more frequent than the development of cutaneous lesions, affecting about 6% of people undergoing lithium compound therapy. All kinds of alopecias can be found. In diffuse alopecia, loss of hair is distributed evenly over the entire scalp. The onset occurs several weeks or months after commencement of the lithium therapy. Patchy alopecia presents as single or multiple rounded patches without desquamation or erythema. Sometimes patchy alopecia (alopecia areata) progresses to complete alopecia (alopecia totalis). A microscopic examination of the hair can eliminate physical or

Table 62.1 *The variety of cutaneous effects (most very rare) reported during lithium therapy*

Acneiform eruptions
Follicular keratosis
Folliculitis
Lichenoid stomatitis with a characteristic infiltrate of T lymphocytes
Lichenoid lesions
Oedema of the lower limbs
Perioral dermatitis
Porokeratosis of Mantoux-like lesion
Pretibial ulcerations
Pruritus, localized or generalized with excoriations, thickened skin or lichenification
Pruritus dermatitis resembling early dermatitis herpetiformis
Psoriasis
Purpura and vasculatis
Reticulated and confluented papillomatosis
Sclerotic plaques
Seborrhoeic dermatitis
Urticaria, lupus-like syndrome
Verrucous hyperkeratosis on the scalp and the back
Warts
Zerosis, ichtyosis

chemical injury. The proportion of plucked hairs in the anagen and telogen phases of the hair cycle may be very significant. Body hair can be affected as well as scalp hair but this is less common.

It has been shown that lithium accumulates in hair, but hair lithium content is not directly relevant in causing alopecia. The mechanism of hair loss is in fact unclear: a direct toxic effect may be involved or it may be an indirect phenomenon (e.g. in association with hypothyroidism). The hair usually regrows despite continuing therapy on lithium. In other cases, the regrowth appears only when lithium has been discontinued.

Nail alterations

Lithium therapy can produce clinical and histological nail changes similar to those occurring in psoriasis or actually in association with this disease. It has also been reported that occasionally lithium therapy may induce a rich golden colour in the nail plate distally. The lesions involving the nail area disappear after the lithium therapy has been discontinued. They have little clinical significance other than, perhaps, acting as a reminder to the clinician that cutaneous effects may occur with lithium therapy and increased vigilance is warranted.

Bibliography

Bloomfield,F.J. and Young,M.M. (1983) Enhanced release of inflammatory mediators from lithium stimulated neutrophils in dermatitis. *Br. J. Dermatol.*, **109**, 9–13.

Heng,M.C.Y. (1982) Cutaneous manifestations of lithium toxicity. *Br. J. Dermatol.*, **106**, 107–109.

Lambert,D., Beer,F., Gisselman,R., Bouilly,D. and Chapuis,J.L. (1982) Manifestations cutanees des therapeutiques par le lithium. *Ann. Dermatol. Venereol. (Paris)*, **109**, 19–24.

Mortimer,P.S. and Dawber,R.P.R. (1984) Hair loss and lithium. *Int. J. Dermatol.*, **23**, 603–604.

63. Bone

Nicholas J.Birch

Since lithium is chemically rather similar to magnesium and calcium (see Section 4, pp. 19–22), the biochemistry of lithium has been investigated in relation to these two elements. Most of the mineral content of bone is calcium and there is a very large amount also of magnesium. It is therefore not surprising that we find lithium is accumulated in bone following administration to both experimental animals and patients.

The demonstration of accumulation of lithium in bone led at one time to some disquiet as to the possible effects of lithium on bone metabolism, and, in response to this expression of concern, investigators in the UK, from the MRC Mineral Metabolism Unit at Leeds General Infirmary and the Biological Research Laboratory of Leeds Dental School collaborated with a group from the Leeds University Department of Biochemistry to study in detail a number of aspects of bone lithium in man and animals. They concluded that although lithium was accumulated in bone it had no long-term deleterious effects. The situation is, however, somewhat confused because the majority of lithium patients are in fact post-menopausal females. Since this group already has a tendency towards osteoporotic change, this must be disentangled from the effects, if any, of lithium.

Lithium in Bone

The first experiments were carried out on 18-month-old female rats which had received lithium since wean-

Table 63.1 *Bone lithium content in rats treated with lithium in their drinking fluid (Experiment 1), in rats treated with lithium and then having their lithium withdrawn (Experiment 2) and in control animals receiving water alone (means; n = 6)*

	Age (days)	Lithium administration (days)	Water administration (days)	Bone lithium (mmol/kg)
Experiment 1	540	540	–	0.78
Experiment 2	540	540	42	0.35
Control	540	–	540	0.19

ing. Bone lithium was determined in one group, whilst in another group the lithium administration was discontinued for 42 days before bone was sampled. An age- and sex-matched control group was also sampled at the same time. The results of this work are summarized in *Table 63.1*. It is clear that lithium is accumulated in bone and also it appears that a significant proportion of this lithium is held fairly tightly since even after 42 days of discontinuation of treatment there is still a significant lithium concentration in the bone. It is also interesting to see that the control animals who have received no lithium at all, apart from what is in their diet normally, have in fact accumulated a significant lithium load. This may indicate that bone normally picks up whatever lithium is around in food. This detoxifying role of bone is well known with other metals.

Results similar to those in *Table 63.1* have been found in samples taken for diagnostic purposes from elderly lithium-treated patients. There is therefore no doubt that lithium accumulates in bone but the evidence suggests that much of this accumulated lithium, perhaps as much as 50%, is associated with bone water and is lost as soon as lithium treatment is discontinued.

Effects of Lithium on Bone

The accumulation of lithium in bone is only important in a practical sense if it has an adverse effect on either bone structure or bone metabolism. In order to determine whether or not this is so, studies have been carried out both on rats and on lithium-treated patients. Tony Horsman of the MRC Mineral Metabolism Unit at Leeds, UK, carried out bone density measurements of rat bone and hand radiographs of patients taken

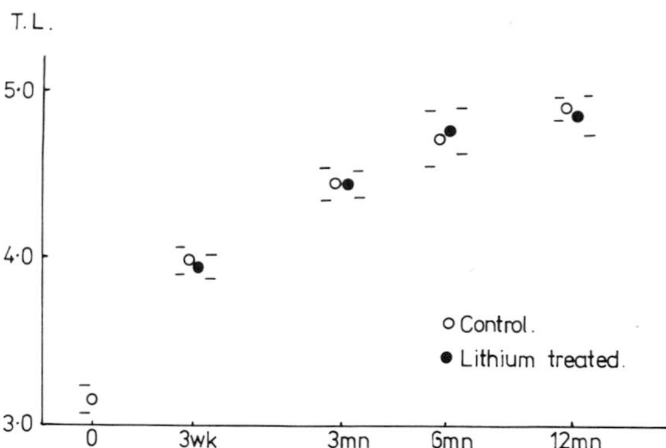

Figure 63.1 Lack of effect of lithium on bone length in rats treated with lithium for up to 1 year when compared with matched controls (means ± SD; n = 10). TL, tibia length (cm).

under standard conditions. The bone density of the femur (the long bone of the leg) in the rat, and the radiographic density of the second metacarpal (the long bone in the hand) were measured. The rat femur and the human metacarpal are approximately equal in size and therefore the same measuring technique was used. Using Vernier calipers on the illuminated radiograph plate it is possible to measure the dense outer or cortical bone and to measure also the total width of the bone and the width of the marrow cavity. Making the assumption that the bone shaft is cylindrical it is possible to calculate the cortical area.

In a group of 100 female rats studied over a period of 1 year there was no significant difference between the lithium treated and control animals in any of the measures. Growth of the animal and increase in bone size were exactly the same in the two different groups (*Figure 63.1*). It therefore seems unlikely that lithium is affecting bones adversely.

In a study of 74 lithium-treated patients, hand radiographs were obtained twice with an intervening period of about 2 years. There was found to be a clear difference in many of the patients between the first and the second radiographs but when compared with the very large control series available to Tony Horsman it is clear that the decrease in bone density shown in the lithium series is within the range expected for a group of similar age structure.

It therefore appears that lithium is not a hazard to bone in patients receiving the drug. The one caveat which might be made is that there is the possibility that in subjects with developing bone a more significant effect may be seen because of the deposition of lithium in the bone mineral as the bone is mineralized. For this reason it is appropriate to urge caution in the use of lithium in children and adolescents. However, there is no direct evidence on this point and as always the risks should be weighed against the possible benefit of treatment.

Bibliography

Birch,N.J. (1974) Lithium accumulation in bone after oral administration in rat and in man. *Clin. Sci. Mol. Med.*, **46**, 409–413.
The original paper describing lithium retention in bone.

Birch,N.J., Greenfield,A.A. and Hullin,R.P. (1977) Lithium therapy and alkaline earth metabolism: a biochemical screening study. *Psychol. Med.*, **7**, 613–618.
Presents a biochemical study of measures which might be expected to alter should there be any bone defect. No effect of lithium was found.

Birch,N.J., Horsman,A. and Hullin,R.P. (1982) Lithium, bone and body weight studies in long term lithium treated patients and in the rat. *Neuropsychobiology*, **8**, 86–92.
Results of a long term patient study and bone density measures in the rat are outlined in this article.

64. Muscle

Ulrik Baandrup, Steen Christensen and Jens Peder Bagger

Our knowledge about the effects of lithium on muscle is only fragmentary, the information having often been collected from experimental animals and under non-physiological conditions. Add to that the individual differences which exist, some probably on a genetic basis, and it becomes evident that details from experiments may be difficult to put into a clear-cut perspective. It is not possible to review here in any detail the many physiological studies which have been undertaken to elucidate the transport mechanisms and effects of lithium on smooth, skeletal and heart muscle; however, major aspects will be dealt with and particular consideration given to morphological changes in the heart muscle.

Lithium Transport and Effects on Muscle Metabolism

There is strong evidence that lithium ions have a direct activating effect on the sodium pump and are themselves transported into the muscle fibres. The calculated ratio of lithium influx to efflux constants for muscle is increased from 1.8 to 4.2 by lithium therapy in man, so that the muscle levels of lithium rise to four times the plasma levels. This suggests that lithium therapy inhibits the ionic exchange or counter transport system in human muscle, as it does in erythrocytes.

It has been observed that lithium reduces the number of acetylcholine receptors in denervated skeletal muscle of rats. In normal muscle it reduces the number of cholinergic receptors at neuromuscular junctions. These changes are relatively specific effects of lithium on the turnover of cholinergic receptors probably due to increased receptor degradation.

Lithium has also been shown to have an anti-histaminergic effect. This effect is mediated by a direct action on guinea-pig smooth muscle, or by a diminished response to adenosine caused by Na–K-pump inhibition in rabbits.

Lithium has been reported to enhance glucose uptake in brain and muscle and to increase glycogen content in these tissues. In experiments on rat muscle lithium inhibited phosphofructokinase, an effect also observed in brain tissue but not in the liver.

In heart muscle from the rat lithium was found to induce changes in cellular calcium distribution which are associated with stimulation of sugar transport, an observation which supports the hypothesis that the increased availability of cytosolic calcium regulates the activity of the sugar transport system in muscle.

Smooth muscle

An anti-histamine-like effect of lithium on smooth muscle has proved beneficial, in therapeutic dose levels, in the treatment of manic-depressive patients who also suffer from asthma. Another clinical effect via smooth muscle may be the lowering of blood pressure which has been observed to occur in some categories of hypertensive patients. Isolated side effects from smooth muscle have not been described but are in any case likely to be obscured by symptoms from other organs during lithium intoxication.

Skeletal Muscle

The effects of lithium on skeletal muscle are represented first and foremost by varying degrees of weakness and tremor (ranging from fine tremor to ataxia and incoordination). While the mild symptoms may develop within the limits of therapeutic lithium concentrations, the more severe reactions emerge when this concentration is exceeded. In chronic treatment the symptoms may persist but their frequency decreases substantially within the first year of treatment.

Aggravation of myasthenia gravis has been reported on several occasions in patients receiving lithium treatment, and it has been suggested that it is a result of prolonged inhibition of the rate of synthesis of acetylcholine and a decrease in its evoked release, even though its release during resting conditions initially may be enhanced via increased calcium influx. Theoretically, lithium may thus accentuate the defect in neuromuscular transmission present during spontaneous myasthenic episodes.

In rats and humans, however, a marked reduction has been shown in clinical myotonia, together with an increased ability to perform activities, and a reduction in recordable electrical myotonia. The plasma lithium level necessary to achieve this marked improvement was, however, 2.3 mmol/l and was associated with excessive sedation.

Acute/subacute painful proximal myopathy causing myalgia, cramps, myokymia or weakness have been described in lithium treatment but the mechanisms or the pathology are not known.

Heart Muscle

The heart muscle can be regarded as skeletal muscle with one major difference; i.e. the automatic depolarization of the myocardial cells, associated with rapid changes in ion fluxes over the cell membrane. Lithium may replace sodium during the generation of an action potential but is extruded at only 10% of the rate of sodium and therefore accumulates in cardiac muscle cells.

Therapeutic concentrations of lithium in individuals without cardiovascular disease have only benign and reversible effects on the cardiovascular system (see Section 58, pp. 213–218, for a detailed account). Lithium has also been listed among drugs suspected of causing toxic myocarditis; however, a search in the literature reveals only three cases of myocarditis occurring in patients as a possible consequence of lithium administration. In a study of morphological aspects of lithium-induced cardiotoxicity in rats under different time and dose regimens, three different rat models were used: rats with chronic renal failure due to lithium administration for 8–16 weeks after birth; normal, adult rats treated with lithium for 16 weeks; and newborn rats exposed to lithium in their prenatal life. Morphological changes were found only in 57% of the male rats with lithium-induced uraemia after lithium administration for 16 weeks postnatally. The changes consisted of areas with myocytic degeneration and necrosis associated with infiltration of lymphocytes and histiocytes. The morphological picture is different from the myocardial changes associated with chronic renal failure, where pericarditis is a constant finding and the myocytic changes less pronounced. *Figure 64.1* shows lithium-induced morphological changes in heart muscle.

Lithium can partially replace intracellular potassium in the heart cells. Myocardial degeneration and even necrosis have been documented in animals with severe potassium depletion, and hypokalaemia has been suggested as the cause of myocarditis in man. However, hypokalaemia is unlikely to be the cause of the myocardial changes demonstrated in this study, since normal plasma potassium values were found in the lithium-uraemic rats.

No explanation has so far been found for the male dominance in lithium-uraemic myocarditis in this study, since the plasma levels of lithium and urea were not different among male and female rats. It is interesting, however, that myocarditis and pericarditis induced by another agent, coxsackievirus B, is also known to occur in male rats and humans, predominantly.

From these studies it seems that myocarditis may be a consequence of persistent high plasma levels of lithium as maintained in the rats with lithium-induced renal failure; it is possible that cardiotoxic effects of lithium may be potentiated by concomitant renal failure.

Summary

Lithium interacts at several levels and in various ways with (neuro)muscular organ systems. Except for possible aggravation of myasthenia gravis, the most serious muscle side effects are related to the heart muscle. The acute cardiotoxic effects are dose dependent, reversible and harmless to the patients as long

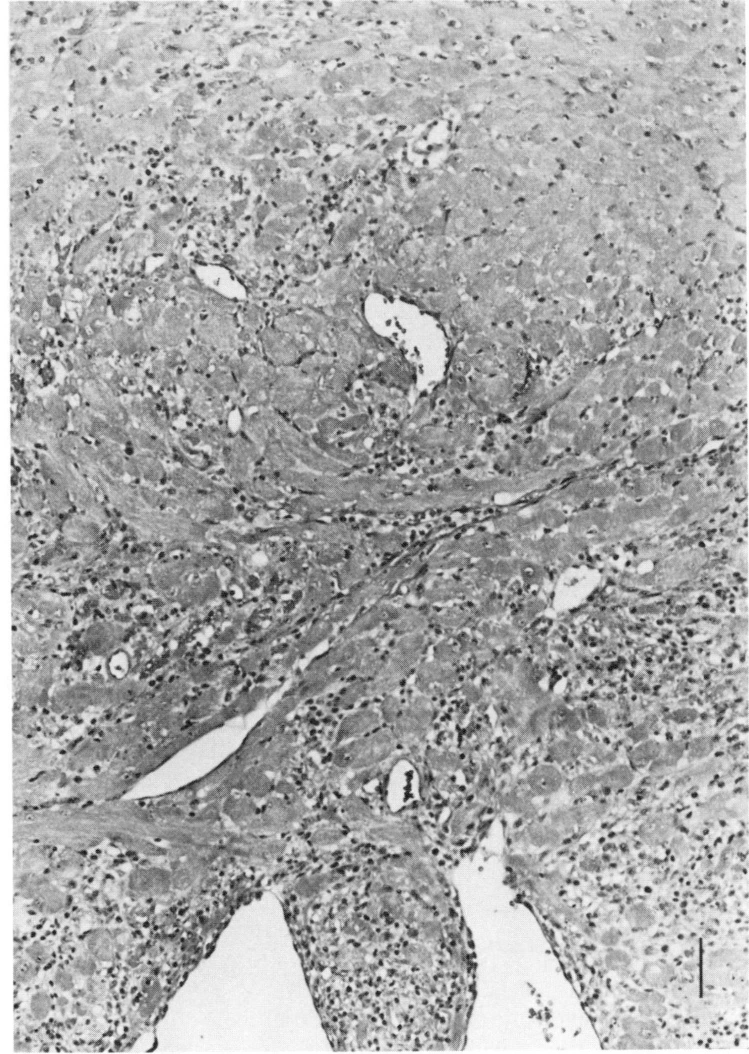

Figure 64.1 A micrograph showing lithium-induced myocardial changes. This section of the left ventricle of a rat shows cellular infiltration (histiocytes, lymphocytes) and corresponding muscle cell degeneration and necrosis (haematoxylin-eosin; 1 bar = 50 μm).

as plasma lithium levels are maintained in the therapeutic range levels. The cardiovascular side effects of alternative psychotherapeutic agents, such as tricyclic antidepressants, are probably more pronounced.

If pronounced indications exist for use of lithium in patients with heart disease, factors interfering with the renal lithium clearance (heart failure, salt restriction, diuretics) must be identified and appropriate dose adjustments considered. If lithium has to be used in patients with cardiac arrythmias, ECG monitoring is essential to detect any possible, although unlikely, aggravation of the arrythmia (pp. 213–218). Although toxic myocarditis has been demonstrated in animal models, there is at present no evidence that carefully controlled lithium therapy should produce irreversible morphological or functional damage to the myocardium.

Bibliography

Baandrup,U., Bagger,J.P. and Christensen,S. (1985) Myocardial changes in rats with lithium-induced uraemia. *Acta Pathol. Microbiol. Immunol. Scand. Sect. A*, **93**, 317–322.

Bibliographic references to other work on lithium and its myocardial effects are given in this article which deals with *in vitro* changes in rats showing clear signs of lithium toxicity.

Brumback,R.A., Gerst,J.W. and Staton,R.D. (1981) Effects of lithium on clinical and experimental myotonia. *Clin. Neurophysiol.*, **52**, 128.

A short paper but one which is useful in putting together clinical and experimental work on the effects of lithium on muscles.

Neil,J.F., Himmelhoch,J.M. and Licata,S.M. (1976) Emergence of myasthenia gravis during treatment with lithium carbonate. *Arch. Gen. Psychiatry*, **134**, 702.

Myasthenia gravis is an exceptionally rare accompaniment of lithium treatment and this brief report is therefore of special interest.

Sampson,S.R. and Weiss-Rotem,C. (1982) Relaxant effects of lithium on guinea-pig tracheal smooth muscle *in vitro*. *Br. J. Pharmacol.*, **75**, 287–291.

In this paper details are given of a typical study using a muscle preparation *in vitro* to study lithium effects.

Tosteson,D.C. (1981) Lithium and mania. *Sci. American*, **244**, 130–137.

A succinct and most readable paper on lithium transport.

65. Respiration

F.Neil Johnson

Effects of lithium on the control of breathing are seldom included in lists of lithium side effects. In fact, very little is known about the frequency with which respiratory effects are associated with lithium therapy, though there are one or two interesting indicators in the literature that such effects can occur under appropriate circumstances.

Non-toxic Patients and Normal Volunteers

A group of investigators led by Drs Peter Szidon and Edward Wolpert, working at the Michael Reese Hospital in Chicago, USA, reported in 1983 on a case of an elderly woman who experienced an episode of acute respiratory failure at a time when her serum lithium level was only 0.5 mmol/l. No reason for this could be discovered but the authors of the report considered the possibility that lithium might have interfered with ventilatory adaptation to an increase in the airways resistance since the patient, a smoker, suffered from stable chronic obstructive lung disease. They therefore organized a trial which involved giving placebo and lithium (0.8–1.2 mmol/l serum levels) to a group of normal, healthy volunteers, using a double-blind cross-over design, and then testing the subjects' ventilatory compensation under various added inspiratory loads. They found that lithium led to a diminished compensatory response.

Two years later, research workers from the same group gave details of a second episode of respiratory failure in the same patient they had described earlier. Respiratory distress was alleviated by withdrawal of lithium.

Respiratory Distress in Lithium Intoxications

In 1981 Dr A.Criado and his colleagues of Madrid, Spain, presented details of a 52-year-old female patient who was admitted to hospital with acute respiratory failure (tachypnoea with progressive dyspnoea) secondary to pulmonary oedema which, in its turn, was probably related to myocardial depression. The patient had a serum lithium level of 3.15 mmol/l (27.6 mmol/l in the urine), i.e. well into the toxic range. The most recent report of acute respiratory failure associated with lithium intoxication has come from Drs P.G. Lawler and J.R.Cove-Smith of the intensive therapy unit of the South Cleveland Hospital, UK. Two patients, one a 52-year-old woman and the other a 27-year-old man, were both admitted to intensive care with lithium toxicity (serum levels of 4.5 mmol/l and 4.9 mmol/l, respectively). Both developed respiratory failure and adult respiratory distress syndrome was the proposed diagnosis in each case.

Clinical Implications

There is no suggestion that respiratory function needs to be routinely monitored in all patients receiving lithium therapy; however, the possibility that lithium may act as a respiratory depressant could well have implications for patients who already have airways obstruction. Certainly when respiratory failure occurs in association with serum lithium levels well into the toxic range, the recommendation of Lawler and Cove-Smith that intermittent positive pressure ventilation should be instituted at an early stage, should be acted upon without hesitation.

Bibliography

Lawler,P.G. and Cove-Smith,J.R. (1986) Acute respiratory failure following lithium intoxication. *Anaesthesia*, **41**, 623–627.
Advice is given on the management of adult respiratory distress syndrome occurring during lithium intoxication.

Weiner,M., Chansow,A., Wolpert,E., Addington,W. and Szidon,P. (1983) Effect of lithium on the responses to added respiratory resistances. *N. Engl. J. Med.*, **308**, 319–322.
Presents the first account of a patient with respiratory failure during lithium treatment. Details are also given of a study showing respiratory depression effects of lithium in normal volunteers.

66. Brain and Nervous System

M.Elena Sansone and Dewey K.Ziegler

The adverse effect of lithium on the human nervous system was described as early as 1898 by Dr Louis Kopilinski, in two patients. In his cases the weakness and tremors that followed lithium ingestion completely resolved within a matter of days. Fifteen years later a more detailed account of the evolution of neurotoxic signs and symptoms was provided by Dr S.A.Cleaveland who reported self-experimentation with lithium. He took 8 g in four divided doses over a 28-h period. Dizziness appeared 2–4 h after the first dose, followed by blurred vision, tinnitus, generalized weakness and marked tremors in about 18 h. Severe vertigo, disturbed sleep, exaggeration of weakness and tremors were noted after the fourth dose. Although weakness and tremors lasted for 5 days, there were no associated gastrointestinal symptoms. Since these two accounts, there have been numerous reports describing the effect of lithium on the central and peripheral nervous system. *Table 66.1* lists the toxic effects which may involve the nervous system.

Table 66.1 *Effects of lithium on the nervous system*

Minor
- Central nervous system
  - decreased concentration and comprehension
  - impaired short term memory
  - restlessness and anxiety
  - depression
  - fine rapid tremors
- Peripheral nervous system
  - easy fatigue
  - slowing of nerve conduction

Serious
- Central nervous system
  - declining cognition and mental status
  - gait disturbance
  - movement disorders
    - choreoathetosis
    - myoclonus
    - Parkinsonism
  - seizure
  - cerebellar signs
  - pseudotumour cerebri
  - neuroleptic malignant syndrome
- Peripheral nervous system
  - myopathy
  - axonal neuropathy
  - myasthenic syndrome
  - potentiation of neuromuscular blockers
  - exacerbation of underlying neuromuscular disease

Normal Subjects and Patients with Huntington's Chorea

Dr Lewis Judd and his colleagues, working at the University of California, USA, compared the effects of a 14-day course of lithium with those of placebo in 24 normal male volunteers. Serum levels obtained within 10 h of the last dose ranged from 0.7 to 1.37 mmol/l with a mean of 0.91 mmol/l, levels generally considered as lying within the therapeutic range. Performance assessed on a battery of tests suggested that lithium had some effect upon cognitive and motor functions but not verbal creativity and aesthetic judgement even at non-toxic blood levels.

In the same group of normal subjects, lithium had significant effects on affect, mood and personality as measured by tests which also revealed problems of lethargy and exhaustion, confusion, inability to concentrate, feelings of negativism and depression, agitation, anxiety, tension and restlessness, shakiness and nausea.

In patients with pre-existing dementia, lithium can further reduce cognitive functions. Dr M.Aminoff and his colleagues demonstrated with test doses of lithium a reversible but significant reduction of cognition in nine patients with Huntington's chorea. Scores on the Wechsler Adult Intelligence Scale were significantly lower during lithium therapy than after placebo administration.

Dr M.H.Branchy and his colleagues conducted

neurological examinations on 36 psychiatric patients who had been receiving maintenance treatment with lithium for at least 6 months and had therapeutic blood levels. The subjects comprised 11 males and 25 females, 33 manic depressive and 3 schizoaffective, with a mean age of 46.1 years. They had not taken neuroleptics for at least 6 months. Twenty-four of the 36 patients (60%) manifested fine and rapid tremors of mild to moderate intensity. Only three had mild cogwheel rigidity. The occurrence of tremor or rigidity was not related to the duration of treatment. On the other hand, Drs Baron Shopsin and Samuel Gershon reported cogwheel rigidity frequently occurring in patients maintained on lithium; however, it is unclear if their patients had had previous neuroleptic treatment.

These minor effects on cognitive and motor functions can easily be mistaken for more serious neurological syndromes. The tremor may be misdiagnosed as essential tremor, hyperthyroidism, anxiety or even Parkinsonism. The disturbance in cognitive function can simulate early dementia from one of many causes, or depression.

Neurotoxicity

Neuromuscular disorders

Lithium-induced myopathy has been reported in a 62-year-old woman on maintenance therapy. The disorder was manifested by severe proximal muscle weakness producing inability to arise from a lying or sitting position, impairment of consciousness, cerebellar syndrome and myoclonus. The serum lithium level was greater than 2 mmol/l. Mental status and abnormal movements improved within 2 weeks but normal strength did not return until 11 months after discontinuation of medication. The patient, however, was left with a persistent cerebellar dysfunction. The case was confirmed by electro-myography and muscle biopsy but the mechanisms responsible for lithium-induced myopathy remained unexplained.

Acute polyneuropathy and myasthenia gravis-like illness have also been attributed to lithium. In the former, severe generalized weakness, respiratory depression, areflexia and sensory loss have accompanied other clinical signs and symptoms of neurotoxicity. The neuropathy is of an axonal type as indicated by electromyographic studies. It is reversible. In the myasthenic syndrome episodic weakness of extremities along with slurred speech and difficulty in swallowing generally improve with rest and remit totally with discontinuation of lithium. The syndrome has been reported to respond to the anticholinesterase agent, edrophonium hydrochloride (Tensilon®).

The relationship of this entity to true myasthenia gravis is uncertain because acetylcholine receptor antibodies were not measured and repetitive nerve stimulation was not done.

The above neuromuscular syndromes clearly indicate the vulnerability of the anterior horn cell, peripheral nerve, neuromuscular junction and/or muscle to the toxic effect of lithium. The potential danger of exacerbating an underlying or pre-existing neuromuscular disorder must therefore be carefully weighed against the benefits of the drug in the treatment of mania.

Encephalopathy

Encephalopathy may appear 24–72 h after an acute overdosage or at any time during maintenance therapy. The first symptoms with acute overdosage as seen in suicidal attempts are distractibility, poor memory, disorientation, incoherence, poor concentration and impaired judgement. Gastrointestinal symptoms of nausea, vomiting and diarrhoea usually precede the encephalopathy. As the condition worsens, involuntary movements may appear in the form of asterixis, myoclonus or choreo-athetosis. In some patients Parkinsonian features, suggested by mask-like facies, rigidity and bradykinesia, develop. Progressive decline of mental status, together with decerebrate posturing and generalized seizures, is indicative of a more serious state of neurotoxicity.

The encephalopathy that occurs during maintenance therapy usually appears insidiously and may be often unrecognized as lithium-related. The serum lithium can be within the therapeutic range. The signs of impaired cognition are similar to those following acute overdosage. It may slowly progress over days or weeks and may be accompanied by involuntary movements, ataxia and dysarthria. In some patients, however, it may be precipitated by an increase in lithium dose. A variety of other stimuli can also be operative: addition of neuroleptic agents, increased ambient temperature, reduced food and fluid intake, salt restriction, diuretic agents, infection or an intercurrent medical illness that leads to decreased lithium excretion.

Lithium-induced encephalopathy, as noted, does not

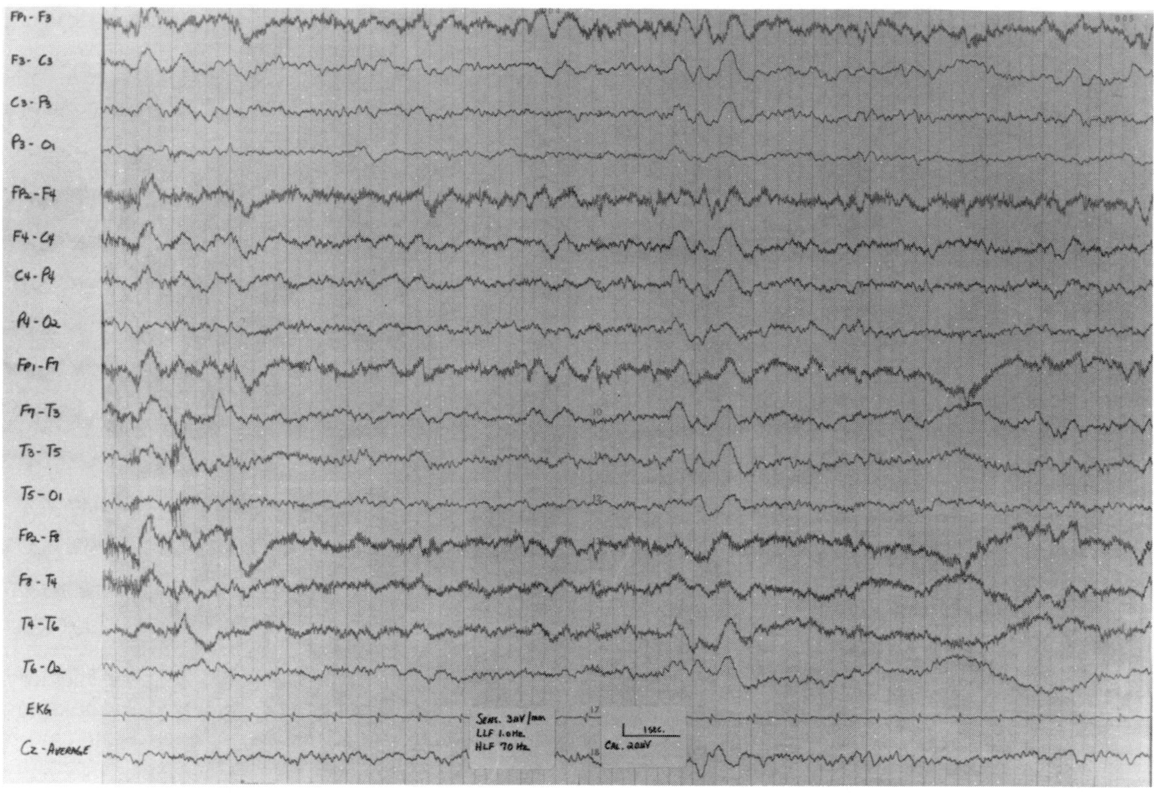

Figure 66.1 A 44-year-old man on several years of lithium therapy for manic-depressive illness had confusion, diaphoresis, rigidity, hyperreflexia and elevated 12-h serum lithium of 1.4 mmol/l on October 24, 1983. On November 1, 1983, his serum lithium was 0.2 mmol/l and his EEG was abnormal showing intermittent generalized high voltage 1.5–2 Hz delta and a background rhythm of 7 Hz.

correlate with serum levels but has been noted to correlate better with electroencephalographic changes. In patients with minimal signs of neurotoxicity, the EEG shows minor asymmetries of alpha frequency or increase in 4–6 theta activities. In those with moderate to severe neurotoxicity as suggested by lethargy and ataxia, the EEG abnormalities consist of increasing episodes of intermittent high amplitude diffuse delta (below 4 Hz) waves with accentuation of previous focal abnormalities. Although the EEG is a sensitive indicator of central nervous system toxicity, similar changes can be seen in a variety of neurological disorders such as encephalitis or cerebral hypoxia. *Figures 66.1, 66.2* and *66.3* show EEG records of a 44-year-old man whose serum lithium varied from 1.4 mmol/l to 0.5 mmol/l as a result of withdrawal of lithium to deal with a neurotoxic state and its subsequent reinstatement to therapeutic but non-toxic levels.

Lithium-induced encephalopathy is usually reversed by reduction or withdrawal of the drug. In some cases, however, it may rapidly progress and follow a fatal course despite discontinuation. If the patient survives, he may be left with neurological deficits persisting for months or years after the episode of intoxication. To date, there are in the region of 22 reported cases with persisting neurological sequelae (though this has to be set against the many thousands receiving maintenance treatment). Deficits include short term memory impairment, dementia, choreo-athetosis, 3 Hz resting tremor and cerebellar syndrome. The latter is the most predominant sequela and consists of scanning speech, intention tremor, ocular dysmetria, and appendicular and truncal ataxia.

It is believed that individual variations in sensitivity may be responsible for persistent neurological deficits. Drs I.Donaldson and J.Cuningham reviewed all cases of lithium encephalopathy resulting in permanent deficits. There was no correlation with duration of lithium therapy, daily dose, maximum serum lithium

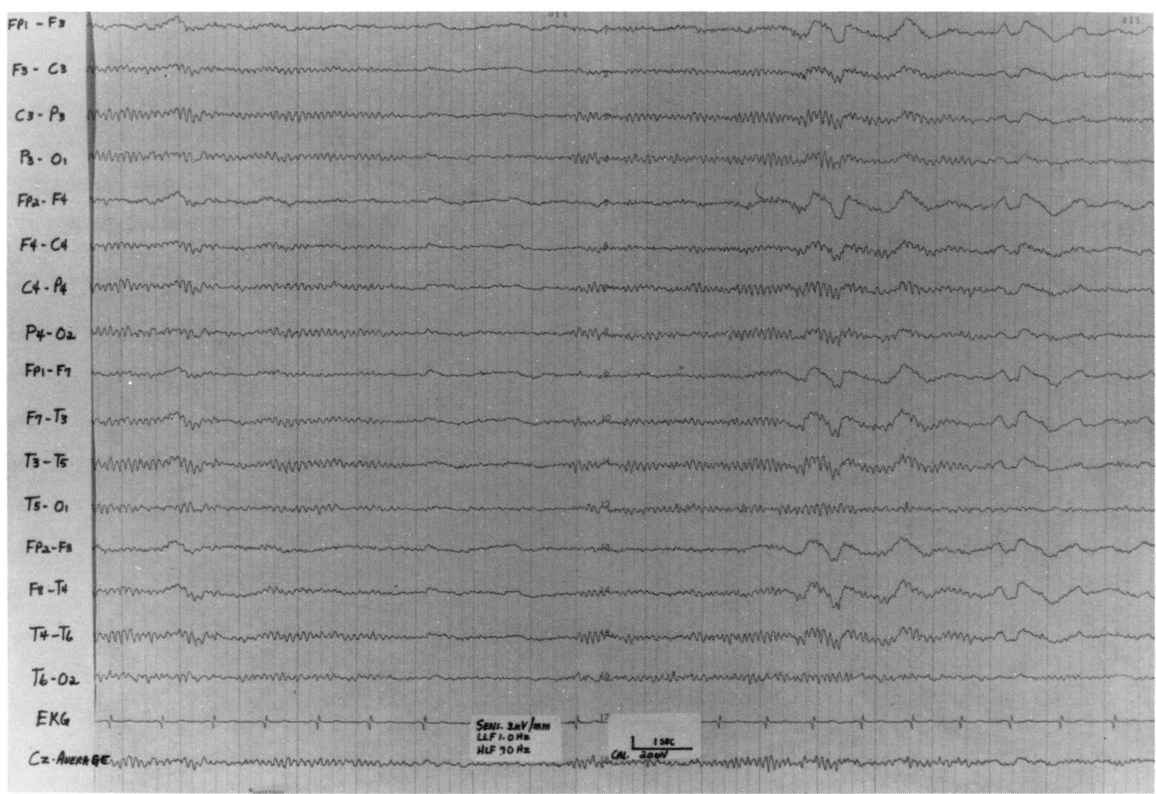

Figure 66.2 On December 22, 1983 he was less confused and his serum lithium was 0.7 mmol/l. EEG was improved with the appearance of 10 Hz alpha but intermittent generalized 1.5–2 Hz delta continued.

concentration, psychiatric diagnosis or age. In this study there was a female:male ratio of 4.7:1. According to the authors, this may simply reflect the greater number of females treated with lithium.

Pseudotumour cerebri

Lithium can also, though extremely rarely, cause pseudotumour cerebri. This condition, a diagnosis of exclusion, is manifested by recurrent headache, papilloedema, increased intracranial pressure with normal cerebrospinal fluid, and slit-like ventricles on computed tomographic head scan. It has been described in five patients during maintenance therapy in whom blood levels were not elevated. Discontinuation of lithium in four cases resulted in complete resolution of symptoms. The exact mechanism of lithium-induced increased intracranial pressure is unknown. However, it has been proposed that lithium may inhibit the sodium–potassium pump causing intracellular brain oedema which, in turn, may lead to impairment of cerebrospinal fluid absorption across the arachnoid villi. If left untreated, the syndrome can lead to permanent visual loss.

Neuropathology of Lithium Toxicity

There is a non-uniform uptake of lithium by various parts of the brain. In one report of two patients who died on the third and fourth days of lithium therapy, lithium was present in the cerebral grey and white matter, cerebellum and pons, with the concentration of lithium in the pons being twice that of the cerebrum and cerebellum, and one-and-a-half to two times that in serum. In another report of two fatal cases, toxic concentrations of lithium were found in all parts of the brain with the cerebral white matter and brainstem showing the highest concentration.

Microscopic studies of brain changes have been few. In one fatal case, changes noted were: (i) reduced

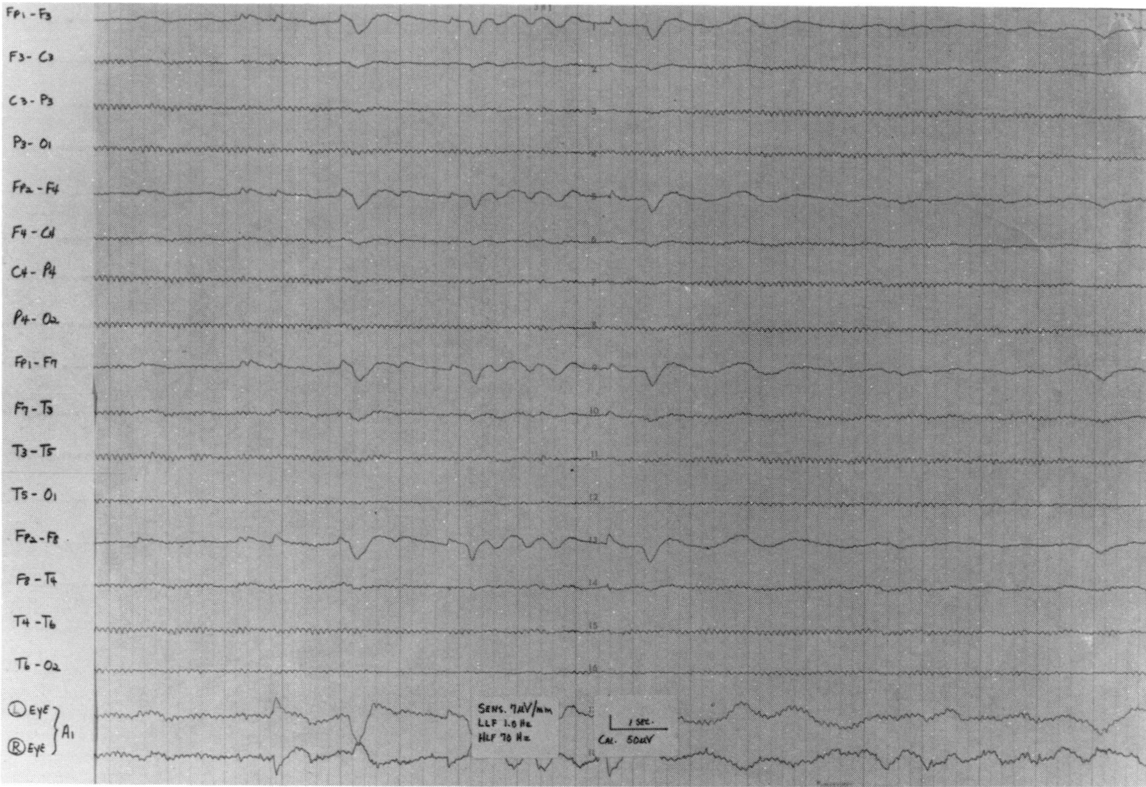

Figure 66.3 On January 4, 1984 his serum lithium was 0.5 mmol/l and his mental status, neurological examination and EEG were normal.

granule and Purkinje cells in cerebellum; (ii) gliosis in dentate nuclei, inferior olives and red nuclei; (iii) cytoplasmic vacuoles in the cells of the supra-optic nucleus. There were no significant changes in the nigro-striatal system.

In experimental studies on non-human primates, ultrastructural changes described by Dr K.Akai and his co-workers included dilatation of the endoplasmic reticulum in nerve cells and oligodendroglia in the cerebral cortex (frontal and temporal lobes), hypothalamus, putamen and medulla; and alterations of dense core vesicles in the basal ganglia, brainstem and hypothalamus. Changes were most severe and diffuse in animals that received the highest dose of lithium for the longest period of time. Since there is a lack of reports on clinicopathological correlations in man, it is unclear as to whether or not mortality is related to severity of pathology, nor has it been determined in man whether severity of pathology parallels the amount and duration of brain exposure to toxic concentration.

Treatment of Neurotoxicity

Minor side effects during maintenance therapy can be minimized by reduction of lithium dose. Severe signs and symptoms warrant immediate and complete withdrawal of the drug. In the event of acute overdosage, prompt haemodialysis is the treatment of choice. The length of exposure to toxic levels determines the outcome. According to the study by Drs H.E.Hansen and Amdi Amdisen from the Institute of Psychiatry of Aarhus University, Denmark, patients with the shortest exposure and mildest symptoms before haemodialysis have a fast and complete recovery. With the onset of coma, there is a greater chance of death or permanent deficit.

Haemodialysis rapidly lowers serum lithium. However, prolonged haemodialysis (12 − 16 h) is recommended to prevent rebound in serum levels. If haemodialysis is stopped prematurely, redistribution of lithium occurs due to non-uniform uptake of the ion by various organs, with the potential of re-entry into the brain resulting in recurrent and prolonged toxicity.

Bibliography

Donaldson,I.M. and Cuningham,J. (1983) Persisting neurologic sequelae with lithium carbonate therapy. *Arch. Neurol.*, **40**, 747–751.
A brief, but comprehensive, survey of long-term neurological side effects following lithium therapy.

Sansone,M.E.G. and Ziegler,D.K. (1985) Lithium toxicity: a review of neurologic complications. *Clin. Neuropharmacol.*, **8**, 242–248.
A useful overview of the main types of central nervous system effects of lithium.

67. Special Sense Organs

F.Neil Johnson

Since lithium quite clearly affects behaviour, in manic-depressive patients, in normal volunteers and in animals (Section 67, pp. 246–252), one has to consider the possibility that the action may be at the level of the sense organs. If the reception of sensory information (visual, auditory, olfactory, etc.) is altered, behavioural responsiveness will also change.

At the present time there is relatively little information on this topic, and most of what is available stems from isolated case reports. Of the major special senses, hearing, gustation and olfaction appear not to be influenced by lithium: at least the literature fails to yield any evidence that they are. Only vision is affected, and then only in some individuals on some occasions. Indeed, some reports have failed to record any visual effects even when a particular effort was made to search for them.

A group of investigators at the University of Wisconsin Center for Health Sciences, USA, were unable to determine any ocular effects of lithium in 13 healthy volunteers. A wide range of parameters was studied but no changes attained statistical significance. Similarly, a group of investigators from the Ophthalmic Hospital of Lausanne, Switzerland, were unable to find any evidence of ocular lesions traceable to lithium in 73 patients, according to a report issued in 1981.

Despite these negative findings, however, enough evidence of ocular effects can be found scattered in the literature to justify the conclusion that a watch kept on the eyes of lithium patients may not always be wasted effort.

Effects on the Eye

There are isolated instances of patients with incipient senile cataract whose sight suddenly worsened following lithium treatment, and of cases of unilateral or bilateral exophthalmos apparently unrelated to thyroid function but linked temporally to lithium therapy. An increased eye irritation, possibly due to the direct effect of lithium ions in the tears, has also been noted in five out of 21 patients according to one very brief report. The condition responded to decongestant eye drops.

In 1980 Dr Paolo Pesando of the University of Parma (Italy) Institute of Ophthalmology reported the occurrence of bilateral papilloedema in a patient who had received lithium carbonate treatment for 5 years (serum levels being below 1.2 mmol/l throughout). This was the second such report, the first having appeared 7 years earlier. Of course, it cannot be established with any certainty that lithium was the causal agent, but Pesando and his colleagues feel that papilloedema should be regarded as 'a certainly infrequent but definite possibility' in lithium therapy. Some support for this view was forthcoming in 1985 with a further report from the Geisinger Medical Center in Danville, Pennsylvania, USA, of three patients with similar lithium-related conditions. In view of this, the suggestion of regular fundoscopic examinations for patients receiving lithium may need to be considered sympathetically.

In 1982 there was the first reported case of photophobia coincident with high serum levels of lithium (1.6 mmol/l). The patient, a 32-year-old woman, kept her eyes shut in normal light and experienced pain from an ophthalmoscope light. The condition resolved when lithium was withdrawn and then restarted at a lower dose. It is possible that there may be some link between this and the fact that dark adaptation processes appear to be inhibited in volunteers treated with lithium, or with a further report that in eight normal healthy subjects lithium-induced changes have been seen in the electro-oculogram (EOG). These findings were intrepreted as suggesting an effect of lithium on the outer segments of photoreceptors and the retinal pigmented epithelium which are the sites of the corneofundal potential which lies behind the EOG.

Structural changes in the eye have not been reported in humans, but mice receiving lithium in their drinking water over an 8-day period were found to show variations in base corneal cells in terms of size, shape, pigmentation with aggregation of the nuclei, and mitotic figures in the absence of inflammation.

Pupil diameter may be reduced in patients receiving lithium as compared with pre-lithium sizes, according to a recent report from Italy.

Visual Effects Secondary to Action on the Eye Musculature

If the muscles which control the movement of the eye are affected by lithium, this might lead to visual impairment. Since lithium-induced muscular tremor is a well-known side effect, it is not, perhaps, surprising that there should have appeared a few reports of visual disturbance related to impairment of muscle control.

Downbeat nystagmus, causing blurring of vision was complained of by a patient in whom it was accompanied by high serum lithium levels (1.6 mmol/l) and hypomagnesaemia. Treatment consisted of withdrawal of lithium and oral magnesium supplements. A second patient with downbeat nystagmus had levels of 1.1 mmol/l and 0.96 mmol/l. Perceptual acuity seems not to be affected by lithium, except in cases in which nystagmus leads to a blurring of vision. There has been one report of oculogyric crises (a spasmodic, upwards deviation of the eyes) in a 38-year-old man with a serum lithium level of 1.24 mmol/l. However, no lithium effects could be determined on visually stimulated saccadic eye movement in a careful study carried out in the University of Vienna Psychiatric Clinic, Austria.

Clinical Implications

It seems clear from these reports that responsible administration of lithium requires that the physician should at least be aware of the possibility of some ocular effects of lithium, though the question of whether routine examinations are really necessary must be a matter for individual physicians to answer for themselves. It should, however, be borne in mind that there is some evidence that lithium has a tendency to concentrate, and remain, in the lens of the eye, appreciable traces (0.33 mmol/l) being detected in the eyes of dogs as long as 8 months after the termination of lithium administration which had continued for 25 months. One does not yet know what implications this and future findings may have for the regard which must be paid to the ocular effects of lithium.

Bibliography

Ullrich,A., Adamczyk,J., Zihl,J. and Emrich,H.M. (1985) Lithium effects on ophthalmological-electrophysiological parameters in young healthy volunteers. *Acta Psychiatr. Scand.*, **72**, 113–119. A clear account of recent work on lithium effects on visual processes and report of an impairment of dark adaptation.

68. Mental Functioning

B.Müller-Oerlinghausen

Members of the general public who do not have specialized knowledge about psychoactive drugs often think that nearly all such agents have similar sedative or 'dampening' effects, resulting in a 'zombie'-like state; and the expression 'being drugged' has become popular. However, this is a very over-simplified and inadequate point of view, probably resulting from experience with hypnotics or sedatives which have been taken in single or repeated doses by themselves or by friends and relatives. In fact, various classes of psychotropics possess quite different patterns of mental effects, and in addition these effects may also differ depending on whether the drug is given to a healthy volunteer or to a patient with a mental illness.

Thus, so-called antidepressant drugs, e.g. imipramine, will produce a mixed state of sedation and eventually increased irritability in a healthy volunteer, whereas in a depressed patient the drug, if given continuously, will within the first few days relieve the sleep disturbances and anxiousness, and later on, after about one or two weeks, lead to improved mood, more drive, fewer suicidal thoughts, better concentration, etc. Neuroleptics, e.g. haloperidol, result in a completely different pattern of mental and behavioural changes.

Does Lithium Produce Mental Effects?

In contrast to the drug classes mentioned above, lithium does not possess any special reputation for producing mental effects. There are several reasons for this puzzling phenomenon. First, lithium salts are never prescribed or taken as single doses, so there does not exist the same general expectancy as surrounds the effects of a sleeping pill or a neuroleptic drug. Second, since many physicians have never experienced claims by patients concerning unbearable or at least troublesome mental side effects of lithium, they do not bother to ask patients specifically about any such effects; they merely look upon lithium as a prophylactic drug, which by some unknown, and probably biochemical, mechanism inhibits the occurrence of depressive or manic relapses. Within such a simplistic way of thinking it is often overlooked that lithium, in addition to its prophylactic effect against periodic aggressiveness, has well-proven acute anti-manic and anti-depressive effects (though the latter seem to occur only in special, but ill-defined, patient populations). Those lithium researchers who invented the notion 'normothymic' for this special class of psychotrophic agent, which for more than a decade had only one representative, i.e. lithium, obviously knew better; 'normothymic' implies a constant effect of normalizing, i.e. improving the patient's mood, or rather his global mental functioning.

The existence of mental effects of lithium must, indeed, be postulated on logical grounds, because otherwise the established prophylactic effect of lithium could not be explained, at least not within a psychological context. Some investigators obviously consider mental processes as epiphenomena of the 'underlying', allegedly essential, physical (physiological, biochemical, etc.) processes. Such a reductionistic view of the living world and of human beings is nourished by a strong belief in a future where any psychological and psychiatric reasoning may finally be reduced to biochemical or molecular-pharmacological terms.

Such a view actually belongs to a 19th century way of scientific thinking which is not supported by modern developments in philosophy or theories of science. Although there may be statistical correlations between the likelihood of occurrence of certain processes in biochemical terms and those in psychological terms, a mental phenomenon can never, for a variety of generally accepted logical reasons, be deduced from a biochemical phenomenon. However, many investigators in the medical field constantly confuse statistical correlations with causal relationships, whilst on the other side, many psychologists appear to be completely disinterested in the fact that psychotropic drugs are eminently suitable tools with which to study changes in experience and behaviour. Thus, the impact of psychology on our understanding of the psychopharmacology of lithium is, in the main, regrettably weak, though there are one or two exceptions from this critical statement (e.g. in the scientific work of the editor of this book, Dr Neil Johnson, the essentials of which will be discussed later, and in the work of Dr Detlef Kropf of the Free University of Berlin, FRG) (p. 250).

Hundreds of interesting biochemical effects of lithium have been reported, yet it is very hard to find structural analogies between them and those effects on pathological experience and behaviour in which psychiatrists are primarily interested. The observation of effects of lithium on the behaviour of experimental animals and on the experience and behaviour of healthy human volunteers or psychiatric patients appears much more likely to provide the kind of findings which can be interpreted in a structural analogy to the therapeutically desired clinical effects in psychiatric patients.

The existence of mental effects of lithium is still a controversial issue. This derives partly from the fact that the effects of lithium are obviously subtle, not always easily detected by either the patient or the attending physician, and partly from the fact that clinicians have been mostly interested in the problem of whether mental *side effects* of lithium interfered with a favourable course of prophylactic treatment, whereas far greater scientific (and practical) interest lies in the possible role of such effects in providing theoretical models of mental function and dysfunction.

Behavioural and Mental Effects in Animals and Humans

Animal experiments

Within the context of this book, the effects of lithium in animals cannot be described in detail; there is far too large a body of findings on the topic. Although they must be interpreted cautiously due to methodological problems which do not allow a direct transfer of these findings to the situation of lithium-treated human beings, two main findings may be mentioned which very likely relate in some way to the effects of lithium in humans.

First, it has been shown under various experimental conditions that lithium reduces spontaneous as well as elicited aggressiveness in various animal species.

Second, it has also been demonstrated that in non-toxic doses lithium does not produce a general sedation. It possesses only little influence on the spontaneous behaviour of animals, such as rats, whereas it has a clearly inhibitory influence on exploratory behaviour such as rearing, sniffing etc., which occurs if an animal is brought into a new environment. From this observation it has been suggested that lithium reduces the animals' responsiveness towards environmental stimuli, indicating a changed central analysis of sensory information. A further development of these findings has been a model in which the central effect of lithium is related to a change in the processing of sensory information.

Effects in healthy volunteers and patients

It has already been stated that the effects of lithium on normal psychic functions are not very marked. Thus, for example, no clearcut evidence exists for impaired performance in driving a motor vehicle under the influence of lithium. One of the methodological problems which interferes with any attempt to determine the psychological effects of lithium is that long-term effects can be studied only in patients, not in healthy volunteers. In patients, however, the difficulty arises as to how drug effects should be discerned from changes brought about by mild subdepressive or hypomanic mood swings. Another problem lies in the fact that a primary impairment of a single mental function, such as memory, can finally result in a state of increased well-being (e.g. fewer depressive ruminations). It also seems that lithium influences certain mental processes in a non-unidirectional way; in other words, it depends on the initial, pre-lithium state what the final outcome will be when lithium is given.

In view of the now extensive literature on the subject, only a few examples of lithium effects on mental functions can be mentioned here.

Aggressiveness. There is strong evidence that lithium decreases aggressiveness in persons with pathologically increased aggressive behaviour. Irritability, hostility and anger can be reduced in such patients, even in cases where neuroleptic drugs, such as haloperidol, have proved unsuccessful. It may well be that this effect is related to a reduced response towards environmental stimuli. On the other hand, it should be noted that, according to some theories, the pre-morbid personality of depressive patients is, among other features, often characterized by hostility, higher irritability and so on. It appears not unlikely, therefore, that reduction of aggressiveness is also related to the prophylactic effect of lithium in patients with manic depressive psychosis.

Mood. Whereas the effects of lithium on aggressiveness seem to be undirectional, this seems not to be the case in regard to lithium effects on mood and feelings. If lithium is administered to healthy volunteers for 2 weeks, they may sometimes become more depressed, more agitated, more anxious and tense. If, however, patients are treated with lithium or if lithium is withdrawn after long-term treatment, various and opposite changes of mood can occur. In one investigation, those patients who were not dysphoric and depressed before lithium, became so after administration of lithium, whilst patients who were dysphoric and depressed before treatment showed a reduction of these mood qualities. It has also been reported that feelings such as joy or sadness show a certain flattening and reduction under the influence of lithium. The significance of such changes for the psychological economy of a patient is unclear and probably depends very much on the specific pre-morbid personality. Lithium may increase or reduce the scope or the degrees of freedom of a subject.

The same holds true for eventual changes of personality. Some findings indicate that long-term lithium treatment may induce some loss of characteristics of the so-called typus melancholicus or, in other words, a decrease of obsessive-compulsive traits. From a psychoanalytical point of view, it could be speculated that a primarily quantitative change of the perception of external or internal stimuli results in a qualitative change in psychodynamic processes.

The awareness of such changes by the patient himself or his relatives may lead to quite opposite consequences: if the changes are considered as a predominantly negative development, this may reduce compliance with treatment and the patient may ask for the treatment to be stopped. On the other hand, many patients regard a reduction of hyperemotionality, of extreme orderliness, and obsessiveness, as some form of progress. The housewife may have no more feelings of guilt if she leaves the dishes for washing until the next day. Another patient may feel much more relaxed if confronted with some unexpected unplanned events in the daily routine. One married patient remarked that for the first time he and his wife could get along in a relaxed and normal way.

Patients during the free interval between episodes of mood disorder may express a mood of 'lack of energy' or 'increased fatiguability', but such complaints may occur in striking contrast to an actual objective improved efficiency occurring at the same time.

Cognitive functions. Neurological studies indicate that lithium does not in any way induce a general sedation. In contrast, it counteracts the marked decline of vigilance normally occurring under resting conditions, to a rather rigidly restricted spectrum of subvigilant stages (in this context 'vigilance' has a neurophysiological meaning). This effect is interesting, because it indicates a reduction of degrees of freedom on this descriptive level.

Several studies have demonstrated a slightly reduced concentration in lithium-treated healthy volunteers. With regard to the common occurrence of concentration deficits in depressed patients, it is difficult to judge the clinical significance of this finding. Visual perception is changed in a very special way, because only the perception of complex stimuli is impaired. This phenomenon occurs particularly if the experimental subject does not know which kind of mixed stimuli will appear next. In other words, the recognition and resolution of visual stimuli is not modified in lithium-treated patients if the subject can rightly expect that all stimuli will be of the same type. However, if this routine situation changes, and complex and simple stimuli occur in a randomized order, lithium treatment results in a change of performance. On the other hand, lithium significantly increases the threshold for visual perception, no matter what kind of stimuli are presented. It should be emphasized, however, that lithium does not show a uniform inhibitory effect, but a differential one, either improving or worsening visual perception. From other experiments it can be deduced that the subjective persistence of a visual stimulus is shortened under lithium, an effect which may lead to reduced interaction with other stimuli and thereby to an improved capability of structuring visual perception.

Memory disturbances have been reported from time to time in anecdotal form, though controlled experiments in patients have provided contradictory results. However, some evidence exists that the transfer of information from short-term memory to long-term memory can occur.

Artists, scientists and patients of other professions requiring a very high level of mental functioning, may fear a loss of creativity under the influence of lithium. To clarify this issue, Professor Mogens Schou, from Aarhus University in Denmark, has evaluated detailed interviews on this subject with selected patients. According to his findings and those of many other experts in this field, it can be concluded that here too lithium does not possess a unidirectional effect. There may be patients who are aware of a reduced creativity and who, therefore, would like to stop lithium. However, there seem to be more patients who, whilst possibly still missing the joy of their former mild hypomanic episodes, are nevertheless clearly aware that the quality of their artistic or scientific output during such episodes was not up to standard. They realize that, in the long run, their creativity and steady working level is much higher under successful long-term lithium prophylaxis than under conditions in which a productive phase is disrupted again and again in an unexpected way by depressive or manic episodes. In addition, several artists have clearly stated that, in contrast to a popular belief, their creativity is by no means optimal during hypomanic episodes, but rather at the very beginning of depressive episodes. This again should warn against premature conclusions or criticisms concerning an alleged general impairment of mental functioning based on a false belief in a non-specific dampening effect of lithium long-term treatment.

Psychological Models of Lithium

From what has been said, it is clear that lithium does indeed possess mental effects, not only in depressed or manic patients, but also in euthymic subjects. The question then arises as to whether or not such observed changes tell us anything about the mechanism of the prophylactic action of lithium salts. In other words, is there a way of explaining the prophylactic effect of lithium in strictly psychological terms? Surprisingly,

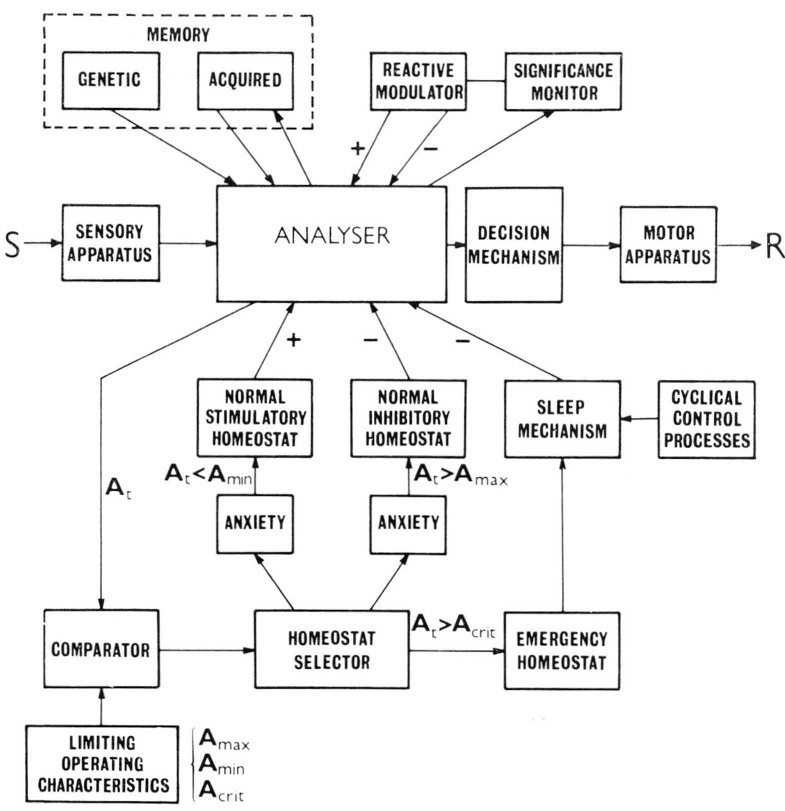

Figure 68.1 Outline of a psychological model of manic-depressive illness put forward by Johnson [Johnson,F.N. (1984) *The Psychopharmacology of Lithium*, Macmillan, London]. Lithium is suggested to act upon the sensitivity of the central analysing mechanism. The model is complex in its specifications and the reader is referred to the original source for a full and detailed explanation.

few investigators have embarked on this theoretical approach. One is Dr Neil Johnson, the editor of this volume, the other is Dr Detlef Kropf, psychologist of the lithium research group in West Berlin. It is self-evident that a psychological model of the mode of action of lithium possesses plausibility only if it is based on an explanation or description of depression and mania in psychological terms, and both these investigators have extended their discussion of the psychological basis of lithium action to encompass a psychological explanation of the conditions which lithium is used to treat.

The theoretical frame of the model proposed by Johnson is a stimulus-response construct, based on cybernetic principles, in which changes in a hypothetical 'analyser' of the sensory input play a decisive role. Details are depicted in *Figure 68.1*. The sensitivity of the analyser can fluctuate within a certain range; a homeostat will start to operate in order to inhibit or stimulate its sensitivity. In patients with affective psychosis it is assumed that the homeostatic processes fail, resulting in over-assessment of the significance of sensory input (mania). As a consequence, however, an emergency homeostat will come into play which drastically reduces the analyser's sensitivity, resulting in stimulus *under*processing and depressive symptomatology. Independently, anxiety levels might also influence the system, e.g. by inhibiting the normal functioning of the homeostat. Thus, in this model depression will always occur as a consequence of manic symptomatology. To explain the action of lithium within this theoretical frame, it is postulated that lithium impairs the efficiency of the stimulus over-assessment in the case of a non-functioning homeostatic apparatus. This effect of lithium, however, is restricted to stimuli of around threshold intensity.

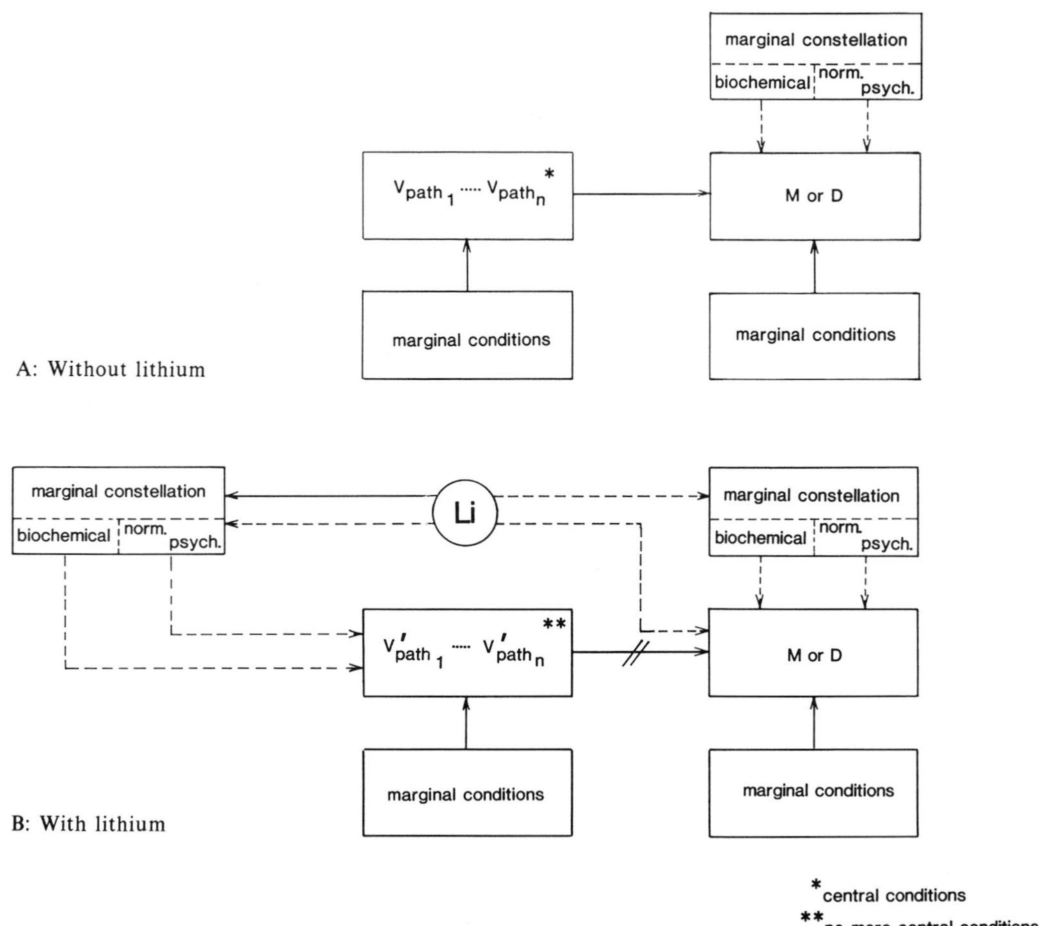

Figure 68.2 Outline of a psychological model of lithium prophylaxis put forward by Kropf [in Müller-Oerlinghausen,B. and Greil,W. (1986) *Die Lithium-Therapie – Nutzen, Risiken, Alternativen*, Springer-Verlag, Berlin]. The figure illustrates indirect effects of lithium. It is assumed that lithium changes one or more pathological variables (V_{path_1} V_{path_2}, ... V_{path_n}) which function as necessary conditions for (i.e. are conditionally related to) the onset or exacerbation of rudimentary manic (M) or depressive (D) conditions. In addition there are postulated to be marginal conditions related in a conditional way to D or M, and marginal constellations (biochemical or normal psychological states) which are merely associated with (but not conditionally related to) M or D. Lithium is held to act directly upon marginal constellations and indirectly on other elements of the model. The pathological variables, V_{path_1} etc., are changed into other variables, V'_{path_1}, V'_{path_2}, ... V'_{path_n}, which are no longer conditionally related to M or D.

Without going into detail it can be said that experiments in animals as well as observations in humans provide support for this model. Particularly, the finding by an Italian group of lithium researchers, that lithium acts much better in those patients with a natural sequence of mania followed by depression than in those with depression followed by mania, would be in accordance with Johnson's theory postulating a primacy of the manic state.

A somewhat different approach has been taken by Dr Kropf, whose model is a phenomenological one based on a specific interpretation of empirical observations in manic and depressed patients and taking into account certain postulates of epistemiology and classic Aristotelian logic. It presents alternative ways of psychological reasoning, all of which are valid from a theoretical point of view, but at the same time makes very clear what kind of logical consequences are implied in particular assumptions. Thus, e.g. suppose we define 'pathological' and 'normal' as two distinct qualities or entities, then depressive or manic symptomatology cannot be deduced from *normal* mental phenomena on logical grounds. If we want to assume such a duality of pathological and normal, and if we assume (what is empirically reasonable) that there exists a special pre-morbid personality of manic-depressive patients, then it must also be assumed that the specific manic or depressive processes already manifest themselves in subtle or rudimentary form in pre-morbid experience and behaviour. And since, for logical reasons, they cannot be based upon normal psychic processes, they must necessarily either have been existent from birth or they must have been generated spontaneously. The question, then, is, how can the pathological character of these pre-morbid processes be described? Kropf has presented a theory which focuses on what he calls the 'weakness of structurizing'. This means, that a person has only a restricted capability to build up the contents of experience and behaviour in a fully differentiated way, to abolish them gradually, and to demarcate different processes, from each other. Lithium must interfere with the origin or development of these pre-morbid processes, or with their exacerbation into manifest psychosis. This could be brought about directly, that is by suppressing the origin or exacerbation of manic/depressive processes or indirectly by influencing the impact of certain conditional variables or of marginal constellations. *Figure 68.2* presents an example of these relationships (which can be very complex). In this figure, the pathological variables V_{path} are a central condition for the occurrence of mania or depression. Lithium changes these pathological variables (for example an increased speed of special cognitive functions, or an increased anxiety level) in the pre-morbid personality in such a way that they lose their central conditional character. In other words, they lose their ability to trigger a manifest manic or depressive episode. Of course, there can be other influences of lithium on marginal constellations (e.g. of sleep) as well. Such marginal constellations, as well as a certain pathogenic set or context of pathological variables, may differ from individual to individual, but also from one time to another within the same individual. This may explain why the efficacy of lithium can differ inter- and intra-individually.

Bibliography

Johnson,F.N. (1984) *The Psychopharmacology of Lithium*. MacMillan, London.
A comprehensive and up-to-date compilation of empirical findings and theoretical reflections on the mental effects of lithium and its mode of action in psychological terms.

Müller-Oerlinghausen,B. and Greil,W. (1986) *Die Lithium-Therapie – Nutzen, Risiken, Alternativen*. Springer Verlag, Berlin.
A comprehensive textbook on lithium treatment, written in German, characterized by presenting different approaches to the mode of action of lithium including a quite sophisticated outline of the philosophical and psychological approach by Dr Detlef Kropf, and also a chapter on the psychoanalytical view of lithium prophylaxis. Both this book and that by Johnson will be useful for non-medical readers as well as those medically qualified, but not for someone without any academic training in psychology, philosophy or science.

69. Sexual Functioning

Sergio Luís Blay

Sexual dysfunction is a rarely described side effect associated with lithium treatment. The clinical features can range from mild, transient, insignificant disturbances, to severe and troublesome sexual impairment. Psychological and marital implications can be important associated events that may lead the patients to discontinue their lithium treatment. Despite the low frequency of reports in the literature, it is possible that lithium-related sexual problems may be more common in practice and it is important that the psychiatrists should be aware that they may occur.

The majority of the communications concerning lithium-induced sexual impairment refer only to its presence in men. However, this difference in the incidence in the two sexes may be more apparent than real, and could be related partly to a differential tendency to voice complaints to the psychiatrist concerning matters of sexual functioning.

Clinical Features

The onset of this side effect occurs at the beginning of lithium therapy, usually within 1 month after the first lithium intake, and arises at regular maintenance serum levels ranging from 0.5 to 0.9 mmol/l.

The disorder may be limited to a brief period, and may have a spontaneous remission after 2 or 3 months after the beginning of lithium intake, or it may become a chronic and stable manifestation with little variability over time during lithium treatment.

The small number of case reports which have been

published concerning sexual dysfunctions associated with lithium treatment deal primarily with male patients with bipolar illness who developed sexual impairment while in treatment. When placebo was administered instead of lithium, sexual functioning was promptly restored.

Sexual dysfunctions due to lithium therapy can be classified according to their main clinical features as involving either disturbances of sexual interest (libido) or disturbances of sexual functioning.

Disturbances of sexual interest

Little is known about the effects of lithium on the loss or decrease of sexual interest. Much of the information available comes from clinical case reports. Many psychiatrists note that patients with affective disorders, while under lithium treatment, may develop an inhibition of sexual desire. The cause of this change is not known. However, the general flattening of affective response due to lithium therapy may be an important factor associated with the suppression of sexual interest. In addition, it is possible that this factor may be of importance in causing certain patients to resist compliance with long-term treatment proposals, or to drop out of treatment, and may explain the use of lithium salts in inhibition therapy for abnormal sexual behaviour.

The initial symptomatology may be vague, so an accurate estimation of the exact time of onset is difficult. The clinical picture is characterized mainly by a persistent inhibition of sexual interest.

Disturbances of sexual functioning

Lithium can produce unwanted disturbances in sexual functioning. The literature on the subject includes few reports, and refers almost exclusively to male sexual impairment. The clinical features of inhibited sexual response may occur in the phase of excitement, consisting mainly of difficulty in achieving and maintaining penile erection. Other manifestations may include an objective delay or a failure to achieve ejaculation.

Although these two major types of impairment have been described, the clinical reports indicate that the main clinical feature is related to impaired erection. Unless sexual activities are unimportant to the patient, the individual usually develops varying degrees of anxiety and apprehension associated with the decline of his sexual performance. A strong psychological reaction often results, and frequently the patient avoids further contacts. The dynamics of the structure of a couple's relationship is almost invariably affected.

Mechanisms

Clinical pharmacological studies of lithium have suggested it has a mild sympatholytic role both on peripheral and presumably on central adrenergic mechanisms. The consequence of this pharmacological action may explain the production of this unwanted side effect.

Diagnosis

As not all sexual dysfunctions in patients receiving lithium preparations are attributable to the drug, an extensive assessment of the patient's sexual life is recommended. The diagnosis of lithium-induced sexual impairment disturbances can be established when a patient is free of manic or depressive episodes; if the patient develops this side effect it may be presumed to be independent of the underlying affective disorder.

Assessment and Treatment

The fundamental issue underlying the management of lithium-related sexual impairment is related to prevention. A proper selection of patients who take lithium on a long term basis may obviate the risk of side effects involving sexual functions. Thus, a careful clinical assessment must be completed before drug treatment begins.

Assessment of the disorder

When sexual functions are impaired due to lithium therapy, the clinician should perform a detailed assessment of the patient's sexual activities before and after treatment. Marital conflicts may arise as a result of these sexual dysfunctions. In assessing sexual issues, the clinician must be careful to place them within the context of the role of sexuality in the patient's life, the dynamics of the couple, and the severity of the affective disorder. Patients with severe affective disorder could be particularly willing to tolerate adverse side effects in order to control affective episodes, and informed and sympathetic understanding on the part of the sexual partner may go a long way to minimizing the seriousness of the condition.

Treatment

The physician should direct efforts towards eliminating or reducing the severity of the side effects and to maintaining effective control in preventing depressive or manic episodes as well. Some therapeutic strategies can be suggested.

Careful control of lithium serum levels is wise, because sexual impairment could be a transient and benign side effect resulting from tissue adaptation to rising lithium levels and any sudden change in the prescription of lithium should be avoided; spontaneous remission may occur within 2 or 3 months after the beginning of treatment. Attempts to decrease lithium serum levels could be a useful procedure, since sexual effects due to the therapy could be dose-dependent. When lithium therapy must continue and sexual impairment persists, an on-off medication schedule can be designed, in order both to provide prophylaxis and reduce sexual impairment. Caution must be taken in the follow-up of these patients, since the effectiveness of this procedure in preventing or attenuating recurrences in bipolar illness is not certain, though it is in line with recent suggestions that a continuous-administration schedule may not be really essential (see pp. 99–105). Alternative therapeutic approaches may be considered if sexual dysfunction becomes intolerable. Tricyclic antidepressants and antipsychotic agents are usually the drugs of choice for lithium substitution. This procedure should be used in a thoughtful manner in each case. This decision should take into account the development of new side-effects associated with long-term treatment with antidepressants and neuroleptics, as well as the risks and benefits of lithium replacement. The effects of carbamazepine on sexual functioning are not known; this may be worth trying in place of lithium.

As a general rule, better therapeutic results can be achieved if a good doctor–patient relationship is established and if the sexual partner actively participates in many of these therapeutic decisions.

Acknowledgement

Thanks are due to Dr Ladislau Ruy Ungar Glausiusz of the Department of Psychiatry of the Escola Paulista de Medicina, for his helpful comments and criticisms.

Bibliography

Blay,S.L., Toledo Ferraz,M.P. and Calil,H.M. (1982) Lithium-induced male sexual impairment: two case reports. *J. Clin. Psychiatry,* **43**, 497–498.
Describes a controlled study and treatment procedures.

Vinarova,E., Uhlir,O., Stika,L. and Vinar,O. (1972) Side effects of lithium administration. *Activ. Nerv. Sup.*, **14**, 105–107.
This article reports on the role of lithium and the occurrence of sexual impairment.

Part IX

THE MODERN CONTEXT

70. The Economics of Lithium Therapy

Robin G.McCreadie

The Production of Lithium

The element lithium occurs as a readily available natural salt (pp. 19–22); it is cheap to produce in a formulation suitable for human consumption, and it cannot be patented. It is thus clear that profits to be made from this drug will not be great, and it is therefore not suprising that although five pharmaceutical firms produce lithium in the UK, four of them are relatively small (see *Table 70.1*).

If a product can make little profit, then it is likely that it will not be widely advertised. This is borne out by a review of all drug advertisements in the 5 years from March 1981 to March 1986 in the *British Journal of Psychiatry*, the leading journal for psychiatrists in the United Kingdom (see *Tables 70.2* and *70.3*). Lithium products accounted for only 3% of the total number of advertisements in this journal. The most widely advertised individual drugs were Prothiaden®, Clopixol® and Depixol®. Priadel® and Litarex® came 19th and 26th out of a total of 34; Phasal®, Camcolit® and Liskonum® were not advertised at all. In contrast, Smith, Kline and French the very large firm which manufactures Liskonum, advertised Stelazine® (used in the treatment of schizophrenia) 33 times. Although all trained psychiatrists are aware of the existence of lithium they are presumably no less immune to the powers of advertising than other people, and this being so it is not unreasonable to suppose that if lithium were more widely advertised, it would probably be more widely used.

The economics of production may have more serious consequences in Third World countries. Dr Sergio Blay, a psychiatrist in Sao Paulo, Brazil, believes that because of low profits there is a great risk that lithium might be withdrawn altogether from the market in developing countries. Indeed, in some areas he believes lithium production has been kept going due only to strong pressure from national psychiatric associations and government mental health policies.

The Cost of Lithium

The cost of different lithium products to the consumer, i.e. the National Health Service in the UK, or the patient if he receives the drug on private prescription, is shown in *Table 70.1*, the information for which is taken from the March 1986 issue of the *Monthly Index of Medical Specialties (MIMS)* (the cost to hospital pharmacists is slightly less). In an attempt to assess the national cost per annum a review was carried out in 1982 of all patients receiving lithium in South-West Scotland. It was found firstly that the average daily dose was 800 mg and so the average daily cost of lithium was therefore about 7–8 pence. Secondly, 77 people in every 100 000 of the general population (i.e. about one in every 1300) were taking lithium. This is very similar to the findings of Dr G.Bucht in Sweden and Dr Ian Glen in Edinburgh, UK, where 1 in a 1000 of the population were taking lithium. If these figures hold good throughout the United Kingdom, then at any given time about 40 000 people are taking lithium: the approximate annual cost of lithium at *MIMS* 1986 prices is thus about £1.1 million.

Table 70.1 *Lithium preparations in the UK and their respective costs*[a]

Trade name	Generic compound	Tablet formation	Pharmaceutical firm	Cost per tablet
Priadel	Lithium carbonate	400 mg*	Delandale Laboratories	3.7p
Liskonum	Lithium carbonate	450 mg	Smith, Kline & French	3.9p
Camcolit	Lithium carbonate	250 mg and 400 mg	Norgine	2.7p 3.7p
Phasal	Lithium carbonate	300 mg	Lagap	3.2p
Litarex	Lithium citrate	560 mg	CP Pharmaceuticals	3.6p

[a]Information from *MIMS* (May, 1986) Medical Publications Ltd, London.
*A 200 mg preparation has recently become available.

Table 70.2 *Advertising of major groups of psychiatric drugs in the British Journal of Psychiatry between March 1981 and March 1986*

Group	Number of adverts	%
Antipsychotics	221	35
Antidepressants:		
Tricyclics	99	16
Tetracyclics	71	11
MAOIS	33	5
Other	53	9
Benzodiazepines	69	11
Antiparkinsonians	33	5
Lithium	17	3
Anticonvulsants	17	3
Others	10	2
Total	623	100

Table 70.3 *Advertising of the top 10 individual drugs, and of Priadel and Litarex, in the British Journal of Psychiatry between March 1981 and March 1986*

Rank	Drug	Number of adverts	%	Type of drug
1.	Prothiaden	60	10	Tricyclic antidepressant
2.	Clopixol	46	7	Antipsychotic
3.	Depixol	42	7	Antipsychotic
4.	Norval	41	7	Tetracyclic antidepressant
5.	Stelazine	33	5	Antipsychotic
6.	Parnate	33	5	MAOI
7.	Modecate	33	5	Antipsychotic
8.	Merital	32	5	Novel antidepressant
9.	Bolvidon	30	5	Tetracyclic antidepressant
10.	Anxon	25	4	Benzodiazepine
19.	Priadel	13	2	Lithium salt
26.	Litarex	4	1	Lithium salt

There were no advertisements for Camcolit, Phasal or Liskonum.

If lithium were not available, patients might receive alternative maintenance therapy. This would cost approximately the same as lithium for out-patients; for example maintenance antidepressant therapy with, say, amitriptyline 75 mg daily, would cost 7.5 pence per day, and with an oral antipsychotic, such as chlorpromazine, 6 pence per day. If both drugs were used in combination, maintenance therapy would of course be more expensive. Hospital pharmacists pay substantially less for both these drugs; the cost of maintenance therapy to in-patients therefore would be considerably less than if they received lithium.

Table 70.4 *Length of inpatient stay before and after the introduction of lithium, according to a survey in South-West Scotland*

Hospitalization characteristic	Duration
Mean lenth of time on lithium	4.6 years
Mean length of stay before introduction of lithium	25 days per year
Mean length of stay after introduction of lithium	11 days per year
Reduction in length of stay	14 days per year

The Cost Benefits of Lithium

It is very difficult to assess the cost benefits of lithium, and what follows must be highly speculative. The survey carried out in South-West Scotland looked at the course of the patient's illness before and after the patient started on lithium. After the introduction of lithium, there was a substantial reduction in the number and length of admissions to inpatient care, and in the number of ECT administered to patients. There was, however, no change in the amount of time patients spent on antidepressant or tranquilizing drugs.

Table 70.4 shows that the average length of in-patient stay dropped from 25 days a year before lithium was introduced to 11 days a year after its introduction; i.e. each year a patient spent on average 14 days less in hospital. The cost of in-patient care in March 1986 at the Crichton Royal Hospital, the psychiatric hospital serving South-West Scotland, was £290 per week. This is probably typical for psychiatric hospitals in the UK, and if so, the saving in in-patient costs per year for the 40 000 patients receiving lithium is approximately £23 million. Against this saving of course must be balanced the cost of lithium, serum lithium estimations and out-patient care. It is noteworthy, however, that in South-West Scotland a third of patients well maintained on lithium were receiving care only from their general practitioner (see pp. 124–127).

In 1979 Dr A.Reifman and Dr R.J.Wyatt from the National Institute for Mental Health in Washington tried to assess the economic impact of lithium in the USA. Not only did they assess the costs of lithium and the saving in in-patient costs, but they tried to examine the 'productivity' of manic-depressive patients before and after the introduction of lithium. Since the onset of affective illness can be at the height of a patient's career, the impact of loss of wage can be dramatic, financially crippling the patient and his or her family. Taking into account all these factors, they estimated that in the 10 years from 1969 to 1979 the United States saved at least $2.88 billion in medical costs, and gained $1.28 billion in production. They believed these estimates of savings, while speculative, were extremely conservative.

The Cost to the Patient

In 1983 Dr M.A.Launer from Burnley, UK, writing in the *British Medical Journal*, highlighted what was for him an important gap in the benefits system. A patient of his, although well on lithium and grateful for being so, was paying a substantial sum of money for prescriptions for lithium carbonate. An individual prescription in the UK costs a patient £2.20 and a yearly 'season ticket' £33.50 (May 1986 prices); this is, in fact, more than the cost of a year's supply at *MIMS* prices (e.g. Priadel £27, Liskonum £28). The patient pointed out that if she needed lithium for life then it would be reasonable for this drug to be exempt from charges—much as drugs for epilepsy are exempt. Paradoxically, groups which are totally exempt from prescription charges in the UK include the young, the pregnant and pensioners—the very groups that are not likely to be taking lithium. Should lithium for manic-depressive disorders be added to the list of conditions which are exempt from prescription charges?

Conclusion

The economics of lithium therapy is a neglected area. As a medication, lithium is probably under-advertised, and therefore possibly under-used. Further research into its cost benefits is required. More detailed information might persuade the UK government to add it to its list of drugs exempt from prescription charges.

Bibliography

McCreadie,R.G. and Morrison,D.P. (1985) The impact of lithium in South West Scotland. *Br. J. Psychiatry*, **146**, 70–80.
A detailed study of the usefulness of lithium in a geographically discrete part of the UK.

Reifman,A. and Wyatt,R.J. (1980) Lithium: A brake in the rising cost of mental illness. *Arch. Gen. Psychiatry*, **37**, 385–388.
A speculative, but detailed, assessment of the economic benefits of lithium in the US over a 10-year period.

71. Cost Effectiveness of a Lithium Clinic

Eric D.Peselow and Ronald R.Fieve

It is estimated that approximately 15% of the general population have a mental disorder. In the United States it is suggested that mental illness can cause an economic loss equivalent to 10% of the gross national product. The lithium clinic described in Section 34 (pp. 127–129) has been used to serve as a primary prevention measure to diminish the undesirable mood state that would lead to this economic loss.

In order to evaluate exactly how cost effective a lithium affective disorders clinic is in terms of dollars spent for direct care, a detailed study was undertaken at the Foundation for Depression–Manic Depression in New York, USA.

From a total number of 750 affective disorder patients, 113 were selected who had been treated in the affective disorders clinic for at least 3 years. For these patients (who included 32 bipolar I patients, 35 bipolar II patients, 24 cyclothymics, and 22 unipolar patients) the treatment represented their first sustained prophylactic outpatient follow-up. All of these patients were maintained on lithium alone for 3 years, with a neuroleptic or antidepressant added for brief periods of time if an affective disorder occurred. From an initial diagnostic interview, it was learned that none of the patients had ever received lithium for greater than 3 months in the 3 years preceding entry into the clinic, and in all cases the lithium was given during an acute affective episode. None of the patients had received pharmacotherapy for sustained periods of time following the alleviation of affective symptoms (generally receiving pharmacotherapy only during an acute manic or depressive episode which required hospitalization or outpatient treatment and discontinuing the medication within a month following the resolution of acute symptoms).

For all of these patients, information was obtained as to the number of affective episodes that required hospitalization or outpatient pharmacological treatment before lithium therapy in the preceding 3 years and compared with the number of hospitalizations and outpatient episodes that occurred during the 3 years on lithium treatment. An affective episode was defined as a major bipolar or unipolar episode according to both RDC and DSM III criteria and requiring additional pharmacotherapy. For the purposes of this evaluation, both manic and depressive episodes were calculated for bipolar I patients before and after lithium, and depressive episodes for unipolar, bipolar II, and cyclothymic patients before and after lithium treatment. Bipolar II and cyclothymic patients usually seek treatment for depression in 85–90% of cases; the fact that they are generally not troubled by hypomania made it difficult to calculate retrospectively the number of hypomanic episodes in the 3 years preceding lithium treatment.

Table 71.1 evaluates affective episodes and hospitalizations both before and after lithium treatment. As can be seen, all groups had fewer affective episodes and hospitalizations in the 3 years of lithium therapy than in the 3 years prior to the initiation of lithium therapy, though this difference was statistically significant only for the bipolar I and bipolar II patients. For the total group of 113 patients, 81 had fewer affective episodes on lithium, 21 had the same number before and after lithium treatment and 11 had more episodes on lithium as opposed to before treatment.

Table 71.1 *Frequency of affective episodes requiring hospitalization or outpatient treatment before and after lithium treatment*

Diagnosis		Inpatient		Outpatient	
	n	Before Li	After Li	Before Li	After Li
Bipolar I	32	45	13	72	39
Bipolar II	35	32	5	50	18
Cyclothymic	24	–	–	58	30
Unipolar	22	19	7	30	14
Total	113	96	25	210	101

Avoidance of Hospitalization Costs

Table 71.2 evaluates the cost effectiveness of lithium for this patient group. Using the assumptions that a hospitalization for an affective episode averaged 20 days at a cost of $250 per day, and estimating outpatient therapy for an affective episode to cost $50 per visit over an average 4-week treatment, the results clearly show the cost effectiveness of lithium. The overall cost for treating affective illness in terms of hospitalization or outpatient visit prior to lithium therapy was $522,000 as compared with $145,200 on lithium therapy. If one then subtracts the total number of visits that the 113 patients actually made during euthymic periods in the 3 years on lithium, the total cost of which was $188,800, the total savings for lithium therapy over 3 years was $188,000.

Avoidance of Productivity Loss

Just as important as hospital costs, is productivity loss as a result of an affective episode. Lithium therapy provides a way of maintaining normal functioning for productive individuals without interfering in any substantive way with their personality or creative achievements, and without severe side effects. The work of A.Reifman and R.J.Wyatt, reported in 1980, and the Medical Practice Information Project report in 1979 bear this out. Under the latter, it was estimated

Table 71.2 *Cost effectiveness (in US dollars) of lithium treatment assessed in 113 patients for a 3-year period before lithium treatment and a 3-year period on lithium*

Diagnosis	*n*	Pre-Li		Post-Li		Balance in favour of Li
		Inpatient	Outpatient	Inpatient	Outpatient	
Bipolar I	32	225,000	14,400	65,000	7,800	166,600
Bipolar II	35	160,000	10,000	25,000	3,600	141,400
Cyclothymic	24	–	11,600	–	6,000	5,600
Unipolar	22	95,000	6,000	35,000	2,800	63,200
Total	113	480,000	42,000	125,000	20,200	376,800

that had the total number of bipolar patients gone untreated in 1976, the economic loss to society (both medical costs and productivity loss) would have been $1,000,000,000. With lithium therapy, the total cost to society (hospital costs, productivity loss, and outpatient treatment for stabilization) was $441,000,000, or approximately half the estimated cost without treatment. It was further estimated that had these bipolar patients received optimum care, the cost would have been reduced to $285,000,000. Thus, one can appreciate the roles played by both lithium and a specialized lithium clinic in reducing costs to society.

Bibliography

Cusano,P.R., Mayo,J. and O'Connell,R.A. (1977) The medical economics of lithium treatment for manic depressives. *Psychiatry*, **28**, 169–170.

One of the first articles to address the issue of the economic benefits of lithium therapy, this is still well worth reading as an introduction to the topic.

72. The Status of Lithium Therapy in Psychiatry

F.Neil Johnson

For reasons which are not always easy to understand, the subject of lithium therapy sometimes arouses antagonistic passions in some psychiatrists. Probably these are vestigial responses left over from the early days of the clinical use of lithium when the medical and scientific literature carried exchanges of quite extraordinary acrimony between investigators of the new drug and a small number of others who chose to label it a 'scientific myth'. Added to this, reports of toxicity and some fatalities arising from overdose have been given importance and prominence quite out of proportion to the frequency with which they have occurred. All drugs are toxic if given in sufficient quantity and all have side effects of one kind or another (often more unpleasant than any which has ever been reported to occur with lithium).

Fortunately, the emotional rejection of lithium as a treatment mode is observed less and less frequently and tends to be limited to those who have failed to keep abreast of the medical literature. The younger generation of psychiatrists seem more than happy to embrace lithium therapy as an important and valuable tool in combating mental illness.

Clinical Status

It is now fair to say that lithium therapy has taken a secure and respected place amongst the range of available psychiatric treatments. It is not a wonder drug—but then few are. It is, however, highly effective if properly prescribed for an appropriate condition, and if treatment is carried out in accordance with certain very simple, but essential principles.

One measure of the degree to which lithium has now become fully assimilated into modern psychiatry is the ease with which clinicians now take the decision to combine lithium treatment with some other medication. It may not always be a particularly wise thing to do, but at least it indicates that the old fear of lithium is at last fading into a proper perspective.

The twin advantages of therapeutic efficacy and economic benefits (pp. 257–261) ensure that lithium therapy will continue to occupy its position as a leading treatment modality in therapy for a long time, a position which can only become strengthened as more is learned about the kind of administration regimens (once a day, for example) which enable maximum clinical effectiveness to be achieved with a minimum number of problems.

Research Status

Whatever happens to lithium as a therapeutic agent, its title to a prime place in basic biochemical and physiological research will remain secure. As one of the alkali metals, it will always be of interest whenever investigations are carried out on excitable tissues. Its ability to modify just about every physiological system that one cares to name, makes lithium a most interesting research tool. Research primarily directed towards an understanding of the clinical actions of lithium has frequently led to fundamental discoveries about biological control processes, and that will never be forgotten.

Lithium is extraordinary in the way it has attracted, and continues to attract, the attention of individuals from so many different fields. It is unusual to see clinicians, biochemists, physiologists, virologists, psychologists and so many others from all branches of the biomedical sciences, showing an interest in chemistry, physics and the other sciences, yet that is exactly what happens at every congress or symposium at which lithium figures as a major topic.

There can be few who would deny that lithium has come to occupy a central place in biomedical research, or who would predict an early change in the situation.

Bibliography

Johnson,F.N. (1984) *The History of Lithium Therapy*. Macmillan, London.
The prologue to this book presents an assessment of the impact of lithium on modern psychiatry.

73. Information and Education about Lithium: the Lithium Information Center

Margaret G.Baudhuin, Judith A.Carroll, James W.Jefferson, John H.Greist and Bette L.Hartley

Today in 1987 there are more than 15 000 items of literature about lithium and its biomedical applications. Of these, more than half have been written and published since 1980. It is virtually impossible for an individual health care professional or other interested person to keep up with this rapidly growing body of literature. It is imperative, however, that people who want to have the latest information about lithium therapy should be able to find it and use it. Several books have been published which have attempted to review either the whole field of lithium therapy or specific—usually research oriented—topics. Such books serve a useful purpose in pulling together and digesting the enormous amount of material which appears in a bewildering array of technical journals. However, the pace at which research advances necessarily means that all books become dated and cannot be relied upon as sources for the most recent findings. It is necessary to have some kind of system for providing research workers, clinicians, and other interested parties with a means of gaining access to original reports and particularly to those which have most recently appeared.

The Lithium Information Center

The Lithium Information Center, established at the University of Wisconsin, USA, in 1975, was developed for this purpose. Its founders' original plan was to establish a database so that they would have easy access to the information they needed to carry out their work in the area of lithium therapy. Today, however, the Lithium Information Center is much more than a simple, in-house information service. Over the years it has become a comprehensive source of bibliographic information about lithium therapy, and staff members now process more than 1500 information requests each year from all over the world.

Lithium Library

At the Center, all references to literature relating to the biomedical applications of lithium are collected and stored in a computerized database called the Lithium Library. Information specialists at the Center are able to search the database and retrieve bibliographic information about very specific aspects of lithium therapy.

The Lithium Library contains references to a full spectrum of published and unpublished materials dating from 1818, one year after the element lithium was discovered. Included are references to journal articles, books, book chapters, meeting proceedings, pamphlets, government documents and all other forms of published materials. The Center also collects and enters into the database unpublished case reports and manuscripts for papers that are in press or prepublication form. New references are added daily, and over 1000 references are added each year. These references are located by several means including the Center's own bibliographic research as well as through subscriptions to various current awareness services such as Ascatopics® and BIOSIS®. References are also obtained through the continuous review of the more generalized bibliographic services such as MEDLARS®, Psychological Abstracts, Excerpta Medica, etc. *Table 73.1* provides a complete list of lithium subtopics that are represented in the database.

Table 73.1 *Subject areas monitored at the Lithium Information Center*

1. Lithium treatment of manic depression and other psychiatric disorders.
2. All non-psychiatric medical uses of lithium.
3. Alternatives to lithium treatment for manic-depression.
4. History of lithium in medicine.
5. Industrial exposure to lithium.
6. Environmental exposure to lithium.
7. Lithium in experimental psychology.
8. All related subtopics including lithium's:
   —chemistry and pharmacology;
   —effects on metabolic and cellular processes;
   —mechanism of action;
   —proper administration and dosage;
   —recommended monitoring procedures;
   —contraindications, side effects and toxicity;
   —interactions with other drugs.

Most of the literature is technical, but patient information and other non-technical materials are included.

Number and sources of requests

Since its inception the Lithium Information Center has received more than 8000 requests for information from all over the United States and more than 35 other countries. In recent years the center has been receiving more than 1000 requests each year, and in both 1985 and 1986 more than 1500 requests were processed. Anyone can contact the Center to request information. Requests have come from physicians, psychologists, pharmacists and other medical professionals, researchers, medical libraries, pharmaceutical companies and other industries, patients and their families, and other interested individuals. Computer searches can be requested by phone or mail. Although most searches can be conducted within 24 h, urgent requests are often processed immediately over the phone. For individuals who have a computer, telephone, and modem, direct computer access is also available.

Support and fees

The Lithium Information Center has been supported in part by public and private grants and contributions but also relies upon user fees. Although fees for a particular search vary according to the complexities of the search and the volume of information generated, the average fee charged is $15.00. The Center also charges a small fee for duplicating services when copies of materials (subject to copyright law) are requested. Remote access users are charged an hourly rate and are also responsible for long distance charges incurred while connected by phone to the Center's computer.

Lithium Index and Lithium Consultation

The Lithium Library is only part of the total Lithium Information Center operation. Two other computerized information services, the Lithium Index and Lithium Consultation, have also been developed. The Lithium Index is a collection of summaries. Each summary is a review of the literature regarding a specific subtopic of lithium therapy. There are currently 125 summaries in the Index on topics as general as lithium and bipolar disorder and as specific as 'low dose' lithium therapy. Existing summaries are updated periodically as new information becomes available, and entirely new summaries are added to the existing collection when appropriate. The summaries, which provide a good background and overview of the various subtopics to which they pertain, are often mailed along with bibliographic information when they are relevant to an inquiry.

The Lithium Consultation is an interactive computer program which can be helpful to physicians faced with making decisions about using lithium with specific patients and how this therapy might be managed. Through a series of questions to the physician, the computer collects information about the patient. Patient selection, proper administration of lithium, and management of side effects are some of the areas that are covered by the Lithium Consultation.

The Lithium Index and Consultation were natural outgrowths of the Lithium Library as the directors and staff recognized the extent to which the information stored could be useful to health care professionals and researchers everywhere. With the computerized reference file as a base, it was felt that the concise, accessible Index summaries would be a way in which many requests for information could be handled more expeditiously. The rationale for the Lithium Consultation was similar in that it was designed to meet the needs of an important segment of the user population: physicians seeking specific help with active cases. These three services allow the Center to serve a broad clientele.

Publications

In recent years the mission of the Lithium Information Center has been expanded to include several independent objectives. The first has been the preparation of publications to make the Center's original mission of disseminating high quality bibliographic information that much easier to achieve. The Center's booklet, *Lithium and Manic Depression: A Guide*, for example, has been a very successful method of providing information to patients and their families. The guide (first published in 1982 and revised periodically) has been helpful in the effort to make the lithium literature accessible to more people. To those without a medical background, the literature had been virtually inaccessible because of its technical nature. Only a few non-technical publications were available before 1982. The guide, written in a less technical style, is a distillation of the literature and provides easy access to the information that patients and other laypersons need. A similar booklet, for the non-professional, *Carbamazepine and Manic Depression: A Guide*, has recently been published. This guide will be helpful to patients who are using carbamazepine, an alternative to lithium in the treatment of manic depression. The *Lithium Encyclopedia for Clinical Practice*, a published version of the Lithium Index, has been very useful to those with a professional background. It is to health care professionals what *Lithium and Manic Depression: A Guide* is to patients and laypersons. The *Encyclopedia* was first published in 1983, and a second edition in 1987.

Research

A second important development in the Center's mission is in the area of research. Having kept records of information requests for several years, staff members at the Center are able to recognize areas in which there is a great deal of interest but little or no information. In some cases this has led to in-house research projects. Studies of lithium and the eye, and lithium and exercise are examples. In other cases, it has helped in planning for the future of research at the Center. The Lithium Information Center should certainly be viewed as a good source of ideas for research that could be done in the area of lithium therapy.

Patient-oriented activities

Finally, the Lithium Information Center has become a referral centre. Patients are interested in locating qualified health care professionals and facilities close to where they live. Some are interested in locating support groups. Physician referrals are made based on a large store of contacts that have been made over the years by the Center's directors and other staff members. In addition, the Center maintains a list of self-help groups which offer support and information to people with bipolar and other affective disorders.

The Lithium Literature

Maintaining the Lithium Library will always be central to the Center's function, and a closer look at the content of the database provides an interesting profile. Of the more than 15 000 pieces of literature cited in the Lithium Library over 1300 were published in both 1983 and 1984 and approximately 1200 appeared in 1985. More than half have been published since 1980. This is remarkable when one considers that before 1970 fewer than 1400 publications were available to those who wanted to learn more about the biomedical uses of lithium (*Figure 73.1* provides a breakdown of lithium publications by year). This rapidly expanding literature has taken several notable turns over the years and today has many interesting characteristics.

Since treatment of acute mania and maintenance of remission in bipolar disorder are the two principal areas in which lithium is used, a large percentage of the literature pertains to these subjects. Other psychiatric applications in which lithium is not the primary therapy, such as unipolar disorder, schizophrenia, and aggression also account for a substantial portion of the lithium literature. In fact, lithium has been used in at least 25 different psychiatric disorders, making lithium in psychiatry the largest single area that is reported in the literature.

There are several areas outside psychiatry in which lithium has shown promise as a therapeutic agent. One of the most heavily investigated of these is neurological disorders. For example, there are reports that lithium has been used with success in the treatment of chronic headache conditions and other forms of pain. Parkinson's disease, tardive dyskinesia, movement disorders, epilepsy, and organic brain syndrome are several other neurological disorders for which lithium has been tried with varying degrees of success. These subjects are also well accounted for in the literature. In all, there are more than 20 neurological disorders for which lithium has been used at least experimentally and reported in the literature.

Another area of interest which has become a trend in the literature is in the field of haematology/im-

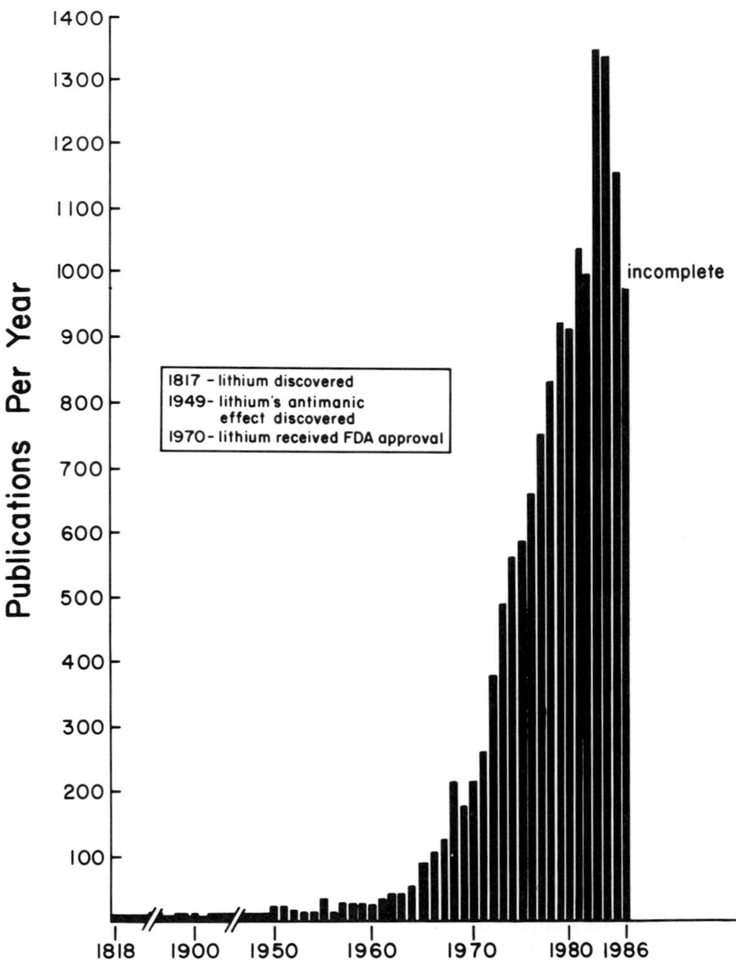

Figure 73.1 The rise in the numbers of articles published on biomedical aspects of lithium from the date of its discovery to the present time.

munology (two separate areas which overlap in investigations regarding immune system deficiencies). The first articles dealing with the possibility of using lithium to treat neutropenic disorders (low white blood cell count) began appearing in the late 1970s, several years after the first reports that elevated white blood cell count was a benign side effect of lithium use. Today there are close to 900 references relating to this subject in the Lithium Library. Almost 75% of these references are documents that have appeared since 1980, clearly indicating a significant recent trend. One of the most frequently studied subtopics of this area has been the use of lithium in cancer patients who have developed reduced white blood cell count as a result of chemotherapy or radiation treatments. Interest in this area has even been extended to such recent developments in the medical world as acquired immune deficiency syndrome (AIDS) and herpes virus infections.

In addition to these areas of major concentration in the literature, there are a few areas of application which do not account for a significant portion of the lithium literature but are still very interesting. These would include reports about lithium as a therapy for hyperthyroidism, asthma, syndrome of inappropriate antidiuretic hormone (ADH) secretion, and colitis.

A second significant area represented in the lithium literature concerns the contraindications and side effects of lithium use. Although there are side effects about which very little has been written (e.g. lithium-induced hair loss, peripheral neuropathy, papilloedema), other side effects have been heavily investigated. For example, at least 1700 articles deal with lithium and its effects on the kidney, the most studied side effect. Lithium and thyroid function, lithium's neurological effects including lithium toxicity, and the use of lithium during pregnancy are three examples of side effects which have also been given substantial attention in the literature. In addition, there are almost 2000 articles about beneficial and harmful drug interactions. Approximately 30% of the literature deals with lithium's side effects, contraindications and interactions with other drugs.

Although some areas of lithium therapy have been given continuous attention over the years (lithium's mechanism of action, for example, about which there are close to 800 references), important new considerations have emerged from time to time. Most recently, three very interesting and notable topics have come to the surface. Dose reduction, for instance, seems to be a very important new consideration in the literature. Can patients be maintained at lower serum lithium levels thereby reducing the likelihood of harmful side effects? Almost 80% of the articles on this subject have been published in the 1980s.

Related to reduced dosage is the idea of discontinued use. Some physicians have experimented with the discontinuation of lithium therapy employing either intermittant application or total discontinuation. The question seems to be whether or not patients who have used lithium for several years can be taken off the drug suddenly or gradually and not experience significant manic or depressive relapses. More than half of the references about this subject that the Lithium Information Center has on file appeared after 1982.

Newer alternatives to lithium for people who do not respond to, or cannot tolerate lithium therapy, is a third important development in recent lithium literature. Of the alternative drugs that have been considered, several, including the leading newer alternative, carbamazepine, have been given considerable attention. This interest is so recent, in fact, that well over half of the references on file are to documents that have appeared after 1984.

This body of literature is, then, a most dynamic and important one. Its history is long but one that shows significant growth in recent years, stimulated by ever increasing and broadening experimentation with the drug and by the growing interest of health care professionals, researchers, patients and other interested individuals. Some people who have either clinical or research backgrounds are served fairly well by this literature. They are able to use it to continue their own work and to identify areas in which more work needs to be done. However, there is still a great deal that is not known about lithium and its biomedical uses, and the information that is available today is not very accessible or useful to patients and other individuals who do not have sufficient backgrounds in either clinical practice or biomedical research. So it seems that information specialists in this and perhaps a multitude of other medical information areas face the double problem of not having enough information for biomedical professionals and of finding ways of making what is available more accessible and useful to the lay population.

Some Lithium Information Center publications, the guides mentioned earlier, for example, are a step in this direction, but the need becomes greater every day as more and more patients become interested in their own medical problems and the medical alternatives available to them.

Those engaged in the process of reporting about biomedical experimentation and new developments in clinical practice should be more responsive to this problem. In cases where reporting must be highly technical or lose its effectiveness, information specialists should either create or encourage the creation of information that can be understood and easily used by the lay population.

Finally, and perhaps most important, the general public should be made aware of these opportunities to find out what they want to know, and they should be strongly encouraged to take advantage of the resources that are available to them.

Acknowledgement

This work was supported by funds from the Lithium Corporation of America and the Wisconsin Cheeseman.

Bibliography

Bohn,J. and Jefferson,J.W. (1987) *Lithium and Manic Depression: A Guide*. Board of Regents of the University of Wisconsin System (Lithium Information Center), Madison, Wisconsin.
A patient guide to lithium treatment for manic depression intended for those who have no background in clinical science.

Greist,J.H., Jefferson,J.W., Ackerman,D.L., Baudhuin,M.G., Erdman,H.P. and Carroll,J.A. (1985) Lithium Information Center: The Lithium Library Revisited. *J. Clin. Psychiatry*, **46**, 327–331.
A recent article describing the Lithium Information Center.

Jefferson,J.W., Greist,J.H., Ackerman,D.L. and Carroll,J.A. (1987) *Lithium Encyclopedia for Clinical Practice.* 2nd Edition, American Psychiatry Press, Washington, DC.
A book containing summaries of the literature on various subtopics of lithium therapy. The book is written for individuals who have a medical background.

Medenwald,J.R., Greist,J.H. and Jefferson,J.W. (1987) *Carbamazepine and Manic Depression: A Guide.* Board of Regents of the University of Wisconsin System (Lithium Information Center), Madison, Wisconsin.
A patient guide to carbamazepine treatment for manic depression intended for those who have no background in clinical science.

74. The Future

F.Neil Johnson

Predicting the future is an activity to be engaged in with caution, if at all; one risks appearing at best uninformed, and at worst misinformed. Prediction of the immediate future, however, may be somewhat less risky than trying to see what lies 10 or 20 years ahead, and on the whole it seem fairly safe to say that we are unlikely to witness much change in the pattern or style of lithium usage over the next 2–5 years.

In the first place there is the natural conservatism of the medical profession to be reckoned with. After all, if an ill-founded notion like the uric acid diathesis (see pp. 24–28) can persist for 20 or more years as a determinant of clinical procedures following its discrediting in the scientific literature, it is certain that lithium therapy, which rests on much more secure foundations, can count on at least as long again. There will, however, be changes and one can perhaps see where they might arise.

Administration Regimen

The recent work on administration schedules seems to have established that once a day administration has no therapeutic disadvantages over a divided dosage procedure, and may indeed have distinct advantages in terms of reduced danger of long-term unwanted effects and increased compliance with the medication regimen. We may expect, therefore, to see the pattern of administration shifting towards the single daily dosage format.

Dosage Levels

There has been a steady drift of opinion about the serum lithium levels regarded as acceptable in long-term maintenance treatment, and modern practice is to keep levels as low as possible. We may see levels of 0.5–0.7 mmol/l being regarded as typical, rather than the levels of 0.8–1.2 which are frequently quoted. To a large extent, however, the question of serum levels cannot be taken out of context of administration regime. If one is giving a single daily dose, the 12-h serum level may be less important than if a divided dose is given, because serum levels will fall appreciably before the next dose is given. If the dosing were to become even less frequent (say once every second or third day) then serum peaks would, perhaps, cease to have any clinical significance.

It has to be said, of course, that the evidence for a difference in renal side effects between once-a-day and twice-a-day regimens has yet to be supported by findings from a definitive test involving random allocations of the two regimens to patients, and one looks forward to such a study being performed in the near future.

Formulations

Even though with a once a day administration regimen the serum peak may have reduced importance, the *rate* at which the peak is attained could be crucial. Rapid rises in serum levels are likely to be accompanied by adjustment side effects (nausea, for example), and can be avoided by the use of controlled release formulations which slow down the release rate. This must not, however, occur at the expense of low bioavailability. Product formulations will have to take these considerations into account.

There may also be developments in the way in which lithium salts are packaged (in capsule form rather than tablets, for example), though it is likely that the salts used will continue to be the carbonate, citrate or sulphate since tests of others have not shown them to have any advantages.

Treatment Combinations

In view of the attention currently being directed towards the relative efficacy of lithium used alone and in combination with other agents, this seems an area where clinical recommendations may change in coming months. This is particularly important in cases of resistance manifested to treatments given singly.

The combination of lithium therapy with social or psychological support has been found to be associated with good outcome, and there is much to be done to identify and capitalize upon the factors which may be at work here.

Alternatives to Lithium

The introduction of carbamazepine as a medication against affective disorders has raised once again in an acute form the question of alternatives to lithium therapy. Given that, when properly used, lithium is as safe as most, and safer than many other agents utilized in psychiatry, there would not appear to be much to be gained from actively seeking alternatives.

Non-psychiatric Uses

Exciting developments in the employment of lithium to stimulate leukocyte production or to inhibit viral replication augur well for a proliferation in the general medical uses of lithium. The more such-non-psychiatric applications are investigated, the more we will learn about the physiological and biochemical effects of lithium, and such information may, in its turn, feed back into our models of lithium action in affective disorders.

Concluding Remarks

Just as it could not have been predicted that John Cade would stumble upon the anti-manic potential of lithium, so too is it impossible to say that some far-reaching discovery will not be made next week, next month or next year, that will completely transform our approach to lithium therapy and the management of the affective disorders.

Until and unless that happens, we must persevere with attempts to refine and improve the way in which we present lithium therapy to our patients, so as to increase its efficacy whilst reducing any disadvantages which it might possess. In addition, we should seek to overcome the resistance of those individuals who, through prejudice, ignorance (or, in some cases, both) would deny the availability of lithium to the many thousands of patients who would benefit from its application.

Lithium is a cost-effective treatment, eminently suitable for use in countries where economic considerations are paramount in determining the availability of medical service, and we must make all efforts to ensure that its benefits become extended to such regions.

There can be no doubt that, at a clinical and at a research level, lithium has transformed modern psychiatric practice, and the impact that it has had will be felt whatever the future holds for its continuation or otherwise as a viable treatment modality.

Bibliography

Johnson,F.N. (1984) *The History of Lithium Therapy*. Macmillan, London.
This book concludes with an attempt to extend the historical trends in lithium therapy into the future.

INDEX

Index